Morocco
Handbook

with Mauritania

Anne & Keith McLachlan

Footprint Handbooks

Sweet water shall be in her streams
And there, drink shall not be denied us.
And the sound of flowing waters
shall swell in the silence: ...

Michel Vieuchange, 1930

Footprint Handbooks

6 Riverside Court, Lower Bristol Road
Bath BA2 3DZ England
T 01225 469141 F 01225 469461
E mail handbooks@footprint.cix.co.uk
www.fooprint-handbooks.co.uk

ISBN 0 900751 90 8 ISSN 1363-7479
CIP DATA: A catalogue record for this book is
available from the British Library

In North America, published by

📖 PASSPORT BOOKS
a division of NTC/Contemporary Publishing Company
Lincolnwood, Illinois USA

4255 West Touhy Avenue, Lincolnwood
(Chicago), Illinois 60646-1975, USA
T 847 679 5500 F 847 679 24941
E mail NTCPUB2@AOL.COM

ISBN 0-8442-4866-5
Library of Congress Catalog Card
Number: 96-72520
Passport Books and colophon are registered
trademarks of NTC Publishing group

Every effort has been made to ensure that
the facts in this Handbook are accurate.
However travellers should still obtain
advice from consulates, airlines etc about
current travel and visa requirements and
conditions before travelling. The authors
and publishers cannot accept responsibility
for any loss, injury or inconvenience,
however caused.

Maps: a number of frontiers in the area
covered by this Handbook are disputed.
Our maps are not intended to have any
political significance or purport to show
authenticated international borders.

Cover design by Newell and Sorrell; cover
photography by Dave Saunders

Production: Design by Mytton Williams;
Typesetting by Jo Morgan, Ann Griffiths and
Melanie Mason-Fayon; Maps by Sebastian
Ballard, Kevin Feeney and Aldous George;
Charts by Ann Griffiths; Original line drawings
by Geoff Moss; Proofread by Rod Gray and
David Cotterell.

Printed and bound in Great Britain by
Clays Ltd., Bungay, Suffolk

Contents

The authors

Anne McLachlan

Anne McLachlan has had a long acquaintance with Morocco and its many experiences, initially helping to manage a series of research expeditions to Tanger and the Sous regions in the 1970s and 1980s. Andalusia is her second home within sight of the Rif Mountains of Morocco. Though deeply involved with travel in the Moroccan south in recent years, with visits to the desert interior and the far south coastlands, she continues to travel throughout the whole country on a regular basis. Anne's background as a professional geographer and geologist enable her to give a particularly sharp insight into Morocco's wonderfully varied landscape and topography. Her lifetime involvement with the Middle East as editor of regional economic and political journals offers strength in these important facets of this large and still far too little known country.

Anne also manages a truly international team of co-researchers who keep the *Footprint Handbook* fully up-to-date from sources in Morocco and elsewhere.

In preparing this volume of the *Handbook* she has visited the growing tourist facilities in southern Morocco, to see the sites where desert 4WD travel vehicles, mountain walking and trekking facilities are increasingly available. A special effort has been put into making more maps, site plans and key information on the Moroccan life style in this edition of the *Handbook*.

Keith McLachlan

Keith McLachlan has travelled widely in North Africa since 1958, when he first traversed the central Sahara and undertook field research into the region's cultural life in desert oases on the rim of the Sahara. He spent his professional career at the School of Oriental & African Studies with a specialism in North Africa and the Middle East, in recent years as head of the SOAS Geopolitics and International Boundaries Studies Centre. Now emeritus professor, he maintains links with the academic community but is giving more time and travel to the *Footprint Handbooks*, including the *Morocco Handbook*.

Keith's interest in Morocco began in a search for Morocco's ancient and famous underground water channels which formerly (and even today in some locations) provide water for home and irrigation. His book *Qanat, Kariz and Khattara* (ed. with Beaumont & Bonine) is still one of the few on this subject. But the remarkable diversity of the terrain and the wealth of Moroccan culture captured a wider and continuing interest. Keith serves on the executive committee of the Society for Moroccan Studies and is a frequent traveller in Morocco, not least in Taroudant and the Sous, his long standing favourite area for relaxation and cultural browsing.

Introduction and hints

THE *Morocco Handbook* is the intelligent guide for both the traveller and businessman in both Morocco and Mauritania. It offers serious attention to the unique nature of these countries together with up-to-date information from a long-term team of professional specialists. The *Handbook* has a wealth of practical information on travel conditions and how to live with them in a minimum of fuss. There is continuous coverage through Morocco and Mauritania in a guide which, though specific to one major country, is highly conscious of the overall regional setting of Morocco in North Africa and the western Mediterranean.

The *Morocco Handbook* makes use of recent and first hand experience in the area to give a thorough picture. It covers with a knowing but light hand the economic and political situations so that the traveller can appreciate the strengths and weaknesses of the country. Importance in the *Morocco Handbook* is laid on understanding the local society as a key to behaviour and practice. Most problems arise from lack of appreciation of local social custom and can be avoided with a little care while there is so much that is fascinating in these very colourful communities for travellers with some knowledge of how things work.

The *Morocco Handbook* contains detailed material on what accommodation is available, both spartan and luxurious. There is information, too, on living with the local environment and climate. Special attention is given to travel conditions and to the requirements of desert safaris. In addition the *Morocco Handbook* contains detailed guides to sites of towns, scenic, historical or gastronomic interest.

The *Morocco Handbook* has a variety of uses – it covers themes as diverse as recreation and topography on the one hand and archaeology/arts/society on the other to enable the traveller to follow not only the standard tourist routes but also to explore off the beaten track either in an organized party or as an individual.

Morocco is a country made for travelling. It possesses an enormous surface area with all the variety of climates and plant life that occurs at the junction of the Mediterranean Sea and the Atlantic Ocean where the Sahara meets with the sub-tropics. To cap it off there is a vast variety of topography from the High Atlas to the deserts in the south – from mountain valleys and coastal beaches.

A wealth of cultures also come together in Morocco. Berbers are present in great numbers as a genuine surviving race with thriving communities. Their crafts, dress and housing is quite different from anything elsewhere in the world. A second world is that of the Arabs, who live as principally an urban and coastal culture in tandem with the Berbers, bringing with them the Arabic language and Islam as a religion. As a bonus, the French colonial legacy is still powerful in the towns. The French language is widely spoken. Morocco thus has elements familiar to Europeans/North Americans, offsetting the exotic local lifestyles.

Tourism in Morocco is a serious business and has been so for a long while. It abounds with good hotels and wonderful travel facilities for sea sports, golf, trekking, mountaineering and desert travel. Morocco has ready and cheap access by air and ship as well as excellent means for internal travel. Overall, this is a vigorous country for the seasoned traveller and a first class introduction to the exotica of Northwest Africa for the novice.

Mauritania is included in the *Morocco Handbook* since it is easily accessed from southern Morocco and forms a natural continuation of Morocco to the south. It is a little-travelled country but is a delight for the serious traveller and a starting point for the west-east trans-Saharan explorer. Its wild beaches and empty inland areas are looked at in detail in the *Morocco Handbook* in what is a unique guide for the visitor to this fragile desert state.

Anne & Keith McLachlan
London

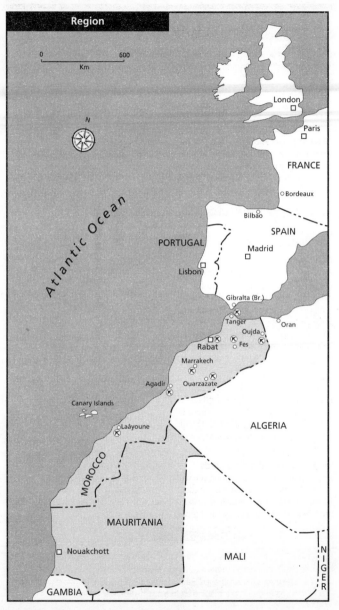

Region

0   600
Km

N

Atlantic Ocean

London

Paris

FRANCE

Bordeaux

Bilbao

SPAIN

PORTUGAL

Madrid

Lisbon

Gibralta (Br.)

Tanger

Oujda

Oran

Rabat

Fes

Marrakech

Agadir

Ouarzazate

Canary Islands

Laâyoune

ALGERIA

MOROCCO

MAURITANIA

Nouakchott

MALI

GAMBIA

NIGER

How to go

General note The advice given below represents a regional summary of more detailed information provided in the **Information for travellers** section of each country entry.

BEFORE TRAVELLING

DOCUMENTS

Passports
All foreign tourists are recommended to have a passport that is valid for the whole of the period of stay. This avoids unnecessary contact with the bureaucracy. Depending on the origin of the passport some countries may require visas. Details are given in each country section.

Special permits
Certain zones, particularly adjacent to borders and in areas of conflict have restricted access and travel there is permitted only with military approval. Details of sensitive areas are given in the relevant country section.

Identity & membership cards
If you are in full-time education you will be entitled to an International Student Identity Card (ISIC), which is distributed by student travel offices and travel agencies in 77 countries. The ISIC gives you special prices on all forms of transport (air, sea, rail etc) and access to a variety of other concessions and services. Contact ISIC, Box 9048, 1000 Copenhagen, Denmark, T (+45) 33939303.

HEALTH
See main section, page 489.

MONEY

Travellers' cheques
TCs can be honoured in most banks and *bureaux de change*. US$ are the easiest to exchange particularly if they are well-known like Visa, Thomas Cook or American Express. There is always a transaction charge so it is a balance between using high value cheques and paying one charge and carrying extra cash or using lower value cheques and paying more charges. A small amount of cash, again in US$, is useful in an emergency.

Some countries have a fixed exchange rate – wherever the transaction is carried out. Other countries have a varied exchange rate and, to a greater or lesser degree, a black market. See the appropriate country sections and be sure you know what you are doing before you get involved.

Don't lose your passport

Keep a firm hold on your passport. Samuel Romanelli carelessly lost his passport and found himself stranded with no resources in Morocco for 4 years. That was, however, in 1787 and things have improved. Read more of his adventures in 'Travail in an Arab Land' recommended in our reading list in **Information for travellers**.

Exchange rates (January 1997)					
	US$	**£**	**Ffr**	**DM**	**Ptas**
Mauritania (Ouguiya)	141.68	236.33	26.08	87.98	0.89
Morocco (Dirham)	9.00	15.02	1.65	5.59	0.07
Spain (Peseta)	134.29	224.00	24.72	83.35	

WHAT TO TAKE

Travellers tend to take more than they need though requirements vary with the destination and the type of travel that is to be undertaken. Laundry services are generally cheap and speedy. A travel-pack, a hybrid backpack/suitcase, rather than a rigid suitcase, covers most eventualities and survives bus boot, roof rack and plane/ship hold travel with ease. Serious trekkers will need a framed backpack.

Clothing of light cotton or cotton/polyester with a woollen sweater for evenings, more northern regions, higher altitudes and the clear desert nights. Comfortable shoes with socks as feet may swell in hot weather. Modest dress for women including (see page 13) a sunhat and headscarf. See hints in country sections.

Checklist

Air cushions for hard seating
Earplugs
Eye mask
Insect repellent and/or mosquito net, electric mosquito mats, coils
Neck pillow
International driving licence
Photocopies of essential documents
Plastic bags
Short wave radio
Spare passport photographs
Sun hat
Sun protection cream
Sunglasses
Swiss Army knife
Tissues/toilet paper
Torch
Umbrella (excellent protection from sun and unfriendly dogs)
Wipes (*Damp Ones*, *Baby Wipes*)
Zip-lock bags

Those intending to stay in budget accommodation might also include:
Cotton sheet sleeping bag
Money belt
Padlock (for hotel room and pack)
Soap
Student card
Towel
Toilet paper
Universal bath plug

Health kit

Antacid tablets
Anti-diarrhoea tablets
Anti-malaria tablets
Anti-infective ointment
Condoms
Contraceptives
Dusting powder for feet
First aid kit and disposable needles
Flea powder
Sachets of rehydration salts
Tampons
Travel sickness pills
Water sterilizing tablets

GETTING THERE

AIR

It is possible to fly direct to several destinations within Morocco from Europe, from the Middle East and most adjacent African countries and additionally from USA, Canada and Brazil. More details are given in the **Information for travellers** sections. General airline restrictions apply with regard to luggage weight allowances before surcharge; normally 30 kg for first class and 20 kg for business

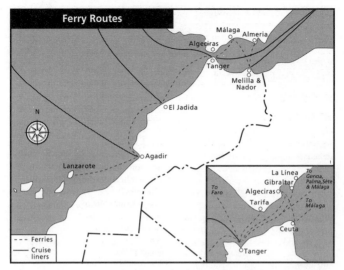

Ferry Routes

Málaga Almeria
Algeciras
Tanger
Melilla &
Nador
El Jadida
N
Agadir
Lanzarote

La Línea
Gibraltar
Algeciras
Tarifa
To
Faro
To
Genoa,
Palma, Sète
& Málaga
To
Málaga
Ceuta
Tanger

--- Ferries
— Cruise
    liners

and economy class. An understanding of the term 'limited' with regard to amount of hand luggage varies greatly. The major destinations are the national capitals and the tourist airports. The scheduled flying times from London are Rabat 2½ hrs, Tanger 2 hrs, and from Paris are Nouakchott 5 hrs. Package tours which frequently offer cheaper flight-only deals generally operate smaller planes which take longer.

Discounts

It is possible to obtain significantly cheaper tickets by avoiding school vacation times, by flying at night, by shopping around and by booking early to obtain one of the quota of discounted fares. Group discounts apply in many instances.

Airline security

International airlines vary in their arrangements and requirements for security over electrical items such as radios, tape recorders and lap-top computers (as does the interest of the customs officials on arrival and departure). Check in advance if you can, carry the items in your hand luggage for convenience and have them wrapped for safety but available for inspection. Note that internal airlines often have different rules from the international carriers.

Note

This *Handbook* outlines further details on air links to and from each country, arrival and departure regulations, airport taxes, customs regulations and security arrangements for air travel in the **Information for travellers** sections.

SEA

Ferries Numerous ferries operate across the Mediterranean carrying both vehicles and foot passengers. Prices vary according to the season. Details are given in the **Information for travellers** sections along with rail and road entry points.

ON ARRIVAL

APPEARANCE

There is a natural prejudice in all countries against travellers who ignore personal hygiene and have a generally unkempt appearance. Observation of the local people will show, where they can afford it, their attention to cleanliness and neatness. The men attend the office in suits with a white shirt and tie or a newly pressed native garment and the women beneath their veil are very well dressed. All persons other than manual workers will be fully dressed. Scantily clad visitors, other than round the hotel pool, show insufficient consideration for their host country. In a hot climate it is eminently sensible and certainly more comfortable to copy the locals and cover the body.

BARGAINING

Bargaining is expected in the bazaars. Start lower than you would expect to pay, be polite and good humoured, enjoy the experience and if the final price doesn't suit – walk away. There are plenty more shops. Once you have gained confidence, try it on the taxi drivers and when negotiating a room (see box, page 28).

BEGGARS

Beggars are a fact of life. It is unlikely that they will be too persistent. Have a few very small coins ready. You will be unable to help many and your donation will most probably be passed on to the syndicate organizer! In the most visited areas of Morocco the tourist police move the mobile beggars on.

CONFIDENCE TRICKSTERS

The most common 'threat' to tourists is found where people are on the move, at ports and railway and bus stations, selling 'antiques', 'gems', offering extremely favourable currency exchange rates and spinning 'hard luck' stories. Confidence tricksters are, by definition, extremely convincing and persuasive. Be warned – if the offer seems too good to be true that is probably what it is.

COURTESY

Politeness is always appreciated. You will notice a great deal of hand shaking, kissing, clapping on backs on arrival and departure from a group. There is no need to follow this to the extreme but handshakes, smiles and thank yous go a long way. Be patient and friendly but firm when bargaining for items and avoid displays of anger. Be very careful never to criticize as officials, waiters and taxi drivers can understand more than you think. See page 28 on how to deal with the bureaucracy. **However** when it comes to getting onto public transport, forget it all and be ready to push.

DRUGS

Ignore all offers of drugs. The Rif area of Morocco is one area particularly noted for this. It is more than likely that the 'pusher', if successful, will report you to the police.

FIREARMS

Firearms including hunting guns may not be taken into any of the countries covered in this book without prior permission.

MOSQUES

Visitors to mosques (where permitted) and other religious buildings will normally be expected to remove their shoes and cover-all garments will be available for hire to enable the required standard of dress to be met.

PERSONAL SECURITY

Travellers are unlikely to experience threats to personal security. On the contrary, followers of Islam are expected to honour the stranger in their midst. However basic common sense is needed for the protection of personal property, money and papers. Use hotel safes for valuable items as hotel rooms cannot be regarded as secure and when travelling, carry valuables as close to the body as possible, and where convenient, in more than one place. External pockets on bags and clothing should never be used for carrying valuables. Bag snatching and pick pocketing is more common in crowded tourist areas. It is obviously unwise to lay temptation in the way of a man whose annual income is less than the cost of your return airfare. **NB** It is wise to keep a record of your passport number, TCs number and air ticket number somewhere separate from the actual items.

POLICE

Report any incident which involves you or your possessions. An insurance claim of any size will require the backing of a police report. If involvement with the police is more serious, for instance a driving accident, remain calm, read the section on how to deal with the bureaucracy (see page 28) and contact the nearest consular office without delay.

PRISONERS ABROAD

Prisoners Abroad, a UK charity, was formed to help people who fall foul of the law in foreign countries, where sentencing can be much harsher than at home. If you or a friend do get into trouble, you can contact Prisoners Abroad at 72-82 Rosebury Ave, London EC1R 4RR, T 071 833 3467, F 071 833 3467 (F +4471 833 3467 if outside the UK).

TIPPING

Tipping in Morocco is a way of life – everyone expects a coin for services rendered or supposed. Many get no real wage and rely on tips. In hotels and restaurants the service has probably been included so a tip to the waiter is an optional extra. It does no harm to round up the taxi fare, and a handful of small coins eases the way.

WOMEN TRAVELLING ALONE

Women face greater difficulties than men or couples. Young Muslim women rarely travel without the protection of a male or older female, hence a single Western woman is regarded as strange and is supposed to be of easy virtue – a view perpetuated by Hollywood. To minimize the pestering that will certainly occur, dress modestly, the less bare flesh the better (see page 21), steadfastly ignore rude and suggestive comments directed at you but aimed at boosting the caller's ego, avoid any behaviour which would aggravate the situation, and keep a sense of humour. Single men often attract greater attention from customs officials and are more liable to receive unwelcome propositions.

WHERE TO STAY

HOTELS

There is a very wide range of accommodation. In the major cities and the popular tourist resorts, the top quality hotel chains are represented. The best offer top class accommodation with the full range of personal and business facilities while the cheapest are spartan and most frequently sordid. Availability of accommodation for visitors varies from country to country. While Morocco is organized in this respect, the traveller in Mauritania will experience greater problems in finding a place to lay his head. The peak season when there is greatest pressure on accommodation varies on the country and the latitude and the relevant country section gives details.

Prices for the top class hotels are on a par with prices in Europe while medium range hotels are generally cheaper in comparison. In almost every case, the advertised room price, that charged to the individual traveller, is higher than that paid by the package tourist and it may be worth bargaining. The six categories used in this *Handbook* are graded as accurately as possible by cost converted to American dollars. Our hotel price range is based on a double room with bath/shower in high season and includes any relevant taxes and service charges but no meals. Normally the following facilities will be available and are therefore not repeated in the descriptions.

Abbreviations in the listings: a/c = air conditioning, T = telephone, Tx = Telex, F = Facsimile. Bath denotes bath and/or shower.

AL US$75+ This is an international class luxury hotel as found in the capital, large cities and major tourist centres. Good management ensures that **all** facilities for business and leisure travellers are of the highest international standard.

A US$75+ An international hotel with choice of restaurants, coffee shop, shops, bank, travel agent, swimming pool, some business facilities, some sports facilities, air conditioned rooms with WC, bath/shower, TV, phone, mini-bar, daily clean linen.

B US$60-75 Offers most of the facilities in **A** but without the luxury, reduced number of restaurants, smaller rooms, limited range of shops and sport. Offers pool and a/c, WC, shower/bath.

C US$40-60 These are the best medium range hotels found in the smaller towns and less popular areas of larger cities. Usually comfortable, bank, shop, pool. Best rooms have air conditioning, own bath/shower and WC.

D US$20-40 Might be the best you can find in a small town. Best rooms may have own WC and bath/shower. Depending on management will have room service and choice of cuisine in restaurant.

E US$10-20 Simple provision. Perhaps fan cooler. May not have restaurant. Shared WC and showers with hot water (when available).

F under US$10 Very basic, shared toilet facilities, variable in cleanliness, noise, often in dubious locations.

Ungraded hotels – too primitive to reach the standard of **F** – but may be cleaner and more interesting than **F**.

CAMPING

Provision varies. It is permitted at certain hostels; enlightened countries have both government and private sites, often with guards; beach camping depends on location and/or gaining permission. Often the difference between a cheap hotel and paying for a campsite is minimal. Assess the security of any site you choose and where possible ask permission to avoid any unpleasantness.

YOUTH HOSTELS

These are found in Morocco as part of the International Youth Hostel Federation. They differ according to location and size, provide a common room, sleeping provision in dormitories, a self-catering kitchen and often budget meals. There is no maximum age limit, persons under 15 should be accompanied by an adult. Permission is necessary to stay more than 3 days in one hostel. Most hostels are open 1000-1200 and 1700-2200. Prices are given in the **Information for travellers** section.

FOOD AND DRINK

FOOD

Restaurants Given the variations in price of food on any menu our restaurants are divided where possible into three simple grades – ♦♦♦ expensive, ♦♦ average and ♦ cheap. Bearing in mind the suggestions in the Health section (page 489) on food best avoided in uncertain conditions, a wide choice still remains. Forget the stories of sheep's eyes and enjoy the selection of filling, spicy and slightly unusual meals. For the less adventurous, Western style food (other than pork) can be found in most hotels.

DRINK

The most common drink is tea without milk, in a small glass, probably with mint. Coffee is generally available too. Bottled soft fizzy drinks are found even in small settlements and are safer than water. Beer and local wine are widely sold. Where available imported wine and spirits are very expensive. *Bottled water* is an essential part of every traveller's baggage.

Wines, beers and spirits in Morocco

Moroccan wines are disappointing in both their limited availability and their quality. The great French tradition of wine-making which established itself so well in Tunisia and, until recently, in Algeria, is but slightly represented in Morocco.

Vines grow well enough in the favourable climate, producing modest amounts of table grapes and a minor volume of feedstock for wine making. Most table grapes were originally grown on a small-scale by Moslems but the main crop for wines was produced by French settler farmers, whose lands have now reverted to Moroccan ownership and to changed cropping patterns that exclude the grape. Moroccan wine output has fallen from more than 1 million hectolitres to less than half a million in recent years.

The Moroccan growing areas are Meknes, Oujda-Berkane and greater Casablanca where abundant water for irrigation and light soils are available. The bulk of Moroccan wine is produced by the Sincomal Company, whose selection is available in most good hotels and restaurants.

Fairly reliable reds are Cabernet Président and Toulal, though both these and other Moroccan reds are on the heavy side. The white and rosé wines are very palatable when taken well cooled.

Moroccan beers – Flag Special, for example, are cheap and light. But keep clear of imported spirits which are very expensive in the major hotels and bars.

WATER

Be prepared for shortage or restriction of water, never regard tap water safe to drink. Bottled water is cheap and easily available. See Health, page 489.

GETTING AROUND

AIR

Domestic airlines link the main towns and run to published but infinitely variable schedules. They are especially recommended to cover the considerable distances and to avoid hot dusty road travel. Safety records vary.

ROAD

Conditions vary from excellent dual carriageways to rural roads and unnerving one vehicle wide and farflung roads which are a rough, unsurfaced *piste*. Problems include blockage by snow in winter, floods in spring and sand at any time.

Buses, the main mode and cheapest means of transport, link nearly all the towns. Air-conditioned coaches connect the biggest cities and keep more strictly to the timetable. Smaller private vehicles require greater patience and often work on the 'leave when full' principle. Book in advance wherever possible. Orderly queues become a jostling mass when the bus arrives. Inner city buses are usually dirty and crowded and getting off can be more difficult than getting on. Sorting out the routes and the fares makes taking a taxi a better option.

Taxis The larger, long distance grand-taxis are good value, sometimes following routes not covered by service buses and almost always more frequent. They run on the 'leave when full' principle and for more space or a quicker departure the unoccupied seats can be purchased. In general these taxis are 25% more expensive than the bus. Inner city taxis are smaller, generally colour-coded, may have a working meter, and can also be shared.

CAR HIRE

Cars can be hired, with varying degrees

of difficulty. They are not cheap and the condition of the vehicles often leaves much to be desired. The problems of driving your own or a hired car are two fold – other drivers and pedestrians.

HITCHHIKING

This is really only a consideration in outlying places not served by the very cheap public transport. Here, eventually, a place on a truck or lorry will be available, for which a charge is made.

TRAIN

Rail networks are limited, are slow and generally more expensive than the alternative – the bus. First class is always more comfortable; offering air-conditioning and sometimes sleeping accommodation. Cheaper carriages can be crowded and none too clean. Train travel offers the advantage of views available only from the track.

LANGUAGE

While Arabic is the official language, many people have as their first language one of the many dialects. Berber and French are widely spoken in Morocco and Mauritania and in all tourist areas some English or French will be understood. Spanish is useful in parts of Morocco. See **Language for Travel**, page 478 for a simple vocabulary.

Radio frequencies

The BBC World Service (london) broadcasts throughout the region. Frequencies are shown below.

| Country | KHz | Transmission times (GMT) | |
		Summer	Winter
Morocco	17705	0900-1615	0700-1615
	15070	0700-2315	0700-2030
	12095	1500-2315	1500-2315
Mauritania	17790	0700-1530	0700-1530
	15400	0430-1130	0445-1130
	15400	1500-2315	1500-2315
	15070	1500-2315	1500-2030

Writing to the editor

Many people write to us - with corrections, new information, or simply comments. If you want to let us know something, we would be delighted to hear from you. Please give us as precise information as possible, quoting the edition and page number of the Handbook you are using and send as early in the year as you can. Your help will be greatly appreciated, especially by other travellers. In return we will send you details about our special guidebook offer.

For hotels and restaurants, please let us know:

- each establishment's name, address, phone and fax number
- number of rooms, whether a/c or air-cooled, attached (clean?) bathroom
- location - how far from the station or bus stand, or distance (walking time) from a prominent landmark
- if it's not already on one of our maps, can you place it?
- your comments - either good or bad - as to why it is distinctive
- tariff cards
- local transport used

For places of interest:

- location
- entry, camera charge
- access - by whatever means of transport is most approriate, eg time of main buses or trains to and from the site, journey time, fare
- facilities - nearby drinks stalls, restaurants, for the disabled
- any problems, eg steep climb, wildlife, unofficial guides
- opening hours
- site guides

Horizons

The people of North Africa principally follow Islam, which is similar to Judaism and Christianity in its philosophical content and Muslims recognize that these three revealed religions (religions of the book *Ahl Al-Kitab*) have a common basis. Even so, there are considerable differences in ritual, public observance of religious customs and the role of religion in daily life. When travelling through Islamic countries it as well to be aware that this is the case. The Islamic revivalist movement has in recent years become strongly represented in North African countries.

Travel, tourism and foreign workers are common throughout the region so that the sight of outsiders is not unusual. Tourists attract particular hostility, however. They are seen as voyeuristic, short-term and unblushingly alien. Tourists have become associated with the evils of modern life – loose morals, provocative dress, mindless materialism and degenerate/Western cultural standards. In many cases these perceptions are entirely justified and bring a sense of infringed Islamic values among many local people, most of whom are conservative in bent. Feelings are made worse by apparent differences in wealth between local peoples whose per head income is US$530 in Mauritania, US$1,030 in Morocco, and foreign tourists living on an average of US$17,500 per head in the industrialized states. Tourists, whose way of life for a few weeks a year is dedicated to conspicuous consumption, attract dislike and envy. Muslims might wonder why a way of life in Islam, seen as superior to all other forms of faith, gives poor material rewards vis-à-vis the hordes of infidels who come as tourists.

The areas where sensitivity can best be shown are:

The dress code

Daily dress for most Moroccans is governed by considerations of climate and weather. Other than labourers in the open, the universal reaction is to cover up against heat or cold. For males, therefore, other than the lowest of manual workers, full dress is normal. Men breaching this code will either be young and regarded as of low social status or very rich and westernized. When visiting mosques, *medressa* or other shrines/ tombs/ religious libraries, men wear full and normally magnificently washed and ironed traditional formal wear. In the office, men will be traditionally dressed or in Western suits/shirt sleeves. The higher the grade of office, the more likely the Western suit. At home people relax in loose *jallabah*. North Africans will be less constrained on the beach where Bermuda shorts and swimming trunks are the norm.

For women the dress code is more important than for men. Quite apart from dress being tell-tale of social status among the ladies of Fes or of

The practice of Islam: living by the prophet

Islam is an Arabic word meaning 'submission to God'. As Muslims often point out, it is not just a religion but a total way of life. The main Islamic scripture is the Koran or Quran, the name being taken from the Arabic *al-qur'an* or 'the recitation'. The Koran is divided into 114 *sura*, or 'units'. Most scholars are agreed that the Koran was partially written by the Prophet Mohammad. In addition to the Koran there are the hadiths, from the Arabic word *hadith* meaning 'story', which tell of the Prophet's life and works. These represent the second most important body of scriptures.

The practice of Islam is based upon five central tenets, known as the Pillars of Islam: Shahada (profession of faith), Salat (worship), Zakat (charity), *saum* (fasting) and Haj (pilgrimage). The mosque is the centre of religious activity. The two most important mosque officials are the *imam* – or leader – and the *khatib* or preacher – who delivers the Friday sermon.

The **Shahada** is the confession, and lies at the core of any Muslim's faith. It involves reciting, sincerely, two statements: 'There is no god, but God', and 'Mohammad is the Messenger [Prophet] of God'. A Muslim will do this at every **Salat**. This is the prayer ritual which is performed five times a day, including sunrise, midday and sunset. There is also the important Friday noon worship. The Salat is performed by a Muslim bowing and then prostrating himself in the direction of Mecca (Arabic *qibla*). In hotel rooms throughout the Muslim world there is nearly always a little arrow, painted on the ceiling – or sometimes inside a wardrobe – indicating the direction of Mecca and labelled qibla. The faithful are called to worship by a mosque official. Beforehand, a worshipper must wash to ensure ritual purity. The Friday midday service is performed in the mosque and includes a sermon given by the *khatib*.

A third essential element of Islam is **Zakat** – charity or alms-giving. A Muslim is supposed to give up his 'surplus' (according to the Koran); through time this took on the form of a tax levied according to the wealth of the family. Good Muslims are expected to contribute a tithe to the Muslim community.

The fourth pillar of Islam is **saum** or fasting. The daytime month-long fast of Ramadan is a time of contemplation, worship and piety – the Islamic equivalent of Lent. Muslims are expected to read one-thirtieth of the Koran each night. Muslims who are ill or on a journey have dispensation from fasting, but otherwise they are only permitted to eat during the night until "so much of the dawn appears that a white thread can be distinguished from a black one".

The **Haj** or Pilgrimmage to the holy city of Mecca in Saudi Arabia is required of all Muslims once in their lifetime if they can afford to make the journey and are physically able to. It is restricted to a certain time of the year, beginning on the 8th day of the Muslim month of Dhu-l-Hijja. Men who have been on the Haj are given the title *Haji*, and women *Hajjah*.

The Koran also advises on a number of other practices and customs, in particular the prohibitions on usury, the eating of pork, the taking of alcohol, and gambling.

The application of the Islamic dress code varies. It is least used in the larger towns and more closely followed in the rural areas.

Islamic diets

Islam has important rules governing what things may be eaten by the faithful. The Koran specifically forbids the eating of the flesh of swine and the drinking of wine. Other rules dictate how an animal may be slaughtered in proper Islamic manner and ban the consumption of meat from any carcass of an animal that perished other than in the approved way. Any food made of animal's blood such as black pudding or boudin is strictly excluded from the diet of a good Muslim.

The ban on wine has been interpreted as a total outlawing of all alcohol. In practice, local traditions have led to relaxations of the ban from place to place. Some areas, such as much of Turkey forbad Muslims from trading in alcohol but not necessarily from drinking it. Indeed the sufi poets used wine as a metaphor for liberty and the ecstasy of truth – and perhaps often as a real stimulant to freedom of the soul! As the poet Hafez wrote:

"From monkish cell and lying garb released,
Oh heart of mine,
Where is the Tavern fane, the Tavern priest,
Where is the wine?"

In Morocco sufism was more a puritanical road to spiritual understanding, especially among the Berbers so that the tradition of wine was never well developed here.

Travellers are unlikely to be disconcerted by Islamic taboos on food. The range of good and palatable foods is infinite (see section of food in **Information for travellers**, page 457). Fasting is a pillar of Islam, as originally of Judaism and Christianity. It demands that Muslims desist from eating, drinking and smoking for the month of Ramadan during the hours of daylight. The Ramadan fast, always followed by the faithful in Morocco, is now rigorously enforced.

tribal/regional origin, decorum and religious sentiment dictates full covering of body, arms and legs. The veil is increasingly common for women moving in public as a reflection of growing Islamic revivalist views. There are many women who do not conform, including those with modern attitudes towards female emancipation, professional women trained abroad and, remarkably, many Berber women or women with genuinely nomadic or semi-nomadic lives such as the Touareg. The religious minorities – Jews in Morocco for example – do not wear the veil. Jewellery (see page 62) is another major symbol in women's dress especially heavy gold necklaces.

The role of dress within Islamic and social codes is clearly a crucial matter for the people of Morocco. While some latitude in dress is given to foreigners, good guests are expected to conform to the broad lines of the practice of the house. Thus, except on the beach or 'at home' in the hotel (assuming it is a tourist rather than local establishment), modesty in dress pays off. This means jeans or slacks for men rather than shorts together with a shirt or tee-shirt. In Islamic places such as mosques, where entry is permitted, or *medressa*, hire *jallabah* at the door. For women, modesty is slightly more demanding. In public wear comfortable clothes that at least cover the greater part of the legs and arms. If the opportunity arises to visit a mosque or *medersa* open to tourists such as the Hassan II Mosque, *jallabah* and slippers are available for hire at the

The inner sanctum – realities of the harem

🦞 Hollywood and the popular image have vested the 'harem' with a fanciful aura that fails entirely to approximate to reality. Perhaps the fact that women in urban great houses and the courts of rulers in North Africa and the Middle East were contained within a protected zone, forbidden to all males but the patron and his eunuch managers, gave the harem a certain mystique to inquisitive Europeans. Architecturally, too, the marvellous apartments with their geometrical *zellij* fascias, spacious rooms and wonderful plaster arches such as the Palace of the Pasha of Marrakech (see page 312) have an alluring atmosphere of quiet and peace. In the same way the gardens set out for the ladies of the harem to take exercise remain fine monuments to the use of sheltered space. The gardens of the harem in the Alcazaba in Seville give an impression of just how serene these cultivated town gardens could be. The romantic side of the harem and those – generally young men of good but undisclosed royal antecedents – who sought to find their loved ones locked within its fortresses is possibly a legacy of the tales of *A Thousand and One Nights*, which early found their way into western literature in romanticized and bowdlerized forms.

In the 19th century a number of European artists such as Delacroix, Roberts and Gleyre were attracted to North Africa by the exotic images of a different and colourful culture. Eugene Delacroix was born in France in 1798 and is known as the most influential French painter of the Romantic School. Before his death in 1863 he had travelled in Morocco and Algeria, accompanying the mission of the Compte de Mornay to the Court of the Sultan of Morocco, which travels inspired a series of heroic paintings such as *The Fanatics of Tangier*. The harem it was, however, that took prime attention, as Paul Lenoir wrote – "... during the 19th century, the harem, the bath and the guard to the seraglio remained amongst the most popular manifestations of Orientalism in painting and literature". Delacroix's *Les Femmes d'Alger* is clear evidence of this abiding passion.

Inevitably it stayed that the Ottoman seraglio and the Islamic harem were widely painted by Europeans in North Africa. Paintings of women in the bath house such as the *Harem in the Kiosk* and the *Moorish Bath* by Gérome did much to give graphic pictures of the subject. In Great Britain, there was also a flurry of orientalist painting, poetry and other literature, with JF Lewis (1805-75) particularly concentrating on the subject of the harem. He travelled in Morocco and Spain and later lived in Egypt for many years. His watercolours have a particular attraction and were widely acclaimed in their day. In addition to *The Hareem* of 1854, pictures like *The Intercepted Correspondence* with its portrayal of richly elaborated backgrounds in the oriental house and images of Islamic domestic action in the harem, set the tone of interest in the West. The works of the European orientalist artists and their romantic preoccupation with women of the seraglio has been roundly attacked by feminists but, for better or worse, remains the dominant influence on mental pictures of the harem.

The harem in Islamic society was and is an urban rich man's way of interpreting the words of the Koran "good women are obedient, guarding the unseen because God has guarded them". In the harem women are kept totally unseen and unable to defile themselves. In all Muslim houses, rich and poor, the women's part of the establishment is forbidden to outsiders, although in many cases in the houses of the ordinary people the harem is no more than a section of the house separated only by an imaginary line or *hoddud* across the floor space. Women themselves, who might circulate throughout the house, withdraw to their quarters when a stranger is about. Even in contemporary North Africa there are women's movements that propagate the notion that the greater the seclusion and veiling of women, the more their purity and religious/social standing. Segregation of men and women in public places is a growing feature of Islamic society: the harem is merely a reflection of that same feature in the rich and conservative. In the geography of the family the male has sole access to the world beyond the door of the house and women must stay within according to the teachings of recent Islamic theologians such as al-Mawdudi.

Of course, the containment of women in a harem also had an important function in a community where purity of ancestry permeated traditional tribal and extended family groups. The worst slur on a man's origins could be eliminated where all the women of the family were kept permanently separated from male company of any kind but that authorized by the senior male. The limitations on a female mixing outside her own house were once defined as "a woman should leave her house only on three occasions – when she is taken to the house of her husband, when her parents die and when she is carried to her own grave".

The harem was populated by the ladies of the house, usually the wives of an extended family. Given that families were large and that any one man could marry four wives, the harem in a noble house would be very large. Additionally, unlimited numbers of concubines could be brought into the harem without benefit of matrimony. The religious sanction for concubinage has always been disputed but it was practised widely regardless of this. The number of women in a harem of a major ruler could be as high as 300. In effect, a large house and its harem even in rural Morocco had a great variety of people within it and women could socialize freely within that group. Similarly, visiting groups of women would be met and entertained by the women of the house.

In Samuel Romanelli's book *Travail in an Arab Land* (see Further Reading on page 471) there is an interesting story of how this custom was used by illicit lovers. The man would visit his loved one's house wearing female dress, leaving women's slippers at the door to indicate that there was a lady visitor. When the husband/father returned, he would see the slippers and, as is the custom, wait outside so that he should not accidentally come across the visitor unveiled. On departure of the 'guest', the husband does not dare to ask who it is who departs, well secluded behind the veil!

A vicarious pleasure in the larger houses and palaces was watching events through a *mashrabia* or wooden grill protecting the women's quarters. By a paradox, it was often the wives of the richest men of traditional social inclination who saw least of the world and who literally saw few visitors, went visiting little themselves and whose only outings were to the *hammam*.

The harem as a Moroccan version of the Ottoman seraglio is no more. But its key elements survive in the main cities such as Fes, Meknes and Marrakech and in small towns throughout the kingdom. Segregation of the sexes in the home is common unless families are thoroughly westernized. A significant number of women are cloistered in their homes and veiled outside it. Women's rights in law are gradually increasing but in traditional households change is very slow, impeded as much by a rising tide of Islamism as by neglect by the authorities.

Meanwhile, the architecture of the Moroccan house continues to reflect the need for exclusive areas for women. Read *The Harem* by Fatima Mernissi (Bantam 1996) for a Moroccan woman's view of her childhood in seclusion and the frustration of the women trapped within the home. A look at the magnificent provision for the women of the harem in the past is still possible at the El-Bahia Palace in Marrakech, where a harem and special quarters for the visir's favourite wife were in use until 1900 (see description and plan on pages 457).

Moroccan Arab geographers: Al-Idrisi – map maker extraordinary

Among the first useful maps of the known world, the Idrisi planisphere and map, was made by Abu Adballah Mohammed Al-Hammudi, known as Al-Idrisi, in approximately 1154 AD when his book *The Pleasure of Excursions* was published. Al-Idrisi was born in Ceuta in 1100 of a noble line reaching back to the Prophet Mohammed. He travelled throughout the Muslim world during his early life, studying in Cordoba, Marrakech and Constantine also venturing to Iberia, France, England and parts of Asia Minor.

In 1145 Al-Idrisi was invited to the court of Roger II of Sicily and was there commissioned to prepare a silver planisphere of the earth, seas, rivers, cities and other natural features. His labours took 9 years, amalgamating all the then available knowledge on the seven parts of the world from Greek, Persian and Arab sources.

Amazingly the maps, though not the silver planispheres, survive to the present day and are still used as sources in long-running arguments about, for example, the original name of the Persian/Arab Gulf. Al-Idrisi died, it is thought, in Ceuta in 1166.

Modern Morocco makes little of its early heroes – Ibn Battuta, Ibn Khaldun and Al-Idrisi – despite the acclaim for them abroad. They serve, however, to remind the traveller in Morocco and the Islamic world that they are heirs to a famous local tradition.

Idrisi's Map of the World - A French version of 1883

doors. Elsewhere full covering of arms and legs and a head scarf is necessary. Offend against the dress code – and most Western tourists in this area do to a greater or lesser extent – and risk antagonism and alienation from the local people who are increasingly fundamentalist in their Islamic beliefs and observances.

Forbidden places

Do not enter mosques in Morocco, except the new mosque in Casablanca. In other places dedicated to religious purposes behave with decorum – refrain from shouting, unseemly laughter and take photographs only when permitted. Outsiders have spent much time and ingenuity in penetrating Islam's holiest shrines. People who are clearly non-Muslim will be turned away by door keepers from places where they are not wanted. Those who try to slip past the guardians should be sure they can talk their way out of trouble !

Good manners

Islam has its codes of other practices and taboos but few will affect the visitor unless he or she gains entry to local families or organisations at a social level. A few rules are worth observing in any case by all non-Muslims when in company with Muslim friends. (i) Do not use your left hand for eating since it is ritually unclean. If knives and forks are provided, then both hands can be used. (ii) Do not accept or ask for alcohol unless your host clearly intends to imbibe. (iii) If eating in traditional style from a common dish, use your right hand only and keep your feet tucked under your body away from the food. (iv) Never offer pork or its derivatives to a Muslim visitor. Buy *hallal* meat killed in accordance with Muslim ritual and/or provide a non-meat dish. Do not provide alcoholic drink.

Religious festivals and holidays

The Islamic year (Hejra/Hijra/Hegira) is based on 12 lunar months which are 29 or 30 days long depending on the sighting of the new moon. The lengths of the months vary therefore from year to year and from country to country depending on its position and the time at sunset. Each year is also 10 or 11 days shorter than the Gregorian calendar. The Islamic holidays are based on this Hejarian calendar and determining their position is possible only to within a few days.

Ramadan is a month of fasting (see below). The important festivals which are public holidays (with many variations in spelling) are *Ras el Am*, the Islamic New Year; *Eïd al-Fitr* (also called Aïd es Seghir), the celebration at the end of Ramadan; Eïd al-Adha (also called Aïd el Kebir), the celebration of Abraham's willingness to sacrifice his son and coinciding with the culmination of the Haj in Mecca; *Mouloud*, the birthday of the Prophet Mohammed.

The Muslims consider Friday to be their Sabbath and services in the mosques on this day are more important and better attended. Holy days and feast days are taken very seriously. The 'day of rest' is Sunday, a legacy from colonial times. Most shops, except those in tourist areas, are closed on that day.

Approximate dates for 1997:

12 Jan	Beginning of Ramadan
8 Feb	End of Ramadan
18 Apr	Festival of Sacrifice
7 May	Islamic New Year (Anno Hegira 1418)
16 Jul	Prophet's Birthday

During **Ramadan**, the 9th month of the Muslim calendar, the faithful abstain from eating between dawn and sunset for the period until an official end is declared to the fast and the start of the festival of the Eïd Al-Fitr. During the fast, especially if the weather is difficult or there are political problems affecting the Arab world, people can be depressed or irritable. The pace of activity in official offices slows down markedly. Travellers have to manage in these conditions by leaving even more time to achieve their aims and being even more patient than usual. If you have a choice, stay out of Morocco during Ramadan and the Eïd Al-Fitr. Travel, services and the atmosphere are all better at other times of year. Travel facilities immediately before and immediately after Ramadan are often very congested since families like to be together especially for the Eïd Al-Fitr.

BUREAUCRACY AND THE POLICE

North Africa is Islamic in religion, oriental in civilization and despotic in political tradition. Governments rule by fear, a culture of populism and political manipulation. They are changed most often by force and violence (see political risks, page 29). Travellers in Morocco should remember these facts in dealing with the local civil and military administrations.

Travellers will not be put off by these 'facts of life'. It is important, though, to adapt to the local ethos and to learn to live with it wherever you are. The quality of the civil service varies greatly throughout the region.

There are a number of quite clear rules in handling situations in these areas:

Avoid trouble The main areas of difficulty affect relations with the bureaucrats, police and other officials. To avoid trouble bear in mind:

(i) Documents: do not lose your passport and ensure that all travel documents are in order. Passports are lost but they are also traded for cash/drugs and officials can be very unsympathetic. Long and often expensive delays can occur while documents are replaced. Keep all forms such as landing cards and currency documents together with bank receipts for foreign exchange transactions.

Caveat Emptor – don't bargain on a bargain

Haggling is a normal business practice in Morocco and Mauritania. Some modern economists might feel that bargaining is just a way of covering up high-price salesmanship within a commercial system that is designed on every side to exploit the consumer who has no legal protection. Even so, haggling over prices is the norm and is run as an art form, with great skills involved. Bargaining can be great fun to watch between a clever buyer and an experienced seller but it is less entertaining when a less than artful buyer such as a foreign traveller considers what he/she has paid after the game is over! There is great potential for the tourist to be heavily ripped off. Most dealers recognize the wealth and gullibility of travellers and start their offers at an exorbitant price. The dealer then appears to drop his price by a fair margin but remains at a final level well above the real local price of the goods.

To protect yourself in this situation be relaxed in your approach. Talk at length to the dealer and take as much time as you can afford inspecting the goods and feeling out the last price the seller will accept. Do not belittle or mock the dealer – take the matter seriously but do not show commitment to any particular item you are bargaining for by being prepared to walk away empty handed. Never feel that you are getting the better of the dealer or feel sorry for him. He will not sell without making a very good profit! Also it is better to try several shops if you are buying an expensive item such as a carpet or jewellery. This will give a sense of the price range. Walking away – regretfully of course – from the dealer normally brings the price down rapidly but not always. Do not change money in the same shop where you make your purchases, since this will be expensive.

Do not bargain on getting a bargain, be content with a purchase that pleases, at a price you are prepared to pay.

(ii) Prices: understand what prices are being asked for taxis, meals and hotels. Do not accept 'favours', like 'free lunches' they do not exist. In Morocco, for example, shop owners will attempt to give you gifts. At best these are used as a lever to get you buy other items expensively or can lead to disputes over alleged non-payment for goods. It is also a matter of discretion how you handle friendly relations with locals who invite you home for a meal/visit. In Libya, only hospitality will be involved and the same will largely be true in Algeria. But in Morocco in particular, commercial or other motives might arise in the form of pressure to buy a carpet, to deal in drugs or to pledge help for a visa to Europe. Be genial but firm in these situations. Or use local ways out – promise to look at the matter *ba'd bokhra enshallah*, ie later!

(iii) Drugs: do not get involved in buying and selling drugs. It is an offence to handle drugs. Penalties can be severe including jail sentences in dismal prison conditions. In Morocco especially *agents provocateurs* can sell drugs and then inform the police.

(iv) Politics: keep clear of all political activities. Nothing is so sensitive as opposition to the régimes. By all means keep an interest in local politics but do not become embroiled as a partisan. The *mokharbarat* (secret services) are singularly unforgiving and unbridled in taking action against political dissent.

(v) Black Market: make use of black market currency only when it is private and safe.

(vi) Driving: keep to driving regulations and have an appropriate international licence. Bear in mind that the incidence of traffic accidents is high and that personal rescue in the event of an accident can be protracted and not necessarily expert.

(vii) Antiquities: trading in antiquities is everywhere illegal. Most items for sale such as 'Roman lamps' and ancient coins are fakes. Real artifacts are expensive and trading in them can lead to confiscation and/or imprisonment.

Keep cool Remain patient and calm whatever the provocation. Redress against officials is next to impossible. Keep the matter from becoming serious by giving no grounds for offence to officials. Be genial and low key. Aggression and raised voices do little to help. Where you feel you are right, be smilingly persistent but not to the point of a break down in relations.

Get help Getting help can often be cheap or free. Start off with agencies used to foreigners, namely travel agents, airline offices and hotels. They will have met your problem before and might offer an instant or at least painless solution on the basis of past experience. They will know the local system and how it works. They act as free translators. Friends who are either locals or who live locally can act as translators and helpers. They will often have networks of family and acquaintances to break through the bureaucratic logjams. Last, and only last, turn to your embassy or consulate. Embassies are there principally to serve the needs of the home country and the host government, not the demands of travellers, though they have ultimate responsibility for official travel documents and, at their own discretion, for repatriation in cases of distress. Treat embassy and consular officials calmly and fairly. They have different priorities and do not necessarily feel themselves to be servants for travellers in trouble.

INTERNAL SECURITY

Political risks are not necessarily higher in North Africa than in other parts of the 'developing world' but they do exist. To an extent the situation of security in each state in the area is tolerable for the individual traveller for most of the time. The following section outlines what signs of difficulty can be spotted to give advance warning of problems.

What to do if unrest occurs

It is wise in circumstances of political uncertainty for a foreigner to be very discreet:

1. Stay in your hostel or hotel.
2. If the telephones are working, get in touch with your embassy or consulate so that your location is known.
3. Conserve any rations you might have.
4. Do not join in any action by locals. Your motives could be misunderstood.
5. Make contact in your hostel or hotel with other foreigners so that you can form a mutual-assistance group.
6. Listen carefully to the advice given by local hostel or hotel officials.

There is no real science for assessing political risks. Any traveller who intends to be travelling in Morocco for a protracted period should check with his/her national authorities on the advisability of visiting the area. In the UK, the relevant Foreign and Commonwealth Office T 0171 2333000 desk will give you the latest assessment from their embassies overseas. If you are deeply concerned, where possible phone your national embassy direct and ask for the press/information officer. Otherwise, take an interest in trends in the countries you intend to visit before leaving home. Some newspapers can be very helpful in this area notably the *Financial Times*, *Le Monde*, and the *International Herald Tribune*.

MAURITANIA

The political fate of Mauritania is closely linked to that of its neighbours, particularly Morocco and the issue of the Western Sahara. A continuing weakness of Polisario will diminish strains on Mauritania from the threat of Saharois ascendancy. Internally, Mauritania is in the course of democratisation which seems to be partially succeeding. The main coastal sites offer the traveller only problems normal in developing countries. Inland, security is less absolute.

MOROCCO

It is an irony that the monarchy in Morocco is in its way far more legitimate as a government than other so-called popular régimes in the region. The king stands as a successor to a powerful tradition of leadership within Islam. The issue of fundamentalism in Islam has less damaging and possibly less serious implications in Morocco than elsewhere in the region. The king transcends the sectional interests of Arabs and Berbers and has separate lines of appeal to the common man and the bourgeoisie. Morocco is none the less politically a vigorous country and opposition movements are also strong. In so far as the king is able to co-opt powerful political interests to his side or to balance rival factions one against the other, he survives. He has acute dilemmas which are causes of instability. The question of the Western Sahara is unsettled, awaiting a UN referendum to gauge self-determination by the inhabitants of the area. Any hint of a loss of the area would be unsettling. The king has to co-operate with the industrialized countries, notably the USA, in order to secure arms, financial aid and diplomatic support. Yet the USA has policies towards the Arabs, including the Iraqis, which are deeply unpopular with the Moroccan masses. Similarly, the régime has to maintain good relations with Western Europe to ensure the flow of investment funds and tourists at a time when some European countries are pursuing policies against their Moroccan migrant workers. Within Morocco, government success or otherwise in job-creation and lifting the standard of living, while also managing to keep foreign creditors and the demands of the IMF satisfied, creates constant strains.

Deep tensions exist, therefore. Riots over costs of food occurred in 1984. There were (mainly orderly) mass street demonstrations in major cities in 1990 at the time of the UN Desert Storm operation against Iraq in Kuwait. Several assassination attempts have been made against the king, though some years ago. Morocco can thus be described as being in a state of stable equilibrium but one where, because of the key role of one individual, the king, rapid change is always possible. In sum, the political risk for the traveller in Morocco is comparatively small if the guidelines above are followed.

The history of North Africa

HUMAN SETTLEMENT IN NORTH AFRICA

Human settlement in North Africa is very ancient, dated as early as 35,000 BC. The region was inhabited by Neanderthal Man – a Caucasoid population, similar to those which were to appear in Asia and Europe at that same time.

The Sahara began to desiccate some 10,000 years ago and divided the Caucasoid populations of North Africa from the Negroid populations of W and Equatorial Africa. The original agricultural mode of production which had been the basis of settlement there was gradually replaced by nomadic pastoralism which, by around 4000 BC, had become the preserve of two groups, the Libyan-Berbers in the E part and the ancestors of the modern Touareg in the W. North African populations, all classified as part of the Hamito-Semitic group which stretched E into Arabia, soon became sub-divided into the Berbers in the W, the Egyptians in the E.

GREEKS AND PHOENICIANS

The North African coastal area became the arena for competition between those Mediterranean civilizations which had acquired a naval capacity – the Greeks and the Phoenicians. Indeed, this became the future pattern and resulted in the history of the region being described in the terms of its conquerors.

Explorers in North West Africa

The exploration of the Sahara came as a by-product of European interest in the NE of Africa of the search for the source of the Nile and in the NW of the great Arab trade routes into the famed city of Timbuktu. Remarkably the first serious attempts to cross the Sahara took place as late as the 19th century when the colonial powers of Western Europe used their new science and industrial power to spread their influence into the 'unknown continent'.

In 1822 the E Sahara was first crossed by a British group of three explorers starting from Tripoli in Libya – Dixon Denham, Hugh Clapperton and Walter Oudney. In the E the first traveller of note was Captain George Lyon who travelled to Tajarhi in 1819 soon after followed by the Scotsman, Alexander Laing, who went from Tripoli to Timbuktu in 1825 but died on his return in 1826. The Frenchman Réné Caillié managed to reach Timbuktu in 1828 from W Africa and returned alive but only after suffering terrible hardships travelling via the great trade route through Arouwane, Taoudenni, Tagounite and Marrakech, a journey of 3,250 km.

Few explorers used Morocco as their starting point since it was thought that the W route around the Sahara was better done by ship than overland. Morocco, too, was regarded as unruly and unpredictable while Libya was well known through a succession of excellent British consuls in Tripoli. Early explorers like Dr Davidson found their medical knowledge no benefit, having to treat hordes of people for their ailments – including the Sultan's harem of 250 women. Davidson eventually left for Timbuktu via S Morocco in 1834 but, like so many European explorers in NW Africa, never finished his journey.

The central Sahara was seen to have more mystery and better route ways – which was certainly true in the sense that there were fewer Touareg tribes with their bandit traditions occupying its hinterland. Morocco came to prominence only with the imposition of French colonial control. Henri Duveyrier (1840-1892) used Morocco as his base in the exploration of the Atlas Mountains and the Touareg country beyond. His researches into the social structure of the Touareg

We do know, however, that the Greek and Phoenician settlements on the coast provoked a response from the nomadic communities of the desert – the Garamantes around the Fezzan in Libya, the Nigritae around Tuwat in modern Algeria and the Pharusii who were located in the Western Sahara. These communities appear to have specialized in warfare based on charioteering and they began to raid the new coastal settlements. At the same time, they also controlled trans-Saharan commerce - one of the major reasons why the Phoenicians, at least, were so interested in North Africa. As a result, they also engaged in trade with the new coastal communities, particularly those created

by the Phoenicians.

The Greeks had begun to colonize the Egyptian and eastern Libyan coastline as part of their attempt to control Egyptian maritime trade. The Phoenicians, by now being harried in their original Lebanese home base of Tyre by the Assyrians and Persians, created a new and powerful maritime commercial empire based on Carthage, with outlying colonies to the W, right round to the Moroccan Atlantic coast at Lixus (Larache).

THE ROMAN EMPIRE

Control of North Africa passed on once again, this time to the rapidly expanding city-state of Rome. Control of the

formed the foundation on which all later work was built. Later Charles de Foucault (1858-1916), a French vicomte and soldier, lived among the Touareg as a hermit. He was highly regarded by the Touareg, translated their language, *Tamashek* into French but ultimately died, murdered by his Touareg servant.

Gerhard Rohlfs (1831-1896) was a German explorer who travelled extensively in the Atlas Mountains of Morocco in 1862-64, in the disguise of a travelling Arab. He had learned Arabic in the French Foreign Legion and successfully crossed the Sahara Desert on a number of occasions. As late as 1930 Michel Vieuchange travelled incognito to Smara (see box on page 405) and the Dane Knud Holmboe wandered through North Morocco through to Libya. His book *Desert Encounter* (Harrap, 1931) is a classic of Saharan exploration.

With the institution of the French Protectorate, the army of occupation undertook systematic exploration of Morocco. Some military expeditions were bent on military conquest and many came to grief in the Sahara like the Flatters expedition which in 1880 was all but wiped out in a sad episode of mismanagement and ineptness ending in cannibalism and death in 1881 in the Algerian Sahara. Slightly later the amazing General Laperrine in service in North Africa in the years 1901-20 organized a mobile camel (mehari) force of a few hundred men and soon made French command of the Sahara complete without, proverbially at least, firing a shot in anger. Typically, however, Laperrine died in the Sahara on a failed attempt at making aviation a new means of desert transport.

There remain, despite the French success in exploration, many areas of extreme S Morocco that the present-day explorer can travel in where few have been before. The arrival of albeit limited numbers of people travelling in 4WD jeeps, however, means that you will have to waste no time in getting out there if you wish to beat the rush of mass Saharan tourism and get a taste of real Saharan exploration. A range of organizations offer travel in the remote desert and mountain areas of Morocco, including *Explore Worldwide*, *Exodus* and *Guerba Expeditions*. (See Rounding up, page 476.)

Ptolemaic Kingdom of Egypt passed to Rome because of Roman interest in its agricultural produce and Egypt became a province of Rome in 30 BC. Cyrenaica had become a Roman province in 74 BC. Conflict with Carthage had begun much earlier because of its interest in Sicily which, for Rome, was of vital strategic importance. Although Carthage was expelled from Sicily in 201 BC, Rome still feared Carthaginian power and the city was eventually razed to the ground in 146 BC, after 3 years of warfare. The fertile plains around the city, a hinterland which had been its agricultural base and part of the Carthaginian Empire, were then converted into the Roman province of Africa. The difficult problem of border security for Roman administrators was solved by creating the *limes*, a border region along the desert edge which was settled with former legionaries as a militarized agriculturalist population. Thus, although the border region was permeable to trade, resistance to tribal incursion could be rapidly mobilized from the resident population, while regular forces were brought to the scene. The *limes* spread W from Egypt as far as the Moroccan Atlantic coast. In S Tunisia, the *limes* were reinforced by a ditch – the *fossia regia*.

By the beginning of the Christian era, North Africa had been organized into four Roman provinces: Proconsular Africa, Numidia, Mauritania Caesariana

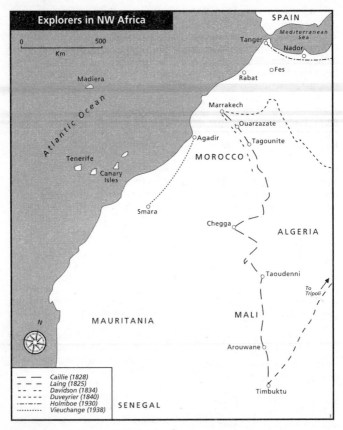

Explorers in NW Africa

SPAIN

Mediterranean Sea

Tanger

Nador

oFes

Rabat

Madiera

Atlantic Ocean

Marrakech

Ouarzazate

oAgadir

Tagounite

MOROCCO

Tenerife

Canary Isles

Smara

Chegga

ALGERIA

Taoudenni

To Tripoli

MAURITANIA

MALI

Arouwane o

N

Timbuktu

SENEGAL

0   500
Km

— — — Caillie (1828)
– – – Laing (1825)
– ·· – Davidson (1834)
– · – · Duveyrier (1840)
– · – · Holmboe (1930)
·········· Vieuchange (1938)

and Mauritania Tingitania. It had also become a major source of food for Rome and a major centre of Roman culture as the sedentary Berber populations themselves were Romanized. North Africa, including Morocco had, in short, ceased to be culturally part of Africa and was, instead, now part of the Mediterranean world. In addition to the commercial and cultural interpenetration of North Africa and Rome, this cultural interaction was intensified by two other factors. First, the region had long been in contact with Greek culture and, indeed, through

the Phoenicians, with the culture of the Levant. Secondly, as a result of the destruction of the kingdom of Judea in 70 AD, large numbers of Jews migrated into North Africa and Judaism intermixed with Berber culture to a significant extent, as contemporary Jewish traditions in Morocco make clear.

CHRISTIAN NORTH AFRICA

North African Christianity became the major focus of the development of Christian doctrine. The Coptic Church became the major proponent of Monophysitism after the Council of Chalcedon in 451 AD; Donatism dominated Numidia; and Tunisia was the home of the greatest of the early Christian fathers, St Augustine. At the same time, official Christianity in Egypt – the Melkite Church – combined with the Coptic Church to convert areas to the S of Egypt to Christianity.

Political evolution, however, did not mirror the growth of Christian influence. In the 5th century, as the Roman Empire crumbled, North Africa was invaded by a Teutonic tribe based in Spain, the Vandals, who by 429 AD, had conquered as far as E Cyrenaica. The Vandal period in North Africa was one of considerable prosperity and apart from religious observance, they to a large extent left North African society to its own devices. The Vandals were no more capable of controlling the desert Berbers than the Romans had been. They gradually lost control of the more distant regions to the major Berber confederation, the Zenata. Mauritania also broke away as an independent state.

Byzantine control, of Tunisia at least, was restored by the Emperor Justinian and his general, Belisarius, in 533 AD. However it was unpopular, not least because of the onerous taxation system necessary to cover Byzantium's heavy military expenditure as it tried to confront the Sassanids in Asia as well as maintain its position in the Mediterranean. Hence when, a little more than a century later, Byzantine rule in Africa was threatened by the expansion of Islam, there was little enthusiasm to support its continuation in northern Africa.

THE ISLAMIC PERIOD

In 642 AD, 10 years after the death of the Prophet Mohammed, Arab armies, acting as the vanguard of Islam, conquered Egypt. To secure his conquest, the Arab commander, Amr bin al-As, immediately decided to move W into Cyrenaica where the local Berber population submitted to the new invaders.

Despite a constant pattern of disturbance, the Arab conquerors of Egypt and their successors did not ignore the potential of the region to the S. Nubia was invaded in 641-42 AD and again 10 years later. Arab merchants and, later, bedouin tribes from Arabia were able to move freely throughout the S. However, until 665 AD, no real attempt was actually made to complete the conquest, largely because of internal problems within the new world of Islam. Then, after two feints SW towards the Fezzan, an army under Uqba bin Nafi conquered Tunisia and set up the first Arab centre there at Kairouan in 670 AD. 4 years later, the Arabs in Kairouan were able to persuade Kusayla, the leader of the Berber confederation which spread right across Tunisia and modern Algeria as far as the Oued Moulouya in Morocco, to convert to Islam. Shortly afterwards, Uqba bin Nafi, in a famous expeditionary raid to scout the unsubmitted areas to the W, swept across North Africa along the northern edge of the Sahara desert as far as the Atlantic coast of Morocco, into the land of the Sanhadja Berbers who dominated the major Western trans-Saharan trade routes.

These early conquests were ephemeral, being based on two mistaken assumptions. The first was that the new conquerors could afford to ignore the isolated Byzantine garrisons along the North African coast, because they would eventually collapse due to their isolation. The Byzantine navy, in fact, supplied them by sea. The second was that the Ommayyad Arab commanders and administrators now imposed on North Africa ignored the promises of equality of treatment given to Berber converts and thus encouraged a major rebellion, led by Kusayla. Arab control of Kairouan was lost and the Arab conquest of the Maghreb had to be undertaken again.

The first Arab move was against Kusayla, who was killed in 688 or 689

Chronology of Moroccan history

10000 BC	Probable first human settlement at Casablanca.
1800 BC	Stone circles set up at sites such as Msoura.
1500 BC	Cave paintings of High Atlas.
1100 BC	Arrival of the Phoenicians at trading posts along the Moroccan coasts and the diffusion of the Phoenician script and new craft skills.
400 BC	The Mauritanian Kingdom established in NW Africa.
149-146 BC	Carthage is destroyed and Rome increases its role in trade and political life in Mauritania (Morocco).
25 BC-23 AD	King Juba II appointed to rule Mauritania from Volubilis.
42 AD	Roman armies occupy the region.
44 AD	Rome assumes control in Morocco as far south as present-day Rabat. Country is named Mauritania Tingitania.
285 AD	Roman withdrawal from south.
249 AD-253 AD	Roman withdrawal to Ceuta and Tanger.
429 AD	End of Roman intervention in Morocco.
683 AD	Arab invasion of North Africa led by Uqba bin Nafi.
704 AD	Tanger conquered by armies of Musa bin Nusayr.
711 AD-732 AD	Arab conquest of Iberian peninsula.
788 AD-792 AD	Idrissid period of settled government.
809 AD	Establishment of the city of Fes by Idriss II.
828 AD-1042 AD	Disintegration of the Idrissid state.
921 AD	Fatimid hegemony in Morocco.
1042 AD-1147 AD	Almoravid Dynasty from Morocco is based in Marrakech under Abdullah Ibn Yasin.
1130 AD-1163 AD	Almohades Dynasty emerged from reformist movement led by Mohammad Ibn Tumart.
1147 AD	Almohades under Abd al-Mumin set up their capital in Marrakech after defeating last of Almoravids.
1184-1199 AD	Yacoub al-Mansur spreads Almohades rule in Iberia.
1213 AD	Almohades defeated in Spain.
1247 AD	Assassination of last of Almohades.
1248 AD	The Merinid Dynasty flourishes in a golden age 1331-1358 but declines thereafter into chaos and corruption by 15th century.
1465 AD	Wattasid visirs run the state.

AD. Then after a further delay caused, once again, by unrest in the Levant, a new army moved northwards against Byzantine centres in Carthage and Bizerta, where the last remaining garrison was defeated in 690 AD. The Arab conquest came up against determined Berber resistance, this time in the Algerian Aures where the core of the Berber Zenata confederation was led by al-Kahina, a Judaized or Christianized Berber priestess. Once again the Arabs retreated to Cyrenaica, returning to the attack only in 693 AD. In 697 AD, al-Kahina was killed and her forces defeated in a battle at Tubna in the Aures which marked the start of a permanent Arab presence in North Africa.

The city of Tunis was founded to prevent further Byzantine encroachment at neighbouring Carthage and, under Musa bin Nusayr, Arab armies swept westwards to conquer Tanger in 704 AD. There they came to terms with the sole remaining Byzantine governor in North Africa, Julian of Ceuta, a Christian potentate who paid tribute to the new Muslim governor of neighbouring Tanger, Ziyad bin Tariq, in order to be confirmed in his post. 7 years later, Ziyad, with help from Julian who had maintained links with the Visigoth rulers of Spain, organ-

1471 AD	Tanger falls to the Portuguese.
1492 AD	Fall of Granada to Castille.
1520 AD	Saadians take control of Taroudant.
1525 AD	Saadians win Marrakech.
1542 AD	Portuguese expelled from Agadir and Safi.
1578 AD	Battle of the Three Kings and the rise to power of Ahmad al-Mansur as leader of the Saadians.
1578-1603 AD	Primacy of al-Mansur. Empire extends into W Africa.
1630 AD	Alawite movement takes over in Tafilalet.
1672-1727 AD	Mawlay Isma'il pushes Spanish back to Ceuta and Melilla. Stops Ottoman Turks in the east.
1817 AD	Corsairing banned.
1844 AD	French army enters NE Morocco in pursuit of Algerian resistance leaders.
1856 AD	Anglo-Moroccan Treaty of Tanger.
1860 AD	Spanish occupation of Tetouan.
1902 AD	French occupation of Touat.
1907 AD	French occupation of Casablanca.
1911 AD	French occupation of Fes.
1912 AD	Imposition of French Protectorate.
1921-26 AD	Rebellion in the Rif under Abd al-Karim.
1929-61 AD	Mohammad V king of Morocco.
1942 AD	WW2, start of Operation Torch as Allied forces land in Morocco.
1956 AD	Morocco becomes an independent state.
1961 AD	King Hassan II comes to the throne.
1969 AD	Spanish withdrawal from Sidi Ifni.
1970 AD	New Constitution promulgated.
1970 AD	Polisario Movement for independence begins in Western Sahara.
1975 AD	The Green March into the Western Sahara.
1978 AD	Mauritania withdraws from Western Sahara.
1989 AD	Morocco joins Maghreb Arab Union (UMA) with Algeria, Libya and Mauritania.
1991 AD	Moroccan contingent in Saudi Arabia with UN Alliance forces to protect Holy Shrines.
1994 AD	GATT Conference in Marrakech.

ized the Muslim invasion of the Iberian peninsula, starting at Gibraltar. By 732 AD, Muslim forces had conquered virtually all of Spain and Portugal and had even crossed the Pyrenees. The Muslim advance was stopped at or near to Poitiers by Charles Martel and, although, for the next 4 years, large parts of Provence were ravaged by marauding Muslim armies, the Muslim presence in Europe effectively ceased at the Pyrenees.

THE EARLY ISLAMIC PERIOD

Despite their victory, the Ommayyads soon became very unpopular in North Africa where the egalitarian and revolutionary doctrines of the kharejite movement – that the caliphate should be elective, that a caliph who failed to uphold Islamic principle could be dismissed by the Muslim community and that sin automatically disqualified those involved from being considered to be Muslims – began to take root. Kharejite missionaries arrived in Kairouan in 719 AD and, within 30 years, the Berbers had become such enthusiastic supporters that they launched a rebellion against the Ommayyads at Tanger in 739-40 AD.

Although the rebellion was crushed,

kharejism survived and, given the difficulties facing the Ommayyads in the Middle East where they were threatened by a new opposition, North Africa was left to its own devices. Ibadi kharejism gained the upper hand in Tripolitania and Sufri kharajism became dominant in southern Tunisia, while the core of Tunisia was left in the hands of the Fihrids, an Ommayyad Arab military caste now effectively abandoned by the Ommayyad caliphate in Damascus. The Ibadis eventually expanded their control throughout Tunisia and forced the Sufris westwards in 758 AD.

In 750 AD, the Ommayyad caliphate was destroyed by the Abbasids who rejected Ommayyad ideas of Arab superiority and supported the early Shi'ite schismatic movement against the Sunni Muslim majority. 8 years later, the new Abbasid caliphate reconquered the old Arab province of *Ifriquiya* (modern Tunisia), but was unable to extend its authority further westward. In any case, the Abbasids did not have the resources to maintain a close control on such far-flung provinces and, by 800 AD, the Abbasid caliph in Baghdad, Harun al-Rashid allowed his governor in *Ifriquiya*, Ibrahim bin al-Aghlab, virtual autonomy. In effect, therefore, the Aghlabites became an independent dynasty in Tunisia until their downfall in 909 AD. The Aghlabites brought prosperity and high culture to Tunisia and, in 827 AD, began the Muslim conquest of Sicily.

The Aghlabites had to share North Africa with three other separate political authorities. After being expelled from Tripolitania, the Ibadis set up a separate state under Ibn Rustam at Tahert in central Algeria, which maintained close links with the Ibadi centre of Basra in southern Iraq. The Sufri Berbers of the Beni Midrar established their own state, based on their control of trans-Saharan trade, at Sijilmassa in southern Morocco. In the heartland of Morocco the Idrisids appeared, a new dynasty which,

although not kharejite in belief, nevertheless was able to capture Berber support by claiming to be directly descended from the Prophet Mohammed. But, because they had supported a Shi'ite rebellion against the Abbasids (who, once they had won control of the caliphate, rapidly abandoned Shi'ism in order to gain support for the Sunni majority) they had been forced to flee westwards into North Africa, an area outside Abbasid control. The founder of the dynasty, Idris bin Abdullah, arrived there in 788 AD. His son, Idris II, founded Fes in 809 AD and the dynasty survived until it was crushed by the Fatimids in 921 AD. Nonetheless, the Idrisids are the original founders of the modern Moroccan state and thus still have an influence even today.

THE GREAT DYNASTIES AND THEIR SUCCESSORS

The failure of the Abbasid caliphate to retain control of North Africa paved the way for a series of local dynasties to take control.

(1) **The Fatimids** The first of the great dynasties that was to determine the future of North Africa did not, however, originate inside the region. Instead it used North Africa as a stepping stone towards its ambitions of taking over the Muslim world and imposing its own variant of Shi'ite Islam. North Africa, because of its radical and egalitarian Islamic traditions, appears to have been the ideal starting point. The group concerned were the Isma'ilis who split off from the main body of Shi'ite Muslims in 765 AD.

The Fatimids took control over what had been Aghlabid *Ifriquiya*, founding a new capital at Mahdia in 912 AD. Fatimid attention was concentrated on Egypt and, in 913-14 AD, a Fatimid army temporarily occupied Alexandria. The Fatimids also developed a naval force and their conquest of Sicily in the

Moroccan Arab geographers: Ibn Battuta – man of myth and miracle

As the Islamic empire settled down after the period of great conquests, there was a surge of interest in all the new peoples and lands now within its boundaries. Beginning in the 9th century learning was formulated by a new breed of Arab Geographers. New maps were drawn of the known world, such as that by Al-Idrissi, and gazetteers of places written up by men like Abu Abdallah Ibn Battuta. Ibn Battuta was born in Tanger in the first half of the 14th century, probably of Berber origin. He was a Muslim and began his travels with the pilgrimage to Mecca in 1325. He wandered the world for a quarter of a century, meeting the elite of theologians, men of science and travellers wherever he went.

He served as a judge in Persia and India and travelled to China as an ambassador for the Sultan of Delhi. He finally returned to Morocco in 1355 bringing his notes of his extensive travels, though these were sadly depleted by his loss of manuscripts during scrapes and adventures. He wrote his excursions as the *Rihla* – a geography/gazetteer of places, myths and miracles. He may be seen as a wonderful story-teller, mingling facts about distant countries with anecdotes and wild fancies. He has tales of killer animals made tame and holy men producing feasts from thin air. Despite the poetic licence shown by Ibn Batutta the *Rihla* is amongst the most comprehensive and entertaining books of its kind and it remains a valuable source of information on a period which otherwise is little documented.

Ibn Battuta underwent a religious renaissance in Delhi when he narrowly escaped death at the hands of a despotic sultan. He increasingly held to Sufi views in which the magical and paranormal were mixed with Islamic theology.

mid-10th century provided them with a very useful base for attacks on Egypt.

After suppressing a kharejite-Sunni rebellion in *Ifriquiya* between 943 AD and 947 AD, the Fatimids were ready to plan the final conquest of Egypt. This took place in 969 AD when the Fatimid general, Jawhar, finally subdued the country. The Fatimids moved their capital to Egypt, where they founded a new urban centre, al-Qahira (from which the modern name, Cairo, is derived) next to the old Roman fortress of Babylon and the original Arab settlement of Fustat.

The Fatimids' main concern was to take control of the Middle East. This meant that Fatimid interest in North Africa would wane and leave an autonomous Emirate there which continued to recognize the authority of the Fatimids, although it abandoned support for Shi'ite Islamic doctrine.

(2) **The Hillalian invasions** Despite

Fatimid concerns in the Middle East, the caliph in Cairo decided to return North Africa to Fatimid control. Lacking the means to do this himself, he used instead two tribes recently displaced from Syria and at that time residing in the Nile Delta – the Beni Sulaim and the Beni Hillal – as his troops. The invasions took place slowly over a period of around 50 years, starting in 1050 or 1051 AD, and probably involved no more than 50,000 individuals.

The Beni Sulaim settled in Cyrenaica, although, two centuries later, factions of the tribe also moved westwards towards Tripolitania and Tunisia. The Beni Hillal continued westwards, defeating and destroying the Zirids in a major battle close to Gabès in 1052.

The Hillalian invasions were a major and cataclysmic event in North Africa's history. They destroyed organized political power in the region and ensured the break-up of the political link between Muslim North Africa and the Middle East. They also damaged the trading economy of the region. There was a major cultural development too for the Hillalian invasions, more than any other event, ensured that Arabic eventually became the majority language of the region.

(3) **The Almoravids** The power vacuum left in the wake of the Hillalian invasions was filled by religious revivalism amongst the Lamtuna tribe, under the influence of a religious scholar, Abdullah ibn Yasin. He transformed the lackadaisical religious observance into a dynamic, inspiring, fully integrated and committed Islamic community. He called his new community the *dar al-murabitun* – the House of the people of the *ribat* (the Muslim equivalent of a monastic retreat, dedicated to preparation for *jihad*), now corrupted to 'Almoravid'. In 1053 AD, the Almoravids captured Sijilmassa.

Religious commitment spurred them on. Ibn Yasin was succeeded by Yusuf Ibn Tashfin who led the Almoravids to victory over most of western North Africa as far as Algiers and over the southern half of Spain between 1060 AD and the end of the century. The Almoravids managed, however, to offend established religious leaders and the Sufi orders (mystical religious orders) of North Africa by their religious intolerance and rigidity. They also failed to check Christian expansionism in Spain. As a result, when a major rebellion against their authority began close to their capital of Marrakech in 1125 AD, it was not long before they were overthrown.

(4) **The Almohads** The Almohads (from *al-muwahhidun* – the unitarians) also began as a religious revivalist movement, this time amongst the Masmouda Berbers of the High Atlas close to Marrakech. They were inspired by a religious leader from the Hargha tribe of the Masmouda, located in the Anti-Atlas mountains, Muhammad ibn Tumart, who was born in 1080 AD. He studied in Spain and the Middle East before returning to Morocco, where he sought support for a revivalist movement designed to purify Islamic doctrine and practice.

The Almohads were organized on a tribal basis and, when Ibn Tumart died in 1130 AD, the most capable tribal leader, Abd al-Mumin, took over. In 1145 AD Abd al-Mumin crushed the Almoravids and, 2 years later, occupied the two leading cities of Fes and Marrakech, the latter of which became the Almohad capital.

The Almohads first moved against the Christian *Reconquista* in Spain, where they held the Christian advance towards Granada and Seville, although the ruler of Murcia managed to remain independent until 1172 AD. The more important move was against the growing threat of the Normans in the central Mediterranean. By 1160 AD, the Almohads had expelled the Normans from North Africa and had united the region under a single political authority.

The Almohad state was sapped by its essentially tribal political structure where those excluded from power had every interest in destroying the state. Also, the cultural environment in North Africa was changing as sufism – Islamic mysticism – became increasingly popular and undermined the religious supremacy of the Almohades. Even worse, the strength of state was sapped by a series of rebellions on its borders. One of the most important in this respect was the long war between the Almohades and the Beni Ghaniya from the Balearic Islands. The result of these problems was the grant of greater freedom to the regional governors in outlying areas while the central authority at Marrakech concentrated on trying to confront rebellious tribes.

In 1207 in *Ifriquiya*, the son of the Almohad governor, Abu Hafs Umar, a close associate of Ibn Tumart, created an independent Hafsid state which governed Tunisia until the Ottoman occupation in the 16th century. In a similar fashion, control of the Central Maghreb devolved on the Beni Zayyan clan of the Beni Abd al-Wad in 1233 AD. However it was the Beni Marin, who created the Merinid state in Morocco, who sealed the fate of the Almohads. The Beni Marin were a Zenata Berber tribe of pastoralists located in the lower Moulouya valley and around Figuig.

(5) **The successor states** The disappearance of the Almohads brought the era of the great unifying North African dynasties to an end. Thereafter power reflected the division of the region, rather than its unity. There was also a change in direction and influence, as Christianity and Europe increasingly dominated the North African horizon, as did the Mediterranean as a zone of conflict. Yet the experience of the Fatimids, the Hillalian invasions, the Almoravids and the Almohads did leave an important monument behind.

In the 14th century Ibn Khaldun, one of the world's earliest and greatest sociologists, investigated the social origins of the great Islamic dynasties. He concluded that their success and decline was based on two factors: one, tribal rulers, supported by the social and ethnic solidarity of their groups, acquired strength and power but, once in power, suffered a loss of collective commitment, undermined by urban life and culture. Within three generations, ruling groups became corrupted and weak so that they were replaced by a new elite of uncorrupted tribes – and it in turn would become effete and itself fall to the next wave of tribal invasion. Ibn Khaldun's theory of the circulation of tribal rulers proved to be a telling and accurate analysis of Moroccan and North African history (see page 121).

The Merinids Merinid expansionism was related to two factors: first a desire to take complete control of Trans-Saharan trade, for the Moroccan route was losing importance to those routes to the E, and, second, to counter growing Christian influence in Spain and in the Mediterranean. In 1291 AD, during the Merinid period, Castilla and Aragon came to an agreement to divide the North African world between them, in terms of commercial and diplomatic penetration. Castilla concerned itself exclusively with Morocco, while Aragon, by now the dominant trading power in the western Mediterranean, handled the Hafsids and the Zayyanids. The Merinids feared that they would not be able to exclude direct Castillian interference nor protect the remnants of the Muslim Empire in Spain. Indeed, all that was left was the Nasrid state in Granada which had been founded in 1238 AD and was to provide a final flowering of Islamic art in Spain. The Nasrid state was a useful buffer for the Merinids, although the Nasrids themselves were very ambivalent about Merinid support and often allied themselves with Christian powers for protection.

In the end, the Merinid state could not support such expansionist policies and their internal quarrelling made them easy prey for Portuguese aggressiveness. When Portugal occupied Ceuta in 1415 AD, Merinid prestige immediately declined and over the next 50 years the situation worsened as the Merinids faced threats from the Portuguese and their successors, the Wattasids (their former visirs).

They also had to face a new development in Morocco, the rapid growth of the Sufi cults which had developed in power and prestige after the discovery of the tomb of Idris II in 1437 AD. Political legitimization now increasingly became a function of Sharifian descent (genealogical descent from the Prophet Mohammed) or of attachment to a Sufi order. The Merinids and the

Wattasids failed both tests and, when the Portuguese occupied Ksar al-Kabir in 1458 AD, Tanger in 1471 AD, Larache in 1473 AD and Azzemour in 1486 AD, the final collapse of the dynasty was merely a matter of time. The Merinid role as defenders of the state had been taken up by Sharifian and Sufi groups. It was the latter who ultimately took over the state.

The Hafsids The new Hafsid state saw itself as the legitimate successor to the Almohads and its ruler as caliph. The claim was widely accepted, even in the Middle East, because the foundation of the Hafsid state coincided with the Mongol invasions which destroyed Baghdad and the last vestiges of the Abbasid caliphate in 1250 AD. But in reality, the Hafsid state lacked the social and political cohesion of its predecessor. Thus its long history was marked by the constant interplay of internal conflict between different members of the Hafsid family and with Arab and other tribal leaders who sought supreme power. Like the Merinid state, it also had to integrate increasing numbers of Muslims and Jews emigrating from al-Andalus.

It had to deal with an ever greater Christian threat. This came in two forms: direct aggression, such as the 8th crusade, led by the French King Louis IX, which besieged Tunis unsuccessfully in 1270 AD, and commercial penetration. In the early part of the 13th century, the great Italian trading cities of Pisa, Genoa and Venice, together with the French of Provence, obtained trading and residence rights in *Ifriquiya*. The most important example of commercial penetration came from Aragon. The Aragonese had created a major trading empire in the Western Mediterranean and, after 1246 AD, Aragon had an ambassador in Tunis, the Hafsid capital. This was followed by mercantile representation after 1253 AD. After Aragon annexed Sicily in 1282 AD, this commercial hegemony was backed by military dominance as well.

By 1318 AD Aragonese influence was on the wane and Hafsid fortunes revived. The Hafsid state was, nonetheless, a Mediterranean state rather than one with its attention directed towards Africa or the Middle East. Its finances increasingly depended on piracy. By the end of the 15th century Hafsid influence had declined once again. Spain, the new threat to the Mediterranean Muslim world, annexed Tripoli in Libya and Bejaa in Western Algeria in 1510 AD, as the first move in a widening penetration into the Maghreb. The Hafsids lingered on until 1574 AD, when the Ottoman Turks destroyed their state.

The Zayyanids The Zayyanid state, based at Tlemcen, was always a buffer between the Hafsids and the Merinids. It suffered from internal struggles for leadership among the three Zenata tribes that dominated it; it controlled a major trans-Saharan trade route; and it was dominated, first by the Merinids and later by the Hafsids. The Zayyanids, like the Hafsids, could not resist the Ottoman invasion of North Africa and disappeared at the start of the 16th century.

THE OTTOMANS IN NORTH AFRICA

The arrival of the Ottomans in North Africa was the last invasion of the region before the colonial period began in the 19th century.

EVENTS IN MOROCCO

The 16th century was dominated by events outside the Ottoman sphere of control. The Merinid state in Morocco eventually collapsed when confronted with a Sharifian Dynasty, the Saadians, who conquered Marrakech in 1525 and Fes 29 years later. They were able to resist too close an Ottoman embrace, particularly after Portuguese influence was eliminated. Morocco became, under the

Sadis, a powerful Muslim state entering into close relations with other nations, even in Europe, where a close relationship developed with Elizabethan England. The matter of trans-Saharan trade was resolved by the Saadians conquering Timbuktu, the S terminal of the traffic and the African Empire of Gao. A 4,000-strong army, of which half were Christians, took Timbuktu in 1591 and for the following 30 years Morocco controlled the southern gold trade. The conquest was abandoned in 1618 AD.

The Saadian Dynasty fell into decline and political power in Morocco was seized by a series of powerful Sufi orders. The result was the growth of a series of petty states ultimately overwhelmed by the Alawite Dynasty. The Alawites were a Sharifian community that had been living in Sijilmassa since the 13th century.

Mawlay Isma'il, who reigned until 1727, set the Alawite state on firm foundations. He removed the European presence from the Moroccan coastline, except in Ceuta and Melilla, and forced back Turkish incursions from the E. He based his claim to power on his Sharifian status, a claim which has been astutely exploited by his predecessors to underpin their legitimacy, even when much of Morocco – the *bilad as-siba* – lay outside the area under their control – the *bilad al-makhzan*. The Alawite success was to be enduring, for the dynasty still rules Morocco today.

During the remainder of the 18th century, the Alawites concentrated on retaining their power. The Sultanate had to ensure that Turkish ambitions to expand into eastern Morocco were curbed and come to terms with the growth of European power. By the start of the 19th century, the Sultanate abandoned its traditional support for corsairing, banned in 1817, just one year

Pirates of Barbary

The pirates of Barbary occupy a notable place in the annals of Mediterranean life and history. The pirates of Morocco were slightly less well known than the famous names such as Dragut and Barbarossa who worked out of Algiers and Tunis. Even Tripoli in the days of the Karamanli pashas and their corsair ships attracted reprisals from the USA. Morocco had its moments, however, as important for piracy in the 19th century, especially in the period 1830-60. The pirates lived off the commercial shipping moving across the Mediterranean Sea. It was an easy prey – largely unarmed and justified by the Muslim corsairs on grounds that the traders were infidels and thus fair game.

Moroccan pirates were particularly effective against coastal Spanish shipping travelling to Melilla on the southern Mediterranean shore and to the nearby ports. Some 80 Spanish ships were attacked in 1856 to the fury of the Spanish governor of Melilla. Virtually any ship becalmed off the Rif coast drifted haplessly into the pirate coast and made seizure of cargo vessels an undemanding occupation. The Moroccan government was far from the country's northern coast and was in no position to end piracy, even if it wished (which is doubtful). Meanwhile, the French were struggling to keep British influence out of Morocco and the rivalry of these two states meant that no coordinated action was taken against the pirate havens. Finally, it was the Moroccan central government in the late 19th century, pressured by the maritime powers who ended piracy by controlling the ports from which the corsairs sailed.

As travellers will see for themselves, the Rif coast with its tall cliffs and hidden bays looks still to be wonderful 'pirate' country.

after the last Christian slaves had been released. A few years later came France's invasion of Algeria and, in 1844, Morocco was defeated by French troops pursuing the great Algerian resistance leader, the Emir Abd al-Qadir. The defeat was a tremendous shock to Morocco, as its leaders realized they could no longer ignore the European threat. From their base in Tangier, the European consuls made ever greater demands on the Sultanate for commercial contact and, in 1856, Britain and Morocco signed an open-door treaty.

Spain, still present in her enclaves of Ceuta and Melilla, resented British influence over the Sultanate and 4 years later, on the pretext of tribal incursions into its territory, successfully fought a short border war with Morocco. Although the Sultanate survived, in 1880 it was forced to permit extra-territorial rights to Moroccan citizens employed by the European powers – the so-called 'protegé' system.

By the start of the 20th century a new sultan, Abd al-Aziz, was on the throne. Reform was once again being looked for under pressure from the British. The 1903 reforms provoked resistance throughout Morocco and in any case by 1904, the British had agreed to leave Morocco in French hands. Events accelerated as Morocco incurred foreign debt and mortgaged its customs revenues to pay off the loans. France, at that stage, began a slow penetration into Moroccan territory. Touat was occupied in 1902, Casablanca in 1907 and Fes in 1911. In every case, furious tribal resistance to French moves only provoked further French advances. Spain, too, began to move into northern Morocco, a zone allocated to her by a secret agreement with France in 1904. The Treaty of Fes of 1912 instituted a Franco-Spanish 'protectorate' over the state.

THE OTTOMAN OCCUPATION

The Ottoman occupation of North Africa was a by-product of Ottoman-Venetian competition for control of the Mediterranean, itself part of the boundless expansionism of the Ottomans once they had conquered Constantinople in 1453. The Ottoman attack was 2-pronged, involving their newly acquired maritime power to establish a foothold and then backing it up with the janissary, land based forces that formed the empire's troops. The decrepit Mamluk Dynasty in Egypt fell to the Ottomans in 1517 and a new, centralized Ottoman administration was established there.

Ottoman interests were soon attracted westward and a maritime campaign was launched on the North African coastline. It was carried out mainly by privateers, attracted both by the religious confrontation between Christian powers in Southern Europe and Islam in North Africa and by the growing practice of corsairing. In the wake of the *Reconquista* in 1492, Spain began to prepare for a veritable crusade against North Africa. 2 years later Spain and Portugal, with Papal blessing, divided their future spheres of influence in North Africa between them and, 3 years later, the Spanish occupation began with the conquest of Melilla.

The Ottoman moves on North Africa were precipitated by the privateering activities of the Barbarossa brothers, Uruj and Khayr al-Din. The Ottomans eventually occupied Tunis permanently in 1574. Before this, however, they had gained a hold over Libya. Khayr al-Din Barbarossa occupied Tajura, on the coast close to Tripoli, in 1531 and was consequently able to threaten the precarious hold of the Knights of the Order of St John of Jerusalem on Tripoli itself. They had just occupied Tripoli and Malta at the request of Charles V of Spain, but were forced out of Tripoli altogether by the Ottomans in 1551. For

270 years North Africa, except for Morocco, was an Ottoman preserve.

COLONIALISM IN NORTH AFRICA

The colonial experience throughout North Africa took many different forms. It involved four European states: Britain after WW2, in part of Libya; Italy in Libya up to WW2, together with residual interests in Tunisia; Spain in northern Morocco and in the Sahara desert to the S of the country; and France, which controlled Tunisia, Algeria and most of Morocco, as well as the southern part of Libya after WW2. Colonialism took different forms, as well. In Algeria and Libya full colonial occupation was instituted, with a degree of integration into the administration and political structures of the metropolitan power. In Tunisia and Morocco, a form of protectorate was instituted whereby the colonial power was present as a tutor, with the object of modernizing political structures and the economy before restoring full Independence.

Colonialism came to Morocco far later than it did to its two Maghrebi partners. Indeed, the colonial period only lasted 44 years in Morocco and the country was not fully pacified until

Lyautey – a Frenchman in Morocco

The Moroccans and the French share a love-hate relationship of each other. The Moroccans dislike the memory of the colonial yoke imposed by France in the 19th century and resent the immense intrusion both economically and culturally of France in present day affairs. Yet many educated Moroccans speak French almost as a first language and look to France as a source of political inspiration. More than a million Moroccans work in France. This paradox can be attributed to the first half of the 20th century and the formidable military figure – Marshal Hubert Lyautey (1854-1934), first French Resident General in the years 1912-25.

Hubert Lyautey was born in Alsace. He suffered from a spinal deformity caused by a fall in childhood but that never impeded his progress as an army officer and as a social reformer. His career in North Africa began in Algeria in 1880. It was not until he had served in France, Italy and Indochina that he moved to North Africa again in 1903. His first contact with Morocco was in putting down border raids by tribal groups into Algeria. There he occupied part of Béchar and refused to withdraw despite orders to do so from Paris. He remained a man of action and moral principle, deeply committed to civilizing North Africa and Morocco in particular. He saw his mission as bringing peace and security to the Moroccan people, which he was able to achieve during the occupation of Morocco which began in 1912. In that year the French established a protectorate over Morocco under the terms of the Treaty of Fes of 30 March. He faced a serious military situation with the city of Fes under siege by tribesmen. He defeated the insurgents after bitter house-to-house fighting and, with a free hand from Paris, eventually set up a working administration for the whole of Morocco.

His main weapons were security and freedom for the local population. He was a great success in Morocco, laying down a civil service, legal system, transport network and all the infrastructure of a 20th century state, modernizing while retaining the best of the old. His legacy in Morocco was considerable and many of the institutions of contemporary Morocco date from Lyautey's time. He is criticized for introducing the inflexibilities of the French bureaucratic service to Morocco but he deserves praise for his honesty, even-handedness and dedication during his time in Morocco where he was for 12 years the effective ruler.

1934, just 22 years before Independence was granted. In addition, the initial colonial experience was less severe in Morocco than in either Tunisia or Algeria, largely because it was carefully controlled by one man, Marshal Hubert Lyautey (see box, page 45). Apart from a short break during WW1, he remained in charge of Morocco until his final recall in 1925. Lyautey was determined to preserve traditional Moroccan political institutions whilst modernizing them and tried to avoid major violence in pacifying tribal rural Morocco, preferring instead a mixture of coercion and persuasion. Nonetheless a 500,000-strong settler colony, controlling around 800,000 ha of land eventually formed in the French zone of Morocco.

Northern Morocco, was occupied by Spain and the Spanish army experienced serious difficulties in controlling

---

The Spanish enclaves in North Africa

Just as the Arabs had swept into the Iberian peninsula during their great period of expansion (711-1212 AD), the Spanish *Reconquista* (1212-1492) had a momentum that, along with the growing wealth of the Spanish Empire, led it into a crusade into Africa. In 1492 the King of Castille permitted the Duke of Medina Sidonia to claim West Africa by force of arms. Imperial ambitions were mixed with religious expansionism against the Muslims. As a result of these aims, Spanish military expeditions seized a variety of cities and towns along the North African coast – Algiers, Asilah, Bugie, Larache and Tripoli. In practice, Spanish attention moved rapidly away from Africa to the New World of the Americas and ultimately the Pacific Ocean. Only five minor holdings remained in North Africa – Ceuta, Melilla, Peñon de Velez de la Gomera (Badis), Peñon de Alhucemas (al-Nakur) and Islas Chafarinas, the latter three being no more than groups of islets. Politically and culturally, these *presidios* became largely detached from Morocco and survive as little fragments of provincial Spain in Africa (see Ceuta, page 135 and Melilla, page 162).

The effective integration of the five *presidios* into metropolitan Spain has not prevented the contemporary Moroccan state from reviving claims to sovereignty, using the same arguments for change that Spain itself deploys into its claim to Gibraltar from the British, including historic rights. The people of the Moroccan Rif have their own tribal and traditional claims to the enclaves, bred by 400 years of episodic warfare against the Spanish fortresses.

That the Moroccan struggle for repossession of the *presidios* has been muted is only explicable by understanding that, first, Morocco has its hands full already in the territorial conflict with the Polisario in the Western Sahara and, second, that the Government of Morocco has more important political objectives in Western Europe than fighting for the small prize of the Spanish enclaves. A close relationship with the EU is vital if Morocco is to continue to achieve rapid economic growth and construction of a permanent crossing of the Strait of Gibraltar would certainly be impossible if a major dispute were to exist with Spain. There is some gratification for Morocco in the changing demography of Ceuta in particular, where the element of Arab-Berber ethnic stock is growing quite rapidly while the number of those of Spanish extraction permanently resident in the enclave is static or falling.

Meanwhile, Spain is happy to hold on to its *presidios*, since Ceuta is still a major national port and the five possessions as a whole give Spain a very strong strategic influence over the world's third most busy strait.

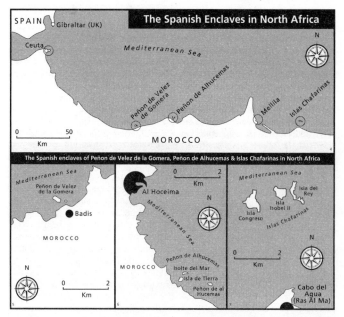

The Spanish Enclaves in North Africa

The Spanish enclaves of Peñon de Velez de la Gomera, Peñon de Alhucemas & Islas Chafarinas in North Africa

the Rif. In 1921, a major anti-colonial war broke out under Abd al-Karim, which eventually required a combined Franco-Spanish army of 500,000 to suppress it in 1926. The last embers of resistance in the Spanish zone were put out only in 1927. Spain was also granted control of the southern Moroccan province of Tarfaya under a 1904 agreement with France but effectively occupation of this and the Western Sahara took place only after 1934.

In the aftermath of the Rif War, the first stirrings of nationalist resistance appeared. The movement sprang into public prominence in 1930. WW2 and the Allied occupation of Morocco in 1942 had ended the myth of French omnipotence and in 1944, with secret support from the Sultanate, Istiqlal, a movement demanding full Independence, was formed.

Riots in Casablanca in 1947 persuaded Sultan Mohammed V openly to support Istiqlal; which he did during a speech in Tanger. Popular support for Independence and for the Sultan as the symbol of Morocco's political integrity burgeoned, and in Mar 1956, Morocco became an independent state. Spain hurried to follow the French example, retaining control only of its towns on Morocco's Mediterranean coast, the enclave of Sidi Ifni (which it abandoned in 1969) and the colony of the Western Sahara which, it claimed, had never formed part of Morocco historically.

Until 1960, **Mauritania** had no independent national existence. Instead it was traditionally divided between the nomadic populations of the Sahara desert and the sedentary populations of the Senegal River valley. Population pressures in the Sahara had, however, consistently forced excess population northwards into Morocco. Indeed, as with the Lamtuna in the 11th century, these northward migrations could have profound political significance, for it generated the empire of the Almoravids. The Zenata Berber tribes of the Sahara were intermingled from the 13th century onwards with Arab migrants, particularly the Beni Hassan. These Arab tribes effectively Arabized the Saharan populations and gave them their characteristics as the Moors of Mauritania. By the 17th century, the Arab tribes dominated their Berber neighbours and in 1674, the latter were symbolically subjugated to their Arab victors as Zawaya tribes.

For the history of the region after Independence, see individual country entries: Morocco, page 84; Mauritania, page 412.

Wildlife

The area covered by the book divides itself into two climatic regions, the Mediterranean and the Desert, with transitional areas between the two extremes. Within these zones, however, is a wide variety of habitats. The sea areas may be enclosed like the Mediterranean, or subject to tidal influences as in Atlantic Morocco. Coastal wetlands include deltas, salt marsh and estuaries, while inland lakes and reservoirs provide freshwater sites. The *maquis* and the *garrigue* contrast with the agricultural areas, while mountain ranges such as the Atlas provide their own climate, delaying flowering and shortening seasons. Even the desert areas provide contrasts with the sands (*erg*), gravels (*reg*) and rock (*hammada*) interspersed with the occasional oasis.

Many of the habitats mentioned above are under threat, either from pollution, urbanization, desertification or advanced farming techniques. Fortunately, in some countries such as Morocco, the conservation movement is gaining pace and many National Parks and Nature Reserves have been created and programmes of environmental education set up. In other countries, regrettably, wildlife is still regarded as a resource to be exploited, either for food or sport.

In both the Mediterranean and Desert regions, wildlife faces the problem of adapting to drought and the accompanying heat. The periods without rain may vary from 4 months on the shores of the Mediterranean to several years in some parts of the Sahara. Plants and animals have, therefore, evolved numerous methods of coping with drought and water loss. Some plants have extensive root systems; others have hard, shiny leaves or an oily surface to reduce water loss through transpiration. Plants such as the *broom* have small, sparse leaves, relying on stems and thorns to attract sunlight and produce food. Animals such as the *addax* and *gazelle* obtain all their moisture requirements from vegetation and never need to drink. Where rain is a rare occurrence, plants and animals have developed a short life cycle combined with years of dormancy. When rain does arrive, the desert can burst into life, with plants seeding, flowering and dispersing within a few weeks or even days. Rain will also stimulate eggs to hatch which have lain dormant for years. Many animals in the desert areas are nocturnal, taking advantage of the cooler night temperatures, their tracks and footprints revealed in the morning. Another adaption is provided by the *sandfish*, which is a type of skink (lizard) which 'swims' through the sand in the cooler depths during the day. Perhaps the most remarkable example of adaption is shown by the *camel* (see box, page 432). Apart from its spreading feet which enable it to walk on sand, the camel is able to adjust its body temperature to prevent sweating, reduce urination fluid loss and store body fat to provide food for up to 6 months.

MAMMALS

Mammals have a difficult existence throughout the area, due to human disturbance and the fact that many of the species are not well adapted to drought. Many have, therefore, become nocturnal and their presence may only be indicated by droppings and tracks. Some mammals common in northern Europe can, nevertheless, be seen in the Mediterranean environments and these include *fox*, *rabbit*, *hare*, Red, Fallow and Roe *deer* and at

least three species of *hedgehog*. Despite widespread hunting, *wild boar* are common wherever there is enough cover in deciduous woodlands. *Hyenas* and *jackals* still thrive in many areas, but the attractive *fennec* is frequently illegally trapped. Typical woodland species include the *red squirrel* (the grey variety from North America has not been introduced), *garden dormouse*, which readily hibernates in houses, *pine* and *beech martens* and the *polecat*. The cat family, once common, is now rare, but the *lynx* hangs on in some areas. The *leopard*, once formerly common, is now extremely rare, but is occasionally seen in some isolated regions, to the panic of local people. There are at least three species of *gazelle* in North Africa, the Dorcas Gazelle preferring the steppes, the Mountain Gazelle inhabiting locations over 2,000m especially where there is juniper forest, and the Desert Gazelle locating in the *reg* of the northern Sahara. There are over 30 species of *bat* in the area, all but one – the Egyptian Fruit Bat – being insectivorous. Recent ringing has shown that bats will migrate according to the season and to exploit changing food sources. Many species of bat have declined disastrously in recent years due to the increased use of insecticides and disturbance of roosting sites. Desert rodents include the large-eyed *sand rat*, the *gerbil* and the *jerboa*. Many, sadly, find themselves in pet shops.

REPTILES AND AMPHIBIANS

Tortoises are widespread in North Africa. The best distributed is *Hermanns tortoise* which can reach a maximum size of 30 cm. *Pond terrapins* are small fresh water tortoises and can be found in all the Mediterranean habitats. Both tortoises and terrapins are taken in large numbers for the pet trade. There are over thirty species of lizard in the area, the most common being the *wall lizard*, which often lives close to houses. *Sand racers* are frequently seen on coastal dunes, while

Birdwatching in Morocco

👣 For birdwatchers, Morocco must be the nearest thing to heaven. There is a great variety of habitats in this large country, craggy coasts, sandy coasts, remote islands, lakes and wetlands and deserts of stone and sand, forests and scrub, plains and mountains so it is not surprising that the list of bird species seen here is one of the longest produced for any European or Mediterranean country. A number of companies produce specialist tours for ornithologists (see Rounding up, page 476).

Sea coast (map locations 5, 6, 7, 17) As the coast of Morocco extends for over 3,500 kms, spans a considerable latitude and includes a range of habitats from inaccessible rugged cliffs through lagoons and salt marsh to extensive sandy beaches opportunities for observing sea birds and associated waders abound. Look out for – Marbled Duck, Moroccan Cormorant, Crested Coot, Turnstone, Ringed Plover and Oyster Catcher (both winter visitors), Audouin's Gull, White-eyed Gull, Sandwich Tern, Redshank, Dunlin, Black-bellied Plover and Eleonar's Falcon which breed on sea cliffs near Essaouira.

Wetlands and lagoons (map locations 3, 5, 11 and 12) are very popular for birds and watchers alike. In the reeds at Oued Massa look out for – Reed Warblers, Herons and Crakes and the Bald Ibis (should you be so fortunate), Greater Flamingo, Coot, Pochard and Osprey coming as winter visitors, White Storks, Spoonbills, Avocets, Ruddy Shelduck, Terns and the Black-headed Bush-Shrike. At the mouth of Oued Sous further finds could include Audouin's and Slender-billed Gulls, Roseate and Lesser Crested Terns.

High Atlas (location 8) offers in addition to splendid views sights of the Red Billed and Alpine Chough, Lammergeier, Black Redstart, Shore and Horned Lark, Dipper, Booted Eagle and Golden Eagle which both nest here, Goshawk and Crimson-winged Finches.

The Cedar Forest (location 4) provides opportunities to see the Great Spotted or Pied Numidian Woodpecker, Scops Owl, Short-toed Eagle, Red Crossbill, Long-legged Buzzard, Levaillant's Green Woodpecker, Moussier's Redstart, Short-toed Treecreeper and the tiny Firecrest and Blue Tit, both resident breeders.

The Argan Forest (location 13) only found in Morocco (and Mexico) is the habitat of the Crested Lark, Moussier's Redstart, Barbary Partridge and raptors such as Tawny, Short-toed and Booted Eagle, Dark Chanting Goshawk and Lanner.

Mamora Forest (location 1) between Rabat, Kenitra and Meknes an excellent spot for those with business in the capital but a little time to indulge in birdwatching. Look out for Roller and Spotted Fly Catcher both summer visitors, Turtle Dove which visits here to breed, Hoopoe, White Stork, Black-Headed Bush Shrike, Black Shouldered Kite an uncommon resident and other raptors.

The **Desert/Steppe** border provides a surprisingly long list of birds to see. Barbary Partridge, Houbara Bustard, Red-rumped, White-crowned Black and Desert Wheatear, Temminck's Horned Lark, Black-bellied, Crowned, Pin-tailed and Spotted Sand Grouse, Trumpeter Finch, Cream-coloured Courser, Dupont's Lark (the least common lark in Morocco), Hoopoe Lark, Blue-cheeked Bee-eater.

Desert regions have a surprising amount of animal life. Mourning Wheatear, Hoopoe Lark, Barbary Partridge, Desert Sparrow, Desert Warbler, Desert Wheatear, Desert Lark, Bar-tailed Desert Lark, Desert and Red-rumped Wheatear, Desert Eagle Owl, Egyptian Vulture, Lanner Falcon.

Migrants (location 2) The huge migrations across the Strait of Gibraltar in spring (Mar-May) and autumn (Aug-Oct) are certainly the most memorable sights. Over 250 species have been counted in the Strait. The migrations of the raptors and storks are most spectacular but smaller birds such as swallows, larks and finches also make this journey, in even greater numbers. The best time to watch the migrations is in the morning a couple of hours after sunrise through to mid afternoon – depending on the thermals. Taking positions adjacent to Jbel Kebir or Jbel Musa will assist but the migration is visible along the whole length of coast from Cap Spartel to Ceuta.

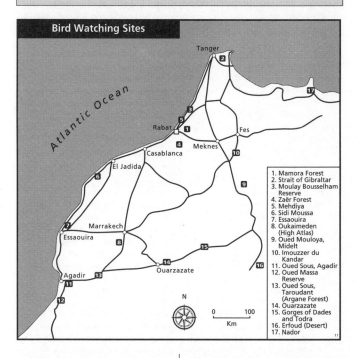

Bird Watching Sites

Atlantic Ocean

Tanger

Rabat

Fes

Casablanca

Meknes

El Jadida

Marrakech

Essaouira

Ouarzazate

Agadir

N

0   100
        Km

1. Mamora Forest
2. Strait of Gibraltar
3. Moulay Bousselham Reserve
4. Zaër Forest
5. Mehdiya
6. Sidi Moussa
7. Essaouira
8. Oukaimeden (High Atlas)
9. Oued Mouloya, Midelt
10. Imouzzer du Kandar
11. Oued Sous, Agadir
12. Oued Massa Reserve
13. Oued Sous, Taroudant (Argane Forest)
14. Ouarzazate
15. Gorges of Dades and Todra
16. Erfoud (Desert)
17. Nador

sand fish and *sand swimmers* take advantage of deep sand to avoid predators and find cooler temperatures in the desert *reg.* The *ocellated lizard* is impressive in size, growing to 20 cm. *Geckoes* are plump, soft-skinned, nocturnal lizards with adhesive pads on their toes and are frequently noted near houses. The *chameleon* is a reptile with a prehensile tail and a long sticky tongue for catching insects. Although basically green, it can change colour to match its surroundings. *Snakes* are essentially legless lizards. There are some thirty species in the Mediterranean areas alone, but only the viperine types are dangerous. These can be identified by their triangular heads, short plump bodies and zig-zag markings. The *horned viper* lies just below the surface of sand, with its horns projecting, waiting for prey. *Sand boas* stay underground most of the time, while other species twine themselves around the branches of trees. Most snakes will instinctively avoid contact with human beings and will only strike if disturbed or threatened. For what to do if you are bitten by a snake (see page 494).

MARINE LIFE

The Mediterranean is a land-locked sea and it is only in the extreme W near the Strait of Gibraltar that there is any significant tidal range. Without strong tides and currents bringing nutrients, the Mediterranean is somewhat impoverished in terms of marine life. Fish and shell fish, nevertheless, have figured prominently in the diet of the coastal people for centuries, with *sardines*, *anchovies*, *mullet*, *sole*, *squid* and *prawns* being particularly popular. *Tuna* and *swordfish* are also widely caught. Over-fishing, leading to the depletion of stocks, has become increasingly problematic. Marine mammals, such as the *common dolphin* and *porpoise* are frequently seen in the Strait of Gibraltar. Some whales are occasionally found in the western Mediterranean, having strayed through from the Atlantic. These are most likely to be *minke* or *fin whales*.

The North Atlantic Ocean marking the western boundary of Morocco and Mauritania is, due to a strong upwelling movement, a mixture of warm surface water and the cold Canaries current. This mixture attracts both tropical and cold water fish, and in addition to the *sardines* and *tuna* on which the fishing industry is based there are *sea bream*, *skate*, *red mullet*, *tarpon*, *sea bass* and *conger eel*. *Dolphins* are a common sight.

BUTTERFLIES AND MOTHS

Because of the lack of vegetation on which to lay eggs, butterflies are scarce in the steppe and desert areas. The Mediterranean fringe of North Africa, in contrast, are often rich in species, some quite exotic. The life cycle – mating, egg production, caterpillar, pupa, butterfly – can be swift, with some species having three cycles in 1 year. some of the butterflies are large and colourful, such as the *swallowtail* and the *two-tailed pasha*. The most common butterflies in the early spring are the *painted ladies*, which migrate from North Africa northwards, often reaching as far as Britain. Other familiar species include the *Moroccan orange tip*, *festoon*, *Cleopatra* and *clouded yellow*. Moths are also widely represented, but as they are largely nocturnal they are rarely seen. Day flying moths include the *Burnet* and *hummingbird hawk moths*. The largest moth of the area is the *giant peacock moth*, with a wingspan of up to 15 cm.

BIRDS

Neither the Mediterranean nor the desert areas are particularly rich in resident bird species, but both can be swollen temporarily by birds on passage. Four categories of birds may be noted. Firstly, there are the **resident** birds which are found throughout the year, such as the *crested lark* and the *Sardinian warbler*. Secondly, there are the **summer visitors**, such as the *swift* and *swallow*, which spend the winter months S of the Equator. **Winter visitors**, on the other hand, breed in northern Europe but come S to escape the worst of the winter and include many varieties of wader and wildfowl. **Passage migrants** fly through the area northwards in spring and then return southwards in increased numbers after breeding in the autumn. Small birds tend to migrate on a broad front, often crossing the desert and the Mediterranean Sea without stopping. Such migrants include the *whitethroat*, plus less common species such as the *nightjar* and *wryneck*. Larger birds, including *eagles*, *storks* and *vultures*, must adopt a different strategy, as they depend on soaring, rather than sustained flight. As they rely on thermals created over land, they must opt for short sea crossings. One route uses the narrow Strait of Gibraltar, while the more easterly route follows the Nile Valley, Turkey and the Bosphorus.

Within Morocco there is a number of typical habitats each with its own assemblage of birds. The Mediterranean itself has a poor selection of sea birds, although the rare *Audouins gull* always excites 'twitchers'. Oceanic birds such as *gannets* and *shearwaters*, however, enter the Mediterranean during the winter. Wetland areas, such as the Oued Massa near Agadir, contain numerous varieties of the heron family such as the *night heron* and *squacco heron*, while *spoonbill*, *ibis* and both *little* and *cattle egrets* are common.

Flamingoes breed in a number of locations when conditions are right. Waders such as the *avocet* and *black winged stilt* are also typical wetland birds. The wetland species are augmented in the winter by a vast collection of wildfowl. Resident ducks, however, are confined to specialities such as the *white-headed duck*, *marbled teal* and *ferruginous duck*. On roadsides, the *crested lark* is frequently seen, while overhead wires often contain *corn buntings*, with their jangling song, and the colonial *bee-eaters*. Mountain areas are ideal for searching out raptors. There are numerous varieties of *eagle*, including *Bonelli's*, *booted*, *short toed* and *golden*. Of the *vultures*, the *griffon* is the most widely encountered. The *black kite* is more catholic in its choice of habitat, but the *Montagu's harrier* prefers open farmland.

The desert and steppe areas have their own specialist resident birds which have developed survival strategies. Raptors include the *long-legged buzzard* and the *lanner*, which prefer mountain areas. Among the ground-habitat birds are the *Houbara bustard* and the *cream coloured courser*. *Dupont's lark* is also reluctant to fly, except during its spectacular courtship display. The *trumpeter finch* is frequently seen at oases, while the insectivorous *desert wheatear* is a typical bird of the *erg* and *reg* regions.

We are grateful to Rowland Mead for providing us with this information.

Travel and survival in the desert

TRAVELLERS AND THE NATURE OF DESERTS

For those travellers staying in well regulated accommodation in good hotels, the realities of the desert can be disguised for as long as electricity and pure water supplies are sustained. Much of the informa-tion in the following section can thus be ignored, though not with total impunity. Trips into the desert even by the most careful of tour operators carry some of the hazards and a knowledge of good practice might be as helpful on the beach or tourist bus as for the full-blooded de-sert voyager.

There is a contemporary belief that the problems of living and travelling in deserts have been solved. Much im-proved technology in transport together with apparent ease of access to desert areas has encouraged these comfortable ideas. The very simplicity of the prob-lems of deserts, lack of water and high temperatures, make them easy to under-estimate. In reality, deserts have not changed and problems still arise when travelling in them, albeit with less regu-larity than 20 or so years ago. One aspect of the desert remains unchanged – mis-takes and misfortune can too easily be

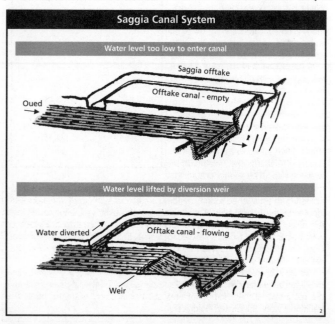

Saggia Canal System

Water level too low to enter canal

Saggia offtake

Offtake canal - empty

Oued

Water level lifted by diversion weir

Water diverted

Offtake canal - flowing

Weir

2

Making the desert bloom

🐾 Most of Morocco away from the Atlantic coast and the high mountains receives an annual rainfall of less than 300 mm. The S of the country is very arid. For agriculture to survive in these low rainfall areas, irrigation is necessary and a great deal of time and effort is lavished on finding, storing and distributing water for irrigation and household purposes.

There are some, if not enough, imaginative and large scale modern irrigation projects built by the government and funded by foreign aid programmes. These are usually based on reservoir storage of water such as the Barrage Sidi Ben Abdallah on the Oued Bou Regreg E of Rabat. For the most part, however, irrigation is small scale and uses traditional technology. The three main systems that you will see are the *saggia* – an open canal taking water off a running stream. A low dam or diversion weir is built across a *oued* lifting the water level slightly so that water can be led off into a canal which begins at the dam or weir and drops down the side of the valley enabling water to be fed to the fields below the level of the canal. A fine example of the canal is the Saggia Taffelagt in Taroudant. The *saggia* runs from a spring in the Oued Sous for 7 km E of Taroudant into the gardens that surround the town to the N. It has been modernized but is not well maintained. It nonetheless provides water for many of Taroudant's 45,000 inhabitants.

The *khattara* is an ancient but clever means of tapping into the water table in alluvial fans or *oued* beds underground. Water is then taken through a narrow inclined tunnel to the surface sometimes many kilometres from the source of the water. There are several *khattara* still in use in the region W of Erfoud and in the Sous valley near Taroudant and the shallow well – usually no more than 10 or so metres deep, water from which is lifted by goat skin bag or hoist.

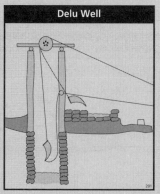

Delu Well

In dry areas of Morocco social organization was designed to protect and share scarce water supplies. Tribal councils or *jama'a* were set up to appoint local irrigation officials for the benefit of the whole group. They would ensure that the canals were maintained properly and that each member got his share of water according to established sharing systems. Traditional systems of irrigation were ignored by the French colonial administration, whose aims were to provide high technology water use mainly for European farms. In consequence local practices were by-passed and facilities allowed to decline. In the late 1960s the Moroccan Government began a land reform and tried to improve local irrigation works but with only limited success.

While in Morocco look out for these fascinating local irrigation systems and their intricate water distribution works, especially in the dry lands of the S and the mountain villages. Taroudant area still has working examples of all the traditional water supply technologies.

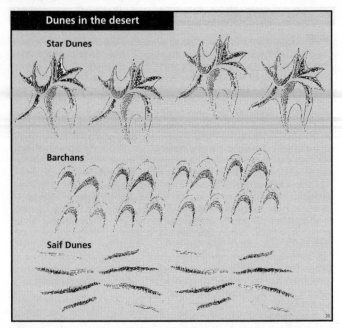

Dunes in the desert

Star Dunes

Barchans

Saif Dunes

fatal.

Desert topography is varied. Excellent books such as Allan JA & Warren A (1993) *Deserts: a conservation atlas*, Mitchell Beazley, show the origins and constant development of desert scenery. In North Africa, desert and semi-desert is the largest single surface area and so has an importance for travellers rarely met with elsewhere. Its principal features and their effects on transport are best understood before they are met on the ground. The great *ergs* or sandseas comprise mobile dunes and shifting surface sands over vast areas. Small mobile *barkhans*, which are crescent shaped, can often be driven round on firm terrain but the larger transverse and longitudinal dunes can form large surfaces with thick ridges of soft sand. They constantly change their shape as the wind works across them. While not impassible, they can be crossed only slowly and

with difficulty as can the rougher parts of the S Atlas zones of Morocco. The *oued* beds which penetrate much of the Sahara, *serirs* and gravel plains provide good access for all-terrain vehicles.

The main characteristic of the desert is its **aridity**. Aridity is calculable and those navigating deserts are advised to understand the term so that the element of risk can be appraised and managed with safety. CW Thornthwaite's aridity index shows water deficiency relative to water need for a given area. There is a gradient from N to S throughout the region, of rising temperatures, diminishing rainfall and worsening aridity. Aridity of the desert is thus very variable, ranging from the Mediterranean sub-tropical fringe to a semi-arid belt to the S and a fully arid desert interior. In basic terms, the further S you are the more dangerous the environment. Do

Moroccan sands

👣 Morocco is not rich in sand dunes. They have to be looked for with some diligence! The main areas of dunes occur in the S of the country with the most accessible sand seas at Merzouga, near Erfoud (Erg Chebbi) and the Draa Valley by Mhamid at the southern end of the surfaced road. Smaller sand areas such as that N of Rissani do exist but are, at least by Saharan standards, very modest in extent and height. Mauritania is better endowed with dunes in its northern territories, especially at Draa Malichigdune where sand masses of more than 100 km long occur.

Dunes form under various wind conditions. Barchan or crescent dunes tend to be found where a steady wind blows from one direction and where the volume of loose quartz sand is limited. The sand in the horns of the crescent is blown ahead of the main mass of the dune as it migrates across the usually flat landscape. Ridge dunes occur at right angles to the direction of the wind, though other theories for their form are proposed by the experts and are known as linear or in Arabic *saif* dunes. They are only lightly developed in Morocco but in Mauritania and in other desert lands can be several kilometres in length and rise to 170m high. Typical of some of the greatest sand masses in the Sahara are the sand seas such as the Great Easter Erg of Algeria or the Murzuq sand sea in SW Libya, where sand sheets and dune formations are both found covering large surface areas. In Morocco there are occasional star dunes, in which wind prevails from different directions or is erratic in direction, giving what appear to be multiple crescent shaped dunes in the shape of a star when seen from above. The star dunes can become centres of massive sand accumulation as in northern Mauritania and Algeria, with altitudes of 300m and a length of 1 km.

The mobility of dunes varies. The largest move perhaps no more than a metre each year. Barchans can, especially if of low altitude, travel more quickly – at up to 50m per year. Mobile dunes create a hazard for transport since roads can be covered quickly in high wind conditions. Elsewhere, cultivated lands can slowly be inundated with sand.

Stabilizing sand dunes is a difficult matter. The large dune systems are unstoppable and man's attempts to halt their advance have rarely succeeded for long. Smaller dunes can be stabilized by planting them with a close graticule of drought resistant grass or other plants, which once established can be inter-planted with desert bushes and shrubs. This process is slow and expensive though generally very effective even in very dry conditions. More cheap and dramatic is to build sand fences to catch moving sand, tar-spraying dunes or layering dunes with a plastic net. The results are less aesthetically pleasing than using the traditional vegetation cover system and are less long-lasting unless combined with planting, though in the driest areas of the Sahara these are the only possible methods of fixing mobile dunes.

Sand dunes

not assume that conditions on the coast properly prepare you for the deep S. The Sahara is also very varied in its topography, climate and natural difficulties posed for the traveller. Rapid transition from rough stone terrain to sand sea to salt flat has to be expected and catered for.

For practical purposes, aridity means **no moisture and very high temperatures**. The world's highest temperatures are experienced in the Sahara – over 55°C. Averages in the S desert run in summer at more than 50°C in the shade at midday. In full sun very much higher figures are reached. High temperatures are not the only difficulty. Each day has a large range of temperature, often of more than 20°C, with nights being intensely cold, sometimes below freezing. In winter, air temperatures can be very low despite the heat of the sun and temperatures drop very rapidly either when the sun goes down or when there is movement from sunlight to shade, say in a deep gorge or a cave.

Increasing aridity means greater **difficulty in water availability**. Scientists define the problem in terms of water deficits. Morocco as a whole and the deep Sahara in particular are very serious water deficit areas. Surface waters are lacking almost everywhere. Underground water is scarce and often available only at great depths. Occasional natural see pages of water give rise to oases and/or palmeries. They are, however, rare. Since water is the key to sustaining life in deserts, travellers have always to assume that they must be self-sufficient or navigate from one known water source to another.

Isolation is another feature of the Sahara. Travellers' tales tend to make light of the matter, hinting that bedouin Arabs will emerge from the dunes even in the most obscure corner of the desert. This is probably true of the semi-desert and some inland *oued* basins but not a

correct assumption on which to build a journey in the greater part of the Sahara. Population numbers in the desert are very low at only one person per 20 km sq, and most of these are concentrated in small oasis centres. Black top road systems are gradually being extended into and through the Sahara but they represent a few straggling lines across areas for the most part without fixed and maintained highways. Once off the main roads, travellers can part from their escorts and find no fixed topography to get them back on course. Vanishing individuals and vehicles in the Sahara are too frequent to be a joke. To offset this problem read on.

The most acute difficulty with off-road emergencies is finding the means of raising assistance because of isolation. Normal preventative action is to ensure that your travel programme is known in advance by some individual or an institution to whom regular check-in is made from points on the route. Failure to contact should automatically raise the alarm. Two vehicles are essential and often obviate the worst problems of break-down and the matter of isolation. Radio communication from your vehicle is an expensive but useful aid if things go wrong.

Bear in mind the enormous distances involved in bringing help even where the location of an incident in the desert is known. Heavy rescue equipment and/or paramedical assistance will probably be 500 km or more distant. Specialist transport for the rescuers is often not instantly available, assuming that local telecommunications systems work and local administrators see fit to help.

LIVING WITH THE CLIMATE

Living with desert environments is not difficult but it does take discipline and adherence to sensible routines at all times. It is an observed fact that health problems in hot and isolated locations take on a greater seriousness for those involved than they would in temperate climates. It is still common practice with Western oil companies and other commercial organisations regularly engaged at desert sites to fly ill or injured persons home as a first measure in the knowledge that most will recover more rapidly without the psychological and environmental pressures of a desert site. Most health risks in the desert are avoidable. The rules, evolved over many years, are simple and easy to follow:

1. **Allow time to acclimatise** to full desert conditions. Conserve your energy at first rather than acting as if you were still in a temperate climatic régime. Most people take a week or more to adjust to heat conditions in the deep Sahara.

2. **Stay out of direct sunlight** whenever possible, especially once the sun is high. Whenever you can, do what the locals do, move from shade to shade.

3. **Wear clothes to protect your skin** from the sun, particularly your head and neck. Use a high Sun Protection Factor (SPF) cream, preferably as high as SPF15 (94%) to minimize the effects of Ultraviolet-B. Footwear is a matter of choice though many of those from the temperate parts of the world will find strong, light but well ventilated boots ideal for keeping sand, sun, venomous livestock and thorns off the feet. Slip on boots are best of all since they are convenient if visiting Arab encampments/housing/religious sites, where shoes are not worn.

4. **Drink good quality water** regularly and fully. It is estimated that 10-15 litres per day are needed by a healthy person to avoid water deficiency in desert conditions, even if there is no actual feeling of thirst. The majority of ailments arising in the desert relate to water deficiency and so it is worth the small effort of regular drinking of water. Too much alcoholic drink has the opposite effect in most cases and is not, unfortunately, a substitute for water!

5. **Be prepared for cold nights** by having some warm clothes to hand.

6. Stay in your quarters or vehicle if there is a **sand storm**.

7. **Refrain from eating dubious foods**. Deserts and stomach upsets have a habit of going hand in hand – 'gyppy-tummy' and 'Tripoli-trots' give a taste of the problem! Choose hot cooked meals in preference to cold meats and tired salads. Peel all fruit and uncooked fresh vegetables. Do not eat 'native' milk-based items or drink untreated water unless you are absolutely sure of its good quality.

8. **Sleep off the ground if you can**. There are very few natural dangers in the desert but scorpions, spiders and snakes are found (but are rarely fatal) and are best avoided.

TRANSPORT AND COMMON SENSE IN THE DESERT

The key to safe travel in desert regions is reliable and well equipped transport. Most travellers will simply use local bus and taxi services. For the motorist, motorcyclist or pedal cyclist there are ground rules which, if followed, will help to reduce risks. In normal circumstances travellers will remain on black top roads and for this need only a well prepared 2WD vehicle. Choose a machine which is known for its reliability and for which spares can be easily obtained. Across the whole of North Africa only Peugeot and Mercedes are found with adequate spares and servicing facilities. If you have a different type of car/truck, make sure that you take spares with you or have the means of getting spares sent out. Petrol/benzene/gas is everywhere available though diesel is equally well distributed except in the smallest of southern settlements. 4WD transport is useful even for the traveller who normally remains on the black top highway. Emergencies, diversions and unscheduled visits to off the road sites become less of a problem with

Instruments for navigation in the desert

The Arabs are thought to have been amongst the great navigators and certainly the Middle East and North Africa were the sources of invention of many means of navigation such as by the stars. Its people invented a fascinating range of instruments for determining locations and directions, most notably the astrolabe. It was the Babylonians who as early as 1700 BC used systems of numbering, algebra and geometry and who combined their mathematical knowledge to develop astronomy to a fine art by 100 BC. Further expansion of mathematics by the Greeks, notably in the 8th and 7th centuries BC by individuals such as Pythagoras and, later, Archimedes.

The Arabs were very early students of mathematics and algebra (the English name of which was derived from the Arabic *al-gebit*) was widely developed, a book on the subject by Mohammed ben Moosa being printed in the 9th century AD at the instigation of the Caliph Mam'un. Most importantly the Islamic period witnessed the tabulation of information, much of it of direct value to navigation in difficult or featureless desert terrain. The astrolabe, invented by the Greeks was perfected by the Muslims as an accurate fixer of angles. The earliest known astrolabe was manufactured in the Iranian city of Esfahan in 984 AD. The astrolabe was made from a circular brass plate, some as large as 500 mm diameter, with a movable pointer or finger called an alidade pinned at the centre of the plate. The astrolabe would be suspended from a ring and the angle to a given star or planet fixed from gradations marked on the rim of the plate which could indicate latitude and even time of day. Instruments of this kind were often wonderfully ornate, often those in Morocco originating in Iberia such as the one made for the visir of Ibrahim ibn Said at Toledo in 1066.

One of the earliest references to use of a magnetic compass in navigation was in the Middle East in the 13th century. The sun compass is still a useful instrument for desert navigation. With this the direction of the sun is picked out on a form of gnomon on a plate that gives an approximation of N.

The arrival of satellite aided navigation and location systems has finally made safe desert travel possible – but not in all cases. The local knowledge of the Touareg in S Morocco is still invaluable, especially in sand sea areas, where electronic devices might tell you where you are geographically speaking but not how to escape the maze of sand.

Astrolabe of Toledo 1066   Astrolabe of Esfahan 1715

all-terrain vehicles. Off the road, 4WD is essential, normally with two vehicles travelling together. A great variety of 4WD vehicles are in use in the region, with Toyota and Land Rover probably found most widely.

All vehicles going into the southern areas of Morocco should have basic equipment as follows:

1. Full tool kit, vehicle maintenance handbook and supplementary tools such as clamps, files, wire, spare parts kit supplied by car manufacturer, jump leads.

2. Spare tyre/s, battery driven tyre pump, tyre levers, tyre repair kit, hydraulic jack, jack handle extension, base plate for jack.

3. Spare fuel can/s, spare water container/s, cool bags.

For those going off the black top roads other items to include are:

4. Foot tyre pump, heavy duty hydraulic or air jack, power winch, sand channels, safety rockets, comprehensive first aid kit, radio-telephone where permitted.

5. Emergency rations kit/s, matches, Benghazi burner (see page 62).

6. Maps, compasses, latest road information, long term weather forecast, guides to navigation by sun and stars.

Driving in the desert is an acquired skill. Basic rules are simple but crucial.

1. If you can get a local guide who perhaps wants a lift to your precise destination, use him.

2. Set out early in the morning after first light, rest during the heat of the day and use the cool of the evening for further travel.

3. Never attempt to travel at night or when there is a sandstorm brewing or in progress.

4. Always travel with at least two vehicles which should remain in close visual contact.

Other general hints include not speeding across open flat desert in case the going changes without warning and your vehicle beds deeply into soft sand

or a gully. Well maintained corrugated road surfaces can be taken at modest pace but rocky surfaces should be treated with great care to prevent undue wear on tyres. Sand seas are a challenge for drivers but need a cautious approach – ensure that your navigation lines are clear so that weaving between dunes does not disorientate the navigator. Especially in windy conditions, sight lines can vanish, leaving crews with little knowledge of where they are. Cresting dunes from dip slope to scarp needs care that the vehicle does not either bog down or overturn. Keep off salt flats after rain and floods especially in the winter and spring when water tables can rise and make the going hazardous in soft mud. Even when on marked and maintained tracks beware of approaching traffic. One of the editor's friend's car was hit by the only vehicle which passed him that day on a 500 km drive in S Libya!

EMERGENCIES

The desert tends to expose the slightest flaw in personnel and vehicles. Emergency situations are therefore to be expected and planned for. There is no better security than making the schedule of your journey known in advance to friends or embassy/consulate officials who will actively check on your arrival at stated points. Breakdowns and multiple punctures are the most frequent problem. On the highway the likelihood is always that a passing motorist will give assistance, or a lift to the nearest control post or village. In these situations it is best simply remain with your vehicle until help arrives making sure that your are clear of the road and that you are protected from other traffic by a warning triangle and/or rocks on the road to rear and front.

Off the road, breakdowns, punctures and bogging down in soft sand are the main difficulties. If you have left your travel programme at your last stop you will already have a fall back position in case of severe problems. If you cannot make a repair or extricate yourself, remain with your vehicle in all circumstances. Unless you can clearly see a settlement (not a mirage) stay where you are with water, food and shelter. The second vehicle can be used to search for help but only after defining the precise location of the incident. In the case of getting lost, halt, conserve fuel while you attempt to get a bearing on either the topography or the planets/stars and work out a traverse to bring you back to a known line such as a highway, mountain ridge or coastline. If that fails, take up as prominent a position as possible for being spotted from the air. Build a fire to use if and when you hear air activity in your vicinity. Attempt to find a local source of water by digging in the nearest wadi bed, collecting dew from the air at night. If you have fuel to spare it can be used with great care both as a means of attracting attention and a way of boiling untreated water. A *Benghazi burner*, two crude metal cones welded together to give a water jacket and space for a fire in the centre can achieve this latter purpose. As ever in Morocco, be patient and conserve your energy.

Jewellery and dress

JEWELLERY

Morocco today boasts a distinctive culture whose abundance of styles of dress and adornment almost defies description. The dynamic history of the region has produced imaginative traditional designs mixed with foreign elements leading to a range of decoration few re-

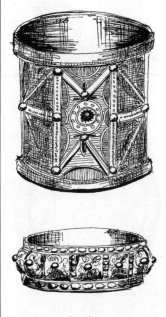

Bracelets

One of the many styles of Khamsa
or Hand of Fatima

Anklets or *Khul-Khal*
(always worn in pairs)

gions in the world can rival. Influences from the Phoenicians, Greeks and Romans, Arabs and Andalusians have each contributed subtly to the immense range of jewellery found in this part of the world.

Although some urban dwellers have adopted Western attitudes to dress and decoration, at times of festivals and especially for marriage ceremonies, traditional dress and elaborate jewellery that has changed little since the Middle Ages is still worn. The increase of tourism, while in some cases destroying traditional values, is in fact promoting and preserving crafts, especially jewellery making, by providing an eager and lucrative market for ornaments that was rapidly declining. Unfortunately, with the changes of cultural values, changes in fashion and style also occur and large quantities of old, exquisite silver jewellery have been destroyed to provide raw materials for new pieces.

Throughout Morocco there is a division of tastes and wealth between towns where gold is favoured and the countryside where silver predominates. Basically, traditional styles continue to be popular and, especially in the Maghreb, jewellery tends to become more traditional the further S one goes. A general shift can be discerned away from silver towards gold which is now believed to be a better investment.

Despite a whole field of inspiration being forbidden to Muslim jewellers, that of the human form, they developed the art of decorating jewellery in ways that eventually merged to become a distinctive 'Islamic' style. Using floral (arabesque), animal, geometric and calligraphic motifs fashioned on gold and silver with precious and semi-precious gems, coral and pearls they worked their magic.

According to Islamic law, silver is the only pure metal recommended by the Prophet Mohammed. For the majority of Muslims this sanction is felt to apply

Silver pendant -
Lizard, a talisman against the evil
eye on a Hand of Fatima

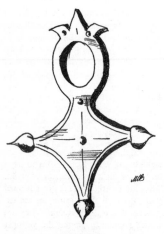

Agades Cross

only to men who do not, as a rule, wear any jewellery other than a silver wedding ring or seal ring.

Every town has its own jewellery *souq* with larger centres providing a greater range of jewellery. There is almost always a distinction between the goldsmiths and the silversmiths and there are also shops, which produce jewellery in brass or gold plate on brass for the cheap end of the market.

Jewellers also sell silver items in the cheaper end of the tourist market which is very popular as 'ethnic' jewellery. Gold and silver jewellery is usually sold by weight and, although there might be an additional charge for more intricate craftmanship, this means the buyer must judge quality very carefully.

The **earring** is by far the most popular and convenient ornament throughout North Africa. It appears in an infinite variety of styles with the crescent moon shape being the most common. This is closely followed by the **bracelet** or **bangle** which is also very much part of a woman's everyday wardrobe.

Most of the jewellery is worn both as an **adornment** and as an indication of social status or rank. It generally has some symbolic meaning or acts as a charm. Jewellery is usually steeped in tradition and is often received in rites of passage like puberty, betrothal and marriage. In North Africa, women receive most of their jewellery upon marriage. This is usually regarded as their sole property and is security against personal disaster.

Many of the **symbols** recurrent in North African jewellery have meanings or qualities which are thought to be imparted to the wearer. Most of the discs appearing in the jewellery represent the moon which is considered to be the embodiment of perfect beauty and femininity. The greatest compliment is to liken a woman to the full moon. Both the moon and the fish are considered as *fertility symbols*. The cresent is the symbol of Islam but its use actually predates Islam. It is the most common symbol throughout the region and acquires greater Islamic significance with the additon of a star inside. Other symbols

The Talisman

The 'evil eye' is a powerful force in the local societies of North Africa. It is believed that certain people have the power to damage their victims, sometimes inadvertently. Women are thought to be among the most malignant of possessors of the evil eye – a factor associated with the 'impurities' of the menstrual cycle. Even a camera can be considered as an alien agent carrying an evil eye – so only take photographs of country people where they are comfortable with the idea and be exceptionally careful in showing a camera at weddings and above all funerals. Envy too is a component of the evil eye and most conversations where any praise of a person or object is concerned will include a *mashallah* or "what god wills" as protection against the evil spirits that surround human kind.

Major victims of the evil eye are the young, females and the weak. Vulnerability is seen to be worst in marriage, pregnancy and childbirth, so that women in particular must shelter themselves from the evil eye. Uttering the name of Allah is a good defence against the evil eye. Alternatively amulets are used, this practice originating from the wearing of quotations from the Koran written onto strips of cloth which were bound into a leather case which was strapped to the arm. The amulet developed as a form in its own right, made of beads, pearls, horn or stone brought back from a pilgrimage. Amulets also have the power to heal as well as to protect against the occult.

In contemporary North Africa, medicine, superstition and ornament combine to give a wonderful array of amulets worn for both everyday and specific use.

frequently seen are the palm and the moving lizard both of which signify life and the snake which signifies respect.

Amulets are thought to give the wearer protection from the unknown, calamities and threats. They are also reckoned to be curative and to have power over human concerns such as longevity, health, wealth, sex and luck. Women and children wear amulets more frequently as their resistance to evil is considered to be weaker than that of a man.

The most popular amulets are the *Hirz*, the Eye which has always had mystical connotations and the *Khamsa* or hand. The *Hirz* is a silver box containing verses of the Koran. The *Khamsa* is by far the most widespread of the amulets. It comes in a multitude of sizes and designs of a stylized hand and is one of the most common components of jewellery in the region. This hand represents the 'Hand of Fatima', Mohammad's favourite daughter. Koranic inscriptions also form a large section of favoured pen-

dants and are usually executed in gold and also heavily encrusted with diamonds and other precious stones.

Coins or *mahboub* form the basis of most of the traditional jewellery, seen in the spectacular festival and marriage ensembles worn in Morocco. Each area, village or tribe has its own unique and extraordinary dress of which jewellery, be it hundreds of coins or huge amber beads, forms a fundamental part.

Among the more interesting items are **anklets** called *khul khal*, worn in pairs and found in a great variety of styles. They are mostly of solid silver fringed with tiny bells. Fine examples are expensive due to their weight. They are losing popularity among the younger generation as they are cumbersome to wear with shoes and because of their undertones of subservience and slavery.

Moroccan jewellery, especially that of Fes and Tanger, shows a clear Andalusian influence in the intricate flowing floral/leafy patterns. Floral networks of filigree enhanced with enamelling are a speciality of Essaouira, while more geometric designs are found in Meknes.

In Morocco *Essaouira* and the Imperial cities are all jewellery centres and *Tiznit* is the place to find Berber jewellery.

Marie-Claire Bakker contributed the text and most of the illustrations for this section.

DRESS

First time visitors to the countries of North Africa will be fascinated by the variety and colour of the garments worn as 'everyday' wear. This section, contributed by Jennifer Scarce, Curator of Eastern Cultures, National Museums of Scotland, sketches in the background and attempts an explanation of what is being worn and why.

The dress traditions of Morocco are striking and colourful evidence of a rich cultural heritage. Here, as in all societies, dress is a powerful form of cultural expression, a visual symbol which reveals a wealth of information about the wearer. Dress also reflects historical evolution and the cumulative effects of religious, ethnic and geographical factors on a society.

It is hardly surprising that the many influences which have shaped North African history have produced an equally diverse dress culture in which elements from antiquity, the Islamic world and Europe are found. The heritage from earlier times is a rich blending of decorative motifs and drapery. Carthaginian material culture drew upon local tradtions of colourful geometric ornament, which is still seen in Berber clothing and textiles. Greek and Roman fashions have survived in the striking dress of the inhabitants of the deserts and mountains of Morocco, where draped and folded garments are fastened with elaborate jewelled pins (see Jewellery page 62) and buckles. The Arabs introduced a different dress tradition, influenced by the styles of Egypt and Syria. Here the main features were loose flowing robes and cloaks, wrapped turbans and headcovering which combined a graceful line, comfort and modest concealment. The establishment of Islamic cities encouraged a diverse range of professions and occupations – civil and religious authorities, merchants, craftsmen – all with their distinctive dress. Within cities such as Fes and Marrakech specialist trades in textiles, leather and jewellery supported dress production. Widening political and commercial relations stimulated new elements in dress. Jewish and Muslim immigrants from Andalucía in the 15th century introduced styles influenced by Spanish tradition which survived in the full-skirted tight-waisted dresses of Moroccan Jewish women.

The Ottoman Turks introduced another feature into city dress, in the form of jackets, trousers and robes of flamboyant cut and lavishly embroidered decoration. Finally European fashion, with emphasis on tailored suits and dresses entered the North African scene.

One of the more rewarding pleasures of a visit to Morocco is the opportunity to see the intricate pattern of mixed dress styles which reflect an adjustment to economic and social change.

The widest range is seen in urban environments where European styles mingle with interpretations of local dress and the clothing of regional migrants. Men have adopted European dress in varying degrees. The wardrobes of civil servants, professional and business men include well-cut sober coloured European suits, which are worn with toning shirts, ties and smart shoes. Seasonal variations include fabrics of lighter weight and colour and short-sleeved shirts and 'safari' jackets. Casual versions of this dress code, including open-necked shirts, are seen in more modest levels of urban society. Blue jeans, blouson jackets, T shirts and

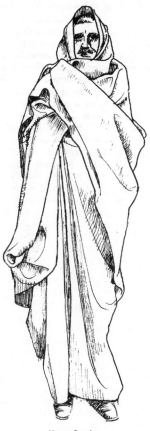

Ksa or Barakan

trainers may be worn equally by manual workers and students.

Men's city dress alternates between European and local garments according to taste and situation. Traditional dress is based on a flexible combination of loose flowing garments and wraps which gives considerable scope for individuality. One of the most versatile garments is the *jallabah*, an ankle length robe with long straight sleeves and a neat pointed hood, made in fabrics ranging from fine

wool and cotton in dark and light colours to rough plain and striped homespun yarn. Elegant versions in white may be beautifully cut and sewn and edged with plaited silk braid. A modern casual version has short sleeves and a V-shaped neck and is made of poly-cotton fabric in a range of plain colours. Professional men may change from a suit into a *jallabah* at home, while working class men may wear a plain or striped *jallabah* in the street over European shirt and trousers.

The more traditional interpretation of dress can be seen in the medinas. Here the *jallabah* is worn with the hood folded at the the back or pulled up and draped over the head. In the past a fez or turban was worn under the hood and a white cotton high-necked shirt with long sleeves and loose white trousers gathered just below the knee were worn under the *jallabah*.

A handsome and dignified garment worn by high ranking state and religious officials is the *caftan*, another long robe with very wide sleeves and a round neck. The cut and detail, such as the use of very fine braid around the neck and sleeves and along the seams, are more formal than those of the *jallabah*. The modern *caftan* has narrower sleeves and is worn in public by men of an older and more conservative generation.

Traditional dress may be completed with the addition of drapery. Examples include the *selham* or *burnous*, a wide semicircular cloak with a pointed hood and the *ksa*, a length of heavy white woollen cloth which is skilfully folded and wrapped around the head and body in a style resembling that of the classical Roman toga.

Headcoverings are a revealing indication of status and personal choice. A close fitting red wool felt pillbox cap, a *fez*, was normally worn alone or neatly wrapped with a turban length. Currently they are seen more often on older

Museums

👣 Morocco has a wealth of interesting material on display in the museums. Archaeology is well represented by the museums in Tetouan (mosaic of the Three Graces) and Rabat (bust of Cato the Younger); in Fes at Dar Batha are displays of superb ceramics and the Oudaïas museum in Rabat an exceptional display of carpets. Check the relevant town sections too for the sumptious Dar Si Said museum in Marrakech and the sublime Dar Jamai museum in Meknes. Moroccan art is well represented by the palatial Dar el Makhnzen in Tanger while the museums of enthnography have a particular interest to visitors wishing to understand the dress and culture of Morocco.

men both in traditional and European dress.

Footwear is a distinctive product of Morocco's longstanding leather industry. Shoes (see page 238) usually in bright yellow or white, are made of fine leather. They are close fitting, have a long pointed toe and are worn with the back folded under at the heel.

Women's town dress is also a mixture of traditional and modern European forms and depends on wealth, status and personal taste. In the larger cities where women are employed in business and professions, European clothes are worn, cleverly accessorized with scarves and jewellery. Longer skirts and long-sleeved blouses are worn, being a more modest form of European dress.

Traditional dress is remarkably enduring especially in the cities of Morocco among women of all classes. The most important garments are the *caftan* and *jallabah* of the same basic cut and shape as those for men. The *caftan*, as worn in the past by wealthy women, was a sumptuous garment of exaggerated proportions made of rich velvet or brocaded silk embroidered with intricate designs in gold thread. The modern *caftan* is usually made of brightly coloured and patterned light-weight fabric and edged with plaited braid. The shape is simple and unstructured with a deep slit at each side from waist to hem. Variations can be found in texture and colour of fabric, changes in proportions of sleeves and

length of side slits. The *caftan* in its many variations is always worn as indoor dress and can suit all occasions. Traditionally it is worn as an everyday garment belted over a long underskirt. A light shawl may be draped around the neck and the hair tied up with a patterned scarf. Women who normally wear European dress to work often change into a *caftan* at home. Very chic versions of the *caftan*, combined with modern hairstyles and accessories, are worn as evening wear at private and official functions.

Outdoor dress in Morocco offers different solutions to the traditional requirements of modesty and concealment. Moroccan women wear a long straight *jallabah*, in a variety of materials and colours and usually slit from knee to ankle, over a *caftan*. There are two versions of the hood, a small one neatly folded at the back which functions more as a collar, or a large one which is pulled tightly over the face over a rectangular veil which conceals nose, mouth and chin. This traditional outdoor dress is worn with backless soft leather slippers or European sandal style shoes.

While the balance between contrasting dress codes is subject to subtle changes of emphasis in everyday life, the rituals of marriage still require a conspicuous display of traditional dress, jewellery and cosmetics for both bride and female guests. The city of Fes offers one of the most distinctive wedding ceremonies where the bride, robed in layers of magnificent brocaded garments and shawls and adorned with a gold crown hung with strings of pearls and with intricate patterns drawn with henna on her hands, is transformed into a splendid icon.

Regional dress, though less varied than in the past, is a striking visual record of the complex ethnic patterns and harsh living conditions of the rural areas. Particularly in Morocco, the tradition of the Berber tribes both settled and nomadic, is still retained in their handsome and brilliantly coloured draped garments. Extremes of heat and cold mean that adjustable layers of loose clothing and protective headgear such as a swathed turban or a straw hat are essential.

In rural areas the men's hooded *jallabah* is the most common, usually of homespun wool in unbeached white, blue or beige and brown stripes. It may be worn over another *jallabah*. Head coverings may be a closefitting knitted cap, a loosely wrapped white turban, or a tall pointed hat with a wide flat brim plaited from reeds, palm fibre or dried grass. Berber men used to drape a *haik*, a heavy cloak in coarse plain or striped wool, over their garments. In the S, the Touareg men still wear brilliant blue robes and conceal their heads and faces with turbans and veils as an extreme precaution against the sun, wind and sand.

Women's dress is considerably more varied and depends on a combination of colourful drapes. The basic garment of the Berber women is an *izar*, a long straight piece of cotton or wool in a series of colours ranging from white or black through to vivid reds, purples and yellows. The *izar*, worn over a *caftan*, is folded in half to envelope the body and is fastened at the shoulders with heavy silver pins or brooches. (See Jewellery, page 62). It can then be further draped, belted and adorned according to local usage. Striped woollen cloaks may be worn over the *izar*. Large turbans bound with cords and scarves, elaborately plaited and coiled hair, and much chunky silver jewellery traditionally complete this form of dress. Some of the most spectacular examples of Berber female dress are seen among the tribes in the High Atlas mountains, where heavy striped cloaks, are worn together with towering head-dresses adorned with skeins of wool and silk threaded with silver chains and pendants. The effect is completed by boldly tattooed and rouged faces.

Other easily identifiable forms of regional dress include the large black *haiks* with which women in the S conceal themselves and the red and white striped skirts and shawls and large straw hats of the country women of Chaouen in Morocco.

In their different ways, **state ceremonies** and tourism encourage the survival of local dress. The soldiers guarding the tomb of King Mohammed V in Rabat wear a dashing scarlet uniform based on Turkish style jackets and trousers worn with a swirling *burnous*.

In tourist areas doormen, porters and waiters are garbed in white *jallaba* and scarlet *fez*, watersellers in traditional dress and gaily decorated broad-brimmed hats roam the streets, displays of Berber dancing are arranged and tourists are encouraged to purchase 'local garments' and participate in versions of local festivals. The souqs in these resorts are festooned with *caftans* and leather slippers.

At another level, North Africa's impressive cultural heritage is taken very seriously and many museums have displays of traditional dress which can be enjoyed by both local and foreign visitors (see Oudaias Museum, Rabat, page 101).

Morocco

MOROCCO is certainly Europe's nearest African neighbour with glimpses of settlements and traffic clearly visible across the Strait of Gibraltar. Yet Morocco is a very different world. In its 703,000 sq km there are long, sandy beaches for the sun-loving watersports enthusiasts, towering snow capped mountain ranges with ski resorts, expanses of barren desert for the intrepid traveller, ancient cave drawings and striking Roman ruins for the historian along with crowded, colourful weekly markets, troglodyte dwellings, primitive pastoral agriculture and quaint mud-built *ksour*. There is the pink Morocco of the spring almond blossom, the green Morocco of the geometric olive tree plantations, the creamy/white dwellings and the deep black Morocco of the Saharan night. The senses record the mixed spices in the *souq*, the smell of mint tea and of donkeys, and taste of *tagine* and the sound of the *muezzin* calling the faithful to prayer. Morocco is not a place to look at, it is a country to be absorbed.

BASICS

OFFICIAL NAME al-Mamlakah al-Maghribiyah (kingdom of Morocco)

NATIONAL FLAG Red background with a green pentacle in the centre

OFFICIAL LANGUAGE Arabic

OFFICIAL RELIGION Islam

INDICATORS *Population*: 26.9 million. *Urban population*: 49%. *Religion*: Muslim (mainly Sunni) 98.7%, Christian 1.1%. *Birth rate*: 28 per 1,000. *Death rate*: 6.0 per 1,000. *Life expectancy*: 67 men, 71 women. *GNP per Capita*: US$1,030.

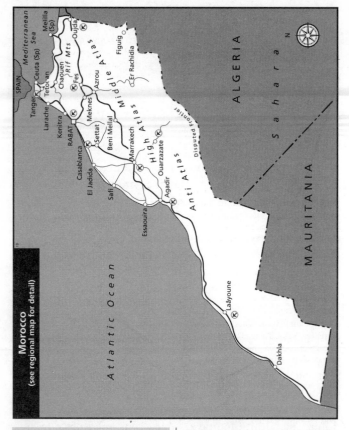

THE LAND

GEOGRAPHY

Morocco at 458,730 sq km is only a fifth the surface area of Algeria or Libya and is slightly smaller than Spain. Morocco has 703,000 sq km if the Moroccan controlled territory of Western Sahara is included.

Borders

Morocco has a 1,835 km coastline from Saidia on the Algerian frontier to La Gouera on the border with Mauritania, of which a fifth lies on the Mediterranean and the rest faces the Atlantic. The main sea-ports are Nador, Tanger, Kenitra, Mohammedia, Casablanca, El Jadida, Safi, Essaouira, Agadir, Tan-Tan, Laayoune, Dakhla, Mdiq and Asilah. Border problems affect both the Western Sahara where Moroccan occupation is challenged by the Saharois and the SE where the line with Algeria in the region of Tindouf is not firmly settled. Morocco itself has long-standing claims to the Spanish enclaves of Melilla and Ceuta. Frontier posts are at Zouj Béghal, Figuig,

Beni-Ounif, Bab Sebta, Beni-Ansar and Aïn Ben al-Mathar. The border disputes periodically affect freedom of transit for travellers, through military action in the Western Sahara and occasional but temporary frictions elsewhere. Currently the borders with Algeria are closed.

Main regions

Morocco is a country of great variety of topography in which huge mountain chains lying SW to NE dominate the relief (see map, page 72). Morocco certainly is a land of mountains for 100,000 sq km of its surface area is above 2,000m in altitude. The High Atlas alone has over a dozen summits which exceed 4,000m. The crescent of the Rif rises sheer from the Mediterranean, few areas lying below 1,500m and the limestone peaks rising to 2,492m in Tidirhine and 2,448m in Jbel Tidiguin, not far from Ketama. Together with its outlier, the Jebala, these mountains all but seal off the rest of Morocco from coastal North Africa. This is the best watered range in the country. Cedars cover the sides of the mountains and pines and holm oaks cover the crests. There is even heather on the moorlands on the wetter N facing slopes. To the S lie the Atlas Mountains in three great chains – the Middle Atlas, the High Atlas and, in the S, the Anti-Atlas.

The Middle Atlas is in parts well wooded and fertile having rainfall to support its forest and moorlands. It is made up of two separate masses with different configurations and reaching different altitudes.

To the W between Kenitra and Ifrane lies a limestone plateau area, the valley thick with oaks and the lower slopes clothed with cedars. In this gently undulating region there are numerous small mountain lakes and small waterfalls. In winter snow blocks many routes. To the E the land is higher, the Jbel Bou Ibane reaching 3,190m. The terrain is very rugged with many slopes almost precipitous. Bou Naceur is 3,343m and Gaberaal is 3,290m.

The great mass of the High Atlas extends for more than 650 km with 400 peaks over 3,000m. It acts as a huge barrier dividing the better watered Atlantic and Mediterranean areas of the country from the extensive desert regions. To the W is a high massif where very old rocks, resistant to erosion, rise to a height of 4,165m at Jbel Toubkal to the S of Marrakech. In the centre is the limestone massif of Azilal and Ouarzazate. The highest point is Ighil M'Goun at 4,071m. This massif is incised with deep, very spectacular gorges and valleys while the rivers are dammed to form large lakes. The slopes which are rainfed have a cover of pine and juniper. To the E is the chalky plateau lying between Imilchil and Midelt. Jbel Ayyachi at 3,737m is the highest peak. The cedars which clothe the slopes are very old.

The Anti-Atlas is another soaring range. It extends for 400 km. The highest peak, directly E of Irherm, is Adrar-n-Aklim reaching 2,531m. There is an eastern extension, Jbel Saghro with high summits Amalou n'Mansour 2,712m and Fengour 2,516m and Jbel Ougnat, while at the western extremity is the Atlantic Ocean. There is minimal vegetation on the mountains compensated for by, surprisingly fertile and surprisingly green, oases.

The Sirwa (Siroua) is the connection between the High and Anti-Atlas ranges. It is a vast volcanic outcrop of great height. The ancient black basaltic lava produces a rugged landscape with deeply carved valleys radiating from the central point of 3,304m.

The country's richest agricultural area is in the plain of the Gharb and the inland basins around Fes and Oujda. The coastal region aligned along the Atlantic between Rabat and Essaouira and limited to the E by the High and Middle Atlas forms a broken plateau of 210m average height. To the E of the High Atlas and S of the Middle Atlas is the W fringe of the High Plateau which run in fuller form through Algeria. To the S of the Anti-Atlas is the Sahara desert.

Morocco on the map

🐾 Morocco takes its name from the Arabic Maghreb Al-Akhtar meaning land of the furthest W. It has long been represented on maps mainly because it was part of the Mediterranean trading world. The first map of Morocco was by the Greek Hecataeus of Miletus in 500 BC in which the Gates of Hercules (The Straits of Gibraltar) are shown in accurate form (see maps below). He was followed by Herodotus, whose map of the world included Morocco as part of 'Libya'. This remarkably faithful representation of the Mediterranean was the base map on which other later geographers made their would-be improvements. In 150 AD Ptolemy, working from Alexandria, produced another advanced map of the world including Morocco's (named as Mauritania) Mediterranean coast with some accuracy but rather misinterpreted the W African river systems running to the Atlantic Ocean (see maps below). Arab cartography made a useful contribution to map-making in the early period (see box Al-Idrisi – Map maker Extraordinary, page 26). Al-Idrisi made one of the first recognizable maps using the Arabic script. Ibn Hawkal in 1086 produced a deviant view of the Mediterranean based on

The world according to
Hecataeus of Miletus

Ptolemy -
map of North-West Africa

The chains of the Atlas Mountains both by scale and height tend to present problems for communications. Travellers should plan their journeys through the limited number of passes such as those at Tizi-n-Test and Tizi-n-Tichka in daylight to maximize enjoyment of the scenery. Heavy snows and landslides can disrupt transport through these passes from time to time in the winter and early spring. In most years mountain snows melt away by Jun.

Traditional regional loyalties are influenced largely by the topographic divisions of the country and comprise (1) The Rif mountains in the N, (2) the agriculturally rich Rharb plain with Meknes and Fes, (3) the Haouz (region) of Marrakech, (4) the Sous which takes in the valley of the Oued Sous and the adjacent lands of the Anti-Atlas and (5) the Tafilalt desertic areas of E Morocco. Racial, tribal, linguistic and historical elements give these regions distinctive flavours among which there is both rivalry and co-operation.

The average altitude for the country as a whole is 800m above sea level, making Morocco the most mountainous in North Africa.

There is a complex set of river systems, the majority running to the sea

traveller's tales, showing Morocco as part of a country with vast river systems facing a rather rotund depiction of Iberia, el-Andalus (see maps below).

From the 18th century the Western Europeans began to manufacture good quality maps with the Kingdom of Morocco clearly demarcated. The activities of the British Admiralty, forever seeking better quality navigational charts and their European maritime rivals in the colonization of Africa, ensured excellent charts of coastal locations. Scientific mapping of the interior of Morocco awaited the coming of the French Protectorate.

Even at the present, access to modern map series at scales better than 1:250,000 is poor, if slightly improving, and can be accomplished only through prolonged bureaucratic processes in Morocco itself, though some original French maps at scales of 1:50,000 can still be obtained through map sellers in Paris. For walkers there are one or two 1960s map sheets at 1:50,000 for sites such as Jbel Toubkal that can be got in second-hand bookshops in the UK. For car travellers the best map is probably the 1:1,000,000 folding road map of Morocco published by Robertson McCarta Publications (see Maps, page 473).

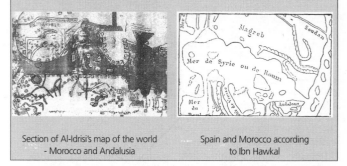

Section of Al-Idrisi's map of the world
- Morocco and Andalusia

Spain and Morocco according
to Ibn Hawkal

from the high mountain zone. In the NE the Oued Moulouya takes its origins in the Middle Atlas and collects the streams of the E Rif before reaching the Mediterranean at Saidia. The Rif proper is drained by a series of fast flowing streams to the Mediterranean such as the Oued Bou Frah and the Oued M'Ter but to the S, surface water runs to the Sebou and its tributary the Ouerrha and thence to the Atlantic near Kenitra. The Jebala is drained by the Loukkos and its tributaries to the Atlantic coast at Larache. The Oum er Rbia drains the vast areas of the Middle Atlas around Beni Mellal and the coastal plateau with the Oued Tensift taking flows from the area immediately to the S from the Marrakech basin. In the S of the country two important rivers, the Sous and the Draa run from sources in the High Atlas towards the Atlantic. On the E side of the High Atlas, streams such as the Rhéris and the Guir run S to inland drainage basins.

There are considerable variations in flows of streams in Morocco depending on the level of rain and snow fall in winter. The larger streams drawing their sources in the higher mountain areas flow for most of the year with snow melt persisting through as late as Jul but many oueds elsewhere are short-lived.

CLIMATE

As is to be expected with a country as large as Morocco, there is a wide range of climatic types. The N coast falls into the Mediterranean climatic zone, though the usual régime of mild wet winters and warm dry summers is affected by the proximity of the Atlantic from which depressions move across N Morocco, bringing heavier and more reliable rainfall than in much of the rest of the Mediterranean basin. The Atlantic coast in the S feels the moderating influence of the ocean even in summer thanks to the cold Canaries current which drifts S along the littoral.

Away from the coasts, high altitudes and the influence of the Sahara make for a complex set of microclimates. In general, movement S and E brings the effect of the Sahara nearer, including higher daytime and lower night temperatures together with greater aridity. Increasing altitude in the Atlas reduces temperatures and also means very cold nights in exposed areas and higher risks of rain and snow in the months of Nov-Mar. Winters can be bitterly cold and wet throughout the Middle and High Atlas. Marrakech averages only 16°C in Jan but 33°C in Jun. Rabat on the coast has temperatures in Jan of 19°C against 25°C in Jun. Rainfall has great importance since the majority of people still rely on agriculture for a living. The rains in recent years have been above average and agriculture has thrived but periods of extreme drought are frequent and mean disaster for rural peoples. Rabat on the Atlantic coast receives an average of 530 mm of rain while Marrakech, further S and in the foothills of the High Atlas, receives only 230 mm. In the SE arid desertic conditions prevail. Rain is often in the form of heavy showers, some with intense thunder and lightning which can occur in the N at any season of the year. In Apr 1995, for example, there was an entire week in the Rif punctuated by thunder storms. During storms there is a high risk of flash floods, with oued beds carrying violent spates for short periods.

The prevailing winds are from the Atlantic Ocean and variably W. Occasional S winds from the desert known as the *shergui* bring high temperatures, very low relative humidity and dust storm conditions, a miserable combination for the traveller. In the Tanger area and the Strait of Gibraltar a 'levanter' wind from the E can bring misty and cold conditions at any time of the year.

FLORA AND FAUNA

Morocco is a country of great contrasts; regional variations in climate, vegetation and relief are striking and these differences help to account for the unusually diverse and profoundly interesting flora and fauna.

Semi desert scrub is widespread, giving a green hue to wide expanses after the spring rains. In regions even less likely to receive precipitation the vivid desert flowers appear at very infrequent intervals. On the steppes the clumps of alfalfa grass help to stabilize the fragile soils and sage bush appears here too, an ungainly plant but able to withstand the wind, the cold and the drought. The soft pink flowered tamarisks hold back the sand while handsome oleanders flower white and red in the *oueds*. By contrast the hills facing to the moist air of the oceans produced thickly wooded areas, holm oaks, cork oaks, drought resistant cedars, thick trunked junipers. Pistachio trees grow wild in the Atlas, the southern plains support the argane found only here and in Mexico and the wild almond which ought to be the national tree produces its own breathtaking version of 'snow' in the early spring. The scented *maquis* of the Mediterranean region of Morocco completes the picture.

Morocco has the greatest diversity of birdlife N of the Sahara, with 460 species, of which 11 are threatened. Migratory birds making use of the thermals to cross the narrow Strait of

A Moroccan view of wildlife

Most of this wildlife is sufficiently elusive to evade most casual visitors. It is regrettably not elusive enough, however, to evade those determined to exploit it and very quickly the visitor will encounter shops offering stuffed lizards, tortoises which have been converted into banjo-like musical instruments, purses and bags of snake skin, together with innumerable furs from fennecs, genets and wild cats. Young boys will offer chameleons, tortoises and lizards for sale at the roadside. Not only is the purchase of these items by visitors directly contributing to the steady decline of Morocco's wildlife heritage, but it is also illegal to export or import such items or creatures without special permits.

It is also often difficult for the westerner to understand the role that folk-beliefs and myths have in the Moroccan's interactions with wildlife. A visit to a traditional medicine stall will reveal many cures and magical preparations based upon animal parts. These beliefs are very widely held. Virtually all reptiles are feared and most are killed on sight – even harmless species. With an increasing human population, these traditional practices are imposing an ever greater drain upon wild fauna.

Snake charmers are common in some cities, notably, in Marrakech in Djemaa El Fna (see page 302). The most favoured species used for this 'entertainment' are the Egyptian cobra (*Naja haje*) and the Puff adder (*Bitis arietans*). Incredibly large numbers of these snakes are collected to supply the trade, with serious ecological consequences for other wildlife. Removing the snakes, for example, enables the rat population to expand. The mouths of charmer's snakes are often stitched closed, preventing them from both biting and feeding. The monkeys which are also there for 'entertainment' are imported. They, like the drugged lion cubs (now banned), have a short life. With so much natural wildlife to observe this exploitation is unnecessary and responsible visitors should not, therefore, encourage these practices.

Gibraltar include huge storks and vultures and smaller (by comparison) buzzards and eagles. Bright coloured bee-eaters and blue rollers, pink flamingos and the striped hoopoes are distinctive sightings for untrained eyes.

Morocco also has a reptile fauna which is among the richest to be found anywhere in the Mediterranean region. The whole of European continent only supports 60 species of reptiles, whilst Morocco alone has over 90. You will, however, see few lizards and very few snakes as many are nocturnal and most shun areas inhabited by man.

The mammalian fauna of Morocco is also very diverse, and features genets, jackals, striped hyena, wild cats, fennecs, gerbils, jirds and jerboas, as well as the famed Barbary Apes of the Middle Atlas, wild boar still common in the Rif, the endangered Orcas gazelle and Oryx. The

forests of the Middle Atlas also harbour a few surviving leopards, watch how you go. Most of these animals are sufficiently elusive to evade most casual visitors.

Insects are a different matter. There are beautiful butterflies and a multitude of moths both in evidence when the spring flowers are in bloom. There are flies both large and small, bees, wasps, mosquitoes, these are not elusive and can at times be too attentive. In addition there are scorpions (see box, page 180).

Because of the high number of endemic, unfamiliar, species which are likely to be encountered and the unique variety of habitats, visitors to Morocco with an interest in natural history are advised to prepare themselves well in advance. Virtually no information on such topics is presently available within the country itself. Most of the books on wildlife recommended on page 471 can be obtained in Europe and the USA.

National Parks

Morocco has a number of National Parks, among the most important of which, internationally, is the Oued Massa National Park to the S of Agadir. In addition to being the haunt of the endangered Bald Ibis and a wide selection of water and wetland bird (see page 50), it also has an interesting reptile and mammalian fauna due to its geographical position which comprises tropical, Mediterranean and Saharan elements. Toads, frogs, terrapins, skinks and lizards abound. The Egyptian Cobra is reported in the vicinity (Bergier and Bergier, see page 473). There are ground squirrels and foxes too but our favourite is the Egyptian mongoose with a tuft on the end of its tail.

AGRICULTURE

Land use

Morocco, excluding Western Sahara, has proportionately more economically useable land than any other country of North Africa. Land use in 1991 was given as:

Land use	(%)
Arable and orchard	22.2
Meadow and pasture	46.8
Forest and woodland	20.1
Other uses	10.9
Total	100.0

Source: *Encyclopaedia Britannica*

Feeding the people – Morocco's dilemma

A population of 26.5 million growing at a rate of 2% means that Morocco has an extra half a million mouths to feed every year. By 2025 there will, according to the World Bank, be 41 million Moroccans. Yet Morocco currently has only 10.1 million ha of fertile land under cultivation. What prospects lie ahead for this country of beautiful landscapes but limited water supply? Few Moroccans are employed in modern agriculture and the production food is well below national needs. Cereal imports run at 3,650,000 tonnes/year and are increasing rapidly; food imports cost more than US$1,000 million each year.

The outlook for the immediate future is fairly good. Farm output in Morocco is still above the rate of population increase. The more distant future offers a less rosy prospect. Standards of living are rising and demand for more and better quality food is also going up. The land base is deteriorating as farmers push cultivation to the most marginal of areas where heavy rains soon carry away thin and fragile soil. Morocco is not another Dakota Dust Bowl in the making but a large rim around the existing cultivated area is increasingly at risk of severe damage. Meanwhile, many poorer farmers and young men aspiring to a better standard of living are drifting to the towns. In bad rainfall years like 1993-95, the drift is more rapid.

In Morocco's favour is its immense potential for growing foods and expensive market garden produce for the rich EU market, with which Morocco has improving trade relations. So far this opening has been scarcely used as a result of poor support for exporters in Morocco and obstruction by bureaucracy. The enormous range of climates in Morocco give opportunity for diversifying crops into the most exotic directions if undoubted local farming abilities can be profitably channelled. Agricultural exports are currently worth US$1,000 million, which figure could be at least doubled and thus the imports of basic cereals easily covered despite a growing population. So far, the farming community has been the Cinderella of the family – poorly funded, short of care and in need of encouragement. And not a prince charming in sight!

The 10,200,000 ha of land under cultivation carry crops of cereals, including wheat, barley and maize, sugar beet, citrus fruits, potatoes, tomatoes, olives and beans. Hill areas of the interior are intricately terraced for agricultural purposes, otherwise the main areas of cultivation are the plains and river valleys.

Land tenure

Moroccan land tenure conditions are dominated by large landlords, communal lands and religiously endowed land known in Morocco as *habous*. The landlord class is well entrenched politically and largely coopted by the régime with support and favour. No reform of tenure conditions has been attempted and large estates farmed by landlords using daily-paid labour or share croppers are the norm except for pockets of small landlords in the Sous and other limited areas. The land is very densely populated, forms of tenure apart, and more than

Berbers – the Ethnic Enigma

Morocco's population is made of Berbers and Arabs. Berbers constitute about 30% of the total according to official statistics but Berber blood probably runs in the veins of most Moroccans. The Berbers are the 'natives' or 'Libyans' of ancient North Africa, having been there since recorded history. The Berber community produced the great Egyptian king Sheshonq of the 22nd Dynasty. Their ethnic origin is unsure. Most authorities see them as Caucasian folk, with uniform racial and linguistic features. The independence and survival of the Berbers makes Arab rulers uneasy and so there is a great tendency in the modern period for the new nation-states in North Africa to stress their Arab rather than their Berber racial origins. In 1971, for example, the Libyan leader claimed, without benefit of evidence, that all Berbers were 'Hamitic' and that they originated in southern Arabia. In Morocco and Algeria modern language policies by governments tend to be pro-Arabic and unhelpful to Berber at school and administrative levels.

The survival of Berber as a culture is a miracle of tenacity. They were beaten in a military sense in the 7th century and overwhelmed politically by the invading Arabs in the 12th century. Yet their language is still used widely in Morocco and elsewhere in North Africa. Many Berbers have quite distinct racial characteristics such as light skin and blue eyes – even fair hair. Their survival is as result of strong social unity within a tribal structure (see box, Ait 'Atta, page 367), and traditions of marriage within the tribe or the extended family. In some Berber villages of Morocco, Arabic is not an adequate *lingua franca*, especially among the older generation and the womenfolk, whose only language is Berber. Berber design and crafts are to be found in jewellery and rugs, while dress is another dimension of Berber individuality (see Dress, page 66).

Berber is a spoken language but for the most part was not written down and had no written alphabet until recently. Instead, history and folklore are passed on through a tradition of spoken narrative. Berbers attach themselves to Islam and to the rule in Morocco of the Shareefian monarch. They therefore generally do not seek Berber political independence (there are exceptions). Even so, a growing sense of nationalism is apparent, expressed in emphasis on Berber cultural identity and a gradually growing modern Berber literature.

In Morocco do not make the colonial mistake of playing Berber against Arab. It will not work and could cause ill-feeling. But do enjoy the great individuality of the Berber communities and their rich traditions in arts and crafts.

The Jewish Tradition in Morocco

The Jewish Diaspora in North Africa dates back at least to the 1st century BC when a large portion of the estimated 5 million Jews outside Palestine lived in Alexandria. There were Jews in Sale in Morocco, dealing in gold at the time of King Solomon. In 320 BC the Egyptian Pharaoh moved some 30,000 Jews to the frontiers of his empire including Sinai, Libya and W Egypt to act as a defensive wall against external attack. In 200 BC there was a campaign in Morocco for the conversion of Berber tribes to Judaism and in the same period many Jewish immigrants appear to have undergone a process of Berberization. A large Jewish community grew up at Carthage during its era of success as a trading centre.

The destruction of the Second Temple and much of Jerusalem by the Romans in 70 AD and the Jewish revolts of 115 AD added to the flight of Jews from their homeland. Many Jews fled to join the existing overseas communities in North Africa.

Large concentrations of Jews were to be found at Sale and Volubilis after 70 AD as is attested by remnants of Jewish tombstones from this period discovered at Volubilis. By the 4th century AD a close network of connections developed between the Jews of Morocco and the Jews of Spain. Jews in the Roman Empire suffered from occasional persecutions in the 4th, 5th and 6th centuries. Moroccan Jewry was affected by further immigration, this time from Spain, in the 7th century. The coming of the Arab conquest in North Africa found a fluctuating but numerous and prosperous Jewish population in Morocco. The Jews specialized in trade with small communities living in small towns serving the trans-Saharan routes. The founding of Fes in Morocco and Kairouan in Tunisia brought new opportunities for Jewish financiers and craftsmen, who mainly enjoyed political protection and religious toleration under the Almoravids (1042-1147), with a new Jewish community growing at Marrakech. The Almohads (1147-1248) were more fanatically Muslim and forced conversions of the Jews were widespread.

Expansion of the Catholic kingdom of Castille in Spain led to Christian persecution of the Jews and many educated and skilled families fled to Morocco, Tunis and elsewhere in North Africa after 1391. This was particularly notable after the introduction of the Spanish Inquisition in 1481 and the expulsion of the Jews from Spain in 1492 and Portugal in 1496. The quality of arts, crafts and culture in those areas that received the Jewish immigrants was greatly enriched. Jews

40% of people still live off farming. The country has experienced a steady drift of people from the land for some years, especially from the Rif and Atlas mountain zones where farming is made difficult by the hostile environment and limited material rewards. The above average rainfall of recent years had eased some of the strains in these communities but the respite will not be permanent, as the drought conditions of 1995 indicate.

Potential

Morocco has a number of important advantages over other countries of North Africa. It is comparatively well-watered over large areas. It has a vigorous and innovating agricultural community. The climate is generally kind, with potential for growing a wide range of crops such as citrus, flowers and early vegetables in demand in nearby Western Europe. The climate, varied terrain and rich heritage also open up possibilities for tourism. The endowment of raw materials is generous, giving Morocco a substantial role as a producer of phosphates, semi-precious stones and non-ferrous minerals. All these resources offer the basis for

were later gathered together in special quarters of the major towns and cities, in Morocco called *mellah* following the example of Fes, where the Jewish quarter was located close to the palace for protection.

Two Jewish cultures lived side by side in Morocco – the older rural farming communities of the mountain areas and the sophisticated urban Jews. This situation was unique to North Africa and especially Morocco. Small groups of Jews were also in subsistence farming in Zliten in W Libya until 1948. Urban Jews were heavily concentrated in industry and trade, many very poor and living in new centres at Marrakech, Rabat and Safi.

By the 1840s the heavy taxes borne by the Jews and periodic violence against them led to a slow growth of emigration to Palestine. The situation of the Jews in Morocco changed dramatically with growing European influence and, in 1912, the establishment of the French Protectorate. The event was marked by an attack by Moslems on the Jewish quarter of Fes. The Jews strongly associated themselves with the colonial power and became increasingly detached from the mass of Moroccans. Further upsets were to follow – the French Vichy government imposed Fascist controls on North African Jews in 1940-42. By 1948 there were approximately 265,000 Jews in Morocco and Tanger. In that same year the State of Israel was formed. Emigration by Jews to France and Israel accelerated, encouraged by Zionist organizations so that in 1956 all Jewish emigration was stopped by the Moroccan Government, a ban that remained until 1961. Emigration persisted and by 1966 the number of Jews in Morocco had fallen to 55,000 and 10 years later to 17,000.

The departure of so large a community from Morocco was damaging and cannot, unlike in other Arab states, be put down to oppression and mistreatment alone since the Jews were largely integrated into Moroccan society at large. Perhaps the Europeanization of the Jewish middle class under the French Protectorate undid many of the established Jewish-Moroccan links, while the new opportunities in the 'Promised Land' of Israel were used to attract the rest of the Jewish population out of Morocco.

It remains that Morocco is still one of the few Arab countries with an open policy towards the Jews and Israel. No real grudges are harboured at the government level.

industrial processing. In many ways Morocco is currently in the throes of urbanization and modernization and seeking to make the best of its natural advantages to accommodate a 27 million population rapidly increasing at 2.4% each year and support a US$20.3bn foreign debt.

CULTURE

PEOPLE

The **population** of Morocco was estimated in 1995 at 26.98 million, of which half was male. Although the crude birth rate has fallen sharply in recent years to 28 per 1,000 population, potential fertility is high, as improved medical facilities enable improvements in the child survival rate. At the same time, death rates are also down to 6 per 1,000 and life expectancy, now 69 years on average, will improve to swell the total population.

Morocco is an intermixture of Arab and Berber peoples. The two sections have intermarried over many centuries so that there are few pure residual groups. Differentiation at the present day is more linguistic that ethnic. The

Mohammed V – architect of independence

Among the most frequently recurring street names in cities and towns of Morocco is 'Mohammed V'. Mohammed V lived from 1909-1961, was sultan of Morocco from 1927 to 1957 and king until 1961. Although he was the third son of the sultan, Moulay Yusuf, he was selected by the French Protectorate in Morocco to succeed his father. He was, however, no less a nationalist than his older brothers and effectively made a stand against French colonial policies such as separate laws for Arabs and Berbers which he saw as divisive. He became a continuing symbol of Moroccan nationalism and anti-colonialism, much to the annoyance of the French authorities.

During his long reign, Mohammed V was politically astute. He encouraged the mood of Moroccan nationalism without involving the monarchy in active opposition to the French. He sustained the monarchy at the centre of Moroccan political affairs. During WW2 he correctly chose to support the allies and met US President, Roosevelt. The independence movement gained strength during the war as the colonial power was overrun by the German army and lost authority in the eyes of the Moroccans, although Morocco was never occupied. With some encouragement from the USA and helped by the strong move to decolonization elsewhere in the world after WW2, Mohammed V increased his calls on the French to give up their protectorate. He passively resisted the French by refusing to sign administrative orders and by siding always with nationalist sentiment across the Arab world.

The French sent him into exile in 1953 after a protracted period of tension. He returned to Morocco and the throne in 1955 on condition that the French would negotiate their departure and thereby an end to the Protectorate. Mohammed V became the first king of Morocco in 1957 but thereafter gave up his powers to his son, who later ascended the throne as Hassan II in 1961. While in other countries of the Middle East and North Africa the end of colonialism was marked by war and destruction, Mohammed V in Morocco achieved independence without spilling blood, maintained the advantages of the French connection and launched an independent Morocco as a force for peace and reason in the Arab world.

principal Berber-speaking areas are clustered in the mountainous areas of the country, reflecting the retreat of the Berbers to regions of refuge during the Arab invasions. For convenience there are three main Berber areas where somewhat different forms of Berber are spoken – *Rifian* in the N mountain zone, *Amazigh* among the communities in the Middle Atlas and *Chleuh* in the Sous and adjacent areas of the High Atlas Mountains. The Arab inhabitants came in waves of adventurers and conquerors in the long period of invasions, including those of the Beni Hillal and Beni Sulaim between the 7th and 12th centuries. The important Jewish community, some locally based among rural Berbers, was reinforced from Iberia during the flight of Jews after the *reconquista* by highly educated and talented urban groups. Many Jews left Morocco after the foundation of the Jewish state of Israel in 1948. Trade with trans-Saharan Africa in goods and slaves introduced Negro blood, while Morocco's Mediterranean connection brought in traders from as far away as Malta and, in the late 19th century and 20th century, settlers from France, Germany and Spain.

Hassan II

The King of Morocco, Hassan II, is one of the longest lasting monarchs of the Middle East and North African region. He was born the first son of Mohammed V in July 1929. He, like most of the Moroccan elite of the day, was educated in France but is profoundly Muslim and nationalist in attitude. He is the scion of a line that comes from the blood of the Prophet Mohammed and as such he is a significant Islamic religious figure in his own right. Like his father, his domestic aims have been to keep the country under central control and the monarchy in charge of the centre.

It has not been an easy task. There were attempts to overthrow the king in 1971 and 1972, one of them when his aircraft was attacked by an airforce jet. His personal and political survival on this occasion added greatly to his charisma. Hassan II essentially rules as well as sits on the throne. He is actively and directly involved in managing the country without formal opposition under a system known as 'guided democracy'. The king suspended the constitution, which in its original 1962 form called for a constitutional monarchy, in 1965. A new constitution in 1970 was a failure and a further draft constitution was adopted in 1972. Elections were held in 1977 but, in practice, the king works without a parliament, much to the dismay of his political opponents who see King Hassan as an autocrat. Among the many successful policies pursued by the king which account for his continued popularity and power in Morocco were the Green March of November 1975, when many thousands of Moroccans responded to his call to march into and claim the W Sahara. The march was in close tune with nationalist wishes and earned him a special place, like his father who won independence from France, in the nation's affections. He has since contained and generally out-manoeuvred the political opposition, established his sons as his potential successors and set up a government that Moroccans understand and can live with. In foreign affairs the king has balanced his links with France by opening a window to the entire EU and seeking closer ties with the European economy. He is well favoured by the USA and the Western nations and has had generous treatment in aid and diplomacy. Morocco's ability as a moderate régime to deal with all sides in the Middle East and in its home territory of North Africa continues to defuse antagonism and to profit state and monarchy alike.

It is a comment on the king's success that Morocco without the guidance of Hassan II seems to be an incomplete concept.

Much of the population is concentrated in the coastal cities and plains. Approximately half the population now lives in cities, the great concentrations being in Casablanca with 2.9 million, Rabat with 1.2mn, Fes with 564,000 and Marrakech with 550,000 (1993 official figures). Areas of heavily settled land with 60-95 people per sq km are found round the Mediterranean and N Atlantic shores, notably in the Rif, Jebala, the Rharb plain and the coastal plateaux and valleys as far S as the Sous. Densities decline rapidly inland. Other than the great cities of Marrakech, Meknes and Fes, the inland area carries low population densities, averaging between 20-60 per sq km. The E and S of the country is sparsely settled with less than 20 people per sq km.

The population is fairly young on average. More than 36% of people are under the age of 15, 50% are under 20 and a mere 6% over 60. Educational progress has increased adult literacy rates to 50%. Some 37% of Moroccans enjoy the benefits of secondary and 1% tertiary education. Morocco is the poorest of the Maghreb states with average personal incomes estimated at US$1,030 in 1993. National income is maldistributed. The income of rural people is very low – less than US$250 per year in many cases and the urban poor, crowded in shanty areas, are little better off. Nutrition levels are improving, however, and aided by continued good rainfall there is a fragile air of prosperity to the country at the present time.

HISTORY SINCE INDEPENDENCE

Morocco became independent on 3 March 1956 through the efforts of Sultan Mohammed V, who was determined that the Sultanate should be the supreme political power within independent Morocco. The only competitor for control of the newly independent country was the Istiqlal party. Although Istiqlal formed the first government of independent Morocco, the monarchy sought to widen political representation to balance its influence. The Royal Palace favoured the Mouvement Populaire, a rural-based, pro-Berber and royalist movement but continued to collaborate with Istiqlal until, in 1959, the party itself split, with a new, more radical wing becoming a separate political party, the Union Nationale des Forces Populaires, under Mehdi Ben Barka. This provided the monarchy with the opportunity to dominate the political process by arbitrating among the different political parties.

The government had to contend with a series of rural rebellions. The most serious of these which occurred in the Rif was crushed by Morocco's new army. Central government distrust of the Rif as a result of the rebellion still persists today.

King Mohammed V died unexpectedly in 1961 and was succeeded by his eldest son, Crown Prince Hassan. The new king had long been groomed for government, with an education both in Arabic in Morocco and in French at Bordeaux and with experience of government, both as an army commander and as premier in the period just before his father's death. Although the Sultanate has been traditionally powerful because of the religious legitimization of its occupant as Amir Al-Muminin (Commander of the Faithful), King Hassan II, like all new Sultans, faced immediate threats to his survival on the grounds of his personal competence. The new monarch sought to introduce limited parliamentary democracy within a constitutional monarchy. The experiment was not very successful and came to an end in Nov 1963, only a few months after it had been begun.

For the next 7 years King Hassan ruled without parliament, and Morocco was placed under a 5 year state of emergency. A new constitution, designed to increase the role of pro-Royalist parties, was promulgated in 1970 but the parliament elected in the subsequent elections was dissolved. A coup attempt against the king took place on the king's birthday on 10 July, 1971, involving an army-backed attack against him and his guests at his summer palace of Skhirat, just outside Rabat, and a simultaneous military attempt to take over the government. Both prongs of the plan failed, in the case of the attack on the king, largely because of his personal courage. The ringleaders were killed or later executed and widescale purges of army and government took place.

The coup highlighted the serious problems of growing corruption and ostentatious amassing of wealth within the administration. Economic conditions inside Morocco had also worsened. The government attempted to respond to both types of complaint, but on 26 August, 1972, units of the airforce attempted unsuccessfully to shoot down the king's aircraft. Once again, King Hassan survived largely because of his

Pan-Arabism

Feelings of Pan-Arabism are strong in Morocco despite the mixed Arab and Berber population of the country. The Pan-Arab movement established grass roots as opposed to an intellectual tendency in the country as early as the mid-1940s.

The Moroccans have generally identified themselves either with issues such as the Algerian struggle for independence and the Palestine cause as Arabs or, as in the case of the Moroccan Berbers, have been sympathetic as fellow Muslims. These Pan-Arab convictions and the attitude to Islam as the religion of "the people" has created a barrier that has stood against the spread of fanaticism or the adoption of political Islam on levels similar to those in Algeria, for example. There is, however, a degree of solidarity with other North African states against the world as a whole. At the Pan-Arab level there is also a deep awareness of a common destiny among the ordinary people. During the Iraqi invasion of Kuwait, a great deal of spontaneous popular support was apparent for Saddam Hussain for his perceived pursuit of unification of the Arab world and apparent defeat of Western interests.

The Moroccan government's policies of alignment with Western Europe run contrary to Pan-Arab sentiment but also have a deal of national support principally for economic if not cultural reasons, though this twin orientation of the country – E to the Arab world and N towards Europe – is now part of a cultural confusion that Moroccans have yet to resolve. The visitor has to take into account both factors and be sensitive to Moroccan feelings towards the rest of North Africa whilst benefiting from Moroccan knowledge of Western habits and values.

personal bravery. On this occasion it was established that the person responsible for both this attack and the coup attempt the preceding year was the minister of defence, General Mohammed Oufkir.

THE WESTERN SAHARA ISSUE

King Hassan tried to rally support throughout the monarchy by reviving Morocco's claim to the Western Sahara. In 1974 Morocco began a diplomatic campaign to force Spain to evacuate the region. Inside the Western Sahara, a national movement, the *Polisario Front*, founded in 1973, had widespread support. Morocco persuaded the UN to place the competing claims for the Western Sahara to the International Court of Justice in The Hague. The Court determined in 1975 that Morocco did not have a sustainable claim of full territorial sovereignty. Morocco nonetheless assumed that the Court had backed its claim and, in a massive display of popular support, organized the **Green March**, a demonstration involving 350,000 Moroccans, to the border of the Western Sahara. Spain acquiesced in a secret deal and created a temporary tripartite administration in the Western Sahara between Morocco, Mauritania and Spain itself. The Polisario Front with Algerian and Libyan support was not prepared to accept Moroccan occupation and moved around 30,000 Sahrawi into refugee camps in Algeria and undertook a guerrilla war to liberate the Western Sahara. Although the Polisario Front succeeded in forcing Mauritania to abandon its occupation in 1978 (Morocco simply moved forces in instead) and in forcing Moroccan forces back into the major towns, it was not able to end Morocco's hold on the region. Starting in 1980, Morocco slowly won back control over virtually all the territory.

Morocco: the big borrower

Morocco has experienced something of an economic renaissance in recent years. Part of the miracle arose from genuine reform of the economy, including privatization of sections of industry and devolution of real authority over development to the provincial centres. But the process was aided by a strong flow of foreign loans to help keep the economy afloat. By 1993 Morocco owed US$20,300 million to overseas lenders and possibly a further US$5,000 million in debts to trade suppliers without Moroccan Government guarantee. For a country without oil wealth, the total debt was a great burden, requiring occasional rescheduling of debt to put off the date of repayment, the biggest in 1983 but with other debt repayment delays since that time.

Morocco signalled its renewed dependence on foreign credit and investment in 1993 when a loan of US$25 million was raised in Europe to pay for new investment in regional utilities such as transport and industries including cement production. Borrowing has persisted and in 1996 no less than US$1,600 million was raised abroad to fund the privatization and modernization of the large coal-fired power station at Jorf Lasfar near Casablanca. Another four loans worth US$190 million were given to Morocco by the World Bank in 1996 for education, health and employment projects.

For Morocco it is important that foreign interest in investment and lending continues as a means of financing the massive structural and other changes needed if the economy is to sustain its admirable rate of growth and living standards for ordinary Moroccans are to keep on rising.

Morocco – borrowing abroad

External Debt US$mn	Annual Interest Payments US$mn	Debt as % Exports	Debt as % GNP	Average rate of interest
21,400	1,020	32	73	7

Source: World Bank, 1995

By the end of the decade, the UN had stepped in, with a proposal for a referendum over self-determination which was formally accepted by both sides. Morocco, however, made it clear that it would not abandon control of the Western Sahara.

MODERN MOROCCO

GOVERNMENT

Morocco remains officially a constitutional monarchy. The system in use is one chamber, a House of Representatives, which is summoned and dissolved by the king at will. In theory, the House of Representatives can bring forward its own legislative programme but this can effectively be vetoed by the king who can also issue laws for endorsement through popular referendum. The king is commander of the armed forces. Four main political parties exist but those which fail to accept the central role of the monarchy are suppressed. The palace has attempted to recruit more support among the previously alienated intellectual classes and universities aided by improvements in living standards and promises of political liberalization.

The autocracy of the centre has been somewhat modified recently by the grant of limited autonomy to local administrations – city, town and region – and to the regional offices of the ministries so that decision-making can genuinely reflect local sentiments. Governors are appointed by the king. Administration in the Western Sahara is in the hands of the military.

Despite successes in foreign policy, King Hassan has not yet been able to democratize the political system without endangering the position of the monarchy. It remains to be seen to what degree he will be prepared to relinquish power after the forthcoming elections, in the face of considerable domestic political pressure to do so. The king's position has been rendered more malleable by the misjudgement of the popular mood his government had made during the war against Iraq in 1991. Moroccans generally had opposed the US-led Multinational Coalition, although the Moroccan government had initially supported it. Nonetheless, King Hassan has proved to be a consummately skilful political operator in the past and will, no doubt, show an equal sureness of touch in dealing with current problems.

ECONOMY

Traditional agriculture

Almost 40% of the labour force in Morocco is engaged in agriculture, by far the majority in traditional farming. In the traditional sector there are many peasant proprietors with smallholdings but most are tenant farmers. It is estimated that 33% of farmland is owned by 3% of the farmers. Much of the area of private land is under traditional tenancies with holdings of less than 10 ha. Forms of nomadism persist in a few areas but there is an increasing tendency for livestock to be herded by shepherds rather than entire families on the move and for former nomadic groups to become settled. Similarly, the traditional valley cultivation areas of the high mountains are being deserted as the low returns and high demands on manual labour are rejected by people seeking higher incomes in the towns. Despite these changes, traditional farming remains the backbone of the economy, heavily involved with cereal growing and vegetable production in which the country, unusual for North Africa, is mainly self-sufficient. Peasant farmers and herders also own the bulk of the country's 16.3 million sheep, 4.7 million goats and 2.9 million cattle and a heavy concentration of fodder production results from this.

Modern agriculture

Modern farming is limited to the fertile plains of the Gharb, Marrakech and other smaller areas, much originally developed as medium-to-large scale enterprises by French settlers. The French have now been replaced by Moroccan owners, some of whom have also invested in reclaiming land elsewhere to take advantage of new irrigation water or modern farming methods. Most large scale farms produce export crops with concentration on citrus, where Morocco has been successful in breaking into Western European markets, sugar beet and specialist early vegetables such as potatoes and soft fruits. The modern farms have taken the largest share of newly provided irrigation water and state credits to the detriment of the small traditional units. There are some 9 million ha under cultivation with approximately 800,000 ha under irrigation. Farm output has expanded in recent years, helped by good rainfall:

Agricultural Output

('000 tonnes)	1994
Sugar beet	3,144
Wheat	3,523
Barley	3,720
Oranges	955
Potatoes	875
Olives	560
	Source: *FAO*

Morocco has a major *fishing* industry, the 1993 catch being 607,000 tonnes and efforts are being made to develop the industry with foreign aid. Morocco is the world's largest producer of sardines. The over-exploited *forests* yielded

The 'sacred aunt' of the Moroccans – the date palm

🐾 Morocco, open to the climatic shocks of the Atlantic Ocean was never the home of the date palm in the way that its neighbours in Algeria and Tunisia have been. Even so, dates are important parts of the Moroccan diet and each year some 62,000 tons of dates are produced (against 265,000 tons in Algeria and 86,000 tons in Tunisia), mainly in southern parts of the country.

The prophet Mohammed called on the Islamic faithful to protect the date palm, which he called their 'sacred aunt' because of its many uses as a food, building material and provider of shade (see below). The Swedish naturalist Carl Linnaeus rendered homage to the beauty and generosity of the palm tree when he classified it in the order of Principes, 'The Order of Princes'. The green and yellow foliage of the date palm is also a fine decoration in the otherwise vegetationless squares and avenues of many Moroccan cities. In the southern oases of Morocco, the palm is the tree of life, its fruit, leaves and wood the basis of the local economy. The Latin name of the date palm, *Phoenix dactylifera*, may be translated as 'the Phoenician tree with fruit resembling fingers' and Morocco's top variety of date, the *majhoul*, has a delicate translucent appearance. The *majhoul* sells for MD40 per kilo. Morocco produces 14 different varieties of dates.

The date palm is a close relation to the grasses. The tree has neither branches nor twigs. Its trunk is in fact a stem: it has no bark; being simply covered by the base of the old fallen leaves. A cross-section of a palm trunk reveals a multitude of rigid tubes containing sap bearing vessels, rather than the annual growth rings of a true tree. Due to the activity of a single bud hidden at the heart of the palm leaves, this trunk grows continuously.

The *phoenix dactylifera* grows to 23m. The top delicate, pinnate leaves grow to some 5m long. Flowers spring from the axils of the leaves and today most cultivated palms are hand pollinated. The date fruit (trees bear fruit at 5 years old) is a berry – with one long seed or pit and an individual palm can have up to 1,000 dates in one bunch. The dried fruit contains by weight 50% sugar and a little protein and fat. Date palms can live for up to 100 years, though the older trees become ragged in foliage and gradually yield less fruits.

In the wild state, the young palm tree tends to resemble a hedgehog due to the uncontrolled development of buds at the base of the initial trunk. If severed with skill, these buds can be planted elsewhere. There are both male and female trees. Broadly speaking, a male tree can pollinate some 50 female trees. To ensure maximum fruit production, the farmer will place a sprig of male flowers next to the female flowers – or should he have only a small orchard, he will not grow any male trees at all, preferring to buy male sprigs at the market.

In March or April, the tiny green date is round like a marble. Its future is uncertain: if the hot winds from the S are too fierce, it may be blown from the tree before its time. During the summer, the date reaches full size, becoming smooth and yellow, rich in vitamins but bitter to taste. In the heat of the summer and autumn, the fruit slowly matures on the tree, softening and turning an amber colour, deep brown or black, depending on the variety. The date sugars change as well and, little by little, the date dries out and becomes a preserved fruit if left on the tree. For the oasis dwellers, the date is so precious that they have a name for each stage of its growth. The date palm may produce up to 100 kg of dates annually for a whole century. However, in order to do this, it needs manure and a lot of

water, anything up to 300 litres a day!

The future of the date palm is not assured. The growth of tourism in the S and E oasis villages of Morocco has offered farmers new ways of making a living and farming is losing its dominance so that the oasis gardens are tending, although at a slower rate than in other North African countries, to fall into decay. The date is no longer a providential food for oasis dwellers and the date palm orchard is now limited to the top producing commercial varieties. Meanwhile, Moroccan palm groves have been ravaged by the *bayoud* fungus, control of which is not yet established. It is estimated that now over 60% of the Moroccan palmeries are affected by the *bayoud* disease. This is a kind of fungus which spreads through the roots from infected trees and is perhaps initially spread by spores. The tree dies within a season. If grubbed out it leaves a gap for the wind and sand to penetrate, if left there is encouragement for the disease to spread. There are some attempts to find a cure or ways to prevent the spread of *bayoud* – but time goes by and damage to the palmeries is continuing.

The palm tree provides many essentials for its owner. The trunks are used to support roofs of houses, strengthen walls and in slices are used to make doors. One or two trunks make an adequate bridge over an irrigation channel, and with pieces cut out can be used as steps. The fibres on the trunk are removed and used as stuffing for saddles while the base of the palm frond, stripped of its leafy part, makes a beater for the washer woman and a trowel for the mason. Palm fronds are used to make baskets and a variety of mats. Midribs can be used to make crates and furniture. Leaf bases are used for fuel and fibre for packing. The sap is drained and consumed as a rough but intoxicating beer or even as a distilled liqueur. This practice is banned for Muslims, who are forbidden alcohol and in any case drawing the sap can also kill the tree and is therefore discouraged by the authorities. The flesh of fruit which is rich in sugar and vitamins is eaten by man and the stone is eaten by the camel. Date stones can even be ground and used to supplement coffee. Best quality fresh dates are a delicacy for the rich. Dried and pressed dates stay edible for long periods and can be taken on journeys or used to sustain the nomads in their wanderings.

2,009,000 cu m of timber in 1993 though a great deal of indiscriminate cutting is used to produce firewood.

Energy/petroleum

Morocco has very poor domestic sources of fuel. Its small reserves of oil in the Rharb are being run down very rapidly and, despite intensive exploration, few discoveries have been made. Oil production was 83,600 barrels in 1992 with natural gas at 23,987,000 cu m. There is some generally low grade coal available, 1992 output being 576,000 tonnes. Other than natural gas, internal output is inadequate to satisfy demand of 1,791,000 tonnes of coal and 47,500,000 billion barrels of oil, the balance of which is imported. Increasing use is being made of hydroelectric power to support a total electricity consumption of 11,257,000,000 kwh. Much hydroelectric potential remains to be developed. The Meskala gas fields remain under-exploited as a result of cash shortages and technical difficulties.

Economic policies and plans

Morocco has put little reliance on economic planning and its experiences have been generally negative. In the 1960s there was an attempt in the national plan to foster rapid industrialization, mainly using state monopoly agencies. Other plans have tended at various times to be sectoral, providing for agriculture, industry or energy as separate entities but rarely extending, as was claimed, to an integrated national economic plan on the French model on which they were supposedly based. The indicative 1988-92

The Maghreb-Europe pipeline

Morocco took on a new role in 1996 – as a pipeline transit country for the Maghreb gasline. The gasline originates in Algeria at the long-established Hassi R'mel field in the Ghardaia area of the country. It has an overall length of some 1,250 km on its journey through Algeria and along the northern rim of Morocco under the Strait of Gibraltar through to Spain and Portugal. The line enters Morocco at Aïn Beni Mathar, 83 km S of Oujda. By the year 2000 approximately 10,000 million cu metres of natural gas will pass through the pipeline on its way to southern Europe.

A reward to Morocco for its part in the project will be royalties paid in gas delivered at a rate of 300 million cu metres/year. Morocco will also buy in extra gas if it can as a means of solving some of its domestic energy supply problems.

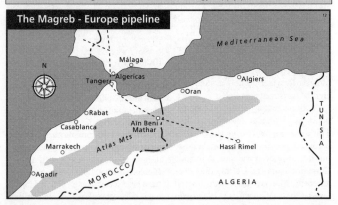

The Magreb - Europe pipeline

Moroccan textiles

Morocco produces a good range of textiles. Dyeing silk and wool for carpets and textiles in a traditional form goes on to the present day in established cities from Marrakech to Fes. *Caftans* are manufactured, together with lace items and a range of embroidered cloths for table and personal adornment. The best of Moroccan textile work is seen in women's wedding dresses, though Morocco has no wonderful display like that at the Dar Cheriat Museum in Tozeur, Tunisia. Interesting *burnouses* (heavy woollen cloaks), *gandouras* (smocks), *jallabahs* (long light shifts) and *caftans*, can still be bought for very reasonable prices at bazaar shops in the souqs and holiday shopping boutiques. The country is also famous for its modern textile manufacturing. In 1994, 12% of all exports worth MD4,400 million were textiles and accessories.

In Morocco there is a growing trade in the labour intensive parts of the modern clothes producing cycle, exporting items back to the main factories in Western Europe for finishing. Some controversy was caused recently in Western Europe by allegations that child labour was being exploited in Moroccan factories.

A traditional Moroccan design for textiles

development plan achieved economic growth at 4% per year in real terms (see also Economic Trends, page 92). Current policies are designed to cultivate privatization of state enterprises, private investment in modern industry, transport and communications. Special incentives apply to investment by foreign interests in Morocco for which tax holidays and preferential treatment are offered.

A key element in Moroccan economic policy is alignment towards the EU. This arose originally from the close relationship between Morocco and France but has since been widened to include Germany, Spain and UK and the EU as an entity. Morocco has sought special terms of association with the EU to gain access for its products and labour. The anti-North Africa sentiment in France and elsewhere has not deterred the Moroccan government from continuing to look for closer commercial links with the EU.

Industry

Is now as important a contributor to national income as agriculture, being valued at MD44,636 million in 1993. It provides only a modest proportion of employment, however, with 15.5% against 39.2% in agriculture. A large segment of industry is still French-owned despite an accelerated programme of Moroccanization. Processing of agricultural products is a major activity, including olive pressing, flour milling, vegetable and fruit canning and milk treatment. There has been increasing success with using phosphates and other minerals as raw materials for domestic industrial use rather than simply for export. Phosphates in particular are the basis for a set of industrial developments related to phosphoric acid and other chemicals. Construction materials, above all cement, form another area of rapidly growing industrial activity. There is a strong traditional craft manufacturing industry located in the major cities, especially Marrakech, Meknes, Fes and Tanger. World famous for design and quality are leather goods, hand-woven rugs and textiles, pottery and metalwork.

Industrial Production 1994

	(tonnes)
Cement	6,324,000
Olive oil	56,000
Wine	40,000
Automobiles	20,150*
Refined sugar	508,000
	* Units

Source: *Encyclopaedia Britannica*

Economic trends

The war in the Western Sahara contributed towards Morocco's growing economic crisis. The government had, in 1976, decided to make an accelerated push for development in the hope of diffusing the growing social tensions which had contributed so much to the domestic political unrest of the early 1970s. Morocco pushed ahead with ambitious development plans using borrowed funds. However, by 1983, the costs of development, together with those of the war, had created an impossible situation.

Economic Structure

	(%)
Agriculture	14.3
Mining	2.0
Manufacturing	18.0
Utilities	7.7
Other services	53.3
Construction	4.7
Total	100.0

In Sep 1983, Morocco had to reschedule its debt in the face of a worsening economic crisis and, despite the likelihood of the need to impose severe austerity measures, turned to the IMF for help. It had already had to face growing domestic discontent and there was every sign that this would recur. Indeed, the IMF economic restructuring plans, which insisted on the removal of consumer price subsidies on staples, such as sugar, flour and cooking oil, produced precisely that effect in Jan 1984. Riots swept the country and the government was forced to rein in its planned austerity measures. Since then the Moroccan government has plotted a very careful economic course, balancing off the need to satisfy its foreign creditors against domestic tensions. Its foreign debt rose from US$11bn in 1983 to around US$20bn in 1993. Morocco has also benefited from aid from the World Bank and from official aid donors, mainly in Europe. The result has been that the economy has been liberalized, the state sector is being dismantled and many observers now expect Morocco to begin slightly more rapid economic growth.

Symbolic of Morocco's desire for modernization has been a privatization programme, in which US$2bn of state companies will be handed over to private enterprise by 1995. Convertibility of the dihram for international transactions began in 1994. In Apr 1994 the GATT (General Agreement on Tariffs and Trade) annual meeting was held in Marrakesh when Morocco officially joined the organization. Despite some criticism that membership of GATT will impede domestic economic growth, accession to membership was seen as endorsing Morocco's growing maturity as a developing economy.

Main economic indicators

Despite a brief surge in the value of national output in the late 1980s, the Moroccan economy is now growing only

Economic indicators				
	1989	**1991**	**1993**	**1994**
GDP (MD billion)	140	...	247	252
Imports (MD billion)	48	56	62	66
Exports (MD billion)	35	38	34	37
Balance of Trade (MD billion)	-14	-13	-29	-29
Inflation (1985=100)	117.9	138.1	153.6	161.3
Foreign Debt (US$ billion)	19.9	21.2	20.3	...

Source: IMF, *Encyclopaedia Britannica*

modestly at 2% per year. Personal incomes have tended nonetheless to stagnate. Unemployment is officially put at 11% but, with seasonal unemployment and underemployment taken into account, a much larger number is less than gainfully employed. Inflation rose sharply in 1990-95 to close on 7% per year. Morocco's trade performance has been dismal, with a large deficit on current account.

Rabat and environs

RABAT AND SALE may lack for travellers the exotic appeal of Fes, Marrakech or Tanger, but these two cities have an impressive architectural legacy which reflects their long and turbulent histories. The massive but incomplete Hassan Tower, the Kasbah des Oudaias overlooking the river and sea, the ruins of the Merinid necropoli of Chellah, and the Abul Hassan Medersa with its intricate carving, are some of the most important and rewarding sites in Morocco. The medinas of Rabat and Sale are small and easy to explore, with beautiful houses and public buildings, and interesting markets and shops. The French built *ville nouvelle* (new town) retains much of the ambience of the colonial capital city, and has a surprisingly relaxed atmosphere. It is a comfortable and convenient place to stay, and perhaps a better first-stop than Casablanca.

RABAT

Pop 1,220,000 (1993); *Alt* 65m; *Best season* Fine all year round, as the humid summer, with high Jul and Aug peak temperatures, is relieved by sea breezes.

"They call Rabat the Pearl of Morocco. It stands high on the steep southern bank of the Bouragrag where the green river lashes the blue sea, above cactus-grown ochre rocks, a long rambling line of white and yellow, everywhere dominated by the huge grey Tower of Hassan." Rankin, Reginald, *In Morocco* (1908).

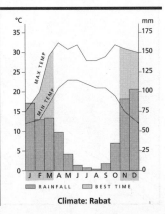

Climate: Rabat

HISTORY

City of Old and New

The name 'Rabat', a shortened and corrupted form of 'Ribat al-Fath', literally a 'monastery of conquest', indicates an initial role as a religious retreat and fortification. The city, located on the bank of the Oued Bou Regreg, with the kasbah on a promontory overlooking both the Atlantic Ocean and the estuary, lies opposite its historic rival, Sale. Rabat, capital since 1912, is Morocco's second largest city. The ambitiously extensive city walls laid out by the third Almohad Sultan Abu Yusuf Ya'qub al-Mansur now enclose, with the river and the sea on the remaining sides, the kasbah, the old medina, and the core of the *ville nouvelle*, the old and new directly alongside each other unlike the more common French pattern found in Fes, Marrakech and Meknes, where the new town was built some distance from the medina.

Early origins

Sala Colonia and the Ribat The first settlement of this area was probably outside the present city walls, on the site of the later Merinid mausoleum of **Chellah**. There is conjecture of prior Phoenician and Carthaginian settlement, but it is with the Roman **Sala Colonia** that Rabat's proven urban history began. Accorded municipal privileges, Sala Colonia was the most southwesterly town of the Roman Empire for the 2 centuries they ruled it, a trading post on the Oued Bou Regreg (which has since changed course), and a defensive settlement, located close to the line of frontier outposts,

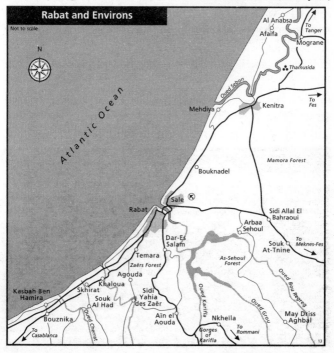

Rabat and Environs

running through the modern-day suburbs to the S of the city.

Sala Colonia was then occupied by Berbers from the 8th to the 10th century, but their heretic Kharajite beliefs represented a challenge to the orthodoxy of the inland Muslims. In the 10th century the Zenata tribe built a fortified monastery, or *ribat*, on the site of the current **Kasbah des Oudaias**, as a base from which to challenge the heretics on both sides of the river, and their supporters, the powerful Berghouata tribe. This led eventually to the abandonment of Sala Colonia.

Rabat under the Almohads

The *ribat* was used by the Almoravid Dynasty, but it was the Almohad Sultan Abd al-Mumin who redeveloped the settlement in 1150, transforming it into a permanent fortress town with palaces, the main mosque which still stands, reservoirs, and houses for followers, and using it as an assembly point for the large Almohad army. However, it was his grandson, Ya'qub al-Mansur, who from 1184 carried out the most ambitious programme of development, with his dream of Rabat as one of the great imperial capitals. He ordered an enormous city to be built, surrounded by extensive walls. These walls were probably completed by 1197, and ran along two sides of the city, broken by four gates, most notably the **Bab er Rouah**. A grid of broad streets, residential quarters, a covered market, public baths, hotels, workshops and fountains were built, along with a new gateway to the medina. A bridge to Sale, and its **Grand Mosque**, were also constructed.

Yet the most impressive monument from this period, the Hassan Mosque, was never completed. Projected to be the largest mosque in western Islam, the vast minaret never reached its full height, and little more than pillars remain of the rest. Ya'qub al-Mansur's death in 1199 led to the abandonment of the project. Rabat then fell into decline, some of it destroyed in fighting between the Almohads and Merinids, so that Leo Africanus, visiting in 1500, found only 100 or so houses, two or three inhabited quarters, and very few shops. As Rabat declined under the Merinids, Sale prospered. The dynasty's most noteworthy contribution to Rabat was the funeral quarter on the **Chellah** site, with its impressive mausoleums, but even that was eventually neglected.

Piracy and Andalusians

Rabat's fortunes did not revive until the 17th century, when the Atlantic Ocean became more important to international trade, and corsairing, or piracy, boomed. For a time Rabat was the centre of this piracy, with 'the Sallee Rovers' of historical repute more likely to have been based here than in present-day Sale. Robinson Crusoe was a fictional captive of 'a Turkish rover of Salle'.

Rabat also benefited from the flow of Muslims leaving Spain during the Inquisition. First rejected by Sale, the Hornacheros settled in the Rabat kasbah in 1609, and the other Andalusians in the Rabat medina in 1610. The medina they settled in was considerably smaller than the city Ya'qub al-Mansur had envisaged, as indicated by the 17th century rampart, which, when built, demarcated the extent of the settlement, and now runs between the medina and the *ville nouvelle*. The area beyond this rampart was used for agricultural purposes, and most of it remained undeveloped until the arrival of the French. The Andalusian influence can be observed in the medina, in the regularity of the street plan, in the motifs on doors, and in the past and present styles of decorative arts and crafts.

A fierce rivalry existed between the Hornacheros and the Andalusians, both of which had set up autonomous city-states, and the period 1610 to 1666 was marked by intermittent strife between the three towns of the Bou Regreg estuary. By 1627 these were united under the control of the Hornacheros as the Republic of the Bou Regreg, a control against which the Andalusians frequently rebelled, most notably in 1636. The Republic lost its independence in 1638. In 1641 the three cities were united, and in 1666 were brought under the authority of the Alawite Sultanate, when Moulay al-Rachid captured the estuary.

The principal background to these conflicts was the struggle for control over the gains from piracy, a profitable activity. Piracy was a form of trade, but also fed off trade, and the legal, illegal and governmental aspects were often closely linked. Rabat was popular with corsairs, many of whom originated in the Mediterranean, because, unlike several other ports, it had not been occupied by Europeans.

Alawite Capital

Under the Alawites, Rabat changed considerably. Trade and piracy were taken over as official functions, the profits going to the state. The port declined, replaced initially by Mogador (Essaouira). Moulay al-Rachid took over the kasbah, expelling its residents and strengthening the walls, and built the **Qishla** fortification to overlook and control the medina. However Sultan Moulay Ismail, most closely associated with Meknes, ignored Rabat, and broke the power of the corsairs.

From 1768, Mohammed Ibn Abdellah had a palace built in Rabat, and since then the Alawite Sultans have maintained a palace there, making the city one of their capitals. Increased trade with Europe in the 19th century temporarily revitalized Rabat's role as a port, but it was gradually supplanted, perhaps because of the shallow mouth of the Bou Regreg and the poor harbour facilities which were inadequate for larger boats, but also because newer towns and cities, notably Casablanca, were more easily controlled by Europeans. In 1832 the rebellious Oudaia tribe were settled in the abandoned kasbah,

giving it its current name, whilst the kasbah continued to be administered separately from the medina until the 20th century.

Rabat in the 20th century

The French landed in Rabat in 1907, and occupied it until 1912, when the Protectorate was officially declared. Fes was initially chosen as the capital, but as it remained a centre of dissidence and rebellion, and the inland areas remained insecure, Rabat was its replacement, formally confirmed in 1913. The first Resident-General, Lyautey, with his architect Henri Prost, planned and built the majority of the new capital, the *ville nouvelle*, both within and outside Ya'qub al-Mansur's walls, leaving the medina much as they found it. Rabat's economy today is primarily based on its role as Morocco's capital, with massive numbers on the government pay-roll. The economic growth of the city has continued to attract migrants from the countryside, with population growth outstripping the supply of housing. Thus Rabat today is a city of extremes, with streets of ostentatious and luxurious villas not far from crowded, decrepit and insanitary tin-shack slums, or *bidonvilles*.

ACCESS Air Regular buses from **Airport Mohammed V** in Casablanca to Rabat, taking 90 mins, cost MD50. Tickets are sold at the booth outside the front entrance of the airport, from where the buses depart, to both Casablanca and Rabat. The buses arrive in Rabat outside the *Hotel Terminus*, Ave Mohammed V, beside the station. Grand-taxis, which also leave just outside the airport, are expensive as they cannot be shared. The local **Rabat-Sale airport**, T 727393, 10 km from Rabat off the P1 Sale to Meknes road, has daily flights from Casablanca and Paris and a weekly flight (Fri) from Tetouan. For the town centre follow the signs to Sale, cross the river and continue up Ave Hassan II. There is a train service into town from the new station.

Train The main railway station, **Rabat Ville**, T 767353, is on Ave Mohammed V, in the city centre, close to the main hotels.

There are luggage lockers, but they are often all occupied. There is another station, **Rabat Agdal**, T 772385, in rue Abderrahman El Ghafiki, closer to the university, the newer ministry buildings and residential areas, but otherwise not convenient. All trains from Marrakech, Oued Zem, El Jadida and Casablanca stop at both stations, as do some of those from Tanger, Meknes, Fes and Oujda.

Road From Tanger and N the P2 brings the traveller through Sale, as does the P1 from Meknes, Fes and E. To get to Rabat, from the roundabout near the Bab Mrisa, cross the Pont Moulay Hassan and turn right, up to Ave Hassan II. From Casablanca and the S on the P36, turn right along Ave An-Nasr, and into the walled city via Bab er Rouah. **Bus** The principal bus terminal, for both CTM buses and those of the private lines, is inconveniently located at Place Zerktouni, 3 km out from the centre. Catch a No 30 bus to Ave Hassan II, or a petit-taxi for about MD15.

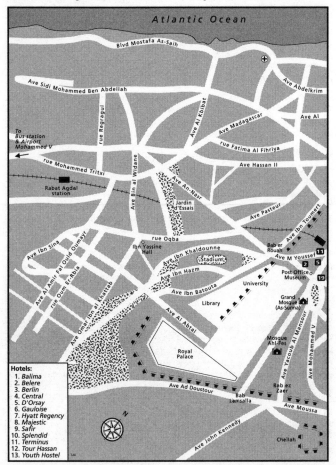

Hotels:
1. Balima
2. Belere
3. Berlin
4. Central
5. D'Orsay
6. Gauloise
7. Hyatt Regency
8. Majestic
9. Safir
10. Splendid
11. Terminus
12. Tour Hassan
13. Youth Hostel

PLACES OF INTEREST

ROUTES THROUGH THE CITY

The **Kasbah des Oudaias**, the **medina** and the **Chellah** have to be explored on foot. Start at the kasbah, carry along Tarik al Marsa to the **Hassan Tower** (4) and the **Mohammed V Mausoleum** (5). From there follow Blvd Bou Regreg, Ave Tariq Ibn Ziad and Ave Moussa Ibn Nos-

sair to the **Chellah**. Enter the *ville nouvelle* by **Bab ez Zaer** to the **Sunna Mosque** (1). Turn along Ave Moulay Hassan and through **Bab er Rouah** (3) to view it from the outside. Pass down Ave Ibn Toumert, past **Bab el Had** to **Bab el Alou**, and right into the medina. Turn right down Blvd Mohammed V and carry on through the medina to Ave Hassan II. Those with transport must park here and explore the medina and the *ville nouvelle*. Blvd Mo-

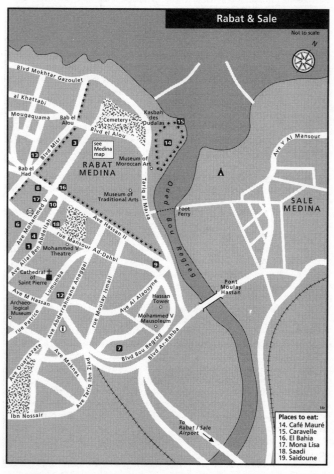

Rabat & Sale

Places to eat:
14. Café Mauré
15. Caravelle
16. El Bahia
17. Mona Lisa
18. Saadi
19. Saidoune

hammed V is the only drivable road in the medina, Ave Mohammed V in the *ville nouvelle* is one way S from Ave Hassan II to the post office.

THE WALLS AND GATES

Rabat has three sets of walls: the Almohad wall around the kasbah, the 5 km of Almoravid wall around much of the city centre dating from the 12th century, and the wall now separating the medina and the *ville nouvelle* built by the Andalusians in the early 17th century. The walls are mainly built of *pisé* or *pisé*-cement and, whilst they have inevitably been considerably repaired, strengthened and adapted, they are much as they were originally. There are four gates still standing in the Almoravid wall: **Bab el Alou, Bab el Had, Bab er Rouah** and **Bab ez Zaer**. **Bab er Rouah** is the most important and impressive of these, but **Bab el Had** is worth seeing. Located at the intersection of Ave Hassan II and Ave Ibn Toumert, the substantially remodelled **Bab el Had** has a blind arch and is flanked by two 5-sided stone towers. Currently you pass through two chambers, at different levels. A number of traditional scribes work in this area.

Bab er Rouah, also known as the 'Gate of the Winds', at Place An-Nasr, can best be approached along Ave An-Nasr from outside the walled city, when its scale and beauty is most obvious. The gate is now used as an exhibition gallery, and is only open when exhibitions are being held, so it is well worth taking any opportunity to see inside it. The arch of the gate is framed by a rectangular band of Kufic inscription. Between the arch and the frame there is a floral motif, with the scallop symbol on either side. The arch itself, with an entrance restored by the Alawites with small stones, is made up of three different patterns, of great simplicity, producing the overall effect of a sunburst confined within a rectangle. The entrance passage inside follows a complex double elbow. This, combined with the two flanking bastions outside, indicate that the gate was defensive as well as ceremonial.

KASBAH DES OUDAIAS

The Kasbah des Oudaias, originally a fortified *ribat*, later settled by Andalusians, is both beautiful and peaceful, and well worth a visit. It can be reached along rue de Consuls through the medina, Blvd el Alou along the N of the medina, or by Tarik al Marsa along beside the Oued Bou Regreg. There is a number of entrances to the kasbah, but the best is by the imposing **Bab al-Kasbah** gateway at the top of the hill. At this point avoid the unofficial guides as the kasbah is very small and quiet and easily explored without assistance.

Bab al-Kasbah was located close to the **Souq el-Ghezel**, the main mediaeval market, whilst the original palace was just inside. The gateway was built by Ya'qub al-Mansur in about 1195, inserting it into the earlier kasbah wall built by Abd al-Mumin, and it did not have the same defensive role as the **Bab er Rouah**. The gate has a pointed *outrepassé* arch surrounded by a cusped, blind arch. Around this there is a wide band of geometric carving, the common *darj w ktaf*. The two corner areas between this band and the rectangular frame are composed of floral decoration, with, as in the **Bab er Rouah**, a scallop or palmette in each. Above this are more palmettes, a band of Koranic lettering, and on top a wide band of geometric motifs. There would originally have been a porch roof. The entrance to the kasbah is via stairs and through two rooms, a third room being closed to the public. The inside of the gate is also decorated, though more simply.

Inside the gate, the main street, rue al-Jama, runs past the **Kasbah Mosque**, dating from 1150, the time of Abd al-Mumin, the oldest in Rabat. Due to the crowding of surrounding properties it is hard to get any real idea of this building.

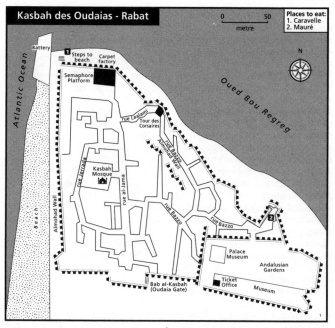

Kasbah des Oudaias - Rabat

Places to eat:
1. Caravelle
2. Mauré

The minaret, complete with very decorative arches was substantially rebuilt in the 18th century. It leads to the semaphore platform, where there is a carpet factory. This gives an excellent view over the sea, the Oued Bou Regreg with its natural sand-bar defence, and Sale. Steps down from the platform lead to the *Caravelle Restaurant*, in a small fort built by an English renegade, known as Ahmed el Inglise, and the popular, but not too clean, kasbah beach.

Coming back from the platform take the second on the left, rue Bazzo. This narrow and cobbled street with steps winds down through the whitewashed Andalusian-style houses to the bottom of the kasbah, directly into the *Café Maure* alongside which is a small but beautiful Andalusian style garden, developed by the French, which is also a pleasant place for a rest. On the other side of the garden is a section of the

Museum of Moroccan Arts also known as the Oudaias Museum, Souq el Ghezel, T 731512, exhibiting traditional dress and jewellery from many regions of Morocco. This opulent building of the 17th century palace, which Moulay Ismail once used as his Rabat residence, now houses the main museum collection, open 0830-1200, 1500-1830, except Tues, entrance fee MD10, with arms, instruments, jewellery, pottery, musical instruments and carpets. The carpet collection deserves particular attention. There are many of the fine carpets, defined by the number of knots per square metre (see Handmade carpets, page 328) using traditional motifs and natural fibres and dyes. There are coarser Berber floor and seat coverings, brighter and very distinctive. It is a good place to visit before you purchase elsewhere. The rows of illuminated Korans are an unusual display.

The reconstruction of the interior of a typical Moroccan house is well worth examination. It is a spacious setting, low divans covered in silk covers with gold embroidery, large fine weave carpets, piles of brocade and silk cushions in brilliant hues, intimate alcoves and a huge central salon. This is worth seeing just for the interior, and the decoration of the building. There are reception rooms around a central courtyard. In particular seek out the palace baths, the *hammam*. The garden here is very pleasant, again in the Andalusian style. The flower beds are intended to be quite formal but the plants grow beyond the confines of the borders on to the paths. The water features are designed to increase the cooling effects of the shady plants.

THE MEDINA

Most of the buildings in the medina date at the earliest from the arrival of the Andalusian Muslims in the 17th century. The Andalusian character of the buildings and decoration sets the medina apart from those such as Marrakech. Whilst Rabat medina is smaller and more limited in the range of markets, shops and buildings than Fes, Marrakech and Meknes, and less distinct in its way of life, its accessibility, size and the simplicity of its grid-like street pattern make it a good first experience of Moroccan medinas. Physically close to the *ville nouvelle*, the medina is very different in the design of buildings and open space, and the nature of commerce and socialization. It as an interesting and safe place to wander, with little risk of getting lost or hassled. Blvd Mohammed V is one of the major arteries of the medina, but the second right, **rue Souika**, and its continuation **Souq es Sebbat** are the main shopping streets, with an unusually wide range of shops and a number of traditional cafés for such a small area. Souq es Sebbat, originally where the shoes were made, is easily recognized by its roof of woven straw and

Laughing horse made in bronze, found at Volubilis and now in Rabat Museum

reeds. A great deal of leather work is on sale here, in particular worked leather for bags and the soft leather *baboushes* (see page 238). The mosque of Moulay Slimane at the junction of rue Souika and rue Sidi Fatah was constructed in 1812. The **Grand Mosque**, on rue Souika, is much restored Merinid, the minaret of which is decorated with polychrome glazed earthenware tiles. Just opposite the **Grand Mosque**, on a side turning, is the interesting stone façade of a fountain, now a bookshop, but dating from the 14th century reign of the Merinid Sultan Abu Faris Abd al-Aziz.

Souq es Sebbat leads down to the river, past the *mellah* on the right. The *mellah* is the former Jewish area, still the poorest area of the medina, with small cramped houses and shops, and narrow streets. It was built in 1808 by Moulay Slimane. Originally there were 17 synagogues, those remaining have become dwellings or storehouses. It is a triangular zone, bound by rue Ouqasson (the continuation of rue des Consuls), the medina wall, and the river. As in many Islamic cities, Jews were kept in one

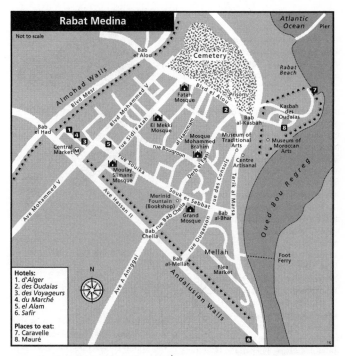

Rabat Medina

Not to scale

Atlantic Ocean   Pier

Rabat Beach

Bab el Alou

Cemetery

Almohad Walls

Blvd Mesr

Prisons

Blvd el Alou

Fatah Mosque

Blvd Mohammed V

Bab al-Kasbah

Kasbah des Oudaias

Bab el Had

Bab al-Kasbah

El Mekki Mosque

al Hammam

rue Sidi Fatah

Museum of Traditional Arts

Museum of Moroccan Arts

Central Market

Mosque Mohammed Brahim

rue Bouqroun

Centre Artisanal

rue Souika

Derb el Asissi

Tarik al Marsa

Moulay Slimane Mosque

Ave Mohammed V

Ave Hassan II

Souk es Sebbat

rue des Consuls

Oued Bou Regreg

Merinid Fountain (Bookshop)

rue Bab Chella

Grand Mosque

Bab al-Bhar

rue Ouqasson

Bab Chella

Mellah

Foot Ferry

Bab al-Mellah

Flea Market

Andalusian Walls

Ave A Anggal

N

Hotels:
1. d'Alger
2. des Oudaias
3. des Voyageurs
4. du Marché
5. el Alam
6. Safir

Places to eat:
7. Caravelle
8. Mauré

area, for both protection and control, and so that they would be easily accessible to the seat of power to carry out tasks Muslims could not perform. There are few Jews left in the *mellah*, most having emigrated to Israel. The streets around here now support an interesting *joutia*, or flea market.

Turning left off **Souq es Sebbat** one can follow the rue des Consuls to the kasbah. This road was where many European consuls and important merchants lived until 1912. Rue des Consuls is now lined with the more expensive shops selling silk embroidery, curiosities, souvenirs, traditional Moroccan items in copper and leather and carpets. There is a carpet market on the street on Tues and Thur mornings. Turn right at the end of rue des Consuls and you are

in Tarik al Marsa. On the left is the **Museum of Traditional Arts**, open 0830-1200, 1500-1830, entrance fee MD10, with crafts and arts. Opposite is the **Centre Artisanal**, with fixed prices for looking at, or buying, craft products.

THE HASSAN TOWER AND MOHAMMED V MAUSOLEUM

The Almohad **Hassan Tower** dominates the skyline of Rabat, and even unfinished it is an impressive building, testimony to Ya'qub al-Mansur's unfulfilled vision of his imperial capital. It overlooks the Oued Bou Regreg and Sale, and can be reached most easily by Blvd Bou Regreg, or by turning right at the end of Ave Hassan II.

The building of the mosque was abandoned on Ya'qub al-Mansur's death in 1199, leaving most of the minaret, but just part of the columns and walls. All the portable parts, tiles, bricks and the roofing material, have been taken for use in other buildings. The remains of the mosque were excavated and reconstructed by the French and Moroccans. The mosque would have followed a T-shape, with the main green-tile roof section between the minaret and the modern mausoleum. The *mihrab* (prayer niche) would have been in the S *qibla* wall, where the mausoleum is, and therefore was not properly orientated towards Mecca. It is also unusual to find the minaret opposite the *qibla* wall.

The incomplete minaret of the Hassan Mosque stands at 45m. When completed, it would have been 64m, four times as high as it was wide, with the lantern making it 80m, five times as high. This is in keeping with the classic North African minaret style, as with the **Koutoubia** in Marrakech (page 298). It is decorated with geometric designs, there being no inscription or floral decoration, but their scale and clarity of execution makes them clearly discernible from a distance. Each of the faces has a different composition, interweaving designs, arches and windows. The common Moroccan motif of *darj w ktaf*, resembling a tulip or a truncated *fleur de lys*, and formed by intersecting arcs with superimposed rectangles, is present, notably on the N and S upper registers.

Adjacent to the **Hassan Tower** is the **Mohammed V Mausoleum**, dedicated to the first king of independent Morocco and father of the current king, and dating from 1971. The mausoleum is constructed on the site where Mohammed V, returning from his exile in 1955, gathered thousands of his people to thank God for giving independence to Morocco. The tomb chamber, but not the mausoleum's mosque, is open to non-Muslims, and shows a number of traditional Moroccan motifs and techniques of religious architecture, with a carved

Head of King Juba II worked in bronze, found at Volubilis and now in Rabat Museum

and painted ceiling, the carved marble tomb, and the *zellij* tiles (mosaic) on the walls. Open 0800-1830 daily, entrance free.

THE CHELLAH

The Chellah, entrance MD10 for visitors and MD5 for residents of Rabat, is reached by going past the main **As-Sunna Mosque** in the *ville nouvelle*, and carrying on S down Ave Yacoub al Mansour and through the **Bab ez Zaer**, entrance MD10, residents MD5. There are five sides to the Chellah, all different lengths and 20 towers. This walled Merinid necropolis was built between 1310 and 1334, approximately on the site of the Roman town of **Sala Colonia**. The second Merinid Sultan, Abu Yusuf Yaqub built a mosque and Abul Hassan, the Black Sultan, then built the enclosure wall and the gate. The Roman ruins at the lower level of the **Chellah** enclosure have been excavated, and include a forum, baths, shops and a temple. These are not open to the public.

The gate is smaller and less impressive than the Almohad **Bab er Rouah**. It is decorated with carving, and coloured marble and tiles, with an octagonal tower on either side above which is a square platform. The entrance is on the elbow pattern and you turn right through three chambers, before walking out into a wild and lush garden. To get to the mausoleum take the wide path to the bottom, where it stands on the right, the Roman ruins on the left. On the far right are the tombs of local saints, surrounding a pool.

The door into the **Merinid mausoleum**, facing the Roman ruins, opens into the mosque of Abu Yusuf Yaqub, which consists of a small courtyard, followed by a 3-aisled sanctuary. The arched doorway on the left has the remains of floral and geometric *zellij* in five colours. Entering the sanctuary the *mihrab*, is straight ahead. A door to the right leads to an area including the remains of the mosque's minaret, and a pool. From this one enters the area of tombs, including those of Abul Hassan and his wife Shams al-Dawha. The remaining area of the mausoleum is taken up with the *zaouia*, or mosque-monastery, of Abul Hassan. This includes a minaret, and a ruined funerary chapel, with very intricate carving, notably on the exterior of the S wall. The main part of the *zaouia* is a rectangular courtyard with a small mosque at one end, and surrounded by small cells. It had a pool surrounded by a columned arcade, the bases of the columns still discernible. The *mihrab* has some intricate stucco carving. The tiles on the upper portion of the minaret are perhaps recent, but the original effect would have been a bright tiled structure.

THE VILLE NOUVELLE

This contains some fine examples of French colonial architecture, which in Morocco incorporated an element of local design tradition, and is called *Mauresque*. Note particularly the main post office (PTT Centrale) and the Bank al-Maghrib, both on Ave Mohammed V. This main boulevard is wide and particularly impressive in the evening, when it is crowded with people out for a stroll. Off to the left, opposite the railway station, is the **Catholic Cathedral of Saint Pierre**. Below the station is the Parliament building. Just past the *Hotel Terminus* is a small postal museum exhibiting stamps. The 18th century but much restored **As-Sunna Mosque** dominates the view up Ave Mohammed V. To the left of the mosque is the **Archaeological Museum**, 23 rue el Brihi, T 722231/ 701919/ 702224. Open 0830-1200, 1430-1800, closed Tues. Entrance MD10 (residents MD5). This was built in 1932 and enlarged a few years later. It has housed the National Museum collections since

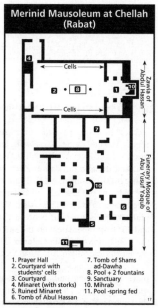

Merinid Mausoleum at Chellah (Rabat)

Zawia of Abdul Hassan

Cells

Cells

Funerary Mosque of Abu Yusuf Yaqub

1. Prayer Hall
2. Courtyard with students' cells
3. Courtyard
4. Minaret (with storks)
5. Ruined Minaret
6. Tomb of Abul Hassan
7. Tomb of Shams ad-Dawha
8. Pool + 2 fountains
9. Sanctuary
10. Mihrab
11. Pool -spring fed

1986. This is a very important museum with the best collections in the country. It certainly must be visited. The section covering pre-history has human remains from 4000 BC. There are pieces of pottery, jewellery and metalwork from the Mauritanian forbearers. The examples from the Roman period are first-rate. The Hellenistic bronzes include a very realistic dog from **Volubilis**. Here too, again from Volubilis, is the bronze statue of an attractive naked Roman youth. His head is crowned with ivy and the face has a most tranquil expression. Perhaps the most striking statue from Volubilis is the bronze horse, dating from the time of Hadrian. The thick short mane is very distinctive and the turn of its head indicates its spirit and nobility. Really a most magnificent and memorable item. From Volubilis is a bronze armrest bracket in the form of a mule. It looks very fierce, with flaring nostrils and open mouth. It is known as the mule crowned with vine leaves or sometimes the drunken mule. The 'Heads of Young Berbers' in marble are as fresh as if newly carved.

The best of mosaics from **Volubilis** are on display here, though there are still 30 left at the site.

The **Natural Science Museum** is part of the Ministry of Energy and Mining. Here there is a reconstruction of a sauropod dinosaur. The skeleton of this creature which is almost 15m in length was discovered in 1979 in the Azilal region of the High Atlas.

The **Postal Museum** was opened in 1970. It belongs to the PTT which has brought together this small and very interesting collection of instruments once used by their service. The items range in size from a post van to an envelope and between are telegraph machines, belinographs which reproduced photographs over long distances and the Baudot telegraph with printer. Among the postage stamps on show is Morocco's first official stamp from May 1912 but the collections of more recent stamps

will catch the collector's eye. Philately is a good export earner. To the right of the **As-Sunna Mosque** is the vast palace complex, where King Hassan II spends part of the year. It is not possible to go beyond this point up the central avenue of the complex. Construction of the **Royal Palace** began in 1864. It is surrounded by a wall cut by three gates. Inside the complex is an open space known as the *mechouar*. Here stands the **Ahl-Fas Mosque** where the King leads prayers each Friday when he is in the capital.

The new **Lalla Soukaïna Mosque**, built in 1989, in quarter Hay Riad is recommended. After all, all the mosques need not be old. The gardens are pleasant with scented laurels and herbs. There is no entrance into the mosque for non-muslims but the custodian will light up centre so one can see through the glass doors to the yellow and green ceramic basins.

FESTIVALS

Rabat is the best place for the state festivals, the *Coronation* on 3 Mar, the *Green March* on 6 Nov and *Independence Day* on 18 Nov.

LOCAL INFORMATION

Price guide

Hotels:

AL	over US$75	D	US$20-40
A	US$75	E	US$10-20
B	US$60-75	F	under US$10
C	US$40-60		

Places to eat:
♦♦♦	expensive	♦♦	average
♦	cheap		

● **Accommodation**

In summer hotels can fill up early. There are not many good, cheap hotels in Rabat. The budget hotels in the medina, for which prices can be very flexible, are in general best avoided. The centre of the *ville nouvelle* provides a wide range of good hotels. **AL** *Hotel Hyatt*, Aviation Souissi, T 771234, F 773039, 220 rm, 28 suites, former Hilton, luxurious, set in an extensive park on the road out past the **Chellah**, rather far from the city centre, but offers everything, including a business centre, mini golf-course, art gallery, pool and *hammam*; **AL** *Hotel de la Tour Hassan*, 26 Ave de Chellah, T 733816, F 725408, 158 rm, convenient location, a Protectorate period building which is perhaps the most atmospheric but least modernized of the top class hotels, excellent restaurants, conference room, popular nightclub and bar, no pool; **AL** *Hotel Safir*, Place Sidi Makhlouf, T 731091, F 725408, convenient, at end of Ave Hassan II overlooking the river and Sale, built around a courtyard in an approximation of a Moroccan palace, quite luxurious, pool, most other facilities and services; **A** *Rabat Chellah*, 2 rue d'Ifni, right in centre of town and a few metres from Plaza de la Mezquita, all rooms with bath and luxurious decorations, restaurant, grill, bar and café.

C *Hotel Belere*, 33 Ave Moulay Youssef, T/F 709801, conveniently located nr the station.

D *Hotel Balima*, 173 Ave Mohammed V, BP 173, across from the station, T 707755, 708625, F 707450, popular café-bar, restaurant, snack bar, salon de thé, nightclub, formerly top hotel in Rabat, a faded grandeur, reasonably priced; **D** *Hotel d'Orsay*, 11 Ave Moulay Youssef, nr station, T 761319, convenient, less interesting than *Balima*.

E *Hotel Central*, 2 rue Al Basra, T 767356, beside the *Balima*, well-run hotel, very good and crazily decorated double rooms, singles not so good, one of the best cheap options for sharers; **E** *Hotel des Oudaias*, 132 Blvd el Alou, nr the kasbah, T 732371, convenient for sightseeing, and well-fitted, one of the few respectable hotels in the medina; **E** *Hotel Gauloise*, 1 rue Hims, off Ave Mohammed V, T 723022, 59 tatty rm; **E** *Hotel Majestic*, 121 Ave Hassan II, T 722997, cheap and rec; **E** *Hotel de la Paix*, 2 rue Ghazza, T 722926, 732031, not very friendly, some rooms no bath, no communal shower; **E** *Hotel Splendid*, 24 rue Ghazza, T 723283, good rooms, friendly staff, pleasant courtyard with meals from restaurant opp.

F *Hotel Berlin*, 261 Ave Mohammed V, T 703435, cheapest in the *ville nouvelle*. There are a number of small, cheap hotels in the medina; **F** *Hotel des Voyageurs*, best of these three, *Hotel du Marché* and *Hotel d'Alger*, are all on rue Souq Semara, second left off Ave

Mohammed V, tatty; **F** *Maghreb al Jedid*, *Hotel El Alam*, best of these three, and *Hotel Marrakech*, all on rue Sebbahi, right off Ave Mohammed V, tatty and cheap.

Camping: is an inconvenient option in Rabat, the two nearest sites being Sale and Temara (see page 116).

Youth hostel: 34 rue Marassa, Bab el Had just inside the medina, T 725769, 60 beds, bed/breakfast MD35 for IYHA members, kitchen, basic and friendly, you can make an identity card here, with a photograph and your passport. Train 1.2 km and bus 150m.

● **Places to eat**

Most higher quality restaurants are located within the walled *ville nouvelle*. A range of fairly cheap restaurants is to be found throughout the city, but the budget options, small Moroccan canteens and café-restaurants, are located in the medina, along Ave Mohammed V, rue Souika, rue Sidi Fatah and adjacent streets. This is also a good area to wander and sample juices, pâtisseries, snacks and sandwiches, particularly from the *laiteries* that make sandwiches to order.

◆◆◆ *Justine's*, in *Hotel Hyatt*, Souissi, T 771234, reservations required, very expensive, prestigious, with a large range of European dishes; *El Andalous*, in *Hotel Hyatt*, Souissi, T 771234, reservations required, vast selection of Moroccan dishes, live music; *La Couronne* in *Hotel de la Tour Hassan*, 26 Ave de Chellah, T 721402, reservations rec, high standard international cuisine, good value and very good service, music in the evening; *El Mansur*, in *Hotel de la Tour Hassan*, 26 Ave de Chellah, T 721402, reservations rec, very good Moroccan food, particularly the *pastilla* and the *tagines*, with the option of eating at low tables, Moroccan music accompanies the meal; *Kanoun Grill*, in *Hotel Chellah*, 2 rue d'Ifni, T 764052, reservations rec, a big menu of good Moroccan food, particularly grilled.

◆◆ *Le Relais du Père Louis*, Zankat Ibn Haoqual, behind the *Hotel Balima*, T 769629, good Moroccan and French food, licensed; *Les Fouquets*, 285 Ave Mohammed V, T 708007, good Moroccan food and service, specializes in fish, licensed; *Hotel Balima*, 173 Ave Mohammed V, continental cuisine on the terrace or inside, but better for drinks; *La Mamma*, 1 Zankat Tanto, Italian food; *Café Restaurant Saadi*, 81 bis Ave Allal Ben Abdellah, T 769903, good Moroccan meals, licensed; *Hong Kong*, 261 Ave Mohammed V, Vietnamese/Chinese food.

♦ *Café Anaouil*, Ave Moulay Abdellah, good *tagines*, salads and juices, European food also; *Mona Lisa*, Passage Derby, 258 Ave Mohammed V, reasonable *tagines*, Moroccan food, salads; *Restaurant Saidoune*, mall off Ave Mohammed V, opp *Hotel Terminus*, very good value Lebanese restaurant, friendly, and with some tasty dishes; *Restaurant El Bahia*, Ave Hassan II, in the wall nr junction with Ave Mohammed V, Moroccan food in a courtyard, good value, erratic service; *Restaurant de l'Union*, 260 Ave Mohammed V, medina, cheap but unexciting meals; *Restaurant de la Jeunesse*, Ave Mohammed V, medina, cheap snacks and meals; *Elfarah Restaurant*, 10 Zankat Sidi Mohammed El Ghazi, third right off Ave Mohammed V, medina, Moroccan canteen: cheap, basic, clean and good, set lunch, *harira* and *brochettes* in the evening; *Café Taghzout*, rue Sebbahi, similar as above in nearby street.

Quick list by type of food served:

Australian: *Le Kangaroo Grill*, Hotel Sheherazade, rue de Tunis.

Chinese: *La Pagoda*, 13 rue de Baghdad.

French: *La Caravelle*, Borj de la Kasbah des Oudaias; *Le Crépuscule*, 10 rue Laghouat; *L'Eperon*, 8 Ave d'Alger; *Le Provençal*, Ave Hassan II.

Italian: *La Mamma*, 6 rue Tanta; *Pizzeria Napoli*, 8 rue Moulay Abdelaziz; *Va Bene*, Hotel Hyatt, Aviation Souissi.

Japanese: *Fuji*, 2 Ave Michlifen, Agdal.

Lebanese: *Dada*, 36 Ave de France, Agdal.

Moroccan: *Dinarjat*, opp the Kasbah des Oudaias La Clef, junction rue Harim and Ave Moulay Youssef; *La Koutoubia*, rue Pierre Parent.

Vietnamese: *Le Mandarin*, 100 Ave Abdelkrim al Khattabi; *Delicacies of Asia*, 17 rue Oqba.

Fastfood: *Dairy Queen*, junction Ave de France and rue Oum-Erbii; *McDonalds*, 1 Ave Al Amir Moulay Abdullah; *Hollywood Diner*, 26 rue Oqba, Agdal; *La Graille*, 66 rue Aqba; *Pizza Hut*, Gallery Commercial, Marjane.

Cafés, Pâtisseries & Glaceries: there are many good cafés, pâtisseries and glaceries on or nr Ave Mohammed V, two of the best being *Salon de Thé Lina*, 45 Ave Allal Ben Abdallah, n0r the French consulate, very French (a smoke-free café with excellent pâtisseries), and *Le Petit Poucet*, on Ave Mohammed V. The *Café Maure* in the Kasbah des Oudaias

serves mint tea and pastries, good views, waiters in traditional dress, a pleasant place to while away the time. There are excellent stand-up juice bars in the medina.

● **Bars**
Piccadilly Piano Bar, in *Hotel Hyatt Regency* popular for those who can afford it, nightly jazz band on patio by pool; *Hassan Bar*, in *Hotel de la Tour Hassan*, similarly expensive, with dated charm; *Hotel Balima*, 173 Ave Mohammed V, one of the most popular places to drink a beer or coffee, particularly during the evening promenade; *Baghdad Bar*, Zankat Tanto, belly-dancing awaits you.

● **Banks & money changers**
ABM, 19 Ave Allal Ben Abdallah, T 724907; **Banque al Maghrib**, Ave Mohammed V, T 763009; **Banque Marocaine de Commerce Exterieur (BMCE)**, 241 Ave Mohammed V, T 721798, the best for change (cash, TCs and VISA/Mastercard) for which it has a separate door (open 0800-2000 weekdays, 1000-1200 and 1600-2000 weekends); BMAO, Ave Allal Ben Abdellah, T 769980; **Credit du Maroc**, Ave Allal Ben Abdellah, T 721961; **Wafabank**, Ave Mohammed V, T 721181/82.

● **Cultural centres**
American, 41 Ave Allal Ben Abdellah; British, 6 Ave Moulay Youssef; French, rue Gandhi; German, 10 rue Jebli; Italian, 204 Zankat Agora; Spanish, rue Mohamed El Fakir.

● **Embassies & consulates**
Algeria, 46-48 Ave Tarik Ibn Ziad, T 765474; Austria, 2 rue Tiddas, T 764003; Belgium, 6 Ave de Marrakech, T 764746; Canada, 13 bis rue Jaafar Assadik, Agdal, T 672880; Denmark, 4 rue de Khemisset, T 767986; Egypt, 31 Ave d'Alger, T 731833; Finland, 16 rue Khemisset, T 762312; France, 3 rue Sahnoun, T 777822; Germany, 7 rue Madnine, T 765474; Greece, 23 rue d'Oujda, T 723839; Israel, Ave Beni Znassen, T 657680/1; Italy, 2 rue Idriss El Azhar, T 766598; Japan, 70 Ave Al Ouman al Mouttahida, T 674163; Kuwait, Ave Imam Malek, Km 4.3, T 754588; Libya, Zankat Chouaib Doukally, T 766863; Mauritania, 6 rue Thami Lamdour, off Ave John Kennedy, T 770912, 756817; Netherlands, 40 rue de Tunis, T 733512/3; Norway, 4 Zankat Jaafar As-Sadik, Agdal, T 673871/2; Portugal, 5 rue Thami Lamdouar, T 756446; Saudi Arabia, 43 Place de l'Unité Aficaine,

T 730171; **Senegal**, rue Cadi Ben Hammadi Senhadji, T 754171; **Spain**, 3 rue Madnine, T 768988; **Sweden**, 159 Ave John Kennedy, T 759313; **Switzerland**, Square Berkane, T 706974; **Sudan**, 9 rue de Tedders, T 761368; **Tunisia**, 6 Ave de Fes, T 730576; **Turkey**, 7 Ave de Fes, T 762605; **UAE**, 11 Blvd Al Alaouiyine, T 730976; **UK** (also used by **Australia, Ireland** and **New Zealand**), 17 Blvd de la Tour Hassan, T 731403; **USA**, 2 Ave de Marrakech, T 762265.

● **Entertainment**

Rabat has little of the entertainments one might expect in a capital city, particularly late at night.

Art galleries: *Galerie Arcanes*, 130 Blvd el Alou, T 735890; *Galerie L'Atelier*, 16 rue Annaba; *Galerie Le Manoir*, 7 rue Baitlahm; *Galerie Marsam*, 6 rue Oskofiah; *Galerie Moulay Ismail*, 11 Ave Bin Al Ouidane; *Galerie Bab Rouah*, Ave de la Victoire.

Cinemas: the four biggest cinemas are easily found, three in Ave Mohammed V, and one at the junction of Ave Allal Ben Abdallah and rue al-Mansur ad-Dahbi which has perhaps the best range of films. Most films are in French.

Cultural Centres: *Alliance France/Morocco*, rue Benzerte with instruction in Arabic and French; *American Language Centre*, 4 rue de Tabner with library; *British Council*, 36 rue de Tanger; *Institute Français*, 2 rue Al Yanboua; *Italian Cultural Centre*, 2 rue Laghouat; *Russian Cultural Centre*, 12 Ave de la Victoire; *Egyptian Cultural Centre*, 12 rue Hussein I; *Goethe Institute*, 10 rue Jebli, noted for its musical concerts.

Discos and nightclubs: the most rec is *Queen's Club*, Hotel de la Tour Hassan, 22 Ave de Chellah, very popular, open from 2230, entrance MD50; otherwise try *Biba* or *Jefferson* in Ave Patrice Lumumba, or the *Balima* in Ave Mohammed V. *Amnesia*, 18 rue Monastir, T 701860, entrance MD100, frequented by more affluent Moroccans and Europeans; *Day and Night*, Ave du Chellah, entrance MD35, has a more African style; *Fifth Avenue*, Ave Bin al-Ouidane, entrance MD60, music and an entertainment; *La Kasbah*, large red house on the right on the coast road out of Rabat, Fri night is very busy, T 749116.

Hammams (Public baths): on Ave Hassan II, beside the *Rex*, or for residents at the *Hyatt Regency*.

Theatres and concert halls: *Theatre Mo-*

hammed V, rue Al Kahira, has a range of plays and concerts. The various national cultural centres, such as the Russian Cultural Centre in Ave Moulay Abdellah and the British Council in rue Tanger, advertise and promote events. Check *Al Bayane*, *L'Opinion* or *Le Matin* newspapers for other listings.

● **Hospitals & medical services**

Ambulance: T 15.

Chemists: *Pharmacie du Chellah*, Place de Melilla, T 724723, and another on rue Moulay Slimane, *Pharmacie de la Préfecture*, Ave Moulay Slimane opposite town hall, if not, look in any chemist's door for details or T 726150 for the name of the night chemist.

Hospital: *Hôpital Avicenne*, Ave Ibn Sina, T 773194, 774411.

● **International organizations**

The *Rotary Club* meet at the *Hotel Hyatt*, Aviation Souissi, T 671234; *Lions Club* headquarters at junction of rue d'Oujda and rue de Tunis, T 720403; *UNICEF* in Agdal at junction of rue Oum-Errabi and rue Oued Baht.

● **Laundry**

Most hotels will do your laundry for you for an arranged price. Otherwise try *Rabat Pressing*, 67 Ave Hassan II.

● **Library**

British Council, 36 rue Tanger, BP427, T 700836, free entry, reference books, novels, some books on Morocco, magazines and newspapers, Sky News on the TV, small café; *George Washington Library*, 35 Ave el Fahs, also has some newspapers. Libraries, mainly in French include: *Librairie Papeterie Kalila Wa Dimna*, 344 Ave Mohammed V, T 723106; *Librairie Populaire*, 4 rue Ghazza (was 18 Juin), T 738867; *Librairie Tahiri*, Residence Kays opp Marché de l'Agdal, T 778287; *Livre Service*, 40-46 Ave Allal Ben Abdallah, T 724495; *Librairie du 6 Novembre*, Ave Fald Ould Oumeir; *Librairie Basta*, Place Othman Ben Affane.

● **Places of worship**

Catholic: Cathedrale Saint Pierre, rue Abou Inan, T 722301, mass is said on Sat at 1700 and Sun at 0900 and 1100. Church of St Francis, rue Soekamo, T 724380, mass in Spanish on Sat at 1900 and Sun at 1030. Church Pie X, 40 rue Jaafar as Sadik, T 670250, mass on Sun at 1000.

Jewish: Synagogue Talmuch Torah, 9 Ave Moulay Ismail, information, T 724504; Synagogue Berdugo, rue Dar el Beida.

Medressa – education for Islam

👣 "Learning is a city, one of whose gates is memory, the other is comprehension", – an Arab saying.

The *medersa* in North Africa, is a college of higher education in which Islamic teachings lead the syllabus. It was an institution originated in Persia and developed in the West in the 13th century. The construction of places of advanced learning was a response by orthodox Sunni Islam to the growth of Shi'ite colleges but they soon became important centres in their own right as bastions of orthodox Islamic beliefs. Subjects other than theology were taught at the *medressa* but only in a limited form and in ways that made them adjuncts to Sunni teachings and acceptable to a very conservative religious hierarchy. Unfortunately, therefore, the *medressa* became associated with a rather uninspired and traditional academic routine in which enquiry and new concepts were often excluded. Knowledge and its transmission sadly fell into the hands of the least academic members of the theological establishment. The poor standards of science, politics, arts and ethics associated with the Arab world in the period since the 13th century is put down to the lack of innovation and experiment in the *medressa*, a situation which has only very recently begun to break down in Sunni Islam. It can, however, be argued that formal Islam needed firm basic teachings in the face of rapidly expanding popular Islam and its extravagant Sufi beliefs.

The short-comings of the *medressa* in creative teaching terms was in part compensated for by the development of the buildings themselves. They were mainly modelled on the Medersa of Bou Inania at Fes (page 272), founded under Sultan Abu Inan (1348-1358), itself based on designs from Syria. The main courtyard *sahn* is edged with cloisters/galleries separated from the *sahn* by ornate screens of wood. The mosque is to the E and the long *qibla* wall has a deeply set *mihrab* (see plan, page 272). The Merinids founded seven *medressa* in Fes during the 14th century.

Entry is restricted for non-Muslims, though at the Medersa of Bou Inania of Fes (page 272) visitors are allowed into the mosaic paved courtyard even if not to the mosque and when the repairs are completed the roof terrace of the Atterin Medersa (see page 275) will once again allow views of Fes. Meknes has its own

Protestant: Temple, 44 Ave Moulay Abdellah, service: 0945; Evangelical Church, Ave Allal Ben Abdallah, opp the French consulate, T 723848.

● **Post & telecommunications**
PTT Centrale, Ave Mohammed V, 0800-1200, 1400-1830. Rue al-Mansur ad-Dahbi, just off Ave Mohammed V, opposite the post office has a permanent facility for telephoning and collecting letters. Check with staff that previous call is cleared before using cabin.

● **Shopping**
Bakers/Confectioners: *Pâtisserie Gerber*, 258 Ave Mohammed V, lovely Moroccan sweet cakes; *La Génoise*, Blvd Wad Akrech, opp Dar Es Salam school, French cakes at reasonable

price; *La Comédie*, 269 Ave Mohammed V, a mouth-watering selection.

Books & maps: the *American Bookshop* at the American Language Center in rue Tanger has a very useful selection of novels, guidebooks and books on Islam and Morocco, all in English. There is an English language bookshop at 7 rue Al Yamama, T 706593, behind the railway station, which sells a large selection of new and second-hand paperbacks. For books in French there are a number of well-stocked bookshops in Ave Mohammed V, such as *Kahla wa Dimna*, and Ave Allal Ben Abdellah. Bookshops in Ave Mohammed V stock simple maps of Rabat or Morocco. For hiking maps go to the **Division de la Cartographie**, 31 Ave Moulay al Hassan, T 765192, which

Bou Inania Medersa (see page 240) and the Medinid Abul Hassan Medersa in Sale should be noted too.

"Let your eyelids enjoy my splendid beauty – you will find a marvellous virtue to chase away cares and sadness", reads one of the many carved inscriptions in the 16th century Ben Youssef Medersa in Marrakech (see page 307) which is the largest *medersa* in North Africa and also considered one of the finest. Originally a Merinid foundation but remodelled in the 16th century its fine architectural works are reflected in the arcaded courtyard with intricate mosaic work, lace-like carved stucco weathered to a faint rose coloured patina and finely worked cedar beams.

Nicolas Clinard, a French humanist, left an account of his time studying in Fes in the 16th century. Writing about the religious scholars he says: "The faqirs do not show off their wealth even if they are rich, and they do not consider it dishonourable to walk in the streets unaccompanied by servants, just like our Parisian doctors with a breviary under the arm and mud on their shoes".

Clinard also tells us about the teaching methods in use: on learning the Koran, he writes that the young students "impress into their memory a book they do not understand". The basis of the different subjects – Arabic language, the Koran, law, astronomy and mathematics – were treatises written in verse or rhymed prose, which facilitated the task of committing them to memory. Ibn Malik's Alfia (treatise in a thousand verses) was the essential grammar book. The emphasis on memorizing texts in a society without masses of printed material bore fruit later on in the educational process. Debate was enriched as all could readily refer to a common body of material, and literary discussions were common. With his basic studies completed, the student might return to his home town – or continue the quest for learning in a *medersa* elsewhere. However, the student seeking material wealth would go for legal studies: detailed knowledge of the law according to the Malekite rite was a precondition for a successful public career.

Moroccan *medressa* were until quite recently used for student accommodation and even for teaching but the traditional life has now disappeared and the *medressa* remain as intriguing monuments to an educational past where religious belief and education were tightly linked.

sells official maps if it is not being too bureaucratic, advertises as having maps of all scales suitable for driving and for rambling, orders taken.

Hairdressers: *Salon Isis*, Residence Kays, Agdal; *Institute Jade* in Hotel Hyatt; *Le Look*, 81 Ave Allal Ben Abdallah. All provide services for men and women.

Markets: local markets are on Thur at Sale, Ave du 11 Janvier, Fri at Bouznika, Sat at Temara, Sun at Bouknadel and Skhirat. In Rabat medina the vegetable market is best on Sun, and carpets in rue des Consuls on Tues and Thur morning. Agdal Market, off Ave des Dades, to the W of the university is noted for its good quality fruit and vegetables, it is, however, a long way to travel. The Municipal Market, clearly marked off Ave Hassan II after the gate into the *mellah*, also has good fruit and vegetables and a splendid selection of fresh aromatic herbs. In the *ville nouvelle* there is an underground vegetable and fruit market at Place Moulay al Hassan, with excellent flower sellers above ground outside. Supermarkets for easy shopping, **Makro** (with items in large quantities) and **Marjane** both on the road to the airport.

Modern shops: there are a range of large shops on Ave Mohammed V and Ave Allal Ben Abdellah. It should be possible to get most things you need here.

Moroccan shops: use the **Centre Artisanal** (Coopartim) in Tarik al Marsa to get an idea of the range, then go out and bargain in the small boutiques in the medina, on or just off Ave Mohammed V, rue Souika, **Souq es Sebbat** and rue des Consuls. There are a number of larger shops, in the *ville nouvelle*, on Ave Mohammed V, or in the malls just off, where the high prices may be negotiable.

Newspapers & magazines: there are three or four boutiques on the pavements of Ave Mohammed V stocking a full range of British, American, French and international newspapers and magazines. However the best is perhaps inside the main railway station. The international edition of *The Guardian* arrives in Rabat about 1800.

Sports clothing & equipment: *Delta*, Ave Al Amir Moulay Abdallah, supplies for golf too; *Filo*, 105 Ave Hassan II; *Suchart*, 4 rue Mamounia for riding equipment.

● **Sports**

Fishing: *Underwater Hunting Club*, BP 368 Rabat, T 778553.

Flying: *Aéro-Club Royal Aerodrome*, T 724222.

Golf: *Royal Golf Dar Es Salam*, 12 km from Rabat on rue de Zaers, T 755864/5, F 757671, is the largest and most famous course in Morocco, with 45 holes, Red course 6,702m par 73, Blue course 6,205m par 72, Green course (9 holes) 2,170m par 32, fees approx MD500 per day; there is also the smaller Golf Club du Souissi, T 750359. For information: *Moroccan Royal Federation of Golf*, 2 rue Moulay Slimane, T 755960.

Hang gliding: at Rabat-Sale airport. Contact 21 bis Ave Allal ben Abdellah, Passage, Karrakchou, Rabat, T 708347.

Horse-riding & polo: the *Royal Polo Equestrian Club* is at the Royal Golf Dar Es Salam, rue de Zaers, T 734692. *Club Equestre Al Foursane*, at Aïn el Aouda, some 27 km S of Rabat, insurance MD130, 1 hr MD100, 2 hr MD150, closed Sun; *Club Equestre Yquem*, on the coast road 20 km S of Rabat, just across Oued Yquem, offer riding on the sands.

Hunting: Ministry of Water and Forest deal with hunting, T 727694.

Jogging: there is a special track nr the Dar el Salam golf club, through a forested area, courses of 800m, 1,500m and 3,000m.

Swimming: the main beach in Rabat is that below the kasbah, which is popular but not too clean. That at Sale is similar, and both have dangerous currents from the river. It may be worth going further afield, to the Plage des Nations, Temara or Skhirat (see page 116 and page 117). Try the pools at Royal Golf Dar Es Salam, the *Hotel Hyatt Regency* or the *Hotel Safir*.

Tennis: *Club des Cheminots*, Agdal, T 770048; *Club El Wifak*, rue de Zaers, T 754539; *Hotel Hyatt*, Aviation Souissi; *Olympique Marocain*, 2 rue Ibn Khaldoun, T 771872, seven courts; *Riad Club*, rue Abdelaziz Boutaleb, Agdal, T 722776, six courts; *Stade Marocain*, Ave Haroun Rachid, T 771903, seven courts.

Walking & climbing: information from Alpine Club 19, Blvd de la Resistance, T 727220.

Watersports: Yacht Club de Rabat, Quai de la Tour Hassan, T 720254; Fath Union Sport, Port de Rabat, T 733679; Olympique Marocain, Quai Léon Petit, T 725123; information from Yachting Federation, Ave Ibn Yassine Bellevue, Agdal, BP332, T 771782. Yachting on Lac de Rabat, where there are winds of up to force 4 or 5.

● **Tour companies & travel agents**
Afric Voyages, 28 bis Ave Allal Ben Abdellah, T 709646/47, 706833; *First International Tours*, 32 Ave Ben Khattab, T 775060; *Gharb Voyages*, 289 Ave Mohammed V, T 767311; *La Royale*, Immeuble Montfavet, Place Mohammed V, T 707031; *North Africa Tours*, Residence El Minzah, rue Kadira, T 769747, F 762298; *Rainbow Travel*, 1 rue Derna, Place Pietri, T 762563, 702579; *Safir Voyages*, Hotel Safir, Place Sidi Makhlouf, T 731093; *TAK Voyages*, 1 bis Ave Ibn Sina, Agdal, T 771684; *Wagons-Lit Tourisme*, 1 Ave Amir Moulay Abdellah, T 709625; *Welcome Voyages*, 29 Ave d'Alger, T 702871/72, F 702873. *Air France*, 281 Ave Mohammed V, T 707066; *Iberia* 104 Ave Mohammed V; *Royal Air Maroc* Ave Mohammed V, T 709766, 9 rue Abou Faris Almarini, T 709700, reservations: T 708076, 709710.

● **Tourist offices**
National Tourist Office at corner of Ave al Abtal and rue Oued Fes, T 775171/79; **Office du Tourisme**, 22 Ave d'Alger, T 730562; **Syndicat d'Initiative**, Ave Patrice Lumumba, T 723272, not very useful.

● **Useful addresses**
Archaeological centres: *Archaeological Institute* (Institute National des Sciences de l'Archeologie et du Patrimoine), Bab Zaer, Ave President Kennedy, PO Box 503, Souissi, Rabat.

Fire: T 15.

Garages: *Concorde*, 6 Ave Allal Ben Abdellah; *Garage Citroen* (SIMA), at the junction of rue de Congo and rue de Senegal.

Language centres: *American Language Center*, rue Tanger, it may also be possible to arrange Arabic lessons here; *British Council*, 36 rue Tanger, BP427, T 760836.

Motoring club: 45 Ave Patrice Lumumba.

Police: rue Soekarno, behind the PTT Centrale, T 19.

● **Transport**

Local Buses: run all over the city, many originating from Ave Hassan II, nr **Bab el Had**, or just past Parc du Triangle de Vue. Six and 12 go to Sale, 17 to Temara, 1, 2 and 4 for the **Chellah**, get off at **Bab Zaer**. The main bus terminal for all buses is at Place Zerktouni, 3 km from the centre, to the W of the city in the direction of Casablanca. Catch a petit-taxi there, or a No 30 bus from Ave Hassan II. Current buses – Casablanca: 10 a day (1½ hrs), Tanger: 2 a day (5 hrs), Meknes: 3 a day (4 hrs), Fes: 6 a day (5½ hrs). **Grand-taxi**: shared between six passengers, run from the bus station for distant locations, and for local locations, such as Temara, Skhirat, Sale and Bouknadel, from the stand on Ave Hassan II, just past the Parc du Triangle de Vue. **Petit-taxis**: in Rabat are blue. They are some of the best in Morocco, nearly always metered, and often shared. They can be picked up anywhere, most easily at the stand on Ave Hassan II, close to the junction with Ave Mohammed V. Alternatively, T 720518, 730311. Sample fare from Ave Mohammed V to Hassan Tower, MD10. A Rabat petit-taxi cannot take you to Sale, which has its own taxis. **Car hire**: **Avis**, 7 Zankat Abou Faris el Marini, T 767503, 769759, Tx 31029, also at Rabat-Sale Airport; **Budget**, Rabat-Ville Railway Station, T 767689; **Citer**, *Residence el Minzah*, rue el Kahira, T 722731; **Hertz**, 467 Ave Mohammed V, T 709227, 707366, Tx: 31977, also at Rabat-Sale Airport; **Holiday Car**, 1 bis Ave Ibn Sina, T 771684, 771351; **Inter Rent-Europcar**, 25 bis rue Patrice Lumumba; **La Royale**, Immueble Montfavet, Place Mohammed V, T 763031.

Air Buses to Airport Mohammed V run from in front of *Hotel Terminus*, Ave Mohammed V. Tickets can be bought at the kiosk for MD50. Departures: 0500, 0630, 0830, 1000, 1230, 1530 and 1830, journey time 90 mins. For Rabat-Sale airport, T 727393, 730316, follow the P1 Sale-Meknes road. Daily direct flights

to Paris and Casablanca, 1 a week to Tetouan (Fri).

Train **Rabat Ville** station, T 767353, Ave Mohammed V, departures – Casablanca: 35 daily between 0437 and 2337; **Marrakech**: 8 daily between 0437 and 2337; **El Jadida**: 1957, **Oued Zem**: 0815, 1527, 1930; **Meknes and Fes**: 9 daily between 0752 and 2349; **Taza** and **Oujda**: 1047, 1522, 2141, 2349; **Tanger**: 0748, 1327, 1656 and 0155; **Aeroport Mohammed V**: 11 daily between 0512 and 1900. **Rabat Agdal** station, T 772385, rue Abderrahman El Ghafiki, departures – Casablanca, Marrakech, El Jadida and Oued Zem: as above, 4-6 mins later, Meknes, Fes, Oujda and Tanger: as above 6-8 mins earlier.

SALE

History

Sale, pronounced and often written as Salé, is Sala or Sla in Arabic, after the Roman Sala Colonia. Sale was founded in the 11th century, and its Great Mosque dates from 1163-1184. The town was embellished and fortified by the Merinids in the 13th century, becoming an important commercial centre. Great rivalry, even armed conflict, has existed between Rabat and Sale, although they were united in the Republic of the Bou Regreg. Up until the 17th century Sale had enjoyed long periods as the more important of the two cities, being known for religious learning and piety. In the 20th century Rabat has outstripped Sale, the latter becoming more and more a dormitory settlement for the former, with little of its own economic activities. While Rabat is known as the city of gardens Sale is perhaps the city of sanctuaries. Sale is worth a day-trip from Rabat to visit the beautiful **Abul Hassan Medersa** and explore the medina and the *souqs*, which are far more traditional than those of Rabat, and less visited by tourists than Fes or Meknes.

Places of interest

Bab Mrisa means 'Gate of the Little Harbour'. This was originally the sea gate of the medina, as there was once a chan-

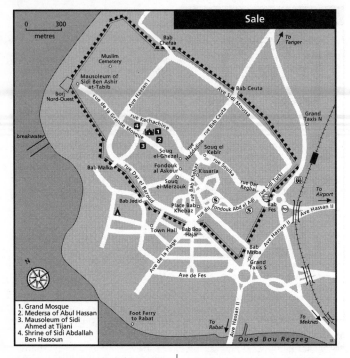

Sale

0   300
metres

To Tanger

Bab Chafaa

Muslim Cemetery

Bab Ceuta

Mausoleum of Sidi Ben Ashir at-Tabib

Borj Nord-Ouest

rue de la Grande Mosque

rue Kechachine

Ave Hassan I

Ave Sidi Moussa

Grand Taxis N

breakwater

4 **1**
2
3

Haddadine
rue Bab Ceuta

Souq el-Kebir

rue Souika

To Airport

Bab Malka

Souq el-Ghezel

Fondouk al Askour

Kissaria

rue Dar Regbaz

rue Sidi Turki

Bab Jedid

rue Dar el Baroud

Souq el-Merzouk

rue Bab Hebaz

Bab Fes

Pol

Place Babo Khebaz

rue du Fondouk Abd el Aji

Ⓢ
Ⓢ

Ave Hassan II

Town Hall

Bab Bou Hajar

Ave de la Plage

Bab Mriba

Ave Hassan II

Grand Taxis S

Ave de Fes

Ave Hassan II

To Meknes

Foot Ferry to Rabat

To Rabat

Oued Bou Regreg

N

1. Grand Mosque
2. Medersa of Abul Hassan
3. Mausoleum of Sidi Ahmed at Tijani
4. Shrine of Sidi Abdallah Ben Hassoun

nel running to it from the river. The gate is easily found, dominating as it does the approach to Sale from Rabat, on the left side. This gate is very large, its *outrepassé* arch opening of 11m in height sufficient to allow access to the sailing boats of the day. Bab Mrisa was built by the Merinid Sultan Abu Yusuf in the 1270s. However in style it is closer to the Almohad gates, with the triangular space between the arch and the frame covered with floral decoration centred on the palmette, with the use of the *darj w ktaf* motif down the sides. Originally it had a porch. Alongside the tower there are two tall defensive towers. It may be possible to get access to the top of the gate. A custodian guards a small door on the left, inside the gate, which gives access to a small garden leading to a round tower. From this tower

walk back along the top of the rampart to the gate. There is another similar sea gate, the next gate around the wall to the left.

Abul Hassan Medersa This *medersa*, or religious school (open 0800-1200, 1430-1800), is the most important building to visit in Sale, being the only *medersa* in this region. It was built by the Merinid Sultan Abul Hassan the Black Sultan and finished in 1342. To reach it follow the city walls around to the left from Bab Mrisa to a small square at Bab Bou Hajar, alongside a park. Just beyond this there is an area where cars should be parked. Take the small lane off to the far right at the end of this area. Take the first left, then the first right. 200m later, just after the lane passes under a house, turn left. The particularly large **Grand**

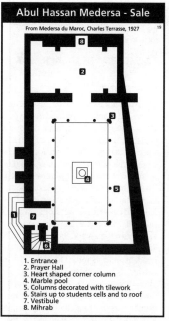

Abul Hassan Medersa - Sale

From Medersa du Maroc, Charles Terrasse, 1927

1. Entrance
2. Prayer Hall
3. Heart shaped corner column
4. Marble pool
5. Columns decorated with tilework
6. Stairs up to students cells and to roof
7. Vestibule
8. Mihrab

Mosque in front was built by the Almohad Sultan Abu Yusuf Ya'qub in the late 12th century, although the minaret and door are both modern. Just beyond the mosque is the tomb of Sale's patron saint, Sidi Abdallah Ben Hasson. The *medersa* is to the left of the mosque.

Note at the entrance to the beautiful Merinid doorway the intricate decorations, with complex designs of inscription around a cusped, interlaced arch, below a green tiled roof resting on cedar. The *medersa* is quite small, with a courtyard surrounded by a gallery, its columns decorated with *zellij* mosaic tiling. The walls above the columns are decorated with geometric and floral motifs, whilst the ceilings of the ground floor have panelled wood in geometric patterns. There has been restoration to both the wood carving of the prayer hall ceiling and the stucco, but much is original, and in good condition. The decoration

which covers almost all the *medersa*, is finely executed. To reach the upper floors, return to the entrance and climb the stairs. These are the students' cells, which seem tiny and ill-lit, but give an insight into the nature of *medersa* life. From the roof is a view of Sale, and beyond it, Rabat.

The Medina Sale medina is small and easy to explore. Walking in any direction you are likely to arrive at the *souqs*, the **Grand Mosque** and **Abul Hassan Medersa**, or the city walls. The **Mausoleum of Sidi Ben Ashir at-Tabib** is located close to the W wall of the cemetery that lies between the medina and the sea. This 14th century Muslim saint was famous for curing people, and the sick still visit his tomb for its curative powers. This is a very striking building, quite tall, brilliant white in contrast to the blue sky and the background of ochre of the city walls. Adjacent, in the walls, cannon still point defensively out to sea.

The **Fondouk al Askour** is worth seeing for its decorated portal. From **Bab Bou Hajar** follow rue Bab al-Khabbaz, and take the fourth lane on the left past the park, which is obstructed by three concrete posts. This leads to a textile *souq*. After 120m the *souq* passes under an arch. On the right is the *fondouk*. It was originally built in about 1350 as a *medersa* by Abu Inan, son of Abul Hassan. It was later a merchants' hostel. The door is surrounded by a partially restored *zellij* mosaic of the *darj w ktaf* pattern. Above this is a panel of *zellij* with the traditional eight pointed star motif, and above that a row of nine niches carved into a plaster panel. Inside there is a courtyard with two storeys of arcades around it.

In this area there are some interesting *souqs*, which are perhaps more traditional than those of Rabat, and worth exploring. This textile market is **Souq el-Merzouk**, while **Souq el-Ghezel** is the wool market. There are stone-masons and carpenters in rue Kechachine, and blacksmiths and brassworkers in rue Haddadine. The **Souq el-Merzouk** is noted for its jewellery and embroidery. The medina of Sale is also noted for a procession of multicoloured candles, or thick poles bearing various representations, which occurs every year on the afternoon before the Prophet's birthday, Moulid an-Nabi. This proceeds through the town, culminating at the **Tomb of Sidi Abdallah Ben Hassoun**. He is the patron saint of Sale and this is the most venerable of the sanctuaries in the city. It is also the most picturesque with a most curious dome and an exterior gallery decorated with polychrome tiles. The seafaring past of the city is particularly visible in this event, with the men in pirate costumes.

Local information
● **Accommodation & places to eat**
Very few travellers stay in Sale, as there are few hotels, and the city is easily accessible from Rabat. There is the cheap **E** *Hotel des Saadiens*, by the bus station. *Camping de la Plage* is by the river and the sea, with toilets, showers, pool, shop, laundry, electricity for caravans, petrol 300m just 100m from beach and on a plot of nearly 4 ha. There is a number of small and cheap café-restaurants just inside both main gates, and along rue Kechachin. *Café Marhaba* nr the SGMB bank is also rec.

● **Shopping**
Handicrafts: the artisans of Sale are as talented as their neighbours and good quality goods are available. Look at the pottery (some is very distinctive), the tooled leatherware, ironware (though this is a bit difficult to transport home), carpets (perhaps not the best place to buy these), fine embroidery, drapery and, for the beach, rush matting.

● **Transport**
Local Bus: to get to Sale take a bus No 6 or 12 from Ave Hassan II in Rabat, a grand-taxi from the stop on the same street, or walk down to the quay below the kasbah and take a rowing boat across the river, from where you can walk up to **Bab Bou Hajar**. Rabat petit-taxis are not allowed to cross the river. Once in Sale it should be possible to explore most of the centre on foot, but if not, the city has its own petit-taxis. If you have your own transport, go along Tarik al Marsa, Ave Hassan II or Blvd du Bou Regreg and cross the bridge below the **Hassan Tower**. It is possible to walk this route in about 30 mins.

EXCURSIONS FROM RABAT

NORTHWARDS
The **Mamora Forest**, to the NE of Rabat, is a peaceful area of cork and eucalyptus trees, a pleasant change after the bustle of Rabat. It has been calculated that half the cork oaks of Morocco are found here. The eucalyptus is also exploited and there are plantations of pine and acacia. The Mamora wild pear is the only other tree found in the region. It is tall, up to 15m and has white flowers for a long time in spring. There are *dayats* in the region and in wetter years these attract the White Stork. The forest provides for both residents and victors. The Spotted Flycatcher is a summer visitor, as is the magnificent blue Roller. The Turtledove, visiting from the S, is declining in numbers as hunting continues, by man rather than the raptors. It lies off the road to Meknes. Turn off left at Sidi Allal Bahroui. Return via the P2 and P29.

The **Jardins Exotiques** are about 20 km NE from Rabat, on the P2, and the 28 bus route. These 4 ha of garden are the work of a French horticulturalist, François, in the 1950s. There are over 1,500 species and varieties of plants from Morocco and all over the world, laid out with pools, bridges and summerhouses, often in the manner of one particular area. There are two marked circuits for visitors. The longer circuit takes 1-1½ hrs and the shorter about 45 mins. Entrance adult MD5, child MD3. They are well-worth a visit and are open from 0900-1830.

The **Plage des Nations** is at Sidi Bouknadel, about 25 km NE of Rabat. It is very popular with the affluent, and more a family beach than those of Rabat-Sale, but the currents can be dangerous. Take the bus No 28 from Sale, and walk the 1 km from the turning, or share a grand-taxi, also from Sale. The **C** *Hotel Firdaous*, T 780407, has a bar, restaurant, pool and is rec. Further on Mehdia and Kenitra can be visited as an excursion from Rabat, by train, bus or car (see page 191).

EASTWARDS

Bou Regreg Dam Cross the Oued Bou Regreg to Sale and take the P1 eastward towards Fes and Meknes. After 18 km turn S on the S204 to Arbaa Sehoul for 7 km. Here there is access to the lake and some popular picnic areas.

SOUTHWARDS

Temara is 14 km from Rabat, off the P36. Bus 17 from Ave Hassan II goes to the town and the ruins of a kasbah. The beach is a 4 km walk to the W. This is a favourite weekend and holiday destination for the people of Rabat for the beach is long, sandy and, being washed by the Atlantic tides, is clean. There are two hotels, **D** *Hotel La Feloque*, T 744388, 23 rm, restaurant, bar, pool, tennis, and **E** *Hotel Casino*. *Camping de Temara*, the first from Rabat on the coastal road; *Camping la Palmeraie*, T 749251, 3 ha site, 100m to beach, bar, snacks, restaurant, groceries, showers, laundry, petrol 600m, electricity for caravans; *Camping Gambusias*, 100m from beach, bar/restaurant, showers; *Camping Rose-Marie* at Ech Chiahna, S of Temara Plage, small site, 100m from beach, snacks, restaurant, showers, laundry, electricity for caravans. There is also a number of popular discos. Temara Zoo has a varied collection of animals and some very beautiful birds. Crowded at weekends, is open from 1000 to sunset. People in Rabat who insist on really fresh fish travel out here to make their purchases.

Skhirat is 31 km from Rabat and is clearly signposted off the P36, P1 and RP36. There are two trains from Rabat-Ville each day, at 0730 and 1855, taking 17 mins. Skhirat town has little of interest itself beyond a Sun *souq*. The palace near the beach was the scene of a bloody but unsuccessful *coup* attempt in Jul 1971. Skhirat beach is upmarket, as are the restaurants and hotels nearby, incl **C** *La Kasbah*, Rose Marie Plage, T 749133, F 749116, 42 rm, pool, tennis, restaurant, bar, parking, and the rec **D** *Amphitrite Hotel*, Km 28, route de Rabat, T 742317, 36 rm, restaurant, bar, pool, tennis.

Tanger and the western Mediterranean Coast

TANGER (Tangier) is a city which reflects its position at the crossroads of Africa and Europe, the Mediterranean Sea and the Atlantic Ocean, as well as its historical experience as an international zone. It is a shabby and bustling city, full of character. Ceuta and Melilla are Spanish enclaves, other towns such as Chaouen, Ouezzane and Tetouan reflect the Andalusian input into the area, whilst Al Hoceima is a more recent Spanish input, that of the 20th century protectorate. The Mediterranean Sea coast is a succession of large, characterless resort complexes and small, isolated, idyllic fishing villages. The Rif, inland, is a wild mountain range with a history of rebellion and a controversial role in hashish production.

The Phoenicians and Carthaginians established trading posts here. The Romans made it a capital city. It was invaded by the Vandals and Visigoths and occupied by the Arabs. The Portuguese took the town before the Spanish. The English came later before Moulay Ismail's troops overran it. What a history!

Of the ancient city nothing remains. Descriptions are full of 'it is possible that' and 'probably be' and even the few antique pieces unearthed are disappointing from a dating and workmanship point of view. The limits of the city have been defined, using the position of necropoli. It extended W to Mendoubia, S to Bou Kachkach and NW to Marshan but don't go and look for there is nothing to see.

TANGER

"Tangier is a foreign land if ever there was one. And the true spirit of it can never be found in any book save Arabian Nights ... the streets are oriental – some of them 3 feet wide, some 6, but only two that are over a dozen; a man can blockade the most of them by extending his body across them. Isn't it an oriental picture?" Twain, Mark, *Traveling with the Innocents Abroad*.

(*Pop* 266,346 (1982); *Alt* 75m) Tanger has a highly individual character, a product of its location at the gate to the Mediterranean Sea and at the meeting point of Africa and Europe, and of its recent historical past, notably as an international city from 1923 to 1956, when its tax-free status and reputation attracted many writers, artists and other famous Westerners, as well as a sizeable banking industry. Tanger also had fame as a gay resort. It remains today a lively city, popular with travellers, including those arriving or just visiting from Spain, interesting to explore, and with a wide range of restaurants and entertainments. A recent cleansing of the city when the King proposed a visit has improved the area. The beach is popular and the resort area extends E adjacent to the new promenade. The city is now an important passenger port and tourist resort. Tanger is well worth a visit, particularly for the **Kasbah**, former residence of Sultans, and the **Medina**, a small and complex maze of houses, shops and narrow, steep streets.

Overseas visitors

In Tanger it is almost impossible not to recall the numerous celebrated figures that once visited the city. They are part of the official and unofficial hard-sell, and are closely bound up in the history and the buildings. Visitors include English diarist Samuel Pepys, film stars Marlene Dietrich and Errol Flynn, writers Oscar Wilde, Brion Gysin, Allen Ginsberg, Joe Orton (*Entertaining Mr Sloane*), Paul Bowles (author of *The Sheltering Sky* and numerous short stories set in North Africa), Ian Fleming, Jack Kerouac, William Burroughs, Richard Hughes (*High Wind in Jamaica*), James Leo Herlihy (*Midnight Cowboy*), Tennessee Williams, painter Francis Bacon, and French composer Camille Saint-Saën, as well as the Woolworth heiress Barbara Hutton, Truman Capote, Winston Churchill, Ronnie Kray, Gertrude Stein and the photographer Cecil Beaton. The French painter Eugène Delacroix visited in 1832, and Henri Matisse in 1912, both completing many paintings of Tanger. This expatriate population has since declined, and Tanger can now seem to be resting on its former glories and notoriety.

Modern European Artists in Morocco

The orientalist artists and writers of the 19th century were confronted with sights and scenes of what appeared to be a startlingly different culture. They recorded what they saw for an audience at home that was eager to catch glimpses of these unknown lands. By the end of the century, a new breed of artists found their way to the new territorial possessions that their countries had acquired

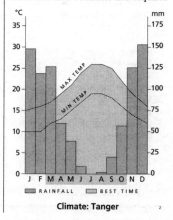

Climate: Tanger

Tanger skyline

in the great grab for colonial purposes. France was the power in Morocco and it was to Morocco or the Moroccan inspiration that many of the great French and other artists went – Matisse, Renoir and Fromentin, among others – though this time to indulge their art and their own senses rather than to convey impressions of exotic lands.

Henri Matisse (1869-1954) first visited Morocco in 1906 and again in 1912 by which time he was an established representative of the Fauvre school of modern painting. Matisse was much attracted by the strong light of the Mediterranean region and set up his home in the S of France, principally the French Riviera. After a short visit to Algiers in 1906 when his famous *Blue Nude – Souvenir of Biskra* was painted, he returned to North Africa 6 years later on two separate visits, this time to Tanger. It is thought that he found in Morocco both an escape from the dull colours of northern Europe but also a release from the Cubist trends in French art, with which he had no truck. During his first sojourn in Tanger he painted *Moroccan Landscape*, full of strong colours and of a direct, rich and simple layout. His later visit in 1912, in Morocco's dry season, saw the painting of *The Palm Leaf – Tanger* and *Moroccan Garden*, designed to bring out the parched nature of the landscape. Matisse produced other paintings of Moroccan subjects – perhaps *La Porte du Casbah* and *Zohrah, La Marocaine* being best known. Even after his return to France, Matisse produced some fine paintings with Moroccan influences clearly visible, such as *Les Marocains* in 1916.

Auguste Renoir (1841-1919) never set foot in Morocco but produced to order a wonderful *Jewish Wedding* based on a description by Delacroix of a wedding ceremony in Tanger. It remains one of the most evocative pictures of North African Jewish society in the 19th century and offsets the dismal stories of the miserable and dull nature of life for minorities in Morocco in that age.

Frank Brangwyn (1867-1956) was a Briton who travelled widely in the Orient, including visits to Tanger in 1893, when he painted the memorable *A Trade on the Beach* of a beach market. Many other artists used the marvellous colours and scenes in Morocco to develop their experience and technique from amateurs such as Winston Churchill to professionals such as Albert Besnard.

Today, keen painters can still take advantage of a brilliant Moroccan landscape and highly individualistic local architecture and dress to develop their expertise through an accompanied tour through organizations such as The Prospect Music and Art Tours, 454-458 Chiswick High Road, London W4 5TT, T 0181 995 2163.

Paul Bowles and the Tanger Literati

Do not be misled! The literary tradition of Tanger does not match up with that of Alexandria or even Palma Majorca by duration or depth. But it is remarkable that an English language tradition exists at all in the city which, after all, is oriented towards Arabic and French.

The beginning of the real Tanger literary tradition was that of the early author-travellers such as Mark Twain who remarked on the Tanger money-changers in his book *Traveling with the Innocents Abroad* in the 19th century. The official written sources on Tanger were written by the Consuls and none more than John Drummond Hay, whose materials in the British Public Records Office are a great source of information on Morocco in the second half of the 19th century.

Authors of international stature formerly or currently resident in Tanger are few. Paul Bowles is an American who has written a number of useful books based on his travels, observations and translations from local languages (as in the novel *A Life Full of Holes* by Mohammed Mrabet). Bowles has lived in Tanger since 1931. His book *The Sheltering Sky*, on an Algerian theme, was produced as a film, while *Their Heads are Green* includes aspects of Moroccan local music. Other contemporary authors - Joe Orton and William Burroughs, for example - have been birds of passage through Tanger but never part of a coherent literary circle. Scholars such as David Hart, author of *Dadda 'Atta and his Forty Grandsons*, Richard Pennell, author of *A Country with a Government and a Flag: the Rif War in Morocco*, and George Joffé, author of articles on Walter Harris, have close connections with Tanger and the country at large but are not permanently resident in Morocco.

Early History

Perhaps the oldest city in Morocco, Tanger was active as early as 1600 BC.

There was a Phoenician settlement here. Roman mythology ascribes its founding to the Greek giant Anteus, son of Poseidon, god of the earth, and Gaia, goddess of the earth. Anteus challenged Hercules, Hercules killing the giant and having a child by the widow, Tingis. Hercules pulled apart Spain and Africa to give this son, Sophix, a city protected by the sea. King Sophix named his city Tingis. Tanger was known to the Phoenicians, Romans, Vandals and Byzantines and has always been important in view of its strategic location commanding the Strait of Gibraltar. The Romans made it at one point capital of their North African provinces, and controlled it until 429 AD. Later, the Vandals and Byzantines struggled to control the city. Arabs took the city in 706 AD. Tanger remained at the centre of conflict between the major Arab and Berber Dynasties.

Mediaeval History

Tanger achieved commercial importance in the Mediterranean sphere during the 1300s. In 1332 perhaps one of the most influential sources of thinking in modern archaeology, Ibn Khaldun (Abu Zayyed Abdelrahman Ibn Khaldun) was born in Tunis. He served as a high official in the administrations in Morocco, Muslim Spain and Algeria, where, at the age of 43 he began writing his introduction to history – the *Moqaddimah*. He developed a segmentary analysis of Muslim society in which he saw a cycle of rise and fall of dynasties. In simplified form, he proposed that strong tribes from the interior would seize power from the sedentary powers of the cities and inject life and inventiveness into society before becoming gradually weakened by the stresses of urban politics and the temptations of the flesh pots of the city. Meanwhile, the tribal areas would once again throw up a vigorous tribal group, first to challenge and then finally take over the cities, deposing the former ruling family. The mechanics of social and political change and the causes for them outlined by Ibn Khaldun became the first serious secular interpretation of history and society. It is the modern anthropologist's 'segmentary theory', a much contested tool of contemporary sociology.

Ibn Khaldun was also a great travel and gazetteer-writer and is known more usually as among the truly outstanding Arab Geographers rather than as an anthropologist. He is known to have crossed via Egypt and his beloved Cairo to Mecca and Damascus, during the siege of which Ibn Khaldun met Timur (Timurlane the Great) in 1400. Ibn Khaldun spent his latter years in Cairo.

Ibn Khaldun is associated with the end of a golden age of thought and innovation in the Muslim world when new crops, cultivation practices and the arts reached their zenith. Sadly, his ideas of social evolution only reached Europe in the 19th century and full recognition of his immense intellectual gifts only fully absorbed by the West in the 20th century. It is ironic that in an increasingly hardline Islamic world at the end of the 20th century Ibn Khaldun is, as a non-religious theorist, much under-rated even in the Arab countries.

Tunis was conquered by the Portuguese in 1471, became Spanish in 1578 and Portuguese in 1640. The city was part of English King Charles II's dowry when marrying the Portuguese Catherine of Braganza in 1661, but the English departed in 1684, destroying the kasbah as they left. Sultan Moulay Ismail rebuilt the town after the English left.

Modern History

In the 19th century Tanger became a popular base for European merchants and housed a large European colony, as well as the focus of political competition between expansionist European powers. In 1923 the city became a tax-free International Zone controlled by a 30 member international committee. The city was reunited with Morocco in Oct 1956 but its tax-free status was maintained until 1960. Since Independence, Tanger has declined in international economic importance, but has also rapidly developed its tourist industry.

NB Hassle and guides

A drawback of Tanger is that the hassling of tourists can be constant and very skilled. If you need a guide, it is better to wait until you can get to the Tourist Office or one of the larger hotels to arrange an official guide. This should keep away the unofficial guides who will otherwise approach at any opportunity. However if you are accompanied by an official guide (or indeed an unofficial guide) you will pay an undeclared commission every time you purchase something. There is also considerable pressure to buy hashish, grown in the nearby Rif mountains. It is unadvisable to succumb to this pressure, in view of the often close links between the dealers and the police. Deterring the attentions of unofficial guides, drug dealers or others will take incredible patience, politeness and firmness. A much more minor problem is that a number of streets have two names: the original and still widely used French name and the newer Arabic name found on the street signs. A few have a third Spanish name.

ACCESS Air Tanger's Boukhalef airport is 15 km SW of the city, T 935129, 934717, on the P2 road to Rabat. Entry formalities slow as tourists and nationals are not separated. Catch bus 17 or 70 from the terminal to the Grand Socco (Place de 19 Avril 1947), or take a grand-taxi MD70 by day MD105 after 2100 in winter and 2200 in summer. (Rates displayed on wall by customs.)

Train Arriving by train from Marrakech, Casablanca, Rabat, Meknes and Fes the traveller stops first at Tanger Ville, and then at Tanger Port. The former is convenient for the city and its main hotels.

Road The P2 from Rabat brings the driver into Tanger along rue de Fes. The S704 from Ceuta twists along the coast and feeds into Ave Mohammed V, as does the P38 from Tetouan. **Bus**: CTM buses arrive at the terminal in Ave des Forces Armées Royales, adjacent to the port gates and Tanger Ville railway station. Private lines arrive at the terminal at the end of rue de Fes.

Sea Trasmediterranea and Limadet, T 933626, jointly run the car/passenger ferry service from Algeciras, Spain. Hopefully passports will have been stamped on the boat. In the terminal there is a *bureau de change* for cash and TCs, as well as a ticket office for trains. Hydrofoils from Algeciras and more traditional ferries from Gibraltar dock close by. Just outside the terminal is Tanger Port railway station for immediate departure to Asilah, Meknes, Fes, Oujda, Rabat, Casablanca and Marrakech, as well as a rank for both kinds of taxis. Negotiation over prices will be necessary but hard.

Places of interest

The Kasbah is constructed on the highest point of the medina. Follow rue d'Italie and rue de la Kasbah and enter by Porte de la Kasbah. From the medina, follow rue des Chrétiens from the Petit Socco, and then rue Sidi Ben Rassouli to Bab el Assa.

There has been a similar construction on the site of the kasbah since Roman days, and it was the traditional residence in Tanger of the Sultan and his harem. It was burnt to the ground by the English as they left in 1685. More recently, during the hey-day of Tanger as an international city, the kasbah was considered a fashionable address for people such as the novelist Richard Hughes (who lived at 'Numéro Zero, Le Kasbah, Tanger').

The **Musée de la Kasbah**, T 932097, open 0930-1300, 1500-1800, closed Tues, is in the former palace of the kasbah, the **Dar al-Makhzen**, and includes Moroccan arts and antiquities. The palace was built by the Sultan Moulay Ismail in the 18th century, and was used as the Sultan's palace up until 1912, when Sultan Mawlay Hafid, exiled to Tanger, lived there, alongside his extensive harem. The palace is itself worth seeing, with an impressive central courtyard. The **Museum of Moroccan Arts** is housed in the prince's apartments. Note the painted wooden ceilings, sculpted plasterwork and exquisite mosaics. This is truly a magnificent setting for the displays. The museum has a wide range of carved, and painted woods, carpets and textiles. Items of note are the firearms from the N enhanced with delicate marquetry; pottery decorated with flowers and feathers also from the N; unique carpets from Rabat. The Fes room is certainly outstanding firstly for the room itself with its intricate wall and ceiling carvings and secondly for the ancient ceramics from Fes and Meknes, centuries old dishes embellished with brilliant colours ranging from golden to the renowned Fes blue. In the Fes room too are dazzling silks, and illuminated manuscripts of the finest calligraphy, all superbly bound.

The former kitchens of the palace is now the Museum of Antiquities. On display are bronzes and mosaics from the Roman sites. A major item is the famous mosaic known as 'The Voyage of Venus' found at Lixus. This quite spectacular mosaic shows Venus in a vessel propelled by oars with nymphs (in and out of the water). The colours and the countenances of the major figures are still remarkably clear. Many of the artefacts relate to the history of Tanger and the surrounding region. In Room 3 which is devoted to ancient funeral rites is a life-size replica of a Carthaginian tomb and a number of lead sarcophagi.

The garden of the palace is worth exploring, a beautiful mature Andalusian arrangement, with fragrant plants. The ancient necropolis incorporated into the garden is a very good reproduction. As you leave the palace stop at *Le Detroit* for a drink and pastries, and an impressive view of the city and sea.

To the left of the palace is the **Museum of Ethnography and Archaeology**. In front of the palace is the Place de la Kasbah, where criminals were once punished or executed. Note the **Grand Mosque** adjacent to the port. In the sea wall a gate leads out onto a belvedere with excellent views of the seascape. On the other side of the Place de la Kasbah, just outside the kasbah gate on rue Sidi Hassani, is the **Musée International d'Art Contemporain**. Also nearby is **Villa Sidi Hosni**, former residence of Barbara Hutton, the American heiress whose Tanger life is famous.

The Medina Lying below the kasbah, and running from the Grand Socco (Place de 19 Avril, 1947) down to the port, the medina is focused on the Petit Socco, and is full of narrow, twisting streets and old houses, many of which are now shops, hotels or restaurants catering for tourists. It is a quarter which

has captured the imagination of numerous European and American writers, with the stories of Paul Bowles amongst the most evocative. It is easy to get lost here, so it might be advisable for the visitor with limited time to take an official guide. Unaccompanied, unofficial guides will hawk for business continuously.

The Grand Socco is where the medina begins. Nowadays it is a busy place, but no longer a thriving market square with street entertainers and food stalls. It now has a few fruit shops, cheap restaurants, and several cafés. Note the tiled minaret of the **Sidi Bou Abid Mosque** (1917) on the corner of the Grand Socco and rue Sidi Bou Abid. On Thur and Sun Rifi Berber women sell all

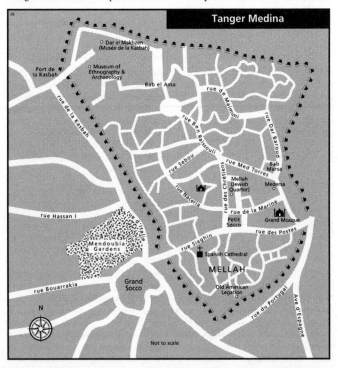

The American Connection – Malcolm Forbes

Tanger has a long connection with the USA. Not only was the Sultan of Morocco the first to recognise American Independence in 1776 but the USA's first building abroad taken over in 1821 – continuously occupied – is the America Legation Building in Tanger (see page 97). In the 20th century overall diplomatic relations have developed at a serious level, not least given the importance of Morocco as a base for the occupation of North Africa by Allied troops during WW2 and its role as a moderating influence on Arab policies in more recent years.

A manifestation of this US connection is the ownership by the US millionaire Forbes family of the famous regional governor's palace, the Mendoubia, in Tanger (see page 96) Malcolm Forbes purchased the Mendoubia Palace in 1970 and visited the city frequently, not least for the sexual freedoms it afforded him. He created a magnificent collection of 115,000 lead soldiers in Tanger, now on public show. The display includes the famous battle scenes of the Battle of the Three Kings at Kasr Kebir in 1578 in Morocco, when the Portuguese army was all but wiped out and the King of Portugal and two Moroccan Sultans died in the fray. Other dioramas are the Battle of Waterloo in 1815 and the Battle of the Somme in 1916.

Mendoubia Palace was the scene of reputedly a US$2.5 million 70th birthday party in 1989 when representatives of a rather middle aged jet-set were flown into Tanger for the celebration. Malcolm Forbes died in 1990 but the Forbes magazine empire maintains the Mendoubia Palace still. It is well worth a visit for its fine position in the *Marshan* area and for its shady gardens of palms and other fruit and ornamental trees.

sorts of wares in rue de la Plage (rue Salah Eddine El Ayoubi). Along rue d'Angleterre they also sell woven blankets. On the rue Bourrakia side of the Grand Socco, the arch with Arabic on it leads in to the **Mendoubia Gardens**, quiet but unimpressive, and normally closed. These gardens were formerly part of the residence of the Mendoub and contain 30 bronze cannons, the remains of old French and British warships. The **Mendoubia Palace** is the former residence of the Sultan's representatives on the International Commission.

Rue Siaghin, the old silversmiths' street, running from the Grand Socco to the Petit Socco, is still an important commercial area of the medina, and the easiest route by which to enter the main area of the medina. To the right of rue Siaghin, is the *mellah*, the Jewish quarter. One also passes the **Spanish Cathedral**, now boarded up. Rue Siaghin leads into the Petit Socco, which lies at the heart of the

medina. This market square was once bigger, but now seems strangely cramped. It is surrounded by a number of famous but primitive *pensiones*, and the *Café Central*, formerly a café-bar attracting the likes of William Burroughs, Allen Ginsberg and Jack Kerouac, but now with no alcohol sold in the medina it is just a fairly ordinary café with a pleasant terrace to watch life pass by.

Below the Petit Socco, the **Grand Mosque** lies in between rue de la Marine and rue des Postes. This is built on the site of a Portuguese cathedral, although that had been predated by a mosque and, probably, a Roman temple. Opposite is a 14th century *medersa*. Also on rue des Postes (rue Mokhtar Ahardan) is the *Pensión Palace*, where Bertolucci filmed *The Sheltering Sky*, based on the Paul Bowles' novel.

The **Old American Legation**, 8 Zankat d'Amerique, T 935904/935317, open 0930-1200, 1600-1830, is the oldest

American diplomatic property, given to the US by the Moroccan Sultan in 1821 and used as a Consulate until 1961. It holds the dubious distinction of being the only historical monument to have remained in its possession since the birth of the American Nation. From rue des Postes turn right after the *Hotel Mamora* into rue Ikiredj, through a confusing region at the heart of the medina, into rue de Four, right into rue Haybender, and left into rue d'Amerique. It is now a museum and study centre on display is a letter from George Washington to Moulay Abdullah and a collection of mirrors, also a good collection of prints including works by Lecouteux and Ben Ali r'Bati who was the first Moroccan 'naif' painter. Note also the building's classic architecture.

Tanger's *ville nouvelle* has little of great interest but it is a pleasant place to explore. Place de France (Place de Faro) has a good view of the bay, with the famous *Café de France* alongside, where wartime agents met and made deals.

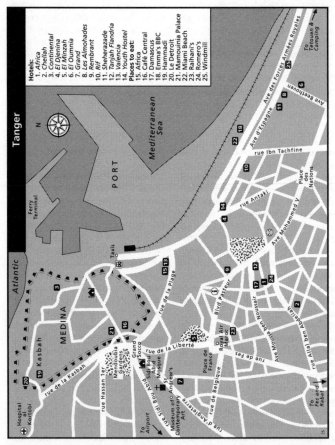

Hotels:
1. Africa
2. Chellah
3. Continental
4. Continentina
5. El Minzah
6. El Oumnia
7. Grand
8. Les Almohades
9. Rembrant
10. Rif
11. Sheherazade
12. Tanjah Flandria
13. Valencia
14. Youth Hostel

Places to eat:
15. Africa
16. Café Central
17. Damascus
18. Emma's BBC
19. Hammadi
20. Le Detroit
21. Mamounia Palace
22. Miami Beach
23. Raihani's
24. Romero's
25. Windmill

The Drummond Hay family in Tanger

In the small Derbyshire village church of St Margaret at Carsington there is a commemorative wall panel to Henrietta Auriol Chandos Pole Gell 'daughter of Edward William Auriol Drummond Hay', who died in Tanger on 17 September 1832. This plaque is a reminder of the depth and closeness of British relations with Tanger over a long period of consular service by the Drummond Hay family, father and son, in Tanger between the years 1829-1886. Edward William Auriol Drummond Hay arrived in Tanger in August 1829 as Consul-General in Morocco. He ran Anglo-Moroccan affairs until 1845 as a competent manager. It was the difficult time of the Algerian insurrection against the French fought at that stage, with no little help from the Moroccan sultan, out of Moroccan territory. Great Britain tried to bolster Moroccan independence against French and Spanish colonial aggression without a resort to arms but with only moderate success.

In 1845 Consul Hay died in Tanger and was succeeded by his talented son, John Drummond Hay, who remained as Consul General, later chargé d'affaires, at Tanger for 41 years. He became an admirer of Morocco and did all that he could to secure good links between the British and Moroccan courts. He was famous for his honesty, directness and love of Morocco. He was a benign influence in the sultan's counsels, looking to keep the Moroccans within the independent traditions of the Sultanate. Perhaps the modern European visitor to Morocco can learn a great deal about good relations from this dedicated man who had a true affection for Morocco and its peoples.

Blvd Pasteur is the main shopping and business street of the new town. Rue de la Liberté is also worth wandering along, perhaps stopping off at the *Centre Culturel Français*'s Galerie Delacroix if it has an exhibition. In Bit el Mal, which was originally the treasury, there is on show an ancient coffer belonging to the Royal Treasury.

At 50 rue d'Angleterre, **St Andrew's** is an Anglican Church consecrated in 1905, with architecture and internal decoration modelled on Moorish Granada. The key is kept by the friendly and helpful groundsman, Mustapha, who will unlock the church and give you a guided tour. Note the Arabic inscriptions of the Lord's Prayer and Gloria at the altar end. Memorials and graves, both inside and outside, feature a number of important former residents of Morocco, including 19th century British consul Sir John Drummond Hay, early 20th century *Times* correspondent Walter Harris, Caid Sir Harry McLean,

Scottish adviser to Sultan Mawlay Abd al-Aziz, and Emily Keane, 19th century wife of the Sherif of Ouezzane.

Nearby, the **Musée d'Art Contemporain de la Ville de Tanger**, 52 rue d'Angleterre, T 938436, has a wide selection of the more important painters of Morocco, but is not very impressive on the whole, entrance MD10. Originally this was the English consulate.

Forbes Magazine Museum of Military Miniatures, Palais Mendoub, rue Shakespeare, just W of the stadium, T 933606, F 934328, open 1000-1700, entry free, closed Thur. Malcolm Forbes, American magazine owner, set up this museum of over 115,000 toy soldiers in a former residence of the Moroccan Sultan. Some of these figures re-enact the famous battles of history, from Waterloo to Dien Bien Phu. The clever use of lighting and sound effects gives realism to the displays. Other armies stand in show cases. Here 600 statuettes bear silent homage to the Battle of the Three

Emily Keene – wife of the Shareef of Wazzan

A Moroccan prince, Abdel-salam ben Alarbi, was dispatched by the Sultan Moulay Hassan to London in 1877. He was unusual in that he was, as a shareef, a descendent of the Prophet, a powerful influence in northern Morocco as a relative of the Sultan, and, interestingly, married to an English woman, Emily Keene. The shareef had taken Emily Keene as a wife in 1873 in Tanger. Miss Keene was born in Lambeth, the daughter of a prison governor in England who came to Tanger as a lady's companion, met the shareef, and after a short courtship married him in the British Legation in Tanger. Emily thoroughly adapted to life in Morocco, becoming best known as the mother of the Shareef's two sons – Moulay Ali and Moulay Ahmad – and as a benefactor of the poor and de-prived of the region.

Kings (see Forbes box, page 125). Essential for the enthusiast, a pleasant change for others. The gardens are magnificent.

The **beach** and the clubs alongside it were previously known as an expatriate zone where anything was permissable and a good time easily available. The clubs are a shadow of what they once were but still offer a range of drinking, eating and dancing opportunities. Try *Emma's BBC*, *The Windmill* or *Miami Beach*. The beach is popular, particularly with Moroccans in Jul and Aug. There is no shortage of more relaxing, less crowded and cleaner beaches either way along the coast.

Tanger is a splendid place for watching the birds which migrate across the Strait of Gibraltar – the easiest crossing place between Europe and Africa. Literally hundreds of species make use of the thermals to cross N in spring and S in autumn, the flocks of huge storks and vultures being the most impressive sight.

Local information

NB There is a shortage of water in Tanger due to poor rainfall. Be prepared for the supply to be cut at any time.

Price guide

Hotels:			
AL	over US$75	**D**	US$20-40
A	US$75	**E**	US$10-20
B	US$60-75	**F**	under US$10
C	US$40-60		

Places to eat:			
♦♦♦	expensive	♦♦	average
♦	cheap		

● **Accommodation**

AL *Hotel El Minzah*, 85 rue de la Liberté (Zankat el Houria), T 935885, F 934546, 100 rm with bath, pricey but central, dates from the 1930s, beautiful gardens set around an Andalusian courtyard, convenient for exploring the medina, two restaurants, wine bar, coffee bar, tea room, mini-club, tennis, pool, extensions in progress will increase to 153 rm and improve facilities; **AL** *Hotel Les Almohades*, Ave des Forces Armées Royales, T 940431, F 946317, 138 rm, nr the beach, most with sea views, luxurious, 4 restaurants, bar, nightclub 'Up 2000', pool, sauna.

B *Hotel Ahlen*, Km 5 Route de Rabat, T 9350001/2, F 9350003/5, low line hotel, all on 2 floors, 2 bars plus poolside bar, 350 beds, all rooms have bath, heating, phone and private balcony, mini suites have in addition a/c, TV, minibar, suites have in addition a spacious living room, 3 restaurants and a snack/grill, Olympic pool plus children's pool, water polo, table tennis, tennis, horse riding, disco, 2 shops, free parking, airport and port are 5 km, free shuttle bus to beach club, Fantasia tents with capacity for 1,000 spectators; **B** *Hotel Rembrandt*, Ave Mohammed V, T 937870/2, centre of the new town, luxurious and prestigious, restaurant and popular bar, garden, pool; **B** *Tanjah Flandria Hotel*, 6 Ave Mohammed V, T 931231/936285, F 934347, centre of the new town, 5 mins from beach, all rooms a/c, bath, phone and radio, 170 rm, comfortable, 2 restaurants, piano bar, disco (2100-0300), sauna (men: 1200-1400, 1900-2100, women: 1000-1200), art gallery, bank, pool, garage; **B** *Tarik*, Route de Malabata, T 940363, F 940944, situated directly on the fine, sandy beach, 154 rm with bath and balcony, wind surfing, sailing, boating, tennis, minigolf, table tennis, volley ball, disco.

C *Africa Hotel*, 17 rue Moussa Ben Noussair, T 935511, 86 rm, comfortable and lively, bar, pool, restaurant, nightclub; C *Hotel El Oumnia*, Ave Beethoven, T 940366, pleasant hotel in this category, pool, international restaurant; C *Hotel Sheherazade*, Ave des Forces Armées Royales, T 940500, 146 rm, close to the sea, pool, private beach, bar and terrace, tennis, fishing, horse riding, water skiing and wind surfing, separate a/c and central heating, high standard of furnishings, disco; C *Solazur*, Ave des Forces Armées Royales, on beach next to bay, just a few minutes from the ferry and the railway station, 360 rm with bath, telephone and radio, 2 restaurants, disco, sauna and massage, tennis, 10 storey hotel, good sea views from most rooms.

D *Chellah Hotel*, central position, 47-49 rue Allal Ben Abdallah, T 943389, 180 rm not all with a/c, 10 suites, good value, disco, tea room, guarded parking; D *Hotel Marco Polo*, Ave d'Espagne, T 938213, 9 rm, German run, restaurant and bar, overlooking the sea.

E *Continental Hotel*, 36 rue Dar Baroud, in the medina, T 931024, Tx 33086, by far the best cheap option, has fallen on hard times but is being renovated, convenient, with a sea view, historic decoration, restaurant; E *Hotel El Djenina*, 8 rue El Antaki (rue Grotius), just off Ave d'Espagne, T 936075, 21 rm, rec; E *Hotel El Muniria*, rue Magellan, incl the *Tanger Inn Bar*, both popular, numbering William Burroughs, Kerouac and Ginsberg among former residents; opp is the E *Hotel Ibn Batouta*, 8 rue Magellan, T 937170, with restaurant; E *Mansora Hotel*, 19 rue des Postes, T 934105, only good hotel in the centre of the medina; E *Hotel Rif*, 152 Ave des Forces Armées Royales, T 937870, central position nr ferry and train station, good views to sea, hammam, pool; E *Valencia*, 72 Ave d'Espagne, junction with rue de la Plage (Zankat Salah Eddine el Ayoubi), T 930770, 45 rm, clean but basic, no restaurant.

F *Hotel Grand Socco*, rue Imam Layti, behind the Grand Socco, is cheap, dirty and noisy, but convenient; *Petit Socco* (Place Souq Dakhil) is the heart of the medina and its *pensiones* have a history, but they may be poorly equipped, try F *Pensión Mauritania*, T 934671, which has a cold shower; or just off, on rue des Postes (Ave Mokhtar Ahardan) F *Pensión Palace* is good; in the *ville nouvelle* there are cheap and basic *pensiones* in rue de la Plage, where prices

do not seem to be fixed, but many do not have showers, incl F *Royal*, *Madrid*, *Le Detroit*, *Playa* and *Atou*, the last being particularly cheap, whilst *Le Detroit* is rec.

Youth hostel: T 46127, 8 rue El Antaki, Ave d'Espagne, 60 beds, overnight fee, MD20-25, advanced booking essential, station 800m, bus 100m. Good reports given on this hostel, clean and well run.

Camping: camping sites are not much cheaper than a budget hotel and rather far from the city. *Camping Miramonte*, on extension of Ave Sidi Mohammed, T 937138, is 3 km W from the city, on bus routes 1, 2 and 21, site of 3$\frac{1}{2}$ ha, beach 1 km, bar/snacks, pool, showers, laundry, petrol at 400m; *Camping-Caravaning Tingis*, T 940191, is 6 km E, well-equipped but 2 km from the beach on site of 6 ha, beach 800m, restaurant and grocery shop, pool, laundry, showers, petrol at 400m; *Sahara* site of 2 ha, beach 300m, bar, restaurant, groceries, shower, laundry, first aid. Also recommended are *Tingis-Sna*, E along Bay of Tanger, just beyond the *oued*; *L'Helice Ripal* on the road to Asilah; *El Manar* on Malabata Rd. *Robinson Plage Camping*, 8 km E by Caves of Hercules, good but far out on the Atlantic coast, take the Boughaz minibus.

● **Places to eat**

◆◆◆ *El Erz*, *Hotel El Minzah*, 85 rue de la Liberté, T 935885, reservations rec, popular restaurant with a wide range of European dishes, often with music; *El Korsan*, *Hotel El Minzah*, 85 rue de la Liberté, T 935885, reservations rec, Moroccan food amid traditional decor and music.

◆◆ *Brenda's*, Ave du Prince Moulay Abdellah, is a cheap English restaurant; *Restaurant Chez Bernard*, off Blvd Pasteur nr the *Hotel Rembrandt*, Spanish menu dominated by fish; *Damascus*, 2 bis Ave du Prince Moulay Abdellah, T 934730, Moroccan food, bar and tea room; *Dar Tajine*, rue du Commerce, high-class Moroccan meals, some tour parties; *Restaurant El Mabrouk*, rue Ahmed Chaouki, off Place de France, has very reasonably-priced set menus with good Moroccan food; further up the same road *Raihani's*, T 934866, also has reasonable menus with excellent Moroccan cuisine, *Restaurant le Detroit*, Ave du Prince Moulay Abdellah, Spanish food, cheaper than nearby Romero's; *Restaurant Hammadi*, 2 rue de la Kasbah, opp junction with Paseo del Docteur Cenarro, T 934514,

A Moroccan feast for the senses

The western fascination with the vivid and diverse colours of Morocco has a short history beginning with the first European travellers there in the 19th century. For a number of artists – not least Matisse (see box 'Modern European Artists in Morocco', page 119) – the Cherifian Empire was to be of prime importance. For the French romantic painter Eugène Delacroix, the scenes and colours witnessed during an early visit to Morocco were to shape his whole career.

Before his journey to Morocco, the well-read Delacroix had travelled only in literature – apart from a brief stay in London in 1825 where he had become familiar with watercolour techniques, as yet little used in France. It was the speed and immediacy of watercolour that was to enable Delacroix to record so much of what he was to see in North Africa.

Delacroix arrived in Tanger in Jan 1832, a member of a diplomatic mission to the Sultan Moulay Abd Al-Rahman. (France had taken Algiers in Jul 1830, and one of the results had been a wave of resentment against French interests in Morocco.) In diplomatic terms the mission was a failure, with Morocco continuing to support the Algerian Emir Abdel Qader. But for Delacroix, the Moroccan notebooks, a rich mixture of water colours, sketches and jottings, were to be a lifelong source of inspiration.

Shortly after arriving in Algiers, Delacroix wrote back to a friend, "We have landed in the midst of the strangest peoples ... At the moment I am like a man dreaming who sees things but fears that they will escape him". Delacroix sketched the town, the family of Abraham Benchimol, and the French consulate dragoman. In Mar, the Duc de Mornay's suite proceeded S towards Meknes to the meeting with the Sultan – later the subject of one of Delacroix's most important pictures, *Le Sultan du Maroc entouré de sa garde* (1845). Mounted on a richly caparisoned horse, shaded by the imperial parasol, Moulay Abd Al-Rahman moves forward amidst a throng of courtiers and guards. In the background are the ramparts of Meknes. The painting is one of the earliest pictorial representations of a Muslim court – important given the reticence to portray the human form prevalent in Islamic art.

In the 1820s, the youthful Delacroix had painted scenes of cruel carnage, inspired by the struggle for Greek independence. The 6 months of the Moroccan journey was to be his only contact with the Orient: his palette became warmer and lighter. "Come to Barbary", wrote Delacroix to a friend in 1832, "You will feel even more the precious and rare influence of the sun which gives each thing a penetrating life". He discovered what he was to call "Living Antiquity", people who through their closeness to nature had all the nobility of the ancient Romans. (Contrasting the French delegation with graceful Moroccan dress, Delacroix wrote: "... in our corsets, our tight shoes, our ridiculous tight clothes, we are objects of pity.")

Yet, despite the vivacity of the Moroccan notebooks – the lively realism of streetscapes and interiors, the Orient of the majority of Delacroix's great paintings is an Orient of cavalcades and bloody combats, of concubines lounging in cool harems – a world often cruel, sometimes erotic. Although memories of Morocco were a constant source of material for Delacroix's work, the vision that emerges is one of primitive nature where cruel passions are played out – a world through which the painter freed himself from the constraints and morals of classicism, but never really sought to understand. That was left to later painters.

Moroccan meals in 'authentic' surroundings; *L'Ibis*, rue Khalid Ibn Oualid, nr Place de France (Place de Faro), moderately priced but unexciting French restaurant/bar; *Restaurant Mamounia Palace*, 6 rue Semmarin, Petit Socco, T 935099, set menus of Moroccan food with authentic decor and folklore/music; *Negresso*, rue Mexique, a bar, snack-bar and restaurant, offers French, English and Moroccan drinks and food; *Romero's*, 12 Ave du Prince Moulay Abdellah, T 932277, highly rec Spanish cuisine, fair prices but not cheap; try also *Emma's BBC*, Ave d'Espagne, famous and cheap beachside bar-restaurant, open summer only; *La Presse Salon de Thé/Restaurant*, Blvd Pasteur; *Miami Beach*, Ave des Forces Armées Royales, T 943401, 1000-1800, beachside bar-restaurant, gay bar and disco at night; *Windmill*, Ave des Forces Armées Royales, T 940907, oldest beachside restaurant patronized by writer Joe Orton, fish, Moroccan and Spanish food.

◆*Restaurant Africa*, 83 rue de la Plage (rue Salah Eddine El Ayoubi), T 935436, a good cheap option; *Dallas* is a cheap fish restaurant in rue El Moutanabi; *Restaurant Hassi Baida* and *Restaurant Cleopatre* are in the same road and similar; the Grand Socco has several cheap places to eat and the *Café-Restaurant Ataif*; in the medina, there are a number of cheap, basic restaurants, such as *Mauritania* and *Assalam* in rue de la Marine, and *Aladin*, *Grece* and *Andaluz* in rue du Commerce. The latter, at No 7, is particularly good.

● **Bars**
Patio Wine Bar, Hotel El Minzah, 85 rue de la Liberté, T 935885, a wine bar in which to explore the wines of Morocco and overseas, a little pricey; *The Pub*, 4 rue Sorolla, T 934789, food, beer and other drinks in a pub atmosphere; *Caid's Bar*, Hotel El Minzah, 85 rue de la Liberté, T 935885, Moroccan decoration and expensive drinks in an atmospheric and celebrated bar; *Tanger Inn*, 1 rue Magellan, T 935337, small bar popular with expatriates; *Emma's BBC*, Ave d'Espagne, beachside bar; *Number One*, 1 Ave Mohammed V, T 931817, popular with gays.

● **Cafés**
As you leave the palace in the kasbah, stop at the *Salon de Thé/Restaurant le Detroit*, T 938080, which is pricey for food, but good for tea, coffee, pastries and a view of the palace, kasbah and the sea, established by the writer Brion Gysin. *Café de France*, 1 Place de France, has a history as a meeting place of the important and famous, popular with Francis Bacon, William Burroughs, Tennessee Williams and Truman Capote. The *Café Central*, in the Petit Socco, has a similar history, but is now just a nice place to watch the hustle and bustle of the medina.

● **Banks & money changers**
BMCE, Blvd Pasteur, with a *bureau de change*. BMCI 8 Place de France, T 935553. **Banque du Maroc**, 78 Ave Mohammed V, T 935553. **Credit du Maroc**, Agence Grand Socco, rue de l'Italie. Banks are open 0830-1130 and 1430-1630.

American Express: c/o Voyages Schwartz, 54 Blvd Pasteur, T 933459, 0900-1230 and 1500-1900 Mon-Fri, 0900-1230 Sat.

● **Cultural & language centres**
American Language Center, 1 rue M'Sallah; Centre Culturel Français, rue de la Liberté.

● **Embassies & consulates**
Belgium, 124 Ave Mohammed Ben Abdellah, T 931218; **Denmark**, 3 rue Ibn Rochd, T 938183; **France**, Place de France, T 932039; **Germany**, 47 Ave Hassan II, T 938700; **Italy**, 35 rue Assad Ibn Fourat, T 931064; **Netherlands**, 47 Ave Hassan II, T 931245; **Norway**, 3 rue Henri Regnault, T 931245; **Portugal**, 9 Place des Nations, T 931708; **Spain**, rue Sidi Bouabid, T 937000, 935625; **Sweden**, 31 Ave Prince Heritier, T 938730; **Switzerland**, rue Henri Regnault, T 934721; **UK**, 9 rue d'Amerique du Sud, T 935895; **USA**, 29 rue El Achouak, T 935904.

● **Entertainment**
Art galleries: *Galerie Delacroix*, rue de la Liberté; *Tanjah Flandria Art Gallery*, rue Ibn Rochd, behind the *Hotel Flandria*, T 933000.

Cinemas: *Ciné Alcazar*, junction of rue de l'Italie and rue Ibn Al Abbar (Paseo del Doctor Cenarro); *Cinema Rif*, Grand Socco, not very good looking. Preferably look around Blvd Pasteur.

Discos and nightclubs: the continuation of rue Mexique, rue Sanlucar (Zankat El Moutanabi), has a number of clubs/discos incl *Churchill's*, *Scott's* and *Koutoubia Dancing*. Also try the more upmarket *Up 2000* in *Hotel les Almohades*, Ave des Forces Armées Royales, T 940431, built on the roof of a hotel; or *Ali Baba* at *Chellah Hotel*, 47-49 rue Allal Ben Abdellah. *Morocco Palace*, 11 Ave du Prince Moulay Abdellah, T 938614, has belly-dancing until 0100, when it becomes a disco.

Handicrafts Centre: Ave de Belgique, T 931589.

● **Hospitals & medical services**
Ambulance: T 15.

Chemists: *Pharmacie de Fes*, 22 rue de Fes, T 932619, 24 hrs a day; *Pharmacie Pasteur*, Place de France, T 932422.

Dentist: Dr Ibrahim Filali, 53 Ave du Prince Moulay Abdellah, T 931268, speaks English.

Doctor: Dr Joseph Hirt, 8 rue Sorolla, T 935729, speaks English, and will pay calls to hotels.

Hospital: emergencies: T 934242; *Hospital Al Kortobi*, rue Garibaldi, T 931073; *Hôpital Español*, T 931018.

● **Post & telecommunications**
Area code: 9. All numbers are six figs in most cases beginning with the area code.

Post Office: the main post office (PTT) is at 33 Ave Mohammed V, T 935657 (0830-1200, 1430-1800, Mon-Fri, 0830-1200 Sat).

Telephone: international phone (24 hrs) far right of post office. Also telephone from the PTT at the junction of rue El Msala and rue Belgique.

● **Places of worship**
Anglican: St Andrew's Episcopal Church, 50 rue d'Angleterre, T 934633, services on Sun 0830 and 1100 and Wed.

Interdenominational Protestant: American Church, 34 rue Hassan Ibn Ouezzane (rue Léon l'Africain), T 932755, service on Sun 1100.

● **Shopping**
Food: there is a food market between rue d'Angleterre and rue Sidi Bou Abid. The stalls along rue d'Angleterre are not very impressive. There are numerous fruit sellers along rue de la Plage and its side streets. Just off, on rue El Oualili, is another food market.

Handicrafts & antiques: Tanger is not the best place to buy handicrafts, for although it has a large selection, Marrakech and Fes have better access to the different producing regions, and prices will be lower. The pressure to buy in Tanger is intense, with bazaarists and hawkers used to gullible day-trippers and weekend visitors from Spain. The cheapest shops and stalls, with the most flexible prices, will be found in the medina. Shops in the *ville nouvelle* may claim fixed prices but in most this is just another ploy. *Coopartim, Ensemble Artisanal*, rue de Belgique, T 931589, is a

good place to start, a government controlled fixed price shop with a vast range of goods from all over the country, where one can get an idea of prices. Also try *Sahara*, 30 rue des Almouahidine; *Bazaar Chaouen*, 116 rue de la Plage; and in the medina, *Marrakech la Rouge*, 50 rue es Siaghin. For crafts and antiques see the amazing *Galerie Tindouf*, 64 rue de la Liberté, T 931525.

Library: Tanger Book Club, the Old American Legation, 8 rue d'Amerique, the medina, T 935317 (0930-1200, Tues-Sat).

Newspapers & books: foreign newspapers can be brought from shops in rue de la Liberté or outside the post office in Ave Mohammed V. For books in French, and a few in other languages, go to *Librarie des Colonnes*, 54 Blvd Pasteur, T 936955.

● **Sport**
Flying: *Royal Flying Club*, Boukhalef Airport, T 934371.

Golf: *Royal Club de Golf*, Boubana, T 944484, F 945450, 18 hole, 5,545m par 70, fees MD200 per round.

Pétanque: 7 Salle Magallanes, T 935203.

Riding: *Country L'Etrier*, Boubana.

Tennis: *M'Sallah Garden Tennis Courts*, rue de Belgique, T 935203; *Municipale*, Ave de la Paix, T 943324.

Yachting: *Tanger Yacht Club*, the Port, T 938575.

● **Tour companies & travel agents**
Holiday Service, 84 Ave Mohammed V, T 933362; *Wagons-Lit Tourisme*, rue de la Liberté. *Air France*, 20 Blvd Pasteur; *GB Airways*, 83 rue de la Liberté, T 935877; *Iberia*, 35 Blvd Pasteur, T 936177; *Royal Air Maroc*, Place de France, T 935501/2; *Limadet Ferry*, Ave du Prince Moulay Abdellah, T 932649; *Comanov Ferries*, 43 rue Abou Alaâ al Maari, T 932649; *Transtour Ferries*, 4 rue el Jabha al Outania, T 934004.

● **Tourist offices**
Office du Tourisme, 29 Blvd Pasteur, T 938239/40, F 948050, open 0800-1400, Mon-Sat; **Syndicat d'Initiative**, 11 rue Khalid Ibn El Oualid, T 935486.

● **Useful addresses**
Fire: T 15.

Garage: Tanjah Auto, 2 Ave de Rabat.

Police (general): rue Ibn Toumert, T 19; **Police** (traffic): T 177.

● **Transport**

Local Bus: Sh Al Jamai al Arabia, T 946682, Tanger is fairly small and thus it is unlikely that you will want to use local buses. If you do they can be picked up in the Grand Socco or in Ave des Forces Armées Royales outside the port gates. Boughaz minibuses, from just outside the port gate, may be useful to get to the private bus station, or on excursions from Tanger westwards. **Bicycle & motorcycle hire**: Mesbahi, 7 rue Ibn Tachfine, just off Ave des Forces Armées Royales, T 940974, renting bicycles, 50cc and 125cc motorbikes, deposit required for 3 days or more. **Car hire**: Avis, 54 Blvd Pasteur, T 938960, 933031, and at the airport; **Budget**, 7 Ave du Prince Moulay Abdellah, T 937994, and at the airport; **Europcar**, 87 Ave Mohammed V, T 938271; **Hertz**, 36 Ave Mohammed V, T 933322, 934179, and at the airport; **Leasing Cars**, 24 rue Henri Regnault, and at the airport, a little cheaper. **Grand-taxis**: can be picked up from the Grand Socco or in front of **Tanger Ville** railway station, to destinations within or outside of the city. You will need to set a fare with the driver. Tanger's **petit-taxis**, turquoise with yellow stripe, may be cheaper, although that will depend on your skill as the meters are not always operated. For a taxi T 935517.

Air Tanger's Boukhalef airport is 15 km from the city along the P2, T 935129, 934717. Catch bus 17 or 70 from Grand Socco or a grand-taxi. Arrive 1½-2 hrs early. There are direct flights to Agadir, Al Hoceima and Casablanca and direct international flights to European cities including Amsterdam, Barcelona, Brussels, Frankfurt, Gibraltar, London, Madrid and Paris.

Train There are two stations in Tanger, very close together. All trains go from **Tanger Ville**, T 931201, on Ave des Forces Armées Royales in the town centre, some leave just before from **Tanger Port**, beside the ferry terminal. Departures – **Rabat and Casablanca**: 0850, 1700, 2345; **Marrakech**: 0850, 2345; **Meknes, Fes and Oujda**: 1100, 0130. All trains stop at Asilah.

Road Bus: information: T 932415. CTM buses depart from the ticket office near the entrance to the port in Ave des Forces Armées Royales. Current departure times – **Kenitra, Rabat and Casablanca**: 1100, 2230, 2330, 2400; **Souq El Arba du Gharb, Ksar el Kebir, Larache, Asilah**: 1100, 1630, 1800, 2230, 2330, 2400; **Sidi Kacem, Meknes, Fes**: 1800; **Agadir, Tiznit**: 1630; **Paris**: 0500. Private buses, running from the terminal at the end of rue de Fes, go to most destinations and are generally cheaper. Departures: **Tetouan** every 15 mins (1 hr); **Asilah** 0915, 0945, 1100 (30 mins; Larache every hour (90 mins); **Meknes** 0700, 1000, 1300, 1600 (5 hrs); **Fes** 1000, 1600; (6 hrs); **Chaouen** 0545, 0800, 1045, 1300, 1330, 1815 (2½ hrs); **Ceuta** 0730, 0945, 1245 (2 hrs); **Ouezzane** 0900, 1400 (4 hrs). To get to the terminal take a petit-taxi or a Boughaz minibus. **Taxi**: to many destinations take a shared grand-taxi from the bus terminal at the end of rue de Fes. To Tetouan and Ceuta this is a quick, practical and not too expensive option. For excursions from Tanger to the Caves of Hercules or Cap Malabata negotiate for a grand-taxi in rue de Hollande.

Sea Ferry tickets to **Algeciras** can be bought at the Limadet Agents in Ave du Prince Moulay Abdellah, just off Blvd Pasteur, T 932649, at travel agents in Blvd Pasteur, or at the ferry terminal. Trasmediterranea and Limadet jointly operate this car and passenger service 3 or 4 times a day in the summer and 2 in the winter. Passengers from MD196, cars from MD8500. Check in at least 1 hr early, to allow time to collect an embarkation card, complete a departure card, and have your passport stamped. For tickets for the Bland's Line ferry to **Gibraltar** go to Med Travel, 22 Ave Mohammed V, T 935872/3, or to the port. Departures Mon 0930, Wed, Thur and Fri 1430, Mon and Fri 1830 and Sun 1630, single: MD250 (£20), return: MD360 (£27). Day trip MD400. Motos and bicycles MD200. Vehicles up to 6m MD600. Journey takes 1 hr on hydrofoil and 2-2½ hrs on traditional ferry. **NB** Holding a return ticket for a specific sailing is no guarantee you will be allowed on the boat – Bland's excursion customers come first. Tickets to **Sete** can be bought from Voyages Comanov, 43 rue Abou el Alaâ el Maâri, T 932649, F 932320. There is a ferry every 3-4 days. Passenger tickets from MD2720. Car and two passengers from MD3,740.

Single prices for slow ferry from Tanger to Algeciras in pesetas:

Adult	3,000
Child	1,500
Trailer	4,200
Car	9,300
Car and roof-rack	13,500
Van	15,400
Motorbike	2,650
Minivan	44,000

NB At the port avoid all touts selling embarkation cards which are free from the officals. Exchange your ticket for a boarding card at the ticket desk.

Walter Harris – friend of Princes

The Englishman, Walter Harris, was a resident of Tanger and the correspondent of the London *Times*. He was born in London in 1866, the son of a merchant and ship owner of substance. His first visit to Morocco was in 1887 and he moved residence to Tanger in 1889. He became an important source of news and views on Morocco since he was widely read in the *Times* and elsewhere. He built a sumptuous house just outside Tanger in 1894 and a great garden, which was an obsession and which his wife cited as a reason for her divorce from him. Villa Harris is now the home of the Tanger Club Mediterranée and is not open to the public. In the later years of his life he moved into Tanger city itself, Villa Harris falling into the hands of American owners (and at one stage bought by the Woolworth heiress, Barbara Hutton).

Harris as a journalist was very well informed – he spoke excellent Arabic. His viewpoints were easily changed, however, and he successively was pro-British, pro-German and pro-French, depending on his connections at the time. His friendship and admiration of Marshal Lyautey after 1906 heavily influenced his interpretations of events. He wrote a number of excellent books such as *Morocco that Was* (1921), but it is always a risk with flamboyant characters like Harris that their writings tell more of the author than the supposed subject! Certainly, critics of Harris have attacked his support for colonial 'modernity' against rough and 'backward' pre-colonial independence.

Harris had privileged access to all the senior Moroccan nobility and travelled widely in the country. He was the first European in places such as Chaouen. Walter Harris was taken as a prisoner for ransom by Ahmad Bin Mohammed Al-Raisuni in 1903. Al-Raisuni was a successful local chief and bandit who profited by the anarchy after the death of Moulay Hassan in 1894. Harris was released and remained a firm friend of Al-Raisuni. Harris had an ambivalent attitude to the Rif War (see box Abd Al-Karim, page 66). While he deplored the carnage and abuse of the Rifis by the Spanish troops in particular, he would never accept that the Rifis had a genuine case for political independence. He must be seen as a latter day colonialist, always a friend of princes, perhaps for all his sympathies with the Moroccan people. He is buried in Tanger.

ATLANTIC BEACH, THE CAVES OF HERCULES AND ANCIENT COTTA

The excursion W is a rewarding experience, with a dramatic drive en route. The coast of Southern Spain can be easily seen on a clear day from the coast road to the N of the town, a special viewpoint is provided. The options are to negotiate a round-trip price with a grand-taxi driver in rue d'Angleterre, take a Boughaz mini-bus from the port gates, or in your own transport, follow rue Sidi Bou Abid and rue Sidi Amar on to the S701. This goes past Montagne, an exclusive suburb of royal palaces and villas. 11 km from

Tanger is **Cap Spartel**, the extreme NW corner of Africa, with a notable lighthouse, and the *Café-Bar Sol*. This is followed by the long and wild Atlantic (or Robinson) Beach. This is a dramatic place, and swimmers should exercise caution. Nearby is the **C** *Hotel Les Grottes d'Hercules*, T 938765; and the **E** *Hotel Robinson*; as well as *Camp Robinson* and the *Robinson Café-Restaurant*.

The **Caves of Hercules** are natural formations which have been extended by quarries for millstones up to the 1920s. Later prostitutes worked here, and a number of Tanger's rich and famous held parties. The natural rock chambers are open from 1000 to sunset, for a nominal charge. From a window shaped like Africa which overlooks the sea there is an impressive view.

After the Caves of Hercules take a rough farm track off the road to the **Ancient Cotta**. This is a small site, less impressive than Volubilis, centred around a factory for *garum*, or anchovy paste. Also note remains of the temple.

CAP MALABATA, KSAR ES SEGHIR

From Tanger, 10 km E along the S704 road around **Cap Malabata**, are large tourist developments, including the *Club Mediterranée* complex, numerous cafés as well as some excellent beaches used by the people from Tanger. Cap Malabata, where the Atlantic and the Mediterranean meet and it is said the waters (with a little imagination) can be seen as two different colours. Despite this the views are magnificent. By the Oued Melaleh estuary is an old Portuguese settlement. Further on the **Chateau Malabata** is a Gothic folly, inhabited by a Moroccan family.

Ksar es Seghir is a small seaside town 37 km E of Tanger, dominated by the ruined Portuguese castle. The town was named Ksar Masmuda under the Almohads, and Ksar al Majaz under the Merinids, who added walls and gates in 1287. The Portuguese took the town in 1458. The floor of the *hammam* and mosque should be noted, as well as the intact sea gate arch. The **F** *Café Restaurant Hotel Kassar al Majaz Tarik Ibn Ziad*, is basic. There are other cafés and restaurants, including the recommended *Restaurant Caribou, Café Dakhla* to W of town, *Café Dahlia* to E and *Café Lachiri* on bridge (sea food), possibilities for camping, and a splendid beach. Onwards, between Ksar es Seghir and Ceuta, there is a string of beautiful and often deserted beaches. Bus 15 from Grand Socco, Tanger, serves this route. This road is busy on a Sun and very busy in summer. Out of season many places are closed.

Bird Migration

Without doubt this is the best place in North Africa to watch the migrations to and from Europe. Over 250 different species have been counted crossing this narrow strip of water and while the main movements are from Mar-May and Aug-Oct early and late movers ensure that there are always some birds to observe. The stretch of coast from Cap Spartel in the W to Punta Ceres in the E and the advantage of height gained by Jbel Kebir and Jbel Musa provides ample viewing spots. While the massive migration of large raptors (Honey Buzzards, Black Kites and Booted Eagles move in their thousands) is very impressive, other, rarer, raptors such as Merlins and Osprey make this journey. Flocks of the huge White Stork cannot easily be missed. Smaller birds make their migrations too, warblers and wheatears, swallows, larks and finches. The tracks followed are determined by the wind direction and strength.

GIBRALTAR/ALGECIRAS

Excursions take only 75 mins. Day trips cost MD360 to Gibraltar, MD250 to Algeciras. See transport details, page 133.

CEUTA

Ceuta or Sebta in Arabic is a Spanish enclave on the Moroccan coast, administered not as a colony but as a military post or *presidio* and thus an integral part of metropolitan Spain. Ceuta has an excellent strategic position on the Strait of Gibraltar and was occupied by the Carthaginians, Greeks and Romans. After being taken in the Arab conquest, the site was captured by the Portuguese in 1415 but on the union of Spain and Portugal was transferred to Spain in 1581, under whose control it has remained ever since as little more than a military prison. Its later fame arose from its importance as a supplying fortress for Spanish forces during a series of 19th century sieges of the North *presidios*. Fighting near Ceuta in 1859 nearly led to the total loss of the enclave. In 1860 a Spanish military force invaded Morocco from Ceuta in what has been described as 'a wretched affair' which led to the fall of Tetouan. In the 20th century Spain once again became embroiled in a bloody war in northern Morocco (see box, Abd Al-karim Al-Khattabi, page 148), in which it badly lost important battles at Annoual in 1921 and in the Shawin-Tetouan campaign in late 1924. Ceuta ultimately survived this episode thanks largely to Abdelkarim's internal political difficulties and the improved Spanish generalship under Franco. Franco later added to Ceuta's name by launching from there his military expedition to impose his form of law and order on mainland Spain in 1936.

Ceuta today is a small heavily urbanized peninsula, the Punta Almina, on the Strait of Gibraltar. It is a mere 19 sq km with an unexciting 19 km coastline. Monte Hacho is the highest point in the peninsula at 204m, though the adjacent Sierra Cimera which forms the boundary with Morocco rises eventually to 350m.

Ceuta harbour lies tucked into a bay on the N of the peninsula with the town largely packed onto a narrow isthmus lying between Monte Hacho in the E and hills adjacent to the frontier with Morocco in the W. The town itself is Spanish in character with a heavy military presence – the armed forces occupy most of the larger and older buildings including the fortress areas. The shopping streets such as Paseo Revellin and Calle Real concentrate heavily on duty free luxury goods such as electrical items, electronic equipment, perfumes and fashion boutiques, rather like Gibraltar. The town is saved from banality by its good quality areas such as those in the old town around the base of Monte Hacho, and in Paseo Revellin together with individual buildings such as the cathedral and Casa de los Dragones. Recent investments in facilities such as the new Mediterranean theme gardens near the Paseo Espanola covering some 55,000 sq m and the splendid Paseo de las Palmeras pedestrian shopping precinct have added to the charm of the enclave.

Much more than Melilla, Ceuta is, however, a transit port between Spain and Morocco and lacks the air of peace and good taste of its twin enclave. Good restaurants are fewer and, other than the duty free lines, shopping as a whole is less varied.

Places of interest

The **Municipal Museum** on Paseo Revellin is well laid out and attractive. Rooms I and II (see plan) have some fine Punic and Roman amphora (earthenware jars) and display the activities of Ceuta and the sea including the salt making pans on the ancient site of what is now the Parador and the Plaza de Africa. Room III has items relating to underwater archaeology with some well preserved

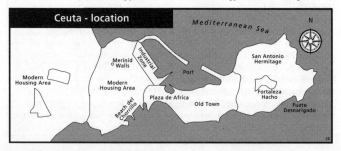

Ceuta - location

Mediterranean Sea

N

Merinid Walls

Industrial Zone

Port

San Antonio Hermitage

Modern Housing Area

Modern Housing Area

Plaza de Africa

Old Town

Fortaleza Hacho

Fuete Desnarigado

Beach del Chorrito

and decorated amphora and pots, a corn grinding wheel and a lead depth sounder. Other rooms (IV and, downstairs V) display mediaeval crafts of Hispanic-Islamic origins. Rooms VII and VIII are given over to scenes and artefacts of the Spanish-Moroccan war (1859-1860) with a wide selection of written sources on the war although exclusively a Spanish view of events. More military materials are on show at the **Legion Museum** on Paseo Colon (Mon-Fri 1000-1400, Sat 1000-1400 and 1600-1800, closed Sun), which celebrates the founding and activities of the Spanish special forces Legion force. There is a variety of armaments, uniforms and military memorabilia on show. The **Cathedral Museum** is situated in the side wall of the cathedral itself off Plaza de Africa. It is open in the afternoons only and has ecclesiastical items in its collection including the highly decorated montage of the *Virgen Capitana*. The **Cathedral** is located in the S of Plaza de Africa and stands on the site of a pre-Muslim church and a mosque from the Arab period. The present building dates principally from the 17th century, though there were large scale renovations in the years 1949-58. It is a large church but other than being cool and tranquil is not magnificent in the way of Spanish cathedrals. The **Church of Our Lady of Africa** is also on Plaza de Africa. The main building dates from the 15th century with many later additions, the largest in the 18th century and is on the site of a former mosque. Its importance was as a great Christian monument in Islamic North Africa, though it has a certain grand baroque air to its ornate interior. The Hotel *La Muralla*, the Parador in Ceuta, well located on Plaza de Africa, has some excellent modern sculptures on show. The **Palacio Municipal** (Town Hall) is a modern building dating from 1926 of interesting design and containing some fine panelling and frescoes by Bertucci. The *Peñon Municipal* (municipal banner) is kept in

the town hall. The centre of the Plaza de Africa is taken up with a large monument to those Spaniards who fell in the country's African wars (1859-60). Note the bronze reliefs of battle scenes by Susillo. The **Church of San Francisco** stands in Plaza de los Reyes, which reputedly contains the bones of the Portuguese King Sebastian.

The city walls form an impressive ring round the city. These Portuguese-built fortifications of forts, towers and curtain walls are at their best adjacent to the San Felipe moat and the Muralla Real. The exterior fortifications are also impressive – Fort (Museum) Desnarigado and Fortaleza del Hacho, though the later, still occupied by the military, is closed to the public. Fortaleza del Haco of ancient foundation, probably Byzantine in origin but strengthened in the Arab period under the Ommayyad Dynasty. It was reconstructed by the Portuguese and redeveloped by the

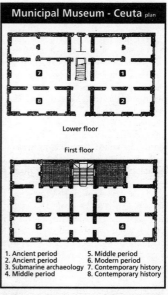

Municipal Museum - Ceuta plan

Lower floor

First floor

1. Ancient period
2. Ancient period
3. Submarine archaeology
4. Middle period
5. Middle period
6. Modern period
7. Contemporary history
8. Contemporary history

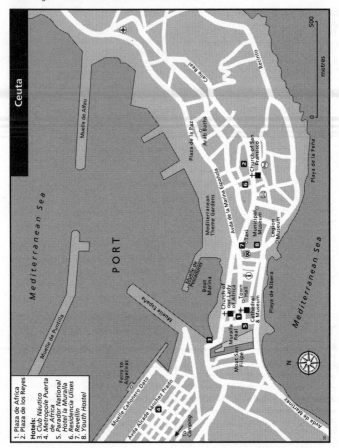

1. Plaza de Africa
2. Plaza de los Reyes

Hotels:
3. Club Náutico
4. Metropole Puerta de Africa
5. Parador National Hotel la Muralla
6. Residencia Ulises
7. Revellin
8. Youth Hostel

Ceuta

Mediterranean Sea

Muelle de Alfau

P O R T

Muelle de Poniente

Muelle de la Puntilla

Muelle España

Ferry to Algeciras

Muelle Cañonero Dato

Avda Alcade Sánchez Prado

To Camping

Calle Real

Recinto

Plaza de la Paz

Arab Baths

Church of San Francisco

Avda de la Marina Española

Mediterranean Theme Gardens

Taxi

Municipal Museum

Legion Museum

Playa de San Amaro

Playa de la Peña

Mediterranean Sea

Boat Marina

Church of our Lady of Africa

Town Hall

Cathedral & Museum

Playa de Ribera

Mont San Filipé

Muralla Real

N

Avda de Martínez

500 metres

Spanish in the 18th and 19th centuries. In the W of the town above Ramparts Pedro La Mata are the Merinid Walls, a 14th century construction on earlier buildings. The ramparts here are spectacular and well worth a visit. The original 2 km walling now remains as a mere 500m run but contains lots of interest, including the old Fes Gate. Adjacent to Plaza de la Paz on Paseo Marina are the ruins of the **Arab baths**, heavily reconstructed but accessible and a useful reminder of the high urban forms of the Arab period.

To the E of the town is a tree covered hill, a pleasant place for a stroll. At the far E edge is an old Portuguese fort. Stop off at the Ermitada de San Antonio, a convent rebuilt in the 1960s. From the walls is a good view of the town.

Local information
● Accommodation

The best and most expensive hotel is the parador **AL** *Parador National Hotel la Muralla*, Plaza Virgen de Africa 15, opp the Cathedral, T 514940, F 514947, 106 rm, pool, bar, nightclub; **A** *Hotel Metropole Puerta de Africa*, Avda Alcalde Sánchez Prado, T 517191; **A** *Hotel Residencia Ulises*, 5 Calle Cameons, T 514540, 124 rm, with pool.

B *Hotel Residencia Africa*, Juan Ignacio Quero Rivero, Muelle Cañonero Dato, T 509470.

C *Hostal Residencia Skol*, Antonio López López, Avda Reyes Católicos 6, T 504161.

The main area to try for cheaper hotels is Paseo del Revellin, Calle Cameons and Calle Real. In Calle Real, try **C** *Pensión Real*, T 511449, 11 rm; **C** *Pensión La Perla*, T 515828, 7 rm; **C** *Atlante*, 1 Paseo de las Palmeras, T 513548.

Also very good in Calle Real is **D** *La Rociera*, T 513559. At the foot of Paseo del Revellin, opp the Banco Popular Español, is the **D** *Pensión Revellín*, T 516762, 16 rm; and **D** *Bohemia* in Calle Cameons, clean, rec.

Youth hostel: 27 Plaza Viejo, T 515148, only open in Jul and Aug. Often crowded but the cheapest place in summer.

Camping: *Camping Marguerita*, T 523706, is located 3 km W of the town. Take the Benzu road and then turn left, at the signs, just after a bar. We have received comments regarding poor facilities and high charges here and have been rec another site closer to the town.

● **Places to eat**
♦♦♦ Try the expensive and rec *La Torre*, 15 Plaza de Africa, T 514949; *Casa Silva*, Calle Real 87, T 513715, expensive array of Spanish fish and seafood dishes, as well as good wine; *El Sombrero de Copa*, Padilla 4, T 518284, seafood specialists; or *Casa Fernando*, at the Benitez Beach, T 514082, good for seafood; *Vincentina*, Alférez Bayton 3, T 514015; *Delfin Verde*, Muelle Cañonero Dato, T 516332; *La Terraza*, Plaza Gilbert 4, T 514029.

♦For a cheaper option, sample some of the *tapas* in a number of the bars. Small cafés with tables outside on Paseo de las Palmeras, *Café Tempo* and *Café Levant* with a better view of the harbour (and the traffic).

● **Banks & money changers**
Banco de España, Plaza de España; Banco Popular Español, 1 Paseo del Revellin.

● **Beaches**
Either avoid the rubbish on the town beaches, or head out W to the more pleasant beach at Benzu.

● **Clubs**
Royal Automovil, Beatriz de Silva 12, T 512722.

● **Entertainment**
Discos: *Bogoteca*, Calle Real; *Coconut*, Carretara del Jaral; *San Antonio*, Monte Hacho.

Festivals: Fiesta de Nuestra Patrona, La Virgen d'Africa, 5 Aug; **Carnival** in Feb.

● **Post & telecommunications**
Plaza de España, T 509275.

● **Useful telephone numbers**
Fire: T 513333.

Police (municipal): T 092. **Police (national)**: T 091.

Red Cross: T 514548.

● **Shopping**
There are numerous shops selling duty-free goods, but the savings are not enormous but shop around for bargains, especially spirits. Fuel is cheaper here than in Morocco. For travellers heading on to Morocco, stock up on Spanish cheese and wine from the local supermarkets. Excellent fresh fish and shell fish.

● **Sports**
Horse riding: Martine Catena, T 511048.

Watersports: Marina has capacity for 300 vessels, weather information, security and dry dock facilities, T 513753; subaquatics, T 513753; windsurfing, enquire at larger hotels.

● **Tour companies & travel agents**
Most of the agencies are on Muelle Cañonero Dato. Try *Viajes Dato*, T 507457; *Viajes Dimasur*, T 503428; *Viajes Flandría*, T 508960; *Viajes Multimares*, T 50 9107; *Viajes Punta Europa*, T 509226; *Viajes Tourafrica*, T 509302. Also *Independencia*, 1, Edificio Inmaculada, T 512074, F 514559.

● **Tourist offices**
Patronata Municipal de Turismo (see map).

● **Transport**
Local Car hire: Africa Car, SL through Flandria Travel Agents, Independencia 1, Edificia Inmaculada. **Taxis**: in Ceuta T 505406, 505407, 505408. **Helicopter**: *Transportes Aereos del Sur* advertise helicopter flights from Ceuta to Jerez and Málaga. Details T 504974.

ACCESS ROAD From Ceuta follow the signposts to Morocco. The frontier post is on the S side of the peninsula, a little way out. Petrol is cheaper in Ceuta than Morocco. For those without transport, pick up a Spanish taxi or take bus 7 from Plaza de la Constitución. There are some long distance Spanish buses, from the bus station on the S coast road in Ceuta, to Casablanca, Al Hoceima and Nador. Tetouan is a better option for finding bus services. From Morocco, drive through Fnideq to the frontier. There are bus and grand-taxi services between Fnideq and Tetouan, and between Fnideq and Tanger. Between the frontier and Fnideq there is a grand-taxi, currently costing MD4. **The Frontier**: passports have to be checked and stamped by Moroccan officials both ways, and there are often lengthy queues. Travellers with their own transport have to have their vehicles registered and their papers, including insurance, registration and licence, checked. This can take some time. Cash can be exchanged on the Moroccan side of the frontier at the Banque Populaire booth.

Sea The Algeciras-Ceuta ferries are cheaper and quicker than those between Algeciras and Tanger, with passengers from MD130 and cars from MD645, taking 80 mins. There are normally six services a day Mon-Sat, five each Sun generally with refreshments available. Tickets can be bought from Trasmediterranea in Muello Cañonero Dato, T 509496, F 509530; from Isleña de Navegación, in the port building, T 509139/40; or from the numerous travel agents around the town centre. The port is in the centre of the town and the main destinations are clearly signposted. The hydrofoil service to Algeciras should be booked in advance at 6 Muelle Cañonero Dato, T 516041. These frequent (6 or 7 daily) Rapido services by catamaran or hydrofoil carry foot passengers only, take 30-45 mins depending on sea conditions and cost 3,000 ptas single.

Single Prices Algeciras to Ceuta on slow ferry (takes 1½ hrs) in pesetas:

Adult	1,800
Child	900
Trailer	5,000
Car	8,250
Car with roof rack	13,500
Van	15,000
Motor bike	1,860-2,800
Minivan	40,000

TETOUAN AND ENVIRONS

Tetouan is the first major centre along the P28 from the border with Ceuta and is considered to be the capital of the Rif. There is a number of appealing resorts between Ceuta and Tetouan and also further round the coast which can be visited en route, or as an excursion from Tetouan.

TETOUAN

Tetouan with a population of 200,000 has a striking location, between the Rif and the Mediterranean Sea. The city is dramatically beautiful with the white buildings of the medina heavily influenced by Andalusian Islamic architecture, often with balconies and tiled lintels. Some impressive colonial architecture is found in the more recent Spanish town. The city is an interesting place to explore, albeit with more noise and hassle than Chaouen and Ouezzane to the S.

Tetouan was founded in the 3rd century BC as **Tamuda**, but destroyed by the Romans in 42 AD. The Merinid ruler Sultan Abou Thabit built a kasbah at Tetouan in 1307. Sacked by Henry III of Castille in 1399 to disperse the corsairs based there, Tetouan was neglected until it was taken over by Muslims expelled from Granada in 1484, bringing with them the distinctive forms and traditions of Andalusian Islamic architecture, still observable in the medinas of Granada and Cordoba. Many of the Andalusians worked as corsairs continuing the tradition. A Jewish community was established here in the 17th century which gave the impetus to open up trade with Europe. Trade with the West continued to boom in the 18th century during the reign of Moulay Ismail. In 1913 Tetouan was chosen as the capital of the Spanish Protectorate in N Morocco which influenced its character and has remained an important regional centre in independent Morocco.

WARNING Tourists to Tetouan must be careful as hashish dealers, pickpockets, and unofficial guides are out in force. It is advisable to pay great attention to one's personal belongings and preferably to avoid having any dealings with people operating in this manner. The tourist office and the larger hotels can arrange official guides.

ACCESS   Air Tetouan's airport, used for internal flights from Rabat, Al Hoceima and Casablanca, is Aéroport Saniat R'Mel, T 971233, 5 km from the city. It is currently being redeveloped. Take a grand-taxi into the city. **Road** The P38 from Tanger, and the P28 from Ceuta to the N and Chaouen, Meknes and Fes to the S, both feed into Ave Hassan I, from where the medina and the centre of the *ville nouvelle* are clearly signposted. **Bus** CTM and most private line bus services arrive at the bus station at the corner of Ave Hassan I and rue Sidi Mandri, close to both Place Moulay el Mehdi and Place Hassan II. The ONCF coach service, for passengers leaving the rail network at Tnine Sidi Lyamani, arrives at Place el Adala. Local buses from the beaches normally drop passengers on Ave Massira or outside the main bus station.

Places of interest

A good point to start is **Place Hassan II**, the focal point of the city and former market, and the best place to stroll or sit in a café terrace in the evening. It is dominated by the gleaming **Royal Palace**, lots of white walls and green tiled roofs, originally from the 17th century but much added to recently, as the place has been redeveloped. Here, in the centre of the square among the palm trees is a smart green and white column surmounted by a flag. Looking on to the square is the Pasha mosque with its distinctive green door and green and brown tiled minaret. Bab er Rouah has also had a face-lift. It is unfortunate that the intricate design of the marble and stone inserts in the actual surface of the square are so often obscured by traffic. Unfortunately parts have been cordoned off and it has lost some of its atmosphere. The

other major centre in the *ville nouvelle* is Place Moulay el Mehdi, along Blvd Mohammed V from Place Hassan II dominated by an impressive golden-yellow **Cathedral**.

Bab er Rouah, in the corner of Place Hassan II, leads into the medina where Spanish influence is still apparent in the whitewashed walls and delicate wrought iron decorations on the balconies. The **medina** of Tetouan is a confusing maze of streets and *souqs*, well worth exploring, although perhaps with the assistance of an official guide. In the *souqs* look out for artifacts with Tetouan's favoured red colouration. Rue Terrafin is a good route through the medina, leading into rue Torres and rue Sidi el Yousti, and out at Bab el Okla. North of rue Sidi el Yousti is an area with some of the larger and more impressive houses.

Souq el Houts, with pottery, meat and fish is to the left of rue Terrafin behind the palace. Here there is a delightful leafy square, pleasant surroundings for admiring the wares. Behind the *souq* is a small 15th century fortress, the **Alcazaba**, now taken over by a cooperative. Take the left-hand of the two N-bound lanes from the **Souq el Houts** and on the right is **Guersa el Kebir**, a textile *souq*, selling in particular the type of striped woven blanket worn by Rifi women. The colours are particularly striking, the red, white and blue striped fabrics on sale by women dressed in the same colours. El Foki market can be found by following your nose – the smell of the bread, traditional, flat, round loaves is impossible to miss. Look out for the L'Usaa Square, extremely brilliant with white houses around a mosaic fountain and a magnificent rose garden.

Further on from this *souq*, leading up to Bab Sebta, is a number of specialist craft *souqs* and shops. Running between Bab Sebta and Bab Fes is rue de Fes, a more general commercial area, although with a number of *souqs* around. From Bab Sebta the road out of the city passes through a large cemetery. Above the medina is the crumbling kasbah, closed to visitors, and nearby a vantage point providing stunning views over the city.

On Place Hassan II, the first alleyway S of Bab er Rouah leads on to the main street of the *mellah*, the 19th century Jewish quarter, where there is a number of abandoned synagogues but few of the original inhabitants. The previous *mellah* is near the Grand Mosque.

The Archaeological Museum, Blvd Aljazaer, near Place Hassan II (0900-1200 and 1400-1800, except Tues), T 967103 or 932097, was built in 1943 and contains a small archaeological collec-

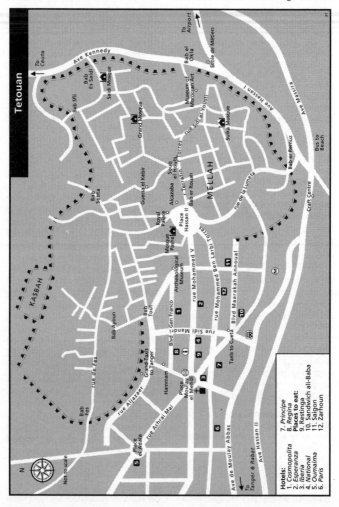

Hotels:
1. Principe
2. Cosmopolita
3. Esperanza
4. Iberia
5. National
6. Oumaima
7. Paris
7. Principe
8. Regina
Places to eat:
9. Restinga
10. Sandwich all-Baba
11. Saigon
12. Zarhoun

tion from the pre-historic and pre-Islamic sites of the northern region of Morocco. Most notable are the Roman statues and mosaics found originally at **Lixus** near Larache and the most notable mosaic is known as the Three Graces, an illustration from Roman mythology (see page 189).

Other rooms display prehistoric tools, bronzes and pottery. Of note here is the Sumarian ex-voto statuette found close to Asilah. Most of the small figures date from the 1st century AD. Note particularly the Roman coins and mosaics. There is also an extensive Spanish library containing over 60,000 volumes.

The Musée d'Art Marocain/Musée Ethnographique, T 970505 (open 0830-1200 and 1430-1730 Mon-Fri, 0830-1200 Sat), Bab el Okla, has been housed here in the former fortress of the Sultan Moulay Abderrahman since 1848. The setting is magnificent and it is hard to concentrate on the displays when the surroundings are so eye-catching. The carpets are worthy of a display in their own right. It contains traditional domestic exhibits and local costume, weapons and Andalusian musical instruments. There has been a major effort to preserve here the best of popular tradition. The displays of the marriage ceremony, very important in any society, are executed with care and taste. Devotées of delicate embroidery will be delighted. Outside, for relaxation is an Andalusian garden. Nearby, the **Ecole de Métiers** (Artisan School) (open 0900-1200, 1430-1730, except Tues and Sat), has craftsmen and students at work on *zelij* tiles, leatherwork, carpentry and pottery.

Local information
● **Accommodation**
Tetouan has **B** *Hotel Champs*, Ave Abdelkhalak Torres, a few kilometres E from Tetouan towards Martil, 68 rm, 12 suites, all with bath, TV, pool, restaurant, protected parking, conference facilities; and **B** *Hotel Malaga* to W of town, both at the more expensive end of the market. **B** *Hotel Safir Tetouan*, Ave Ken-

nedy, T 970144, 5 km from town centre, 100 rm with bath and phone, frequented by package tours, garden, pool, tennis, restaurant, nightclub (2300-0300).

The budget hotels or *pensiones*, in and nr the medina and Place Hassan II, are often primitive and unhygienic. **E** *Hotel Oumaima*, rue Achra Mai, T 963473, central, convenient and respectable; **E** *Hotel National*, 8 rue Mohammed Torres, T 963290, rec and not too expensive, with a café; **E** *Paris Hotel*, 11 rue Chakib Arsalane, T 966750, similar, with garage; **E** *Hotel Principe*, 20 Ave de la Resistance, T 962795, large, clean, not all rooms have hot water; **E** *Hotel Regina*, 8 rue Sidi Mandri, T 962113, a cheaper hotel in the *ville nouvelle*, all 58 rm with bath, no hot water.

F *Pensión Iberia*, above BMCE, Place Moulay el Mehdi, small and cheap with hot water; also good are **F** *Pensión Esperanza*, Ave Mohammed V; and **F** *Pensión Cosmopolita*, 5 Blvd General Franco.

Camping: a number of camping sites at a little distance from Tetouan along the coast, the nearest by the river and beach at Martil. *Camping Tetouan*, site of 6 ha, beach only 200m, bar/snacks, restaurant, shop, showers, laundry, electricity for caravans, petrol at 200m; *Camping Municipal*, at Martil Beach; *Camping Ch'bar*, at Cabo Negro; *Camping Fraja*, at Restinga Smir.

● **Places to eat**
Tetouan does not have any exceptional restaurants. The city is known for its sweets.

◆◆◆ *Hotel Safir Tetouan*, Ave Kennedy, T 967044, well-rec and reliable.

◆◆*La Restinga*, 21 rue Mohammed V, good well-priced Moroccan food with good *tagines*; *Restaurant Marrakech de Tetouan*, in the medina, has good Moroccan food and music, busy at lunch time; *Restaurant Saigon*, rue Mourakah Anual, Moroccan and Spanish food; *Zarhoun*, 7 Ave Mohammed Torres, nr the bus station, Moroccan decor and music, and set Moroccan meals, bar.

◆ *Café-Restaurant Moderne*, 1 Pasaje Achaach, nr the bus station, cheap Moroccan food; *Sandwich Ali Baba*, rue Mourakah Anual, is a popular place for cheap local food; also try the places around rue Luneta and Bab er Rouah.

● **Banks & money changers**
Banque Marocaine, Place Moulay el Mehdi;

BMCE, 11 Ave Mohammed Ibn Aboud (0800-2000 Mon-Fri, 0900-1300 and 1500-2000 Sat-Sun); **BMCI**, 18 rue Sidi el Mandri, T 963090.

● **Embassies & consulates**
Spanish Consulate, Ave Al Massira al Khadra, T 963590.

● **Hospitals & medical services**
Chemist: 24-hr, rue al Wahda, T 966777.

● **Post & telecommunications**
Area code: 9.
Post Office: Place Moulay el Mehdi, T 966798.

● **Shopping**
Try the *souqs*, or the *Ensemble Artisanal*, the government fixed-price shop on Ave Hassan I.

● **Sports**
Al Enara Complex, Torreta el Mers, provides swimming, tennis and basketball.

Golf: *The Cabo Negro Royal Golf Club* is situated at Cabo Negro, T 978303, F 978305, fees MD200/round, open daily (see box, page 463).

Gymnastics: *Saniat Rmel*, Martil Rd, T 974089.

Horse Riding: *La Ferma*, Cabo Negro, T 978075.

Hunting: *Sochanord*, M'Diq, T 974415.

Tennis: *Kabila Tennis*, Tetouan-Ceuta road, T 977051.

Yachting Club: M'Diq port, T 977694.

● **Tour companies & travel agents**
Akersan Voyages, Ave Forces Armées Royales, T 963034; *Hispamaroc*, Ave MV, T 963812; *Maroc Consult*, rue Achra Mai, T 965832.

● **Tourist offices**
Office du Tourisme (ONMT), 30 rue Mohammed V, T 961915, F 961914. **Syndicate d'Initiative**, Blvd Hassan II, Residence Nakhil, T 966544.

● **Useful addresses**
Police: Blvd General Franco, T 19.

● **Transport**
Local Much of Tetouan can be reached on foot. A petit-taxi is a cheap alternative. **Car hire**: *Amin Car*, Ave Mohammed V, T 964407; *Zeite*, Yacoub el Mansour.

Air Aéroport de Sania R'Mel, 5 km away, T 971233, services to Rabat, Al Hoceima and Casablanca; Royal Air Maroc, 5 Ave Mohammed V, T 961260.

Road Bus: the bus station, at the corner of Ave Hassan I and rue Sidi el Mandri, T 966263, has both CTM and private line services to most major destinations. Services to **Fnideq** (for Ceuta, 30 mins), **Chaouen** (1½ hrs), **Tanger** (1½ hrs), **Meknes** (8 hrs) and **Fes** (6 hrs). ONCF also operates a coach service to link up with the rail network at Tnine Sidi Lyamani. Through tickets can be bought from the office at Place el Adala, where the coach also departs from each day at 0650 and 1555. Buses to Martil, Cabo Negro and Mdiq leave from near the old railway station on Ave Massira, those for Oued Laou from the main bus station. **Taxi**: much of Tetouan is quite manageable on foot, but a petit-taxi is a cheap and reasonable alternative. Grand-taxis to Tanger, Fnideq (for Ceuta), Chaouen, the beaches and other places, leave from Blvd Maarakah Annoual or nearby.

Tamuda The ancient ruins of Tamuda lie to the S of the road. It was founded in the 3rd-2nd centuries BC but during the Roman period it disappeared for in the 3rd century AD a Roman camp was built on the site. From here only remains of dwellings have been excavated, no public buildings or religious buildings. Any material from Tamuda is in the Archaeological Museum in Tetouan.

AROUND TETOUAN: THE BEACHES

From Fnideq to Tetouan, the P28 passes through a flat strip of beaches and marshes, and a number of tourist developments. **Restinga Smir**, 22 km from Tetouan, has a long beach and a correspondingly long line of holiday complexes, hotels, bars, restaurants, bungalows and camping areas. Until recently it was still a small fishing village frequented only by a small number of local visitors. Now it enjoys (?) an international reputation. There is, however, sufficient space on the vast beaches for the activities on offer which include horse riding, mini-golf, tennis, underwater fishing as well as windsurfing and of course bathing. It includes a *Club Medit-*

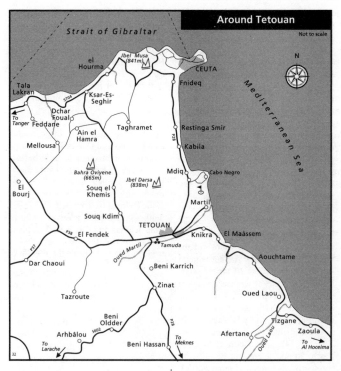

Around Tetouan

Not to scale

Strait of Gibraltar

Mediterranean Sea

N

el Hourma

Jbel Musa (841m)

CEUTA

Fnideq

Tala Lakran

S704

Ksar-Es-Seghir

To Tanger

Dchar Foual

Feddane

Taghramet

Restinga Smir

Ain el Hamra

P28

Kabila

Mellousa

Bahra Oviyene (665m)

Jbel Darsa (838m)

Mdiq

Cabo Negro

El Bourj

Souq el Khemis

Martil

Souq Kdim

TETOUAN

Knikra

El Maàssem

P38

El Fendek

Oued Martil

Tamuda

P27

Dar Chaoui

Beni Karrich

Aouchtame

Zinat

P28

Oued Laou

Tazroute

Beni Oldder

Tizgane

Arhbâlou

S602

Afertane

Oued Laou

Zaoula

To Larache

Beni Hassan

To Meknes

To Al Hoceima

32

erranée, **D** *Hotel Carabo*, T 977070, 24 rm, bar, restaurant, pool, tennis and disco, the rec restaurant *Nuevo Le Chariot* with a sea view and fine sea food, *Al Fraia* campsite or *Camping Andalus* though there are many good campsites to choose from, and the small marina/pleasure port of **Marina Smir**. After Restinga Smir the road passes through **Kabila**, another beach and marina, to **Mdiq**, a small fishing port with some traditional boat construction. Mdiq shares the same coastline and the same clientele as Cabo Negro (see below) and there is a certain feeling of competition. Mdiq is a well established resort offering a range of modern hotels and restaurants (mainly fish of course), nightclubs, swimming pools and the usual selection of water-

sports on the beach. This is certainly a popular family resort which is spreading to the N. The town centre offers banks, a post office and telephones and a number of shops selling handicrafts unlikely to tempt a discerning buyer. Accommodation ranges from **A** *Hotel Golden Beach*, T 975077, F 975096, 86 rm, on beach side opp bus station; **A** *Kabila Hotel*, T 975013, 96 rm, to **E** *Hotel Playa*, T 975166, and a campsite, as well as the *Restaurant du Port* and *Restaurant Al Khayma* in centre of town.

After Mdiq turn for **Cabo Negro** which is 3½ km off the P28. Other names for this cape are Taifor or Ras Tarf. Here the beach is more rugged with the low hills which overlook the sea dotted with small houses. This is a slightly less commercialized region though the number of discos and nightclubs is growing. Riding is very popular here with horses for hire by the hour and day and at times the stables are very evident. The roads through the town follow the contours and rise at various levels up the hill. At the coast there is a small pleasure marina by the jetty. The Royal Golf Club of Cabo Negro is currently only a 9 hole (par 36) course but construction of a further 9 holes is planned. At Cabo Negro is another large *Club Mediterranée* adjacent to the golf course; as well as **D** *Hotel Petit Merou*, T 978115/6, 23 rm, restaurant, bar, disco. The *Restaurant La Ferma*, T 968075, with French food is only 1 km from main road.

Martil, Tetouan's former port, and a pirate base, stands at the mouth of the Oued Martil. It is now another popular resort. There is over 10 km of sandy beach here. Once it was the particular resort of the people from Tetouan who established holiday homes here on the coast but now Martil welcomes visitors from far afield. Stay at **A** *Karia Kabila*, T 975013, 14 route de Ceuta, right on the beach, 90 double rm and 10 suites all with bath, telephone and some with TV, restaurant, snack-bar, disco and 2 pools; **B** *Club Bahia del Sol*, 16 route de Ceuta, adjacent to town and to beach, 300 rm with bath, 2 restaurants, 2 pools, nightclub; **D** *Hotel Etoile de la Mer*, Ave Mawlay al Hassan, T 6776, 30 rm; **E** *Hotel Nuzha*, rue Miramar; *Camping Martil*, by the river or *Camping Oued La Malah* clearly signed further out of town. Municipal Camping at Martil Beach, T 979435, site of 3 ha, beach 10m, showers, laundry, electricity for caravans, petrol at 600m; *Ch'bar*, Martil Rd, Cabo Negro. *Hotel/Café Addiyafa* on right towards Tetouan, is recommended. Buses from Tetouan to Martil, Cabo Negro and Mdiq leave from Ave Massira, near the old railway station.

Oued Laou is 44 km from Tetouan, along the spectacular coastal road, the S608. It is a relaxed fishing village with an excellent beach but only basic facilities. Stay at **F** *Hotel-Café Oued Laou*; **F** *Hotel-Restaurant Laayoune*; or *Camping Laayoune*. Eat at the hotels or food stalls. Note the tiled octagonal mosque. An option from Oued Laou is to drive inland or take a bus to Chaouen.

The road continues along the coast through the villages of **Targa**, **Steha**, **Bou Hamed**, and **Dar M'Ter**. Possibly a more convenient place to stop is the final settlement, **El Jebha**, built by the Spanish. It is another fishing village and beach, with a *souq* on Tues morning. Stay at the **F** *Grand Hotel* or the **F** *Petit Hotel*, neither very good. It is served by buses from Tetouan and Chaouen. A tortuous mountain road, the 8500, takes the intrepid traveller to meet the P39 W of Ketama.

CHAOUEN AND THE NORTHERN RIF

CHAOUEN

(*Pop* 23,563 (1982); *Alt* 600m) Chaouen, 60 km from Tetouan, also called Chefchaouen, is a beautiful blue and whitewashed Andalusian town in the Rif, set above the Oued Laou valley. Chaouen lies below the twin peaks, Jbel ech-Chaouen, that have given it its name 'the horns'. Just nearby is the P28, N to Tetouan and S to Ouezzane, and the P39 E through the Rif to Al Hoceima. Lying within easy reach of Ceuta or Tanger, it is an excellent and peaceful introduction to Morocco. The selling of hashish is a big business here, but persistent refusal should rid travellers of unwanted attentions.

Here you may have your first sighting of the distinctive garments of the women of the Rif, the *fouta* or overskirt usually of red and white vertical stripes and the very large conical straw hat with woollen tassels.

Chaouen was founded in 1471 by Sherif Moulay Ali Ben Rachid, a follower of Moulay Abd es-Salam Ben Mchich, the patron saint of the local Djeballa area whose tomb is nearby, in order to halt expansion further S of the Spanish and Portuguese. The city's population was later supplemented by Muslims and Jews expelled from Spain, particularly from Granada, and for a time the rulers of Chaouen controlled much of N Morocco, whilst the town also grew in importance as a pilgrimage centre.

From 1576 Chaouen was in conflict with, and isolated from, the surrounding area, with the gates locked each night. Prior to 1920 only three Christians had braved its forbidding walls, the Frenchman de Foucauld disguised as a *rabbi* in 1883, Walter Harris, Times correspondent and author of *Morocco that Was*, in 1889, and the American William Summers, poisoned in Chaouen in 1892. In 1920 Chaouen was taken over by the Spanish as part of their protectorate. Until that time the few

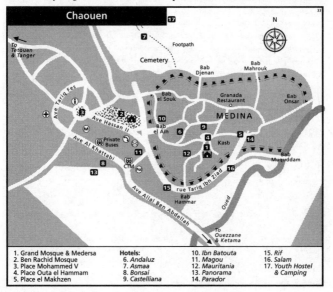

1. Grand Mosque & Medersa
2. Ben Rachid Mosque
3. Place Mohammed V
4. Place Outa el Hammam
5. Place el Makhzen

Hotels:
6. *Andaluz*
7. *Asmaa*
8. *Bonsai*
9. *Castelliana*

10. *Ibn Batouta*
11. *Magou*
12. *Mauritania*
13. *Panorama*
14. *Parador*

15. *Rif*
16. *Salam*
17. *Youth Hostel & Camping*

Europeans who ever visited the town found Jews still speaking 15th century Andalusian Spanish. The Spanish were thrown out from 1924 to 1926, by Abd al-Karim's Rifian resistance movement, but then returned to stay until Independence in 1956.

ACCESS Buses and grand-taxis will drop travellers on Ave Al Khattabi. Walk up through the market alongside to reach Ave Hassan II, then turn right to reach Bab el Aïn and the medina. There are many one-way streets which can be confusing for the motorist.

Places of interest

The Spanish-built new town of Chaouen is small, a pleasant and relaxing place. The centre is Place Mohammed V, with its small Andalusian garden. Ave Hassan II leads to Bab el Aïn and the medina. The market is down some steps from Ave Hassan II, on Ave Al Khattabi. Normally a food market, there is a local *souq* on Mon and Thur.

The Medina of Chaouen is one of the most rewarding to explore, sufficiently small not to get lost, but with intricate

Abd Al-karim – rebel of the Rif

Abd al-Karim (Al-Khattabi) was born in the Rif Mountains of Morocco in 1882. He led a long resistance movement against both Spanish and French occupations of his homeland. He was educated in Spanish as well as Islamic schools. His objective became the establishment of an independent Rifian republic in northern Morocco. He was particularly eager that the Rif should become a state on an Islamic but modern model with a flag and full freedom of action in foreign policy. His difficulties arose on two sides. First, his colonial opponents were well equipped and organized. He mainly faced the Spanish, whose army he defeated at Annoual in 1921 and again in the Shawin-Tetouan campaign in late 1924. Second, he faced the difficulty that the Rif was fragmented into tribal factions, whose allegiance to the concept of a Rifian republic was never sure. Constant political in-fighting between the tribes of the Rif and of adjacent areas of northern Morocco gave Abd al-Karim perpetual problems as he tried to keep his armies provisioned and united. He showed great skills as a diplomat and politician, maintaining tribal loyalty and overcoming tremendous pressures towards disintegration of his command.

His military successes against the Spanish and his encroachments as local tribes joined him deep into French controlled Morocco, almost reaching Fes in 1924 and 1925 brought the European powers to a joint agreement against him. In 1926 the Spanish army, better organized under General Franco, landed on and was heavily reinforced along the Mediterranean coast. The French moved in from the S and by autumn the Rif was surrounded on all sides. By January the area was short of food and there was a growing spate of defections by tribes not directly affiliated to the Rif. In April 1926 a peace conference was convened but failed as a result of Abd al-Karim's failure to return European prisoners. In May the French and Spanish moved into the Rif and, other than a short resistance in Azilaf in the extreme N, collapse came quickly and on 27 May he surrendered to the French commander. He went into exile, first in the French island of Réunion and eventually died in Cairo in 1963.

Abd al-Karim was the forerunner of North African political leaders with strong ideas of statehood and independence. His resistance to European colonisation was well organized and sustained. In many ways he had ideas of sovereignty, justice and political structures that most countries of North Africa still have not achieved.

Rifian headgear

Andalusian architecture, arches, arcades and porches, white or blue-washed houses with ochre tiled roofs and clean, quiet cobbled streets. In the maze of these narrow streets one encounters by chance, fountains, small open squares with shops and the solid ramparts of the kasbah. By car, park in Place el Makhzen and explore the rest on foot. Approaching the medina on foot, enter by Bab el Aïn. From Bab el Aïn a small road leads through to Place Uta el Hammam. This is the main square, lively at night, and surrounded by a number of stalls and café-restaurants, popular with *kif* (hashish) smokers.

The square is dominated by the 15th century kasbah, now the **Musée de Chefchaouen** (including the **Centre d'Etudes et de Recherches Andaluses**) (open 1000-1200 and 1400-1900, 0900-1700 in Ramadan), T 986761. It was built by Pasha Ahmed Errifi. As a prison it housed the Rifi leader Abd al-Karim from 1926. The museum has an exhibition of local costumes, some with very delicate embroidery, tools, musical instruments, pottery, weapons and a collection of decorated wooden caskets. These illustrate the customs and popular art of the region in particular and northern Morocco in a more general way. It is an interesting building, worth climbing to the top for a good view of the town from the roof, and exploring the dungeons and prison cells below. There is a quiet garden constructed in the Andalusian style in which to relax. Note the beautiful **Grand Mosque**, with its oc-

tagonal minaret, beside the kasbah, dating from the 15th century, but restored in the 17th and 18th. Next door is a 16th century **medersa**, unfortunately closed. Opposite the *Restaurant Kasbah*, at No 34, is an old *caravanserai*.

Further on, Place el Makhzen, the picturesque second square, has stalls along the top side, the **Ensemble Artisanal** at the end. Chaouen has a large number of artisans employed in metalwork, leatherwork, pottery and woodwork, amongst other crafts, and is particularly known for weaving the striped Rifi blankets, as seen on country women. It is well worth exploring the *souqs*, many of which are in the alleys S of Place Outa el Hammam.

For swimming there are several popular pools down in the Oued Laou, either walk or get a taxi. A pleasant pool to visit, and rest in a nearby café, is Ras el Ma, above the medina. Leave Place el Makhzen and head out above Bab Onsar.

Chaouen has many sanctuaries for pilgrims and each year thousands of visitors are attracted to pay homage to the memory of Sidi ben Alil, Sidi Abdellah Habti and Sidi el Hadj Cherif.

Chaouen is a good base for *mountain walks*, with some spectacular scenery and plentiful animal and birdlife. Expect suspicious questioning, and be prepared for a long and strenuous day. Taking a guide is well worth considering. In particular look out for the natural spring called Ras El Maa just 3 km out of town in the direction of Jbel Tisouka.

Local information
● Accommodation
B *Hotel Parador*, Place el Makhzen, T 986324, next to kasbah and medina, lovely views, 37 rm with bath, telephone and a/c, safe parking, bar, restaurant, pool, the best in Chaouen, a wonderful central location, comfortable and well-equipped, reservations needed.

C *Hotel Asmaa*, T/F 987158, 94 rm, placed insensitively on a hill above the town, but with an excellent view of the medina and the valley beyond, pool, bar, 2 tearooms, restaurant; **C** *Hotel Bonsai*, 12 rue Sidi Srif, T 986980, small hotel, quieter, being out of town, convenient for bus station; *Hotel Madrid*, Ave Hassan II, T 987496/7, F 987498, good hotel, clean, plenty of hot water, friendly management, breakfast MD25; *Hotel Panorama*, 33 rue Moulay Abderrahman Chrif, T 986615, F 987498, new hotel, quiet as out of town, convenient for bus station, lives up to its name as has good views from the roof.

D *Hotel Magou*, 23 rue Moulay Idriss, outside Bab el Aïn, T 986257, 986275, 32 rm with bath, clean and rec, currently closed.

E *Hotel Ibiza*, rue Sidi Mandri, T 986323, on the entry to the town from Tetouan, a small hotel which is highly rec; **E** *Hotel Rif*, 29 rue Tarik Ibn Ziad, T 986207, bar and restaurant, a friendly hotel with a restaurant and a good view from higher rooms; **E** *Hotel Salam*, 38 rue Tarik Ibn Ziad, T 986239, just below the medina, clean rooms with hot water, breakfast.

The cheap hotels and *pensiones* in Chaouen are often very good, basic but clean and very reasonably priced. The **F** *Andaluz* is clean and friendly with hot water, a few minutes walk from Place Outa el Hammam, follow signs; the **F** *Pensión Castilliana*, signposted just off the main square; and **F** *Auberge Granada*, up rue Targhi from Place Uta El Hammam, are also cheap; **F** *Pensión Mauritania*, 20 Kadi Alami, below the square, is a friendly place with music and a café; **F** *Pensión Ibn Batouta*, clean and quiet, just off the road between Bab el Aïn and Place Outa el Hammam.

Youth hostel and camping: T 986031, with 30 beds, meals available, kitchen, overnight fee MD20 and *Camping Municipal* are together, 2 km above the town nr the *Hotel Asmaa*, follow the signs from the road in from Tetouan, or walk (diplomatically) through the cemetery above the medina. there is a small café, a shop, simple toilets and showers, tents amongst the trees, good view of the valley.

● Places to eat
♦♦ *Restaurant de l'Hotel Magou*, 23 rue Moulay Idriss, rec Moroccan food. More up-market are the *Hotel Asma* and the *Hotel Parador*, the latter with an extensive French-Moroccan menu.

♦There are several cafés and restaurants on the main square, Place Uta el Hammam such as *Restaurant Azhar*, rue Moulay Idris, friendly restaurant nr the *Hotel Magou*; *Restaurant Kasbah*; also try *Restaurant Tissemlal*, 22 rue Targhi, with excellent Moroccan food; *Restaurant Zouar*, rue Moulay Ali Ben Rachid, nr the main square, wide range of cheap Spanish dishes incl fish; *Restaurant La Plaza Grande Kazba*, rue Targhi, cheap Moroccan food nr the main Place Uta el Hammam. For a modestly priced licensed restaurant go to *Restaurant-Bar Omo Rabi*, on rue Tarik Ibn Ziad. *Pâtisserie Magou*, Ave Hassan II, is good for bread and cakes; the *Hotel Parador* and *Hotel Asma* are good for a drink and view.

● Banks & money changers
Banque Populaire, Ave Hassan II; **BMCE**, Ave Hassan II.

● Hospitals & medical services
Chemist: beside the *Hotel Magou*.

● Post & telecommunications
Area code: 09.

Post Office: PTT, Ave Hassan II.

● Tourist offices
Syndicat d'Initiative, Place Mohammed V, open mornings.

● Transport
Road Bus: CTM is just down from Bab el Aïn. Private line buses run from the station next to the market, on Ave Al Khattabi. Buses are often through services and can thus be full. There are several buses a day for **Ouezzane**, 2 daily for **Meknes** (5 hrs), 1 per day for **Fes** (6 hrs), several a day for **Tetouan**, 2 daily for **Al Hoceima** (8 hrs), 2 a week for **El Jebha** (7 hrs). **Grand-taxis**: leave from the bus station on Ave Al Khattabi to most destinations.

THE NORTHERN RIF

The P39 known as the 'route of the crests' from Chaouen to Al Hoceima, is one of Morocco's most dramatic journeys, a route through a succession of small villages with stunning views over the remote valleys and towards the snow-capped Rif Mountains. Care must be taken on this narrow, hill-top road which may be closed by snow in winter. Traditionally this was an area of unrest against central authorities, notably in the Rif rebellion of Abd el-Krim against the Spanish from 1921 to 1926, whilst more recently bandits have preyed on travellers. Today the situation has improved, and the main dilemma is how to replace the production of *kif* (hashish) as the principal economic activity. Despite government programmes and pressures from Europe, production continues. Along this road it will be assumed that all travellers are there for the sole purpose of buying *kif* and the numerous vendors are unlikely to believe anything else, and can be aggressive, so do not stop. There is often close cooperation between the police and the vendors, and sentences can be stiff.

Ketama is the centre of hashish growing and selling. It has grown in importance as a walking resort with access to the mountains which are thickly clothed with cedar. Hunters visit in season looking for wild boar and fowl. It is pleasant in summer due to its altitude but in winter can be snowbound. The small Berber settlements in the surrounding foothills produce a variety of handcrafted goods, particularly woodwork. It is unfortunate that pressure from the *kif* sellers can make it quite a stressful place to stay but it is perhaps the most comfortable along this road, with the **C** *Hotel Tidighine* in the town centre, 67 rm, an old Spanish hotel with tennis, pool, bar and restaurant. Cheaper options are the **F** *Café-Hotel Saada* and **F** *California*.

The S302 runs S from Ketama to Taounate, Aïn Aicha and Fes with views of deep valleys and forested slopes. This road, the *Route de l'Unité*, was built just after Independence by voluntary labour battalions, to link the Spanish Protector-ate of the N with the French Protectorate to the S. To the S, the mountain ranges of the Rif rise to 2,456m at Jbel Tidighine. This district of small settlements at high altitude is accessed along very twisting tracks through the cedar woodlands. This is a very attractive region but care must be taken not to become involved with the *kif*. Products of a less dubious nature include work in wood, leather and wool. This area is well known to hunters of wild boar, hare and partridge.

East of Ketama, along the P39, the Rif becomes increasingly barren. After 12 km 8500 branches off to the left, a 61 km drive to the small coastal resort of **El Jebha** (see page 146). 30 km further there is another road, the 8501 to Torres el Kal'a, a tiny fishing village, with some basic café-hotels (described under Al Hoceima, page 152). Just E of Torres el Kal'a is the site of the port of Badis, destroyed in 1564, and offshore, the small island of Peñon de Velez de la Gomera, still owned by the Spanish. 4 km W of Torres el Kal'a is a campsite near Kalah Iris one of the most beautiful Mediterranean beaches.

Back on the P39 the next stop is **Targuist**, 65 km W of Al Hoceima and 30 km inland is at 110m in the Oued Rhis/Oued Takarat watercourse, a more peaceful alternative to Ketama, and a safer place from which to explore the mountains. There are many walks and rides in the cedar forests here. This is where Abd al-Karim finally surrendered. Stop at **F** *Hotel Chaab* or **F** *Hotel Café-Restaurant El Mostakbel* by the square where the buses stop. Visit the small handicraft centre. There are fairly regular buses and grand-taxis to Al Hoceima.

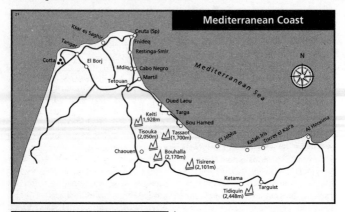

Mediterranean Coast

THE MEDITERRANEAN COAST

AL HOCEIMA

(*Pop* 60,000; Tanger 300 km, Melilla 170 km, Algerian border 250 km) Al Hoceima (previously Alhucemas), is a beautiful though not overly developed resort. The attractiveness of its location makes a visit well worthwhile though the difficulty of approach by road reduces the flow of casual visitors. The beauty of the natural features makes it an attractive resort. The clear Mediterranean within a natural horseshoe-shaped bay provides deep but safe water. Nearby there are other coves and sandy beaches an ideal place for watersports. Surrounding it is a fertile plain enclosed on three sides by the foothills of the Rif. The view of the group of small islands is intriguing. They have interesting histories having been fought over by the French, the English and the Spanish for their strategic position rather than their commercial value.

The character of the centre is distinctly Spanish, reflecting input in the protectorate years. Established by the Spanish in 1920 as Villa Sanjurjo, it was built as a garrison to control the Beni Ouriaghel tribe, of which Abd al-Karim was the chief, immediately after the Rif rebellion. To the E of Al Hoceima is the long and less busy beach of the Alhucemas bay, offshore is Peñon de Alhucemas, a remarkable idiosyncrasy of history. This small rocky island, topped by a few buildings and a church, is owned and occupied by Spain and apparently used as a prison. It is completely dependent on Melilla for supplies and even water, and has no contact with the Moroccan mainland, off which it sits like a ship at anchor. It looks just right for a pirates' refuge, which is just what it was.

Places of interest

View the vibrant Place du Rif, from the crazily decorated *Florido Café*. The *souq*, busiest on Thur, is quite remarkable in that all the local peasants and mountain dwellers come from the surrounding plain and from the Rif in their distinctive traditional garments to sell their vegetable produce. The new town of Al Hoceima is dominated by Ave Mohammed V (banks and cafés) which leads down to Place du Marche Verte. Rue Tarik Ibn Ziad to the left has some crumbling Spanish colonial buildings while to the right a road curves down to the main beach (note on the left the intricate and colourful old Spanish school) and the port. The nearest beach is dominated by the *Hotel Quemado* complex, open to non-residents, offers watersports, scuba diving, busy in the summer. There is no shortage of other good beaches nearby. Visit the port area, which includes a fishing port (some good fish restaurants) as well as a naval port closed to visitors. There is the daily fish auction to attend, fish and shell fish, every afternoon. A relaxed place to wander with gardens to stroll in, pavement cafés and pleasant palm tree lined promenade. Tourist Festival in Aug.

Local information
● **Accommodation**

The *Club Mediterranée*, lies about 10 mins E of the town, and the *Maroc-Touriste complex* is down from the centre by the beach.

D *Hotel Quemado*, T 982371, or reservations by Maroc Tourist in Rabat T 763915, an

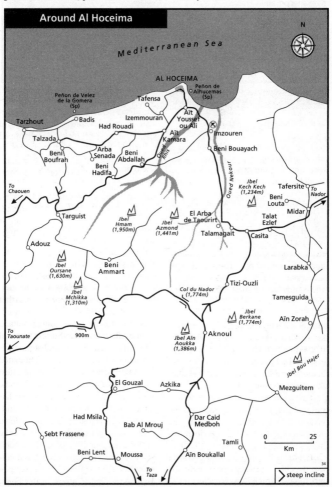

Around Al Hoceima

ugly complex but with an ideal beach location, comfortable rooms, bungalows and villas, restaurant, bar, nightclub, tennis; **D** *Hotel Maghreb El Jadid*, Ave Mohammed V, T 982504, 40 good rm, restaurant, the best option in the town.

E *Hotel Karim*, 25 Ave Hassan II, T 982184, clean and reasonable establishment, bar and restaurant; **E** *Hotel National*, 23 rue Tetouan, T 982141, 16 a/c rm with bath, telephone, breakfast room and TV room.

F *Hotel Florido*, 40 Place du Rif (Sahat Rif), T 982235, a stylish pink and white Spanish building dominating the main square, once the town's casino, friendly, clean, best rooms overlook the square, cold showers, restaurant, café; or as a fall-back the **F** *Hotel de Station*, Place du Rif, basic, cold showers, friendly, convenient for buses; **F** *Rif Hotel*, rue Sultan Moulay Youssef, also rec; or at the camping sites, *El Jamil*, T 982009, 2 km E; *Kalah Iris*, nearby and cheaper.

● **Places to eat**
Expect plenty of fish on all menus. There are few top eating options in Al Hoceima but try ◆◆◆*Hotel Maghreb El Jadid*, Ave Mohammed V, T 982504, with a mixed French, Spanish and Moroccan menu, or *Hotel Karim*, 25 Ave Hassan II, T 982184, French and Spanish cuisine, good for fish. At the port there are several good **fish restaurants** incl ◆◆*Restaurant Karim*, T 982310, licensed; *Restaurant Scorpio Sahara*, T 4410, *Restaurant Chez Mimoune*, and the rougher, licensed ◆ *Bar-Restaurant des Poissons*, most do not speak French. Other economic options in town are *Restaurant Mabrouk* or *Restaurant Al Hoceima* in rue Izzemounen just off Place du Rif, both serving *tagines*.

● **Banks & money changers**
Mainly on Ave Mohammed V, incl Banque Populaire (at No 47), BMCE, BMC and SGMB.

● **Hospital & medical services**
Hôpital Mohammed V, Ave Hassan II, nearby to a number of pharmacists.

● **Shopping**
Markets: Souq is on Tues, fish market each morning.

● **Tourist offices**
Délégation Regionale du Tourisme, Immeuble Cabalo, rue Tarik Ibn Ziad off Place Marche Verte, T 982830 (0830-1200 and 1400-1800), small but friendly.

● **Transport**
Local The town is small enough to explore on foot but for the port or beaches hail one of the blue and beige petit-taxis.

Air The airport, Aéroport Côte du Rif is at Charif al Idrissi, 17 km SE from Al Hoceima, T 982005, with flights to **Amsterdam** (2 a week) and **Brussels** (1 a week), **Tanger** and **Casablanca** (2 a week) and **Tetouan** and **Rabat** (1 a week). **Royal Air Maroc**, T 982063.

Road Bus: all buses leave from Place du Rif, which has ticket booths for the different companies. Most buses leave early in the morning. CTM (T 982273) services to **Casablanca** (2000: 10 hrs), **Nador** (0500, 1230: 7 hrs), **Tetouan** (3 per day), **Targuist** (3 per day); private line services to **Tetouan** (0700, 0800, 1900, 10 hrs), **Nador** (0600, 0955, 1315, 1400, 1530, 1745), **Targuist** (0315, 0700, 0815, 0945, 1900), **Tanger** (0800), **Oujda** (1100, 5 hrs), **Fes** (0315, 0945, 12 hrs), **Ketama** (0315, 0945). **Taxi**: grand-taxis leave from just off Place du Rif, to **Nador**, **Taza** and **Targuist**, amongst other destinations.

Kalah Bonita beach is within the urban area of the town and has a campsite, sports facilities and a café-restaurant with an adequate range of dishes especially if you like fish. The beach of **Sebadella** is also close to the town and boasts over 2 km of fine sand.

Kalah Iris is 60 km to the W and can be considered one of the most attractive beaches of the Moroccan Mediterranean coast. There is a campsite near the village. The village itself depends on fishing as well as tourism.

Torres el Kala stands alongside the site of **Badis**, which was the port for Fes. It was destroyed in 1564 and some undistinguished ruins remain. Offshore the small island of Peñon de Velez de la Gomera is still owned by Spain.

OUEZZANE AND THE SOUTHERN RIF

An alternative route follows the P28 through the cork oaks and coniferous forest from Chaouen to Ouezzane. Look out for Pont de Loukkos, the old border post with café and stalls. However, whilst Ouezzane is a memorable town imbued with the atmosphere of an historic pilgrimage centre, and the scenery E is impressive, the opportunities for visitors are sparse.

OUEZZANE

Ouezzane with a population of 41,000 is 60 km S of Chaouen along the P28, and like the latter has a dramatic hillside location perched on the N facing slopes of Jbel Ben Hellal. A short track from the town (only 3 km) leads up to the peak (609m) and gives a splendid view across towards the Rif. Just 9 km N is Azjem. Here is buried an important Rabbi, Amram Ben Djouane, who came from Andalucia in the 18th century, with impressive views of the rugged Rif Mountains and the verdant valleys between. It is worth visiting en route from Chaouen to Meknes or Fes.

The town was founded in 1727 by Moulay Abdellah Sherif founder of the Tabiya Islamic order. This brotherhood achieved great national prominence from the 18th century when the *zaouia*, or monastery, they had founded in Ouez-

zane, became the focus of extensive pilgrimage activity. Ouezzane had close links with the Sultan's court, which was often dependent on the *zaouia* and its followers for support.

Ironically, in view of the veneration Muslims accorded the *sherifs*, the then *Sherif* of Ouezzane married the Englishwoman Emily Keane in 1877 in an Anglican service, after they had met at the house of the American Consul where Keane was governess, although she later separated from him to live out her dotage in Tanger, where she is now buried in the Anglican Church. The *zaouia's* importance was destroyed by the *sherif's* growing connection with the French.

Ouezzane has importance today in the production of olive oil, and because of its *souq* on Thur, drawing in local farmers and tradesmen.

ACCESS Road The P28 to the N leads to Chaouen and Tetouan, S to Meknes. The P26 is to Fes and the P23 to Rabat and Casablanca. These roads meet at Place de l'Indépendance, the main square. There are numerous grand-taxis to Chaouen, and others to Souq El Arba du Gharb and Meknes. Buses to Chaouen (80 mins), Meknes (4 hrs) and Fes (5½ hrs) pass through Ouezzane, calling at Place de l'Indépendance.

Places of interest

The **medina** of Ouezzane has some of the most interesting architecture in the Rif, with the picturesque tiled roof houses

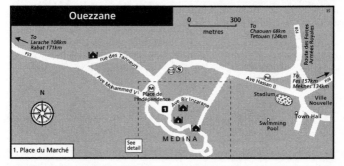

Ouezzane Medina

Hotels:
1. el Elam
2. Grand
3. Horlage

Place de l'Indépendance

Ave Bir Inzarane

Place du Marché

rue de la Zaouia

rue Abdellah Ibn Lamlih

Mosque S'ma des Zaouia

Mosque Moulay Abdellah Sherif

rue Haddadine

Place Rouida

0   100
metres

along winding cobbled streets. The focus of the town is the 18th century *zaouia*, on rue de la Zaouia, a distinctive green-tiled building with an octagonal minaret. Non-Muslims should not approach too close. Nearby are old lodgings for the pilgrims and the decaying Sherifian palace.

Place de l'Indépendance, the centre of the medina, is busiest during the town *souq* on Thur. To get to the permanent craft *souqs*, centred around Place Bir Inzarane, follow rue Abdellah Ibn Lamlih up from Place de l'Indépendance. Ouezzane is particularly known for woollen carpets woven in the weavers' *souq* at the top of the town. The smiths' *souq* is along rue Haddadine. There is a **Centre Artisanale** on Place de l'Indépendance, and another on Ave Hassan II, open 0800-1900.

● **Accommodation** Ouezzane is very limited for hotels, and is perhaps best visited in passing or as an excursion from Chaouen. Choose between **F** *Marhaba*; **F** *Horloge*; and **F** *El Elam*, on Place de l'Indépendance; or the more basic **F** *Grand Hotel* on Ave Mohammed V, although none of these is an attractive option. Eat at the basic café-restaurants on Place de l'Indépendance. *Café Africa*, 10 km N is a good place to stop.

EAST OF OUEZZANE

From Ouezzane, the P26 goes SE as far as Fes-el-Bali. This Rifian village is on the site of the ruined Almoravid 11th century city, the walls of which can still be seen, along with the *hammam*. From here the P26 continues S, 84 km to Fes a long winding route on an adequate road, good surface but poor camber. There are excellent views and a scattering of settlements, their tree lined approach indicating the French influence, providing the essential petrol and drinks, best S of Port du Sebou. Construction of a new barrage on the Oued Ouerrha N of Fes-el-Bali causes some delays. Of note, and perhaps the only reason to take this route, are the unique *white villages* where all the buildings and the straw stacks are plastered with lime and local clay and merge into the landscape. Difficult to photograph. A daily bus from Ouezzane to Fes follows this route. The S304 weaves E through the Rif, 17 km to Ourtzargh, where a side road takes intrepid drivers to the village of Rafsai (Ghafsai), an olive market, from where a track leads to Jbel Lalla Outka, a 1,595m mountain from which there are extensive views over much of the Rif.

The next stopping point is Taounate, an uninteresting town with a large *souq* on Fri. From here it is possible to continue N to Ketama and S to Fes on the S302 (the **Route de l'Unité**). It is a long and tortuous drive to Aknoul from which there is a 39 km drive N to the P39 between Al Hoceima and Nador, and 53 km S to Taza on P1, with grand-taxis.

Eastern Morocco

TRADITIONALLY the domain of nomadic tribespeople, the lands to the east of the Rif and the Middle Atlas mountains have for centuries constituted a frontier region, distinct from the more urbanized and sophisticated areas to the west. Historically these are the marchlands of Morocco, once used as a transit route for invasions and for trade from the East and the Mediterranean. Several dynasties arose from this region, notably the Merinids and the Wattasids, who used it as a base to harrass and eventually conquer the capital, Fes.

As a result of this turbulent past, Eastern Morocco has less in the way of architectural merit and historical interest, however, it will appeal to those in search of a less 'discovered' and more relaxing part of the country, where daily life can be appreciated without the visitor being a constant object of attention.

Away from the coast, Eastern Morocco is noticeably drier than other parts of the country, as the Rif and Atlas Mountains act as a barrier to moist air originating from the Atlantic. The combination of this effect, poor soils, and the results of severe deforestation and overgrazing is reflected in the vast expanses of barren landscapes that predominate E of Taza. In spite of this, there are some excellent areas for mountain scenery and rural life, which offer good hiking opportunities, notably the Jbel Tazzeka just to the S of Taza, and the Beni Snassen Mountains between Oujda and the

sea. The 20 km stretch of coast between Ras Kebdana and the relaxing seaside resort of Saïdia has a wonderfully unspoilt beach, while the peninsula of Cap des Trois Fourches is wild, rocky and windswept. The water temperature along the Mediterranean coast is comfortable to swim in from Apr to Nov. Further S, the Debdou massif is worth exploring, while for lovers of the desert environment and vast horizons there is Eastern Morocco's trump card **Figuig**, a large and interesting oasis settlement in the far SE.

NADOR

Between Al Hoceima and Nador the P39 winds inland through the foothills of the Rif, which are fairly deserted. One can stop at two roadside towns, **Drouiche** with the basic **F** Hotel Es-Salam, and **Mont Aroui**, with the similar **F** Hotel

Hassan. At **Selouane**, a small mining and industrial settlement, there is a fine example of a late 17th century kasbah built by Moulay Ismail. From here the P39 continues inland to Nador and Melilla, whilst the P27 leads off to Berkane, Ahfir, Oujda and Algeria.

By the salt lagoon known as Sebkha Bou Areq, the port of **Nador** (*Pop* about 120,000), is a relaxed settlement with the

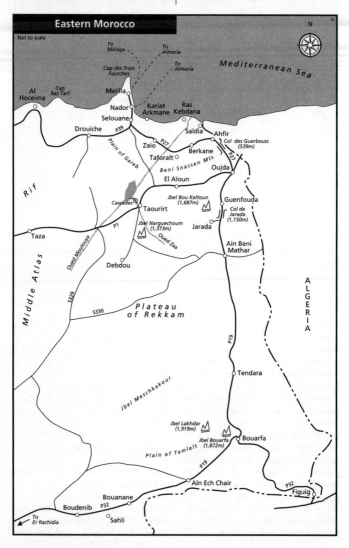

Eastern Morocco

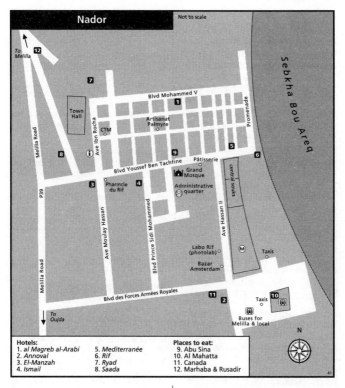

Nador

Not to scale

To Melilla 12

7

Town Hall

Blvd Mohammed V

1

Promenade

Sebkha Bou Areg

Melilla Road

Ave Ibn Rocha

CTM

Artisanat Palmyre

8 i

9

5

6

Blvd Youssef Ben Tachfine

Pâtisserie

Grand Mosque

central souks

P39

3

Pharmcie du Rif

4

Administrative quarter

Ave Moulay Hassan

Blvd Prince Sidi Mohammed

Ave Hassan II

Labo Rif (photolab)

M

Taxis

Melilla Road

Bazar Amsterdam

To Oujda

Blvd des Forces Armées Royales

11 2

Taxis

10

Buses for Melilla & local

N

Hotels:
1. al Magreb al-Arabi
2. Annoval
3. El-Manzah
4. Ismail
5. Mediterranée
6. Rif
7. Ryad
8. Saada

Places to eat:
9. Abu Sina
10. Al Mahatta
11. Canada
12. Marhaba & Rusadir

atmosphere, commerce and transport of a border town, and it is most likely that travellers will pass through only en route or from Melilla. This modern city is now a major port and industrial centre and has a university. It cannot be considered a typical Moroccan town, having a steel plant and a modern harbour with cargo boats always on the move.

The grid pattern of the town makes orientation straightforward. The high street, Blvd Youssef Ben Tachfine, at right angles to the lagoon, cuts right through the centre from the roundabout on the Melilla road to the *Hotel Rif* on the waterfront. The administrative quarter, post office, and the modern Grand Mosque with its unusually tall

and slender minaret are all located on this road. Further down, on the right, is the market complex, a busy, cramped, stifling place, alongside which runs Blvd Hassan II leading to the bus station. To the left of Blvd Youssef Ben Tachfine is an area of small shops and cafés which becomes increasingly residential and whitewashed towards the sea. On the same side, parallel to Blvd Youssef Ben Tachfine is the palm tree and café-lined Blvd Mohammed V connecting the promenade by the lagoon with the town hall. This is the nicest part of town.

Most Nadorians are relatively recent immigrants from the Rif, and many still identify strongly with their rural Berber origins. This element, combined with the proximity of Melilla, and the Mediterranean atmosphere makes Nador an untypical modern Moroccan town. There is a good selection of hotels, and several cheap seafood restaurants.

20 km round the lagoon to the E is a good beach at Kariat Arkmane, where there are also some good fish restaurants, the *Kariat Plage* camping site, watersports and birdwatching opportunities. There is a wide variety of birds here. The acrobatic Sandwich Terns entertain off shore while the Turnstones, Ringed Plover and Oyster Catcher are found at the water's edge or among the rockpools. Some continue to Ras el Ma'a for more birdwatching.

Local information
● Accommodation

C *Club Méditerranée*, Ajdir BP 38, T 982222, Tx 43676, directly opp Peñon de Alhucemas; **C** *Hotel Rif*, 1 Blvd Youssef Ben Tachfine, T 603635, at seaside, restaurant, nightclub, pool and tennis, large and well-equipped; **C** *Hotel Ryad*, Blvd Mohammed V, BP60, T 607715, F 607719, 41 rm, 18 suites, lavish decor, restaurant with Moroccan and international cuisine, 2 bars, café, 24-hr room service; **C** *Mohammed V*, Place de la Marche Verte, T 982371.

D *Hotel Ismail*, 34 Blvd Prince Sidi Mohammed, T 606280, cheaper than *Hotel Mediterranée* and almost as nice, clean and comfortable, but hot water not available round the clock, pleasant staff, nice cafe but no restaurant, rec; **D** *Hotel Mediterranée*, 2-4 Blvd Youssef Ben Tachfine, opp *Hotel Rif*, T 602611, very clean, large hotel, airy, quiet location nr seafront, with balconies and lift, restaurant very clean, attentive cook, menu MD80.

E *Hotel Annoual*, overlooks bus station, substantial price reduction offered, hence good value, insist on good room with hot water, rooms at front are very noisy, large ornate café; **E** *Hotel El-Manzah*, on the corner of Blvd Youssef Ben Tachfine and Ave Moulay Hassan, T 332578, adequately comfortable, centrally located, with a receptionist who speaks English and a guarded parking space, private bathrooms with hot water on request.

F *Hotel al-Maghreb al-Arabi*, situated on street of the same name just off Blvd Mohammed V in the best part of town, very cheap, very simple, but clean; **F** *Hotel Saada*, 26 rue Ibn Rochd, central location, large rambling hotel, fairly clean but rather gloomy.

Camping: *Camping de Kalah Iris*, Circle de Beni Boufrah; *Camping Kalah Bonita*, Plage Bellevue, T 10, 400 places; *Kariat Plage* at Kariat Arkmane, E end of salt lagoon, 2 ha, 20m to beach, bar, snacks, restaurant, grocery shop, showers, laundry, electricity for caravans, petrol at 400m.

● Places to eat

◆◆◆ *Hotel Rif*, T 606535, and *Hotel Ryad*, T 607715, both have international and Moroccan cuisine.

◆◆ Slightly less expensive, with good fish dishes, is *Restaurant Romero*, on the corner of Ave Hassan II and Ave Yacoub El Mansour; *Marhaba*, 2 rue Ibn Rochd nr *Hotel Ryad*, large establishment with a fast service aimed at Spanish day-trippers, wide choice; *Rusadir*, situated next to *Marhaba* but slightly more up-market, speciality is fish.

◆ *Al Mahatta*, is situated above the bus station, very good, spacious and clean, a quality cheap restaurant, terrace has good view over town, lamb tagine MD30; *Abu Sina*, rue Abu Sina, just off Blvd Youssef Ben Tachfine on right, busy small restaurant open at lunchtime, wide selection including fish soup, grilled prawns and paella; *Canada*, Blvd des Forces Armées Royales, very close to bus station, fast service catering for travellers.

There are cheap reasonable restaurants serving Moroccan food in Ave Hassan II, try *Restaurant Centrale* or *Restaurant Kanaria*.

Cafés and pâtisseries: *Pastelaria Elssayah*, 65 Blvd Youssef Ben Tachfine is a bright modern establishment, good for fresh fruit juices; *Pâtisserie Noor*, 43 Blvd Youssef Ben Tachfine, nr mosque, has a good selection of cakes; *Salon de Thé Ismail*, 34 Blvd Prince Sidi Mohammed, next to *Hotel Ismail*, comfortable and quite smart. In addition to those on Blvd Mohammed V, there are also some good cafés on Blvd des Forces Armées Royales, not far from the bus station.

● Banks & money changers
ABM, next to the Grand Mosque.

● Hospitals & medical services
Chemists: *Pharmacie Du Rif*, on corner of Blvd Youssef Ben Tachfine and Ave Moulay Hassan;

Pharmacie Ibn Sina, at top end of Blvd Youssef Ben Tachfine under the arches.

● **Shopping**

Artisanat Palmyre, Calle al-Kaissaria 99, off Blvd Youssef Ben Tachfine; *Bazar Amsterdam*, 230 Ave Hassan II has good selection of handicrafts. There are many small shops selling attractive and cheap bronze jewellery on Calle al-Kaissaria in the heart of town.

Photography: *Labo Rif*, 210 Ave Hassan II, nr bus station.

● **Sports**

Fishing: the mérou (gouper) are said to be of the best here.

Watersports: water skiing, windsurfing, sailing and underwater swimming.

● **Tour companies & travel agents**

Kemata Voyages, 146 Blvd Mohammed V, T 982173; *La Méditerranée*, 47 Blvd Mohammed V, T 982376; *Royal Air Maroc*, 24 Blvd Mohammed V, T 606478.

● **Tourist offices**

3rd Flr, 88 Blvd Ibn Rochd, T 606518, ask to speak to Mr Addouche who is as helpful as possible, given his resources.

● **Transport**

Road Bus: the bus station, a noisy, busy, dirty place is at the end of Ave Hassan II, near the junction with Ave des Forces Armées Royales. CTM buses run to **Tetouan** (0930, 1800), **Al Hoceima** (0900, 1645), **Oujda** (0600, 0800, 0900, 1500), **Tanger** (1500), **Casablanca/Fez/Meknes/ Rabat** (2030 and 2100), **Tetouan** (0930 via Al Hoceima and 1800 via Fes/Meknes). Private lines run to **Beni Enzar** for Melilla known as the 'Nador Bus' departs every 15 mins. If you want a seat be sure to board the bus at the terminal as it fills up rapidly along the way (journey time is 30 mins). Further destinations include **Er Rachidia** (0600, 1830 taking 8 hrs via Missour/Midelt), **Figuig** (0915 taking 9 hrs via Oujda), **Karia Arkmane** (0830 on Wed only, 0900, 1100, 1230, 1400), **Ras el Ma'a/Ras Kebdana** (1100, 1400), **Meknes/Fes** (0500, 0715, 0900, 1030, 1100, 1445, 1600), **Fes** (0200, 0400, 0630, 0800, 1200), **Casablanca** (1700, 1800, 2000), **Guercif** (1220), **Oujda** (14 from 0600-1830), **Tanger** (0415, 1600, 1700, 2130), **Tetouan** (0415, 0530, 0800, 1700, 1800, 1900), **Ceuta** (1900), **Chaouen** (0415, 1900), **Targuist** (0415, 1115, 1700), **Al Hoceima** (10 between 0415-1700), **Rabat** (1900, 2000), **Taza** (1300, 1340), **Taourirt** (1345, 1500, 1515), **Berkane** (1130, 1330), and to **Ketama** and **Bab Taza**. ONCF, the railway company, run a bus at 2000 to **Taourirt** to connect with the trains to **Fes**, **Meknes**, **Rabat** and **Casablanca**. **Taxi**: grand-taxis from beside the bus station, with numerous destinations including **Ahfir** (over 1 hr) and from there to **Saïdia**, to the border with **Spanish Melilla** (MD4), to **Al Hoceima** (MD50), **Meknes** and **Fes**. Taxis for Beni Enzar (border) and other points N depart from the main road nr *Hotel Ryad*. **Boat**: there is a Comanov car and passenger ferry service from Nador to Séte in France, every 4 days from Jun to Sep, tickets and information from Comanov Passages, Immeuble Lazaar Beni Enzar, BP 89, T 06608538, or from the same company in Casablanca, 43 Blvd des Forces Armées Royales, T 03310015/6. The new ferry service between Nador and Almería operated by Ferrimaroc is a nightly service (except Sun) departing from Nador at 2330, arriving in Almería 8 hrs later. Cost is MD240 minimum fare one way for foot passenger. Cabins from MD475 (2 people). Enquiries: Manatours Voyages, 5 Blvd Prince Héritier Sidi Mohammed, Nador or Ferrimaroc Agencias, Almería, T 3450274800.

KARIAT ARKMANE

Situated 20 km to the E of Nador, at the extremity of the lagoon, Kariat Arkmane is a small settlement divided into three separate parts some distance away from each other. The main village, on the lagoon, is a bustling rough and ready sort of place with plenty of well stocked grocery stores. There is a morning fish market behind the square. The weekly *souq* is held on Wed. The modern residential area, is situated about 1 km inland along the road, where you will find the turning to Kariat Plage, which is itself a further 2 km further on, across a stretch of marshlands. Although the swimming is safe and clean here, the beach is at times litter-strewn and gets very crowded in high summer.

● **Accommodation** There are no hotels, but family-sized apartments are available in the large modern block at the beach next to *Restaurante Arena de Oro* for MD350/day in high season and less in the low season. Ask around for other cheaper possibilities.

● **Places to eat** ♦♦*Arena de l'Oro*, a well known quality establishment specializing in fish; ♦*Le Marché Vert*, by the beach is simple, clean and the food is good; ♦*Al-Andalous* is similar, good food in simple clean surroundings.

● **Banks & money changers** Credit du Maroc, in main village by taxi rank.

● **Hospitals & medical services** Chemist: *Pharmacie Centrale* is next to bank.

● **Shopping** There is a well stocked grocery store next to the *Marché Vert*.

● **Transport** Buses for **Nador** are hourly in the morning and at 1600. For **Ras Kebdana/Ras el Ma'a**, at 1130 and 1400. All depart from the main village where there are also frequent Grand-taxis.

RAS KEBDANA

(also known as **Ras el Ma'a**) From Kariat Arkmane to Ras Kebdana is about 40 km and the 8101 winds inland across attractive rolling farmlands and deeply eroded *oued* beds cut into the soft, red sandstone. On the right stand the jagged and wild Kebdana mountains, on the left the sea appears from time to time, and it can be reached on foot by following one of the many dry *oued* beds for 2 or 3 km. There is no beach though, only low, muddy cliffs. The village of Ras Kebdana is entirely devoted to fishing, and is dwarfed by its large modern harbour, beyond which there is a wonderful unspoilt beach stretching for 6 km to the estuary of the Oued Molouya, and beyond that to the resort of Saïdia (see page 169). The view from the headland over the coast and the Spanish-held Chafarines Islands offshore is spectacular. From the breakwater at the far end of the harbour a flight of steps leads up to the lighthouse where a bored sentry may stop you out of curiosity. Take care walking along the crumbling cliff edge. It is possible to walk back along the crest of the headland to the road and down another flight of steps to the back of the village. Unfortunately the headland itself has been somewhat spoilt by military installations.

● **Accommodation Camping**: on the large space behind the beach, no facilities as yet.

● **Places to eat** ♦♦*Café restaurant du Port*, T 605972, large restaurant situated in the middle of the port area, clean and friendly, huge portions of excellent and very fresh fish and prawns make this very good value.

● **Transport** Buses to **Nador**, 0830, 1500; **Berkane**, 1230, 1530. Grand-taxis run from time to time to Kariat Arkmane and Berkane.

CAP DES TROIS FOURCHES

Jutting some 30 km into the Mediterranean, N of Nador, the des Trois Fourches peninsula is rocky, wild and windswept. For the adventurous there is a couple of tiny beaches close to the lighthouse, accessible by a 14 km long rough hilly track from the village of Taourirt N of the border post of Farkhana. Past Taourirt, there is a turning on the left to another tiny beach at Cala Tramontana 4 km away. There are few settlements, only a couple of impoverished hamlets. The scenery along the way to the cape is very beautiful, but there are strong currents around the peninsula and swimming can be dangerous.

● **Transport** Taxis from Beni Enzar or Farkhana as far as they will go, then walk.

MELILLA

Melilla is the main town in the small Spanish *plaza* or enclave, on the Mediterranean coast of Morocco. It stands on the promontory, facing E, just 16 km S of Cape des Trois Fourches and 12 km N of Nador. The enclave is well worth a day's visit. It is a charming small Spanish town of some 80,000 inhabitants, well planned by the architect Don Enrique Nieto in the first half of the 20th century. Shopping is excellent with a fine range of standard goods on sale as well as cheap electronic items and some Moroccan craft goods at set prices.

The original foundation of the site, the port of Rusadir, is Phoenician. The Greeks and Romans were here too. The Spanish captured the town from the

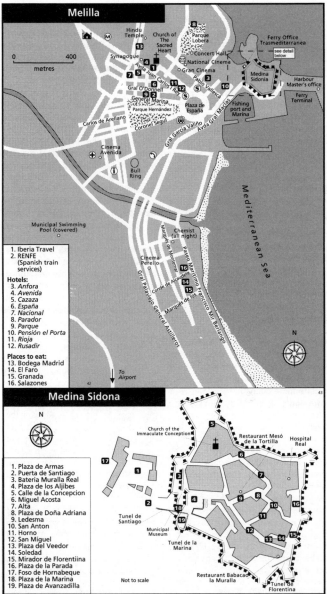

Melilla

Hindu Temple
Church of The Sacred Heart
Parque Lobera
Ferry Office Trasmediterranea
see detail below
Synagogue
Concert Hall
National Cinema
Gran Cinema
Medina Sidonia
Harbour Master's office
Ferry Terminal
Avda Juan Carlos Rey
Pablo Vallesca
Gral O'Donnell
General Marina
Parque Hernández
Plaza de España
Fishing port and Marina
Coronel Segui
Carlos de Arellano
Gral García Valino
Avda Gral Macias
Cinema Avenida
Bull Ring
Mediterranean Sea
Municipal Swimming Pool (covered)
Chemist (all night)
Marqués de Montemar
Cinema Perello
Gral Palahejo General Artillero
Conde de Alcaudete
Paseo Marítimo Francisco Mir Berlango
Marqués de los
To Airport

0   400
metres

N

1. Iberia Travel
2. RENFE (Spanish train services)

Hotels:
3. *Anfora*
4. *Avenida*
5. *Cazaza*
6. *España*
7. *Nacional*
8. *Parador*
9. *Parque*
10. *Pensión el Porta*
11. *Rioja*
12. *Rusadir*

Places to eat:
13. Bodega Madrid
14. El Faro
15. Granada
16. Salazones

42

Medina Sidona

N

Church of the Immaculate Conception
Restaurant Mesó de la Tortilla
Hospital Real
Tunel de Santiago
Municipal Museum
Tunel de la Marina
Restaurant Babacao la Muralla
Tunel de Florentina

1. Plaza de Armas
2. Puerta de Santiago
3. Bateria Muralla Real
4. Plaza de los Aljibes
5. Calle de la Concepcion
6. Miguel Acosta
7. Alta
8. Plaza de Doña Adriana
9. Ledesma
10. San Anton
11. Horno
12. San Miguel
13. Plaza del Veedor
14. Soledad
15. Mirador de Florentiina
16. Plaza de la Parada
17. Foso de Hornabeque
18. Plaza de la Marina
19. Plaza de Avanzadilla

Not to scale

43

Berbers in 1497. The ancient citadel, **Medina Sidonia**, was built on a huge rock which rises out of the sea to the E of the promontory. The modern city is well laid out with its focus at the busy but green **Plaza de España** from which all principal thoroughfares including the main shopping streets radiate. The main bank, Banco de España and the ferry office are here on Plaza de España. To the N is the post office and beyond, up the hill, is the *Parador*. Call in for magnificent views of the city and a cup of coffee. There is a large bull-ring near the tourist office for those who want some Spanish local colour.

The sandy beaches to the S of the town are disappointingly littered.

Places of interest

Medina Sidonia is by far the most interesting place to visit. It is a series of three intercommunicating forts surrounded by a common defensive wall but separated from each other by drawbridges and formal gates. The principal gate **Puerta de Santiago** stands above the Plaza de Armas though the most accessible entrance for those on foot is the **Puerta de la Marina**. Pass through the Cuesta de las Peñuelas to the Plaza de los Aljibes, in one corner of which is the small but welcoming and free **Municipal Museum** (open daily 1000-1400), T 2699158 which also gives access to the Bateria Muralla Real walkway with views across the town. Through the gaps in the defensive wall a row of cannons is prepared to attack the Parador!!! The first floor of the museum is set aside for visiting exhibits. More interesting, on the second floor, the archaeological section has Roman lamps and pottery found locally, Carthaginian coins and a pair of gold earrings each shaped like a dove beside the skull which presumably they once adorned. The top floor has local materials, uniforms and pieces of industrial archaeology, making a statement of the Spanish nature of the settlement.

The 17th century **Church of the Immaculate Conception** stands to the N of the peninsula, approach through Calle de la Concepción or Calle San Miguel. It is worthy of a visit to see some excellent period carving, the statue of Nuestra Senora de la Victoria, the patroness of Melilla whose day is celebrated on 17 Sept, and the cave cut into the rock beneath the church, **Cueva del Conventico**, a type of refuge. All other sites, including the former restaurants Mesòn de la Tortilla and Babacao La Muralla (for gourmets other excellent restaurants can be found in the new town), are subject to closure as the long-term building work funded by the EU progresses. Although it is possible to walk around part of the walls a great deal of the remainder of the old town is either occupied by the military or currently under major reconstruction works.

Local information
● **Accommodation**

A wide range of good but Spanish priced accommodation is available in Melilla.

A *Parador de Melilla*, Avda de Cándido Lobera, T 2684940, F 2683486, 40 rm, 76 beds, telephone, TV, parking, lift, facilities for disabled, credit cards, exchange, a/c, heating, restaurant, coffee shop/bar, seasonal pool, no dogs allowed; **A** *Rusadir*, 5 Pablo Vallescá, T 2681240, F 2670527, 35 rm, telephone, credit cards, a/c, lift, TV.

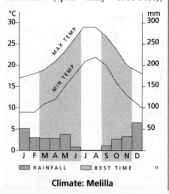

°C / mm

MAX TEMP
MIN TEMP

J F M A M J J A S O N D

□ RAINFALL   □ BEST TIME

Climate: Melilla

B *Anfora*, 16 Pablo Vallescá, T 2683340, F 2683344, 145 rm, garage, lift, a/c, telephone, TV, cycle hire; **B** *Avenida*, 24 Avda Juan Carlos 1 Rey, T 2684949, F 2683226, 78 rm, a/c, TV, telephone, lift, credit cards, bar; **B** *Cazaza*, 6 Jose Antonio Primo de Rivera, T 2684648, 8 rm, rec; **B** *Parque*, 15 General Marina, T 2682143, 28 rm, telephone, not quiet but overlooking the central park; **B** *Rioja*, 10 Ejército Español, T 268709, 11 rm, a friendly atmosphere here.

C *Mirasol*, 31 General Astilleros, T 2674686, 13 rm, bar/coffee shop; **C** *Nacional*, 10 Jose Antonio Primo de Rivera, T 2684540, 30 rm, credit cards, exchange, telephone, bar/coffee shop.

D *España*, Avda de Juan Carlos I Rey, T 2684645, homely; **D** *Miramar*, Paseo General Macias; **D** *Pensión el Porto*, 1 Calle Santiago, T 2681270, facing the port; **D** *Pensión Numéro 7*, Avda de Generalisimo.

Camping: there is a camping site but no youth hostel.

● **Places to eat**
There are many good restaurants despite the (temporary?) closure of those in the old town.

◆◆◆*Zayka*, 32 Montemar, T 2681037, is the most expensive, the food is excellent.

For Spanish food at mainland prices try ◆◆*Los Salazones*, 15 Calle de Alcaudete, and for a good fish selection *Granada*, 30 Montemar, T 2673026, and *Victoria*, 9 General Pareja, T 2677946.

◆ *Casa Martin*, 11 General Polavieja; *El Mesòn*, 9 Avda de Castelar and *El Faro*, 27 Montemar, just 100m from the beach.

There are many bars such as *Bodega Madrid*, 10 Castelar, cafeterias like *La Palma*, 20 Avda Juan Carlos 1 Rey, and ice-cream sellers such as *La Ibense*, Plaza Héroes de España, T 2681188.

● **Banks & money changers**
Banco de España, Plaza de España, T 2683940; **Banco Español de Credito**, 10 Avda Juan Carlos 1 Rey, T 2684348; **Banco Hispano Americano**, 5 Plaza Menéndez Pelayo, T 2673405. Itinerant money changers operate outside the Trasmediterranea office on Plaza de España.

● **Embassies & consulates**
Consul representation: France, Mulle Ribera, T 2681511.

● **Entertainment**
Bull ring: Calle Querol, T 2699213.

Cinemas: *Cine Avenida*, Avda Manuel Fernández Benítez, T 2674300, nr Tourist Office; *Cine Nacional*, 8 Cándido Lobera, T 2681384; *Cine Perelló*, 37 Calle General Polavieja, T 2676267.

Nightclubs: there are 2 on Ctra Alfonso XIII, 2 on Calvo Sotelo, 3 on Mar Chica and 2 on Calle General Polavieja. Enough choice here to while the night away.

Television: Melilla has its own TV station as well as mainland Spanish and Moroccan programmes and its own newspaper, Melilla Hoy, for those with Spanish.

Theatres: *Auditorium Carvajal*, Parque Lobera; *Grand Teatro National*, 8 Candido Lobera.

● **Hospitals & medical services**
Hospitals: *Melilla Commercial Hospital*, Remonta, T 2670000; *Red Cross Hospital*, Avda Duquessa Victoria, T 2684743.

● **Places of worship**
Church of the Sacred Heart, Plaza Menéndez Pelayo, off Avda Juan Carlos 1 Rey. *Hindu Temple*, 13 Avda de Castelar. *Main mosque*, Calle Garcia Cabrelles. *Synagogue*, 8 Calle López Moreno.

● **Post & telecommunications**
Area code: there are numerous public telephone boxes permitting international connections. Melilla code, like Málaga, is 952. Omit the 9 when ringing from outside Spain. When phoning Melilla from Morocco the international code is 0034.

Post Office: is on Pablo Vallescá, T 2681936.

● **Shopping**
The best shopping streets, spacious and clean, are the Avenida Juan Carlos 1 Rey including Plaza de los Héroes de España (crowded with shoppers and socializing groups in the evening), Ejército Español and Calle General O'Donnell.

As with Ceuta there are many duty free shops offering a wide range of electric and electronic items, none very cheap. On Avda Juan Carlos 1 Rey try *Bazar Estilo*, T 2682805 and on Ejército Español, *Arte Arab*, T 2683046. There are shops selling Moroccan craft goods at fairly high fixed prices. Await until arrival in Morocco for the real thing at bargain(ed) prices. The town has several bookshops mainly of course stocked with Spanish language materials. Town maps in a variety of detail are available from Rafael Boix Sola, 23 Avda Juan Carlos 1 Rey, T 2681983. Surf and Windsurf equipment at *Ultrafun*, 36 Calle General Polavieja.

● **Sports**

Watersports: *Municipal Swimming Pool*, covered, Avda de la Juventud. *Marina, Club Maritimo*, Calle Muelle, T 2683659.

● **Tour companies & travel agents**

Include *Renfe* for rail/sea travel, 113 Calle General O'Donnell, T 2683551. *Compañia Trasmediterranea* for ferries, 1 General Marina/Plaza España, T 2681918, F 2682572. *Iberia* for air travel, 2 Calle Cándido Lobera, T 2670386. Iberia at airport T 2673123/2673800. There are independent travel agents incl *Andalucía Travel*, 13 Avda de la Democracia, T 2670730, F 2676598 and *Viajes Melvia*, Pasaje Avenida, T 2688526.

● **Tourist offices**

Oficina de Turismo, Avda General Aizpuru, T 2674013 (open 0900-1400 and 1600-1800 Mon-Fri, 1000-1200 Sat).

● **Useful telephone numbers**

Ambulance: T 2674400.

Fire service: T 080.

Guardia Civil: T 2671300/2671400.

Police: (Local) T 092, (National) T 091.

Red Cross Ambulance: T 2672222.

Weather information: T 2673555.

● **Transport**

Air There are excellent air services from Melilla to the Spanish mainland at Madrid, Málaga and Almería. **Panair** runs BAe146 jets and **Trasmediterranea** flies propeller-driven aircraft in a 30-min 8 flight/weekday (6 flights Sun) service Málaga-Melilla and return, a very comfortable ride. Return prices from Melilla-Málaga are 38,800 ptas. Flights Melilla-Almería and return go on Mon, Tues, Thur and Fri. Melilla-Madrid flights and return run on Mon, Tues, Wed, Thur and Fri. Flight frequencies can vary on a quarterly basis and it is advisable to check in Melilla with the appropriate agency, **Panair**, 2 Calle Musico Granados, T 2674211, **Compañia Trasmediterranea**, 1 General Marina/Plaza España, T 2681918 or **Iberia**, 2 Calle Cándido Lobera, T 2670386. Taxis to/from the airport take 10 mins and cost 600-700 ptas.

Road Bus: there is a cheap and frequent bus service within Melilla, most buses calling at Plaza de España. Most services run on 15-min circuit (Info T 2672616). Taxis are comparatively cheap: pay on the meter. Taxi ranks are to be found at Calle Arturo Reyes, T 2683628, Calle Cándido Lobera, T 2683623, Calle Castilla (Real), T 2673624 and Calle General Marina, T 2683621. Hire cars are available at the airport and from agencies in the town such as Auto-Venta, 3 Teniente Coronel Segui, T 2683633. Hire cars cannot be taken from Melilla into Morocco.

For travel to the frontier take the regular bus from Plaza de España (15-30 mins frequency).

Sea The Trasmediterranea Co runs a regular ferry service to Málaga and Almería from the terminal just off the old town. The crossing takes $7^1/_2$ hrs from Málaga and $6^1/_2$ hrs from Almería leaving Melilla Mon, Tues, Wed, Thur, Fri and Sat at 2300 for Málaga (return 1300 daily except Sun) and at 2330 for Almería (return 1200 daily except Sun 2330) in winter. Summer services from Melilla run to Málaga daily at 2300 (return 2300) and to Almería on Mon, Wed, Fri and Sun at 1000 (return 0200 and 1800) and on Tues, Thur and Sat at 0200 and 1800 (return 1000). Single prices to Málaga for a foot passenger 3,400 ptas and for a private cabin 15,560 ptas. 13,230 ptas for a private cabin to Almería. Other much cheaper rates apply to ordinary deck/public cabin tickets but the margin against the air fare for a half hour flight is close.

Information and tickets from Trasmediterranea, 1 General Marina/Plaza España, T 2681918 in Melilla; Estaciòn Maritima, El Puerto, T 952224391 in Málaga; Parque Nicolàs Salmeron 19, T 950236155 in Almería. The UK agent is Southern Ferries, T 01714914968.

NB Remember to allow an extra time if crossing the border from Morocco to catch the ferry, as Spanish time is 2 hrs ahead of Moroccan time Apr-Sept and 1 hr ahead Oct-Mar.

Crossing the border at Melilla/Beni Enzar

From Melilla: providing there is no queue, the procedure is quite simple. About 100m past the Spanish checkpoint in the middle of the road is a small hut with a blue door and a counter where passports are stamped. Before this is done, you have to fill in a customs form which you obtain from the same office. Then proceed to the barrier and show your passport stamp to the blue-uniformed police officers who will let you through. Coming across from Melilla buses to Nador (MD2.50) leave from the chaotic large open space behind the first block of buildings on the right. Shared Grand-taxis to Nador cost MD4, unshared MD24. **From Beni Enzar**: when leaving Morocco the same procedure applies.

If you are an EU citizen, the Spanish customs are most likely to let you through without delay. The Melilla border is, however, sensitive to drug smuggling and Spanish border police can be demanding if made suspicious by travellers.

If you intend to catch a ferry from Melilla to Málaga or Almería (dep 2330), remember that Spanish time is always 1 or 2 hrs ahead of Moroccan time.

The best time to cross the border in either direction is early in the morning. Crossing the border well before or after the ferry arrives can also help to smooth one's passage. If possible, avoid crossing this border at peak holiday times, especially Easter and Jul-Sept, when up to 4 hrs wait in a queue can be expected. Sometimes, when the border is congested, an unofficial dual system operates, with touts charging money for an 'express' passport stamping service.

Don't bother, there is no guarantee that this will save time.

EASTWARDS TOWARDS ALGERIA

From just S of **Nador**, at **Selouane** which has Sat *souq*, a fine kasbah built in the 17th century by Moulay Ismail and a good 2-star restaurant, the P27 branches off the P39 and goes E across the barren foothills of the Kebdana mountains towards the Algerian border. There are some magnificent views. About 10 km after the small town of **Zaio** the road crosses the Oued Moulouya, which marks the easternmost limit of the former Spanish protectorate, into the plain of Triffa or Saïdia. The attractive **Beni Snassen Mountains** appear on the S, overlooking the plain.

During the period of French administration (1911-1956), this tiny NE corner of Morocco was transformed into one of the richest agricultural areas in the country thanks to the construction of the Triffa Canal diverting water from the Oued Molouya. European settlers or *còlons* were imported to run farms on the same organized model that prevailed in neighbouring Algeria.

One of the most enduring legacies of

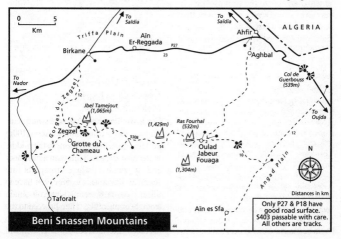

Beni Snassen Mountains

this period are the Beni Snassen vineyards, which produce a good wine of the same name. Since the departure of the *còlons* in the 1950s and 60s, the area has remained industrious and relatively wealthy although there are still wide gaps in income. Over the past two or three decades, many Moroccan expatriates have returned from France, Belgium and the Netherlands to build houses for their families and invest in farming and small businesses.

For the visitor, this small area offers two worthwhile attractions within easy reach of one another: the glorious beach at Saïdia and the wonderfully unspoilt Beni Snassen Mountains to the S of Berkane.

BERKANE

Berkane is a bustling modern agricultural centre with little of historical or cultural interest, however it is a convenient base for excursions to the nearby mountains and there is a good comfortable hotel with a good restaurant. A sharp contrast exists between the leafy, well-to-do end of town close to the administrative and military buildings on the Oujda Road, and the busy crowded dusty streets which characterize the rest. Most facilities can be found on the main artery, Blvd Mohammed V which is also the Nador to Oujda main road. At the western end of this road, before the bridge over the *oued* is a large open space with the main mosque, several cafés and a large weekly market each Tues.

● **Accommodation** C *Hotel Zaki*, 27 Route Principale d'Oujda, opp the municipality building, T 613743, surprisingly smart and stylish little hotel with an excellent restaurant (menu MD96); **E** *Hotel Ennajah*, Blvd Moulay Youssef, T 612914, simple hotel with clean rooms, street noise can be bothersome in early morning, no hot water, there is a café/restaurant below; **E** *Hotel Mounir*, just off Blvd Mohammed V on rue Cheraa, T 611867, a popular and efficiently run hotel, which doubles as a rooming house, with a friendly and helpful owner, self catering possible, hot water generously supplied!

● **Places to eat** ♦♦ *Restaurant des Orangiers*, in *Hotel Zaki*, T 613743, excellent little restaurant, Master Chef Haji Sakhraji, who featured on a BBC food programme in the 1980s runs the kitchen, menu MD95. For a snack try *Sandwich Venisia*, 144 rue Sultan Moulay Mohammed. A cheerful drink and snack with the locals can be sampled in the tiny wine cellar at 21 Blvd Mohammed V opp the post office, probably the best evening entertainment available.

● **Banks & money changers**
BMCE, opp Shell petrol station; **Crédit du Maroc**, 44 Blvd Mohammed V.

● **Hospitals & medical services**
Chemist: *Pharmacie de la Mosquée*, Place de la Grand Mosque.

● **Post & telecommunications**
On Blvd Mohammed V.

● **Tour companies & travel agents**
Oriental Voyages, 94 Blvd Mohammed V, friendly and helpful.

● **Transport**
Road Bus: the CTM offices are located midway along on Blvd Mohammed V next to the Café des Jardins. There is a bus to Oujda at 1030 and one to Fes/Casablanca at 1900 from here. Most other bus services depart from Blvd Moulay Youssef opp Café des Jardins. From here there are hourly departures for Ahfir and Oujda. Buses for Nador stop to pick up every hour on the hour (roughly) by the Grand Mosque. There is normally only one bus for Saïdia at 1400 departing from the same place as the Taxis (see below). **Taxis**: Grand-taxis for Nador, Taforalt, El Aioun and Taourirt leave from the parking space under the tall trees by the Grand Mosque. For Saïdia, the taxis leave from the Saïdia road at the opp end of town (bear left at the roundabout with the emblem in the middle). All other Grand-taxis depart from the main bus stop in Blvd Moulay Youssef.

The Beni Snassen Mountains

Geologically a continuation of the Rif, but very different in atmosphere, this small hassle free mountain range is perfect for gentle hiking and exploration amidst an impressive variety of Mediterranean type vegetation (lavender, pine, almond, orange, oleander, olive, juniper etc) and dramatic rockscapes. The orange and olive orchards which cling to the lower slopes are very prosperous. The necessary terraced cultivation gives a very ordered appearance to the scenery and the bands and blocks of colour change up the gorge. The whole area is riddled with underground caves, most of which remain unexplored. Some of the caves have very fine formations of rede-posited calcium and other shapes formed by water erosion of the limestone. In the Plombo caves there are some very rare prehistoric cave drawings which make the journey really worthwhile. The high-lights are the **Gorges du Zegzel** and the **Grotte du Chameau**, where it is possible to camp. A warm stream flows out of the main entrance of the cave and joins the nearby Oued Zegzel. Inside the cave there are stalactites and an extensive war-ren of unlit passageways. Unfortunately at the time of writing these are closed to visitors, presumably for safety considera-tions. Both sites are easily accessible from Berkane, even on foot, in a couple of hours if one is feeling energetic. The area is inhabited by the Beni Snassen, a sed-entary Berber tribe who, like most other Berber groups in the Maghreb, survived the Arab invasions by taking refuge in the mountains.

The local economy is based around small scale farming, goat-herding and fruit cultivation.

ACCESS There are several ways to ac-cess these mountains. If you are pressed for time, and don't have your own trans-port, the best way is from Berkane via a circular route that takes in the gorges and the caves. This can be done easily in 2 to 4 hrs, either by taxi or by using a combi-nation of taxis, walking and lifts. Taxis from Berkane don't normally pass via the gorges, so you may have to charter one. Make sure the price you agree on is for a return trip including stop-offs. A cheaper option is to do the circuit anti-clockwise by taking a shared taxi heading for Taforalt (20 km) along the S403 and getting off at the pass shortly before the village. From here there is a signposted road winding 9 km to the caves along a very attractive valley of fruit trees and tiny hamlets. From

the Grotte du Chameau you can return to Berkane, a further 10 km downhill, via the Zegzel Gorges. Lifts are easy to come by in this area, but one should always offer to pay.

Eastwards, a rough but very scenic cor-niche road (the 5308) branches off from the Zegzel defile, and runs along the crest of the range for 30-40 km, down to the Angad Plain and on to Oujda. Distances and the most rewarding viewpoints are marked on the map. Back on the P27, the next town after Berkane is Ahfir, a quiet border town. From here there are two op-tions, N to the resort of Saïdia, or S to Oujda by the panoramic Col de Guerbouss (539m).

SAIDIA

The road to Saïdia runs parallel to the Algerian border, at one point through a narrow gorge when all that separates the traveller from Algeria is the narrow but ironically named Oued Kiss. There are areas of fruit production and market gar-dening and large expanses of local vines which produces a reasonably good wine. While Saïdia is located on the coastal plain of Triffa the forested mountains are not far to the S offering pleasant picnic areas, interesting walks with unique views and abundant game for those li-censed to hunt. Saïdia is a pleasant resort popular with Moroccans, which has not yet been overly developed, and perhaps lacks some comforts. It has an old 17th century fortress from the time of Moulay Ismail and a more recent 19th century construction. It is packed in the summer, with no shortage of places to eat, but limited and expensive hotels, some of which are closed in winter, when the place is fairly deserted. There is a 12 km long attractive sandy beach, and a bay which provides a safer area for boating and sailing, and views of the Spanish held Islas Chafarinas and of Algeria. It is an easy place to walk around, with a grid of brightly coloured houses, restaurants and hotels parallel to the beach.

The 20 km between the Algerian bor-der and the estuary of the Oued Mou-

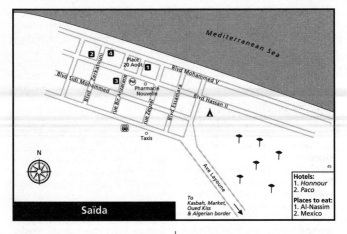

Hotels:
1. Honnour
2. Paco

Places to eat:
1. Al-Nassim
2. Mexico

Saïda

louya is the only section of the Mediterranean coast to have been occupied by France for any length of time. During the low-season, Saïdia feels like an empty film set, waiting for the big show, which in a sense it is; the **Saïdia Music Festival**, in Aug, marks the high point of the year, when virtually the entire population of Oujda and Berkane seems to migrate here to escape the heat.

The tiny square 19th century kasbah, with its intact walls and humble dwellings was all that existed here prior to the 1930s. It was built by Sultan Moulay Hassan to guard against the French. The adjacent market enclosure, which holds a *souq* on Sun, backs onto the Oued Kiss which marks the border with Algeria.

From the kasbah, it is a short walk to the beach through a eucalyptus forest. A new tourist complex is planned here which will include hotels, restaurants, golf courses and a marina. There will be emphasis on self catering in villas, apartments and aparthotels.

● **Accommodation** Hotel options are limited, particularly as many are closed out of season. The central, **C** *Hotel Hannour*, Place 20 Août, T 625115, is the smartest hotel in Saïdia, with a good restaurant and a bar, open Jun-Oct; **D** *Hotel Paco*, Blvd Hassan II, T 625110, 15 rm, comfortable, friendly, family hotel close to the beach, restaurant, open Jun-Oct; **E** *Hotel El-Kalaa*, rue Layoune, T 625123, open all year round. Also *Sherif*, which is also open all year, some distance from the beach. Apartments can be rented cheaply Sept-May if you bargain. The owner of the *Al-Nassim* restaurant may be able to help. There are also several campsites: *Camping du Sit* for families, *Camping Caravaning Al Mansour*, rue de Moulouya, site of 6 ha; *Camping Centre Autonome*, at Saïdia Plage, a site of 8 ha, beach only 200m, bar/snack, grocery shop, pool, showers, laundry, petrol at 500m, electricity for caravans; *Camping Essi*, site of 2½ ha, beach 200m, groceries, showers, laundry, electricity for caravans, petrol 500m.

● **Places to eat** ◆◆*Café/Restaurant Al-Nassim*, rue Bir Anzarane, T 625008, open all year, breezy panoramic salon, very fresh fish, rec; ◆ *Café/Restaurant Mexico*, Blvd Zerkatouni, in the centre, facing the beach, friendly proprietor who speaks English, very good value, open all year. Several standard restaurants on rue Sidi Mohammed, open all year round, incl ◆ *Café Restaurant Plus*. Try ◆ *Café Bleu* in rue Laayoune, relaxed and friendly atmosphere.

● **Banks & money changers** The nearest banks are in Ahfir, 20 km away. In the high summer, a mobile branch service operates in Place 20 Août.

● **Hospitals & medical services** Chemists: *Pharmacie Nouvelle*, Blvd Hassan II.

● **Transport Road Bus**: depart from rue

Layoune to Ahfir/Oujda at 0600, 1000, 1400, 1600; more frequently in the summer. **Taxis**: Grand-taxis leave from rue Laayoune or from the tree-lined road behind and parallel to rue Sidi Mohammed, to **Ahfir** (20 mins), and on to **Oujda**, **Berkane** and **Nador**. Grand-taxis also depart from rue Layoune or from the taxi rank by the kasbah.

OUJDA AND SOUTH TO FIGUIG

OUJDA

History

Oujda, with a present population of 260,000, is the most significant city in the E of Morocco, its essential character determined by its location close to the Algerian border. Traditionally a rather conservative town, Oujda has a rather sophisticated metropolitan feel to it, particularly when coming from other areas of eastern Morocco. The place makes a welcome break from the hassle of other Moroccan cities, as people see few Westerners. Signs of economic hardship are evident, although not overwhelming, but the total collapse in the number of visitors crossing from Algeria since the closure of the border in 1995 has hit the local economy badly and affected morale among the many Oujdans who rely on regional tourism and business for revenue. There are few visitors enjoying the fairly peaceful, comparatively modern medina or taking a day trip to the Sidi Yahia oasis. It is a convenient stopping point for those crossing the border into Algeria or Spanish Melilla, or planning to journey down S to Figuig, in the Sahara. It is a well-equipped city which can be a useful last stop in relative comfort for the determined Saharan traveller. Indeed its privileged geographic position makes it, in more settled times, the centre for Maghreb tourism and the meeting point of routes between Morocco and other countries of North Africa.

Although Roman ruins have been found at Marnia, in 944 Zenata Berbers founded Oujda, strategically located on the main route from Rabat and Meknes to Algeria. It has traditionally been contested by the rulers of Fes, in Morocco, and Tlemcen, in Algeria. Captured by Sultan Youssef Ben Tachfine in 1206, it was a major centre for the Almohads who added to the fortifications. King Merinide Abou Youssef rebuilt the city in 1297, constructing new walls and a kasbah, a mosque and a palace. Later the Ottoman Regency of Algiers gained control of the city, but Moulay Ismail regained it in 1687 and was one of the sovereigns who did most to develop the city. Oujda was acknowledged as part of Morocco by treaties with Morocco, but was occupied by French forces in 1844 after the decisive **Battle of Isly** fought 8 km W of the city, and again in 1859. In 1903 Oujda was the centre of the insurgency by Bou Hamra, and was again taken by French forces from Algeria in 1907. The city was a centre of nationalist activity prior to Independence.

The plain of Angad on which Oujda is situated has as a splendid backdrop the Beni Snassen Mountains lying to the NW. Here there are interesting narrow gorges and caves to explore. From these issue many small streams which provide irrigation for the well kept gardens and orchards. To the S is another high range of mountains, the extension of the Middle Atlas which extends into Algeria.

ACCESS Air Aéroport Oujda-Les Angad is 15 km from the city, off the P27, T 683261. Take a grand-taxi into town. **Train** Oujda is at the E end of the Moroccan rail network. The railway station is on Place de l'Unité Africaine, at the end of rue Zerktouni not far from the town centre. **Road** Oujda is a long haul over the P1 from Rabat, Fes and Taza to the W, which brings motorists over the Oued Nachaf into Blvd Mohammed ben Lakhdar, along with the P19 from Figuig, a hard drive across the Sahara. The P27 from Melilla, Nador and Ahfir enters Oujda along Blvd Abdellah Chefchaouni. From Ahfir continue to Saïdia and the Mediterranean. East to Algeria along the P1 follow Ave

Mohammed V. **Bus**: CTM and other buses run into the Oued Nachef terminal, across the river from the town centre, take a petit-taxi to the town centre. Some CTM buses terminate in Place du 16 Août in the town centre. **Grand-taxis** from Nador, Berkane, Ahfir and the border terminate near Place du Maroc in the town centre, those for Figuig, Bouarfa and Taza stop at the bus station.

Places of interest

Oujda is not a very exciting city to visit for sightseeing. Its small medina is surrounded by the *ville nouvelle*, and is not particularly distinct from it, being a primarily 20th century quarter, with no notable buildings, but is pleasant to wander in. At night the streets are deserted and not very inviting. The area is partly surrounded by Merinid ramparts. Place du Maroc and Ave des Marchés are busy commercial areas with stalls, and with *souqs* alongside. From rue de Marrakech **Bab Ouled Amrane** leads into the *mellah*, Oujda's Jewish quarter.

The most animated part of the old town is around the Bab Ouahab at the end of Ave du Marché, where you will find the fish, meat and vegetable markets. Bab el Ouahab is the main gate to the medina where the heads of criminals used to be placed on poles.

Just outside the Bab el Ouahab is a large area where street entertainers used to perform for large crowds in the evenings. Sadly, the square has now been designated as a parking lot. Some of the former atmosphere can be enjoyed on the far side of Place Bab Ouahab, where there is also a junk market. Inside the gate is a large *kissaria*, or covered market, and a small area of *souqs*, a relaxing place in which to browse and bargain, best on Wed and Sun. The first of these is the busy **Souq el Ma**, or water market where the market gardeners used to come to draw water to irrigate their land is well worth a visit. It stands alongside the **Sidi Oqba Mosque**, with a striking minaret. Nearby is the busy **Souq el Knadsa**,

selling a wide range of traditional items. Turn left from the rue des Marchés, past vegetable stalls, into Place Al-Attarine, with the *koubba* of Sidi Abd el-Ouahab, as well as the 13th century Merinid **Grand Mosque** (one of the city's finest buildings) and **medressa**, built by Sultan Abu Yaqub. Adjacent to the Place is the kasbah, former residence of government officials. On rue el Ouahda is the **French Cathedral**, opening times: Mon-Thur 0700-1800, Fri 1500-1800; Sat-Sun 1200-1800. There are two other gates, of lesser importance but not to be missed, Bab Sidi Aissa and Bab Ahl Jamal.

The modern heart of Oujda is centred around the 1930s municipal clocktower on Place 16 Aôut and the central section of Blvd Mohammed V where the best cafés are concentrated and the evening promenade takes place.

The **Lalla Aicha** gardens are small, pleasant to wander in or relax. They contain the **Lalla Aicha ethnographic museum**, open 0900-1200 and 1430-1730. In the Lalla Meryem Park outside the walls which surround the kasbah one can find a place to rest and relax. Some of the vegetation is quite exotic. Here in the park is situated the **Museum of Traditional Arms**.

Following Blvd de Sidi Yahia 6 km from the medina takes one eventually to the **Shrine of Sidi Yahia** in the oasis of the same name which used to be an important meeting place. This is thought to be the tomb of St John the Baptist, and has been revered by Jews, Christians and Muslims. It is a pleasant area of trees around a stream, popular with pilgrims and visitors, with stalls, a few areas reserved for Muslims, and has two *moussems* (religious festivals) in honour of Sidi Yahia, in Aug and Sep. Take a town bus from Bab el Ouahab, they run every 10 mins and take 20 mins, or a petit-taxi to here from the city centre, perhaps for a picnic.

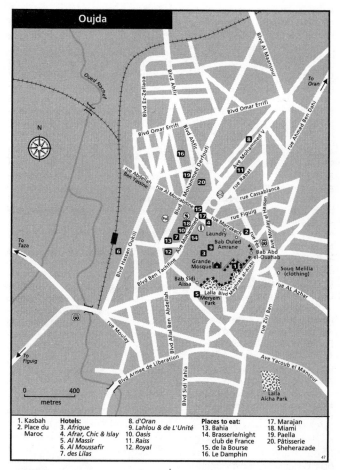

Oujda

1. Kasbah
2. Place du Maroc

Hotels:
3. Afrique
4. Afrar, Chic & Islay
5. Al Massir
6. Al Moussafir
7. des Lilas
8. d'Oran
9. Lahlou & de L'Unité
10. Oasis
11. Raiss
12. Royal

Places to eat:
13. Bahia
14. Brasserie/night club de France
15. de la Bourse
16. Le Damphin
17. Marajan
18. Miami
19. Paella
20. Pâtisserie Sheherazade

47

Local information
● Accommodation

NB Since the closure of the Algerian border in 1995, hotels in Oujda have seen a drastic fall in clientele and a consequent collapse in profits. For the time being, this often means no hot water, darkened corridors, poor plumbing, etc, as hotels struggle to economize. This state of affairs is particularly noticeable in some of the more expensive hotels, where, apart from the *Hotel Al Moussafir*, you can bargain prices down to half the official price.

B *Al Moussafir*, corner of Blvd Abdallah Chefchaouan and Place de la Gâre, T 688202, by far the best hotel in town, newly established as part of the Moussafir chain, airy, 72 semi-luxurious rms with a/c, TV, shower, telephone, professional management, bureau de change, pool, restaurant (menu MD112), parking.

C *Al Massir*, Blvd Maghreb al-Arabi, T 685300, one of several good hotels to have fallen on hard times, gloomy and almost empty at time of writing, no longer part of the Salam chain, it may be possible to obtain a room at a knock-down price if you bargain, pool, tennis, garden, bar.

D *Hotel des Lilas*, rue Jamal Eddine el-Afghani, T 680840, tranquil, clean and friendly hotel, tastefully decorations, central location, reliable hot water, heating, lift, garage, nice café; **D** *Hotel d'Oran*, Blvd Mohammed V, Route d'Alger, T 701001, tastefully decorated, comfortable and friendly family run hotel, very clean, efficient, reliable hot water, heating, all rooms with bath, TV, restaurant, expected to open in 1997; **D** *Hotel Raiss*, Blvd Mohammed V, Route d'Alger, T 703058, newly built, elegant, all rooms with bath, comfortable and very clean, enthusiastic staff, lift, café, TV, garage.

E *Hotel Royal*, 13 Blvd Zerkatouni, T 682284, large, 1930s hotel with 60 good rm, has seen better days, worth bargaining hard, no hot water at time of writing, insist on towels, soap, etc.

F *Hotel Afrah*, 15 rue de Tafna, T 686533, central position, clean and good value, but no hot water at time of writing; **F** *Hotel Afrique* or *Ifriqiya*, 2 Impasse Achakfane Barrani, T 682095, best choice in the medina, located just off rue Mazouzi (jewellery *souq*), clean but very simple, no showers; **F** *Hotel Chic*, 2 rue Ramdane El Gadhi just off Place 16 Août, small and simple, rms rather dark, no private bathrooms or hot water, good value; **F** *Hotel Isly*, 24 rue Ramdane El Gadhi, off Place 16 Août, T 683928, old fashioned French-style establishment, clean and pleasant but rather spartan, no hot water; **F** *Hotel Oasis*, 65 Blvd Mohammed V, T 683214, very similar to *Hotel Isly*, situated just off the main road. Other basic hotels in the medina include *Hotel Lahlou*, 96 rue Mazouzi, T 682122, and *Hotel de l'Unité*, down the narrow rue Ouled Rzine nr the Bab Ahl Jamal.

Camping: the nearest is at Saïdia on the coast (see page 170).

Youth hostel: 11 Blvd Allal ben Abdellah, T 680788, 45 beds, kitchen, meals available, bus 100m, train 500m, overnight fee MD20.

● **Places to eat**
♦♦♦*Brasserie Night-Club de France*, 87/89 Blvd Mohammed V, rather formal French-style establishment serving international cuisine; ♦♦♦*Restaurant Hotel Al Moussafir*, Place de la Gâre, T 688202, quality International and Moroccan food, impeccable service, set menu good value at MD120.

♦♦ *Restaurant Le Dauphin*, 38 rue de Berkane, T 686145, smart but homely fish restaurant, nice ambiance and welcoming owner; ♦♦*Restaurant Paella*, 83 Blvd Derfoufi, cheaper alternative to the Dauphin.

♦ *Allo Pizza*, nr *Sandwich Sindibad*, best choice for pizza eat-in or takeaway; ♦*Marajan*, 9 rue Tafna, Moroccan food, speciality is tagine MD30; ♦*Miami*, 67 Blvd Mohammed V, good for standard Moroccan cuisine; ♦ *Sandwich Sindibad*, 95 Blvd Derfoufi, good quality sandwiches, fruit juices, very popular with the younger crowd, busy, fast service.

Cafés & pâtisseries: the best cafés in Oujda are located in and around the central section of Blvd Mohammed V, try *La Bourse* on Blvd Mohammed V or the *Bon Acceuil*, on Place Jeddah. *Café Bahia* is the smartest, where the invariably male local élite while away the hours discussing business and politics. One of the best places for cakes is *Pâtisserie/Laiterie Sheherazade*, on rue Ben Attia, off Place Jeddah. A local speciality known as *karane* made from chick peas and eaten in a sandwich is sold from stalls on the Ave du Marché.

● **Banks & money changers**
Most banks are on Blvd Mohammed V where both the **Wafabank** and **Crédit de Maroc** have cashpoint machines. Outside normal banking hours, the main branch of the **BMCE** is open until 2200 and on Sat. Otherwise, there is the *Hotel Al Moussafir* bureau de change.

● **Embassies & consulates**
Algeria, 11 Blvd de Taza, T 683740-1; **France**, 16 rue Imam Lechaf, T 682705.

● **Hospitals & medical services**
Chemist: all night on rue de Marrakech, T 683490.

● **Laundry**
There are two or three places on rue Marrakeh. Try *Pressing Centrale*, 115 rue Marrakech.

● **Post & telecommunications**
Post Office: PTT, Ave Mohammed V/Place du Jeddah.

● **Shopping**
More expensive places than the *souqs* in which to shop, but good to sample the range of goods. *Bazar Ali Baba* on 36 Blvd Mohammed V is a good general handicraft store. Also try the artisanat shop at 23 Blvd Mazouzi for Saharan artifacts, basketware, old musical instruments and assorted folk souvenirs. For new

clothes, try the *Souq 'Melilla'*, a huge indoor warren of stalls located opp the Bab Abdel Ouahab. Boulevard Mazouzi in the medina is where all the jewellery boutiques are concentrated. For stocking up on travel food, the grocery shops on Blvd Derfoufi are a good bet.

Photography: *Photomagic*, rue Benattia off Place Jeddah.

● **Sports**
Sporting Tennis Club, T 682545, and **Riding Club**, T 682499.

● **Tour companies & travel agents**
Carlson Voyages, 26 Blvd Mohammed V, opp clocktower.

● **Tourist offices**
Delegation Regionale du Tourisme, Place du 16 Août, BP 424, T 684329 (open 0800-1200 and 1430-1830), unhelpful.

● **Useful telephone numbers**
Fire: T 15.
Police: T 19.

● **Transport**
Local Car hire: cars for rent are hard to find in Oujda and in every case very expensive. **Avis**, 110 Ave Allal ben Abdellah, T 683993, 684618, and at the airport; **Hertz**, 2 Immeuble El Baraka, Blvd Mohammed V, T 683802, Tx 61639, and at the airport. **Taxis**: petit-taxis are red. Watch out for unofficial red vehicles without signs. Taxi from Ave Mohammed V to Oued Nachaf bus station MD5.

Air T 682084. There are flights to Casablanca (6 a week), as well as to Amsterdam, Bastia in Corsica, Brussels, Dusseldorf, Frankfurt, Marseille and Paris. Take a grand-taxi from Place du Maroc. **Royal Air Maroc** has an office at the *Hotel Oujda*, Ave Mohammed V, T 683963-4, as does **Air France**.

Train The train station is on Place de l'Unité Africain, T 683133. Departures to **Tanger** (12 hrs): 0710, 2200; **Taza** (3½ hrs); **Fes** (6½ hrs) and **Meknes** (7½ hrs): 0710, 0945, 1930, 2120, 2200; **Rabat** (9½ hrs) and **Casablanca** (10½ hrs): 0945, 0930, 2120.

A goods train with a couple of supplementary passenger carriages leaves for Bouarfa every Sat at 2200 arriving at 0635 the following morning. It makes the return journey to Oujda at 0920 on Sun arriving at 1701 the same day. Convenient if you are heading for Figuig, especially in summer, when coach travel in the heat can be exhausting.

A question of colour

It takes more than a little imagination but the connoisseur can distinguish five quite different colours of camel. By far the most beautiful and the most expensive is the white camel and it is also claimed to be the fastest though that may just be an excuse to charge a higher price; the yellow beast is a very popular second; the red animal is solid, dependable and known as a good baggage animal; the blue is really black but called blue to avoid the evil eye and as such is not high in the popularity stakes, while a camel which is a mixture of white, red and yellow is just another unfortunate beast of burden.

Road CTM buses leave from 12 rue Sidi Brahim, just off Place du 16 Août, T 682047, to **Fes** (1100), **Nador** (0500, 1000, 1300, 1530) and **Casablanca** (2000, 2030), and from the Oued Nachaf bus station at Place du 3 Mars to Fes (0500, 1100) and **Nador** (0700, 1000, 1300, 1530). Private line buses leave from the Oued Nachaf bus station, T 682262, to **Casablanca** (0430, 0630, 1600, 1700, 1800, 1930, 2030), **Fes** (0500, 0830, 1100), **Meknes** (1430), **Taza** (0400, 0730, 0930, 1200, 1300), **Taourirt** (1400, 1500, 1600, 1700, 1730), **Midelt** (0600), **Figuig** (0600, 1000, 1500 – the earlier the better to avoid the heat), **Bouarfa** (0700, 1700), **Nador** (10 between 0200 and 1315: 2 hrs), **Al Hoceima** (1400), **Berkane** (9 between 0740 and 1315), **Saïdia** (0800, 0900, 1330, 1420, 1610), **Ahfir** (regularly from 0635 to 1740). **Taxi**: grand-taxis to Berkane, Ahfir (40 mins) and the border leave from just off Place du Maroc. For Saïdia change at Berkane or, preferably, Ahfir. Grand-taxis to Taza, Figuig and Bouarfa leave from by the bus station.

THE ALGERIAN BORDER
This border is closed.

SOUTH TOWARDS FIGUIG

The journey S by road is long, monotonous, and very hot and is to be avoided if possible in summer. Only the initial part of the road, climbing up towards the Col de Guerbouss

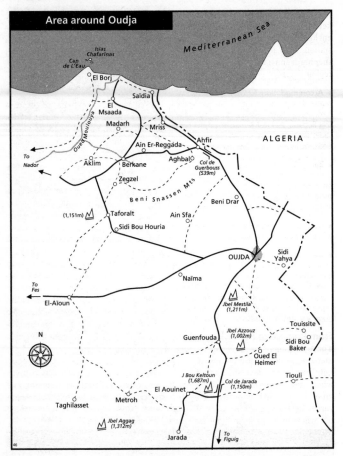

and the mining district of Jerada is green and varied. The rest of the route crosses the eastern edge of the vast Plateauof Rekkam, which extends across into the high plateaux of Algeria. The predominant vegetation here is a low carpet of esparto grass and wormwood stretching to the horizon. Travel by bus is punctuated by numerous frequent stops to pick up and set down shepherds who miraculously survive in this scorched, windswept emptiness. The only towns along the route are Guenfouda, Ain Beni Mathar, Tendrara, and Bouarfa, none of which holds much interest other than their remoteness and an opportunity to rest and buy basic provisions.

BOUARFA

The administrative and garrison town of Bouarfa serves as transport hub for the southeastern corner of Morocco. A stop here is unavoidable for those travelling to/from Er Rachidia. The town is well provided with shops and services. Market day is on Sat and it is held in the large enclosure off to the right below the bus station. It is a major event, attracting shepherds and traders from the whole SE region.

● **Accommodation** F *Hotel des Hauts Plateaux*, situated above the bus station by the mosque, panoramic location at the foot of the Jbel Bouarfa; F *Hotel Tamlatte*, on the high street below the bus station, above a café, clean, well-ventilated rms with attractive tiling.

● **Banks & money changers** The only bank with an exchange facility is the Banque Populaire, some distance from the centre. To get there, turn left at the foot of the high street and then right at the next junction.

● **Hospitals & medical services Chemists**: two pharmacies on the main street.

● **Transport Train** The weekly train from Bouarfa to Oujda leaves at 0920 on Sun and arrives there at 1701. The return journey is the following Sat at 2200 getting into Bouarfa on the Sun at 0635. **Road** Buses from Oujda to Figuig pass through Bouarfa. There are two buses a day to Er Rachidia.

From Bouarfa to Figuig

The route from Bouarfa to Figuig is mesmerizing in its isolation and quality of light, particularly along the final stretch, where the valley narrows. Here the ground is covered with an impressive variety of aromatic herbs, which survive on what little precious moisture is trapped in this dry valley. As a result, the produce of the herds which graze here is very tasty. Dew-fed mushrooms, which grow overnight, are picked by the local shepherds and sometimes sold in Figuig.

FIGUIG

Tucked away in the extreme SE corner of Morocco, right next to the Algerian border, and an incredible 400 km S of Oujda, Figuig is a great place to relax for a few days and enjoy the pristine desert environment. The beauty of the place is not instantly apparent, but some gentle exploration away from the centre of town soon dispels this impression. Its frontier location has given Figuig (*alt* 900m) a strategic significance, and it has often been fought over between the Moroccan sultanate and the powers to the E, most recently in 1963 and 1975, between the armies of Morocco and Algeria. A recent souring of relations between the two countries has resulted in the closure of the border, which has meant even fewer visitors to this least-frequented of the southern oases. There are an estimated 100,000 palm trees but no need to check this figure.

Figuig offers a choice of excursions. One can enjoy its semi desert climate, the nearby historical monuments and the varieties of fauna in the numerous small oases of the region, of which Figuig is one of the best.

The case of the sleeping foetus

Today a Moroccan child is considered to be legitimate if it is born no sooner than 6 months after the marriage and no later than a year after the marriage ends. This is recent legislation. Previously the belief in the sleeping foetus, *raqqad*, had allowed that a woman could be pregnant for up to 5 years.

According to still popular belief, for a reason which cannot be explained, the embryo falls asleep in the womb. It is eventually woken by a spell, divine intervention ... who knows? and begins to develop. During the 'sleep' the embryo shrinks and does not prevent menstruation. Once it begins to expand menstruation ceases. The jurist who founded the Maliki school, the most influential school of law in the Maghreb, is said to have been conceived before his father's death and born 3 years later. To doubt this and the claims of many who say they are the living proof of this condition is to doubt their legitimacy, a gross insult. Shhh ...

Figuig is composed of seven distinct villages situated on two levels: the upper level consists of Ksour El-Oudaghir, which straddles the main road where most shops and facilities are located, and the adjacent villages of El-Maiz, El-Abid, Ouled Slimane, and El-Hammam; the lower plain, or 'Baghdad' as it is known here, supports a large area of palmgroves connected by a network of alleyways, with Zenaga, the largest of the *ksour*, in the middle. The two levels are separated from each other by an escarpment, the Djorf. A platform with excellent views over the lower half of Figuig can be reached by turning right at the bottom of the main street, through the small market enclosure (Fri *souq*), and following a narrow path across fields. On the horizon is a gap between two mountains which marks the Moroccan/Algerian frontier.

Until recently, each of the *ksour* of Figuig was independent, and their history was one of continuous feuding with each other, mainly over the issue of water. Centuries of management and protection of this precious resource have moulded the appearance of each *ksar*, with their watchtowers, high walls, and winding irrigation channels. Of all the *ksour*, Zenaga has the most to offer, being the largest and most distinctive. The centre of Zenaga has a pleasant square with a café and a mosque from where several alleyways radiate into the palmery. El Hammam, to the E with its hot springs used for bathing, and El-Maiz with its vaulted streets and arcaded square are also worth visiting. A good panorama of the Figuig ensemble can be obtained in the evening (for the best light) from the rocky pass situated on the road that encircles Figuig to the W. Another worthwhile excursion is to the Oued Zousfana Valley and the Taghla Pass 4 km to the SE of the administrative centre, from where there are brilliant views. To avoid arousing the suspicions of border guards, it is advisable to notify the police station if visiting the Zousfana and surrounding hills.

Local information
● Accommodation
At the time of writing there is only one functioning hotel in Figuig, the basic *Hotel Meliasse*, next to the petrol station at the entrance to the town, this unfinished construction offers no comforts, and is freezing cold on winter nights. Enquire at the petrol station – it may be possible to camp in the grounds of the attractive *Hotel/Camping Diamand Vert*, T (06)99030, which is expected to reopen in the near future.

● Places to eat
There are no proper restaurants in Figuig, but the following two places do simple meals (eg omlette): ◆ *Café Oasis*, situated in the municipal gardens at the end of the main street, Ave Hassan II. ◆ *Café Moussa*, down in Zenaga new town (take second turning signposted for Zenaga after Hotel/Camping), garden at rear with a stage, where concerts are sometimes held.

● Banks & money changers
Banque Populaire, on the main street.

● Hospitals & medical services
Chemist: on the main street or in Zenaga.

● Transport
Road Bus: buses leave from Ave Hassan II, in front of the *Hotel Sahara*, which operates as the ticket office. There are four buses a day to Oujda 0500, 0645, 0815, 1400 (later service is

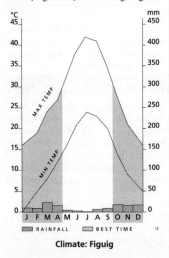

Climate: Figuig

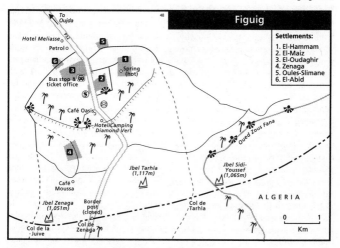

Settlements:
1. El-Hammam
2. El-Maiz
3. El-Oudaghir
4. Zenaga
5. Oules-Slimane
6. El-Abid

irregular) enquire from ticket office and a daily morning service to Er Rachidia.

From Bouarfa to Er Rachidia

With the border closed, there is little choice but to retrace one's steps from Figuig to Bouarfa and from there on to Er Rachidia (or Oujda if you are travelling anticlockwise). The hauntingly dramatic landscape along the P32 more than compensates for the lack of facilities and places of interest along the route.

For the first 70m or so the road runs close to the Algerian border along the broad plain of Tamlelt with little but telephone poles to break the horizon. The first stop is the dusty mud-brick village of Aïn Ech Chair 1 km off to the left, with a tiny café and grocery shop, that comes alive briefly for the twice-daily bus service. Not surprisingly travellers are the object of great curiosity here. 12 km beyond the village, inaccessible from Moroccan side of the disputed border, stands the isolated monument to General Leclerc.

The next settlement is **Bouanane** the first significant palm oasis, situated on the *oued* river of the same name. The village's reddish-brown buildings, gardens and leafy streets make for a pleasant halfway stop; there is an attractive porticoed square with a café away from the main road. North of the town along the bed of the *oued* is the picturesque Kasbah of Takoumit and beyond it a rough network of mountain tracks that can be explored with a 4WD vehicle.

About 35 km further on, on the left, is the mysterious and elusive oasis of Sahli, with its low profile desert architecture seeming to merge into the utterly barren surroundings. The inhabitants of Sahli are regarded as Sharifians, descendants of the Prophet Mohammed.

Boudenib (*Pop* est 15,000) is a rather forlorn and uninviting military town which in colonial times operated as the French military quarters for Southern Morocco. The town has a central garden square where the buses stop. There is only one very basic hotel.

After more desert, the P32 finally joins the P21 (and civilization!) close to the source of the Oued Meski. It is a further 18 km from here to Er Rachidia along a flat and relatively fertile stretch of the Ziz Valley. Er Rachidia is described in detail on page 384.

Scorpions – the original sting in the tail

Scorpions really deserve a better press. They are fascinating creatures, provided they no not lurk in your shoe or shelter in your clothes.

Scorpions are not insects. They belong to the class Arachnida as do spiders and daddy longlegs. There are about 750 different kinds of scorpions. The average size is a cosy 6 cms but the largest, *Pandinus imperator*, the black Emperor scorpion of West Africa, is a terrifying 20 cm long. The good news is that only a few are really dangerous. The bad news is that some of these are found in North Africa.

They really are remarkable creatures with the ability to endure the hottest desert climates, revive after being frozen in ice, and survive for over a year without food or water. They have a remarkable resistance to nuclear radiation, a characteristic yet to be proved of great use.

Scorpions are nocturnal. They shelter during the heat of the day and to keep cool wave their legs in the air. They feed on insects and spiders, grasping their prey with their large claw-like pincers, tearing it apart and sucking the juices. Larger scorpions can devour lizards and small mammals.

Their shiny appearance is due to an impervious wax coating over their hard outer shell which protects them from any water loss. They have very small eyes and depend on their better developed senses of touch and smell. The sensitive bristles on the legs point in all directions and pick up vibrations of movements of potential prey or enemies. This sensitivity gives them ample warning to avoid being seen by heavy-footed humans.

The oft reported 'courtship dance' before mating is merely repeated instinctive actions. The grasping of claws and the jerky 'dance' movements from side to side are a prelude to copulation during which the male produces spermatozoa in a drop of sticky fluid to which the female is led so that they may enter her body. The male departs speedily after the 'dance' to avoid being attacked and devoured.

Scorpions bear live young. After hatching, the young crawl on to the female's back and are carried there for two or three weeks until their first moult. They gradually drop off after that time and have to fend for themselves.

Most scorpions retreat rather than attack. They sting in self-defence. The sting is a hard spine and the poison is made in the swelling at the base. The sole of the bare foot, not surprisingly, is most often the site of a sting, and the advice in the section on Health (**see page 494**) is not to be ignored. The African

fat-tailed scorpion (we do not recommend measuring the size) is described as aggressive and quick-tempered. It is responsible for most of the reported stings to humans and most of the human fatalities in North Africa. The beautifully named *Buthus occitanus*, the small **Mediterranean yellow scorpion** and *Leirus quinquestriatus*, the **African golden scorpion**, also have neurotoxic stings that can be fatal.

Northern and Central Atlantic Coast

THE ATLANTIC COAST has a wide variety of environments, reflecting its great length. At its centre is the immense axis of cities which dominate the country demographically, industrially, economically and politically, from Kenitra in the N, through Sale, Rabat, Mohammedia, to Casablanca in the South. This massive city, the second largest in Africa, has many of the facilities and problems of cities elsewhere in the Third World and is just as typical of modern Morocco as Fes or Marrakech. Elsewhere are a series of walled cities, initially built by the Portuguese, and now often relaxed beach resorts, including Asilah, El Jadida, Safi and Essaouira.

THE NORTHERN COAST

ASILAH

Asilah, also 'Arzila', is a striking fishing port and coastal town of white and blue houses, surrounded by ramparts and lying alongside an extensive beach. As the

> "Surrounded by the still imposing zone of its old, ruinous grey ramparts, covered with lichen that preys upon them, the ancient town, so often captured and recaptured, is quietly dying away in the proud sepulchre of its lofty decaying walls ...."
>
> Montbard, George, *Among the Moors* (1894).

first stopping point S of Tanger about 40 km by road or rail, it provides an excellent introduction to Morocco, in spite of the extent to which tourism dominates. If it is possible, visit in Aug for the cultural festival, the *International Festival of Asilah*.

History

Asilah, the name means *authentic*, stands on a site once occupied by the Phoenicians, who called it *Silis*, or *Zilis*, and later by the Carthaginians, Byzantines and Romans in Anthony's reign. After destruction by the Romans, the town was rebuilt in 966 by El Hakim II, ruler of Cordoba. It was the last stronghold of the Idrissid Dynasty. The Portuguese occupied Asilah from 1471, and built the town's impressive fortifications, and in

1578 King Sebastian landed there on his way to defeat in the *Battle of the Three Kings*. This defeat led to the Spanish absorption of Portugal, and thus of Asilah, but the Portuguese influence on the town is still quite discernible.

The Moroccans recovered Asilah in 1691, under Moulay Ismail. In 1826 Austria bombarded Asilah, then a base of piracy, as did the Spanish in 1860. In the late 19th and early 20th century Ahmed al-Rasouli, the bandit chief who terrorized much of the NW of Morocco, was based in the town, as described by his one time hostage and later friend, Walter Harris, in *Morocco That Was*. Al-Rasouli built his palace in the medina, and from it exercised power over much of the region, being for a time its governor. The Spanish took Asilah in 1911, as part of their protectorate of N Morocco.

ACCESS Train The train station is just to the N of the town, a distance which can be walked, or if heavily laden, travelled in a taxi or local bus. There are frequent trains from Tanger, so this is a practical day excursion. **Road** Just off the P2 from Tanger to Rabat. Buses arrive in the town centre, 5 mins walk from the medina. Grand-taxis take an hour from Tanger, and drop passengers a short walk from the medina, near the bus station.

Places of interest

The **medina** is the main interest of Asilah, a quarter of predominately white and blue buildings, reflecting in their design the influences of Portuguese and Spanish occupation. Note the modern murals on some of the houses in the medina, painted by artists during the festival. The ramparts were built by the Portuguese in the 15th century, and are broken by a number of important gates, including **Bab el Kasbah**, **Bab el Bahar**, 'the sea gate', **Bab el Hamar** 'the land gate', an impressive structure topped with the eroded Portuguese coat of arms, as well as **Bab el Jbel**, 'the mountain gate', and **Bab Ihoumer**. At points it is possible to climb the fortifications for impressive views of the town and along the coast. Within the medina, **Le Palais de la Culture** is a cultural centre converted from the former residence of the brigand Ahmed al-Rasouli, built in 1909 right beside the sea. It is difficult to gain access except during the festival, but it is quite possible to visualize those who incurred al-Rasouli's wrath being made to walk the plank from the palace windows over the cliff front.

The Souq The Thur market attracts farmers from the surrounding area. In addition to the sale of the usual fruit, spices and vegetables, handicrafts distinctive of the Rif region are also on display.

The International Festival of Asilah, a cultural festival which has taken place in Asilah since 1978, involves performers from all over the world. Events throughout the town each Aug attract many spectators.

The **beach** is often windy, frequented by bathers, men touting camel rides, and fishermen, but at times can be quite perfect. The beach stretches beyond the building works to the N of the city, and to the S.

Local information

● **Accommodation**

C *Hotel Al Khaima*, Km 2, Route de Tanger, BP 101, T 917230, F 917566, 113 rm with bath, some with telephones, on N edge of town with restaurant, disco, bar, pool, tennis.

D *Hotel Ouad El Makhazine*, Ave Melilla, T 917090, 917500, 36 rm with a/c, with showers, best hotel in the town centre, restaurant, bar and café, pool and telephone, atmosphere is not exciting; **D** *Hotel Mansur*, 49 Ave Mohammed V, T 917390, 8 rm with bath, is a reliable choice.

E *Hotel l'Oasis*, 8 Place des Nations Unies, T 917186, 12 rm, an old palace with restaurant and bar.

F *Hotel Asilah*, 79 Ave Hassan II, T 917286, 11 rm, reasonable, friendly and central; **F** *Hotel Marhaba*, 9 rue Zallakah, T 917144, nr the medina, adequate and cheap, rooms poorly sound-proofed but with colourful decor; **F** *Hotel Nasr*, Place Zallakah, cheap and basic;

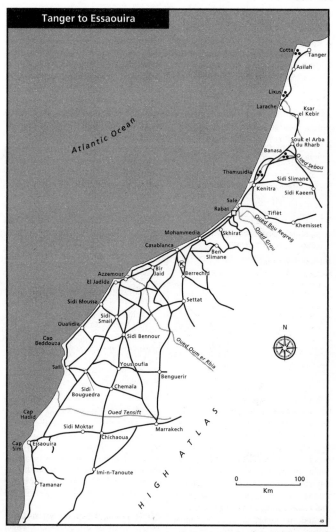

Tanger to Essaouira

F *Hotel Sahara*, 9 rue Tarfaya, T 917185, 24 rm, not very exciting.

Camping: there are numerous camping sites just N of the town along the road to Asilah, incl *Camping International*, site of 1 ha, 5m to beach, showers, laundry, petrol 300m, elec-tricity for caravans, petrol 200m; *Camping Atlas*, 110m to beach, snacks, showers, laundry, grocery, first aid, electricity for caravans; *Camping Ocean*, site of 1 ha, 30m to beach, grocery, showers, laundry, electricity for cara-vans, petrol at 200m; *Camping Echrigui*,

T 917182, with a shop and restaurant; and the adjacent *As Saadi* which is rec.

● **Places to eat**
◆◆*La Alcazaba*, 2 Place Zallakah outside the ramparts, T 917012, an excellent Italian/Spanish restaurant concentrating on fish and seafood dishes; *Casa Garcia*, rue Ya'qub al-Mansur, is also rec for similar food. ◆*El Espignon* and *El Oceano* are both on Place Zallach just outside the ramparts. Several places here sell excellent and very fresh fish dishes.

● **Banks & money changers**
Banque Hispano-Marocaine, Place Mohammed V, T 917321.

● **Hospitals & medical services**
Chemist: *Pharmacie Loukili*, Ave de la Liberté, T 917278.
Hospital: Ave du 2 Mars, T 917318.

● **Post & telecommunications**
PTT, Place des Nations Unies.

● **Useful addresses**
Police: Ave de la Liberté, T 19 or 917089.

● **Transport**
Train Asilah railway station is just outside the town alongside the P2 to Tanger, T 987320, and can be reached by local bus, by either petite or grand-taxi from Place Mohammed V. There are six trains daily to **Tanger**; 4 daily to **Meknes**, **Fes** and **Oujda** and 2 daily to **Rabat** and **Casablanca**.

Road Bus: the bus station is on Ave de la Liberté, T 987354. There are regular bus links with Tanger, Ouezzane, Tetouan, Meknes, Rabat and Casablanca. **Taxi**: grand-taxis which are particularly convenient for Tanger, leave from Place Mohammed V.

LARACHE

Although with less appeal than Asilah, Larache is a relaxed, faded seaside town, with a good beach and not too many tourists, a halfway house between Spanish and Moroccan urban life. The town is easily reached by the P2 from either Tanger or Rabat. The bus station is just off Ave Hassan II.

Larache is called El Araish in Arabic, a name which refers to the vine arbours of the Beni Arous, a local tribe. The occupation of the area dates back to the

Phoenician, Carthaginian and Roman settlement of nearby **Lixus**. Larache was occupied by the Spanish from 1610 to 1689, and as part of their protectorate, from 1911. They then added the harbour and the new town, using it as the principal port of their N Morocco zone. Larache has fruit processing and exporting activities, as well as fishing, but has lost its status as a major port. Amongst a small foreign population a former resident of Larache was Jean Genet, French playwright, now buried in the Spanish graveyard.

Places of interest
On the way into Larache from Rabat, travellers pass **La Cigogne** (also called Castillo de las Ciguenas or Al Fath), a large fort built either by Moulay Ahmed al-Mansur and his Christian slaves in 1578, or during the subsequent Spanish occupation. The 16th century **Kebibat Fortress** is near the port, seeming to rise out of the sea, and now used as a hospital. Ave Mohammed V is the main street of the new town, with gardens on either side as well as a castle on the right and the **Iglesia de Nuestra Señora del Pilar** on the left (as heading to the centre). The circular Place de la Liberation with a fountain, is the heart of the town, lying between the medina and the new town.

Bab el Khemis leads off Place de la Liberation to the medina, a poor quarter but with some architectural appeal. Just inside is the Spanish built market square. There is a number of *souqs* in the medina, notably **Socco de la Alcaiceria**, the cloth market, a picturesque sight, in an otherwise unexciting old town. At the edge of the medina is the **Moroccan National Academy of Music**, built by the Spanish in 1915, near to an **Archaeological Museum**, T 912091, open 0900-1200 and 1500-1730, Wed-Sun. This palace was the home of Sultan Youssef Adbelhak el Merini between 1258 and 1281 and was used by the Spanish for state occasions.

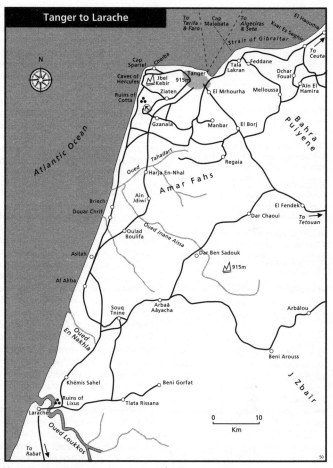

Tanger to Larache

To Tarifa & Faro
Cap Malabata
To Algeciras & Sete
Ksar Es Seghir
El Haouma
To Ceuta
Strait of Gibraltar

N

Cap Spartel
Ghilba
Tala Lakran
Feddane
Dchar Foual
Aïn El Hamira
Caves of Hercules
Jbel Kebir 915m
Tanger
Ziaten
El Mrhourha
Melloussa
Ruins of Cotta
Gzanaïa
Manbar
El Borj
Bahra Puiyene
Atlantic Ocean
Tahadart
Oued
Harja En-Nhal
Regaia
Amar Fahs
Briech
Aïn Jdiwi
Douar Chrit
El Fendek
To Tetouan
Oulad Boulifa
Oued Jnane Aïssa
Dar Chaoui
Asilah
Dar Ben Sadouk
915m
Al Akba
Souq Tnine
Arbaâ Aâyacha
Arbâlou
Oued En Nakhla
Beni Arouss
J Zbaïr
Khémis Sahel
Beni Gorfat
Ruins of Lixus
Tlata Rissana
Larache
Oued Loukkos
To Rabat

0   10
Km

50

Now it displays a range of Moroccan archaeological material, coins, musical instruments, statues. Some of these items are from Lixus. The medina is surrounded by a thick rampart. Through this **Bab el Kasbah** leads through to the ruined mediaeval kasbah.

For the main beach take town bus No 4, or a boat across the estuary. This is an extensive strip of fine beach, with a number of cafés nearby.

Local information
● Accommodation

D *Hotel Riad*, Ave Moulay Mohammed Ben Abdellah, T 912626/29, Tx 33803, a converted former residence of the Duchess of Guise, large well-maintained gardens, good restaurant and bar, tennis and pool, 24 rm, half-board required.

E *Gran Hotel España*, 6 Ave Hassan II/Place de la Liberation, T 913195, is the best cheap option.

F *Hotel Cervantes*, Place de la Liberation, a rather dismal place; the *pensiones* just off Ave Moulay Mohammed Ben Abdellah, **F** *Pensión Es-Saada*; **F** *Pensión Amal*, T 912788; and **F** *Pensión Palmera*; and *Pensión Atlas* in the medina.

● **Places to eat**

◆◆ *Restaurant Al Khozama*, 114 Ave Mohammed V, T 914454.

◆ Cheaper eating options are *La Grotte de Pêche*, 7 rue Tarik Ibn Ziad, a fish restaurant; *Le Medina*, a small Moroccan place in the medina; *Restaurant Oscar*, just off Ave Mohammed V; and *Restaurant Larache*, on Ave Moulay Mohammed Ben Abdellah.

● **Shopping**

Ensemble Artisanal is on the road out to Rabat.

● **Tourist offices**

There is a **Syndicat d'Initiative** on Ave Mohammed V, T 913532.

EXCURSION TO ANCIENT LIXUS

Lixus is perhaps the second most important Roman site in Morocco after Volubilis, and lies just N of Larache on the right bank of the Oued Loukkos. It is about 4 km from the sea and stands on a small prominence known as Tchemich hill which is no more than about 50m above sea level but kept the town out of the water-logged area drained by the *oued*. Immediately after the bridge look out for a sign to Plage Las Rimmel. Some writers located at Lixus the Garden of Hesperides, with the golden apples harvested by Hercules (see box, page 254) to gain his place on Mt Olympus more likely to have been oranges. This is all most unlikely as the first traces of settlement date from around 7th-6th century BC while the oldest building is dated at 4th century BC. There was a 7th century Phoenician and later a Carthaginian settlement here, and after the fall of Carthage a Roman colony, with particular importance under the Emperor Claudius I, when it exported salt, olives and fish. Lixus had a strategic position on the road from Tingis (Tanger) to Sala Colonia (Rabat) and was occupied until the 5th century AD.

To reach the site follow the Tanger road out of the town, take a bus across from the town, or bus No 4. The site is open during daylight hours. It is not enclosed, entry is free. If you wander in someone will come and offer to show you round. The lower town includes several 'factories' for fish salting and the manufacture of *garum* paste. The upper town includes a necropolis complex, with a large sanctuary, with temples, eight have been excavated, dating back as far as the 7th century BC. The largest temple which covers 1,500 sq m is dated to the reign of Juba II. Between the two parts of the site are a bath house with mosaics of Neptune and shellfish, a small semi-circular amphitheatre and theatre.

Beyond Lixus the road to the beach has picnic and camping areas, salt flats and traditional shipbuilding.

KSAR EL KEBIR, ARBAOUA, SOUQ EL ARBA DU GHARB AND MOULAY BOUSSELHAM

Ksar el Kebir means the 'Great Fortress' and stands on the most probable site of the Roman colony *Oppidum Novum*. The exact location cannot be certain and there is not a lot to go on. Two funerary inscriptions were found here, one in Greek and one in Latin, recycled with other 'Roman' ashlar blocks in the construction of the Great Mosque. There was also, but no longer, a bronze statue of a bacchante. In its favour Ksar el Kebir has a number of Roman bits and pieces to the N and W and if the Romans had wanted to cross the Oued Loukkos, where better than here? An 11th century settlement here was expanded and fortified by Ya'qub al-Mansur in the late 12th century. Near the town in 1578 was fought the famous Battle of Three Kings, where King Sebastian of Portugal, Saadian Sultan Abd al-Malek, and a claimant to the throne, former Sultan El Mutawakkil, all died. Moulay Ismail destroyed much of the town in the 17th century. The Spanish occupied Ksar el Kebir in 1911, rebuilding it and calling it Alcazarquivir, and developing it as a military centre. There is a large regional market (Sun) outside the station, as well as permanent *souqs* throughout the town, and a tannery. The town has an Almohad **Grand Mosque**, near to a Merinid *medressa*. **Accommodation F** *Café-Hotel Andaluz*, very basic. *Getting there*: there are six trains a day to Tanger, 4 a day to Fes, Meknes and Oujda, 4 a day to Rabat and Casablanca, and 2 a day to Marrakech.

Arbaoua lies to the W of the P2, the trees providing shade for a popular picnic area in summer, although mosquitoes can be a nuisance. **Accommodation E** *Hotel Route de France*, T (07) 902668, 26 rm with bath, restaurant serves medium range meals, speciality is rabbit. A splendid lunch stop. **Camping**: on a site of 4 ha, has showers, laundry, electricity for caravans, and is convenient for the train station.

Souq el Arba du Gharb is an important market town, with a *souq* each Wed, at the centre of the rich agricultural region of the Gharb, which extends as far N as Larache, and as far S as Kenitra. This region has been important for cereal, and then citrus and vegetable, production.

● **Accommodation E** *Hotel Gharb*, Route de Rabat-Tanger, T 902203, 902441, with a restaurant and bar; also a number of basic hotels and restaurants, but little else.

● **Transport** There are regular trains to Tanger, Meknes, Fes, Oujda, Rabat, Casablanca and to Marrakech, as well as regular

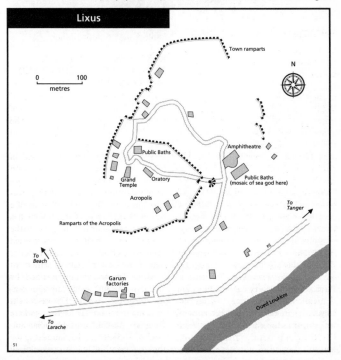

Lixus

0   100
metres

N

Town ramparts

Public Baths

Amphitheatre

Grand Temple   Oratory

Public Baths (mosaic of sea god here)

Acropolis

Ramparts of the Acropolis

To Tanger

To Beach

P2

Garum factories

To Larache

Oued Loukkos

51

Neptune from a mosaic, Lixus

buses and grand taxis to Ouezzane and Moulay Bousselham.

Moulay Bousselham is a small beach resort with a relaxed atmosphere and rough swimming conditions. Although easily reached from Souq el Arba du Gharb, only 44 km along the S216, Moulay Bousselham is bypassed by most tourists. The place is named after a 10th century saint, supposed to have come from Egypt and to have converted the Atlantic Ocean to Islam. He is commemorated in a nearby *koubba*, and a festival, or *moussem*, in Jul. The beach is spectacular but dangerous for swimming, although not bad for fishing. The lagoon, Merja Zerja, is one of Morocco's largest lagoons covering over 30 sq km. This and the surrounding wetlands are a designated reserve offering protection for migrating and over-wintering water birds.

By car it is possible to approach the reserve from the S. Proceed from Souq el Arba du Gharb and after 34 km turn left on the 2301. After crossing the Nador Channel (Canal de Daoura) turn sharp right and park in the village, Daoura Oulad Mesbah. Access to the reserve from Moulay Bousselham is across the Oued Drade which flows to the S of the village. Arrange a lift or hire a rowing boat. Bargain firmly. Be sure to arrange for a return trip with the fisherman who ferries you across. The track down the W side of the lagoon goes through Daoura Roissia and eventually to the minor coast road but provides ample opportunity for peaceful observation. It is estimated that half of the ducks and small waders wintering in Morocco N of latitude 30°N are found here. It will be impossible to miss the Greater Flamingos and Spoonbills and the familiar Wigeon, Mallard, Shoveler, Shelduck and Teal. Sighting a Slender-billed Curlew is less likely. **Accommodation**

D *Hotel le Lagon*, T 902603, with restaurant, bar, nightclub and pool; at the cafés; or at the basic *Camping Moulay Bousselham*, site of 15 ha, bar, snacks, restaurant, grocery shop, pool, showers, laundry, electricity for caravans, petrol at 100m. Eat at *L'Ocean*.

EXCURSION TO ANCIENT BANASA

Banasa, easy access from the S210, is situated to the S bank of the Oued Sebou which was probably bridged at that time. Excavation is not easy as any pre-Roman remains are buried beneath many layers of alluvium deposited by the flooding *oued*. The earliest settlement recorded here was 3rd century BC but the main colony was founded at the end of the 1st century BC by Caesar Augustus. Remains include vestiges of houses (some giving indication of wealthy owners) and baths (five have been found during excavations) and shops. There was a wealth of pottery, mosaics and inscriptions. Banasa pottery was of a distinctive style. The alignment of the streets on a NE-SW

Three graces from a mosaic at Bansa

grid has been discerned with a forum in the centre of the town, but most of the material has been removed and 'recycled'. A discovery here of a number of bronze inscriptions, legal texts, military diplomas and decrees of patronage make this an important site.

A few mosaics have been found on the site. They include an ornamental design with the head of Ocean in the centre from one of the excavated baths; one containing fighting cocks and a bag of money which needs no explanation and a number with marine scenes.

Allal Tazi grew up as the centre of the rice growing area on the marshy land.

EXCURSION TO ANCIENT THAMUSIDA

There are remains of Roman **Thamusida** (Sidi Ali ben Ahmed) on the left bank of the Oued Sebou 18 km from the *oued* mouth, just off the P2 some 10 km N of Kenitra. The most distinctive feature for finding this site is the *koubba* of Sidi Ali ben Ahmed. Access in wet weather is quite a problem. It was in an excellent position, protected from flooding (being on a flattish hillock about 12m above sea level) but accessible from the sea by boats of considerable size making use of the tidal flow and had been settled on and off since prehistoric times. Its first official mention was by Ptolemy. The Roman garrison was established here under the Flavians and monuments have been found dating from that period. These include (the remains of) a temple with three shrines beside the *oued*, the Baths and some dwellings one named, with some lack of imagination, the House of the Stone Floor. The House of Dallage to the E of the complex has the traditional open central courtyard with the *triclinium* at the eastern end and the *exèdre* on the southern side.

The baths, close to the *oued* having been altered and extended a number of times finally covering an area of around 3,000 sq m, the ground plan showing a

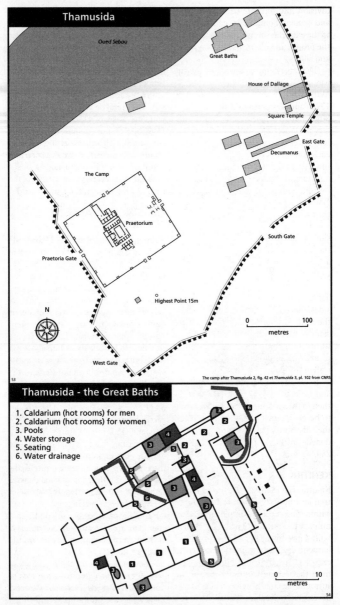

Thamusida

Oued Sebou

Great Baths

House of Dallage

Square Temple

East Gate

Decumanus

The Camp

Praetorium

South Gate

Praetoria Gate

○ Highest Point 15m

N

West Gate

0   100
metres

The camp after Thamusiuda 2, fig. 42 et *Thamusida* 3, pl. 102 from CNRS

53

Thamusida - the Great Baths

1. Caldarium (hot rooms) for men
2. Caldarium (hot rooms) for women
3. Pools
4. Water storage
5. Seating
6. Water drainage

0   10
metres

54

division into separate sections for men and women. Some evidence also points to the existence of fish salting works for the production of *gargum*, an iron works and shops.

The large camp to the SW of the site was constructed at the instruction of Marcus Aurelius. It measures 166m by 139m and is considered to have been large enough to house a substantial military presence. The walls of the fort had four gates, one more or less central in each wall and 14 towers which project inwards. In the centre is the praetorium, a rectangular porticoed courtyard 45m by 30m with rooms on three sides, the NW, SW and SE. In the SW side one of the rooms is larger, is built on a podium and reached by four steps. On the NW side of the praetorium, projecting into the main courtyard, are the remains of a hall constructed at the time of Septimus Severus.

A wall with a number of entrance gates encloses the town on the three land sides, the fourth side being protected by the *oued*. At intervals along the wall are semicircular towers which project outwards. In it construction use was made of existing buildings, such as the SW wall of the camp.

Excavations began in the early 1930s and from these it is suggested that although the settlement could be assumed to be prosperous and quite active into the 3rd century the whole area was abandoned quite suddenly between 274 and 280.

KENITRA

Kenitra (*Pop* 188,194 (1982)) is an industrial and military centre of importance within Morocco. It was a small Moroccan military fort until 1913 when the French built a new town, as well as an artificial harbour used as a military port and to export citrus fruit and other products from the rich agricultural areas of the surrounding Gharb region. The port was developed to replace Larache, in the Spanish zone, and Tanger, in the International Zone. In 1933 the French renamed Kenitra Port Lyautey, after their first Resident-General of the Moroccan Protectorate. US troops landed here in Nov 1942 as part of Operation Torch, and experienced heavy casualties under fire from the port at Mehdiya, but from 1947 the USA returned to establish an important naval base, which they used until 1977. After Independence Port Lyautey was renamed Kenitra. Kenitra is still important as military centre and port. It lies on the P2 from Rabat to Tanger, close to the beach at Mehdiya.

● **Accommodation** C *Hotel Safir*, Place Administrative, T 365600, Tx 91995, good but unexciting, from an established chain with restaurant, bar, nightclub and pool; **D** *Hotel Mamora*, Ave Hassan II, T 363007, 365006, with a good restaurant and bar, nightclub and pool; **E** *Hotel la Rotonde*, 50 Ave Mohammed Diouri, T 363343/4, with a restaurant and bar; as well as cheaper hotels along Ave Mohammed V. **Camping**: *Camping la Chenaie*, T 363373, site of 3 ha, showers, first aid, electricity for caravans, restaurant, grocery shop, petrol 400m.

● **Places to eat** There is no shortage of restaurants on Ave Hassan II and Ave Mohammed V. *Hotel Mamora* and *Hotel la Rotonde* are rec as places to eat and drink.

● **Post & telecommunications** Post Office: Ave Mohammed V.

● **Sports** Flying and gliding: *Royal Aéroclub de Kenitra*, at local airport, T 772183. Horse riding: at *Club Equestre de la Mamora*, the Hippodrome. **Tennis**: at the *Tennis Club de Kenitra*, Ave des Sports, BP 131, T 363160, which has six courts. **Watersports**: wind surfing and yachting organized through *Union Athlétique de Kenitra*, Clos Dublin Kenitra, T 362012.

● **Tourist offices** Syndicat d'Initiative on Ave Mohammed V, T (07) 162277; **Royal Air Maroc**, 435 Blvd Mohammed V, T 376234.

● **Transport** Train From the railway station, T 365095, 363402, trains leave regularly to Asilah, Tanger, Meknes, Fes, Oujda and Marrakech, and there are almost hourly services to Rabat and Casablanca between 0400 and

2309. **Road** The bus station is on Ave Mohammed V.

MEHDIYA

This is the beach for Kenitra, noted for windsurfing but more interesting to visit for its kasbah, and the nearby **nature reserve** around Lac de Sidi Bourhaba. Mehdiya is 11 km from Kenitra, with plentiful grand-taxis and there is a bus service up the P2 from Rabat to Kenitra.

It has been suggested that a Carthaginian trading post was established here in the 6th century BC and that later, around the 10th century the site was occupied by the Berbers. Naval shipyards were established here by the Almohads.

The **kasbah** was built by the Portuguese, and changed greatly by Moulay Ismail. In the 17th century it was used as a governor's palace, but was damaged by the US troops during their 1942 landing. The nature reserve is an extensive area focused on the **Lac de Sidi Bourhaba**, popular for birdwatching, and in the summer, for picnicking. The *koubba* has a festival in Aug. Approaching from Mehdiya the road (S212) goes N or S along the lagoon. The nature reserve is an extensive area focused on the southern section of Lac de Sidi Bourhaba and the adjacent marshes and access is restricted.

The northern section of the lake is a pleasant area for picnicking, either by the water's edge which tends to be marshy or better in the surrounding woodlands. With easy access from Rabat (30 km) and Kenitra this is a popular place in summer. Fortunately for bird watchers interests do not clash as there are few birds at that time of the year. Over-wintering water birds are the main interest (literally thousands of ducks) and/or an April visit for spring migrants. African Marsh Owls are frequently reported. There is a keeper's residence on the E side.

● **Accommodation** D *Hotel Atlantique*, 21 rm, with a popular nightclub featuring live music; F *Auberge de la Forêt*; and *Camping Mehdia*, T 4849, open in the summer with pool, restaurant and shop, site of 15 ha, distance to beach 100m, bar, snacks, showers, laundry, first aid, electricity for caravans, petrol at 20 km, situated N of the town adjacent to Oued Sebou.

● **Places to eat** There are cafés nr the beach. *Restaurant-Café Dauphine* is rec for fish meals.

The Zaër Forest

The region to the S of Rabat, inland from the bustle of the coast roads, is the region known as the Zaër Forest, with picturesque valleys, the amazing Karifla Gorges and rolling hills clothed with cork oak, juniper and acacia. It is really impossible to explore this area without a car. A recommended journey leaves Rabat on the P22, follows the side of the *oued* and passes through the small village of Aïn el Aouda at Km 28. Turn right after a further 11 km towards the cereal farming town of Merchouch, almost immediately crossing the Oued Karifla. At Merchouch turn W along the S106 and across the Karifla gorges to the ancient rest site Sidi Bettache on the old road from Rabat to Marrakech. Enjoy the steep descent and ascent on this hair-raising winding route. Take time to admire the views. The S208 leads N to Sidi Yahia des Zaër and on to Temara. There are numerous small tracks into the forest and down to the streams.

One of the best times to do this tour is the spring to enjoy the fresh flowers and greenery and when the dayats have water. This is the best time too to observe the birds, the summer visitors are beginning to arrive and there are ample sites for breeding. There are numerous larks, warblers and shrikes in the open fields, Spotted Flycatchers and Short-toed Treecreepers in the woods and the road between Sidi Bettache and Sidi Yahia des Zaër is reported the best chance of sighting a Double-spurred Francolin.

Mehdiya Kasbah – Pirate republics and a decaying kasbah

In the 16th century, Al Mamoura, close to today's kasbah at Mehdiya (see page 192), was a small and active commercial port visited by European merchants. Its location on the rich coastal plain just S of the mouth of the Oued Sebou made it an object of interest to the Portuguese, at that time expanding along the African coast after taking Ceuta in the previous century.

King Manuel of Portugal (Manuel the Fortunate) sent out an expeditionary force which took the little town in June 1515, renaming it **Sco Joco da Mamoura**. The Portuguese were quickly defeated and the little port became a lair for pirates and adventurers. By the early 17th century, along with Sale and Algiers, it was one of the leading pirate ports in North Africa, and a source of irritation to the European trading nations. Like Sale (Sala in Arabic), home of a band of renegades known as the Sally Rovers, it functioned as a sort of autonomous republic. For a while Mamoura was ruled by the English adventurer Henry Mainwaring, who later continued his career in the Royal Navy before becoming a member of parliament (1620-1623). And it was also at Mamoura that another adventurer, Saint Mandrier, was captured by Moroccan forces; this enterprising Frenchman later became technical adviser to the Sultan on fortifications and cannon foundries.

The pirate republics of Morocco harmed European trade with the Indies. In 1614, Spanish forces took Mamoura, and on a hillside overlooking the river a new fortress was constructed, named San Miguel de Ultramar, the basis of most of this kasbah still surviving today. In May 1681, this fortress in turn fell to the advancing armies of the Alawite sultan Moulay Ismail. The victory marked the end of the Spanish *presidios*: Larache and Tangiers were subsequently evacuated.

The newly taken fort was renamed El Mahdia, "the citadel delivered". Henceforth the name Mamoura was to be used for the vast cork oak forests to the NE of Sale. Moulay Ismail installed a garrison, strengthened the walls and began works on a new port at the mouth of the Oued Sebou, ultimately abandoned in the late 18th century. A century later, under the French, the fortress was occupied by the military, and it was the scene of clashes between US and French forces during the American Expeditionary Force landings of Nov 1942.

The kasbah at Mehdiya is now largely abandoned – although the mosque with its whitewashed minaret is still used by local people. The smaller of the two entrance gates, Bab el Aon, is of Spanish origin, while the other gate, the grander Bab Jedid (New Gate), flanked by two massive rectangular towers, was erected by Moulay Ismail. From the roof terraces there is a magnificent panorama of the *oued* and ocean to the NW and over to the Lac de Sidi Bourhaba, a protected area to the S. The NW bastion or Borj Bab el Aon is well preserved with some cannons still in place. The most important building, however, is the governor's house, the Dar el Makhzen, which with its great mosaic patio and extensive outbuildings must have been an extremely fine residence in its day. Close to the main entrance are the remains of a *hammam* and a merchants' hostel or *funduq*. The bustle of traders and soldiers in the fortress overlooking the Oued Sebou belongs very much to the past: goats graze on the weeds growing out of the paving and there is no foreign army to menace the great Vauban style bastions and moats.

The valleys too have their bird populations, in particular the magnificent Bee-eaters.

A second route into this attractive area leaves from Ben Slimane, an important market town on edge of the Zaër forest. There are some interesting tracks through this area, suitable for cars. The route recommended in the forest leaves Ben Slimane on the S106 going E, ignore the turn right to El Gara and after 15 km take the next right into the forest. After 16 km turn left to Bir el Kelb and El Khatouat. This is a steep climb up the side of Jbel Khatouat, 830m. At El Khatouat turn W and either the first turn right after 12 km or the second turn right after a further 10 km will take you back to Ben Slimane. The first is slower but more scenic.

CASABLANCA AND ENVIRONS

MOHAMMEDIA

Just to the N of Casablanca, stands Mohammedia, known as Fedala until 1960. In the 14th and 15th centuries it was a thriving port. Its trade with Europe expanded in the 17th and 18th centuries exporting horses and the kasbah was built in 1773 to support this activity. A decline in trade left Mohammedia subordinate to adjacent Rabat. Specializing the handling of petroleum gave it a new lease of life and the oil refinery, opened in 1961, raised its status to one of Morocco's major ports. Industrial activities are centred around a rock salt factory. Its 3 km of sandy beaches makes it a popular recreational area for the people of Casablanca both for a weekend break and a summer holiday haunt.

The distinctive mosque, Jamma

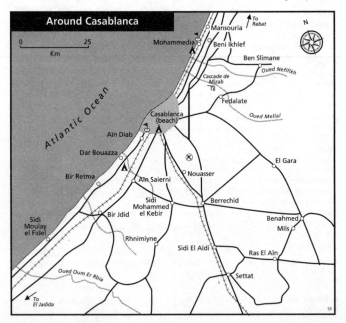

Erradouane, was opened in 1991. There are three doors, in arched apertures, approached by shallow steps across a gleaming white marble courtyard.

● **Accommodation** A *Hotel Miramar*, rue de Fes, T 322021, F 324613, 188 rm, a luxurious place with restaurant, bar, nightclub, tennis and pool; **A** *Hotel Samir*, 34 Blvd Moulay Youssef, T 310770/4, F 323330, 154 rm, good value with all facilities, all rooms have shower, some have balcony, direct telephone, TV and a/c, conference facilities, private parking; **F** *Hotel Castel* and **F** *Hotel Voyageurs* are much more basic. **Camping:** *Camping International Loran*, T 322957, with pool, restaurant and shop, site of 4 ha, beach 100m, bar, snacks, showers, laundry, first aid, electricity for caravans, petrol at 500m. At **Mansouria**, 10 km N up the coast: *Camping Oubaha*, site of 3 ha, only 100m to beach, groceries, showers, laundry, first aid, electricity for caravans, petrol at 600m; *Camping Mimosa*, site of 1½ ha, beach 100m, grocery, showers, laundry, electricity for caravans, petrol 5 km.

● **Places to eat** ◆◆◆The restaurant in *Hotel Samir* is good, but expensive; *Le Frégate*, rue Oued Zem, particularly good for fish; *Auberge des Grands Zenata*, T 352102, midway between Casablanca and Mohammedia, sea food specialities, pricey.

● **Sports** Mohammedia is very well equipped for sports. **Golf:** the course, T 322052, with 18 holes is one of the best in Morocco, despite the high winds, 5,917m, par 72, fees per round MD220, closed Tues, T 324656. There is also a 9-hole course at Ben Slimane 30 km E of Mohammedia, 3,100m par 36, fee per round MD200, T 328793, open every day. **Horse riding:** *Club Equestre*, on Blvd Moulay Youssef. **Tennis:** *Tennis Club de Mohammedia*, nine courts, T 322037. **Watersports:** a number of yachting regattas between Oct and May through the *Yacht Club de Mohammedia*, Port de Mohammedia, T 322331, well-equipped club-house. A watersports centre at the *Ibn Batouta Nautic Base de Mohammedia*. Water skiing is popular here. The beach is good, despite its proximity to Casablanca.

● **Tour companies & travel agents** *Royal Air Maroc*, junction of Ave des Armées Forces Royales and rue du Rif, T 324841.

● **Tourist offices** At 14 rue Al Jahid, T 324299.

● **Transport Train** There are regular trains from Mohammedia to Rabat between 0707 and 0107, to Casablanca Port between 0547 and 2306, and to Casablanca Voyageurs between 0526 and 0033, as well as to all other major destinations. **Road Bus/taxi:** there are frequent bus and grand-taxi services into Casablanca.

CASABLANCA

(*Pop* 2.9 million (1993), unofficial est 6 million; *Alt* 50m; *Best Season* Any time of year except July-Aug which can be humid.) Casablanca is also known as El-Dar-el-Beida, both names meaning 'the white house'. The city is the economic capital of Morocco, the centre for trade, industry and finance, a major port handling a wide range of commodities including phosphates, and by far the largest city in the country, the second largest in Africa after Cairo. Travelling through the city its immense size is impressive, less so the sprawling *bidonvilles*, tin-shack slums, which house much of the city's rapidly expanding population. Casablanca is a city where extreme poverty and wealth co-exist uncomfortably, where crime, prostitution and unrest are more evident than elsewhere in the country. The city does not have the historic monuments of Rabat, Fes and Mar-

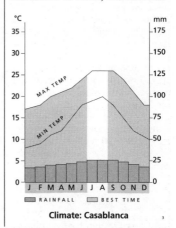

Climate: Casablanca

rakech, and has a noisy westernized air that is unlikely to appeal to many travellers. However, as Morocco's largest city it is an interesting place to see, and is as representative as any of contemporary society.

The port is entirely man-made and consists of two breakwaters, the larger, known as Jetée Delure, being over 1 km in length. A number of cruise liners, mainly European call in here, see **Information for travellers** (page 453).

History

There is believed to have been a Phoenician settlement at Casablanca during the 7th century BC. The discovery of a Roman galley indicates use if not settlement of the area in the 1st century BC. The silver coins found on this vessel are on show at the Banque National du Maroc in Rabat. In the 7th century AD the Berber tribe, the Barghawata, held this area. It was conquered by the Almohads in 1188, and developed by Sultan Abd el-Moumen as a port. In the 14th century the Portuguese established a settlement here on the site of the village of Anfa, but when it became a pirates' base in 1468, they destroyed it, repeating this act in 1515. The Portuguese re-established themselves in the late 16th century, renaming the town Casa Blanca, staying until 1755, when an earthquake destroyed the settlement. The town was rebuilt at the end of the 18th century by Sultan Mohammed Ibn Abdellah, including the construction of the **Grand Mosque**, but it declined in the early 19th century.

In the 19th century, European traders settled at Casablanca, and at the beginning of the 20th century the French obtained permission from Sultan Abd al-Aziz to construct an artificial harbour, which marked the beginning of Casablanca's rapid expansion. The French occupied Casablanca in 1907, and expanded and developed the medina, which from 1918 until the establishment of Israel, became a largely Jewish quarter. In 1915 the French resident-general, Lyautey, and his chief architect, Henri Prost, planned the new city centre which bears a heavy imprint of French planning, with a grid of wide boulevards, large white commercial and residential constructions, and key state buildings designed in a style amalgamating European and Moroccan traditions, known as *Mauresque*. The city has subsequently sprawled far beyond this core, with vast planned projects and unplanned *bidonvilles*. Anfa was the site of the Casablanca Conference of Allied leaders in Jan 1943. Moroccan trade unions developed in Casablanca during the French protectorate, and were important in the nationalist struggle, notably in the riots of 1952 and insurrection from 1953-5.

No part of the Warner Bros 1942 production 'Casablanca' was filmed here.

ACCESS Air Aéroport Mohammed V, T 339100, for most international flight arrivals and the centre of Royal Air Maroc's national network is 30 km to the S of the city at Nouasseur, and there are regular buses price MD25 to the city centre, arriving at the CTM terminal on rue Leon l'Africain. There are also expensive *grand-taxis* costing MD150, MD200 before 0700 and after 2000 and taking 1 hr. The airport has a BMCE bureau de change, open most hours, car hire agencies, and desks for the major hotel chains, as well as a bar, restaurant and post office. An express train direct to Casablanca Ville or Casablanca Port takes 20 mins and costs MD30 economy class.

Train The city has two main stations: Casablanca Port, at the end of Blvd Houphouet Boigny, which is most convenient for the city centre; Casablanca Voyageurs, at the end of Ave Mohammed V, which has more services; and the small suburban station of Aïn Sebaa, to the E of the city.

Road Casablanca is well connected by road, with the P36 from Rabat and the N entering the city centre via Blvd Emile Zola, which leads into Ave Mohammed V; the P8 from Agadir and El Jadida enters via Blvd Brahim Roudani; the P7 from

Casablanca

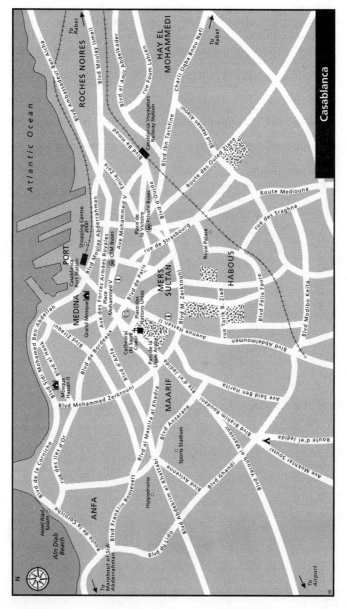

Casa Déco: architectures of the White City

A city of some 4 million people today, Casablanca had barely 40,000 inhabitants at the beginning of this century. However, under the French protectoral administration, it quickly became a magnet for adventurers and speculators of all kinds – and a testing ground for new town planning techniques. The 1917 plan drawn up by Henri Prost, nominated chief city planner by resident general Lyautey, put an end to unbridled speculation, while Albert Laprade, specialist in Moroccan traditional architecture, created a pastiche medina for Muslim notables, the famous Quartier des Habous still visitable today.

However, Casablanca is perhaps best known for its Art Déco buildings. The early period of the Protectorate (from 1912 to roughly 1920) was characterized by building in the neo-Moorish style already widely used in Algeria and Tunisia (see the Hotel Lincoln opposite the Central Market). Later in the interwar period, a local variant of Art Déco took root, using geometric motifs in low relief and wrought ironwork, and occasionally incorporating plaques of Moroccan *zellij* mosaic decoration. Setback terraces on the top storeys and horizontal detailing gave the larger buildings a sculptural quality. The Art Déco aesthetic, strengthened by the success of the 1925 Paris Exhibition of Decorative Arts and Modern Industries, can be traced in buildings as diverse as the Hôtel de Ville – by Marius Boyer, undoubtedly the leading architect of the city, and Paul Tournon's Cathédrale du Sacré Coeur.

One of the first cities to be planned with aerial photography and formal zoning regulations, Casablanca was also one of the first places to see the use of revolutionary construction techniques like concrete formwork. In the early 1930s, streamlining and speed stripes were all the fashion – hence the horizontal window bands of many buildings – and the first mini-skyscrapers appeared, marking a break with the 6-storey apartment buildings. Plot size and land prices (and the enterprising spirit of 'French California') allowed the construction of buildings difficult to envisage in the crowded cities of France. And of course there were numerous adaptations to local conditions: terraces and belvederes, granito floorings for the daily washing of floors, and separate servants' quarters. 1951 saw the completion of Morandi's Immeuble Liberté – 17 storeys high, in the finest ocean liner style.

WW2 saw Casablanca with a population of 700,000. Between 1921 and 1951 the number of inhabitants grew by 85% – due to an exodus from the Moroccan countryside and arrivals fleeing wars of Europe. With rising unrest in the expanding slums (the original *bidonville* or tin can city was in Casablanca), it was essential to improve housing conditions. Planner Ecochard and the Atbat-Afrique team developed the concept of culture specific housing for the masses, ie inward looking, multi-storey patio houses for the poor Muslim communities. However, as André Adam, chronicler of Casablanca's development put it "in her hanging patio, today's woman is like a bird in a cage".

Some observers saw Casablanca as a sort of New York, a city of unprecedented modernity in the Old World. Certainly it had the most up-to-date facilities for work and leisure: office buildings and the great Auto-Hall, modern abattoirs and the International Fair. Cinemas had a key place:theRialto (1930) and the Vox (by Boyer, 1930, now demolished). The construction of the vast new port (against all expert advice) had reduced the beaches - hence the construction of a 300m long municipal pool on the site now occupied by the Great Mosque. A corniche was created at Aïn Diab with pools and restaurants built into the rocks.

With the arrival of the Allies in 1942, and the new US base at Nouaceur, American influence grew. American cinema, and its capital Hollywood (with a similar climate to Casablanca) inspired the city's wealthy families. The new villas of the *zones de plaisance* like Anfa and Le Polo were luxurious and functional according to the tenets of the modern movement. The bourgeoisie, enriched by the war and the influx of capital from France, showed their taste and status in Scandinavian style homes.

Casablanca was always more than just another colonial city – due to Protectorate policy and the populations which moved there. A laboratory for urban planning and a mix of influences, Casablanca somehow captured Jazz Age modernity, the speed and futurist fantasies of the early 20th century with a Moroccan touch. Today the city has a great architectural heritage of which its inhabitants are increasingly aware. The demolition of the Boyer designed Villa El Mokri in 1995 aroused widespread criticism and media interest. A new association, Casa Mémoire, is now working for the preservation of the city's unique heritage of buildings. And the tradition of grand and innovative building is certainly not dead – witness the Grand Mosque Hassan II and the dark, angular mass of the Office Chérifien des Phosphates.

Historic Casablanca architecture – a checklist

1. *Hotel Lincoln* (opposite the Marché central on Blvd Mohammed V) *style arabisant* with features from Moroccan domestic architecture. May soon be demolished.

2. Quartier des Habous, including Mahkamat el Pacha (the Pacha's Court Building which has a definite Lutyens feel to it). Wonderful Albert Laprade designed mini-medina and a symbol of the 'acceptable face' of colonial segregation.

3. *Hôtel de Ville* (architect Marius Boyer) on Place Mohammed V. One of his most important works. Frescoes by the painter Majorelle.

4. Palais de Justice (architect Joseph Marrast, 1915) also on Place Mohammed V. Elegant arcades on this monumental building in the *style arabisant*.

5. PTT or Main Post Office (architect Adrien Laforgue) on Blvd de Paris in *style arabisant*.

6. Gâre de Casa Voyageurs. Train station complete with magnificent clock tower.

7. Cathédrale du Sacré Coeur (architect Tournon), Blvd Rachidi, close to the Parc de la Ligue Arabe. Huge concrete cathedral scheduled to be turned into a cultural centre or gallery.

And numerous anonymous apartment buildings and hotels throughout the city centre. Stroll along Blvd Moulay Youssef, lined with slender Washingtonia palm trees. Many fine villas in the area close to the Parc Murdoch and the Parc de la Ligue Arabe (quartiers Lusitania and Gautier).

Marrakech via Ave Hassan II. **Bus**: CTM buses arrive at the terminal on rue Leon l'Africain, off Ave des Forces Armées Royales, private line services at the square near Place de le Victoire, from here it will be necessary to get a petit-taxi.

Places of interest

There is some confusion with street names as the French is being translated into Arabic but transliterated into Latin script. In general, despite this, streets are still referred to in French.

The City Centre of Casablanca is a bustling place full of life, an example of the diversity of Moroccan society. The buildings are large, dirty, white constructions with balconies and shutters, revealing the predominate French influence on the design, and indeed it has the feel of a European Mediterranean city. The centre piece is the Place des Nations Unies, surrounded by major state buildings designed by the French in the *Mauresque* style, an amalgam of European and Moroccan architecture. This has a square and fountain popularized by western and Moroccan tourists, with crazily-dressed water-sellers wandering through the crowd. On the corner of the 1930s tower (60m) is a siren which is sounded each evening during Ramadan to denote the end of the day's fasting. There is a lights display, 3 nights a week when rainbow-coloured jets of water are sent skywards, accompanied by background music of dubious taste, which brings the city centre to life. Near the square is the pleasant Parc de la Ligue Arabe, the largest green space in Casablanca, with palm trees, arcades and cafés in the shade. It was opened in 1918 and adjacent to that is the exuberant design of **Cathedral de Sacré Coeur**, built in 1930 and now used as a school.

The Medina the site of the old city, is a ramshackle, tatty quarter, dating primarily from the 19th century, and occupied for a while by a Jewish population. It can easily be explored in a couple of hours, entering from Place Mohammed V. The **Grand Mosque** was built by Sultan Sidi Mohammed Ibn Abdellah at the end of the 19th century to celebrate the recapture of Anfa from the Portuguese. The medina is a good place to shop, although real bargains or high quality handicrafts are difficult to find.

The *koubba* of **Sidi Bou Smara** stands in the SW corner of the medina near an old banyan tree. It is said that in the 10th century Sidi Bou Smara (man of the nails) was passing through the town and asked for water to perform his ritual washing before praying. He was thrown insults and stones instead. Undaunted he struck the ground with his staff and there issued from that place a spring which continued to flow. It seems that the inhabitants' earlier inclination to send him away changed to a reluctance to let him go so he settled in the corner of the medina and planted a banyan tree which grew quickly and to an immense size. Here he lived. The banyan tree in the medina is studded with nails driven in by suppliants for the saint's assistance.

The *koubba* of **Sidi Beyliot** stands in the N of the medina. This saint is said to have blinded himself and gone to live with the wild animals finding them preferable to the human race. The animals cared for him and a lion carried him to this resting place after his death. He is appealed to by those needing consolation. Near his shrine is a fountain. Those who drink the water will certainly return to Casablanca.

The remains of **Sidi Allal el Kairouani** and his daughter Lalla Beida are in a shrine on rue Traker to the N of the medina. He was the patron of fishermen and she was known as the White Princess due to the attractive pale colour of her skin. Dar el Beida (House of the White Princess) was the name given to the town in 1770 when it was rebuilt and only later took the Spanish translation Casa Blanca. The story recounts how

Sidi Kairouani, travelling from Tunisia to Senegal, was shipwrecked off the coast here, but rescued by the locals. He sent for his motherless daughter who was not so fortunate. Her ship sank too but she drowned. Her body was carried to her grieving father who buried her facing the sea and left a place beside her for himself.

The Port was constructed at the beginning of the 20th century, and is now a massive complex used for fishing, phosphates, commerce and industry, pleasure boats and cruise ships. There is a shopping centre, Centre 2000, and a number of fish restaurants, beside the port.

Grand Mosque Hassan II was an ambitious project inaugurated Aug 1993, the culmination of 5 years of intensive labour by over 30,000 workers and craftsmen. It stands, as proposed by King Hassan II, at the most western point in the Muslim world. Apart from 50 chandeliers, all the materials and labour is Moroccan. This exceptionally beautiful new mosque has a highly decorative minaret over 200m high, a landmark in the city, from which shines a laser beam, visible over 35 km away, indicating the direction of Mecca. It is huge, in terms of covered area the largest in the world, and has space for 80,000 worshippers as well as a library and a

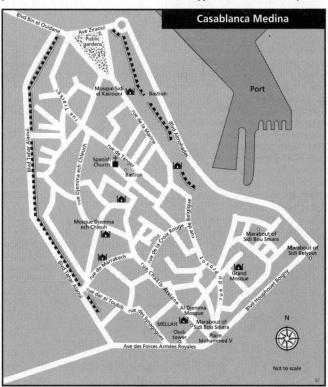

Casablanca Medina

museum. The upper prayer hall has space for 5,000 female worshippers, hidden from the rest of the mosque by a fine example of a carved screen. It is built out over the sea, the water washing against the windows of the ablutions room, the bay windows of the prayer hall (which has a mobile roof allowing it to be opened to the sky) looking over the Atlantic Ocean. The costly operation has been paid for by public subscription. Now support is required for the maintenance and day to day running costs. Non-Muslims may enter as part of a guided tour (at 0900, 1000, 1100 and 1400, entry MD100). The easiest way to get there is by petit-taxi.

The New Medina, an area also called the **Quartier Habous**, or district of religious men, was built in the 1930s to the S of the town. It was an interesting attempt by the French to solve a housing problem and incorporate features of traditional Moroccan house design and community layout with modern streets and utilities. Perhaps they failed, but it is an appealing area nevertheless. Take Bus 4 or 40 from the bus station at the junction of Blvd de Paris and Ave des Forces Armées Royales. Incidentally, the Quartier Habous sells excellent pickles and olives. At the entrance to the New Medina is the church of our **Lady of Lourdes**, remarkable for the expanse of stained glass windows. The church was built in the 1950s and the windows designed by Gabriel Loire. This medina is noted too for the household articles crafted in copper and brass. The large brass trays are purchased by both tourists and locals.

The **Pasha's courthouse**, erected between 1948 and 1952 is today used for administration. It is a mixture of styles, blended into a pleasant building. The central courtyard has marble pillars supporting the highly decorated arches. The plasterwork is very delicate. The central cupola is of carved cedarwood reminiscent of the Hispanic style.

Local information
● **Accommodation**

Price guide

Hotels:			
AL	over US$75	D	US$20-40
A	US$75	E	US$10-20
B	US$60-75	F	under US$10
C	US$40-60		

Places to eat:			
♦♦♦	expensive	♦♦	average
♦	cheap		

Hotels in Casablanca are often booked up early in the day. The lower range hotels are often more expensive than elsewhere in Morocco and unusually can often be of a lower standard of cleanliness. **AL** *Hotel El Mansur*, 27 Ave des Forces Armées Royales, T 313011/2, F 314818, 170 rm, 2 restaurants, coffee bar, bar, health club and pool, overlooked by the new mosque; **AL** *Hotel Hyatt Regency*, Place Mohammed V, T 261234, F 220180, 300 rm, one of the centre-pieces of the town, 5 restaurants, bar, nightclub, health club, art gallery, squash courts and pool; **AL** *Hotel Riad Salam*, Blvd de la Corniche, T 391313, F 391345, 189 rm and 8 suites, a/c, 5 restaurants, bars, nightclub, tennis, pool, sun terraces, conference room and shops, parking, all major CCs, wide choice of cuisine, dinner menu MD230, breakfast MD110 in main hotel restaurant, cheaper menus available in Le Jardin and Pizzeria Venezia; health facilities include thalassotherapy centre 'Le Lido', built in attractive style in a circle around the main pool with many of the low-rise rooms also overlooking a central courtyard and gardens, expensive but rooms are equipped to a high standard of comfort; rec is the best place by the beach; **AL** *Hotel Sheraton*, 100 Ave des Forces Armées Royales, T 317878, F 315136, 306 spotless and well-equipped rm, helpful reception, 5 restaurants, 3 bars, high quality business centre, special meeting room, health club, *hammam* and nightclub; **A** *Hotel Safir*, 160 Ave des Forces Armées Royales, T 311212, F 316555, recently renovated, 310 pleasantly decorated and well-equipped rm, 4 restaurants, 2 bars, nightclub, sauna and heated pool.

B *Hotel el Kandara*, 44 Blvd d'Anfa, T 262937, F 220617, central position, pool; **B** *Hotel Idou Anfa*, 85 Blvd d'Anfa, T 264004/200136, F 200029, 20 mins from airport, pool, conference room, restaurants

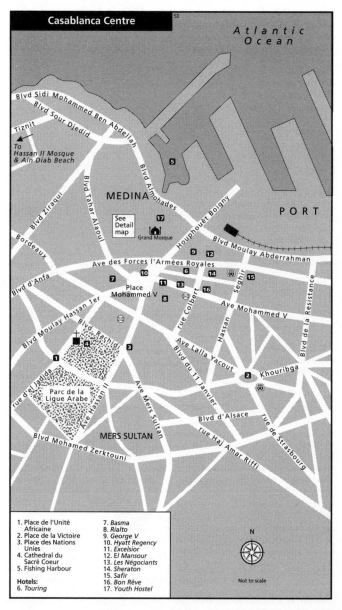

Casablanca Centre

Atlantic Ocean

Blvd Sidi Mohammed Ben Abdellah

Blvd Sour Djedid

Tiznit

To
Hassan II Mosque
& Aïn Diab Beach

Blvd Ziraqui

Blvd Tahar Alaoui

Blvd Almohades

MEDINA

5

PORT

Bordeaux

Blvd d'Anfa

See Detail map

17

Grand Mosque

Houphouët Boigny

Blvd Moulay Abderrahman

9 **12**

Ave des Forces l'Armées Royales

7   **10**   **6** **14**   **15**

Place Mohammed V   **11** **13**   **16**

8

rue Colbert

Ave Mohammed V

Seghir

Hassan

Blvd de la Resistance

Blvd Moulay Hassan 1er

Blvd Rashidi

1 **4**   **3**

Ave Lalla Yacout

Parc de la Ligue Arabe

rue de Jdida

Ave Hassan II

Ave Mers Sultan

Blvd du 11 Janvier

2 Khouribga

MERS SULTAN

Blvd Mohamed Zerktouni

rue Haj Amar Riffi

Blvd d'Alsace

rue de Strasbourg

N

Not to scale

1. Place de l'Unité Africaine
2. Place de la Victoire
3. Place des Nations Unies
4. Cathedral du Sacré Coeur
5. Fishing Harbour

Hotels:
6. *Touring*

7. *Basma*
8. *Rialto*
9. *George V*
10. *Hyatt Regency*
11. *Excelsior*
12. *El Mansour*
13. *Les Négociants*
14. *Sheraton*
15. *Safir*
16. *Bon Rêve*
17. *Youth Hostel*

Anoual and Les Elysees; **B** *Los Almohades*, Ave Hassan I, T 220505, 140 rm, Moroccan style hotel, takes tour groups.

C *Basma*, 30 Ave Moulay Hassan I, T 223323, modern, comfortable.

D *Hotel du Centre*, 1 rue Sidi Belyout, T 312448, fair prices, clean and convenient; *Hotel Excelsior*, 2 rue Nolly, T 200048, 54 rm, 32 with bath, central, with a more illustrious past; **D** *Hotel Plaza*, 18 Blvd Houphouet Boigny, T 221262, 27 rm, satisfactory place with restaurant and bar; **D** *Hotel Windsor*, 93 Place Oued El Makhazin, T 278274, 32 good rm, no restaurant, bar.

E *Hotel Guynemer*, 2 rue Pegoud, T 275764, a friendly, good and clean hotel in a quiet but central location; **E** *Hotel Rialto*, 9 rue Claude, T 275122, fine; **E** *Hotel Touring*, 87 rue Allal Ben Abdullah, T 310216, very good large rooms often with balconies, fills up early.

F *Hotel Bon Reve*, rue Allal Ben Abdullah, T 311439, similar; **F** *Hotel du Perigord*, 56 rue de Foucauld, not very clean but could be worse, central position; **F** *Hotel Genève*, 44 rue du Marché aux Grains, in the medina, is clean and basic; **F** *Hotel Les Négociants*, rue Allal Ben Abdullah, good and cheap.

Camping: *Camping de l'Oasis*, Ave Mermoz, T 253367, this is the nearest, in the direction of El Jadida, take Bus 31, has a site of 1½ ha, 10 km from beach, petrol in 100m, electricity for caravans; in the same direction are *Camping Tamaris*, T 330060, MD8.25 pp/night, at Hajra Kahla about 20 km SW of Casablanca, in a site of 9 ha, only 10m from the beach, has bar, snacks, restaurant, grocery shop, pool, showers (cold?), laundry, first aid post and electricity for caravans; and *Camping Desserte des Plages*, both at rue Azemmour, Km 16.

Youth hostel: 6 Place Amiral Philibert, T 220551, a square in the medina off Blvd des Almohades, nr the harbour, 80 beds, meals available, overnight fee MD30-40 incl breakfast, bus and train 350m, renovated, friendly, airy and well maintained.

● **Places to eat**
◆◆◆ *Al Mounia*, 95 rue du Prince Moulay Abdullah, T 222669, Moroccan food; *Andalus Restaurant* and *Sakura* both in *Hotel Sheraton*, 100 Ave des Forces Armées Royales, T 311194, for local or Japanese food; *Dar Beida*, *Hotel Hyatt Regency*, Place Mohammed V, T 261234, reservations needed, sumptuous restaurant with all Moroccan specialities and music; *La Cambuse* at Aïn Diab, T 367105, noted for fish dishes; *Ma Bretagne*, Sidi Abderrahman beyond Aïn Diab, T 362111, excellent fish and good wine cellar, sea view; *Oriental Restaurant*, Hotel El Mansour, 27 Ave des Forces Armées Royales, T 313011, excellent Moroccan specialities; *Restaurant Wong Kung*, Hotel Hyatt Regency, T 261234, the best Chinese restaurant in Morocco, incl excellent seafood dishes.

◆◆ *Restaurant de l'Etoile Marocaine*, 107 rue Allah Ben Abdullah, adjacent to market, no alcohol; *La Corrida*, 59 rue Guy Lussac, Spanish food; *La Marignan*, 63 rue Mohammed Smiha, excellent Japanese food; *La Tajine*, Centre 2000, by the port, good Moroccan food; *Las Delicias*, 18 Ave Mohammed V, good Spanish restaurant; *Le Petit Poucet*, 8 Ave Mohammed V, licensed French restaurant; *Maharaja Restaurant*, 46 rue Mohammed El Qorri, T 273780, a very good Indian restaurant with alcohol; *Restaurant Saigon*, 40 rue Colbert, T 286007, good Asian food; *Taverne du Dauphin*, Blvd Houphouet Boigny, T 221200, good for seafood.

◆A cheap area for eating is around rue Colbert and rue Allal Ben Abdullah, try *Café Restaurant Anwal*, 116 rue Allal Ben Abdullah, T 319630, standard Moroccan fare; *Café Intissar*, rue Allal Ben Abdullah, reliable; another cheap area is in the medina, with the *Restaurant Widad* a good choice.

Cafés and pâtisseries: Casablanca's reputation for ice-cream is quite without foundation, but for exotic combinations try *Olivier's*, Ave Hassan II. There are some good cafés along Ave Mohammed V, and a popular scene around Place Mohammed V.

● **Bars**
Rick's Bar, in the *Hotel Hyatt Regency* on Place Mohammed V, is not the original, but has marginal curiosity value; *Le Sphinx*, Ave Mohammed V, is a cheaper option; the *Churchill Club*, rue Pessac, Aïn Diab is an expatriate club for English speakers.

● **Airline offices**
Air Afrique, Tour des Habous, Ave des Forces Armées Royales, T 312866; **Air France**, 15 Ave des Forces Armées Royales, T 294040; **British Airways** (Tour Atlas), 57 Place Zellaqa, T 307607; **Iberia**, 17 Ave des Forces Armées Royales, T 294003, Aéroport Mohammed V, T 339260; **KLM**, 6 Blvd Mohammed El Hansali, T 203232; **Lufthansa**, Tour des Habous, Ave

des Forces Armées Royales, T 312371; **Libyan Airlines**, Tour des Habous, Ave des Forces Armées Royales, T 311500; **Royal Air Maroc**, Airport T 912000, 44 Ave des Forces Armées Royales, T 311122, 90 Ave Mers Sultan, T 268712, 44 Place Mohammed V, T 203270, reservations, T 314141; **Swissair**, Tour des Habous, Ave des Forces Armées Royales, T 313280; **Tunis Air**, Direction 10, Ave des Forces Armées Royales, T 273914.

● **Banks & money changers**
ABM, Place du 16 Novembre, T 221275; **Banque du Maroc**, Blvd de Paris, T 224110; **BMAO**, 115 Blvd d'Anfa, T 278828; **Credit du Maroc**, 48-58 Ave Mohammed V; **GMB**, 55 Blvd Abd el-Moumen, T 224134; **SMDC**, 79 Ave Hassan II, T 224114.

American Express: Voyages Schwartz, Ave Moulay Abdellah.

● **Embassies & consulates**
Algeria, 159 Blvd Moulay Idriss I, T 804175; **Austria**, 45 Ave Hassan II, T 266904; **Belgium**, 13 Blvd Rachidi, T 222904; **Denmark**, 30 rue Sidi Belyout, T 316656; **France**, rue Prince Moulay Abdellah, T 265355; **Germany**, 42 Ave des Forces Armées Royales, T 314872; **Greece**, 48 Blvd Rachidi, T 277142; **Italy**, 21 Ave Hassan Souktani, T 277558; **Japan**, 22 rue Charam Achaykh, T 253264; **Netherlands**, 26 rue Nationale, T 221820; **Norway**, 44 rue Mohamed Smiha, T 305961; **Portugal**, 104 Blvd de Paris, T 220214; **Russia**, 31 rue Soumaya, T 255708; **Spain**, 29 rue d'Alger, T 220752; **Sweden**, 88 Blvd Lalla Yacout, T 319003; **Switzerland** (Visa Office), 43 Blvd d'Anfa, T 205856; **UK**, 60 Blvd d'Anfa, T 221653, 223185; **USA**, 8 Blvd Moulay Youssef, T 264550, 224149.

● **Entertainment**
Discos & nightclubs: La Fontaine, Blvd Houphouet Boigny, has belly dancing and music; La Cage, by the port, popular with the youth; Le Balcon, Aïn Diab, a good disco; also try Caesar's in the Hotel Sheraton, 100 Ave des Forces Armées Royales, T 311194.

There are over 50 cinemas in town, a municipal theatre and a casino.

● **Hospitals & medical services**
Ambulance: T 15.

Chemists: Pharmacie de Nuit, Place Mohammed V, T 269491.

Doctors: Dr A El Kouhen, 24 rue Nolly, T 275343, speaks English; Croissant Rouge,

T 340914.

Emergency: SOS Médecins Maroc, T 989898.

Hospital: T 271459.

● **Laundry**
Pressing Mers Sultan, 116 Ave Mers Sultan, T 264194.

● **Post & telecommunications**
Area code: 02.

Post Office: the main PTT is on Place des Nations Unies, for collecting poste restante and good for telephoning, there is another PTT on Ave Mohammed V.

● **Places of worship**
Anglican: Church, 24 rue Guedj, T 365104 (1030, Sun).

Catholic: Eglise Notre-Dame de Lourdes, Rond Point d'Europe, T 220852; Eglise Saint-François d'Assise, 2 rue de l'Eglise, T 300930; Eglise d'Anfa, 13 Ave Jeanne d'Arc, T 361913.

Jewish: Temple Beth-El 67, rue Verlet-Hanus; Synagogue Téhila Le David, Blvd du 11 Janvier; Synagogue Benarrosh, rue de Lusitania.

Protestant: Temple, 33 rue d'Azilal, T 301922.

● **Shopping**
Books: English Forum, 27 rue Clemenceau; American Language Center Bookshop, Blvd Moulay Youssef.

Food: there is a large covered market on Ave Mohammed V which has some excellent and cheap foodstuffs for sale.

Handicrafts: the best fixed price shop, and a friendly place just to look, is the government-run Coopartim in the Grande Arcade Complexe Commerciale, just off Place des Nations Unies, T 269444. There are smaller shops in the medina and along Blvd Houphouet Boigny.

Newspapers: stalls, some selling European papers, on Place Mohammed V and along Ave Mohammed V.

● **Sports**
Archery: Archery Les Compagnons de l'Arc, 25 rue des Flamants, T 277981.

Bowls: La Boule Fédérale, Parc de la Ligue Arabe, T 272868.

Boules: La Boule Fédérale, Parc de la Ligue Arabe, T 272868.

Golf: Royal Golf d'Anfa, 9 holes, T 365355, F 393374, 10 mins from the centre of the city, a prestigious course with a luxurious club-house and a restaurant. See also El Jadida course (page 216) and Mohammedia course (page 195) both 18 holes, par 72. There is also a 9-hole course at Ben Slimane about 50 km NE of Casablanca.

Horse Riding: *L'Etrier*, Quartier des Stades, Route d'El Jadida; *Club Equestre Bayard*, rue Schuman; CAFC, Quartier des Stades, Route d'El Jadida, T 259779, 255005.

Hunting: *Club La Gazelte de la Chaouia*, 21 rue d'Oudin le Romon, T 252911.

Rowing: *RUC*, Jetée Moulay Youssef.

Swimming: the beach is an unadvisable option, there are, however, pools in the Aïn Diab area, try the *Miami* beach club.

Tennis: *Cercle Athlétique de Casablanca*, Ave Jean Mermoz, T 254342, 18 courts; *Cercle Municipal de Casablanca*, Parc de la Ligue Arabe, T 279621, six courts; *Racing Universi-taire de Casablanca*, Clos d'Aviation, Route d'El Jadida, T 254572; *Stade Olympic* Casablancais, Route d'El Jadida, T 254023, eight courts; *Union Sportive Marocaine/Tennis Club de Casablanca*, Parc de la Ligue Arabe, T 275429, eight courts.

Watersports: *Water Skiing Federation*, Port de Casablanca, T 227775.

Yachting: *Société Nautique de Casablanca*, Jetée de Delure, T 225721; Centre National de Voile, Royal Naval Club.

● **Tour companies & travel agents**
Comanov Voyages, 7 Blvd de la Resistance, T 303012, 302006; *Discover Morocco*, 62 rue de Foucauld, T 273519; *Gibmar Travel*, 8 rue Nolly; *Menara Tours*, 57 Place Zellaqa, T 307607, 307629; *Olive Branch Tours*, 35 rue de Foucauld, T 223919; *Sun Tours and Travel*, 75 rue Driss Lahrizi, T 200196; *Transalpino*, 98 Ave Mers Sultan, T 270096; *Wag-

The hammam

🦶 A visit to the *hammam* or Turkish bath is still part of the way of life for many Moroccans.

A ritual purification of the body is essential before Muslims can perform prayers, and in the days before bathrooms, the 'major ablutions' were generally done at the *hammam*. Segregation of the sexes is of course the rule at the *hammam*: some establishments are open only for women, others only for men, while others have a shift system (mornings and evenings for the men, all afternoon for women). In the old days, the *hammam*, along with the local *zaouia* or saint's shrine, was an important place for women to gather and socialize, and even pick out a potential wife for a son.

In the older parts of the cities, the *hammam* is easily recognizable by the characteristic colours of its door. A passage leads into a large changing room cum post-bath rest area, equipped with masonry benches for lounging on and (sometimes) small wooden lockers. Here you undress under a towel. *Hammam* gear today is football or beach shorts for men and knickers for women. If you're going to have a massage/scrub down, you take a token at the cash desk, where shampoo can also be bought.

Next step is to proceed to the hot room. 5 to 10 mins with your feet in a bucket of hot water will see you sweating nicely, and you can then move back to the raised area where the masseurs are at work. After the expert removal of large quantities of dead skin, you go into one of the small cabins or *mathara* to finish washing. (Before doing this, catch the person bringing in dry towels, so that they can bring yours to you when you're in the *mathara*.) For women, in addition to a scrub and a wash, there may be the pleasures of an epilation with *sokar*, an interesting mix of caramelized sugar and lemon. Men can undergo a *taksira*, which although it involves much pulling and stretching of the limbs, ultimately leaves you feeling pretty good. And remember, allow plenty of time to cool down reclining in the changing area before you dress and leave the *hammam*.

ons-Lit Tourisme, 60 rue de Foucauld, T 203051.

● **Tourist offices**
Office du Tourisme, 55 rue Omar Slaoui, T 271177, F 205929; **Syndicat d'Initiative**, 98 Ave Mohammed V, T 221524, 274904.

● **Useful addresses**
Chamber of Commerce: Chambre Brittanique, 185 Blvd Zerktouni, T 256920.

Fire: rue Poggi, T 15.

Garage: Renault-Maroc, Place de Bandoeng.

Motoring Club: Touring Club de Maroc, 3 Ave des Forces Armées Royales (0900-1200 and 1500-1830, Mon-Fri).

Police: Blvd Brahim Rodani, T 19; **Traffic police**: 177.

● **Transport**
Local Bus: the local bus station is at the junction of Blvd de Paris and Ave des Forces Armées Royales, take No 9 for Aïn Diab, No 4 and No 40 for the Habous quarter, No 31 for *Camping Oasis*. **Car hire**: Avis, 19 Ave des Forces Armées Royales, T 312424, 311135, and at Aéroport Mohammed V, T 339072; **Euro Rent**, 3 rue Assaâd Ibnou Zarara, T 254033; **Hertz**, 25 rue de Foucauld, T 312223, Airport T 339181; **Inter-Rent Europcar**, Tour des Habous, Ave des Forces Armées Royales, T 313737; **Inter-Voyages**, 4 Ave des Forces Armées Royales; **Leasing Cars**, 110 Blvd Zerktouni, Y 265331, a cheap option. **Taxi**: Casablanca's red petit-taxis are numerous, efficient and usually metered, hail them anywhere or T 255030. Nowhere in city should cost more than MD12.

Air Aéroport Mohammed V, T 339100 S of the city at Nouasseur connected by trains from Casablanca Voyageurs and Casablanca Port and by buses from inside the CTM terminal on rue Leon l'Africain and grand-taxis outside. Buses leave CTM terminal at 0530, 0630 then hourly from 0700 to 2200. There are flights to/from Casablanca to **Agadir** (at least 2 daily), **Al Hoceima** (2 weekly), **Dakhla** (weekly), **Fes** (daily), **Laayoune** (daily), **Marrakech** (2 daily), **Ouarzazate** (4 weekly), **Oujda** (daily), **Rabat** (daily), **Tanger** (daily), **Tan-Tan** (weekly) and **Tetouan** (weekly). Most major world cities are connected to Morocco through Casablanca. Internal transfers to other cities are not always at convenient times.

Train Departures from **Casablanca Port**, T 223011, 271837, to **Rabat** almost hourly between 0645 and 2035; **Meknes** and **Fes**: 0700, 1850, 2035; **Taza** and **Oujda**: 2035; **Tanger**: 0645; **Aeroport Mohammed V**: 12 a day between 0510 and 2000, takes 40 mins, costs MD20. Departures from **Casablanca Voyageurs**, T 243818, 240800 to **Rabat** almost hourly between 0754 and 0017; **Marrakech**: 0600, 0730, 0914, 1156, 1455, 1652, 1912, 0140; **El Jadida**: 0845, 2055; **Oued Zem** 1000, 1710, 2030; **Meknes** and **Fes**: 0945, 1047, 1225, 1400, 1730, 2235; **Taza** and **Oujda**: 0945, 1400, 2235; **Tanger**: 1225, 1555, 0045; **Aeroport Mohammed V**: 12 a day between 0522 and 2012.

Road Bus: the CTM terminal is at 23 rue Léon l'Africain, off rue Colbert and Ave des Forces Armées Royales, T 268061-7; daily services to Essaouira (5 hrs), El Jadida, Agadir, Tiznit, Beni Mellal, Marrakech, Fes, Tanger and Rabat. Private line buses leave from the terminal on rue Strasbourg, near Place de la Victoire. The following destinations are served daily: **Rabat** (51), **El Jadida** (32), **Mohammedia** (22), **Agadir**, **Fes** (11), **Meknes** (10), **Essaouira** (9), **Marrakech** (6), **Tafraoute** (5), **Ouarzazate** (4), **Azzemour**, *Inezgane*, Tiznit (3), Khenifra, Khouribga, Oued Zem, Kasbah Tadla,

Prickly pears or barbary figs

Opuntia Vulgaris is the Latin name for the prickly pear cactus, with large flat spined leaves, which is used for boundary hedges or less commonly shelter belts to deflect wind from delicate plants.

The attractive flowers of yellow or cyclamen occur on the rim of the leaves from May onwards and provide a bright splash of colour. If your visit occurs in Jul or Aug do not hesitate to try the delicacy, the fruit of the Barbary fig. Obtain them ready peeled from roadside sellers and certainly DO NOT pick them yourself as they are protected by a multitude of fine spines, almost invisible to the naked eye, which can only be removed, painfully, by an expert.

Consume these fruits in moderation as more than two or three can cause constipation.

Safi (takes 4½ hrs, costs MD64, Taza Tetouan, Sefrou (2), Nador, Taroudant, Oujda, Kenitra, Larache (1). Call 'Allo CTM' on (02) 449424 for full details of all services. **Taxi**: grand-taxi to Mohammedia and Rabat from by the CTM terminal.

Sea Boat: Marinasmir, has 7 km of quay, and places for 454 private boats with draught up to 65m, T 306066. **Ferries**: COMANAV, 7 Blvd de la Résistance, T 303012; **COMARINE**, 65 Ave des Forces Armées Royales, T 311941.

EXCURSIONS FROM CASABLANCA

Aïn Diab beach to the SW is well worth a visit. It is one of the better beaches (though still not too clean) close to the city. There are numerous restaurants and expensive hotels, coffee shops and night clubs and bars most of which charge an entrance fee. Most of these charge an entrance fee. Here is the new Sinbad amusement park. Regular bus service, No 9 from town centre.

Beyond Aïn Diab another 3 km along the coast is the picturesque **Marabout of Sidi Adberrahman**, on an outlying rock, reached only at low tide. It is still visited by Muslims (non-muslims are not allowed inside the shrine itself). It is dedicated to an ascetic from Baghdad, said to have miraculous healing powers particularly with regard to psychological and nervous complaints.

Anfa, the site of ancient town, is today a very smart area of Casablanca. Here are luxurious villas set in spacious grounds and with magnificent views. *Anfa* means hill.

El Hank lighthouse stands to the W of Casablanca, built on a rocky headland. It was built by the French in 1905.

Cascades de Mizab are about 24 km along the old road P1 towards Rabat. A popular visit for the people of Casablanca, a place to picnic and relax.

An interesting excursion is to **El Gara** and **Benhamed** through quite a rich farming area, cereals and lots of citrus fruit, which also supplies market garden produce for Casablanca.

ROUTES FROM CASABLANCA

a) to Beni Mellal The road to **Beni Mellal** takes the traveller first S to Berrichid (the centre of an important cereal producing area, with a ruined kasbah and a *moussem* during the Aid el Kebir festival) and then on the P13 past Benahmed with its ruined kasbah lying to the S and on to Khouriibga. This is not one of the most beautiful spots on earth being the centre for phosphate extraction. These are said to be the world's richest phosphate deposits and some 65% of Morocco's annual phosphate production originates here. Oued Zem 33 km further E (once a military post and now an important market town is reached after riding through the mining area. Boujad, known for its striped woollen blankets and as the birthplace of the painter Ahmed Cherkaoui is 22 km further on. It is an old town, founded perhaps in the 11th century with many shrines and a *zaouia* each autumn. **Fkih Ben Salah**, 46 km S of Oued Zem has gained in importance as a market town in the centre of a very fertile region. Here, with the help of irrigation, quality produce is grown – cereals, cotton and fodder crops.

b) to Marrakech The road towards Marrakech, the P7, goes through Berrichid (or take the more restful minor road through Bouskoura) and on to Settat (*pop* 150,000, an industrial town in the rich plain of Chaouia. There are industries associated with agriculture (cereals, cattle and sheep), textiles and chemicals. Off to the E, on the Oued Oum er Rbia, stands **Boulaouane** in the vine growing country which produces the famous, being the most widely consumed, rosé wine. At Boulaouane in a most strategic position in a meander of the *oued* stand the remains of the kasbah built in 1710 by Moulay Ismail for his favourite concubine and enclosed by rectangular crenellated ramparts flanked by seven bastions. Above the arched monumental gateway the date of construction was carved into the architrave. The ruins consist of a well, a tall square tower with arched gateway and part of the minaret. Some underground chambers have been located. The best view of this kasbah is from the S105, the Sidi Bennour to Settat road where it crosses the Oued Oum er Rbia.

c) to Azzemour and El Jadida There are two options for travelling SW towards Azzemour and El Jadida. Use of the inland P8 will accomplish the journey more quickly, this is also the principal bus route, but the coastal S130 is the more pleasant and scenic choice for drivers. This route leaves Casablanca via the Blvd de la Corniche with its busy development of hotels, beach terrace clubs, shops and bars and follows the coast towards the **Marabout of Sidi**

The fortified cities

There are five fortified coastal towns on the Atlantic seaboard, Asilah, Azzemour, El Jadida, Safi and Essaouira.

Asilah The original settlement, now the site of present day Asilah, 'Zilis' or 'Arcila' goes back over 3,600 years and would have been one of the most important cities in the 'Tingitan Mauritania'. The impressive fortifications were built by the Portuguese, their influence still discernible to this day, who used it as a trading centre, occupying as it did, an important position on the gold trade route from the Sahara (see page 181).

Azzemour Originally the Carthaginian trading post of 'Azqama', present day Azzemour came into prominence as a 15th century port trading between Portugal and Guinea. The fortifications date from this time as protection for the traders and as a base from which to attack Marrakech. They were not sufficiently strong to repel the Saadians who took the town in 1541 (see page 210).

El Jadida After the discovery of the new route to the East Indies via the Cape of Good Hope the number of trading vessels looking for safe anchorage along this coast increased greatly. The Portuguese set up a harbour in the sheltered area they called 'Angels' Bastion', or Mazagao. The harbour was fortified with armed cannons prepared for any attack, the ramparts having five large bastions, and the town was considered to be on the best protected site on the Atlantic coast of Morocco. Indeed the Portuguese resisted until the siege which ended in 1769, leaving a destroyed and burning town for Sidi Mohammed Ben Abdullah (see page 212).

Safi Although the harbour where Safi stands today was important in pre-Roman times, the first ramparts which surrounded the town were Almohad. The distinctive sea castle (Dar el Bahr) dates back to 1523. The Portuguese who had been trading in the area since the previous century took the town in 1508 and increased the fortifications, adding this tower to defend the N entrance to the port (see page 219).

Essaouira, previously Mogadar, and known also by the Arabic name of Souirah which means the painting or the picture was even earlier called by the Berber name *Amegdul* which means 'well protected'. The city was founded much earlier than this. In the 1st century BC, King Juba II (also of Volubilis fame) was trading purple dye from here and made this one of his capitals. In the 15th century it was a Portuguese trading post and a fort was built at the entrance to the port in 1506. Later they constructed fortifications round the harbour area for this was one of their three most important bases. The new city and the new fortifications were designed in 1765 by a French engineer/architect for Sultan Sidi Mohammed Ibn Abdellah. There are still cannons which face out to sea, 'protecting' the ramparts (see page 227).

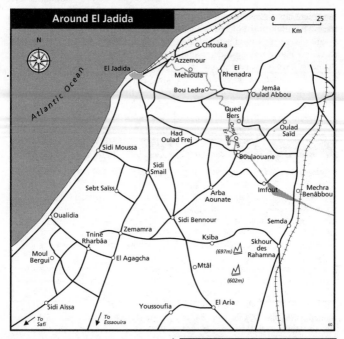

Around El Jadida

Chtouka
Azzemour
Mehioula
El Jadida
El Rhenadra
Bou Ledra
Jemâa
Oulad Abbou
Oued
Bers
Oulad
Saïd
Had
Oulad Frej
Boulaouane
Sidi Moussa
Sidi
Smaïl
Arba
Aounate
Imfout
Mechra
Benâbbou
Sebt Saïss
Oualidia
Sidi Bennour
Semda
Tnine
Rharbâa
Zemamra
Ksiba
Skhour
des
Rahamna
(697m)
Moul
Bergui
El Agagcha
Mtâl
(602m)
Sidi Aïssa
Youssoufia
El Aria

To Safi

To Essaouira

Atlantic Ocean

Abderraham (see page 208). There is ample roadside parking here if you decide to take a closer look at the shrine. After turning left at the renowned *Restaurant A Ma Bretagne* (see page 204), the road swings inland and, although the sea is often tantalizingly out of sight for much of the remainder of the journey to Azzemour, there are regular glimpses of wide, sparsely populated beaches. Approaching Azzemour, the hedgerows become higher with poppies, hibiscus and bougainvillea adding splashes of bright colour; the area is more intensively cultivated, too, with tomatoes and maize much in evidence. Along the route there are camping opportunities at **Tamaris Plage** at Km 16 (see page 204), *Camping Hawaii International*, T 330070/77 at Km 25 and **Plage Sidi Rahad** at Km 29 (45 km from Azzemour).

EL JADIDA AND ENVIRONS

AZZEMOUR

Azzemour is an easy excursion from El Jadida. With a population of 24,774 (1982), Azzemour, only 80 km SW of Casablanca, still partly surrounded by imposing ochre ramparts with several attractively carved bastions often decorated with cannons, is located at the mouth of the Oued Oum er Rbia, 15 km N of El Jadida. From the hill above the bridge on the E side of the river there is a most striking view of the medina with its white, square-fronted, flat-roofed houses stretching along the top of the steep bank opposite. The beach is also one of the best, but the town attracts few visitors. There is a train from here to Casablanca and Rabat at 0827, and buses and grand-taxis to and from El Jadida, and is best visited as an excursion, al-

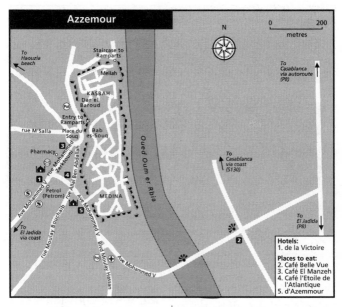

though there is the **F** *Hotel de la Victoire*, 308 Ave Mohammed V.

There was a trading post here called Azama in the Carthaginian period but earlier marble columns dating back to Punic times and Roman coins have also been found in the area. In the 15th century Azzemour was an important trading port on the routes between Portugal and West Africa trading horses, carpets, *jallabah* and *haiks* with Guinea and cereals with Portugal. The Portuguese occupied Azzemour in 1513 as a base from which to attack Marrakech, but under opposition from the Saadians had to withdraw in 1541. The town assumed regional importance under the Saadians, but soon lost ground to the growth of its near neighbour, El Jadida. Azzemour is known for embroidery. The town is sometimes referred to as Moulay Bou Chaib, after its patron saint, who has a *zaouia* above the town. This town on the Oued Oum er Rbia was once noted for the widespread shad fishing

throughout the cooler part of the year. The fish were caught as they went upstream to spawn. Water control barrages have drastically reduced the numbers.

The walls of the old medina can be explored by the rampart walk, with excellent views of the town. The steps are at the NE end of the walls. Via **Bab es-Souq** enter the medina, with its clear Portuguese architectural influences and impressive wooden doors generally round-arched with carved keystones and visit the *kissaria*, or covered market, and the **Sanctuary of Moulay Abdellah Ben Ahmed**. The doors of this house have a particular style, reminiscent of the Portuguese. A passageway to the left leads to the **kasbah**, which also had a role as a *mellah*, or Jewish quarter. In the kasbah, visit the **Dar el Baroud** building, the house of the powder, built within the ramparts between the medina and the kasbah. It is dominated by a tower from which there are views back over the rooftops towards the *oued*. The 16th cen-

tury kasbah gate is a strikingly simple semicircular arch. Climb its tower for a view of the town. Close to the medina the choice of cafés and restaurants includes *Café l'Etoile de l'Atlantique*, a colourful place with a good terrace and *Café El Manzeh* on Ave Mohammed V, close to Place du Souq. You might also try *Restaurant d'Azemmour* for fresh fish or *Café Belle Vue*, a good vantage point for a view of the town. Outside the town is the popular, fine sandy beach of Haouzia, a half hour walk away, with the usual bungalows and cafés, including *Restaurant La Perle* which is signposted from Place du Souq. Haouzia beach, 1½ km from Azzemour is very popular with locals, other Moroccans and international tourists, those who appreciate the cooling sea breeze during the warmer summer months.

EL JADIDA

El Jadida (*Pop* 150,000 (1996)), is a popular beach resort, particularly for Moroccans, and has a faded elegance rather like some English seaside towns. The main historic site of the walled 16th century citadel is, however, distinctly Portuguese in character.

El Jadida is a contraction of '*Al Brija al Jadida*', meaning 'the new little port', but before Independence was known as Mazagao, or Mazagan. The town was the site of an Almohad *ribat*, or fortress, later abandoned. The Portuguese founded a town at Mazagan in 1515, and it became one of their most important bases, holding it after the fall of their other enclaves. Sultan Mohammed Ibn Abdellah retook the town in 1769 and, following reconstruction work begun in 1815 by Abd al-Rahman, it expanded beyond the walls of the Portuguese city. There was a significant influx of Jews from Azzemour in the 19th century, and the town was further developed by the French, as the chief town of the Doukkala region. The town has an important port, with involvement in sardine fishing. The major deep-water port just to the S of the town, at Jorf Lasfar (Yellow Rock) is mainly for the trade in phosphates which are extracted in an area to the S. Artificial fertilisers are manufactured in the town and exported. Raw materials for the petro-chemical industry are also handled here. Each summer there is an influx of Moroccan tourists, particularly from Marrakech. The richest tourist curiosity here is the old Portuguese cistern which dates from the 16th century.

ACCESS Train The train station lies 3 km S of El Jadida off to the W of the P8 (the Marrakech road) and, unfortunately,

is not well signposted from the centre of town. Take a turning to the right after the Petrom service station and just before the railway bridge. Trains are met by a local bus to carry people in the town. **Road** The bus station is S of the centre, along Ave Mohammed V. From here it is a 5-10 mins walk to Place Mohammed V, the focus of the town.

Places of interest

The Citadel was built by the Portuguese from 1513, and its distinctive character was maintained after their departure in 1769 by European and Jewish merchants who settled here from 1815. The quarter is small and relaxed and very easily explored and contains some attractive Portuguese and Jewish houses with decorated, arched doorways, intricately carved wooden eaves and wrought iron balconies. It is well worth taking a walk round the ramparts, access from the right of the main gates, which are surmounted by the escutcheons of the Portuguese kings, were completed in 1541. The **Bastion du St Esprit** is located at the SW corner and from here the walk along the ramparts follows a canal on the S side which is all that remains of the old moat that once surrounded the citadel. From the **Bastion de l'Ange** at the SE corner there is a superb panoramic view of the citadel, the fishing harbour and beach.

Looking N the walls are broken on the coastal side by the **Porte de la Mer**, the old sea gate from where the Portuguese finally left in 1769; many of the other interesting features of the old walled city including a chapel, hospital, prison and Governor's palace and a lighthouse converted into the **Grand Mosque** can be seen from this vantage point. The mosque's minaret was built on the foundations of an old watchtower and has five sides which makes it unique in the Islamic world. The old prison was converted into a synagogue; this building dominates the skyline to the N and the Star of David can be seen clearly high up on the white fronted façade. It is possible to gain entry to this building if you are able to find the guardian with the key but there is little of note to see inside. Beyond the Porte de la Mer, the ramparts walk can be completed via the **Bastion de St Sébastian** and the **Bastion de St Antoine**. From this final section the old Jewish cemetery can be seen to the N outside the city walls. If you choose to make use of the services of a guide for this tour, make sure that the price is negotiated beforehand. Located between the entry gates and the Bastion du St Esprit is the **Church of Our Lady of the Assumption**, a Portuguese construction,

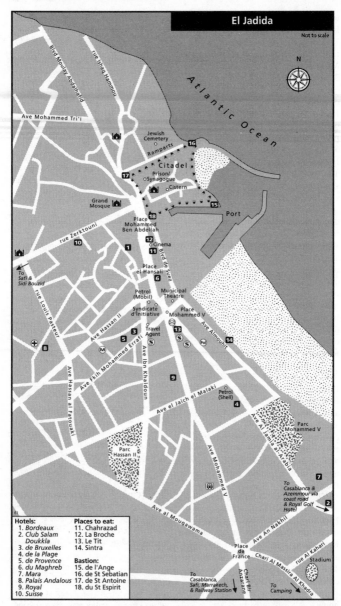

El Jadida

Not to scale

N

Atlantic Ocean

Ave Mohammed Tri'i

Jewish Cemetery

Ramparts

16

Citadel

17

Prison/Synagogue

Cistern

15

Port

Grand Mosque

rue Zerktouni

18

Place Mohammed Ben Abdellah

12 Cinema

10

1

11

Place el Hansali

To Safi & Sidi Bouzid

rue Louis Pasteur

Petrol (Mobil)

Syndicate d'Initiative

Municipal Theatre

Place Mohammed V

8

5

3

Travel Agent

13

Pol

Ave Almoulit

14

Ave Hassan II

Ave Fkih Mohammed Errafi

Ave Ibn Khaldoun

9

Ave el Jaich el Malaki

Petrol (Shell)

4

Ave Hassan al Fatouaki

Parc Hassan II

Parc Mohammed V

Ave Mohammed V

Ave Al Jama al-'Arabia

7

To Casablanca & Azemmour via coast road & Royal Golf Hotel

2

Ave al Mouqawama

Chari Al Massira Al Khadra

Place de France

Chari Al Anza Briz

To Casablanca, Safi, Marrakech, & Railway Station

To Camping

rue Kahari

Stadium

Hotels:
1. *Bordeaux*
2. *Club Salam Doukkla*
3. *de Bruxelles*
4. *de la Plage*
5. *de Provence*
6. *du Maghreb*
7. *Mara*
8. *Palais Andalous*
9. *Royal*
10. *Suisse*

Places to eat:
11. *Chahrazad*
12. *La Broche*
13. *Le Tit*
14. *Sintra*

Bastion:
15. *de l'Ange*
16. *de St Sebatian*
17. *de St Antoine*
18. *du St Espirit*

was restored by the French in 1921, and later converted into a mosque.

The Cistern, a most distinctive feature of the citadel, underground on rue Mohammed Ahehami Bahbai (open 0830-1200 and 1430-1800, entry MD10), dates from the 16th century and was designed originally to store munitions. It served as a fencing school before being used after completion of the town walls in 1541 as a tank to store water for times of shortage. When full, the cistern reportedly held 4 million litres of water. The symmetrical construction has a vaulted roof supported by 25 circular and rectangular pillars, with just one central window in the ceiling, 3½m in diameter, producing a single shaft of light. The floor is covered with a shallow sheet of water, which produces a remarkable mirror-like effect of the shimmering reflection of the roof in the half-light of the cistern. Orson Welles used it in his film of Othello. A less well known film made here is The Harem. In the entrance hall to the Cistern there is a small display of 17th century muskets and other Portuguese weaponry originally found on the ramparts.

Outside the citadel, the other main focus of interest is the area between Place Mohammed V and Place Mohammed ben Abdellah and the immediately adjacent streets. The main shops, banks and restaurants are here, together with cinemas and the Municipal Theatre and the pedestrianized Place el Hansali provides a pleasant alternative to the corniche for a relaxing drink on a café terrace.

The **beach** of El Jadida has a long elegant corniche, flanked by cafés, restaurants and beach clubs but the beach itself is not always clean. A better beach is on the W coast, past the lighthouse, away from the problems of the harbour. This beach is very popular with Moroccan families at weekends.

Market day Wed, held near the lighthouse.

Local information
● Accommodation

Hotels are often heavily booked in the summer, so ring ahead if possible, particularly if arriving late at night. The best are **AL** *Royal Golf Hotel*, Km 7 Route Casablanca, BP 542, T 354170/1/2, F 353473, 220 rm, situated next to the *Royal Golf Club*, new luxury hotel, 2 restaurants, pool, sauna, 2 tennis courts, golf, nightclub, hairdresser and shop, conference room, parking, room price incl breakfast, dinner menu MD200, superbly situated in a secluded location only 100m from the first hole of the golf course and close to Haousia beach, a spacious complex of very attractive whitewashed buildings with beautiful gardens offering all the facilities expected by those seeking luxurious surroundings.

C *Hotel Club Salam Doukkala*, Ave Al Jamia al-Arabia, T 343737/340802, F 340501, 81 rm, a modern, well-equipped, unexciting hotel with restaurant, bar, nightclub, tennis court, pool and on-site parking, a rather unattractive looking concrete building, although ideally situated for those requiring a beach holiday, but some rooms are looking distinctly jaded and hardly offer the facilities and standards of comfort expected of a 4-star hotel, ask for one of the rooms overlooking the sea which offer splendid views towards the harbour and Citadel, the pleasant restaurant also overlooks the beach, dinner tourist menu MD157, breakfast MD48, situated some distance to the SE of the medina, central shops and restaurants on the coastal route to Casablanca, although it is reported that the hotel offers a minibus service into the centre of El Jadida.

D *Hotel Mara*, Ave Al Jamia al-Arabia, T 344170/1/2, F 344379, 28 rm with restaurant, bar, tennis courts and pool, closed temporarily, please check; **D** *Hotel Palais Andalous*, Blvd Docteur de Lanouy, T 343745, F 351690, 31 rm, conference room, parking, charming, good value hotel from the Protectorate period, good restaurant and excellent bar, dinner menu MD120, breakfast MD34, situated a little way out of town off Ave Hassan II close to the *Hospital Mohammed V*.

E *Hotel de Bruxelles*, 40 Ave Ibn Khaldoun, T 342072, 14 rm, parking only, clean and reasonable doubles with bath, convenient central location; **E** *Hotel de Provence*, 42 Ave Fquih Er Rafy, T 342347/344112, F 352115, 16 rm, rec as a good value hotel in this price range, a friendly and popular place with restaurant and bar, dinner menu MD74; **E** *Hotel Suisse*, 145 rue Zerktouni, T 342816, 21 rm, restaurant, parking, reasonable value and quiet.

F *Hotel Bordeaux*, 47 rue Moulay Ahmed Tahiri, T 342356, old but clean, hot showers available; **F** *Hotel de la Plage*, Ave Al Jamia al-Arabi, T 342648, cheap and reliable; **F** *Hotel du Maghreb*, rue Lescoul, just off Place Mohammed V, T 342181, basic and convenient, good low budget option; **F** *Hotel de Provence*, 42 rue Fkih Errafi, T 342347, a good value and friendly place with restaurant and bar; **F** *Hotel Royal*, 108 Ave Mohammed V, T 341100/342839, 38 rm, TV room, games room, gardens, terrace, comfortable establishment with restaurant and bar, well situated for the bus station which is only a short walk up Ave Mohammed V.

At Sidi Bouzid: **D** *Hotel Hacienda*, Centre Balneaire de Sidi Bouzid, T 348311, 12 rm, restaurant, bar, pool, tennis, kiosk, conference room, hairdresser, parking, a more expensive out of town option but with good facilities.

Camping: *Camping International*, Ave des Nations Unies, T 342547, with a restaurant, shop and pool, site of 4 ha, only 500m from beach, showers, laundry and electricity for caravans; *Camping Sidi Ben Zid*, by beach, bus no 2, just 5 km out of town.

● **Places to eat**
◆◆◆*Restaurant Le Tit*, 2 Ave Al Jamia al-Arabia, T 343908, open 1200-1500 and 1900-2300, closed Mon, expensive but good quality, main courses range from MD45-90, CCs Visa and Mastercard, convenient central location.

◆◆ *Restaurant La Provence*, 42 Ave Fkkih Errafi, T 342347, good value French and seafood dishes MD50-60, fixed price menu MD74, a/c, CCs Mastercard and Visa; *Restaurant Ali Baba*, Ave Al Jamia al-Arabia, T 341622, situated on the coastal route to Casablanca, 5 mins' walk from *Hotel Doukkala Salam*, upstairs restaurant with excellent views of the sea and the Cité Portugaise, 3-course menu for MD85, plenty of choice from à la carte dishes, open lunchtimes and 1930-2230, rec but you will need a car or petit taxi from the centre of town; also Café and Pizzeria downstairs. *Chez Chiquito*, fish by the port.

◆ *Restaurant La Broche*, Place el Hansali, small restaurant on 2 floors on a busy square, popular with locals, offering keenly priced choice of dishes and quick, friendly service,

dinner menu mainly fish MD35-80 but you will also find couscous, chicken and other meat courses for MD25-40, also open lunchtimes.

Cafés: *Café Sintra*, on Ave Almouhit has a good open air terrace with sea views; look for other cafés along this stretch of the seafront (guardian controlled street parking available here) and also in and around Place el Hansali.

● **Bars**
One of the best is at *Hotel le Palais Andalous*, Blvd Docteur de Lanouy, T 343745; also try *Hotel de la Plage*, Ave Al Jamia al-Arabi.

● **Banks & money changers**
BMCE Bank, on Ave Fkih Mohammed Errafi; **BMCI Bank**, on Ave Al Jamai al-Arabia; **Credit de Maroc**, **Bank al-Maghrib** and **WAFA** banks on and around Place Mohammed V.

● **Entertainment**
Cinemas: there are two on Place el Hansali.

● **Hospitals & medical services**
Night pharmacies are available at Sidi Daoui, 14 Blvd Moulay Abdelhafid, T 353448 and *Pharmacy Ennour*, 77 Ave Jamal Eddine el Afghani, T 351240.

● **Post & telecommunications**
PTT Centrale, Place Mohammed V.

● **Shopping**
The main traditional shops and stalls are around rue Zerktouni. El Jadida also has a reputation for craftwork in brass; look for this on sale in Place Mohammed ben Abdullah and Palace Moulay Youssef at its junction with rue Zerktouni close to the entrance to the Citadel. Regular street markets are also held to the N of the ramparts nr the Bastion de St Antoine and inside the medina on rue Mohammed Ahchemi Bahbai there are some interesting shops selling clothing, pottery and other tourist goods. A *souq* is held nr the lighthouse on Wed. To find this, take the coastal route to Sidi Bouzid via rue Zerktouni.

● **Sports**
Flying: *Royal Aéro Club*, Airport El Jadidia, T 350582.

Golf: *Royal Golf Club*, T 352251, 6,274m, 18 holes, par 72, green fees MD300 weekday, MD350 weekend, club hire MD75, open every day.

Horse riding: *Real Club Equestre S/C de Tribunal Regional*.

Tennis: *Tennis Club Jedidi*, Parc Hassan II, T 342775, 5 courts.

Yachting: *Association Nautique d'El Jadida*, Port d'El Jadida, T 342718.

● **Tourist offices**

Office du Tourisme, Immeuble Chambre du Commerce, Ave Ibn Khaldoun, T 332724; **Syndicat d'Initiative**, Ave Rafii opp the Municipal Theatre, open each day 0830-1200 and 1430-1830. Only a limited range of information is available here but helpful staff are happy to provide details of hotel accommodation and tourist brochures of a general nature.

● **Transport**

Train There is only one train daily at 0810 to Casablanca where connections can be made to Marrakech, Rabat, Kenetra, Tangier, Meknes, Fez, Taza and Oujda. The train station is far out of the town, and will entail a trip in a petit-taxi, or in the bus which leaves from in front of the citadel ramparts.

Road The bus station is in Ave Mohammed V, approximately 1 km S of Place Mohammed V. Principal destinations are well served with 7 buses daily to Essaouira, first bus is at 0800 and last at 1400; for Marrakech there are buses every hour from 0500 until 1200 midday and then 3 in the afternoon with the last at 1630. For Safi there are regular services beginning at 0400 followed by a further 7 buses with the last at 1830 and the 9 services to Rabat are at hourly or 2 hourly intervals from 0620 until 1730. Casablanca departures begin at 0530 and continue frequently until 1900 and for Agadir the first bus is at 0700 and there are a further 6 departures with the last at 1800. Buses for Oualidia leave at 1000, 1300 and 1500 and for Taroudant at 1600, 1800, 2115 and 2200. Other destinations incl Settat (0500, 0700, 0800 and 1130) and Sidi Bennour departing at 1030, 1330 and 1730.

Excursion to the beaches and Moulay Abdellah (Tit)

The beaches S of El Jadida on the S121 are reached by bus No 2 and grand-taxis. First is Sidi Ouafi and after the more developed Sidi Bouzid, with a bar, café-restaurants and a camp site. Here at Sidi Bouzid the Mediterranean Gulls congregate in their hundreds between Nov and Feb each year. **Moulay Abdellah (Tit)** is a fishing village with an attached site of religious importance, lying 10 km from El Jadida. Tit, meaning 'the source', was founded by Ismail Amghar, an ascetic from Arabia, who settled here in the 11th century. The minaret of Ismail Amghar dates from the Almoravid period, and is almost intact. The place was renamed Moulay Abdellah, after a son of Ismail Amghar who founded a *zaouia* and another mosque here, and built the fortifications. The Almohad *zaouia* attracts many pilgrims to its annual *moussem*, or festival, in Aug. This is one of the major festivals of the Moroccan calendar with up to 200,000 visitors. Thousands of horsemen take part in the parades and displays, magnificent in their skill and their costumes.

Excursion to the Kasbah of Boulâouane

Travelling S on the P8 turn off left after 20 km on the S105. This route crosses a flat, fertile arable landscape of fields divided by low stone walls before reaching the tree-lined entry to Had Ouled Frej, an untidy settlement with the saving grace of having a petrol station in an emergency. Boulâouane is another 19 km from here and areas of low bushy vines planted in the reddish-brown soil become increasingly frequent. The best view is obtained by turning left to the bridge over the Oued Oum er Rbia but access is only obtained by turning right on the S124 towards Sidi Bennour and then left and left again. For more details about the kasbah (see page 211).

Excursion to the gorges of Méhéoula

Also known as the Orangers. Take the road S out of Azzemour turning right just before the Oued Oum er Rbia, and left at the first junction to keep alongside the *oued*. About 9 km from this turn there is a signed turn left (N) giving the best view of this gorge.

CENTRAL ATLANTIC COAST

OUALIDIA

The coastal road from El Jadida to Safi with its 40 km long chain of lagoons is popular with bird watchers during the spring and autumn migrations, particularly between Oualidia and Sidi Moussa and at Cap Beddouza. This is considered to be an important over-wintering location making a winter visit very profitable too for bird watchers. All year there are flamingos, cattle and little egrets, white storks and grey herons and the tiny sardinian warbler. Migrants include the Collared Pratincole and Little Tern while the study of gulls and waders is always rewarding here. Once in a while the Slender-billed Curlew has been spotted. Access is possible by bus, asking to be put down at a suitable place but travel by car gives more flexibility. Once S of the industrial port of Jorf Lasfar, the next 20 km to Sidi Moussa is particularly attractive. At times, the road runs close to the seashore past a series of small, deserted sandy beaches, little bays and inlets dotted with fishing boats. At Sidi Abed there is an opportunity for a café stop; look, too, for *Restaurant La Brise* 37 km S of El Jadida. Beyond Sidi Moussa the route is less scenic, giving intermittent glimpses of the lagoons across the salt marshes and, to the E, views of small settlements tucked into the gentle hill ridge W of the Doukkala plain. This area is intensely cultivated with fruit and vegetables, particularly large quantities of tomatoes under polythene. The main reason, however, to take this road, is Oualidia, 76 km S of El Jadida, 66 km N of Safi, a delightful, picturesque, unspoiled port village set out in a crescent shape round a lagoon which the sea enters through two breaches in a natural breakwater. The skyline on the wooded hillside above the beach is dominated by the **kasbah** built in 1634 by the Saadian Sultan el Oualidia (access via track to right off the S121 opposite the turning to Tnine Gharbia), built by the Saadian sultan El Oualid to

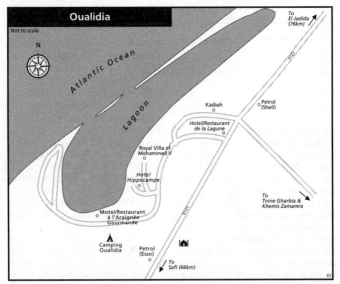

defend the harbour. Below it is the now disused **Royal Villa** built by Mohammed V as a summer palace. The town has a market (Sat), dealing with the local agricultural produce. The lagoon and beach provide an ideal sheltered location for sailing, surfing, windsurfing and fishing or for those just looking to enjoy the peaceful, relaxing surroundings. Early fruit and vegetables are produced here for the nearby main towns and more importantly for export to Europe. The oyster beds are very productive.

- **Accommodation D** *Hotel Hippocampe*, T 346499, 20 rm, small, very relaxed, good restaurant, bar, tennis and pool, beautiful setting above lagoon; **D** *Motel-Restaurant à l'Araigneé Gourmande*, T 366447, F 366144, 14 rm, good restaurant particularly for fish, menu MD65, bougainvillea covered terrace with steps directly to the beach, street parking, friendly, welcoming staff, rooms are clean and spacious, very well appointed, all with balconies, simple, comfortable reception areas, superb location with beautiful views of the lagoon, kasbah and royal villa, rec as good value for those looking for total relaxation by the beach; **E** *Hotel Auberge de la Lagune*, T 346477, 11 rm, has town's best restaurant and bar. **Camping**: *Camping Municipal* and *Camping International de Oualidia*, T 366160, site of 30 ha, bar, snacks, restaurant, grocery shop, hot and cold showers, laundry, petrol at 1 km, electricity for caravans in summer only (MD10/night), other charges per night caravan MD30, tent MD30, car MD2, person MD3.

From Oualidia there is the opportunity to visit the **Kasbah Gharbia** about 20 km to the SE on the S1336. Travelling S from Oualidia the S121 is elevated with the land falling away to the E towards a cultivated plain; to the W there are beautiful views of craggy coastlines, broad reaches of deserted beach and the Atlantic Ocean beyond. Despite the isolated nature of much of this route, you are unlikely to travel far before passing optimistic traders offering bead necklaces and other trinkets for sale. The landscape becomes more barren approaching the rocky headland and green-topped lighthouse at Cap Beddouza, a

dominating, fortress-style building. Formerly known as Cap Cantin, this promontory is believed to be where a shrine to the sea god Poseidon was built in the 5th century BC by the Carthaginian navigator Hanno. The final 30 km of the route into Safi gives many opportunities to see some splendid cliff scenery as the road follows the sweep of the bay towards Cap Safi and then beyond to Sidi Bouzid (see page 221). Make sure that you stop here to enjoy the extensive views of Safi, notably the commercial port and fishing harbour, the Portuguese fortress, medina and Ville Nouvelle on the hill above the old town.

SAFI

With an estimated population of 300,000, Safi is a port and an important industrial centre. While not the most attractive of the coastal resorts, there is a **medina** worth visiting, and it is a convenient stopping point on the way down the coast. Its harbour has been important since pre-Roman times and it was one of the first areas of Morocco to receive Islam. Later it was the site of a *ribat*, or holy fortress. The Almohads surrounded the city with ramparts and built the **Zaouia of Sheikh Mohammed Saleh**. During their reign, Safi had an active intellectual and religious life. The Portuguese had had a trading centre here since 1481 and took control of the town in 1508, building a citadel, repairing the kasbah and building the distinctive Dar el Bahr (Castle of the Sea) in 1523, to defend the N entrance of the port and to be the official residence of the governor. Some of the cannons, cast in Spain and the Netherlands, remain today, 'protecting' the town. The Portuguese left in 1541. The Saadians, in particular Sultan Sidi Mohammed ben-Abdullah, developed the city's trading role, notably in sugar, and built the **Grand Mosque** in the medina. The Alaouite Sultans also added their mark to Safi by erecting religious and scientific schools as well as restoring and reconstructing the old medina which had been neglected by the Portuguese. The Alawites added further buildings and restored the medina. In the 17th century, European countries had a significant trading presence in Safi, and Moulay Ismail was instrumental in developing the city in the early 18th century. Safi had importance as the base of a large sardine fishing fleet, which continues to this day, and, for many years, Safi was the biggest world sardine port. Large schools of sardines are present as a result of the currents of cold water which bathe the coasts S of El Jadida in the summer and more than 30,000 tonnes of fish now pass through the port annually.

The French developed it as a port for exporting phosphate rock, connecting it by rail to the mines around Youssoufia, and from 1964 a new processing complex for Maroc-Chimie to the S of the town on the route to Souira Kédima enabled the export of phosphate fertilizers, as well as unprocessed phosphates, and established Safi as one of the largest ports. The city also has important fish (sardine) processing industries, which provides employment for the women and a reputation for producing some of the best pottery of the country.

In his attempt to prove that ancient Egyptian navigators could have crossed the Atlantic to Central America and founded the Inca and Aztec pyramid cultures more than 4,000 years ago, the Norwegian ethnologist and explorer Thor Heyerdahl set sail from Safi in his papyrus reed boats Ra I (1969) and Ra II (1970). The first attempt failed after 2,800 miles but the second crossing in Ra II achieved a safe landing after 57 days at Bridgetown,

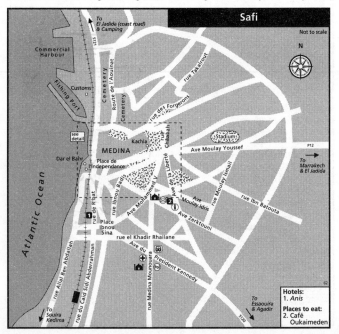

Barbados. Heyerdahl named his craft after Ra, the sun god of Egyptian mythology, who was considered to be the creator and controller of the universe and was depicted with the head of a hawk and a human body.

ACCESS Both the railway station, on rue du Caid Sidi Abderrahman, the continuation of rue de R'bat, and the bus terminal, on Ave du President Kennedy, are to the S of the town centre, which is easily reached by local bus or petit-taxi. A very limited train service links Safi with Benguerir, which is on the line from Marrakech to Settat. The town is on the S121 coastal road from El Jadida and the P12 from Marrakech. Approaching on the main P8 from Casablanca and El Jadida to Essaouira and Marrakech turn along the P12 from Tleta de Sidi Bougedra.

Places of interest

The Medina with its ramparts and large towers, slopes westwards towards the sea and can be entered by the main gate, **Bab Chaaba**. The main thoroughfare which runs from Place de l'Indépendence to Bab Chaaba is rue du Socco, around which are located the main *souqs*. It is a busy, bustling, area with shops and street stalls selling all manner of food, jewellery, cheap toys and plastic goods. Close to the northern wall of the medina near Bab Chaaba is the pottery *souq*, a colourful

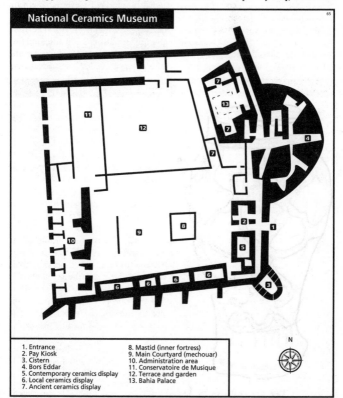

National Ceramics Museum

1. Entrance
2. Pay Kiosk
3. Cistern
4. Bors Eddar
5. Contemporary ceramics display
6. Local ceramics display
7. Ancient ceramics display
8. Mastid (inner fortress)
9. Main Courtyard (mechouar)
10. Administration area
11. Conservatoire de Musique
12. Terrace and garden
13. Bahia Palace

N

alleyway and courtyard crammed with pots and plates displaying a wide variety of local designs. This leads on up some steps to an open courtyard with attractive archways housing some further pottery stalls. Just off the rue du Socco is the **Grand Mosque** with a notable minaret, and behind it a ruined Gothic church built by the Portuguese, and originally intended as part of a larger cathedral. There is also an interesting old *medressa*. On the E flank of the medina is the **Kechla**, which houses the **National Ceramics Museum**, T 463895 (open 0830-1200 and 1400-1800, entry MD10), a large kasbah built by the Saadians, clearly identifiable with its towers and green-tiled roofs. It offers some outstanding views over the medina and the potters' quarter at Bab Chaaba. The entrance opens out into the main courtyard (Mechouar), gardens and a terrace. Displays of ceramics here are divided into three sections, contemporary, local and ancient and, amongst these, are some very

Vase from Safi

fine pieces of Safiot pottery. These lovely pieces are examples of the engraved, stamped, moulded and sculpted decorations used here. The unusual colouring effects are the result of painting on the enamel. The visit should inspire you to visit the local potters where a cruder form of pottery is available and the construction can be observed. On the right of its entrance is a large round tower built by the Portuguese, and within the **Kechla** is the **Bahia Palace**, an 18th century governor's residence flanked by gardens.

Dar el Bahar Just outside the medina ramparts, overlooking the sea, is the Dar el Bahar fort and prison (open 0830-1200 and 1430-1800, entry MD10) built by the Portuguese in 1523. Used by them as the governor's residence it was restored in the 1960s. It is worth entering the building, if only for the view. Entry is under an archway, inscribed 'Chateau de Mer', opposite the *Hotel Majestic*. Just to the left of the pay kiosk is a hammam and to the right is the prison tower. The dungeon area can be clearly seen but it is more interesting to climb the spiral staircase of the tower (narrow and dark in places) for the excellent views of the medina, Kechla and port from the top. After returning to the foot of the tower, access to the ramparts on the seaward side of the fortress is via a ramp. Here can be seen an impressive array of Dutch and Spanish cannons pointing out to sea; castings on two of these show 'Rotterdam 1619' and two others are marked 'Hague 1621'. From the top of the SW bastion there is a further opportunity to enjoy a fine panorama, including the coast southwards towards Essaouira.

Away from the medina, activity is centred around the town's two main squares, the Place de l'Indépendence and Place Mohammed V. Located just to the S of the junction of Ave Moulay Youssef and Bvld du Front de Mer, Place de l'Indépendence is a wide, bustling

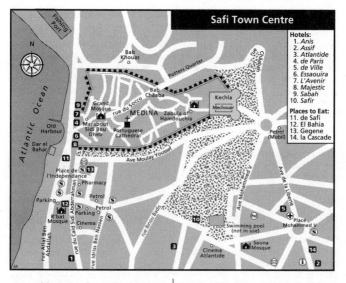

Safi Town Centre

Hotels:
1. *Anis*
2. *Assif*
3. *Atlantide*
4. *de Paris*
5. *de Ville*
6. *Essaouira*
7. *L'Avenir*
8. *Majestic*
9. *Sabah*
10. *Safir*

Places to Eat:
11. *de Safi*
12. *El Bahia*
13. *Gegene*
14. *la Cascade*

street with a central, tree-lined reservation, flanked by shops, banks, cafés and restaurants. Street markets are also to be found here and in the rue d'Rbat to the S. The impressive fortifications of the Dar el Bahar dominate the views at the NW corner of the square. In contrast, on the hill high above the old town, Place Mohammed V is a large, modern paved area somewhat lacking in character, acting as the focal point for the seven streets which converge upon it. The Town Hall is the main building here and the principal post office, the tourist office and the more expensive hotels are close by. However, some of the local cafés manage to add a little colour to an otherwise lacklustre street scene.

The Potters' Quarter at **Bab Chaaba** is worth a visit to watch the craftsmen at work, using traditional processes and materials. The predominate Safi colours are blue and white but the reintroduction of more colourful decorations has increased interest and trade. Safi pottery has an international reputation. Safi also produces the green tiles which are found on many major buildings throughout Morocco. The potters are all located in the same area, away from the old town, as they were a fire hazard.

Beaches

The best local beach is Sidi Bouzid, just N of the town and on the No 15 bus route, with cafés and the very good *Le Refuge* seafood restaurant. Further afield is the Lalla Fatma beach, just past Cap Safi.

Local information
● Accommodation

B *Hotel Safir*, Ave Zerktouni, T 464299/462275, F 464573, 90 rm, restaurant, bar, nightclub, snack bar, conference room and small pool, a modern hotel, with well appointed rooms, some having fine views of the ramparts, medina and harbour, part of an established hotel chain with large, comfortably furnished lounge areas set around a central atrium, with attractive grounds and a terrace close to the pool, suites available at MD690/960, dinner menu MD160, breakfast MD50, parking, major CCs, expensive but rec for those prepared to pay for the full range of facilities.

D *Hotel Atlantide*, rue Chaouki, T 462140/1,

F 464595, 47 rm, restaurant overlooking attractive hotel gardens and sea, bar, handball court, a pleasant, friendly, old style hotel with an air of faded elegance, built in 1920, in a quiet, elevated position close to the centre of Safi new town, rooms are plain but comfortable, about 100m from the *Hotel Safir*, it shares similar excellent panoramic views of the old town and harbour, tourist menu MD118, breakfast MD33, extra 10 rm now being built, renovation of existing rooms and construction of a pool are also planned for the near future, *Cinema Atlantide* next door offers one daily afternoon film performance for hotel guests, parking in quiet street, no CCs; **D** *Hotel les Mimosas*, rue Ibn Zeidoun, T 463208, F 625955, 34 rm, all with bath, 2 suites, restaurant, bar and snack bar, nightclub/discotheque, sauna and pool, tourist menu MD79, breakfast MD20, clean and simply furnished rooms and public areas, convenient for the commercial centre and Place Mohammed V.

E *Hotel Anis*, rue de R'bat, T 463078, Tx 71753, 36 rm, restaurant, close to the Place de l'Indépendence and the medina; **E** *Hotel Assif*, Ave de la Liberté, T 462311, F 621862, 26 rm, restaurant, an old hotel, close to Place Mohammed V, friendly with pleasant lounge areas and clean and comfortable rooms, some with balcony, family room available, tourist dinner menu MD79, breakfast MD20, street parking in front of hotel, extension of further 40 new rm, incl more family rooms, due to open in summer 1996, with spacious restaurant, lift, conference facilities, new rooms, estimated price category **D**, look better equipped, incl TV and telephone, and larger than the older part of the hotel, major CCs.

F *Hotel Majestic*, Place de l'Indépendence (corner of Ave Moulay Youssef), T 463131, 20 rm, shared showers, friendly and clean, no breakfast, public parking 20m. Amongst the other cheap hotels around the medina also try *Hotel de Paris, Hotel/Café L'Avenir, Hotel Essaouira* and *Hotel Sabah*.

Camping: *Camping de Sidi Bouzid*, 3 km N of Safi at Sidi Bouzid, T 462871, site of 6 ha, bar/snacks, grocery shop, pool, showers, laundry, petrol 2 km, electricity for caravans; *Camping Balneaire*, at Kedima, 32 km S, site of 2 ha, beach 3m, showers, laundry, electricity for caravans, petrol at 18m.

● **Places to eat**

Restaurants in the *Hotel Safir* and *Hotel Atlantide* are both rec for good value tourist menus.

Centrally located are ◆◆*Restaurant de Safi*, 3 rue de la Marine, T 610472 and *Restaurant Gegene*, 8 rue de la Marine, T 463369, which specializes in fish and Italian dishes; both are just off the Place de l'Indépendence nr the Wafa Bank. Cheaper places are to be found around the medina. Although out of Safi to the N (a petit taxi or car needed), also try ◆◆ *Restaurant Le Refuge*, Route Sidi Bouzid, T 464354, which has a good reputation for their French cuisine, particularly fish dishes (closed Mon) and *Restaurant La Courniche*, also on Route Sidi Bouzid, T 463584, for Moroccan food and shellfish. Generally, restaurants in Safi do not display menus outside so check inside to be sure of prices and range of food on offer.

Cafés: the *Café Restaurant El Bahia* at the southern end of the Place de l'Indépendence is a very popular spot and offers a good opportunity to sit on the downstairs terrace and watch the world go by. In the area around Place Mohammed V *Café Oukaimeden* on Ave Zerktouni has a pleasant street terrace; other possibilities worth trying incl *Café al-Marjan*, also on Ave Zerktouni and *Café La Cascade* next door to *Hotel Assif* on Ave de la Liberté.

● **Banks & money changers**

BMCE, Place Ibnou Sina and BMCE, BMCI and Banque du Maroc, Place de l'Indépendence. Bank Populaire, Ave de la Liberté, close to Place Mohammed V.

● **Post & telecommunications**

PTT, Place de l'Indépendence and Post Office, Ave Abdellah, at junction of Ave Zerktouni.

● **Shopping**

The best bargain in Safi is pottery, for which the town is celebrated. For lively local shopping try rue du Souq in the medina and rue de R'bat to the S of the Place de l'Indépendence.

● **Sports**

The beach at Sidi Bouzid is known for surfing. There is horse riding at *Club Equestre*, Route de Sidi Ouassel. There are signs to a swimming pool from Place Mohammed V along Ave Moulay Idriss. However, the pool site on Ave Mohammed V next to the public gardens looks distinctly neglected and certainly not used at present. *Royal Aéroclub de Safi* at local airport, T 622614.

● **Tourist offices**

Ave de la Liberté, Ville Nouvelle. Open Mon-Fri 0900-1200 and 1500-1830. The office is in a small portacabin in a side street opp the *Hotel Assif* and, although you will receive a friendly welcome and a willingness to help, only generalized tourist literature about Morocco seems to be available, so expect little by way of specific maps and information about Safi itself.

● **Transport**

Local Bus: no 7 takes you from main bus station into town centre, MD2. **Car hire**: Europcar, Place Ibnou Sina, T 462935.

Train The railway station is to the S of the town, on rue du Caid Sidi Abderrahman, the continuation of rue de R'bat, T 464993. There is one train daily at 0815 to Benguerir, journey time approximately 1 hr, which connects with services to Casablanca, Rabat, Kenitra, Meknes, Fez, Marrakech, Asilah and Tangier. The daily arrival at Safi from all these destinations is at 1846.

Road The bus terminal is on Ave President Kennedy to the S of the town. CTM operates 6 buses daily to **Casablanca**, first bus is at 0430 and the last departure is at 1600. For **Marrakech** its service leaves at 0700 and there are 2 buses daily for **El Jadida** leaving at 0830 and 1430. CTM buses for **Agadir** leave at 1000 and 2300, for **Tiznit** at 1000 and **Essaouira** at 2100. Other operators incl Chekkouri which offers 6 daily buses to **Marrakech**, first bus 0500 and last bus 1700, 6 **Agadir** services, first bus at 0100 and last bus at 2330. **Casablanca** is very well served by Chekkouri with 9 daily buses, first at 0200 and last at 2300 and they also have departures for **Taroudant** at 0400 and **Rabat** at 0130.

SAFI TO EL JADIDA

An option for travelling inland to El Jadida uses the P12 Marrakech exit from the town. Once into open countryside beyond the roadside snack and butchers' stalls on the outskirts of Safi, the first 26 km stretch to **Bouguedra** is through an area of fertile arable farming land. At Bouguedra, which has a few shops, cafés, a Credit Agricole bank and a brick factory but otherwise little else of interest to detain the traveller, turn N on the P8 towards Casablanca. After a further 18 km through more arable country with views of distant hills to the right, the town of **Jemâa-Sahi** is reached. This is quite a

sizeable, well developed town with a good choice of petrol stations, pharmacies and small shops including tyre repairers. There is a reasonable selection of cafés, too, including *Café Ibtissam*, but recommended is *Café Restaurant Oasis*, open all day until midnight, on the right just as you leave the northern end of town. A cool, covered open air terrace looks out on to some very pretty gardens; the welcome is friendly and you can get an inexpensive snack lunch or, alternatively, try the dinner menu MD60 for a starter and steak. Less attractive 33 km further N is the bustling town of **Khemis Zemamra**, a busy place cluttered with sugar beet lorries. A detour can be taken here to **Sidi Bennour** (31 km) by turning right on the S123, an undulating route across a productive farming landscape criss-crossed with irrigation ducts, past grazing camels and local people swimming and washing in roadside pools. The western side of **Sidi Bennour** is a busy, somewhat scruffy area full of roadside market stalls but once the junction with the P9 is reached, the character of the town changes to one of pleasant apartments, shops and pavement cafés. There are petrol stations and banks here. Turn N on the P9, past factories manufacturing pipes and processing sugar beet, for another 21 km to **Sidi Smail**, another large town at the junction of the P8 and P9 where there is a good choice of facilities. The landscape for the remainder of the journey is mainly agricultural but given added variety by roadside traders selling pottery, live pigeons and eggs. On the outskirts of El Jadida, the train station is down a turning to the left immediately after driving under the railway line; the route passes through a residential area before it reaches the large roundabout at Place de France.

SAFI TO AGADIR – VIA CHICHAOUA AND THE HIGH ATLAS

This route is an alternative to the more direct option using the P8 via **Talmest** and **Ounara** and, later in the journey, provides a good opportunity to enjoy some of the fine scenery of the Western High Atlas mountains. Leave Safi on the P12; beyond Sidi Bouguedra the road climbs steadily into the hills for the first part of the 42 km to **Chemaia** and then levels out to give views of high plains in all directions. Petrol is available outside Sidi Tiji. In Chemaia, where there is little of interest to detain the traveller, turn S on the S511 for Chichaoua (63 km). This is a very isolated section (no petrol), travelling across wide plains with flat-topped hills in the far distance, crossing the Oued Tensift after 35 km. Reaching the busy junction with the P10 road to Marrakech offers the chance to refuel and stop at one of the shops or cafés here. **Chichaoua** is noted for the distinctive animal designs of its good quality, brightly coloured carpets. Travelling S on the P40 the impressive peaks of the High Atlas soon comes into sight on the way to Imi-n-Tanoute; a detour off the main road into this busy but unattractive town provides the chance to visit shops and banks but little else. Leaving **Imi-n-Tanoute** the route winds upwards through the pass of **Tizi Maachou** (1,700m) through some beautiful mountain scenery. Beyond the summit there

are fine views of the higher peaks to the E before you reach the reservoir and **Barrage Abdelmoumen**; on the way you will pass many local traders offering bottles of argan oil for sale. A rapid descent to the viewpoint at Ameskroud then follows; it is worth stopping here to enjoy the extensive views SE over the plain towards Taroudant before completing the remainder of the journey to Agadir.

SAFI TO ESSAOUIRA – ON THE COAST ROAD

After the beach resort of Sidi Rosia is **Jorf el Yhoudi** – also known as the Jew's fort. On the coast at **Souira Kédima**, 32 km S of Safi, is a rebuilt/restored Portuguese ribat. It dates from the 1550s. Guides say it was completed in 1521 and abandoned in 1525. It is open to the public. Across the Oued Tensift, the ford having been replaced by a new road and bridge, and beyond Dar Caid Hadji is the more recent Kasbah Hamidouch built in the 18th century by Sultan Moulay Ismail as a fortress to control this region. At one time the river surrounded the building a a moat. It is as splendid building, crumbling turrets and crenelations in abundance. This coastal area is very popular in summer. Good campsite here, see page 224.

Sebaatou Rijal – the Seven Holy Men

From this region in the 7th century seven holy men of the Regada tribe travelled to Mecca. Their mission was to see if the 'Messenger of God' was indeed at that place. Speaking only Tachelait dialect they were astounded to find that the Prophet Mohammed was able to converse with them. He told them who he was and they took instruction from him in the faith of Islam. Eventually they returned to their tribe and preached to their people, converting them all. As the first men to carry Islam to the Maghreb and as men who actually received instruction from the Prophet their shrines are very important. Their *moussem* lasts for over a month, beginning at the coastal shrine of **Moulay Berserktoun**, and continues 12 days later at Akermoud where both **Sidi Bou Bekr** and his son **Sidi Salih** are buried. Other celebrations take place in Zaouia Khourati where the shrines of **Sidi Ali Khouai** and **Sidi Aissa Bou Khabia** are to be found, near the Oued Tensift at the shrine of **Sidi Abdullah Ben Adnas** and at the shrine of **Sidi Quasmin** who is famed for being the first to receive God's call to find the true faith.

The road continues through **Akermoud** with Jbel Hadid (Iron Mountain), 725m, to the E. In this region are a number of white shrines. That of Moulay Bouzerktoun set among the sand dunes is most striking.

ESSAOUIRA

(*Pop* 45,000 (1995); *Alt* 5m) Essaouira is one of the most relaxed of the coastal resorts, with little of the large scale tourist infrastructure found elsewhere, but is understandably popular with independent travellers and surfers. It has a friendly, peaceful atmosphere and an interesting medina. Visitors are attracted in increasing numbers by its mild, temperate weather throughout the year and a fine curving beach. The benefits of a sub-tropical climate tempered by oceanic influences gives rise to temperatures ranging from an average of 16.4°C in Jan to 22.5°C in Aug. Average annual rainfall is 280 mm and falls mainly in the winter months. One of the most appealing aspects of Essaouira is that all the principal tourist sites can be comfortably reached on foot; cars can be left in the parking area to the S of Place Moulay Hassan.

There was a small Phoenician settlement at Essaouira, previously called Magdoura or Mogador, a corruption of the Berber word *Amegdul*, meaning 'well-protected'. The Romans were interested in the purple dye produced from the shellfish *murex brandaris*, which they used to colour the robes of the rich. Mogador was occupied by the Portuguese in the 15th century who built the fortifications around the harbour. The town was one of their three most important bases, but was abandoned in 1541, from when it went into decline. Visited by Sir Francis Drake, Christmas 1577. In 1765, the Alawite Sultan Sidi Mohammed Ibn Abdellah transformed Mogador into an open city, enticing overseas businessmen in with trade concessions, and it soon became a major commercial port, with a large foreign and Jewish population establishing the town as a major centre of trade. The Sultan employed the French architect Théodore Cornut to design the city and its fortifications. In his design Cornut chose an unusual rectangular layout for the main streets, resulting in a very uniform style, and constructed ramparts in the Vauban style. Mogador was shelled by the French in 1844.

Orson Welles stayed here for some time, filming part of Othello at the **Skala du Port**. From Independence the town was called Essaouira, a local name meaning 'little fortress'. In the 1960s Essaouira had a brief reputation as a 'happening place', which attracted hippies, notably the rock star Jimi Hendrix. Essaouira now seems to be emerging from several decades of decline, for on top of fishing, fish processing, a small market and handicraft industries, the town is attracting greater numbers of tourists, notably surfers. Essaouira is still noted for its woodwork cabinet making and inlaid work using the local juniper.

ACCESS Essaouira is connected to Marrakech via the P10, and lies just to the W of the P8 from Casablanca to Agadir. The new bus station is to the N of **Bab Doukkala**, and it is worth taking a *calèche* or petit-taxi as far as the gate to the medina or Ave Mohammed V.

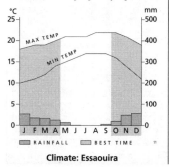

Climate: Essaouira

Places of interest

The Medina enclosed by walls with five main gates, is Essaouira's major attraction. Entering from **Bab Doukkala** the main thoroughfare is rue Mohammed Zerktouni, which leads into Ave de l'Istiqlal, where there is the **Grand Mosque**, and just off, on Darb Laalouj, the **Ensemble Artisanal** and the **Museum of Sidi Mohammed Ibn Abdellah**, T 472300 (open 0830-1200 and 1430-1800, except Fri 0830-1130 and 1500-1830, closed Tues, entrance fee MD10) which houses the Museum of Traditional Art and Heritage of Essaouira and which has an interesting collection of weapons, as well as handicrafts such as woodwork and carpets. This house, once the home of a pasha, has examples of stringed instruments beautifully decorated with marquetry which were used by the musicians to accompany their dances. On display too are documents on Berber songs. Upstairs is the ethnographic collection which is well worth a visit. This collection features a wide range of signs and symbols which play an important role in the traditional craftwork of the artisans of the Essaouira region. These mystico-religious symbols appear in carvings and engravings, in finely crafted filigrees, in tapestries and embroidery and on attractive forms of local jewellery.

Ave de l'Istiqlal leads into Ave Okba Ibn Nafi, on which is located the small **Galerie des Arts Frederic**, at the end of the street a gate on the right leads into Place Moulay Hassan, the heart of the town's social life and although recently repaved and modernized, still with character. The town's *souqs*, are mainly located around the junction between rue Mohammed Zerktouni and rue Mohammed El Gorry, although there is an area of woodworkers inside the **Skala** walls to the N of Place Moulay Hassan, where some fine pieces can be picked up with some good-natured bargaining. At the NE end of rue Zerktouni, close to Bab Doukkala is the **Mellah**, or old Jewish quarter, an area of significant size underlining the importance of the Hebrew population settling in Essaouira at the time of its foundation. Although the

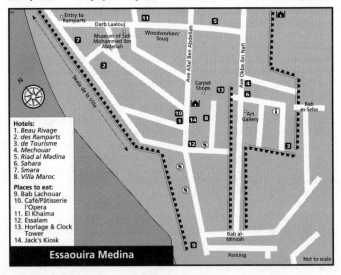

Hotels:
1. *Beau Rivage*
2. *des Ramparts*
3. *de Tourisme*
4. *Mechouar*
5. *Riad al Madina*
6. *Sahara*
7. *Smara*
8. *Villa Maroc*

Places to eat:
9. Bab Lachouar
10. Café/Pâtisserie l'Opera
11. El Khaima
12. Essalam
13. Horlage & Clock Tower
14. Jack's Kiosk

Essaouira Medina

Not to scale

Jewish community no longer remains, it made a substantial contribution to the commercial and cultural development of the town.

The Harbour and Skala Off Place Moulay Hassan is the small but vibrant harbour, which principally supports a fishing fleet, and is worth a visit. It is still possible to see the work of traditional shipbuilders and repairers on the bustling quayside and nearby the lively fish market and open air restaurant stalls serve many varieties of grilled fish, typically prices range from MD10-25. The Sea Gate (the Porte de la Marine) which serves to link the harbour with the medina was built in 1769, it is said by an Englishman converted to Islam, during the reign of Sidi Mohammed Ibn Abdullah. The gateway is built of stone in the classical style and the year of its construction (1184 of the Hegira) is inscribed on the pediment. It is connected to the ramparts on the **Skala**, an old Portuguese sea defence and battery, by a bridge which spans small primitive dry docks. Entry to the **Skala du Port** (MD10) is via a kiosk close to the Porte de la Marine and from the top of the bastion there are extensive panoramic views of the harbour and the offshore islands, the **Isles des Purpuraires**.

Further to the N of Place Moulay Hassan it is possible to get on to the ramparts of the **Skala de la Ville** from rue Skala close to its junction with rue Darb Laalouj. Entry here is free and crenellated walls protect a 200m long raised artillery platform and an impressive array of decorated Spanish and other European cannons. From the tower of the North Bastion there are fine views of the old *mellah*, the medina with its white buildings and blue shutters and the coastline to the N of Essaouira. The woodworkers' *souqs* are situated here in arched chambers underneath the ramparts.

Cemeteries Outside the walls is the Consul's cemetery for British officials who died there converting Mogador into a trading post with strong UK links. Across the road in the Jewish cemetery – if you can find the man with the key – is the resting place of Leslie Hore-Belisha who invented the first pedestrian crossing light.

The **beach** at Essaouira is very beautiful, isolated but fiercely windy. The wind, known as the *alizee*, stirs up a lot of sand, and it is cold for swimming, but ideal for surfing. When walking far along the beach it should be noticed that the incoming tide makes the small stream below Diabat into an impassable river.

Diabat The ruined palace/pavilion below Diabat is worth a detour from a

Grand Mosque | Clock Tower | Mosque | Diabat | Place Moulay Hassan

beach walk, just after the stream which crosses it, but the village of Diabat is dreadfully miserable. The building is said to have been swallowed by the sand after the people of the Sous put a curse on it as their trade was being ruined. The old fort was built by the Portuguese in the 18th century.

Isles des Purpuraires These islands to the SW are a bird sanctuary, particularly for Eleonora's Falcons. It is possible to see these falcons from the end of the jetty using a good telescope. One particular area frequented by the falcons is the mouth of Oued Ksob to the S of the town. This river mouth is also noted for a large colony of Yellow-legged herring gulls and a variety of migrating seabirds including Black, Little, Sandwich, Whiskered and White-winged terns. The *oued* can be reached from a track off the P8 S of the town but access to the sea is not easy. The scrubland in the same vicinity provides sufficient sightings to satisfy any birdwatcher. It is possible to visit the main island, the Ile de Mogador, and the ruins of a prison, by contacting the Tourist Information Office on Place Moulay Hassan. They will direct the visitor to the Province office off Ave Mohammed V where a permit can be obtained for MD50, and will arrange a boat for transport for the 15-min trip, for

a negotiable price. It is understood, however, that there is the prospect of a regular daily ferry service to the islands being established soon.

Local information
● Accommodation

For hotels in Essaouira it is important to get a well ventilated room with windows, and preferably a view of the sea, for the others can be dark, claustrophobic and damp.

B *Hotel des Iles*, Ave Mohammed V, T 472329/74, F 472472, 70 rm of which 46 are bungalow style around a central swimming pool, the only one in Essaouira, remaining rooms are in the old historic hotel built in 1948 which has tasteful period decoration, comfortable public lounge areas, seafood and international restaurants (fine views of harbour and beach), bar, nightclub and secure parking, tourist menu MD180 (3 course), breakfast MD55, friendly, welcoming staff, very convenient location for beach and medina, all major CCs, train reservations can be made here, for those wanting a full range of facilities incl a pool, our recommendation for a category **B** hotel; **B** *Hotel Villa Maroc*, 10 rue Abdellah Ben Yassin, T 473147/473758, F 472806, 17 rm, inside the medina, a converted Moroccan house, beautifully decorated in blue and white with rooms arranged around a central court liberally festooned with plants and greenery, roof terrace with superb views of harbour and islands, suites and an apartment (all for 4 people) are available for supplements of MD360 and MD460 respectively, restaurant for guests only, dinner MD150, breakfast is incl

Place Orson Welles | Harbour | Ramparts | Skela du Port

in the room price, public parking (approx 200m) nr Place Orson Welles, all major CCs, highly rec for the discerning traveller and those looking for a relaxed, informal atmosphere in a small hotel.

D *Hotel Tafoukt*, 98 Ave Mohammed V, BP 38, T 784504/05, F 784416, 40 rm, a reasonable hotel just across the road from the beach but an appreciable walk (about 1 km) from the centre of town, tea room, bar and restaurant but ask for a room with a sea view to get the best from this hotel.

E *Hotel Beau Rivage*, Place Moulay Hassan, T/F 472925, 18 rm, central, rooms available with and without showers, some with balconies overlooking main square, others with sea view, TVs in room may prove to be more decorative than functional, clean, basic and with friendly, helpful management, pleasant TV room, roof terrace with good panoramic views, no restaurant but breakfast (MD14) available from *Café/Patisserie L'Opéra* outside hotel, major CCs, if you are looking for a hotel to soak up the atmosphere of Place Moulay Hassan, this is probably as good a choice as any; **E** *Hotel des Remparts*, 18 rue Ibn Rochd, T 473166, 27 rm on 3 floors, a popular place with friendly staff and a spectacular view from the roof terrace, spacious public lounges, otherwise basic and clean, although avoid rooms reported as rather dark, damp and with poor utilities, no restaurant for evening meals, breakfast MD17, public parking in a restricted area, CCs, Amex; **E** *Hotel Mechouar*, Ave Okba Ibn Nafia, T 784828, 25 rm, in the medina but uninviting appearance and probably not the best value option in this price range,

no breakfast available but restaurant reported as open in the season, major CCs; **E** *Hotel Sahara*, Ave Okba Ibn Nafia, T 472292, 70 rm, in the medina next door to the Hotel Mechouar overlooking the Beffroi, comfortable and central, range of rooms, some pleasant with central heating, cheaper rooms on inner courtyard are darker and less well ventilated, terrace, breakfast MD20, no restaurant for dinner, public parking nr Place Orson Welles 200m.

F *Hotel du Tourisme*, rue Mohammed Ben Messaoud, at the SE corner of the medina, is cheap but some rooms are poorly equipped and damp, not rec; **F** *Hotel Smara*, 26 rue Skala, T 472655, 17 rm, just inside the ramparts in the woodworkers' *souq* N from Place Moulay Hassan, clean and friendly, rooms have wash basins and bidets but showers cost extra and WCs are shared, make sure the room is one of those with a stunning sea view, the others can be damp and dark, no restaurant for evening meals but breakfast available for MD10, with a MD5 supplement for a glass of orange juice!, good roof terrace with a view as good as anywhere in Essaouira, very restricted parking in street, no CCs but is by far the best cheap option.

Hotel Riad al Madina, 9 rue Attarine, 30 rm with bath, new hotel, a conversion of the former Palais de Justice, reputedly once owned by Jimi Hendrix, has potential to be an attractive option with good facilities, well located in the centre of the medina.

Camping: *Camping Municipal d'Essaouira*, along Ave Mohammed V from the medina, small site of 1 ha, just 50m from beach, grocery store, laundry, petrol at 300m, this site does not have a good reputation.

● Places to eat

◆◆◆Chalet de la Plage, 1 Ave Mohammed V, T 472972, F 473419, good fish dishes but also a wide ranging menu offering good choice for tourists, main courses range from MD50-90, with a set 4 course meal for MD90, also open for lunch, make sure of a table which takes full advantage of the attractive terrace directly overlooking the beach; *Chez Sam*, T 473513, in the harbour with fine views of the port, a fish and seafood restaurant and bar, with good food and drink and a distinctive atmosphere, particularly good lobster, although pricey, at MD170 for 3 courses, alternative 4-course menu of the day at MD60, seafood platter at MD100 for two, main courses range from MD45-70, Amex and Diners Club CCs taken here; *Restaurant Riad*, Ave Allal Ben Abdellah, a wide range of Moroccan dishes.

◆◆Restaurant El Khaima, in a small square off Darb Laalouj al Attarin opp the museum, a good licensed restaurant with Moroccan specialities, separate lobster menu at MD180, alternative fixed price menu at MD80, individual main courses cost between MD55-65; also try *Restaurant Bab Lachouar*, at the SW end of Place Moulay Hassan which offers interesting fixed price menus at MD50/60, main dishes range from MD35-45.

◆ By far the best cheap eating option is to sample the freshly caught fish grilled at open air restaurants between Place Moulay Hassan and the port; accompanied by a tomato salad

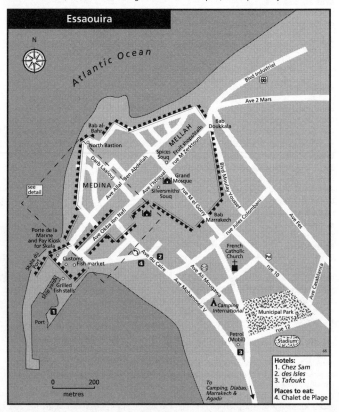

Essaouira

Hotels:
1. *Chez Sam*
2. *des Isles*
3. *Tafoukt*

Places to eat:
4. Chalet de Plage

this makes a meal at a reasonable, negotiated price. The standard of hygiene is not high, however, be warned. *Chez Toufik* will prepare fish you have bought in the market. There are also a series of so-called Berber Cafés off to the left of rue Mohammed Zerktouni as walking towards Bab Doukkala. Other good cheap options incl *Café-Restaurant Essalam*, conveniently situated on Place Moulay Hassan which offers very good value local dishes, couscous at MD40 rec here, open daily from 1200-2300, all the main credit cards taken; and *Mustafa's*, on Ave Allal Mohammed Ben Abdellah. The latter street has a number of cheap places.

Cafés: the best cafés are on Place Moulay Hassan, particularly *Café L'Opéra* and *Chez Driss*, a good place to have breakfast, or watch the evening social life pass by. There are several beachside cafés, ideal for a rest from the wind.

● **Bars**

Try *Chez Sam*, in the harbour; or *Hotel des Isles*; and *Hotel Tafoukt*, both on Ave Mohammed V.

● **Banks & money changers**

Branches of **Bank Commercial du Maroc**, **Bank Populaire** and **Credit du Maroc** (you can change money here Sat morning in addition to normal banking hours) are in and around Place Moulay Hassan.

● **Post & telecommunications**

The PTT is on Ave Lalla Aicha, back from the seafront and Ave Mohammed V. Stamps also available from telephone booths opp *Restaurant Chalet de la Plage*. *Jack's Kiosk* will send a fax for you (MD30/sheet to England).

● **Shopping**

Essaouira is renowned for the fine quality of its cabinet making, marquetry and fine woodwork, in particular the intricate inlays of mother-of-pearl, ebony, lime wood and silver wire in thuya wood. There is plenty of opportunity to choose from an extensive array of trays, boxes, chess sets and furniture and some of the best examples can be purchased from the woodworkers' *souq* under the ramparts of the Skala de la Ville, also try rue Darb Laalouj nr the museum. Silver jewellery, brassware and spices can be found in the *souqs* off Ave de l'Istiqial; look for small woven articles as well as carpets and rugs in the small street which links Place Moulay Hassan with the Beffroi on Ave Oqba ben Nafia. For English books, try *Jack's Kiosk* on Place Moulay Hassan. For

general shopping, rue Mohammed ben Abdallah and Ave de l'Istiqial both offer a wide variety of interesting choices.

● **Tourist offices**

Ave du Caire, open Mon-Fri 0830-1200, but don't expect too much by way of useful information from this rather basic looking office.

● **Transport**

Local Bus: CTM and private line bus services operate from the terminal N of Bab Doukkala, with connections to Casablanca, Safi, Marrakech and Agadir. An ONCF service to Marrakech, to connect with onward trains to Casablanca and Rabat leaves at 0620. **Taxi**: grand-taxis operate from a parking lot beside the bus terminal, and also petit taxis in Ave Oqba ben Nafia opp the Art Gallery.

ESSAOUIRA TO SAFI VIA THE COAST

For the journey N to Safi the main route travels E on the P10 to Ounara and then N on the P8 through the market village of Talmest to Sebt-des-Gzoula. Here there is the option to branch off NW on the P120 or continue N to Bouguedra and then E on the P12. If you are travelling by car, following the coastal route is a much more attractive alternative; make sure, though, that you have sufficient petrol for the 125 km drive as there are no service stations once you leave the main road. Leave Essaouira on the P10 to Marrakech and after about 6 km turn left on a new road (not yet marked on the Michelin map) signposted to Safi. For about 15-20 km this fast stretch of well-metalled road travels through open scrub landscape before descending at Km 244 towards the sea near Cap Hadid to give superb views of Atlantic waves breaking on to a long, windswept beach. For much of the next 35 km there is plenty of opportunity to enjoy the wild, unspoiled beauty of the coastline and the mountains of the Chiadma region to the E. The highest peak in this range is Jbel Hadid (Iron Mountain), 725m. At Km 221 there is a rough track to the left to Plage Bhibhab and, on an otherwise isolated route, *Café Voyager* is passed just before Km 206.

Before reaching the new bridge across the Oued Tensift at Khemis-Oulad-el-Hadj, look for the ruins of **Kasbah Hamidouch**, an 18th century fortress built by Moulay Ismail. The road narrows and deteriorates as it follows the river estuary northwards but improves again at Souira Kédima (see page 226) where the rather dreary looking *Café Echabab* is close to the beach. For the next 15 km the route becomes more elevated with some fine cliff-top scenery before the left turn at the *Café-Restaurant Essaouira*, 17 km from Safi. Much of the remaining journey is through a large industrial complex; on reaching the ring road, best to head for the centre of town as signposting is certainly not Safi's strong point.

ESSAOUIRA TO AGADIR

The road S is set some distance in from the coast. Although Essaouira has extended there are remnants of the argane forest that once covered this area now cut through by the P8 to Agadir. At Km 161 a track goes W to Sidi Kaouki on the coast. After a further 19 km another track leads W to more marabouts. At Simimou a road leads E by the side of Jbel Amardma to Souq el Tnine and Sebt des Ait Daoud, an interesting detour. The road then descends the side of Jbel Amsittene with many bends to cross the two parts of the Oued Iguezoulen, then climbs up the other side. Tamanar is built

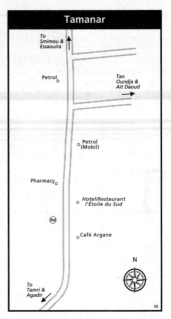

round a large kasbah. A winding road of 21 km leads down to the resort, shrine and viewpoint at Point Imessouane. A steep ascent leads up to Tamri, Cap Rhir offers good views, Paradis Plage is not as pleasant as its name suggests, Taghazout is a fishing village, and Agadir is reached. See page 347 for further details of this coastal stretch.

Meknes, Fes and Central Morocco

T HE REGION of Central Morocco is the pivotal strategic region of the country, through which military and trade routes have always passed, as well as a productive agricultural area. It is thus a region in which power has often been concentrated, and some of the greatest urban settlements have evolved.

Under the Romans power was, for a time, concentrated at the site of **Volubilis**, still the best preserved and most informative site of the period. Nearby, Moulay Idriss, the father of the Moroccan state is honoured in the pilgrimage town of the same name, a memorable settlement, with houses cascading down hills on either side of a large sanctuary. Moulay Idriss founded **Fes** which went on to become an imperial capital, and the undisputed intellectual, spiritual and cultural centre of the country. Today it is full of stunning examples of different periods of Islamic architecture, as well as *souqs*, each with its own speciality, still functioning at the heart of the city. **Meknes**, 522m, lying to the W of Fes, is a quieter city with a pleasant medina and the ruins of Sultan Moulay Ismail's vast capital. To the E of Fes, towards Algeria, Taza and Oujda are regional centres which have held vital strategic roles. To the S of Fes and Meknes lie the Middle Atlas mountains, with peaceful small towns amidst attractive wooded valleys.

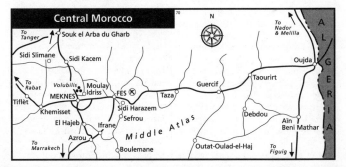

"Very high against the yellow sky show the lines of the superimposed ramparts, the innumerable terraces, the minarets, the towers of the mosques, the formidable embattled kasbahs, and, above a number of fortress walls, the green-tiled roof of the Sultan's Palace. It is even more imposing than Fez, and more solemn". Loti,

MEKNES AND ENVIRONS

From Rabat to Meknes the P1 passes through the Mamora Forest and a belt of fertile, relatively prosperous and unexciting countryside. The only major town en route is Khemisset, with a *souq* on Tues, and a reputation for the best *brochettes* in the small restaurants along the main street. The former imperial capital of Meknes lies between the Middle Atlas and the Cheraga hills. It is an essential stop en route to Fes, with a traditional medina and the ruins of Moulay Ismail's vast imperial city on either side of the huge and brightly tiled **Bab Mansur**. The shrine town of Moulay Idriss and the ruins of the Roman capital of Volubilis, the best ancient site in Morocco, are easy excursions from Meknes.

MEKNES

History

Meknes is a striking town, a fact accentuated by the backdrop of the Jbel Zerhoun, rising to 1,118m, to the N. The wooded foothills, cork oak at a height and cultivated orchards of olives, apples and pear below provide a green background to the white dwellings for much of the year. Meknes is one of the great historic cities of Morocco, pre-eminent during the reign of Moulay Ismail when its vast, and now mostly ruined, imperial city was built. This is memorable more for the impressive size and feeling of space than for the architecture. Another distinct part of Meknes is the historic medina

which includes the intricately decorated **Bou Inania Medersa**, the traditional but vibrant *souqs*, and numerous mosques. The *ville nouvelle* was built by the French on the opposite bank of the Oued Boufekrane, commanding impressive views over the medina and the imperial city. It has a relaxed atmosphere, a calm place to drink a coffee or tea and watch the evening *promenade* pass by.

Early origins Meknes was originally a kasbah from the 8th century, used by the Kharajite Berbers against the Arabs. The town itself was founded by the Zenata Berber tribe called Meknassa in the 10th century and then destroyed by the Almoravids in 1069. A later kasbah was destroyed by the Almohad Sultan Abd el-Moumen in order to build a new grid-patterned medina, some features of which still remain. This city was ruined during the conflict between the Almohads and the Merinids, but was partially rebuilt and repopulated in 1276 under Sultan Moulay Youssef. The Merinids also built the *medersa*.

The Reign of Moulay Ismail The reign of the Alawite Sultan, Moulay Ismail (1672-1727) witnessed the peak of Meknes' glory, as the dynamic Sultan used his immense power as *pasha* to develop the city before his succession to the imperial throne. Meknes was chosen as his capital rather than the rebellious and self-important rivals of Fes and Marrakech. Moulay Ismail is renowned for his ruthless violence, but many of the stories recounted by the guides may be apocryphal. What is certain is that he made a great impression on the visitors to the court from Europe, and Meknes became a kind of Moroccan Versailles, indeed, some suggest that the Sultan was trying to rival Louis XIV, who was building his French palace at the same time. Moulay Ismail conquered and then controlled Morocco and left his mark all over the country, particularly with the kasbahs built by his troops as they paci-

The jeweller's craft

🐾 Jewellers must be masters of many crafts. Those in Morocco certainly are. The many types of metal and insets require great skill.

The engraved jewellery is very popular (see Jewellery, page 62). Here the craftsman prepares his silvered plates and molds them to the shapes required. He then smears them with 'jewellers black', a preparation made from oil and darkened with smoke. When this is dried he removes with a dry tip the lines he intends to work on and eventually the pattern emerges. He sets up his metal on a tripod called a *h'mar el aoued* or 'wooden donkey' and carefully chisels where he had previously drawn. This 3-dimensional work is very skilful, particularly where the work is fine and the ornament small.

Jewellers must also be masters of the art of gilding. In earlier days this process was done with veneers of thin gold leaves or powdered gold mixed with fish glue which was then baked in a small wood fired oven. Today the gilding is done with an amalgam of powdered gold and a mercury base. This is brushed on to the base metal and then heated leaving a small film of gold. This process is repeated many times until the desired thickness of gold has been deposited.

Enamelled jewellery is very popular. Described simply, the shape for the decoration was scraped out of the metal and the liquid enamel was poured in. An alternative method was to place the powder in the desired shape and use fire to vitrify the enamel. In the SW of the country and in the Meknes region jewellers

still prepare their insets in their traditional way. Small enclosures are constructed with silver wires by welding them to the surface of the ornament. These circular and geometric spaces are filled with a dough of enamel paste which is then exposed to heat, care being taken not to melt the silver surround. Colours are obtained from copper (green), lead (yellow) and cobalt (blue).

Neatly shod

Babouches, the traditional footwear, slippers of soft leather with the heel turned in, probably derive their name from the Persian *papouch* which means foot covering. They vary in design depending on whether they are worn by men or women and are worn inside the home or outside. Men's slippers, generally called *balgha*, are lined with sheepskin and have stronger soles of goatskin. They are normally dyed a bright yellow but grey slippers are becoming more common. Women have a greater choice. Outdoor slippers called *rihiya* are most often black or red leather with perhaps an embossed pattern while indoor slippers or those for special occasions, the famous *cherbil*, are in a wide range of bright colours, lighter materials and are heavily decorated. While the sole, the *farracha* is still strong the upper may be only of velvet. The amount of decoration, em-
broidery in pure gold or silver thread, varies as do the stylized designs of leaves, flowers and geometric shapes, all of historic origin. The techniques of slipper making and gold-thread embroidery are associated with the town of Fes. When purchasing look for the craftsman's seal on the heel.

fied the numerous rebellious tribes, but also with an array of mosques, public buildings and medinas.

Moulay Ismail's vision of Meknes was vast, and although much of the *pisé* cement city is in ruins, those walls still standing are testimony to its original scale. The city was built by a massive army of slaves, both Moroccan and Christian, and the Sultan was in particular famed for his barbaric treatment of these people, supposedly interring them in the walls. He built several palaces to accommodate his wives, concubines, children and court, as well as quarters for his army of Abids, black slaves, which was the instrument of his power. The city contained within it all that was necessary for such a large population and military machine, with store houses, stables, armouries, exercise areas, gardens and ponds.

After Moulay Ismail After Moulay Ismail's death Meknes gradually declined. His huge court and army could not be held together without his author-

ity, and his successors Moulay Abdellah and Sidi Mohammed returned the emphasis to Fes and Marrakech. Furthermore the earthquake of 1755 destroyed many of Moulay Ismail's creations. The French revitalized Meknes, appreciating its strategic position in the corridor linking E Morocco and Algeria with the coastal belt around Rabat and Casablanca. They built their *ville nouvelle* apart from the medina and the Imperial City, on the E bank of the Oued Boufekrane, as part of their policy of separate development of Moroccan and European quarters. Meknes was an important army base for the French, and was not neglected in the way that Fes or Marrakech were.

Although Meknes is perhaps overshadowed by its near neighbour Fes, it is today the fifth largest city in Morocco with both tourism and industrial activities, and the centre of a highly productive agricultural region, noted particularly for its wines which are the best in the country.

ACCESS **Train** The main railway station is at Ave de la Basse, T 520017, 520689, but most trains also call at the Al Amir Abdelkader station, E of Ave Mohammed V, both in the *ville nouvelle*. **Road** Coming in from the E from Rabat along the P1, the principal route skirts the medina, crossing the Oued Boufekrane and reaching the *ville nouvelle* at the junction of Ave Moulay Ismail and Ave des Forces Armées Royales. Another route continues into the medina via Bab Khemis. From Fes and the E the P1 leads into Ave de Fes in the *ville nouvelle*. The P6 from Tanger and the N brings the traveller into the *ville nouvelle* along rue de Yougoslavie (Ave Al Moutahadia). **Bus**: CTM buses arrive at the terminal at 47 Ave Mohammed V, T 522583. Private line buses call at the terminal below Bab Mansur.

Places of interest

Guides Meknes is one of the easiest imperial cities to explore independently but there is no shortage of *faux guides* offering their services, often aggressively, in Place el Hedim and nearby. If you need assistance, obtain an official guide from the tourist office or one of the larger hotels. MD100 is a realistic fee.

The Medina: Place el Hedim (the Square of Destruction), opposite **Bab Mansur** is the centre of Meknes' old city, and the best starting point for exploration. This is certainly the biggest open square in the city and was once as busy as Djemaa El Fna in Marrakech (see page 302) with an open air theatre where acrobats and snake charmers performed. Despite its name this is a quiet area, other than the *faux guides* plying their trade, recently paved, set out with unremarkable fountains and surrounded by a few handicraft stalls and cafés. It is a pleasant place to sit. To the left of the square is a crowded, covered food market with vast displays of vegetables and pickles. On the right-hand corner of the square down a few steps is **Dar Jamai**, a 19th century palace, owned by officials at the court of Sultan Moulay Hassan, now the **Museum of Moroccan Arts** open 0900-1200 and 1500-1800, entrance MD10, T 530863. It was built in 1882 to be the residence of the very important Jamaï family, two of the family being ministers to Moulay el-Hassan. It was used as a military hospital after 1912 and only in 1920 used to display Moroccan Art. Exploring the house gives one an insight into the houses and life of the 19th century Muslim élite, with an interesting exhibition of craftwork (wrought iron, wooden sculpture, weaving, leather work, brass and copper wares) and antique household items, porcelain, jewellery and carpets mixing Berber and Andalusian influences, including pottery from Meknes and Fes, and carpets from the Middle Atlas. Once again the embroidery and use of colour are outstanding. The richly painted wooden chests and panels are a distinctive feature of the exhibition. Note also the wall tiles and jewellery. The upstairs includes a furnished reception room. The Andalusian garden planted with cypress and fruit trees indicates the degree of luxury enjoyed by those with wealth at that time.

The souqs Meknes has seven traditional *souqs*, all in the medina, which whilst not quite of the order of those in Marrakech or Fes, are worth exploring. Immediately to the left of the **Dar Jamai** a small entrance leads to the *souqs*. The

Strip of mosaic tile work

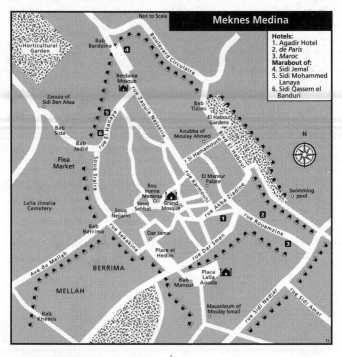

Meknes Medina

Not to Scale

Hotels:
1. Agadir Hotel
2. de Paris
3. Maroc
Marabout of:
4. Sidi Jemal
5. Sidi Mohammed Lanaya
6. Sidi Qassem el Banduri

alley bends around to the right behind Dar Jamai past some undistinguished clothes shops. Just before a carpet shop turn left. The passage, now covered, widens slightly, and continues past a range of shops selling modern goods, a bank, and various minor side turnings. At the junction, on the left, is **Souq Nejjarin** (see below). **Souq Sebbat** is the right hand turning including sellers of *baboushes*, modern clothes and *kaftans*, several tourist and handicraft shops, a *fondouk* on the right, and another on the left before the **Bou Inania Medersa**. A turning on the right opposite the *medersa* leads directly onto rue Dar Smen, a good alternative route to remember.

Although non-Muslims are not permitted to enter the **Grand Mosque** it is possible to view the green tiled roof with

its series of six domes leading up the central nave to the *quibla* wall and the similarly decorated minaret from the neighbouring Bou Inania Medersa. The Grand Mosque, situated in the heart of the medina, is 12th century Almoravid with 14th century alterations. It is one of the oldest in Meknes and also the largest, with 12 doors (one main one and 11 less important).

Bou Inania Medersa The Merinid Bou Inania *Medersa* (open 0900-1200 and 1500-1800), built by Abul Hassan dating from 1345, is the most important building to visit in the medina. It is best approached from Souq Sebbat. The door to the *medersa*, part of a cedar screen, is just past a dome, notable for its ribbed design.

This religious school has 40 cells for

A
journey of
1000 miles
begins with
your first
footprint...

With apologies to
Lao Tzu c.604 - 531 BC

Footprint Handbooks

Win two Iberia flights to Latin America

Welcome to Footprint Handbooks - the most exciting new development in travel guides since the original South American Handbook from Trade & Travel.

We want to hear your ideas for further improvements as well as a few details about yourself so that we can better serve your needs as a traveller.

We are offering you the chance to win two Iberia flights to Latin America. Iberia is the leading airline for Latin America, currently flying to 34 destinations. Every reader who sends in their completed questionnaire will be entered in the Footprint Prize Draw. 10 runners up will win an exclusive Footprint T-shirt!

Complete in a ball-point pen and return this tear-off questionnaire as soon as possible.

1 **Title of this Handbook** _____

2 **Age** Under 21 ☐   21 - 30 ☐   31 - 40 ☐
           41 - 50 ☐   over 50 ☐

3 **Occupation** _____

4 **Which region do you intend visiting next?**
   North America ☐ India/S. Asia ☐ Africa ☐
   Latin America ☐ S.E. Asia   ☐ Europe ☐
   Australia   ☐

5 **Which country(ies) do you intend visiting next?**
   _____

6 **There is a complete list of Footprint Handbooks at the back of this book. Which other countries would you like to see us cover?**
   _____

Please enter your name and permanent address:

Name_____

Address_____

_____

_____

E-mail_____

Offer ends 30 November 1997. Prize Draw winners will be notified by 30 January 1998. Flights are subject to availability.

IBERIA Win two Iberia flights to Latin America

Footprint Handbooks
6 Riverside Court
Lower Bristol Road
Bath
BA2 3DZ
England

Affix Stamp Here

Footprint Handbooks

6 Riverside Court
Lower Bristol Road
Bath BA2 3DZ
T 01225 469141
F 01225 469461
handbooks@footprint.cix.co.uk

Andalucía Handbook

Zimbabwe & Malawi Handbook with Botswana, Mozambique, Zambia

Caribbean Islands Handbook with the Bahamas

Morocco Handbook with Mauritania

Indonesia Handbook

Chile Handbook

Cambodia Handbook

India Handbook

Vietnam Handbook

Thailand Handbook

East Africa Handbook with Kenya, Tanzania, Uganda and Ethiopia

South Africa Handbook

Tibet Handbook with Bhutan

Peru Handbook

Malaysia & Singapore Handbook

Namibia Handbook

Myanmar (Burma) Handbook

Egypt Handbook

Ecuador & Galápagos Handbook

Mexico & Central America Handbook

Laos Handbook

South American Handbook

Tunisia Handbook with Libya

Caid Maclean – Military Advisor to the Sultan

In 1877 Harry de Vere Maclean, a British subject resident in Gibraltar, was employed by the Moroccan Sultan Moulay Hassan to train and manage his small regular army and to oversee the work of Moroccan military personnel who had been trained by the British Gibraltar garrison. Harry Maclean became a trusted servant of the Sultan, a *caid* (of magisterial rank), though incurring the deep suspicion of the French government. Among Caid Maclean's exploits was the transfer in 1891 of an Indian elephant called 'Stoke', which was a gift from Queen Victoria to the Sultan, from Tanger to Meknes. The trip was full of incident as the British and Indian escorts walked the elephant through mountain passes and across deep gorges past the assembled crowds of incredulous rural Moroccans. Sultan Moulay Hassan was reported to have been much pleased with his present.

The efforts of Caid Maclean and other officers from Europe to improve the Moroccan army were lost after the death of Moulay Hassan in 1894. His successor, Abdelaziz, was less talented and less dedicated to maintaining the state. The military and political developments of the reign of Moulay Hassan were frittered away at a time when tribal factions within Morocco were gaining in strength and French claims to bring Morocco within its sphere of influence were becoming more insistent.

its students, on both floors, around an oblong courtyard including a pool, with arcades surrounded by a screened passageway. As with many of the *medressa* there is a good range of decoration, the *zellij* tiling catching the eye, whilst the carving on the beams and screens are also skilfully and beautifully executed. There is a plentiful display of intricate Koranic inscription executed in a range of materials around the walls and pillars.

Turn right to the green and yellow tiled prayer hall. The door is ornamented with *zellij* tiling, as well as the customary and perhaps a little over-the-top stalactite style plasterwork. Note the inscriptions by the *mihrab*. Climb up onto the roof for a view of the medina, including the domed roof of the Great Mosque, the minaret of the Nejjarin Mosque, and other minarets.

Beyond the *medersa* bear right then second left passing a number of handicraft shops, notably selling iron pots and figures decorated with beaten silver thread, to **El Mansur Palace**, a former palace now a carpet shop and called the *Palais des Idrissides*. It is worth entering

to see the impressive stucco and wood carving, and ceiling painting. From here the energetic can continue on into the northern medina.

Souq Nejjarin, includes sellers of textiles, and carpenters, another entrance to the carpet *souq*, and a *fondouk* hardly changed since it was built. This route passes the Almoravid **Nejjarin Mosque**. At the end one can turn left towards the *mellah* or Place el Hedim or right into the dusty and noisy **Souq Sraira**, just inside the city walls, used by carpenters and metalworkers. At the very end, on left, is the 12th century Almohad **Bab Jedid** gate, around which are some interesting stalls selling musical instruments. **Souq Cherchira**, initially occupied by tentmakers runs parallel to Souq Sraira but outside the city walls.

The Mellah To the W of Place El Hedim through a street popular with hawkers of household goods turn left into Ave de Mellah. On the left is the *mellah* a quarter built by Moulay Ismail in 1682 for his large Jewish community, walled off from the Muslim medina. The

Bab Berrima Mosque dates from the 18th century when the *mellah* was becoming increasingly Muslim, as the Jews were moved further downhill into the medina.

Heading SW towards Rabat the city wall is broken by **Bab El Khemis** (**Bab Rih**), built by Moulay Ismail, with a range of different arches, decoration and calligraphy. It is certainly very stylish, with intricate tile work and its floral decoration. This is the only remaining piece of the garden quarter attributed to Moulay Ismail. The rest has gone. It was destroyed by Moulay Abdellah, son of the great Moulay Ismail, who was not pleased by the ironic reception he received from the inhabitants when he returned from an unsuccessful campaign. Through this the Blvd Circulaire leads past the 18th century tomb of Sidi Mohammed Ben Aissa, founder of the important religious brotherhood of the Aissoua, closed to non-Muslims but worth a look from a respectable distance. The Ben Aissa religious fête is still held on *Mouloud*, but is no longer the ritually violent occasion it once was. The Blvd Circulaire continues round to Bab el-Berdaine, the entrance to the N medina.

The northern medina is less frequented by tourists. Either weave through the medina from the *medersa* or the *souqs*, or more easily, enter from the Blvd Circulaire. **Bab Berdaine**, dates from the 17th century, a building decorated by Jamaa el Rouah and flanked by two immense towers. Inside, on Place el Berdaine, is the **Berdaine Mosque**. Travelling S the streets continue through an area of the traditional medina, less spoilt by the demands of tourism, and indicating more clearly the nature of the Islamic City where private and public space are clearly differentiated, commercial areas zoned by function, with each quarter having its own mosque, *hammam* and *four* (bakers), the three most important facilities in the neighbourhood. Eventually one will pass the **El Mansur Palace**, another 19th century house (see above).

Back on the Blvd Circulaire, the next major gate around towards Oued Boufekrane is Bab Tizmi, near to *Restaurant Zitouna*. Opposite Bab Tizmi is the small and quiet **Parc Zoologique El Haboul** (open 1300-1700 Tues-Thur, 1000-2000 Fri-Sun, closed Mon). This zoo is one part of an area of gardens and recreational facilities in the valley dividing the medina and the *ville nouvelle*.

Bab Mansur Meknes is dominated by the monumental gate at the top of the hill in the medina, opposite Place el Hedim. Bab Mansur is claimed by some to be the finest gateway in North Africa. It dates from the reign of Sultan Moulay Ismail, and was completed by his son Moulay Mohammed Ben Abdellah in 1732, and marks the entrance to the huge grounds of his Imperial City. The gate is named after one of the Sultan's Christian slaves, Mansur the Infidel. The huge size is more of a testimony to its Sultan than a reflection of defensive strength, as design is more ceremonial, for example the decorated flanking towers do not have firing posts.

The *outrepassé* arch is surrounded by a blind arch including the *darj w ktaf* motif and colourful *zellij* tiling. The

Tile design - based on a flower

frame is a band of *darj w ktaf* and *zellij* surmounted by inscription, and between the arch and the band is a black tiled area with floral patterns. The overall effect of the main gate is an exuberant and powerful display of the architecture of Moulay Ismail's reign. This has come to be a symbol of Meknes.

The Imperial City of Moulay Ismail is a massive area of crumbling walls and ruins well worth taking a day to explore at leisure. Immediately through Bab Mansur from Place el Hedim there is Place Lalla Aouda, once the public meeting point during the period of Moulay Ismail and now a relaxing and pleasant area to rest. In the far corner is the **Lalla Aouda Mosque**, the story being that it was built by Princess Aouda as penance for eating a peach during the Ramadan fast.

Directly opposite Bab Mansur, in the right hand corner of the square, a space in the walls leads through to a second square, the Mechouar. To the right note the domed **Koubat al-Khayyatin** situated in a small park behind a fence, entrance MD10. A plain building with pleasing simple decor. In the 18th century this was used to receive ambassadors, and later to make uniforms. To the right of this building steps lead down to an underground space, variously explained as a prison or a storehouse. In the wall opposite the small park the right hand gate leads to a golf course. This was originally to have been a lake, but was converted into its present usage by the present king. Behind the golf course is a later palace of Moulay Ismail, the **Royal Palace** or **Dar al-Makhzen**, still in use and now heavily restored, closed to visitors.

The Mausoleum of Moulay Ismail can be reached through the gate to the left of that to the golf course. The Mausoleum, inside, opposite some shops selling over-priced handicrafts, contains the tombs of Moulay Ismail, his wife and Moulay Ahmed. Unusually for religious buildings in Morocco, the Mausoleum is open to non-Muslims who can enter as far as an annex to the mosque section and admire from there the plaster stucco, *zellij* tiling and distinctive and exuberant colouring. The guardian normally allows visitors to take photos of the interior of the mosque from the annex. Entrance free. Close by is the Koubat el Khayatine, the building where Moulay Ismail received foreign ambassadors. Just past the mausoleum is an entrance to **Dar al-Kebira**, Moulay Ismail's late 17th century palace. The palace is in ruins, and occupied by squatters in an ironic statement on Morocco's housing situation, but the nature and vast scale of the original basic structure of the building can be easily discerned. Back out on the road pass under the passage of the **Bab ar-Rih**, a long, arched structure. Follow the walled road, running between the Dar al-Kebira and the Dar al-Makhzen and turn right at the end. Carry straight ahead until the large **Heri as-Souni** building is reached.

Heri as-Souni, also called Dar el Ma, open 0830-1200 and 1430-1830, is a large, impressive structure dating from the reign of Moulay Ismail, used variously as a granary, warehouse and water point, to provide for the court, army and followers in either the normal run of events or in case of conflict or drought, and indicating the scale of the imperial city which Moulay Ismail built. The first, long room exhibits typical furniture, decoration and woodwork from the richer Meknes houses. The second room is surrounded by large storerooms and wells, the latter were used with a donkey-powered system of chain-buckets. Behind this is a vast space originally used as a granary. From the roof there is a good view. To the right is the Agdal basin now storing water for irrigation purposes previously a vital reserve in case of siege. This is a pleasant location as popular at weekends and summer evenings as it was when used by the king's many wives when it was first con-

structed. Nevertheless it is rather stark and lacks integration into the landscape.

Heri al-Mansur Turn right and then take the second left. On the left is the

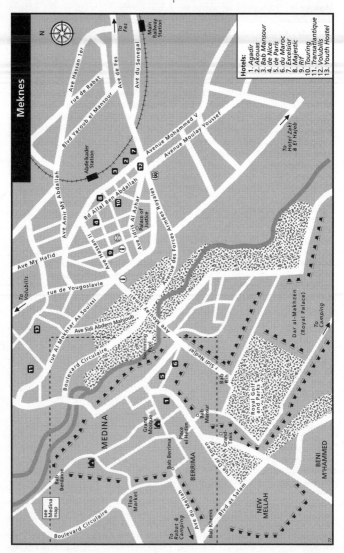

Meknes

Hotels:
1. Agadir
2. Akouas
3. Bab Mansour
4. de Nice
5. de Paris
6. du Maroc
7. Excelsior
8. Majestic
9. Rif
10. Touring
11. Transatlantique
12. Volubilis
13. Youth Hostel

Dar al-Baida or White Palace built by Sultan Mohammed Ibn Abdellah in the 1790s, now a military academy closed to visitors. He also built the **Rouah Mosque** in 1790, with columns from the **Badia Palace** in Marrakech. To the left is a small *medersa* used as a Koranic school. Nearby is a long canal alongside the massive structure of the **Heri al-Mansur**, also known as the **Rouah**. This ruined building, once the stables, reveals much about the size of the Sultan's retinue.

Local information
● Accommodation
B *Hotel Tikida Transatlantique*, rue El Marinyen, T 525051/6, F 520057, central, 120 a/c rm, 2 restaurants and a bar, tennis, 2 good pools, an elegant, stylish and well-equipped hotel with excellent view of the medina, dating from the 1930s.

C *Hotel Rif*, rue d'Accra, *ville nouvelle*, T 522591/4, F 524428, 120 rm, new, comfortable, soundproofed and a/c, Moroccan decor, lively nightclub (2130-0300), 2 restaurants, good bar, TV room, pool, safe parking; **C** *Hotel Zaki*, Blvd Al Massira, city outskirts, T 520990, Tx 41079, 230 a/c rm, 2 restaurants, 2 bars, nightclub and pool, rec.

D *Akouas Hotel*, 27 rue Emir Abdelkader, T 515967, F 515994, new, 52 rm, 2 restaurants, bar, nightclub (2200-0100); **D** *Hotel Bab Mansur*, 38 rue Emir Abdelkader, T 525239/40, F 510741, 76 rm and 2 suites, new, all with carpets and TV, restaurant, bar, nightclub, in *ville nouvelle*; **D** *Hotel de Nice*, 10 rue d'Accra, T 520318, restaurant, bar, centre of *ville nouvelle*, safe parking, good rooms; **D** *Hotel Volubilis*, 45 Ave des Forces Armées Royales, T 520102, bar, nightclub, quite old, conveniently located.

E *Hotel Excelsior*, 57 Ave des Forces Armées Royales, T 521900, 42 rm, another cheap *ville nouvelle* option; **E** *Hotel Majestic*, 19 Ave Mohammed V, T 522033, F 527427, 42 clean rm, excellent value, friendly staff; **E** *Hotel Touring*, 34 Ave Allal Ben Abdellah, T 522351, cheap, respectable, large rooms, café.

F *Hotel du Maroc*, 7 Derb Ben Brahim, off rue Rouamzine, T 530075, 28 rm, the best cheap hotel in the medina, quiet, clean and efficient, cold showers; *Hotel Agadir*, 2 rue Dar Smen (on the small square), T 530141, 18 tiny and basic rm in a bizarre, distinctively decorated rabbit-warren; *Hotel de Paris*, 58 rue Rouamzine, 11 good rm but no showers.

The gates on the left of Heri as-Souni lead to the campsite.

Camping: *Camping Agdal*, 2 km from Meknes centre on the road to Rabat, take buses 2 or 3, there on a 4 ha site is a shop, café, laundry, electricity for caravans, and hot showers, and it is clean and well organized, petrol only 2 km. Camping also at **Moulay Idris** some 30 km N and at **El Hajeb** about 32 km S of Meknes, site of 3 ha, small shop, showers, laundry, electricity for caravans, petrol 100m, convenient for bus routes N and S on P21. *Camping Refuge* at Zerhoun nr Meknes, small site, snacks, showers, electricity for caravans.

Youth hostel: T 524698, Ave Okba Ibn Nafii, 1000-1200, 1600-1700, near the municipal stadium and *Hotel Transatlantique*, 60 beds, MD25-35 per night, kitchen, meals available, bus 25m, train 1.2 km. This is the YHA headquarters in Morocco and is one of the best and most friendly hostels with dormitories around a garden, well maintained.

● Places to eat
◆◆◆ *Restaurant Belle Vue* in *Hotel Transatlantique*, rue El Marinyen, T 525051-6, an extensive international menu, good wines, excellent views over Meknes medina from its *ville nouvelle* hilltop location; *La Hacienda*, Route de Fes outside Meknes, T 521092, highly rec excellent French and international food in a farm atmosphere, nightclub below; *Restaurant Zitouna*, 44 Jamaa Zitouna, T 532083, in style of a Moroccan palace in a medina side-street nr Bab Tizmi, with a Moroccan menu, no alcohol.

◆◆ *Restaurant Bar Brasserie Metropole*, 12 Ave Hassan II, T 522576, international menu, licensed; *Bar Restaurant La Coupole*, Ave Hassan II, T 522483, French/Moroccan menu, friendly, quiet, reasonable food, licensed; *Café Restaurant Camprinoss*, Ave Omar Ibn El Ass (opp the market in the *ville nouvelle*), T 520258, French, Spanish and Moroccan cuisine, unlicensed; *Le Dauphin*, 5 Ave Mohammed V, T 523423, licensed Moroccan restaurant, seafood; *Pizzeria Le Four*, 1 rue Atlas, T 520857, reasonable international cuisine and moderate pizzas in a pleasant atmosphere, good wine.

◆ *Rôtisserie Karam*, 2 Ave Ghana, good chicken, *brochettes* and salads; *Novelty*, Ave de Paris, T 522156, Moroccan food, licensed; *Restaurant Economique* is perhaps the best of several cheap and basic Moroccan restaurants on rue Dar Smen.

Cafés: the aromatic mint tea of Meknes is recommended. Try one of the cafés on rue Dar Smen, or one of the better hotels. In the *ville*

nouvelle try *Cremerie-Patisserie Miami*, Ave Mohammed V.

● **Bars**

Hotel Transatlantique, rue El Marinyen, is an excellent place for a relaxing drink, not least because of the view over the medina; also try the *Hotel de Nice*, 10 rue d'Accra; *La Carav-*

A smooth tale of olive oil

Most of the world's supply of olive oil comes from the Mediterranean Basin and, not surprisingly, most is consumed there. Morocco is one of the leading producers.

In Morocco, at the last count there were some 33 million olive trees under cultivation and 90% were of the same variety – the Moroccan Picholine. Annual olive production is around 350,000 tonnes of which some 80% will be pressed to produce about 53,000 tonnes of oil.

While the best fruits are selected as table olives, those that are smaller than average are picked in Dec or Jan when they are a deep black. This is when lipogenesis is complete, ie the fleshy part is saturated with oil, which with the pit removed amounts to about 18-28% oil.

The harvested berries are washed in tepid water then crushed. Originally the olives were crushed by conical stones moved round on a base by an animal or by hand. Many Roman oil presses remain. In **Volubilis** near Meknes 55 olive presses were found, 16 at **Lixus** near Larache and 15 at **Tingis**, present day Tanger. The resulting paste was placed between mats of grass or straw and then squeezed in a press, the animal walking round to tighten the screw. The resulting oil, dark and thick, is separated off and purified.

Today the hydraulic presses do a better but less picturesque job. The oil is separated from the water by centrifuge, is filtered and kept in airtight vats until bottled. The initial pressing produces 'virgin' oil which, like wines, must be of a particular standard. The residual pulp is pressed again, with hot water, and the result has the unusual name of *lampante*, as this was oil originally used for lamps. Lampante and inferior virgin oils are refined to reduce the acid, colour and smell and the result, refined olive oil, is for food and for industry.

The oil varies in quality and colour, rather like wine. Some oil is a clear yellow, some has a rich golden hue.

Olive oil is classified as:

Extra virgin oil: oil with no flaws, produced from perfect olives which are picked ripe and processed at once. Acidity must not be over 1%. This oil adds flavour and aromatic fragrance to Mediterranean cooking. Like good wine it is rich and delicious.

Virgin olive oil: oil from olives not bruised, damaged or subjected to adverse temperatures. Can only be blended with other virgin oils. Limit of acidity is 1.5%.

Pure olive oil: lacks the quality of the above, being more acid and cheaper.

Olive oil also smooths the economic path as employment is provided in 170 pressing factories and by over 15,000 traditional olive presses or *maasras*, in bottling/canning factories and in transportation.

Olive oil is good for you – being very easy to digest and having little effect on the level of cholesterol in the blood. It is safer too – reaching 210°C – before bursting into flame. No chip pan fires in Morocco.

elle, 6 rue de Marseille; *Bar Continental* and *La Coupole* both in Ave Hassan II.

● **Banks & money changers**
ABM, Angle Blvd Nehru and rue Ali Ben Rahal, T 520015; **Banque du Maroc**, 33 Ave Mohammed V; **BMAO**, 15 Place 2 Septembre; **BMCE**, 98 Ave des Forces Armées Royales, T 520352, bureau de change open every day 1000-1400 and 1600-2000; **Credit du Maroc**, 33 Ave Mohammed V; **SGMB**, Place Al Wahda Al Ifriquia, T 527896; **Wafabank**, 11 Ave Mohammed V, T 521151.

● **Cultural Centre**
Centre Culturel Français, Zankat Farhat Hachad, Ave Hassan II, cultural and social programme.

● **Entertainment**
Discos & nightclubs: *Bahia*, *Rif Hotel*, rue d'Accra (2130-0300); *Cabaret Oriental*, *Grand-Hotel Volubilis*, 45 Ave des Forces Armées Royales. Also at *Hotel Zaki*, Blvd Al Massira, *Akouas Hotel*, 27 rue Emir Abdelkader (2200-0100) and *Hotel Bab Mansur*, 38 rue Emir Abdelkader.

● **Hammam**
4 rue Patrice Lumumba.

● **Hospitals & medical services**
Ambulance: T 15.
Chemists: *Pharmacie d'Urgence*, Place Administrative, T 523375, 0830-2030; *Depot de Nuit: Medicaments d'Urgence*, *Hotel de Ville*, Place Administrative (2030-0830).
Hospitals: Hôpital Mohammed V, T 521134; Hôpital Moulay Ismail, Ave des Forces Armées Royales, T 522805, 522806.

● **Places of worship**
Catholic Church: Notre Dame des Oliviers, Place Poereiam, services Sat 1800, Sun 1030.

● **Post & telecommunications**
PTT Centrale, Place Administrative, 0800-1400, T 0800-2100; also the PTT on rue Dar Smen, in the medina.

● **Shopping**
One of the specialities of Meknes is iron work decorated with beaten silver thread. For this and other specialities try the medina, or the *Ensemble Artisanale*, on the road out to Rabat, 0830-1200 and 1530-1830, with a fixed price shop, bank, and an extensive training centre and individual workshops which visitors will be shown on request.

● **Sports**
Aviation: *Meknes Royal Flying Club*, T 522941; *Delta Plane Municipal* camp site, Agdal, T 524952.

Golf: *Royal Golf Club*, El Mhancha, T 530753, 9 holes, 2,707m, par 36, fee per round MD200, closed Mon.

Riding: *L'Etrier* (Haras Régional).

Skiing: *Skiing Club*, T 524268.

Swimming: *Lahboul Park*, Rond-Point Bou Amer, BP 45, T 520415.

Tennis: *Club de Meknes*, Lahboul Park, Rond-Point Bou Amer, BP 45, T 520415.

● **Tour companies & travel agents**
Wagons-Lit Tourisme, 1 rue de Ghana, T 521995; *Wasteels Voyages*, Ave Mohammed V, T 523062. *Royal Air Maroc*, 7 Ave Mohammed V, T 520963.

● **Tourist offices**
Office du Tourisme (ONMT), 27 Place Bathal'Istiqlal, T 521286, very helpful; **Syndicat d'Initiative**, Palais de la Foire, T 520191.

● **Useful telephone numbers**
Fire: T 15.
Police: T 19.

● **Transport**
Local Bus: bus station, Ave Mohammed V, T 522583/4 for CTM and LN coaches. Buses No 5, 7 and 9 run between the *ville nouvelle* and the medina. **Taxi**: use the light blue petit-taxis.

Train The main station is at Ave de la Basse, T 520017, 520689. Departures for **Rabat** and **Casablanca**: 0409, 0749, 0954, 1144, 1503, 1655, 1927, 2026, 0242; for **Tanger**: 0459, 1346; for **Fes**: 11 a day between 0547 and 0240; for **Taza** and **Oujda**: 0547, 1344, 1549, 1855, 0031, 0240. Some trains also stop at Meknes El Amir Abdelkader station, just below Ave Mohammed V, and closer to the centre of the *ville nouvelle*.

Road Bus: CTM buses to Rabat, Casablanca and Fes (7 a day), Tanger, Ifrane, Azrou, Ouezzane and Er Rachidia (daily) leave from 47 Ave Mohammed V, T 522583. Private line services go from the terminal below Bab Mansur. **Taxi**: grand-taxis which are a particularly good option to both Fes and Azrou, leave from the car park below Place el Hedim, opposite the private line buses. Ask the drivers hanging around for the destination. Grand-taxis for Moulay

Idriss (and then a short walk to Volubilis) leave from rue Yougoslavie.

Agourai, about 20 km S of Meknes, is in the foothills of the Zaiane. Many of the people have names more akin to Europe than to the Middle Atlas. As explanation, Moualy Ismail is said to have given this area to his Christian prisoners for services rendered. This is an important vine growing region producing some reasonable wines.

EXCURSION WEST
FROM MEKNES

Khemisset is in the heart of the Zemmour region, a very busy town in an interesting area of olive plantations and extensive cereal fields. From here there is the opportunity to travel N on the S205 to the Barrage el Kansera or SW on the S106 to the popular inland resort of *Daya er-Roumi*, camping site of 1 ha, swimming in lake (depends on water level), electricity for caravans.

The P1 continues W to **Tiflet**, an important local market town where Oulmés bottled water is produced. Here the spring comes from the banks of the Oued Aguennour at the bottom of a deep canyon. Access to the spring, a drop of 700m is by jeep along a road with hairpin bends and a precipitous drop. Quite an experience. The area is wooded with ancient cork oaks. The bottling takes place some 7 km from the site. At the spring there are baths carved out of the

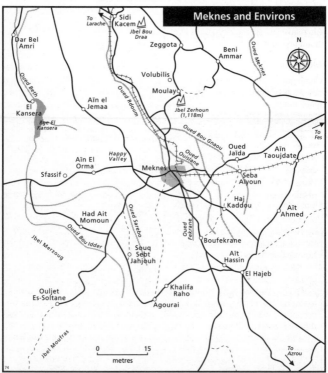

Meknes and Environs

rock where it is possible to bath in water at body temperature. There is a hotel with 46 rooms near the spring and the surrounding area offers hunting and fishing, walking and riding.

EXCURSION TO MOULAY IDRISS AND VOLUBILIS

The shrine town of Moulay Idriss is 30 km to the N of Meknes. Leave Meknes by rue de Yougoslavie in the *ville nouvelle*, and follow the P6 as far as Aïn el-Kerna, and from there the P28 to Moulay Idriss. Take a grand-taxi from rue de Yougoslavie, or from the square below Place el Hedim, to Moulay Idriss. There are also regular buses from below Bab Mansur. The last bus back is at 1900. Volubilis is a clearly signposted 5 km drive from Moulay Idriss, a pleasant walk on a nice day, or a short taxi ride. Alternatively, bargain in Meknes for a grand-taxi all the way.

MOULAY IDRISS

Coming round the last bend from Meknes, Moulay Idriss is a dramatic sight, houses and mosques piled up around two rock outcrops, with the *zaouia*, or sanctuary, in between. The centre of the Jbel Zerhoun region, Moulay Idriss is a pilgrimage centre, including as it does the tomb of its namesake, the great-grandson of the prophet, the town a Mecca in Morocco for those unable to do the ultimate pilgrimage. Moulay Idriss (see box, page 250) came to Morocco from Arabia, after defeat at the Battle of Fakh in 786. In 788 he was accepted as *Imam* by the Berber Aurora tribe at Volubilis, and went on in his short life in Morocco, before he was poisoned in 791, to win over the loyalty of the tribes to the Idrissid Dynasty he established, and to spread further the faith of Islam. This town and Fes were two of his major legacies.

However, the town of Moulay Idriss was mainly developed in the 18th century by Sultan Moulay Ismail, in part using materials lifted from nearby Volubilis, which the Sultan plundered without restraint. Moulay Idriss was closed to non-Muslims until 1912, and even today is primarily a Muslim sanctuary, best visited during the day as an excur-

The 'golden age' of Moulay Ismail

Moulay Ismail became Sultan in 1672 as head of the Alawite Dynasty. His reign is associated with a period of great stability and city building, especially at Meknes, which was his chosen capital. Old sites were cleared so that a new kasbah, stores and gardens could be constructed at Meknes. The military zone of the town was extended to accommodate an army numbering more than 150,000 men. His empire was extensive and no less than 76 garrisons were set up to defend the sultan's interests. He enforced a strong central rule on the country, overwhelming the regional tribal leaders. He was also notably successful against the Europeans, pushing the British out of Tanger in 1674 and the Portuguese from Asilah in 1691.

Moulay Ismail is remembered for his authoritarian rule. He permitted no opposition, putting down any possible source of political challenge ruthlessly. Indeed he is known as much for his cruelty as his tremendous effort at building roads, dams and cities. He also failed to train and introduce a successor to take over after his 53 years of absolute rule. His death was followed by a struggle for the succession during which the country declined into anarchy. For those who wish to see the architectural achievements of Moulay Ismail, go no further than the imperial city in Meknes, where the gates and palaces give a sample of the grand status of the Sultan Ismail.

sion, and although not unfriendly, certainly a place to be treated with cautious respect. A religious festival, or *moussem* is held here in Aug, when the town is transformed by an influx of pilgrims and a sea of tents.

Buses and taxis stop in the main square where there are some basic restaurants and cafés, and below it an open market space. Above it is the **Moulay Idriss Zaouia**, as well as shops for items associated with pilgrimage: rosaries, scarves, candles, and a delicious array of nougats, candies and nuts, taken by Muslims as souvenirs. The sanctuary itself, with its green-tiled roofs, a succession of prayer halls, ablution areas and tombs, is closed to non-Muslims.

Looking up from the square, the medina clings to the two hills, on the left is Khiba, Tasga on the right. The steep paths through either section pass through a fascinating and largely unaltered area of housing. After the steep climb there is a rewarding view over the sanctuary, showing the courtyards and roofs, and the adjacent royal guesthouse. The road through the town, keeping right, leads to a Roman bath just above the stream. Further on, beyond the road, there is a ruined 18th century palace with a good view of the town.

There are no hotels in Moulay Idriss, but there is a camp-site, *Zermoune Belle Vue*, en route to Meknes, whilst opposite the turning to Volubilis the proprietor of

Moulay Idriss – Islamic Missionary in Morocco

🦶 In the early years of Islam in North Africa conquest was achieved by the sword and by inspired commanders such as Uqba bin Nafi who in 682 won Volubilis and northern Morocco and Tarik, who made the first incursions into Iberia in 711 AD. Lightening conquests were superficial and it was left to men of peace to bring Islam in the wake of the Arab armies.

No more dramatic story exists than that of Moulay Idriss, known as the 'Elder' or the 'Great'. He was on the losing side in the battles of the campaign in Iraq in 786 AD when Ali, claimant by blood line to the Islamic Caliphate, was defeated and killed. Moulay Idriss fled to the extreme edge of the then Muslim world (Morocco is still known as Maghreb Al-Akhtar – the extreme west). As a grandson of Ali and the Prophet's daughter Fatimah, he could also claim a direct line from Mohammed himself. He came as a refugee to Morocco in about 787, staying first at Oulili. He set up an Islamic sanctuary/centre or *zaouia* near to Volubilis, close to the town named after him – Moulay Idriss – and began the conversion of the people of the region to Islam. He was very successful and was adopted as a venerable holy man by the entire tribal zone of northern Morocco. He was eventually nominated as sultan and became a very powerful political figure, ruling over a peaceful and constructive period in which the foundations were laid for the new city of Fes.

His emergence as the principal personality in NW Morocco was resented by the Caliph in Baghdad who feared that the area would become one of Shi'ite dissent from the orthodoxy (Sunni Islam) of the centre. Moulay Idriss was poisoned – reportedly at the behest of the Caliph Haroun Al-Rashid – in 791 AD. His mark on the totally Muslim city of Moulay Idriss and on the city of Fes have made him a continuing folk hero and a saint of influence. There is an annual pilgrimage in late summer to the site of his mausoleum, rebuilt with only moderate good taste in the 19th century. The Fassi faithful troop in their thousands to make their penance and seek good fortune in their affairs (see page 249).

The Marabout

The North African landscape is dotted with small white painted buildings scattered about the hillsides, hilltops and cemeteries. These are the burial places of the holy men or *marabouts* (*marabit* in Arabic) though the practice of adopting seers and ascetics is thought to have preceded the coming of Islam. The *marabout* was a religious teacher who gained credibility by gathering disciples around him and getting acknowledgement as a man of piety and good works. *Marabouts* were in many cases migrant preachers travelling to and from Mecca or were organizers of sufi schools. Place names of *marabout* sites are mainly after the names of the holy man interred there usually prefixed by the word 'sidi'. Some sites are very modest, comprising a small raised tomb surrounded by a low wall, all whitewashed. Other *marabouts* have a higher tomb several metres square topped by a dome (*koubba*). In some instances, *marabout* tombs are large house-like structures acting as mausoleums and shrines. Most tombs in rural areas can carry stakes bearing flags in green cloth as symbols of the piety of their donors and as a token of the continuing protection provided by the *marabout*.

Annual processions or pilgrimages (*moussem*) are made to the *marabout* shrines for good luck, fertility and protection against the evil spirits. This is particularly the case where the area around is occupied by a tribe claiming descent from the holy man in question.

In Morocco there are more than 600 pilgrimages each year to *marabout* sites. Look particularly for the tomb of Moulay Idriss in the town of the same name 25 km N of Meknes where the annual pilgrimage takes place in Sept with the participation of high officers of state.

the café allows people to camp. For lunch *Baraka de Zerhoun*, 22 Aïn Smen-Khiber, T 44184, with good Moroccan food at average prices, is recommended.

VOLUBILIS

Volubilis is the most impressive Roman site in Morocco, and whilst much has been removed to adorn other cities over the centuries, or taken to museums such as that in Rabat, the structure of the town, the nature of its society and economy, and the design of the buildings is clearly discernible from the ruins, whilst some floor mosaics are still intact. Lying just below the Jbel Zerhoun and 5 km from Moulay Idriss along the P28, the site which is poorly signed from the road has free parking, a café and ticket office but little else. It can be viewed in a day trip from Meknes but for comfort stay at the **C** *Volubilis*, T (05) 544405/7, F (05) 544408, 52 rm, two restaurants, pool, terrace, excellent views,

just to the N of site. In summer start early to avoid the heat. Admission is MD20, and the site is open from 0800 to sunset. On the way in, note the collection of mosaics and sculptures, an 'open-air museum'.

Archaeological evidence points to the possibility of a Neolithic settlement at Volubilis, whilst tablets found show there was a 3rd century BC Phoenician settlement. In AD 24 it was the Western capital of the Roman kingdom of Mauritania, and from AD 45 to 285 the capital of the Roman province of Mauretania Tingitania. Under the Romans the immediate region was rich agriculturally, with significant production of olive oil, and contained scattered villas. However Volubilis was at the SE extremity of the province, connected to Rome through the Atlantic ports, its weak position necessitating the extensive city walls.

Under the Emperor Diocletian (see

box, page 258), Rome withdrew to the coastal areas, leaving Volubilis at the mercy of neighbouring tribes, but the city survived with diminished importance, notably with Christian and Jewish inhabitants, and later as the Christian enclave Oualila during the 8th century. Moulay Idriss was proclaimed as Sultan in Volubilis but during his reign he gave greater emphasis to Fes, so the city of Volubilis became totally deserted by the 11th century. Volubilis suffered when Moulay Ismail ransacked it to build Meknes, and further in the earthquake of 1755. French excavations and reconstruction began in 1915. The metal tracks on the site date from this work.

From the ticket office the entrance to the city is by the SE gate. A path, with sculptures and tombstones alongside it, leads down to a bridge across the Oued Fetassa. Up on the other side the first important remains in an area of small houses and industrial units is of an **olive press** complex. The mill stones, for crushing the olive stones, and the tanks for collecting and separating the oil, can be seen. Olive presses can be found through much of the city, as olive oil production was an essential element in its economy, as it is in the area today, where many of the same techniques are still used.

Right of the olive press is the **House of Orpheus**, a large mansion. In this building, as in most, some areas will be clearly roped off, and it is advisable to respect this, to avoid the whistle and

Stork on nest - at Volubilis

wrath of the otherwise very friendly guardian. The first entrance gives access to a room with an intricate dolphin mosaic, to a kitchen with a niche for religious figures, and to a paved bathroom and boiler room. Note the complex heating system. The second entrance leads to an open court with a mosaic of the goddess Amphitrite, with living rooms around, including a dining room with an Orpheus mosaic, showing the hero playing his harp. The mosaic from which the illustrated elephant was taken is a rare example of a mosaic depicting the local environment.

Heading further down and then to the right lie the **Baths of Gallienus**, public baths in the manner of a Moroccan *hammam*. Beyond this the large public square in front of the **Basilica** is the **Forum**. In this area are a number of

Mosaic of elephant, House of Orpheus

Know Your Roman Gods

A brief look at the Roman gods mentioned in the buildings and mosaics of Banasa, Lixus and Volubilis. The name of the Greek equivalent is given in brackets. The Romans worshipped gods at various levels. There were everyday gods who protected hearth and home and those like the Triad (Jupiter, Juno and Minerva) on a much higher plain and more likely to be found in illustrations.

Acteon was the son of the god Aristaeus and the daughter of the founder of Thebes. The story goes that while out hunting he saw the goddess Artemis bathing and was changed by her into a stag. He was then pursued by his 50 hounds and killed.

Ariadne, the beautiful daughter of Minos, the king of Crete, fell in love with Theseus and gave him the sword with which he killed the Minator and the ball of thread which he used to find his way out of the labyrinth. There is some problem with the end of the story. Either he abandoned her and she hanged herself ... she was carried off to Naxos and left there to die ... she was carried to Naxos and married the wine god Bacchus (by whom she had 6 children) ... she died in childbirth on Cyprus.

Bacchus (*Dionysus*) was a nature god of fruitfulness and vegetation, especially known for wine and ecstasy. He was the son of Jupiter and a daughter of the King of Thebes who died (blasted with thunderbolts) when the full force of Jupiter's power was released. Jupiter protected their son Bacchus by sewing him in his thigh until he reached maturity. Bacchus worship had great appeal for the women who 'abandoned their families, took to the hills, wearing fawn skins and crowns of ivy and shouting "Euoi", the ritual cry ...'. Early pictures represent him as a bearded man but later he is portrayed as young and effeminate. Bacchic revels were a favourite subject on mosaics.

Diana (*Artemis*) was represented as the twin sister of Apollo and was the moon goddess. She originated as an Italian woodland goddess who was prayed to by women to assist conception and delivery. She was also the goddess of domestic animals. She is also known as Diana the huntress and in Roman art she appears

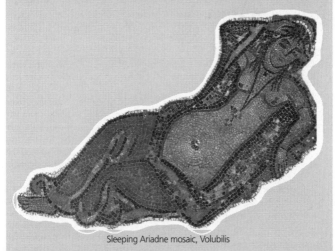

Sleeping Ariadne mosaic, Volubilis

as a young huntress accompanied by a hound or deer.

Eros, the god of love, originally a primeval god, was later taken to be the son of Venus and (perhaps) Jupiter. He was the god not simply of passion but also of fertility. His chief associates were gods representing longing and desire. Quite a trio. He is represented as a beautiful winged youth, sometimes even a child. His golden arrows would inflame the passions of those impaled while his arrows of lead inspired hatred. He often set off two arrows at once, a recipe for disharmony. The plural form Erotes is used.

Hercules was son of Jupiter and a mortal, venerated for his labours and his power to avert evil. He had a very violent nature. He killed his wife and all his children and as penance was set the famous 12 Labours which he seemed to enjoy. After being poisoned by a jealous wife his body was burned on a funeral pyre but Jupiter caught up the immortal part (his soul) and took him to live with the gods. In art and literature he is represented as an enormously strong man, medium height, a huge eater and drinker, amorous and kindly but given to occasional violent outbursts.

Hylas Legend says he was a companion of Hercules on the Argonautic expeditions. He went ashore at Cios to get water and was carried off by the nymphs of the spring. He did not return. Hercules threatened to ravage the land if Hylas was not found and each year, on a stated day, the natives of Cios roam the mountains shouting his name.

Juno (*Hera*) was the goddess of womanhood, of marriage and maternity. She was the wife of Jupiter; the daughter of Time and of Rhea who was the daughter of Sky and Earth; mother of Mars. She was worshipped each year on 1 March as the goddess of women and marriage and at each new moon as the goddess of the moon. She was often portrayed as a matronly figure, of mature proportions, beautiful but rather severe, standing in a chariot drawn by sacred peacocks. She has a difficult private life, being jealous of the various women/goddesses with whom Jupiter associated and their offspring.

Jupiter (*Zeus*) was the chief god, the god of the sky, who had various ways of manifesting himself; as the light bringer, the rain god worshipped at time of drought, the god of thunderbolts thus making all places struck by lightning sacred. The days of the full moon were sacred to him and he was also worshipped at the grape harvest. On a more moral tone he was concerned with the solemnization of oaths and treaties. His amorous adventures caused problems, especially with his wife.

Mars (*Ares*) was second only to Jupiter in importance. Initially he was a god of nature and fertility and protector of animals and crops. Later he became the god of war and protector of Rome. He was regarded as the father of the Romans through his son Romulus.

Minerva (*Athena*) was the daughter of Jupiter. As goddess of handicrafts and industrial life, the professions, art and sometimes war, the fifth day of the Ides of March was her festival.

Nereids were daughters of the sea god Nereus, about 50-100 of them. They were imagined as attractive young girls inhabiting any water (salt or fresh), harmless to mortals.

Orpheus who was the father of song was presented at birth with a lyre by the god Apollo and given instruction in music by the Muses. He could enchant men and beasts with his music and also move rocks and trees. When travelling to look for the Golden Fleece his music put the monsters to sleep and prevented the cliffs from falling. When his wife Eurydice died from a snake bite he followed her to Hades and with his music persuaded hard hearted Pluto to let her return to earth. But he forgot his promise not to look back as they journeyed and he lost her for ever. In his grief he treated all women with contempt, and the story says they tore him to pieces in revenge. The Muses picked up the pieces and buried him at the foot of Mt Olympus and set his lyre in the sky in his memory.

Pegasus was the winged horse which sprang from the body of the slain Medusa. The horse was caught and tamed by Bellerophon by means of a golden bridle provided by the goddess Minerva. Pegasus was a faithful companion but when Bellerophon impiously attempted to ride up to heaven Jupiter sent a gad-fly which stung Pegasus so that he unseated his rider who fell to earth lame and blind. Pegasus was then placed as a constellation in the sky.

Saturn was a fire god and later an agricultural god who taught mortals how to till the land. His name comes from the Latin meaning to sow. He is represented with a sickle in his hand. His wife, Ops, was the goddess of plenty. A useful couple to have around. In his honour a yearly festival, Saturnalia, was held in Dec after the farming year was completed. This was a time of games and feasting when presents were exchanged including especially wax candles and dolls. This took place on 17 Dec and had a direct influence on Christmas celebrations. His name is given to Saturday.

Theseus a legendary hero, son of Aegeus the king of Athens, had numerous adventures, mainly killing cruel and wicked monsters. Being heir to the throne did not prevent him sorting out the fire-breathing bull of Marathon and offered himself as one of the 7 youths and 7 maidens sacrificed each year to the Minator. He killed the Minator (see Ariadne above) and returned home. He unfortunately forgot to change the sails on his ship to white on the return voyage – a signal that he had succeeded. His father, seeing the black sails cast himself into the sea (the Aegean Sea) so Theseus became king. He had many other adventures. He and Hercules captured the Amazon princess Hippolyte, he and Pirithous carried off Helen and later tried to rescue Persephone from Hades, were caught but later rescued by Hercules. An uprising in Athens forced him to Scyros where he was killed. His bones eventually were placed in a temple in Athens.

Venus (*Aphrodite*) was originally a mere goddess of vegetable gardens but later became identified with Aphrodite the goddess of love and beauty. Venus was represented as the highest ideal of feminine beauty. She was honoured too for the belief that Romulus, the founder of Rome, was descended from her son Aeneas.

Mosaics

This is the 'art of decorating a surface with designs made up of closely set, usually variously coloured, small pieces of material such as stone, pottery, glass, tile or shell'.

The first mosaics were constructed of natural materials, pebbles and small stones set in clay, and the colours were mainly black or brown and white. The inclusion of other coloured stones, glass, pottery and shells was introduced at a later date. The production of small, regularly shaped, natural clay and polychrome tiles known as *tesserae* developed even later as designs for mosaics became more complicated.

Although Africa was one of Rome's first overseas provinces the actual process of Romanization was very slow and there were certainly no major developments before the 2nd century AD. The area we know as Morocco, on the western extremity, was not urbanized by the Romans to any great extent. Hence it has fewer sites of Roman settlement and in consequence few examples of mosaics.

Yet, in total, the mosaics of North Africa are more numerous and much better preserved than those remaining anywhere else in the empire due to a combination of climatic conditions and lesser population pressure.

The earliest mosaics in North Africa were very simple and it is assumed that early examples of more elaborate designs were produced by imported labour or constructed in Italy and carried to their final positions. Some very early mosaics were found at Carthage in Tunisia but it was not until local workmen were available to produce mosaics that the practice moved W reaching Lixus and Volubilis in 2nd and 3rd centuries AD.

The wealthy Romans decorated both their private and public buildings with mosaics. These were a luxury item, expensive to produce. Whereas in Rome mosaics had been used to advertise like shop signs in North Africa they were primarily decorative, though their size/sophistication would certainly advertise the wealth of the patron. Generally the finer specimens were in the better, more visited parts of the house and ornamental/geometric rather than pictorial designs were found in less important areas.

There are clear indications that the central part of the mosaics were constructed by 'master' craftsmen while the geometric designs and borders were done by workers who were less well trained, and often produced a poorer standard of work. Subject matter of the mosaics is frequently repeated and similar examples can be found on many different sites. Examples of the pattern being drawn in the underlying clay have been found but are not common. The workmen must have followed some pattern especially where the work was more complicated. The recurrence of identical motifs across a wide area shows that designs were probably chosen from a common stock and not drawn for each building.

The common themes to look out for are: hunting scenes and scenes showing rural life; seasons and seasonal activities; scenes from literature; scenes from mythology. The all important central medallion was set in a circle, square, oval or polygon and was surrounded with a border usually exhibiting a geometric design. Most common were the *gillouche* and Greek key borders (see diagrams). Only Banasa (see page 189), Lixus (see page 186) and Volubilis (see page 251) have mosaics *in situ*. Volubilis has 30, all well worth viewing. Some have been removed to the major museums (see Rabat, page 102, Tetouan, page 141 and Meknes, page 239).

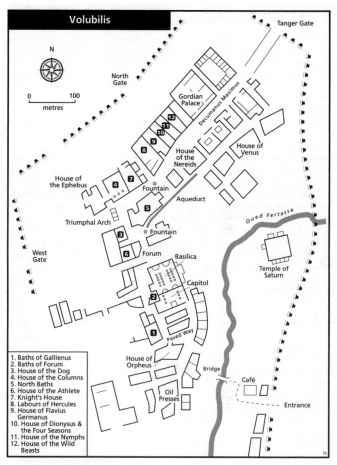

Volubilis

Tanger Gate

North Gate

N

0 ——— 100
metres

Gordian Palace

Decumanus Maximus

House of the Nereids

House of Venus

House of the Ephebus

Fountain

Aqueduct

Oued Fertassa

Triumphal Arch

Fountain

West Gate

Forum

Basilica

Capitol

Temple of Saturn

Paved Way

House of Orpheus

Bridge

Café

Oil Presses

Entrance

1. Baths of Gallienus
2. Baths of Forum
3. House of the Dog
4. House of the Columns
5. North Baths
6. House of the Athlete
7. Knight's House
8. Labours of Hercules
9. House of Flavius Germanus
10. House of Dionysus & the Four Seasons
11. House of the Nymphs
12. House of the Wild Beasts

monuments to leading Roman figures. The **Basilica** is one of the most impressive ruins, with a number of columns intact. This 3rd century building was the court house for the city.

Beside the Basilica is the **Capitol**, also with columns. In the court in front there is an altar, and steps leading up to the temple. This temple is dedicated to Juno, Minerva and Jupiter Optimus Maximus. This building had great state importance, being the place where the council would assemble on great occasions.

Adjacent to the Forum is the **House of the Athlete**, named after the mosaic of an athlete winning a cup. The **Triumphal Arch** dominates the skyline, as well as the **Decumanus Maximus**, the roadway leading to the Tanger Gate. This was built in 217 AD to honour Emperor Caracalla (see box, page 258) and his mother Julia Domna. Originally topped by nymph fountains, and with medallions honouring its dedication, the arch was heavily reconstructed by the French. **Decumanus Maximus** was lined with a columned arcade with small shops, in front of a series of large houses, some containing interesting mosaics.

Starting on the left, from just beside the **Triumphal Arch**, the **House of the Ephebus** was built around a courtyard with a pool. Adjacent is the **House of Columns** and then the **Knight's House** which has an interesting mosaic of Bacchus. The **House of the Labours of Hercules** has a mosaic with individual pictures of Hercules' life, and another of Jupiter. Further up the **House of the Nymphs Bathing** has a mosaic showing nymphs undressing. The largest house on this side, the **Gordian Palace**, is fronted by columns but the remains are quite plain. This may have been the governor's residence from the time of Gordian III (see box, page 258), with both domestic quarters and offices.

On the right hand side of Decumanus Maximus from the Triumphal Arch there is a large public bath and fountains, fed by an aqueduct. Three houses up is the **House of Nereids** with a pool mosaic. Behind this and one up is the **House of Venus** has one of the best array

Mosaic of wind to be seen insitu at Volubilis

of mosaics. The central courtyard pool has a mosaic of chariots. There are also mosaics of Bacchus, on the left, and Hylos and two nymphs, on the right. Nearby is a mosaic of Diana and the horned Acteon. From the House of Venus cross back over the Oued Fetassa to the remains of the **Temple of Saturn**, a Phoenician temple before the Romans took it over. From here, follow the path back to the entrance, perhaps for refreshments in the café after the labours in Volubilis.

The following more detailed descriptions and diagrams will serve to aid interpretation of the other dwellings on this wonderful site.

THE HOUSE OF THE DOG

The House of the Dog is where the famous bronze Volubilis Dog, now on display in the archaeological Museum at Rabat, was found. It is an interesting construction, very little changed or restored, situated close to the Triumphal Arch. The facade is made up of several lock-up shops (2-4) opening on to the street. Central to the frontage is the main entrance (1) to the house. This is paved and leads to a central atrium (7) with a long impluvium or water tank (5), which was fed by rain water from the roof. All the rooms are approached from the atrium. The bronze statue of the dog, found in room 6, is thought to be part of a composite piece, including a figure of a huntsman. The plan of the house, unlike most others at Volubilis, is absolutely true to the Roman pattern, lacking the complex atrium features of the hellenistic-Roman forms of other great houses in the city.

THE HOUSE OF EPHEBUS

The House of Ephebus is located on the W of the site adjacent to the Triumphal Arch and is named after the bronze head

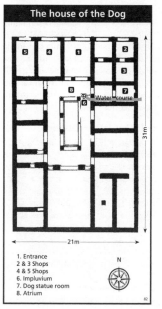

The house of the Dog

Water course

31m

21m

1. Entrance
2 & 3 Shops
4 & 5 Shops
6. Impluvium
7. Dog statue room
8. Atrium

N

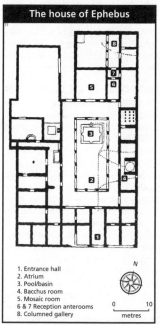

The house of Ephebus

1. Entrance hall
2. Atrium
3. Pool/basin
4. Bacchus room
5. Mosaic room
6 & 7 Reception anterooms
8. Columned gallery

N

0   10
metres

of a young man crowned with ivy leaves (Ephebe was the Greek for a youth of 18-20 years doing garrison duty) found at the site. The bronze is now in the Museum at Rabat. The house is rich in archaeological interest on a site 35 x 50m. Entrance to the house is through a narrow corridor (1), flanked by rooms for shops, which leads to a large peristyle atrium (2). The atrium was well endowed with a columned semi-roof, a mosaic floor and had an ornate pool (3) which served instead of an impluvium. The main rooms lie off the atrium, the most decorated being those on the E side where they are floored in mosaic. Look for the Bacchus room (4) where are to be found a mosaic of Bacchus in a chariot drawn by panthers and a water basin with images of aquatic animals. Room 5 has a fine mosaic, the largest at Volubilis, of varied subjects. Adjacent are corridor reception rooms (6-7) which lead to the columned gallery (8). The W side of the house was occupied by an oil press, a chapel and a necropolis. The house is complex and ornate and belonged probably to a grandee of the city, built in the 3rd century BC.

THE HOUSE OF COLUMNS

To the N of the Triumphal Arch is the **House of the Columns**, so called because of the large number of columns and column remnants discovered on the site. There are three main parts to the house – the master's quarters, a service area and a separate residential section in the SE corner. The usual single room shops face on to the street (1), the one on the SW corner containing a stone basin (2). Enter the master's house from the S door (3) up a stairway to a vestibule (4) and thence to the atrium (5). The atrium contains a circular basin or impluvium and two torso columns to its S side. S of the atrium is a tablinium/triclinium (6). Behind stands a minor atrium (7) where there was formerly a fountain and a set of

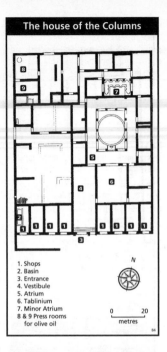

The house of the Columns

1. Shops
2. Basin
3. Entrance
4. Vestibule
5. Atrium
6. Tablinium
7. Minor Atrium
8 & 9 Press rooms for olive oil

N

0   20
metres

84

decorated basins. The NW corner rooms (8 and 9) were concerned with olive pressing. Take note of the ornamented columns still on the site, several cleverly fluted. Unfortunately all the mosaics have been destroyed.

THE KNIGHT'S HOUSE

Although in ruins for the most part, the **Knight's House** is worth a short visit. This is the site where a small bronze horseman was found. Overall the decoration is very rich throughout the house. The facade, as is common at Volubilis, comprises a series of single-cell shops, those on the left of the doorway being two-part (front and back separated by a half wall) units. The main doorway (1) is followed by steps down to a hallway (2) from which a paved vestibule (3) leads into the atrium. To the left is a narrow room with

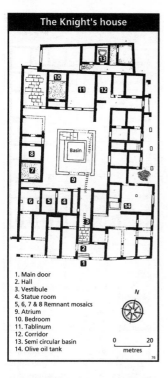

The Knight's house

1. Main door
2. Hall
3. Vestibule
4. Statue room
5, 6, 7 & 8 Remnant mosaics
9. Atrium
10. Bedroom
11. Tablinum
12. Corridor
13. Semi circular basin
14. Olive oil tank

N

0   20
  metres

There is an interesting olive oil tank (14) close to a part of the house used for commerce.

THE NORTH BATHS

One of the largest sites discovered at Volubilis is the **North Baths** area. The entrance is on the N side (1). Note the basin to the left of the entrance. Inside a vestibule (2) leads to the cold bath (3), the steps down to which are still clearly visible. The steam rooms (4 and 5) are in a poor state, with all the upper construction now gone. Room 6 is a cold bath set four steps down, while rooms 7, 8 and 9 were for service staff. Water for the baths is thought to have been drawn from a nearby spring or from the main aqueduct which passes close by. The North Baths are very plain in comparison to the Baths of Gallienus, with no mosaics and little work in marble. Architectural decoration is more in evidence with massive lintels and bas-reliefs in geometric designs.

access to both atrium and vestibule – it was probably once a stairway. Immediately to its left is a room (4) once containing a statuette called Ephebe on horseback. Continuing left into rooms 5, 6, 7 and 8 brings sight of a series of remnants of mosaics, of which only the one in room 7 still shows the its original form. The atrium (9) has a complex square basin and surround but the columns have all been taken away. The bedroom (10) has an anteroom and a partial mosaic of Bacchus (some say Dionysus) looking at the sleeping Ariadne. The room adjacent (11) is the tablinum/triclinium but its mosaics have completely disappeared. A corridor (12) leads into a separate apartment with an ornate semi-circular basin (13).

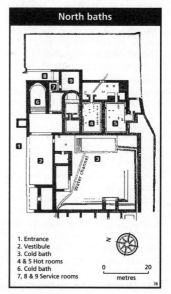

North baths

1. Entrance
2. Vestibule
3. Cold bath
4 & 5 Hot rooms
6. Cold bath
7, 8 & 9 Service rooms

Water channel

N

0   20
  metres

THE HOUSE OF FLAVIUS GERMANUS

The main doorway to the **House of Flavius Germanus** is near the House of the Labours of Hercules fronted by six great columns (1-6). Inside there are four shops (7-10) to the right of the outer door (11). The main doorway (12) leads into a vestibule (13) with a small porter's lodge. The courtyard/peristyle (14) has a domestic altar (15) in its SE corner made of soft sandstone. The altar door carries the inscription " ... MUS I FLAVIUS GERMANUS VSLA" which in full reads in Latin as (Genio) (do)mus T(itus) Flavius Germanus V(otum) s(olvit) l(ibens) a(nimo) which appears to be a dedication to the engineer who constructed the house for Flavius Germanus. The peristyle has 14 columns and off it run the main rooms of the house. Two rooms with mosaics open directly onto the courtyard (16 and 17), the former probably a main bedroom but with little of its decoration remaining. Room 17 also had geometric pattern mosaic on its floor. The ornate mosaics and columns in the room in the SE corner was a bedroom of sorts. Other rooms in the centre of the site were for accommodating service areas and staff. At the very rear of the house (Rooms 18-22) is a row of shops. The water system is simple but interesting. Water enters from the front of the house to the basin in the courtyard and is then drained to the back of the house through the rear shop area.

THE HOUSE OF DIONYSUS AND THE FOUR SEASONS

Immediately to the E of the House of Flavius Germanus is the **House of Dionysus and the Four Seasons**, named after a mosaic still in situ. The portico area has six columns in place, behind which lie four shops, including a possible former entrance to the house (7) and the new door (8) and paved entrance (9). The porter's room (10) is beyond the entrance. Meanwhile, the peristyle (11)

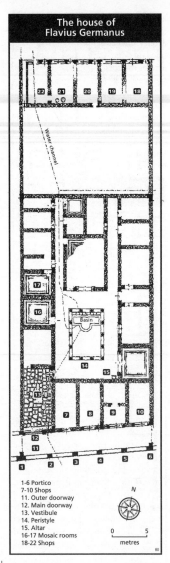

The house of Flavius Germanus

1-6 Portico
7-10 Shops
11. Outer doorway
12. Main doorway
13. Vestibule
14. Peristyle
15. Altar
16-17 Mosaic rooms
18-22 Shops

N

0   5
metres

takes an elongated rectangular shape with a ten-piece colonnade. The main rooms give off the peristyle, including Room 12 which was the triclinium with a mosaic in T-form. The mosaic is intact showing a geometric plan bearing hexagonal shields defined by a blue-black line laid out to form a cross. The service area of the room has a mosaic with two figures in hexagonal lozenges on a white ground including the heads of Medusa and Nemesis. The main mosaic is however one with eight circular medallions set in pairs and joined by smaller elliptical illustrations. Included are mosaics of Dionysus at an altar surrounded by light-hearted depictions of the four seasons,

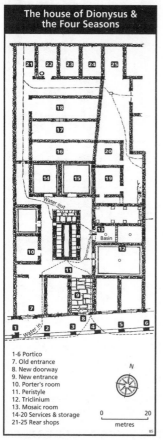

The house of Dionysus & the Four Seasons

1-6 Portico
7. Old entrance
8. New doorway
9. New entrance
10. Porter's room
11. Peristyle
12. Triclinium
13. Mosaic room
14-20 Services & storage
21-25 Rear shops

N

0   20
metres

Four medallions from mosaic at House of Dionysus

and Ariadne seated on a rock. The next door room (13) has a narrow doorway and is divided into two sections by a wall, the floors each side of this internal wall bearing a mosaic of floral designs. Other rooms represent winter quarters, corridors and stores. At the back of the house is a series of service rooms and large commercial stores (14-20) leading to a set of rear shops (21-25).

HOUSE OF THE NYMPHS BATHING

This is a much-altered house where the groundplan is not always clear. It is adjacent to the House of Dionysus and the Four Seasons and has a smaller floor area and is approximately the same size as the next house – the House of the Wild Beasts. The portico is a mere four pillars (1-4), the most easterly one stronger and shared with the House of the Wild Beasts (see plan). Beyond the portico lie two shops (5 and 6), the remnants of a finely sculptured doorway (7) and a long vestibule (8). The main vestibule has as tiny doorway in its N end leading to a secondary hall also with a doorway in the N face, presumably to hide the peristyle (9) from people coming from the street. Room 10 has a split basin at a lower level in Room 11 which might have been part of a former peristyle. To the E is a three-part courtyard in the W containing an ornate pit (12) surrounded by domestic altars. In the N of the courtyard is a single beautiful but incomplete mosaic panel of Diana and Actaeon (13) with a third nymph and a depiction of the tree of Nature. It is suggested by archaelologist that the complex of rooms to the N of the courtyard (14,15 and 16) compise an olive oil storage area. Credibility to this view comes from the nearby paved oil pressing plant (17). A series of small shops (18-21) complete the house to the N side.

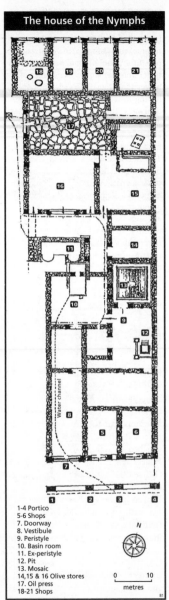

The house of the Nymphs

1-4 Portico
5-6 Shops
7. Doorway
8. Vestibule
9. Peristyle
10. Basin room
11. Ex-peristyle
12. Pit
13. Mosaic
14,15 & 16 Olive stores
17. Oil press
18-21 Shops

N

0   10

metres

HOUSE OF THE WILD BEASTS

This house has scant clear remains and to the present is something of a puzzle to archaeologists. Was it, for example, part of a double house with its neighbour? The portico (1-5) is narrow though bigger than the House of the Nymphs, having to its N three shops (6-8) and a doorway to the main house (9), decorated with pilasters. The vestibule (10) is plain and gives on to the peristyle (11) which has a domestic altar (12) in the SE corner. The peristyle has a central columned basin which takes in the N end the aspect of an atrium. Off the peristyle in its NE corner is a medium sized room (13) with a floor mosaic bearing eight square panels, some with a wild animal depicted within it including a lion, gazelle, jaguar, tigress and bull and some with floral motives. N of the mosaic room there appears to be an apartment complex (14, 15 and 16) succeeded by an oil press area (17,18 and 19). As ever, the N extremity of the house is given over to shops (20-23).

HOUSE TO THE WEST OF THE GORDIAN PALACE

This is a large house by Volubilis standards, its front aligned along Decumanus Maximus and its rear N along Decumanus. It seems likely that the house was attached in some way to the Gordian Palace. The portico has eight columns (1-8) and is backed by four shops and a large and imposing main entrance (9) flanked by two small service doors (10-11), with what seems to be a stairway facing the right hand. The doors open into a rectangular vestibule (12) with matching exit doors (13) to the peristyle (14). The latter is very spacious with the courtyard around the central colonnade and basin, all better proportioned than in the other house in this block. There

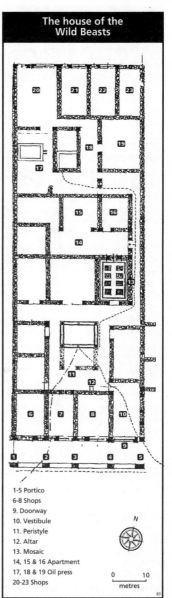

The house of the
Wild Beasts

1-5 Portico
6-8 Shops
9. Doorway
10. Vestibule
11. Peristyle
12. Altar
13. Mosaic
14, 15 & 16 Apartment
17, 18 & 19 Oil press
20-23 Shops

N

0   10

metres

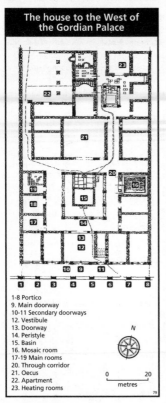

The house to the West of the Gordian Palace

1-8 Portico
9. Main doorway
10-11 Secondary doorways
12. Vestibule
13. Doorway
14. Peristyle
15. Basin
16. Mosaic room
17-19 Main rooms
20. Through corridor
21. Oecus
22. Apartment
23. Heating rooms

N

0   20
metres

79

up of lines of circles of a great variety of decoration. From the top the first line shows a range of black cubes, the second larger circles of similar design enclosing shapes such as the Maltese Cross or mythical birds, as in diagrams above and below. Subsequent lines use similar motifs ending on line nine with rather damaged small circles. Other W rooms off the peristyle, such as (17-19), have fine wall finishes, with floral and other motifs. Room 19 has a raised floor in a form of podium with a paved surface in its NE corner.

The through-corridor is worth noting (20) since it serves a large room (21), so far the largest found at Volubilis. In the N of the corridor there is a secondary courtyard perhaps designed to be used by those who entered the house from the N side. An apartment (22) is thought to have occupied the NW rooms of the house with its own small peristyle, basin and fountain. In the NE corner of the site are what could have been heating rooms (23) for warming the adjacent rooms in winter. Notably, unlike the other houses in this area, there are no shops on the N.

are enough remains of the column bases to show how rich the architectural decoration must have been. The basin (15) is also of good proportions, originally fed from a fountain in the wall. A water trap extension to the basin can be seen built to catch the overflow of the basin and rainwater.

Six principal rooms open onto the peristyle of which the NE one (16) is most interesting. It has columns at the triple entrance doors and inside the walls are well rendered with plaster decorations. On the floor is a mosaic. Together these features suggest that it was the triclinium. The mosaic is made

FES AND ENVIRONS

Fes (also called Fez, and derived from the Arabic word for the pickaxe used in its construction) is a city which will take several days to come to terms with, several days to take in the atmosphere (this does not mean the industrial pollution which hangs over the city although this cannot be ignored), and several days to explore, but is worth giving the time. Spread out over three sites, the two most historic areas are full of memorable buildings, centred around the **Qarawiyin Mosque** and some memorable *souqs*. Fes is also a base from which to explore nearby regions, Bhalil and Sefrou to the S and the springs of Sidi Harazem to the SE, as well as sites further afield, the Middle Atlas resorts of Azrou and Ifrane, and the historic sites near Meknes, Volubilis and Moulay Idriss.

FES

(*Pop* 564,000 (1993); *Alt* 415m)

History of a city at the heart of Morocco

The historic city of Fes lies in the Oued Sebou basin, astride the traditional trade route from the Sahara to the Mediterranean, as well as on the path from Algeria and the Islamic heartland beyond into Morocco. For centuries the dominant axis within Morocco was of Fes and Marrakech, two cities linked by their immense power as well as by their rivalry. Even today, while the coastal belt centred

> Ideas that never change, indeed something resembling an instinct, mean that in Fez there is only one age and one style: that of yesterday. It is the site of a miracle – that of suppressing the passage of time. That has given this city a unique character – unique perhaps in the universe, certainly in the Mediterranean world."
> Tharaud, Jérôme/ Tharaud, Jean, *Fez*, (1930).

on Rabat and Casablanca dominates the country in demographic, political and economic terms, Fes is still seen as the spiritual and cultural capital, and holds an enduring fascination for visitors, as one of the largest historic medina, full of monuments reflecting the different periods of Morocco's imperial and architectural development. Fes has for long supplied the mercantile and intellectual élite of the country, and the *Fassi* (the people of Fes) are to be found in most towns and cities. The *Fassi* are rightly proud of their city and history, and often have a self-confidence quite beyond that of most Moroccans. Perhaps it does not have the immediate friendliness of the villages and towns of the mountains or the desert, but it is a city well worth giving time.

The Three Cities The city is composed of three distinct parts. On either side of the Oued Fes, a tributary of the Oued Sebou, lies Fes El Bali, the oldest part of the city, a medina divided by the river into Adwa al Andalusiyin (the Andalusian quarter on the E bank) and Adwa al Qarawiyin (the Qarawiyin quarter on the W bank). On a plateau just to the W lies Fes El Jedid, containing the royal palace and the *mellah*, which could be

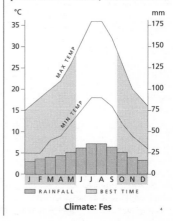

Climate: Fes

described as the new historic city. To the SW, on another raised area, lies the *ville nouvelle*, the modern city built by the French which has taken over many of the political, administrative and commercial functions of Fes.

Andalusiyin and Qarawiyin The first settlement here was the village Medinat Fes founded in 789/90 by Moulay Idriss, the Sultan and saint commemorated in the shrine town bearing his name near Meknes. However the town proper was founded by his son Idriss II as Al-Aliya in 808/9. Muslim families, refugees from Cordoba and surrounding areas of Andalucía soon took up residence in the Adwa al Andalusiyin quarter. Later 300 families from Kairouan in modern-day Tunisia settled on the opposite bank, forming Adwa al Qarawiyin. The **Qarawiyin Mosque**, perhaps the religious centre of Morocco, is the centre of a university founded in 859, including several important *medressa*, and one of the most prestigious of the Arab World. The **Andalusian Mosque** was also founded in this period. The minarets of both major mosques date from 955/6.

Almoravids and Almohads The two parts of Fes El Bali were united by the Almoravids in the 11th century, and as the focus of independent Morocco, Fes became one of the major cities of Islam. In the 12th century the Qarawiyin mosque was enlarged to its present form, one of the largest in North Africa and can take up to 22,000 worshippers. The Almohads strengthened the fortifications of the great city. Under both dynasties Fes was in competition with the southern capital of Marrakech.

The Growth of Fes under the Merinids Fes reached its peak in the Merinid period, when the dynasty built the new capital of Fes El Jedid reflecting its power, containing the green-roofed Dar al-Makhzen still occupied by the monarch, the **Grand Mosque** with its distinctive polychrome minaret dating

Spoken by Idriss II: "O my God, please exhaust our prayers so that this city remains the dwelling of science and of the *fikh*, may it be the place where your Book will be recited and where your prescriptions will be maintained. Also do so that its population be faithful to the *sounna* as long as the city will last".

from 1279, and the *mellah*, to which the Jews of Fes El Bali were moved in 1438. The Merinid Sultans Abu Said Uthman and Abu Inan left a particularly notable legacy of public buildings. Among the achievements of the period are the **Bou Inania Medersa** and other *medressa*, several mosques, and the **Merinid Tombs**. The **Zaouia of Moulay Idriss**, which holds the tomb of Idriss II was rebuilt in 1437. In the 15th century Fes consolidated its position as a major centre for artisanery and trade.

Saadian and Alawite Fes Under the Saadians Fes declined, with a degree of antagonism between the authorities and the people. Their main act was to refortify the city, adding the **South Borj** and **North Borj** fortresses.

Under the Alawites Fes declined further. In 1889 the French writer Pierre Loti described it as a dead city. However the dynasty had added a number of new *medressa* and mosques, and reconstructed other important buildings. The French entered Fes in 1911, but were unable at first to gain full control of the city and its hinterland and thus abandoned plans to make it their capital, choosing Rabat instead. The *ville nouvelle* was founded in 1916, but dates principally from the 1920s. French policies left the historic quarters intact, preserved in their traditional but perhaps stagnant form.

During the 20th century Fes has been overshadowed by the growth of Rabat and Casablanca, and the medina faces critical conservation problems, which a current programme by UNESCO aims

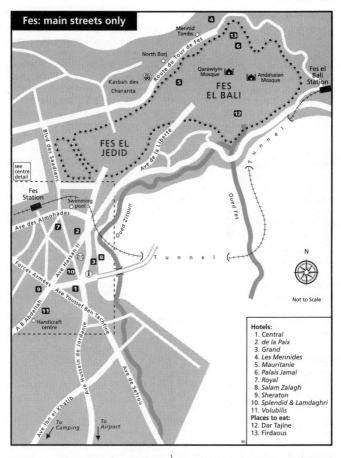

Fes: main streets only

Merinid Tombs

North Borj

Kasbah des Cherarda

Route du Tour de Fes

Qarawiyin Mosque

Andalusian Mosque

FES EL BALI

Fes el Bali Station

FES EL JEDID

Ave de la Liberté

Blvd des Saadiens

see centre detail

Fes Station

Swimming pool

Ave des Almohades

Oued Zitoun

Oued Fes

Tunnel

Tunnel

Ave Hassan II

Forces Armées

Ave Youssef Ben Tachfine

A B Abdellah

Handicraft centre

Ave Ibn el Khatib

Ave Hussein de Jordanie

Ave de Sefrou

To Camping

To Airport

N

Not to Scale

Hotels:
1. *Central*
2. *de la Paix*
3. *Grand*
4. *Les Merinides*
5. *Mauritanie*
6. *Palais Jamaï*
7. *Royal*
8. *Salam Zalagh*
9. *Sheraton*
10. *Splendid & Lamdaghri*
11. *Volubilis*
Places to eat:
12. *Dar Tajine*
13. *Firdaous*

to address. However, there is some controversy over the specific plans, particularly the creation of new openings in the city walls, and the building of two roads into the centre, one up to Talaa Kebira, and the other over the existing course of Oued Fes.

The large and beautiful houses of the historic city are being abandoned by the élite who move to the *ville nouvelle*, or to Casablanca and elsewhere, and often being taken over by poor migrants from the country. With rapidly increasing population densities the houses and the infrastructure are crumbling. There are, however, still many impressive houses, and a walk in Fes El Bali is one of the memorable experiences of a visit to Morocco.

ACCESS Air Aéroport Fes Saiss is 15 km to the S of the city, off the P24, T 624712. Take Bus 16 to the railway station.

Train The railway station is at the end of Blvd Chenguit, in the *ville nouvelle*, T 622501, 625132. Head down this road and slightly to the left into Ave de la Liberté. This joins Ave Hassan II, the main street of the new town, at Place de Florence.

Road Fes lies at a crossroads in Morocco, and is an excellent base from which to plan and carry out the next stage of travels. The P1 W from Meknes, Rabat and Casablanca arrives in the city at the corner of the walls of the royal palace, continue straight ahead for the medina (Fes El Bali), or right into Blvd des Saadiens for the *ville nouvelle*, the P26 N to Chaouen, Tetouan and Tanger and the P1 W to Taza, Oujda and Algeria arrive to the N of Fes El Bali, from where gates enter the old quarter, or the Route du Tour de Fes circumnavigates the city, either way, leading to Fes El Jedid and the *ville nouvelle*. The P24 S to Azrou and Marrakech and the P20 S to Sefrou lead into Place de l'Atlas. Turn left into Ave Allal ben Abdellah, and then right into Ave Hassan II. **Warning** On the routes into the city men on motorbikes often drive alongside motorists to tout for unofficial guide work – it is advisable to ignore them. **Bus**: CTM buses arrive at the terminal on Ave Mohammed V, T 622041. Private buses arrive at the new terminal off the Route du Tour de Fes, just below the N Borj.

Places of interest

Fes has so many rewarding and interesting sites that most visitors will have to be selective. If time is limited, go to Fes El Bali and see the **Bou Inania Medersa**, the **Moulay Idriss Zaouia** and the **Qarawiyin Mosque**, as well as a few of the *souqs* nearby. In Fes El Jedid stroll through the two *mechouars* past the entrance to the **Royal Palace** (**Dar al-Makhzen**). Outside the historic heart of the city go to the **Merinid Tombs** or the *Hotel Les Merinides* for a panoramic and memorable view across Fes El Bali. Fes El Bali can only be explored on foot. It has a complex layout, and it may save time to engage the services of an official guide, as long as the balance between sites of interest and expensive shops is agreed to the visitor's preference. Avoid the numerous unofficial guides and 'students' who will offer their services.

Fes El Bali The best approach to Fes El Bali, the oldest part of Fes, is E along Ave des Français from Fes El Jedid between the Alawite wall on the left and on the right the **Boujeloud Gardens** (Jardins de la Marche Verte), open 0900-1800 except Mon. Rue de l'UNESCO leads right to **Dar el Beida**, a late 19th century palace. The **Boujeloud Mosque** is ahead. Behind the mosque a small road leads to the **Dar Batha**, a 19th century Hispano-Moorish palace set in lovely gardens, and now a **Museum of Moroccan Arts and Handicrafts**, T 634116 (0900-1130 and 1500-1800 except Tues), with an excellent display which includes particularly fine examples of decorative material, such as carved wood, wrought iron, sculpted plaster. There is some very delicate and very colourful embroidery, a selection of carpets which shows the range available and a very interesting display of coins. The delicate Fes pottery is well known and the pottery room is the jewel of this museum. The use of cobalt by a special technique developed in the 10th century produces the famous 'Fes blue' and the

Carved plaster work, stylized Arabic script

examples here are of the best. Here too is a collection of astrolabes.

Bab Boujeloud, marks the entrance into the most historic part of Fes, the medina known as Fes El Bali. Bab Boujeloud itself is a large blue-tiled structure which looks misleadingly ancient.

An earlier version is just to the left, while the current gate was built in the first few years of the Protectorate. The name is derived from *Abu Juloud*, or 'father of soldiers'.

The region of the medina up on the left of the gate is the Kasbah Filala,

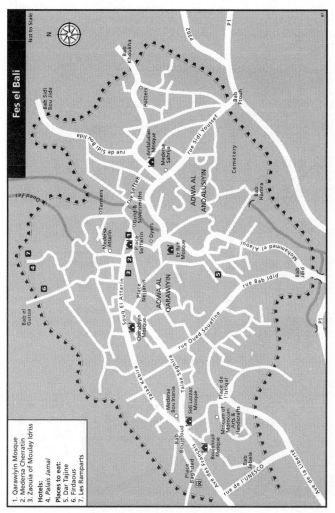

Fes el Bali

1. Qarawiyin Mosque
2. Medersa Cherratin
3. Zaouia of Moulay Idriss

Hotels:
4. Palais Jamai

Places to eat:
5. Dar Tajine
6. Firdaous
7. Les Ramparts

originally occupied by people from the Tafilelt who arrived with the early Alawite kings. **Bab Boujeloud** and the two small squares before and after make up busy area with fruit stalls and throngs of people, including persistent *faux guides*, despite the presence of a tourist police post. Just inside the gate is a square with a few small cafés and restaurants which may offer respite before exploring the medina.

The two minarets visible from the square are the 14th century **Bou Inania Medersa** and the nearer 9th century **Sidi Lazzaz Mosque**.

There are two routes onto the main thoroughfares of Fes El Bali. Talaa Seghira leads to the right. Talaa Kebira, leads to the left, directly past the Sidi Lazzaz Mosque, and the next major building, the Bou Inania Medersa, one of the most important sites in Fes.

Bou Inania Medersa, open 0800-1700 every day except Fri, entrance fee

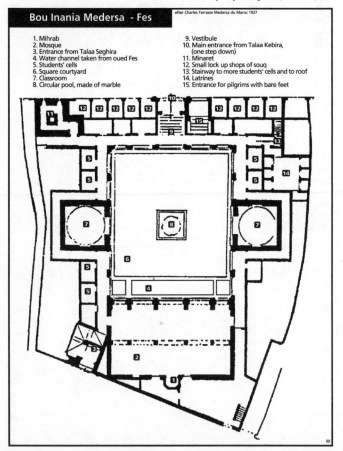

Bou Inania Medersa - Fes

after Charles Terrasse Medersa du Maroc 1927

1. Mihrab
2. Mosque
3. Entrance from Talaa Seghira
4. Water channel taken from oued Fes
5. Students' cells
6. Square courtyard
7. Classroom
8. Circular pool, made of marble
9. Vestibule
10. Main entrance from Talaa Kebira, (one step down)
11. Minaret
12. Small lock up shops of souq
13. Stairway to more students' cells and to roof
14. Latrines
15. Entrance for pilgrims with bare feet

MD10, and one of the most important sites to visit in Fes, was built by the Merinid Sultan Abu Inan between 1348-1358. It is a large and particularly impressive example of the architecture of the period, dating from 1350-5, and until the 1960s was used to accommodate students studying at the university, as well as providing some lessons itself. Entrance is off Talaa Kebira, a small turning between the lock-up shops in the *souq* here. Enter through a highly decorated vestibule roofed by a stalactite dome. Inside the building a channel of water, a tributary of the Oued Fes, separates the prayer hall from the square courtyard. The channel marks the limit for non-Muslims, as the prayer hall is closed, still being used as a mosque. The mosque area has a highly decorated minaret, indicating that it was far more important than most *medressa*, which normally do not have minarets, or even pulpits for the Fri prayer. Indeed, the *medersa* has the status of a Fri mosque, and for a time rivalled the great Qarawiyin Mosque.

The courtyard is decorated with *zellij* tiling, Koranic inscriptions, and some fine carved woodwork, well worth close inspection. Around the courtyard are a number of students' cells, with decorated ceilings, which give an indication of the life led by the students here, studying zealously in often cramped conditions. There are similar cells on the 2nd flr. Take the next flight of stairs up to the roof for a view of the surrounding area and of the minaret.

There used to be a complex water clock built in the wall opposite the *medersa*, dating from the 14th century. This clock is said to have enabled the **Bou Inania Medersa**, visible to both the Qarawiyin Mosque and the Mosque of Fes El Jedid, to signal the correct time for prayer to both. However, as part of the restoration programme this clock was moved to the Qarawiyin. The Merinid latrines or ablution halls are currently being repaired but once reopened it is worth seeing the intricate carving.

Talaa Kebira, the main thoroughfare of Fes El Bali, is only a narrow, crowded, alley way, descending steeply through distinct residential and commercial areas, towards the **Moulay Idriss Zaouia** and the **Qarawiyin Mosque**, the spiri-

The zaouia

The *zaouia* is an important part of the architectural heritage of North Africa. It originated as the name of a small or local mosque but became associated with the spread of sufi orders in the area from the 13th century. It comprises a set of structures to provide a prayer room, a classroom for the teaching of the Koran and accommodation for guests. *Zaouias* were set up by holy men (*marabouts*) whose shrine often makes up part of the site, with a surrounding cemetery. In some cases the *zaouias* developed into monastic establishments with strong attachment to a particular sufi school of mystical Islam.

The Senussi of Libya in the 19th and 20th centuries showed that the teaching tradition of the sufi brotherhood survived and flourished until recently using *zaouias* as centres for religion, education and administration.

In Morocco, the occurrence of *zaouia* is widespread in both the major cities and the smaller population centres. The old medina of Marrakech has two *zaouias* of architectural interest, first the Zaouia of Sidi Bel Abbas (12th century) one of the seven saints of Marrakech (see page 310) and second the Zaouia of Sidi Ben Slimane el-Jazuli (14th century) which also houses the shrines of a further seven holy men of Marrakech (see page 310). Entry by non-Moslems is forbidden to both sites.

Tile design - spider's webb

tual heart of the city. Beware of the heavily-laden mules carrying goods across the city, guided by muleteers crying out 'Balak!' to warn pedestrians. The distinctive character of Talaa Kebira may soon be lost, as a road has been constructed to convey tourists and goods into the heart of the medina. As you descend look out for **Fondouk Talaat Kebira**, still used to sell olives, butter and jam in bulk, and **Fondouk Labatta**, now used by tanners.

Talaa Kebira becomes **rue Cherabliyin** (slippermakers) as it descends, where each afternoon except Fri people hawk secondhand shoes and slippers. The **Cherabliyin Mosque** dates from 1342, the reign of Sultan Abul Hassan, and has a small and attractive minaret tiled in green and white including the *darj w ktaf* motif. On the right is the *Palais des Merinides*, one of the more impressive of the palace restaurants, and worth a look inside even if you cannot afford the food. Note the fountain, and the cedar carving treated with egg white. Further on in rue Cherabliyin is the Aïn Allou area where leather articles are auctioned everyday except Fri. At the bottom of rue Cherabliyin is a crossroads, just before the entrance to Souq El Attarin, the commercial heart of the medina.

Before exploring into Souq El Attarin

turn right to an interesting area of *souqs*. On the left is **Souq al Henna**, a small square around two trees which originally specialized in *henna*, the powder used to dye the feet and hands of women. It now also sells other beauty products (perfume, myrrh and amber), traditional medicines, and some pottery and general handicrafts. On its right is **Merstane Sidi Frej**, a hospital built in 1286 by Youssef Ibn Yacoub but not currently open. On the right of this turning is a carpenters' *souq*, followed by the **Souq Sekhatin**, originally dominated by belts and saddles, but now includes a variety of goods including silverwork.

On **Place Nejjarin** (Carpenters' Square) is the 18th century **Fondouk Nejjarin**, a building of impressive tiles and carving, now being restored by UNESCO. In recent years it accommodated students in a similar way to the city's *medressa*. The 18th century tiled **Nejjarin Fountain**, also being carefully restored, has water which was reputed to cure fever. Nearby Place Nejjarin are the **Souq Kashashin**, where metalworkers operate and kitchenware and clocks are sold, and **Hammam Laraïs**, apparently used by grooms and brides before a pre-marriage trip to the Moulay Idriss Zaouia which can be approached from here, or from Souq al Attarin.

Souq El Attarin at the bottom of rue Cherabliyin, was originally just the spice sellers' *souq*, but is now one of the major *souqs* of the city, with a wide range of goods, and the focus of the commercial area of Fes El Bali. The sunlight filtered through the straw covering over the alleyway combines with the sacks of almonds, peanuts, lentils and peas piled into mountains, sculpted heaps of colourful spices and other goods to create an unforgettable atmosphere. The smells of the spices, saffron, ginger, verbena, cumin, pepper, cloves and orange flower mix to assault the senses (see box, page 487). On the *souq* is the *Dar Saada*, a recommended restaurant for lunch. To the left is a number of small *souqs*, including **Souq Tellis**, **Souq el-Haik**, **Souq Selham** and **Souq El Bali**.

To the right of Souq El Attarin is the **Moulay Idriss Zaouia**. Many shops around the *zaouia* sell candles and other artifacts for pilgrims, the distinctive chewy sweets which are taken home as souvenirs of a pilgrimage, and silverware. The *zaouia* itself is prohibited to non-Muslims, but is encircled by a precinct which is open to all visitors and from here parts of the *zaouia* can be seen by tactful glances through the large unscreened door spaces. Each entrance to the precinct is crossed by a wooden bar, which both marks the limit for animals and forces people to bow as they approach the building. The 18th century building contains the 9th century remains of Idriss II and includes a Louis IV clock. The sultan is considered a saint, and numbers amongst his devotees women, who can be seen in one of the rooms opening on to the precinct. On the way round note that the exterior of the sanctuary includes a circular porthole through which offerings are passed, and the ablutions room. The **Zouag Mosque**, now closed, was apparently for travellers who could not wait for prayers in the *zaouia*.

The Kissaria, off the *zaouia*, is a covered market area dating from the 9th century but rebuilt after most of it was destroyed in a fire this century. The *kissaria* is consequently not the most picturesque commercial area of Fes, but for particular goods is probably more reasonably priced and certainly less frantic than the *souqs*. There are distinct areas of the *kissaria* including those devoted to *babooshes*, thread and jewellery. One of the *kissaria* gates is directly opposite the main entrance to the Qarawiyin Mosque.

The Attarin Medersa (open 0900-1200 and 1400-1800), is a remarkably decorated Merinid building dating from 1323, built by Sultan Abu Said, used to accommodate students from the NW of

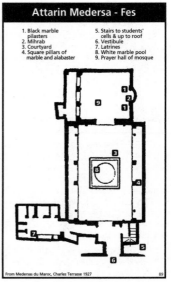

Attarin Medersa - Fes

1. Black marble pilasters
2. Mihrab
3. Courtyard
4. Square pillars of marble and alabaster
5. Stairs to students' cells & up to roof
6. Vestibule
7. Latrines
8. White marble pool
9. Prayer hall of mosque

From Medersas du Maroc, Charles Terrasse 1927   89

Morocco, and functioning as a constituent college of the Qarawiyin University, which instructed students in religious and related subjects.

The courtyard is one of the most elaborately decorated in Morocco, with carved stucco, cedar wood carving, and *zellij* tiling, surrounded by the arches of the two overhanging galleries. A higher circular water container, complete with fountain, stands in the square, white marble pool. The whole is beautifully decorated with tiles. Here, too, is a mixture of square and slender round pillars of marble and decorated alabaster which support, with the help of carved wooden beams, the accommodation for students upstairs. The rather dark prayer hall has a chandelier bearing the name of the *medersa*'s founder and the date. Some of the glass in the small windows which illuminate this prayer hall is the original glass, installed when the *medersa* was built. The niche is on the right, flanked by two pilasters in marble. Note in particular the beautiful bronze faced doors.

As with most *medressa*, the 2nd flr has a succession of students' cells which are interesting to see. From the roof of the *medersa* is one of the best views of the minaret and interior of the Qarawiyin Mosque but at present the terrace is closed.

To the left of the Attarin Medersa is the closed and partially ruined Merinid **Misbahiya Medersa**. On the same route note a cloth *souq*, the central medina's PTT, and the **Fondouk Hayouni**. Opposite the PTT is a branch of *Banque Populaire*, in an historic building with impressive carving and tilework. Further down is the **Tomb of Sidi Muhammad Tijani**, dating from the 13th century, a pilgrimage centre for followers of Tijani, many of whom live in Senegal.

The **Qarawiyin Mosque** at the end of Souq El Attarin, dominates Fes and serves as the focal point of Fes El Bali, the centre of a complex of *medressa*, added mainly by the Merinids, and the most important religious building of Morocco. The mosque was the main building of the Qarawiyin quarter of the city, and owes its original construction to the generosity of a rich emigrant family in 857. It was enlarged in 956 and again most importantly under the Almoravids between 1135 and 1144. The Almohads built a large ablution hall, whilst the Merinids built a timekeeper's room and redecorated the courtyard and minaret, and the Saadians added the pavilion. The original minaret, the oldest in Morocco, dates from 956. There is also the **Borj an-Naffara** tower, used during Ramadan. On the SW side is an Almoravid funeral chapel.

The mosque has 14 doors, 275 pillars and three fountains for ablutions. It includes some elaborate Almohad carving, a 13th century chandelier and an historic wooden pulpit. With space for some 20,000 devotees it is one of the biggest mosques in North Africa. The separate space for women is raised, behind the men. The Qarawiyin was also a very important university, one of the oldest in the Arab world, with professors in law, theology, algebra, mathematics, philosophy, and astronomy. Students often gathered around their teacher in front of a particular pillar. The *medressa* across the city formed part of this university, often accommodating students from a particular part of Morocco, but also from across the Islamic world, attracted by the fame of the university and the reputation and wisdom of individual teachers.

The Qarawiyin Mosque is, however, a frustrating building for the non-Muslim, as it is impossible to get a clear view of the structure, surrounded as it is by the city. Walk around the mosque taking diplomatic glances in where possible, but no photographs.

Behind the mosque, past the stairs used by the *imam* to the Qarawiyin Library, is the 14th century 3-storey **Fondouk Titouani**, which originally provided accommodation for merchants from Tétouan, now used by artisans and a carpet shop, but worth seeing for its carved and panelled interior and for an insight into the way in which *fondouks* functioned. Both this and the nearby *Palais de Fes* restaurant, apparently a former marriage palace, have an excellent view of the Qarawiyin's courtyard and pavilion.

The triangular **Place Seffarin** (Brassworkers' Square) is marked by a tree that is noticeable in views over Fes El Bali from the N or S Borj. On the right is the **Qarawiyin Library** founded in 1349, still operational and with a valuable and ancient collection of books but closed to non-Muslims. It is an atmospheric place, with the sound of copper and other metals being beaten into large pans and cauldrons and the light filtered through the tree.

On the left is the **Seffarin Medersa**, the earliest *medersa*, from the 13th century, a partly ruined building in the style of a *Fassi* house, but with some interesting carving and a small minaret.

Carved plasterwork, decorative Arabic script

Cherratin Medersa Continuing off to the right along Sma't El Adoul (Street of Notaries) around the Qarawiyin, one passes the **Sidi Talouk sanctuary**, and then to the right the Alawite Cherratin Medersa, built in 1670 by Sultan Moulay Rashid, and currently being restored. This is a more modern *medersa* with a different design from the Merinid structures, including three storeys, in order to house a greater number of students, and three arches leading from the prayer hall to the courtyard.

Dabbaghin To get to the tanneries turn left at the Fondouk Titouani entrance into Place Seffarin, into Derb Mechattine. This alleyway leads to the tanneries, or **dabbaghin**, where leather is tanned and dyed in ancient pits, as in time immemorial. Although this is somewhat of a dirty and smelly place, it is a memorable experience for the courageous. Two enterprising individuals have turned their tiny houses into viewing terraces for the tanneries. There is no charge to climb up the steep and narrow stairs for a worthwhile view, but of course the owners have provided handicrafts boutiques on the roof, to tempt you before you struggle back down.

As-Sabbaghin At the end of Place Seffarine one passes a *souq* for silverwork, and then can take a right turn to the dyer's area, As-Sabbaghin, still in use to dye huge amounts of wool and other materials in an array of bright colours. It is a highly photogenic area, but those who work there are well aware of the possibilities for tipping. As-Sabbaghin is beside the notoriously dirty Oued Fes, which the UNESCO programme may cover over to provide another road for vehicular access to the central medina. Currently this only reaches as far as Place Rsif just along the river to the right.

The Andalusian Quarter Cross the Oued Bou Khrareb and follow rue Seftah to the **Andalusian Mosque** with its green and white minaret dating from the same period as the Qarawiyin Mosque but smaller and less important. The minaret dates from the 10th century, and the mosque was enlarged in the 13th century, with an architect from Toledo designing the impressive doorway, surmounted by carved wood.

Adjacent is the **Sahrija Medersa** from 1321-3, built for students studying at the mosque. It is a heavily restored building but there is still some memorable *zellij* tiling and wood carving. Note the scallop motif, much in evidence. The white marble basin after which the *medersa* was named, has been removed from the courtyard. The large prayer hall contained the library against the *qibla* wall at either side of the *mihrab*. The view from the roof of the *medersa* is recommended. Nearby is the **Sebbayin Medersa**, still in use. If you have a guide you could seek out the small **Fondouk Derb Laamti**, restored by Mawlay Hassan I in the 19th century, and of interest because it is still used for accommodation and storage by trading caravans, and also the **Derb Laamti Fountain**. From here, return to the Qarawiyin quarter by rue Sidi Youssef and the El Aouad bridge, noting the potters at work in the area. Alternatively take the No.18 bus from the **Mosque er Rsif** to Place de la Resistance.

Less grand, but very useful, Bab Ftouh has a large wholesale market and a flea market. Nearby is the **Koubba of**

Sidi Harazem which has a *moussem* each spring.

To the N the square **Kasbah des Cherarda** (after the Cherarda tribe), also called the **Kasbah al-Khemis** (after the nearby Thur *souq*). This was built in 1670 by the Alawite Sultan Moulay Rashid, and is now occupied by the Hopital Ibn al-Khatib, university buildings and a school.

View of Fes El Bali There are three excellent vantage points for viewing Fes El Bali permitting one to piece together the places explored or plan visits.

The Merinid Tombs, best approached from Fes El Jedid by car or petit-taxi date from the 14th century. The tombs are ruins, and much of the ornamentation documented by earlier visitors has not survived. A word of caution – this is not a safe place to go alone. Splendid view over town. Nearby is *Hotel Les Merinides*, also with an excellent view. It is a good place for a relaxing coffee, gazing out over the rooftops and minarets of Fes El Bali.

The North Borj is a fortress built by the Saadian Sultan Ahmad al-Mansour in 1582, which, though small, is an interesting example of the fortress architecture of the period. There is a good view of parts of Fes El Bali from the roof. It contains an Arms Museum, T 645241 (closed Tues), which exhibits a diverse display of weapons and military paraphernalia from all periods, including an array of European cannons. Every civilization is represented though the majority off and the finest, exhibits are Moroccan. The collections have been built up mainly as a result of royal donations and include a number of rare pieces. Examination of the exhibits permits a study of the development of techniques in armaments while in themselves these weapons have a splendour as crafted items. Look out for the largest weapon of all, a 5m long cannon weighing 12 tonnes used during the Battle of the Three Kings.

The South Borj provides a different view of Fes El Bali. It dates from the 13th century and is used by the military, but visitors can park beside it to admire the scene. Nearby is a **Son et Lumiere** auditorium, providing a spectacular history of Fes El Bali from this panoramic position.

Sound and Light at Bab Ftouh/Borj Sud Capacity 600 seats in two separate amphitheatres with commentaries in English, Arabic, Spanish and French. The performance takes 45 mins and costs MD200 per person and is organized by Massabih Fes, Ave Hassan II, Fes, T 5931892/3, F 5931894. **Performances**: Feb/Mar at 1900; Apr/May/Jun at 2130; Jul/Aug/Sept at 2200; Oct/Nov at 1900; Dec at 1900. This spectacle of sound and light certainly shows off the architecture of Fes to its best advantage. It clearly points out the places of interest and gives a good background. It is also in itself an entertainment of very high quality and is highly recommended. For further information contact the office in Tour Al Wataniya, Ave Hassan II, T 931892-3.

Fes El Jedid This is the Merinid capital, containing the Royal Palace, now a rather quiet area between the hustle and bustle of Fes El Bali and the modern *ville nouvelle*.

The Vieux Mechouar is the larger of the two open spaces in Fes El Bali. The large door on the W leads to the **Makina**, a desolate structure which has seen better days, originally built in the 19th century as an Italian run arms factory and now used for various functions including a rug factory and youth club. The large gate, Bab Dekkakine, leads onto the Petit Mechouar.

The Petit Mechouar is often bustling with people. On the left a gate leads to Ave des Français and Fes El Bali. Directly in front is a gate to the Royal Palace, the **Dar al-Makhzen**, a Merinid building from the 14th century, at the

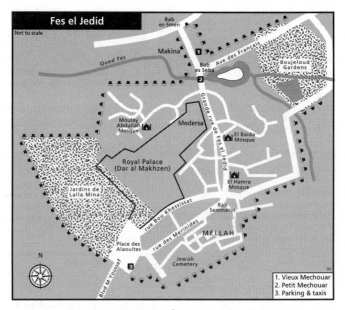

Fes el Jedid

Not to scale

Bab es-5men

Makina

Oued Fes

Ave des Franca

Bab es Seba

Boujeloud Gardens

Moulay Abdullah Mosque

Medersa

Grande rue de fes el jedid

El Baida Mosque

Royal Palace (Dar al Makhzen)

El Hamra Mosque

Jardins de Lalla Mina

Bab Semmarin

rue Bou Khessissat

rue des Merinides

MELLAH

Place des Alaouites

Jewish Cemetery

Blvd M Youssef

N

1. Vieux Mechouar
2. Petit Mechouar
3. Parking & taxis

heart of a large estate closed to visitors. To the right a doorway leads into **Moulay Abdellah**, now a normal area of housing but under the Protectorate a red light district. The 18th century mosque built by Moulay Abdellah stands here.

The Waterwheel and the Grande Rue
In the bottom left corner a gate leads into the rest of Fes El Jedid. Just inside this gate steps lead down to a pleasant walk around the perimeter of Fes El Jedid. It passes a bridge by an old, non-operative waterwheel, and the pleasant *Café Restaurant La Nouria* with the Boujeloud Gardens beyond. The Grande Rue de Fes El Jedid is the main marketing street of the area. Although the shops, many of which sell clothes, are less interesting than Fes El Bali, it is perhaps a more relaxing place to wander. The **Grand Mosque** has a minaret with a simple relief design and a tiled section at the top. The taller of the minarets, green with tiles at the top, belongs to the **El**

Hamra Mosque, dating from 1339. Surprisingly at this point there is a tree growing in the *souq*. At the end of the street is the 20th century **Bab Semmarin**, opening into rue Bou Khessissat.

The Mellah Rue Bou Khessissat with its balconies of wood and wrought iron leads W towards the *ville nouvelle*, past the 16th century Merinid gates to the Dar al-Makhzen. On the left is the *mellah* which includes a number of old synagogues and Jewish public buildings, although the area is now predominantly Muslim. The **Serfati** and **Fassiyin** synagogues now used for other purposes now. The houses are smaller and have a quite distinct architectural style. Below the *mellah* the Jewish cemetery is being restored. Since the beginning of the peace process in the Middle East, Morocco has opened its doors to Israeli tourists. The Jewish heritage of the *mellah* in Fes is now on the itinerary of many Jewish visitors.

Local information
● **Accommodation**

Price guide

Hotels:
AL	over US$75	**D**	US$20-40
A	US$75	**E**	US$10-20
B	US$60-75	**F**	under US$10
C	US$40-60		

Places to eat:
◆◆◆	expensive	◆◆	average
	◆	cheap	

AL *Hotel Jnan Palace Fes*, Ave Ahmed Chaouki, T 653965, 193 rm; **AL** *Hotel Les Merinides*, Borj Nord, T 646040, F 645225, 80 rm, 11 suites, pool, restaurant, bar, night-club, pool, modern, conference room, over-looking the medina with 4 restaurants, 2 bars, the *Nightclub Les Merinides*; **AL** *Hotel Palais Jamaï*, Bab El Guissa, T 634331/3, F 635096, 100 rm, 20 suites, 2 restaurants, bar, popular nightclub, *hammam*, sauna, tennis and a pool heated in winter, a former palace with excellent views of the medina, and a beautiful garden, reservations advisable, this is the best hotel in town but service is slow, breakfast disappoint-ing, certainly not value for money.

A *Hotel Sheraton*, Ave des Forces Armées Royales, T 625002, F 620486, 280 rm, mod-ern, comfortable, in *ville nouvelle*, extensive gardens, 2 restaurants, coffee shop, bar, tennis and pool, used by tour groups hence package tour treatment of all guests, grab your buffet meal before it goes cold, dancer in Moroccan restaurant highly rec.

B *Hotel Sofia*, 3 rue de Pakistan, just off Ave Hassan II, in heart of city, T 624265/7, F 644244, 120 a/c rm and 4 suites, 2 restaurants, 2 bars, nightclub, pool, safe parking.

C *Hotel Splendid*, 9 rue Abdelkarim el Kattabi, T 622148, F 654892, centre of *ville nouvelle*, 70 a/c rm with bath, restaurant, bar, TV room, small pool in courtyard, safe parking, rec; **C** *Hotel Volubilis*, Ave Allal Ben Abdellah, T 621125, F 621125, restaurant, bar, pool, good hotel from the PLM chain with a pleasant garden.

D *Hotel Batha*, rue de l'Unesco, T 636437/9, recently renovated; **D** *Hotel de la Paix*, 44 Ave Hassan II, T 626880, Tx 51636, stylish, in *ville nouvelle* from the Protectorate period with bar and restaurant, a/c, clean and comfortable; **D** *Le Grand Hotel*, Blvd Chefchaouni, T 625511-2, Tx 51631, a 1930s building in centre of *ville nouvelle* with style and atmos-phere, a restaurant, bar, and nightclub; **D** *Hotel Mounia*, 60 rue Asilah, T 624838, Tx 51801, this is a mock kasbah with modern, comfortable rooms, *hammam*, restaurant and a bar; **D** *Moussafir Hotel*, Ave des Almo-hades, T 651902, part of the chain attached to the railway company, efficiently run and comfortable, nr the railway station; **D** *Hotel Olympic*, Ave Mohammed V, T 624529, cen-tral location, restaurant, reasonable and com-fortable.

E *Hotel Central*, 50 rue du Nador, T 622333, big and clean rooms, very cheap; **E** *Hotel Kairouan*, 84 rue du Soudan, T 623590, rea-sonable, nr railway station; **E** *Hotel Lam-daghri*, 10 rue Abasse El Massadi, off Blvd Mohammed V, T 620310, small and highly rec, around a courtyard, with a restaurant and bar; **E** *Nouzha Hotel*, 7 rue Hassan Dkhissi, off Place Atlas, T 640002, recently opened, clean, efficient staff, café, bar; **E** *Hotel Royal*, 36 rue d'Espagne, T 624656.

F *Hotel Mauritanie*, by the **Bab Boujeloud** gate, one of best in medina, clean and with efficient and friendly management; nearby is the almost as good **F** *Hotel Erraha*, nr the bus station; *Hotel Jardin Publique* nr the Bou-jeloud Mosque is a safe bet; in the *ville nouvelle* cheap options are *Hotel Rex*, Place de l'Atlas; *Hotel Regina* and *Hotel Maghrib*, Ave Mo-hammed es Slaoui.

Camping: *Camping du Diamant Vert*, nr Aïn Chkeff, right off the P24, expensive but well-equipped site with shop and restaurant. *Camping Moulay Slimane*, site of 6 ha, res-taurant, groceries, showers, laundry, first aid, electricity for caravans, petrol 200m.

Youth hostel: 18 rue Abdestam Serghini in the *ville nouvelle*, T 624085, 60 beds, kitchen, bus 150m, train 1.2 km, overnight fee MD25, cheap option for those with a YHA card. Will rent space out on the roof if all the dormitories are full. Open only 0800-0900, 1200-1500, 1800-2200.

● **Places to eat**

◆◆◆ *Fes El Bali* has a number of beautiful palaces converted into restaurants, with elabo-rate decoration and sumptuous *Fassi* menus, look out for *pastilla*, not all are licensed; *Res-taurant Palais Tijani*, 51-3 Derb Ben Chek-roune, Lablida, T 633335; a more spectacular setting is *Restaurant Dar Saada*, 21 Souk El Attarin, T 637370-1, convenient for sightsee-ing; also try *Palais Mnebhi*, 15 Souq Ben Safi

Talaa Sghira, T 633893, good Moroccan food; *Dar Tajine*, 15 Ross Rhi, T 634167, fixed Moroccan menus in an exquisitely decorated 19th century palace, try the *pastilla*; *Restaurant Palais des Merinides*, 99 Zkak Roah, T 634028, serves lunch and dinner. Easier to find but pricier are the hotel restaurants: *Al Fassia*, in the *Hotel Palais Jamaï*, Bab El Guissa, T 634331, reservations advisable, one of the best Moroccan restaurants with a vast array of dishes incl quail *tagine*, and traditional Moroccan music; *La Koubba du Ciel*, in *Hotel Les Merinides*, Borj Nord, great cuisine and entertainment with the best view of Fes El Bali.

There are reasonable licensed restaurants in the *ville nouvelle*: ◆◆*Oued de la Biere*, Ave Mohammed V, T 625324, Moroccan and French cuisine, good *tagine de kefta*, clean and relaxed; *Restaurant Mounia*, 11 Blvd Mohammed Slaoui, rue Houceine El Khaddar, T 626661, Moroccan and European food but unlicensed; *Restaurant du Centre*, 106 Ave Mohammed V, T 622823, good Moroccan food; *Restaurant Pizzeria Chez Vittorio*, 21 rue Brahim Roudani, T 624730, good Italian food.

There is no shortage of cheap restaurants in Fes El Bali, particularly nr **Bab Boujeloud**, one

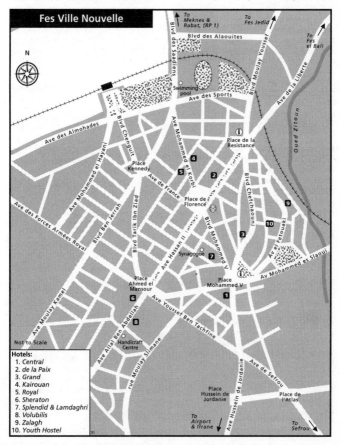

Fes Ville Nouvelle

To Meknes & Rabat, (RP 1)
To Fes Jedid
To Fes El Bali

Blvd des Saadiens
Blvd des Alaouites
Blvd Moulay Youssef
Ave de la Liberté

N

Swimming pool
Ave des Sports
Oued Zitoun

Ave des Almohades
Blvd Chenguit
Ave Mohammed el Korbi
Ave Mohammed el Hayani

Place Kennedy
Ave de France
Place de la Resistance ℹ

Ave des Forces Armées Royal
Blvd Ben Jerrah
Blvd Tarik Ibn Ziad

Place de Florence
Blvd Chefchaouni
Ave Fetouaki

Ave Hassan II
Synagogue
Blvd Mohammed V
Ave Mohammed es Slaoui

Blvd Moulay Kamel
Place Ahmed el Mansour
Place Mohammed V

Ave Youssef Ben Tachfine

Handicraft Centre
Ave Alla Ben Abdellah
rue Moulay Slimane

Not to Scale

Ave de Sefrou
Ave Hussein de Jordanie

Place Hussein de Jordanie
Place de l'Atlas

To Airport & Ifrane
To Sefrou

Hotels:
1. Central
2. de la Paix
3. Grand
4. Kairouan
5. Royal
6. Sheraton
7. Splendid & Lamdaghri
8. Volubilis
9. Zalagh
10. Youth Hostel

of the best is ◆*Restaurant Bouayad*, 26 Bab Boujeloud, T 633432, open 24 hrs, a large and cheap menu incl *pastilla* and excellent *brochettes*. In the *ville nouvelle* one of the best cheap places is **Restaurant Chamonix**, 5 rue Mokhtar Soussi, off Ave Mohammed V, T 626638, Moroccan, European and pizzas; also try **Croque Burger**, 26 Ave Slaoui, T 654029, take away, delivery and eat in burgers and pizzas; *Fes Mondi Sportif*, Tazi Cherti Abdellah, nr intersection of Ave des Forces Armées Royales and Ave Hassan II; *Marrakech*, opp *Hotel Nouzha* off Place Atlas, food of good quality; *Marhaba*, 23 Ave Mohammed V, very good *tagines* and salads; *Chawarma Sandwich*, 42 rue Normandie, reasonable and clean.

Cafés: the best cafés are in the *ville nouvelle*, but the best for watching *Fassi* life are in the medina. In the *ville nouvelle* try *L'Elysée*, 4 rue de Paris; or *Café l'Opéra*.

● **Bars**
A drink in the *Hotel Palais Jamai* is a good break in the medina, the *Hotel des Merinides* has a good view of the city. In the *ville nouvelle* try *Es Saada*, on Ave Slaoui, or *Bar du Centre*, Ave Mohammed V.

● **Banks & money changers**
ABM, Ave Hassan II, T 651515; **BMAO**, Immeuble Mamda, Place de Florence, T 650785; **Banque al Maghrib**, Ave de France, T 625596-8; **BMCE**, Place Mohammed V; **Banque Populaire**, Ave Mohammed V; **Credit du Maroc**, Ave Mohammed V; **SGMB**, Ave Lalla Yacout, T 625011; **SMDC**, 3 Blvd Bir Anzarane, T 642611; **Wafabank**, Ave Mohammed V, T 622591.

● **Cultural centres**
Centre Culturel Français, 33 rue el-Bahrein, T 623921, library and films. **Spanish Cultural Centre**, 5 Blvd Mohammed V.

● **Entertainment**
Disco & nightclubs: *Nightclub Les Merinides*, in the *Hotel Les Merinides*, Borj Nord, T 645225 (2130-0300), a fashionable but expensive place, with drinks from MD50; also try *Nightclub* in the *Hotel Palais Jamai*, Bab El Guissa, T 634331 (2200-0300), similarly expensive but popular with those that can afford it.

● **Hospitals & medical services**
Chemists: there is an all night chemist at the Municipalité de Fes, Blvd Moulay Youssef, T 623380 (2000-0800); during the day try

Bahja, Ave Mohammed V, T 622441; or *Bab Ftouh* at Bab Ftouh, T 649135.

Hospital: *Hôpital Ghassani*, Quartier Dhar Mehraz, T 622776.

● **Post & telecommunications**
The PTT Centrale is at the junction of Ave Hassan II and Ave Mohammed V. Telephone facilities are open 0800-2100. There is another post office in the medina, at Place Batha.

● **Shopping**
Books & newspapers: try the *English Bookshop* of Fes, 68 Ave Hassan II, nr Place de la Résistance. Newspapers from the stalls in Ave Mohammed V.

Handicrafts & Moroccan goods: Fes has for long been one of the great trading centres of Morocco. The *souqs*, *kissaria* and boutiques offer a splendid selection for visitors. Many of the boutiques in the hotels, the *ville nouvelle* and near the important tourist attractions charge inflated prices. The further afield you go, the lower the prices are and the more genuine the claims of regional provinence and antiquity. The large carpet shops, have some incredible goods to sell, but have very experienced salesmen. Look for the blue and white pottery, metalwork, jewellery and carpets.

For antique carpets, jewellery and artifacts, *Maison Berbere*, 4 Riad Jouha, nr the Attarin Medersa, T 635686, is normally a wholesaler, but has an excellent selection at low prices. For new carpets in the medina try *Dar Ibn Khaldoun*, 45 Derb Ben Chekroune Lablida, BP 745, T 633335 or *Palais Vizier*, 35 Derb Touil Blida which give an opportunity to see two restored 'palaces'. Two places where one should be very cautious about the prices and products are *Palais Andalous*, 15 Derb Selma, and *La Bahia*, 3 Bouakda, Zkak Rouamane. For new and antique jewellery, metalware and silverware, as well as *kaftans*, you should not miss a visit to *Dar Kairouan*, 6 Derb el Hammam Joutia, T 633735. Another good place to buy antiques is *Aux Merveilles de Fes*, 11 rue Rahabt el Kaïss, opp the Attarin Medersa, T 633632. For smaller items wander in the Souk El Attarin and nearby *souqs*, with *babouches* best bought from the *kissaria*. For most items the **Coopartim Centre Artisanale**, Blvd Allal Ben Abdellah, T 625654 (0900-1400 and 1600-1900), has a good selection but fixed prices. Fes El Jedid is a quieter but slightly more pricey area to shop in.

● **Sports**

Flying: *Royal Flying Club*, Airport de Fes-Saiss, T 644167.

Golf: *Royal Golf Club*, Route d'Ifrane, T 763849, 9 holes, 3,168m, par 37. Fees per round MD400, hire of clubs MD100, closed Mon.

Riding: at *Club Equestre Moulay Idriss*, Hippodrome Moulay Kamel.

Swimming: in the large hotels, mainly *Hotel Salam Zalagh*, rue Mohammed Diouri, or at the municipal pool, Ave des Sports.

Tennis: at *Sporting Club Fassi*, Clos de la Renaissance, 10 rue Moulay Slimane, T 641512, with five courts or *Tennis Club Fassi*, Ave Mohammed El Kori, T 624272, with seven courts.

● **Tour companies & travel agents**

Azur Voyage, 3 Ave Lala Meriem, T 625115; *Fes Voyages*, 9 rue de Turquie, T 621776; *Number One*, 44 Ave Slaoui, T 621234; *Tak Voyages*, 41 Ave Mohammed V, T 624550, 622455, F 652736; *Wagons-Lits Tourisme*, Immeuble Grand Hotel, T 654464. *Royal Air Maroc*, 52 Ave Hassan II, T 625516-7, reservations T 620456-7.

● **Tourist offices**

Office du Tourisme, Place de la Résistance, T 623460, F 623146; **Syndicat d'Initiative**, Ave Mohammed V, T 625301.

● **Useful telephone numbers**

Fire: T 15.

Garages: Fiat, Ave Mohammed V, T 623435; Renault, rue d'Espagne, T 622232.

Police: Ave Mohammed V, T 19.

● **Transport**

Local Bus: these can be a convenient option in Fes, a ticket costs MD2. No 1 runs from Place des Alawites to Dar Batha, No 3 from Place des Alawites to Place de la Résistance, No 9 from Place de la Résistance to Dar Batha, No 10 from Bab Guissa to Place des Alaouites, No 18 from Place de la Résistance to Bab Ftouh and No 20 from Place de Florence to *Hotel les Merinides*.

Car hire: **Avis**, 50 Blvd Chefchaouni, T 626746; **Budget**, adjacent *Palais Jamaï Hotel*, T 620919; **Europcar-Inter-Rent**, 41 Ave Hassan II, T 626545; **Hertz**, Kissariat de la Foire No 1, Blvd Lalla Meryem, T 622812; airport T 651823; **Holiday Car**, 41 Ave Mohammed V, T 624550, 622455, F 652736; **SAFLOC**, *Hotel Sheraton*, T 931201; **Zeit**, 35 Ave Mohammed Slaoui, T 625510. **Taxis**: red, are a cheap and quick way to get around Fes, can be found around much of the city, and sometimes have meters. Sample fares Bab Boujeloud to Place Mohammed V, MD10; Place Mohammed V to *Hotel Les Merinides*, MD15. Parking can be a problem approaching the medina, so it is perhaps better not to use one's own car.

Air Aéroport Fes Saiss is 15 km from the city, off the P24, T 624712. Flights to Casablanca with connections to internal and international destinations (see page 196), 1 a week to Er Rachidia, as well as direct flights to Marseille

---

Bottled up

Seasoned travellers are easily identified by how quickly they take to the bottle ... of water. On sale in Morocco are three main brands, each different. *Oulmès*, SW of Meknes, gives its name to the only spring of naturally gaseous water found in Morocco. Its source is in the Zaër Zaiane massif, part of the Middle Atlas but the spring emerges near Tiflet, W of Meknes, at the bottom of a deep canyon. The health-promoting trace elements found in this spring water include calcium, magnesium, sodium and iron. *Oulmès*, is sold in small glass bottles and has been on the market for over half a century. From the same area and exploited by the same company comes non-gaseous *Sidi Ali*, not very mineralized, most commonly used as table water and recommended for salt-free diets and mixing milk powder for babies. It is sold in the ubiquitous semi-transparent blue plastic bottles. This is more recent, first marketed in 1977 and now selling more than 500,000 hectolitres each year. The third source, also in the Middle Atlas, and known since Roman times, is the spring at *Sidi Harazem* just 10 km SE of Fes. This also is non-gaseous but contains chlorine and sodium which can be noted in the taste. This too is sold as table water but in smaller quantities than the *Sidi Ali*.

(Wed) and Paris (Sun). To get to the airport take Bus 16 from the train station.

Train The train station is at the end of Blvd Chenguit, T 625001. Departures to **Taza** and **Oujda**: 0400, 0640, 1455, 1715, 2020, 0130; **Meknes**: 11 a day between 0315 and 0145; **Tanger**: 0410 and 1250; **Rabat** and **Casablanca**: 0315, 0700, 0900, 1040, 1410, 1605, 1835, 1930 and 0145.

Road Bus: CTM buses leave from the station on Ave Mohammed V, T 622041, for Beni Mellal at 0630 and 2300, Marrakech at 0630 and 2100, Tetouan at 0800 and 1100, Tanger at 1100, 1800 and 0030, Taza at 1230 and 1830, Oujda at 1230, Nador at 0130, for Casablanca 8 a day between 0700 and 1900, for Rabat 7 a day between 0930 and 1900, and for Meknes 8 a day between 0700 and 1900. Most other private line buses leave from the new terminal off the Route du Tour de Fes, below the N Borj. Buses for the Middle Atlas leave from the Laghzaoui terminal, rue Ksar el Kebir. **Taxi**: grand-taxis leave from Place Baghdadi, except for Sefrou and Azrou which leave from rue de Normandes.

EXCURSION TO MOULAY YACOUB

Moulay Yacoub lies 20 km NW of Fes, a short journey through rolling countryside and some interesting capital intensive irrigated farming. Taxis from Bab Boujeloud stop near the car park above the village and the steep walk down to the pool and hammams has small shops, cafés and a number of cheap lodging. **C** *Hotel Moulay Yacoub*, also called the *Fes Motel*, stands above the village, T 694035, F 694012, 60 rm with TV, bath and terrace, 60 bungalows, restaurant with magnificent views, bar, tennis, pool. A new tree lined road leads down from the hotel to the medical treatment centre using *thermal springs*, with neat gardens, café and practice golf.

EXCURSIONS TO SIDI HARAZEM, BHALIL AND SEFROU

Sidi Harazem In restaurants all over Morocco the mineral water is almost exclusively from Sidi Ali or Sidi Harazem (see page 283). Sidi Harazem was originally buried in Marrakech. The source and spa centre of that name is an easy day excursion being only 4 km along the P1 from Fes, with buses from the CTM bus station and Bab Boujeloud, and grand-taxis from Bab Ftouh. The area around the thermal baths is still very popular for swimming and picnics but the once impressive water courses, pools and spas have been disappointingly neglected. There is too much concrete and the cafés and trinket sellers are not recommended. There is a 17th century *koubba*, and the PLM chain **C** *Hotel Sidi Harazem*, T 690057, F 690072, 62 a/c rm, with health facilities, restaurant and bar.

Bhalil En route to Sefrou, 5 km before the town off the P20, is Bhalil. This small hill village may have had a Christian population before the coming of Islam. Behind the picturesque village are several troglodyte dwellings, with people still inhabiting the caves. The road takes you round the town, giving excellent views on all sides, and two good clean cafés on the outskirts when approaching from the E.

SEFROU

Sefrou is 32 km S of Fes along the P20. It is unlikely to be reached en route, as the P24/P21, via Ifrane and Azrou, is a better route from Fes to Er Rachidia and the S, but is certainly worth visiting as an excursion from Fes or to stay for a few days, as this is one of the most appealing towns in Morocco, an unspoilt historic walled town lying in a beautiful wooded valley, with a calm and genuinely friendly atmosphere. Both buses and taxis arrive and leave from Place Moulay Hassan, by Bab Taksebt and Bab M'Kam, where the road from Fes meets the old town. Buses from Fes leave from Bab Boujeloud and many go on to Er Rachida. Grand taxis from Fes leave from Bab Ftouh.

Although now bypassed by new roads, Sefrou once lay astride the major caravan routes from Fes and the N, to the S and the Sahara beyond, and is an important market-place for the surrounding agricultural region. Sefrou always had a distinctive character due to its Jewish roots, which predated Moroccan Islam, and although converted to Islam by Moulay Ismail, it returned to its status with the migration of Jews from Tafilalt and Algeria in the 13th century. This characteristic lasted until the emigration of Jews to the large cities, Europe and Israel after WW2 and the 1967 Arab-Israeli War. More than any other equivalent small town it has fascinated Western academics, with the anthropologists Geertz, Rosen and Rabinow carrying out reseach here. Recently Sefrou was created a province in its own right, and received new and badly-needed investment, as it was a town declining into shabby anonymity.

The market place below and E of Ave Mohammed V is a relaxed place to wander, best during the Thur **souq**. The town, which is known for olive and cherry production, has a large **Fête des Cerises** in Jun, and other smaller *fêtes* during the year. There is a *moussem*, or religious gathering, for Sidi Lahcen Lyoussi.

Entering from the N the road curves down to the Oued Aggaï, past the Centre Artisanal (0800-1200 and 1400-1900, except Sun) into the busy Place Moulay Hassan. From here Bab M'Kram is the main entrance to the *medina* which lies N of the river and Bab Taksebt the main entrance, over the bridge, into the *mellah*. Both are small, maze-like quarters, but it is difficult to get seriously lost. The *mellah* can also be entered from the covered market place through Bab M'Rabja. Beside a mosque built into the wall, bend right and down the main street, beside small restaurants, butchers, shops and craftsmen, and then left to reach one of several small bridges over the Oued Aggaï. Alternatively, take one of the small side turnings to discover the cramped design of the *mellah*, now mainly occupied by poorer Muslims, with houses often built over the narrow streets.

In the medina, the **Grand Mosque of El Jamaa Kebir**, restored in the 19th century, lies beside the river, and the *souqs* just upstream. In the *souqs*, where bargaining will be less fierce than in Fes, note the silversmiths and the woodworkers. Past the *souqs* is the **Zaouia of Sidi Lahcen ben Ahmed**. In the medina there is a clearly discernible difference in the design of the quarter, reflecting the strict regulations and conditions under which Jews in the *mellah* lived. Sefrou is quite remarkable, however, in that the *mellah* is as large as the medina.

Ave Moulay Hassan crosses the Oued Aggaï, where there is a *Syndicat d'Initiative*, T 660380, past the Jardin Publique, which has a swimming pool and continues as Ave Mohammed V, the main street of the unexciting new town, with the Post Office, and a few shops and simple café-restaurants, the *rôtisseries*, for grilled chicken, being one of the places. Take time to explore. Turn into rue Ziad by the post office, past hotel Sidi Lahcem Lyoussi and continue uphill on the black top road. Camping is signed to the left but continue up to the koubba of Sidi Bou Ali, white walls and distinctive green tiled roof. There is a café, a few stalls and a magnificent view. Another small excursion beginning S of the river leads W to the small waterfall grandly known as the cascades.

● **Accommodation** The two best places to stay are the **D** *Hotel Sidi Lahcen Lyoussi*, off Ave Moulay Hassan, T 660497, 24 rm, a dated but comfortable place with a restaurant, bar and pool; and **F** *Hotel les Cerises*, Ave Mohammed V, T 661528, a large, impersonal but cheap hotel; there is also the **F** *Hotel Lafrenie*, Route de Fes, T 662030, a small *pensiones*. Follow rue Ziad, by the post office on Ave Mohammed V, to a campsite, *Camping de Sefrou*, T 660001, 2 km from the town, in site of 4 ha, bar/snack, grocery, showers, laundry, petrol at 2 km, and on a fork off that road, the **F** *Hotel-Café Boualserhim*, by the green-roofed **Koubba of Sidi Bouserghine**, Sefrou's patron saint.

The olive – a symbol of harmony and of plenty

Even before the arrival of the Romans in what is now Morocco the people there knew how to graft the olive tree, *oleo europeae sylvestris*, to improve its productivity. But it was under the Romans, in the 2nd and 3rd centuries AD, that olive cultivation spread across North Africa from Morocco to Libya. Today the olive tree is an integral part of the Mediterranean landscape and in Morocco is cultivated from the Rif mountains in the N to the valley of the Oued Sous at Taroudant in the S. Today, crossing this region by air the chequer-board pattern of cultivation is very distinctive. On the ground the endless hectares of these trees is even more impressive. The regular arrangement of the trees is known as quincux, one at each corner of a 10m square and one in the middle leaving room for machinery and adequate nourishment.

The olive is a sub-tropical, broad leaved, evergreen tree, both fire and drought tolerant and resistant to decay. It grows 3-12m high and many trees are said to survive to between 80-100 years in age. The leathery, lance-shaped leaves, growing in pairs are dark green above and silvery below. From the tiny white flowers which bloom in the late spring and are wind pollinated, the green olive fruits develop. Fruit setting is erratic, in less than perfect conditions trees may fruit only in alternate years.

In Morocco the olive is the principal fruit crop, 33 million trees covering over 350,000 ha. The main zones are the plateaux of Taza, Fes and Meknes where the annual rainfall is adequate and the inner plains of Beni-Mellal, El Kelaa and the Haouz around Marrakech where irrigation is required. Traditional cultivation of older trees by family labour produces about 15-20 kg per tree. However, in the mountain regions such as the Zerhoun by Moulay Idris or Amizmiz in the foothills behind Marrakech the topography, climate and land ownership are obstacles to improving production techniques. Modern cultivation described above can yield 50 kg. Harvesting appears quite brutal as the branches are struck to remove the fruits but must be done with care as bruised fruit cannot be sold for table consumption nor used to produce the best oil. 20% of the olives are sent to bottling factories while the rest are destined to produce olive oil.

The olive was considered an important tree. It was sacred to the goddess Minerva (see box, Know Your Roman Gods, page 253) and a crown of olive leaves was the reward given to victors in the Olympic Games. The olive branch, synonymous with peace and plenty was Noah's first indication of the receding flood.

EXCURSION TO VALLEY OF OUERGHA

The triangle formed by the S302, S304 and the P26 makes an interesting tour. Aïn Kansera stands off the road to the right before the track to the Barrage of Idriss 1st is reached. This large lake in the Oued Inaouena is some 20 km in length and stores water for Fes. It is a popular picnic site. At Tissa there is an important annual gathering of horses and their riders. Aïn Aicha is an important regional market in the Oued Ouerrha. Take time to visit picturesque Rafsai, 10 km beyond Ourtzarh. Jbel Messaoud 825m can be reached from Ourtzarh and affords fine views over the valley and the Rif.

Return to Fes travelling S on the P26. Where Tnine stands on the E of the road, Moulay Bouchta stands on the W, a venue for the annual horse and rider *moussem*.

TAZA AND ENVIRONS

TAZA

The town is divided into three quite separate parts, the area around the railway and bus station, the *ville nouvelle* around Place de l'Indépendence, and the quiet medina on the hill. Unfortunately its most impressive historic buildings are closed to non-Muslims.

History

Taza (*Pop* 77,216), is a modest market town which has in the past achieved considerable regional importance under successive dynasties. The town has been settled since Neolithic times, and has gained importance with its highly strategic location in the Taza Gap, between the Rif and the Middle Atlas. The town was developed by the Meknassa tribe of Berbers, and was an important but finally unsuccessful fortification against the advance of the Fatimids from the E. The Almohads under Sultan Abd el-Moumen captured the city in 1141-1142, making it their second capital, and used it to attack the Almoravids. The Almohads built a mosque and provided much of the city's fortifications.

Taza was the first city taken by the Merinids, who added considerably to the Almohad city. Its important defensive role continued under the Merinids and the Saadians, and was again pivotal in the rise to power of the Alawites, who further extended and fortified the city, later using it as a defence against the French threat from the E.

The eccentric pretender, Bou Hamra, proclaimed himself as Sultan here in 1902 and controlled much of E Morocco until 1912, when he was caught and killed. He was known as a wandering miracle-maker, travelling Morocco on a donkey. Taza was occupied by the French in 1914, and became an important military centre.

ACCESS Taza is well connected by road and rail. The railway station, private bus station and grand-taxi rank are N from the centre of the *ville nouvelle*, Place de l'Indépendence, beyond walking distance. Buses, taxis and car parking in Place Moulay Hassan in the medina.

Places of interest

The *ville nouvelle* for hotels, restaurants, banks and other services is a quiet place centred around the old French buildings on Place de l'Indépendence.

The older buildings are in the small attractive medina perched on the hill 3 km away from the railway station and 2 km from the centre of the new town. From the bottom of the hill there is an interesting short cut to the kasbah via a flight of steps which provide remarkable views. Beyond this point, further along the main road on the right, are the **Kifane el-Ghomari** caves, inhabited in Neolithic times.

The transport hub of the old town is Place Moulay Hassan, just outside the main entrance to the *souq*, where the post office, bank, cafés, teleboutique etc are to be found. The focus of the old quarter is the main street, with a number of names but commonly called the Mechouar from end to end, which runs behind Place Moulay Hassan along the entire length of the medina from the Andalusian Mosque behind Place Moulay Hassan to the Grand Mosque at the opposite end of town by the Bab er Rih gate. Between the two mosques are the various *souqs*. These, which are noted for jewellery and carpets of the Aït-Benhaddou Berber tribes, are not aimed at tourists, and are refreshingly hassle-free. There is also an interesting second-hand section to the right past the main entrance. A tour of the ramparts is certainly to be included in the itinerary.

Turning left just past the main gate to the *souq* by the *Cinema Friouato* is the jewellery section. From here you can turn left along a very straight and narrow section of road towards the Andalusian Mosque, or right toward the

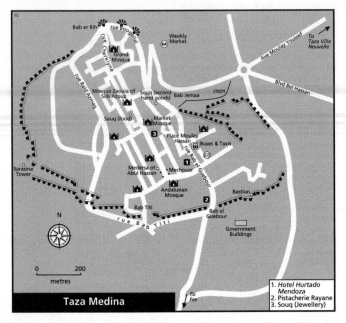

Taza Medina

1. *Hotel Hurtado Mendoza*
2. *Pistacherie Rayane*
3. *Souq (Jewellery)*

Grand Mosque. Following the latter route, the food and spice *souq* (see box, page 487) is off to the left, behind the broader section of the mechouar. Further along, one can perhaps gain a glimpse of the Zaouia of Sidi Azouz and note its beautiful wall-basin by the door. It is difficult to gain a good view of the Grand Mosque. The mosque, including its existing minaret, was built by the Almohads in the second half of the 12th century, with further elaboration by the Marinids in the late 13th century, and the Alawites in the 17th. As in the case of the Koutoubia mosque in Marrakech (see page 304), the minaret follows the classic proportions of 1:5. Only Muslims can view the beautiful chandelier bearing 514 oil lamps which lights the mosque.

To the right of the grand mosque, down a steep passage, you reach a section of the ramparts, with good views over the surrounding countryside, Taza Bas, and the Rif mountains beyond. Below the walls is an area where the weekly market is held. The walls were originally laid out by the Almohads and repeatedly improved since. Following the ramparts anticlockwise note the Almohad Bab el Rih gate, and the circular Sarasine Tower further on, also dating back to Almohad times.

In the opposite direction is the Andalusian Mosque with its 12th century minaret. Just before, on the right, stands the 14th century Medersa of Abul Hassan, named after a Marinid sultan. This is closed, but the exterior shows a carved lintel in cedar wood, and a porch roof overhanging the road. At the end of the Mechouar, in a lane to the right of the mosque, Zankat Dar al-Makhzen, there is the former house of Bou Hamra the pretender.

Local information
● Accommodation

D *Hotel Friouato*, Ave de la Gare, T 672593, 58 rm, top hotel in town, bar, restaurant, tennis and pool, but inconveniently located between the medina and the *ville nouvelle*, to get there turn left at the foot of the steps that climb the hill to the old town, this hotel has seen better days and capacity outstrips demand but good for a drink in the large peaceful garden.

E *Grand Hotel du Dauphine*, at the centre of the town on junction of Ave de la Gare and Place de l'Indépendence, T 673567, 26 rm, some with shower but no communal shower for those without, comfortable, rec bar and restaurant, dating very obviously from the Protectorate period, visitor's comment – "plus points are comfortable large rooms, faded charm and central location; downside the peeling paintwork, poor plumbing and surly staff"; **E** *Hotel de La Gâre*, situated at the main crossroads nr the station, T 672448, the best cheap option in the new town, adequate standard of cleaning, friendly owners, nice café, teleboutique next door, best rooms are on the first floor, cold showers only.

Cheaper and more basic options incl **F** *Hotel de la Poste*, Place de l'Indépendence, T 672589, by the CTM office above a café, simple and adequate, tiny rooms, at times very noisy; **F** *Hurtado Mendoza* (alias *Hotel Etoile*), Rue Moulay Hassan, opp the post office, only hotel in the old town, pretty Andalusian style courtyard, nicest rms are on the upper floors, which are better ventilated and have good views from the balcony, no showers, the proprietor, Mr Mendoza, is Spanish and lives on the premises with his Moroccan wife and children; and *Hotel Guillaume Tell* on Place de l'Indépendence, basic and not very clean.

Camping: at *Zeitoun*, off Ave de la Gare en route to the medina, campsite of 5 ha, advertised with snack bar, laundry, showers, electricity for caravans is not rec.

● Places to eat

♦♦♦ The *Hotel Salam Friouato*, T 672593, has reasonable, unexciting meals. A better option is the **♦♦***Grand Hotel du Dauphine*, junction of Place de l'Indépendence and Ave de la Gare, T 673567, huge '50s' dining hall, good value if you don't mind a limited menu (sometimes only steak and chips), beer available.

♦ *Café Restaurant Majestic*, Ave Moham-med V, Moroccan food, and on same street *Restaurant Azzam* and *Restaurant des Gouts*; *Snack Bar Youm Youm*, behind *Hotel de la Poste* on Blvd Moulay Youssef, cheap fastfood mainly serving kebabs (*brochettes*).

Cafés: *Pâtisserie des Festivités*, 1 Blvd Mohammed V, just off Place de l'Indépendence, cosy salon at rear, good for breakfast and cakes. *Café Andalous*, in the old town where terrace overlooks the animated Place Moulay Hassan, fascinating place to sit and observe. *Café el-Ghissani*, opp *Café Andalous* by the main entrance to the *souq*, popular café, good for people-watching. *Café des Jardins*, Ave Ibn Khatib, with very relaxing atmosphere, situated in the municipal gardens on route to the old town, terrace with views, closed at night.

● Banks & money changers
Wafabank, Place Moulay Hassan, in the old town; *BMCE*, Ave Mohammed V, in the new town.

● Laundry
Gentleman Pressing, Ave Mohammed V.

● Post & telecommunications
Rue Moussa Ibn Noussair, near Place de l'Indépendence.

● Shopping
Pistacherie Rayane, 5 Ave Moulay Hassan, situated by the entrance to old town sells factory-fresh nuts, a fraction cheaper than elsewhere.

Photography: *Photolab Ennceiri*, Ave Moulay Youssef, off Place de l'Indépendence.

● Tour companies & travel agents
Taza Voyages, Ave Mohammed V; *Bennani Voyages*, Place de l'Indépendence, changes money on Sat 1000-1200.

● Tourist offices
Closed down.

● Transport
Local Taxi: it is advisable to take one of Taza's light blue petit-taxis between Place de l'Indépendence and the railway station (MD3-5), or the medina (MD5). There are also town buses.

Train To Oujda (stopping at Guercif and Taourirt), 0613, 1644, 1742; to **Tanger** (8 hrs): 0959, 0141; to **Fes** (2 hrs); Meknes (3 hrs); and **Casablanca** (7 hrs): 0036, 1050, 1300, 2254; **Marrakech**, 0036, 1050. Make sure you get in the right carriage.

Road Bus: CTM buses leave from their office on Place de l'Indépendence to **Oujda** at 1500 and **Fes/Meknes/Casablanca**, 0700, 1430, 2200, 2330. Other companies operate from near the railway station, turn right at the end of Ave de la Gare. Regular services to **Oujda/Guercif/Taourirt**, at 0600, 0700, 0900, 1000, 1100, 1200, 1300, 1530, 1600 (4 hrs), **Fes** generally every half hour, between 0500 and 1800 (2 hrs), **Nador** at 0700, 0800, 1100, 1300, 1400 (4 hrs), other services to **Al Hoceima** (4 hrs), **Aknoul** (1 hr). **Taxi**: grand-taxis leave from the transport cafés by the bus station to **Oujda** (2½ hrs), **Fes** (1½ hrs), **Al Hoceima**, **Nador**, amongst other places. For the Jbel Tazzeka (see below) they leave from the old town.

EXCURSION ON THE TAZZEKA ROAD

To the S of Taza and the P1 lies the **Jbel Tazzeka National Park** in an area of outstanding mountain scenery. This is a region of oak forest with a rich undergrowth supporting several species of resident and migratory birds. The Black-shouldered Kite, a quite rare raptor, is found here. The S311 winds its way through this area from S of Taza, rejoining the P1 31 km further W. This is an excursion primarily for those with their own transport, but it may be possible to bargain for a grand-taxi part of the way, from the rank by the railway station. En route travellers should stop at the waterfalls, the **Cascades de Ras el Oued**, and further on, the **Dayat Chiker**. Nearby is the **Gouffre du Friouato**, an immense series of caves, dominated by a 180m deep underground bowl, worth exploring with a torch. After the caves, continue on to the Bab Taza pass from which a rough and challenging track goes N up to the Jbel Tazzeka, where there are incredible views of the surrounding mountains. After, or avoiding, the Jbel Tazzeka the road continues through the narrow gorge by the Oued Zireg and back to the P1. The map shows distances between major points and the quality of the roads. Excursions S to Immouzer du Kandar and the Dayats of Aaoua, Afourgan and Ifra see page 338.

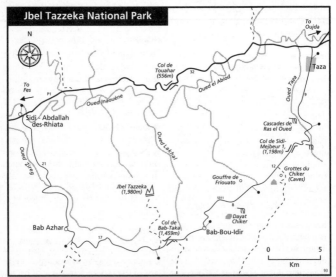

Lying N from Taza is a section of the Rif mountains that can be visited easily in one day. Although less dramatic and tamer than the mountains further W, it is a pleasant trip if you have your own transport, particularly on market days (see below) which make for more entertaining halts. If you are heading for Nador the S312 is more scenic than routes further E. The road branches off from the P1 2 km to the E of Taza station, and after 20 km reaches the village of Aïn Bou Kellal, which has a large bustling market on Sat. It is important to arrive early to enjoy the event at its best (and coolest!).

The next village along the way is Jbarna, which has a market on Sun. Thereafter the road begin to climb more steeply, and mature Aleppo pines begins to appear. Some 5 km past Jbarna the road joins a stretch of the upper Oued Msoun which is very pretty. Near the top of the pass, a road to the E signposted to Mesquitem follows the *oued* downstream back to the P1 (see Msoun, page 291) while to the W a less well surfaced track leads to El Gouzat and S alongside the Oued el Hadar back to the P1. Either makes an interesting excursion but these are not short distances and would require planning.

Continuing N the small administrative centre of Aknoul is disappointing. There are hardly any shops and no place to stay, only a petrol station and two banks on the main road. If you are passing through on a Tues, however, its worth stopping for the *souq*, which draws a colourful crowd from the surrounding mountains. Shortly after Aknoul there is the turning for the S304 which leads precariously westwards into the Rif heartland over the Col du Nador. There is a permanent *sureté* roadblock at this T-junction. Expect a courteous but thorough routine check. The next 18 km are scenic and high, reaching 1,300m. But this is nothing to the towering Jbel Berkane on the E (1,774m) and the Rif massif to the W, over 2,000m. It is not until the town of Tizi-Ouzi (Mon *souq*) is reached that the road descends, very rapidly, towards the plains and Casita. This is a speedy 21 km but watch out for the *oued* bed just before reaching the main road.

CASITA

This is little more than a junction town on the P39 with a 'it happened yesterday' feel about it. It is located just inside the former Spanish zone of influence. There are buses to Nador and Al Hoceima every hour, so there is little reason to stay unless you are heading back to Taza, in which case you may have to wait some time for public transport. A bus departs at 1500 back to Taza. If you are stuck here the only acceptable option is the basic Hotel Andalous opposite the Taza Road, above a simple café/restaurant.

● **Transport Local Taxis**: from Taza taxis to Aknoul/Casita/Al Hoceima depart from the rear of the long taxi queue behind the transport cafés nr the station. Waiting for a taxi to fill up can take some time.

From Taza to Oujda Msoun

20 km to the E of Taza along the P1, is the fortified farming village of Msoun. Built around 1700 in Moulay Ismael's reign to guard the approaches to the strategic Taza Gap, it is still inhabited by members of the semi-nomadic Houara tribe. The village has a shop, post office and even a tea-house. The compact, walled settlement stands isolated on a hillside, clearly visible from the main road where there is the convenient Motel-Restaurant Casbah, and a petrol station. It is possible to walk to the village from here, just 2 km.

GUERCIF

An unremarkable modern agricultural town noted for its olives and shoe industry. In the 14th century, Guercif became a stronghold of the Beni Ouattas tribe, who later overran Taza and replaced Merinids to form the Ouattasid dynasty. The main part of town, which lies to the S of the main road, is centred around Blvd Mohammed V, its solid 19th century mosque, and two adjacent squares: the central square, which functions as a commercial and transport hub, and the Place Zerkatouni with the public gardens and post office. The railway station is reached via a driveway from the opposite side of the main road. Market day is Sun.

● **Accommodation E** *Hotel Howary*, Ave Moulay Youssef, T 625062, a busy small hotel on the Oujda Road near the railway station, rooms are very variable, and the plumbing is unreliable, you may have to ask for clean bed linen but staff are friendly and helpful; **E** *Hotel/Restaurant des Voyageurs*, Rue Ibn Battuta, between the mosque and the main road, a faded piece of colonial France frozen in time, atmospheric, threadbare, large rooms, nonchalant staff, in spite of the name, no restaurant. A large new hotel, as yet unnamed, is due to open in 1997 opp the Shell petrol station on the Oujda road. **Camping**: a site of 1½ ha, with restaurant and small shop, laundry, and electricity for caravans. Convenient for the train station.

● **Places to eat** The best eateries are the group of transport cafés known as "*le complex*" on the main road, the meat used for the brochettes is very fresh, direct from the in-house butcher. *The Place Centrale* has several snack places and grocery stores catering for travellers. **Cafés**: *Café Nahda* is a small friendly efficient place on the corner of rue Mohammed V and rue Ibn Battuta near the mosque. The café opp is also good.

● **Banks & money changers** Banque Populaire, on market square; BM and BMCE, nr Shell petrol station on Oujda Road.

● **Hospitals & medical services Chemists**: *Pharmacie centrale* on the market square.

● **Transport Train** Taourirt/Oujda 0430, 0712, 1745, 1837; Taza/Fes/Casablanca 0948, 1204, 2157, 2335. Bus: CTM Oujda 1600; Fes 1400; Midelt 0800, 1000; Er Rachidia 0800. The CTM Offices are located between the central square and Place Zerkatouni. Private lines: Taourirt/Oujda and Taza/Fes every half hour during the day from the central square. Nador 0700, 0730, 0930, 1200, 1500, 1830. Er Rachidia 2100 departs from "le complex" on the main road.

Excursions from Guercif

A road with a surface varying between poor and bad leads SW into the Middle Atlas for about 45 km. It eventually reaches the small settlement of Bourached. This is not the object of the exercise. About 5 km before Bourached a path to the E leads by a tributary of the Oued Moulouya to the main river and back N, keeping to the western bank, to Guercif. A track of similar quality surface leads steeply N to Saka and a small lake but there is not alternative return route.

From Guercif to Midelt

About 4 km E from Guercif towards Oujda is the turning for the S329, a long, straight narrow road that follows the middle reaches of the Oued Moulouya parallel to the Atlas mountains.

It is a little used route, ideal for those wishing to head S as quickly as possible. Note that Café/Snack Bar des Voyageurs on the P1 is the last place for refreshments until Outat Ouled el Hadj, another 200 km. Petrol stations are also few and far between on this route, and there is only one hotel, at Missour (250 km). Initially barren and uncultivated, the landscape becomes attractive around the farming village of Mahirija, with the Debdou massif on the E. However, this green respite soon disappears entirely as the route enters the vast semi-desertic territory of the Rekkam Plateau, Morocco's "empty quarter". From here until Outad Ouled El Haj much of the road follows the path of a dismantled railway line used by the French in their arduous campaign to conquer the tribes of the middle and upper Moulouya in (1913-1923). Note the viaducts and the remains of former stations along the way. The snowclad peaks of the Middle Atlas are a constant presence throughout the length of this route. The Rekkam is

Asses, donkeys and mules

🐾 There is a certain amount of confusion when naming the normally overladen and generally undernourished beasts of burden found in the countries of North Africa. While there can be no confusion as to what is a **horse**, *Equus caballus*, or even an **ass**, *Equus asinus*, despite the fact that it is most commonly called a **donkey**, a **mule** requires some definition.

The term **mule** can refer to any hybrid but as a beast of burden it is the offspring of a male donkey (jack) and a female horse (mare), while the offspring of a male horse (stallion) and a female donkey (jenny) is correctly termed a **hinny**.

A mule is a horse in the middle with a donkey at either end. It has longer ears, and a thinner mane and tail than its mother and carries the typical 'cross' markings on the shoulders and back. The hinny is less popular, being nearer the size of a donkey and has the shorter ears and thicker mane and tail of its father.

A mule is stronger than a horse, has a much longer working life under the right circumstances, can withstand extremes of temperature without long-term ill effects, is less vulnerable to sickness and can survive on a very limited diet. Mules are noted for being surefooted and for being fast and accurate kickers. Mules are generally considered to be infertile though instances of offspring are recorded.

The Algerian wild ass originally roamed the Atlas Ranges. The Romans carefully preserved them on mosaics but are held responsible for their demise. The Nubian wild ass, of a distinctive reddish hue, roamed the semi-desert areas between the River Nile and the Red Sea shores. It survived into the 20th century.

The Egyptians used asses. Illustrations from 2500BC show us that even then these domesticated beasts were carrying loads and passengers out of all proportion to their size. They also had mules which are thought to have first been bred around 1750 BC. Models of this hybrid were found in the pyramids and a mule drawing a chariot is depicted on a vase found in Thebes.

The Romans placed heavy reliance on the mule, for riding, to draw carts and farm implements and to carry equipment. To assist copulation they devised a wooden cage with a ramp to enable the shorter jack ass reach the taller mare.

Facts The Food and Agriculture Organization's (FOA) latest figures place Morocco second (800,000) and Algeria third for mule populations in Africa.

---

criss-crossed by *oueds*, and the road is frequently interrupted by *oueds*, generally with no water that require slowing down to a snail's pace as they are very bumpy. Beware of sudden deviations caused by flash floods. The first small town is Outat Ouled El Hadj, attractively situated with Jbel Bou Naceur (3,340m) in the background, and the Oued Moulouya running through the centre, which is leafy and compact. There is a *souq* on Mon in the enclosure by the river. Unfortunately the attractions stop here, and the inhabitants are not particularly welcoming. Transport

connections are poor (Bus: Guercif/Nador 0930. Missour/Midelt/Er Rachidia 1500). Make sure you don't get stuck here, as there is no accommodation. A much better option is to proceed to the next town, Missour which has a good hotel.

MISSOUR

A tranquil rural town with a high proportion of donkeys and unpaved roads that comes alive for the weekly market. Though unaccustomed to foreigners, the people are helpful. There is an excellent medium-priced hotel here. Most of the commercial activity in Missour is concentrated behind the central section of the main boulevard. If you are lucky enough to be here on a Wed, there is a large local *souq* situated on the hill by the water tower, past the new mosque. The lower part of the market is disappointing, but the top end of the main enclosure has the fruit and vegetable market, and a separate area beyond encloses the livestock market. The latter is the most interesting part. Both enclosures have tea tents where you can have breakfast. There is a good view of the town and the mountains from the adjacent hill.

● **Accommodation** D *Hotel Baroudi*, Blvd El-Bassatine, T 0558 5651, take the dirt track by the Credit Agricole bank and follow the signs to a veritable oasis of a hotel with a swimming pool and a large garden where a couple of mischievous semi-wild monkeys roam, beautiful, restful atrium, good restaurant (menu around MD75), very nice staff, prices negotiable.

● **Banks & money changers** Banque Populaire, on the main road.

● **Hospitals & money changers** Chemist: *Pharmacie Echifa*, opp the new mosque.

● **Useful addressses** Petrol: at the S end of the main boulevard before the bridge.

● **Transport** All transport arrives and departs from the busy street 2 blocks away from the main road, behind the Bank Populaire. Guercif/Nador 0830; Mdelt/Er Rachidia 1600; Mdelt/Fes 1400.

On to Midelt

Past Missour, the road continues for about 30 km through a still bare but slightly more dramatic landscape that would make a good location for a Western movie. After Tamdafelt, the road runs along an attractive stretch of the Oued Moulouya, with pisé villages and richly cultivated river banks. Two fortified kasbahs built by Moulay Ismael around 1690 AD to guard the imperial route from Fes to Sijilmassa are still inhabited: Saida and Ksabi. The inhabitants of these kasbahs, originally forming an agglomera-

tion of 10 ksours, are mostly descendants of Alawite guardsmen from the Tafilalt. At over 1,000m, the freshness of the air and quality of light in this remote region is exhilarating. After Ksabi the road swings away from the Oued Moulouya and crosses the high plain of Aftis until it joins the P21 15 km E of Midelt (see page 336).

TAOURIRT

Halfway between Taza and Oujda, Taourirt is an important local commercial centre with a large weekly market on Sun. In the past the town functioned as the junction between 2 major trade routes: the E-W trans-Maghreb route and the route from Melilla to the Tafilalt. The centre of town is located around the junction of the P1 and the Debdou road (the ancient caravan route to the S which is packed with shops, garages, cafés and small workshops. The only tangible historical attraction in Taourirt are the remains of the kasbah on the hill 1 km to the NW of the town centre. Unfortunately, the site has been despoiled by electricity pylons and is occupied by the army. But there is an excellent view from here.

There are several excursions around Taourirt that make it worthwhile stopping for a day or two: the mountain village of Debdou and surroundings; the Zaa waterfalls and the Zaa Gorges (see below). For the cave dwellings you will need a guide.

● **Accommodation** F *Hotel Mansour*, on Debdou Road just off main crossroads, large rooms, adequately clean, good café below, no hot water available.

● **Banks & money changers** BMCE, CMD and **Wafabank** next to *Hotel Mansour*.

● **Hospitals & medical services** Chemists: on the road out to Debdou: Al-Jabri; Al-Qods.

● **Transport** Train Oujda 0530, 0800, 1800, 1930 (approximate times). Taza/Fes/Casablanca 0830, 1045, 2030, 2230 (approximate times). **Road** Bus: for Oujda (every half)hour) and Nador (around 5 a day) depart from the

Agip petrol station past the main crossroads. Guercif/Taza/Fes (virtually every half hour during the day and hourly at night) depart from near the Shell petrol station on the same road, as do the Grand-taxis that ply the P1. Grand-taxis for Debdou leave from the rank on the Debdou Road.

Around Taourirt

Zaa Waterfalls Providing there is enough water in the *oued* (unlikely between Aug and Dec), this makes an enjoyable picnic and bathing excursion. Camping is possible. To get here, turn right at the signpost 6 km along the Taza Road. It is a further 9 km to the waterfalls. The track continues to Melga el Ouidane and the large lake known as Barrage Mohammed V. This looks better when it has a good quantity of water. There are a number of picnic spots along the route.

Zaa Gorges As you leave Taourirt on the Oujda road, there is a turning off to the right for the Zaa Gorges (about 12 km). You cannot drive through the narrow defile. Leave the car where the road ends and walk from there. The gorge is deep and very impressive and well worth the journey.

DEBDOU

50 km to the SW of Taourirt, nestling in a verdant bowl formed by the surrounding massif, Debdou is an island of rural tranquillity. The fact that Debdou is on a road "to nowhere" has helped to preserve its own identity. The surrounding area is very scenic and provides good opportunities for walking and exploration. There is an interesting kasbah halfway up the mountainside above the main village. There are no tourist facilities, and transport links are poor. Until the 1960s over half the population of Debdou were Jewish, most of whom were the descendants of Jews from Taza who fled persecution and chaos of Bou Hamra's rule (1902-1908). The "high street" branches off the main road at the entrance to the village and zigzags for about 1 km, past store houses and tiny shops with green shutters, to a square at the top end of the village known as Aïn Sbilia. Overlooking the square is a balcony shaded by 4 huge plane trees. A small sluice gate allows water to flow into a channel bisecting the square below which has a café. It is all very restful, with the locals playing cards and backgammon and drinking mint tea. High above, on a mountain ledge is the still inhabited Kasbah of Caid Ghomriche built by the Beni Merin in the 13th century as a fortress and subsequently handed over to the Beni Ouattas, a related tribe, around 1350 when the Marinids ruled Morocco. Follow the signposted track (2 km) starting from the bottom end of the village. Note the colourful dwelling housing the *hammam* which is still heated by a wood stove. Along the way there are pretty views of the town on the right and the waterfalls high above on the left. Just before entering the kasbah there is a grassy ledge with good views over the valley, and the entrance to a cave. The settlement is a mixture of ancient ruins, small vegetable gardens and mud houses. At the back of the village, past the walls, and a dry moat, is a field where jagged stones stick out of the ground; these are the sunken headstones of ancient tombs. Take care not to trip over them. By crossing the field and turning left for 30m-40m and then sharp right, there is a pathway (1 km) linking up with the main road and the source of the Oued Debdou. The same location can be reached by the main road which swings to the left just before Debdou, and runs along the mountain crest or Gaada de Debdou for 5 or 6 km. There are fantastic views from here and good walking opportunities. Beyond this the road descends from the plateau down into the arid Rekkam plain where it becomes a rough track, eventually leading to Outad Ouled al Hadj (see page 293). Market day is Wed.

● **Places to eat** There are no restaurants in Debdou. Apart from the café at Aïn Sbilia (see above), the only other proper café is at the entrance to the town, at the start of the track leading to the kasbah.

● **Transport Road Bus**: Taourirt 0600 and 1430. **Taxis**: to Taourirt are unpredictable, but most frequent in the morning and early evening. If you don't want to get stuck here, try to leave before 1800.

El Aioun

Founded by Moulay Ismail in 1679, El Aioun has a small kasbah that was restored in 1876 by Sultan Moulay Hassan in response to the threat of French expansion from Algeria. To the S of the town is a cemetery where those who died fighting colonialism are buried. During the first half of this century, El Aioun became a centre of the Sufi Brotherhood of Sheikh Bou Amama, whose *zaouia* is located here. The weekly souk in held on Tues and frequented by members of the local Ouled Sidi Sheikh tribe. The town is situated halfway between Taourirt and Oujda, and within easy reach of the Beni Snassen Mountains (see page 168).

Oujda is described in the section Eastern Morocco (see page 171).

Marrakech, The High and Middle Atlas

A N IDEAL tourist location, Marrakech lies within reach of beautiful High Atlas valleys and arid pre-Saharan plains. The city itself is one of the great Islamic cities of North Africa, with the **Koutoubia Mosque** a memorable building which dominates the city, and the **Djemaa El Fna** square, a place of continual activity and entertainment. Around these the medina stretches, its narrow streets and flat-roofed red houses accommodating a way of life which has retained many characteristics from over the centuries. Within easy reach of Marrakech, the **Ourika valley** and the **Toubkal National Park** are some of the most popular areas of the High Atlas, and there is excellent skiing at Oukaimeden North of Marrakech, where the Middle Atlas mountain range runs up towards Meknes and Fes, with the relaxed Alpine-style resorts of Azrou and Ifrane.

MARRAKECH

(*Pop* 550,000 (1993); *Alt* 470m)
Along with Fes, Marrakech is the most important historic city in Morocco, with the **Koutoubia Mosque** and **Ben Youssef Medersa** among its most distinctive buildings. Marrakech has a memorable beauty, with its palm-lined streets and red earth walls, surrounding a huge medina of flat-roofed, red houses. The High Atlas mountains, snow-capped until Apr, loom above the city, a venue for numerous excursions.

"The *souks* of Marrakech seem, more than any others, the central organ of a native life that extends far beyond the city walls into secret clefts of the mountains and far-off oases where plots are hatched and holy wars fomented – farther still, to yellow deserts whence negroes are secretly brought across the Atlas to that inmost recess of the bazaar where the ancient traffic in flesh and blood still surreptitiously goes on." Wharton, Edith, *In Morocco* (1927).

Above all Marrakech is worth visiting because of the vibrant mass of people that mill around in the unique **Djemaa El Fna** square, with its grill-stalls, traders and entertainers, and the vast network of *souqs*, people that come from all over the surrounding plains, the High Atlas and the Sahara. The character of the city owes much to its continuing role as a trading centre and capital for the S of the country. Tourist hassle which deterred some visitors in the past is now much reduced and the predominant atmosphere is very relaxed, best appreciated from a café terrace beside Djemaa El Fna.

The city of Marrakech, or Marrakesh, takes the Arabic form of 'Marrakch', whilst in some early European maps it appears as 'Morocco City'. The location of the city is particularly impressive. It is situated in the Tensift valley, in the rich agricultural Haouz plain, normally called the 'Haouz of Marrakech'. The city is surrounded by extensive palmeries, into which areas of villas and hotels are gradually spreading. Yet there are also sandy, arid areas near, and even within, the city, which give it a semi-Saharan character. The other dominant landform is the mountains. Arriving from Fes or Meknes one crosses the end of the Middle Atlas range, and from Casablanca or Rabat the dry, sparsely populated Bahira Jbilet. But from most points in Marrakech it is the High Atlas which is the visible mountain range, its often snow-covered peaks appearing to rise from just behind the city. Indeed the popular mountain destinations of the Ourika Valley, Oukaimeden, Asni and the Toubkal Park are easily accessible from Marrakech. Marrakech is also an important crossroads, the focal point of the S, linking roads from Fes/Meknes, Rabat/Casablanca, Safi, El Jadida, Essaouira, Agadir, Taroudant and Ouarzazate/the Sahara, whilst it also has an airport and is the S terminus of the railway network.

Marrakech covers a large area, with distinct zones separated by less populated areas. For the visitor this will entail long walks between the main points of interest and utility in the medina, the French built *ville nouvelle*, and the two gardens of Agdal and Menara, or more probably reliance on taxis, *calèches*, buses or their own transport. The long, wide tree-lined boulevards of the *ville nouvelle*, a number of which are focused on the beautiful **Koutoubia Mosque**, give the city an impressive feeling of spaciousness, which contrasts with the equally impressive density of the medina.

Marrakech is Morocco's fourth largest city, with a population including Arab, Berber and mixed elements, whilst many of its residents are immigrants from surrounding rural regions, and further S. The economy of the city includes administrative activities and modern shops and services, whilst it has for many centuries been an important regional market for trade in agricultural produce and other goods. There is still a wide range of handicraft production and small-scale industry, particularly in the medina. There are a number of fac-

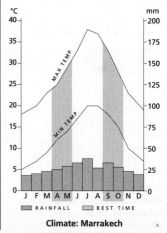

Climate: Marrakech

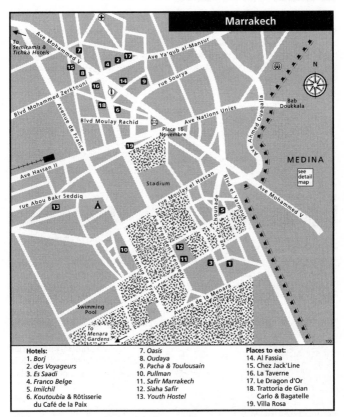

Marrakech

Hotels:
1. Borj
2. des Voyageurs
3. Es Saadi
4. Franco Belge
5. Imilchil
6. Koutoubia & Rôtisserie
du Café de la Paix
7. Oasis
8. Oudaya
9. Pacha & Toulousain
10. Pullman
11. Safir Marrakech
12. Siaha Safir
13. Youth Hostel

Places to eat:
14. Al Fassia
15. Chez Jack'Line
16. La Taverne
17. Le Dragon d'Or
18. Trattoria de Gian
Carlo & Bagatelle
19. Villa Rosa

tories and industrial units, notably in agro-processing. However the city's economy and employment are heavily dependent on tourism, Marrakech being one of the major tourist attractions of Morocco. Furthermore many of the city's large unemployed or under-employed labour force supplement their incomes by casual work with tourists, their unwanted attentions having in the past given Marrakech a bad name.

History

Almoravid origins Although Marrakech has probably been occupied since Neolithic times, it was first founded properly in 1062 by the Almoravids, as a base from which to control the High Atlas mountains. A kasbah, Dar al-Hajar, was built close to the site of the Koutoubia Mosque. Under Youssef Ben Tachfine Marrakech was an important capital and marketing centre, with the building of several mosques, palaces and the city's famous walls, as well as the development of extensive gardens and an irrigation system. The city attracted leading mediaeval thinkers from outside Marrakech.

Marrakech under the Almohads Marrakech was taken by the Almohads in 1147, who almost totally destroyed and then rebuilt the city, making it the capital of their extensive empire. Under the Almohad Sultan Abd el-Moumen the *Koutoubia Mosque* was built on the site of Almoravid buildings, with the minaret added by Ya'qub al Mansur. Under the latter Marrakech gained palaces, gardens and irrigation works, and again became a famous centre for musicians, writers and academics, but on his death it declined and fell into disarray.

Merinid neglect and Saadian revival Whilst the Merinids added several *medressa* to Marrakech, Fes received much of their attention, and was preferred as capital, although from 1374 to 1386 Marrakech was the centre of a separate principality. Marrakech was revitalized by the Saadians from 1524 with the rebuilding of the *Ben Youssef Mosque*, and the construction by Ahmed al-Mansur Ad-Dahbi of the *El Badi Palace* and the *Saadian Tombs*. Marrakech also became an important trading post, due to its location between the Sahara and the Atlantic.

Alawite Marrakech The Alawites took control of Marrakech in 1668. In the early 18th century the city suffered from Moulay Ismail's love of Meknes,

Muslim cemeteries

One of the lasting monuments in Islam is the *maqbara* or graveyard. All are different, ranging from undefined rocky areas near villages, where unnamed head and foot stones are barely distinguishable from the deserts surrounding them, to the elaborate necropoli of Cairo and Fes where veritable cities of the dead are established. In all cemeteries bodies are interred with head towards the *qibla* – Mecca.

In Morocco graveyards often contain a series of simple whitewashed mud brick tombs of holy men or *marabouts*, around which his disciples and their descendants are laid. At Fes there is a large and complex example of a long-used cemetery at Bab Ftouh, where stylized mausoleums, tombs and graves are densely packed in. Even more ornate and walled cemeteries occur in cities elsewhere.

Muslim graveyards in Morocco have no flowers unless they grow wild and by chance. Instead of buying flowers to ornament family graves on their routine weekly visit, relatives will often give a simple dish to the poor to provide a meal for the children. The Bab Ftouh cemetery is used as a public prayer ground on feast days.

Important or noble families have private cemeteries. Most frequently, they are part of a complex of religious buildings – schools or mosques – with separate rooms or a distinct domed area. There is a fine mausoleum of this kind at the Saadian Tombs in Marrakech (see page 311).

Death and funerals are times for noisy outbreaks of wailing and crying. In traditional families, the approach of a person's death is signified by wailing, increased on actual death by the addition of the mourning neighbours and relatives. Occasionally in villages the body is laid in a large room where funeral dances are performed by wailing women, singing the praises of the deceased. Corpses are washed and wrapped in a simple shroud for interment. Mourners follow the cortege to the cemetery often in large crowds since every person who walks 40 paces in the procession has one sin remitted. At the graveside a *shedda* or declaration of Islamic faith is recited. Urban funerals are more ornate than those in the country districts and the passing of public figures is often accompanied by some pomp.

Paul Pascon – the French Moroccan

🦶 Explaining the Moroccan way of life and economy, especially the problems of modern development they face, is not easy either to the Moroccans themselves or to Westerners. Morocco is geographically so close to W Europe, has such great potential of natural resources yet is so distant from conventional norms of living standards and administrative skills of Europe. The cultural and historical processes that have contributed to this great gap between apparent neighbours need a plausible exposition.

Perhaps the one man qualified to do this task was the French Moroccan, Paul Pascon. He was born in Fes of French colonist farmer stock in 1932 but was never part of the French establishment – his parents being anti-Vichy during WW2. He grew up in a local Moroccan school system and was as much at home in the Arabic as French languages. His advanced education was likewise shared between the University in Rabat and at the Sorbonne in France. He opted for Moroccan citizenship when Morocco became independent in 1956.

Pascon was a rigorous man intellectually. He never sold himself to any single "ism" but worked himself on research into the nature and direction of development of the native Moroccans in the Marrakech region to show how all the components of the rural Moroccan communities – based in soil, water, kinship, culture and politics – work together to make up a singular and intense society. His book *Capitalism and Agriculture in the Haouz of Marrakesh* (KPI, London, 1986) is a classic for those who want to get deeper into the Moroccan way of life. He explains in incisive language the 'hows' and 'whys' of Morocco as neither Moroccan alone dare or European could.

Paul Pascon died in a motoring accident in 1985.

with many of the major buildings, notably the *El Badi Palace*, stripped to glorify the new capital, and a significant shift in power and wealth. The destructive effects of this period were compounded by the civil strife following his death. However, under the Alawite Sultan Moulay Hassan I, from 1873, and his son, Marrakech gained a number of important buildings and reestablished its prestige. From 1898 Thami el-Glaoui and his family controlled the city as a powerful *pasha* with considerable autonomy from central control. A number of leading merchants built palaces in the city.

The French took control of Marrakech and its region in 1912, crushing an insurrection by a claimant to the Sultanate. The French built the *ville nouvelle*, Gueliz, in the 20th century, but Marrakech stagnated in comparison to the coastal cities of Casablanca and Ra-

bat. In recent decades the city has grown enormously, with the authorities developing its tourist appeal and capacity, as well as its role as a conference centre.

ACCESS Air Aéroport Marrakech-Menara, T 430939 and 447903, is 5 km to the SW of the city near the Menara Gardens. It has a *bureau de change* open until 1800. Road 6010 leads to the city, the routes are clearly signposted. There are taxis from the airport, MD50 by day, MD90 after 2100 as well as bus No 11.

Train The railway station is in Gueliz, on Ave Hassan II, T 447768, 447947. There is usually no shortage of taxis waiting for the arrival of trains, although fixing a reasonable rate may be difficult for the new arrival. Most hotels in the *ville nouvelle* or the medina should be reached for MD5-10, and MD8-15 at night. Alternatively take bus No 3 or 8 from outside the station along Ave Hassan II and Ave Mohammed V, to the medina.

Road The P10 from Essaouira and Agadir enters the city along Ave d'Essaouira

and Ave Hassan II, into Gueliz, and at Place 16 Novembre turn right along Ave Mohammed V for the medina. On the approach along the P9 from Safi (via the P12) and El Jadida cross the roundabout for the medina, and turn right along Ave Mohammed Abdelkrim Al Khattabi for Gueliz. From the P7 from Rabat and Casablanca turn right along Ave Allal Al Fassi for the medina, for Gueliz continue ahead. The P24 from Fes and Meknes skirts the N ramparts, from Bab Doukkala follow the outside of the walls to reach Djemaa El Fna and the centre of the medina, turn along Ave des Nations Unies for Gueliz. From the P31 from Ouarzazate follow the ramparts round to Bab Doukkala. Route 501 from Taroudant reaches Marrakech at a roundabout near Bab Rob, pass through the gate for the medina, turn left for Gueliz. **Bus** All long-distance buses arrive at the Gare Routière at Bab Doukkala, T 433933, from where taxis and bus No 3 or 8 can easily be taken. CTM services for Agadir and Casablanca also call at the office in Gueliz, in Blvd Mohammed Zerktouni. ONCF buses from Laayoune and Agadir arrive at the railway station in Ave Hassan II.

Places of interest

Main areas of interest Marrakech is clearly divided into the large historic city, the medina, and the *ville nouvelle*, Gueliz. The focal point of the medina, and indeed of the whole city, is the **Djemaa el Fna**, an open place full of street entertainers and food sellers, adjacent to which are the most important markets, as well as numerous hotels, restaurants, cafés and shops. This is a good base from which to explore the historic sites of the medina. The gates in the city walls are also important centres, notably **Bab Rob**, **Bab Doukkala** and **Bab el Khemis**. The major thoroughfare of the Gueliz is Ave Mohammed V, and the evening promenade along its length is very popular. There is little to see in the Gueliz but it is a pleasant place to wander or rest in a café. The **Menara Gardens** are to the S of Gueliz, the **Agdal Gardens** directly to the S of the medina. On the E side of Marrakech, across the Oued Issil, is the **Palmerie**.

It is worth attempting to coincide a visit to Marrakech with the **National Festival of Popular Art**, an extravagant mixture of music, dance and folklore displays. The exact date in the summer for this varies annually so check with a tourist office.

Djemaa El Fna The Djemaa El Fna is

unique in Morocco, perhaps the greatest pull for tourists, yet still a genuine social area for the Marrakchi people, and those flooding in from the surrounding regions, with much aimed solely at Moroccans. It is a large irregular space full of people hawking their goods or talents and others watching, walking, talking and arguing. Its activity never seems to finish, and at each point of the day has a distinctive character. It is particularly memorable during Ramadan when the day's fast ends. Whatever the time of the day or year, Djemaa El Fna is somewhere that the visitor will return to again and again, responding to the magnetic pull that affects locals as much as tourists, to mingle with the crowd or watch from the terrace of the *Café de France* or *Café-Restaurant Argana*.

Djemaa El Fna means 'assembly of the dead', and may refer to the traditional display of the heads of criminals, executed here until the 19th century. In 1956 the government attempted to close down the square by converting it into a corn market and car park, but soon reverted it to its traditional role. Visit it during the day to explore the stalls and

collections of goods spread out on the floor: fruit, herbs and spices, clothes, shoes, electrical goods and handicrafts, as well as the snake charmers and monkey tamers, who pose for photographs. Return in the evening to watch and listen to the folk-healers, dancers, musicians, boxers, acrobats and storytellers that crowd the square, each with a throng of people gathered around. Those with courage may sample the food from the stalls, but it is wise to eat only what is cooked on request. Try the excellent freshly-squeezed orange juice from one of the stalls surrounding the square.

WARNING It is wise to take extreme caution with pickpockets, and to deal

Wish I could remember

For those with a poor memory a visit to the tomb of Ibn el-Arif in Marrakech is recommended. Local tradition goes that students needing to improve their memory should walk around the wooden tomb of the saint and then consume raisins picked up with the point of a reed pen. We wish we could remember where it was ...

Minarets

The minaret (*ma'dhana*) evolved to provide a high point from which the prayer leader (*muezzin* or *mu'adhdhin*) could make the call (*adhan*) to the faithful to their devotions five times each day. Construction of minarets to give a vantage point for the *muezzin* began in Damascus at the end of the 7th century AD. The earliest minaret that has survived is the one at the Great Mosque in Kairouan, Tunisia, built in the years between 8th-9th centuries.

The minarets of the Moroccan mosque are quite different from those elsewhere in the Islamic world in shape and architectural effect. They developed in very sophisticated forms (see box, page 308) as, for example, the Koutoubia in Marrakech and the Giralda tower at Seville Cathedral. The shape of Moroccan minarets is thought to have come from models taken from Christian churches in Syria, with their square towers and arcaded windows. The original brick-built minarets in Morocco used finely worked panelling showing interlaced arches. The passage of time saw the expensive kiln brick medium dropped in favour of stone and finally rough random stone laying covered with a plaster rendering. These white painted towers have been augmented in the recent past by what has become a standard modern equivalent, reproduced in new urban and country settlements, alike. It is plain and repetitive – scarcely a description of the more traditional and characterful minarets – but serves its purpose (see box, page 308), preserves its basic Moroccan character and remains a principal topographic marker in the landscape.

patiently with the numerous unofficial guides, 'students', or 'friends' that will seek business.

The Koutoubia Mosque dominates the whole of Marrakech, a landmark throughout much of the medina, and around which the French laid out their road network. It is clearly visible as, unlike the Qarawiyin Mosque in Fes, it is set apart from the dense areas of historic building, and has a tall minaret, of over 65m. According to legend as this structure overlooked the harem, only a blind muezzen was allowed to climb it to call the faithful to prayer. However it is a memorable structure with both elegance and simplicity in the design. The name, meaning the 'Bookseller's Mosque', reflects the trade which used to go on in the immediate surrounds.

The Koutoubia Mosque is at the end of Ave Mohammed V, close to the Djemaa El Fna. In viewing the site it is wise to be extremely careful, as the mosque is closed to non-Muslims and, as the most important in Marrakech, does not welcome close inspection. However it is possible to walk around and through the surrounding areas, where there are some interesting points from which to take photographs.

The site of the mosque is itself historic, with its prior occupation by a late 11th century kasbah, the **Almoravid Fortress**, or **Dar al-Hajar**. This was built by either Youssef Ben Tachfine or Abu Bakr, and formed the focus of the town. The configuration of the walls of this fortress can be seen between the mosque and Ave Mohammed V. The walls are double, each about 1m thick with an irregular gap of some 90-100 cm filled with red clay. There were transverse rocks joining the walls at intervals. Only the outer surface of the wall was faced. It is an impressive structure indicating a highly developed indigenous building capability. At the W extremity of the walls are the sites of a S facing gate and a semi-circular fountain. These were decorated with painted panels (geometrical designs in red paint) from the Almoravid period which are now in the **El Badi Palace**. The fortress ruins are the oldest Almoravid site in the country, and one of the few remaining in Marrakech.

On the corner of the two sections of the wall is **Bab Ali**, named after the son of Youssef Ben Tachfine. This is the ruins of a square tower and entry arch, an entrance into the kasbah. It is suggested that it may have been the place where the Almohads finally defeated the Almoravids.

The successful Almohads destroyed much of the Almoravid city, and in 1147 built a large mosque, located between the kasbah and the later Koutoubia Mosque. The *mihrab* of this mosque was located on its S wall, bordering the existing building, and it is suggested that its location was wrong and led to the mosque's destruction. The two mosques existed for some time together, the bricked-up spaces on the N wall of the Koutoubia Mosque indicating the doors which connected them. However the complex was excessive in size and the older structure fell into disrepair and eventual ruin. The site was excavated from 1948. These excavations also revealed a *maqsura* or screen, in front of the *mihrab*, which could be wound up through the floor to protect the Sultan, and a *minbar*, or pulpit, which was moved into position on wooden rollers. The two cisterns in the centre are probably from a previous Almoravid structure. On the E flank of this mosque was an arcade of which a niche and the remains of one arch remain. Along this arcade runs a paved street where the booksellers worked.

The existing Koutoubia Mosque was built by Abd el-Moumen in 1162, soon after the building of the first mosque. The minaret is 12.5m wide and 67.5m to the tip of the cupola on the lantern, and is the mosque's principal feature, rightly ranked along with the later Almohad structure of the **Hassan Tower** in Rabat (see page 103) and the Giralda in Sevilla. The minaret, with its 1:5 proportions, had great influence on subsequent buildings in Morocco. It is illuminated at night and thus dominates the skyline. The recommended positions for the best photographs are from the SE and SW.

The minaret is composed of six rooms, one on top of the other. The cupola on top of the minaret is a symmetrical, square structure surmounted by a ribbed dome and three golden orbs. These are alleged to have been made from the melted down jewellery of Ya'qub al-Mansur's wife, in penance for having eaten three grapes during Ramadan. The cupola has two windows on each side, above which is a panel of stone-carved *darj w ktaf*. The main tower has a band of hexagonal and square tiles at the top, below which is a different series of arches and windows on each side, including a representation of many Almohad design motifs. The main building itself is fairly plain.

Behind the mosque, on rue Sidi Mimoun, is a small tomb to the Almoravid Sultan Youssef Ben Tachfine, the founder of Marrakech.

The Souqs of Marrakech, many of which retain their original function, and the presence of both craftsmen and traders, are worth at least a morning to explore. It is, however, far from a relaxing experience, with traders continually besieging tourists with pleas of 'just for looking' or similar. It is worth getting an idea of prices before choosing a reasonable trader and getting down to serious bargaining. An unofficial guide is likely to be more trouble and expense than he is worth, and certainly one should not believe the 'Berber market, only open today' line, which is used everyday. **NB** It is important to inspect goods closely, especially anything involving gold, silver or gems, as these are often fakes. The increasing business in antiques often involves new products which have been treated.

The main *souqs* lie to the N of Djemaa El Fna. The entrance is to the left of the mosque. Follow this round to the left and then turn right in the main thoroughfare of the *souqs*, **Souq Semmarin**. Alternatively enter through the small touristic pottery market, further round to the left on Djemaa El Fna. Souq Semmarin is a busy place, originally the textiles market, and although there are a number of large, expensive tourist shops, there are still some cloth sellers. To the left is a covered *kissaria* selling clothes. The first turning on the right leads past **Souq Larzal**, a wool market, and **Souq Btana**, a sheepskin market, to **Rahba Kedima**, the old corn market, now selling a range of goods including traditional cures and cosmetics, spices, vegetables and cheap jewellery, and with some good carpet shops. Walk back onto the main *souq* via a short alley with wood-carved goods. Here the *souq* forks, into **Souq el Attarin** on the left and **Souq el Kebir** on the right.

To the right of Souq el Kebir is the **Criée Berbère**, where carpets and *jallabahs* are sold. This was where slaves, mainly from across the Sahara, were auctioned until 1912. Further on is the **Souq des Bijoutiers**, with jewellery. To the left of Souq el Kebir is a network of small alleys, the **kissarias**, selling Western goods. Beyond the *kissarias* is the **Souq Cherratin**, with leather goods, somewhere to bargain for camel or cow hide bags, purses and belts.

Continuing back on the other side of the *kissarias* is the **Souq des Babouches**, a far better place to buy slippers than in the tourist shops. This feeds into **Souq el Attarin**, the spice and perfume *souq*, which itself leads back into Souq Semmarin. West of the Souq el Attarin is the **Souq Chouari**, with carpenters. From here walk on to a Saadian fountain and the 16th century **Mouassin Mosque**. South of Souq Chouari is the **Souq des Teinturiers**, or dyers' market, where wool recently dyed is festooned over the walkways, the most picturesque area of the medina. Nearby are the blacksmiths' and coppersmiths' *souqs*.

The Almoravid Koubba and Ben Youssef Medersa These buildings are close to each other, to the N of the Djemaa El Fna, see map page 305.

The **Almoravid Koubba** (**Koubba el-Baroudiyin**) dates from the 11th century, and is a rare example of the architecture of this period, the only complete Almoravid building surviving. It dates from the reign of Ali bin Youssef (1107-43), and perhaps formed part of the toilet and ablutions facilities of the mosque which at the time existed nearby.

At first glance it is a simple building, with a dome surmounting a square stone

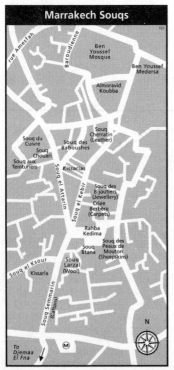

Marrakech Souqs

rue Ameslah

Baroudienne

Ben Youssef Mosque

Ben Youssef Medersa

Almoravid Koubba

Souq Cherratin (Leather)

Souq du Cuivre

Souq des Babouches

Souq Chouari

Souq aux Teinturiers

Kissarias

Souq el Attarin

Souq el Kebir

Souq des Bijoutiers (Jewellery)

Criée Berbère (Carpets)

Rahba Kedima

Souq Btana

Souq des Peaux de Mouton (Sheepskins)

Souq Larzal (Wool)

Souq el Ksour

Kissaria

Souq Semmarin (Carpets)

To Djemaa El Fna

N

The souq explained

The *souq* in the cities and towns of Morocco has distinctive characteristics, for here both Islamic ideas and traditional trading habits have remained strong.

There is a view that the Moroccan/Islamic city has a particular social structure and perhaps even a specific physical shape. Whatever the town, the crafts, trades and goods are located in the *souq* by their 'clean' or 'unclean' status in the Islamic sense. Only 'clean' goods can be sold close to the mosque or *medersa*, for instance perfumes and spices. More valuable objects such as precious metals are on sale near to the main thoroughfares while lesser trades needing more space and cheaper land are pushed to the outer edges. There is, too, a concentration of similar crafts in the same location within the *souq* so that, for example, all shoe sellers are in or near the same street. Souq des Babouches in Marrakech (see page 306) proves this point. Economic principles certainly play an important part too. Thus there is a hierarchy of crafts, modified at times by custom and Islamic practice, which gives the highest priority to book making and gold and silver jewellery production over carpet selling and thence through a graded scale of commodities such as metalwork, ceramics and the sale of agricultural goods ultimately to such low grade crafts as dyeing and tanning of leather.

All goods and *souqs* do not conform exactly to this plan but as you visit the various cities it will be interesting to see how many do.

and brick structure. The dome is quite decorated, however, with a design of interlocking arches, and a star and chevron motif on top. The arches leading into the *koubba* are different on each side. Climb down the stairs to look at the structure close-up. Inside, the ceiling below the dome is intricately carved. It includes an octagon within an eight pointed star, and the use of a range of Almoravid motifs, including the palmette, pine cone and acanthus. Around the corniche is a dedicatory inscription in cursive script. Set into the floor is a small, almost square, basin.

Close by the *koubba* is the large 12th century **Ben Youssef Mosque**, rebuilt in the 19th century. On a side street just to the E of the mosque is the Saadian **Ben Youssef Medersa** (open 0900-1200 and 1430-1800, closed Fri). It is fortunate that this *medersa*, one of the largest in Morocco and one of the few Islamic buildings open to the general public, should be in such a good state of preservation and such a good example of its

kind. It is, perhaps, one of the most attractive buildings in Marrakech with its carved Carrara marble a finely worked cedar wood. It is an impressive example of religious architecture of the period, with strong influences from Andalucía. A boarding school for religious students, each student has a separate cell with a sleeping loft and a window onto the courtyard. It was founded in 1564-5 by the Saadian Sultan Moulay Abdellah, on the site of a previous Merinid *medersa* greatly restored. The *medersa* and since has been greatly is centred around a square courtyard containing a rectangular pool, and with arcades on two sides. The arcades and walls are comprehensively decorated with a variety of different designs and scripts, with use of *zellij* tiling on the arcade floor, walls and pillars. Inscriptions are in Kufic and cursive lettering, interwoven with floral patterns. The inscription, in the prayer hall, dedicated to the Sultan, has been translated as: "I was constructed as a place of learning and prayer

The Mosque – the glory of Islamic architecture

The remarkable development of Islamic architecture took place despite the men of the Arab conquest being essentially unlettered nomads and warriors. To redress the shortcomings of the Arab armies, their rulers imported skilled architects, masons and tile workers from established centres of excellence in the empire – Persians, Armenians and others. Together these strange teams of artisans and their Islamic patrons evolved a wonderful and distinct style of building forms and decoration which is among the great legacies of Islam, especially in its early innovative period.

The mosque was the first and main vehicle of spectacular Islamic architecture, based initially on the mosque constructed by the Prophet himself in Madinah in 622 AD. In the Madinah mosque the worshippers faced north towards the holy city of Jerusalem but changes brought about in the first century after the death of Mohammed saw the *qibla* direction of prayer moved to face Mecca and other elaborations. Key parts of the early mosques which were enduring elements of all mosques built since that time include:

the entrance, normally large and ornate, in the north wall,

the *mihrab*, or niche indicating the *qibla* wall,

the *sahn*, or open courtyard,

the *minbar*, or pulpit,

the *maqsurah*, or wooden screen giving privacy to the ruler or imam,

the *liwanat*, or covered arcades surrounding the *sahn*

the *koubba*, or dome, which was adopted as a roof form in the Dome of the Rock at Jerusalem, from whence Mohammed ascended to heaven.

As the empire extended and grew wealthy, so the architecture of the main Friday mosques, made for mass worship by the faithful on the holy day, became more magnificent as exemplified in the Great Mosque of Damascus, built in the 8th century AD, which also had a square *ma'dhana*, or minaret outside the main building for the *muezzin* to call people to prayer. The minaret of the Great Mosque of Kairouan in Tunisia, constructed in the 8th century, is the oldest minaret still standing. Rabat's 12th century Hassan Tower (minaret) is a fine relic of this great age of mosque building (see pages 83-84). Moorish architecture flourished in both Morocco and Spain in a form that differed from and some would say bettered the rest of the Islamic world. Some of the finest minarets were built in this "western Islamic" style of the 12th century, including the Giralda tower that now stands, slightly modified as the bell tower of Seville Cathedral, and the Koutoubia Tower at Marrakech, the relic of a fine mosque on the site. Both these buildings in proportions, arcading and tracery were to set trends eventually to be reproduced in European Gothic architecture. The delicate features of the style are visible in the illustration below.

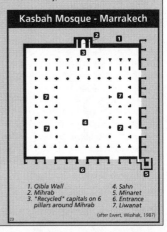

Kasbah Mosque - Marrakech

1. Qibla Wall
2. Mihrab
3. "Recycled" capitals on 6 pillars around Mihrab
4. Sahn
5. Minaret
6. Entrance
7. Liwanat

(after Ewert, Wisshak, 1987)

Note that the heights of these towers (Hassan Tower 45m but originally designed to be 80m, Koutoubia 67.5m and Giralda of the Islamic era 76m) called for great engineering skills and first rate building materials, mainly brick. The Koutoubia in Marrakech is a supreme example of this opportunity to understand just how much W European mediaeval and subsequent ecclesiastical and palace architecture owes to its Saracen and Moorish roots.

The mosque-building era is far from finished as the new Rabat mosque dedicated to Mohammed V, demonstrates. In addition to the great mosques used for public prayer on holy days, there are many local mosques of plain construction, many with architectural modifications to suit regional conditions of climate, culture and the availability of building materials. The basic lay-out even here is uniform, though the ornamentation and wealth in carpets in the *sahn* many well vary.

In Morocco, infidels are not allowed into mosques (with the exception of the new one in Rabat). But access is possible to small mosques in abandoned villages – many of them ancient and of infinite historical and architectural interest. Similarly the ruins of former great mosques and, more often, their minarets are open to all.

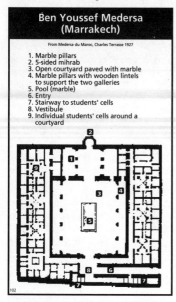

Ben Youssef Medersa (Marrakech)

From Medersa du Maroc, Charles Terrasse 1927

1. Marble pillars
2. 5-sided mihrab
3. Open courtyard paved with marble
4. Marble pillars with wooden lintels to support the two galleries
5. Pool (marble)
6. Entry
7. Stairway to students' cells
8. Vestibule
9. Individual students' cells around a courtyard

102

by the Prince of the Faithful, the descendant of the seal of the prophets, Abdellah, the most glorious of all Caliphs. Pray for him, all who enter here, so that his greatest hopes may be realised."

At the far end is the prayer hall covered with an 8-sided wooden dome. Beneath the dome plaster open work windows illuminate the very attractive tilework. In the *qibla* wall is a 5-sided *mihrab*. Note the stalactite ceiling of the *mihrab*, and the carved stucco walls, in which the pine cone motif is prominent. There are small students' cells on both levels of the building, around separate courtyards. On the second level they often have a tiny sleeping room above, entered by bars on the wall.

On the way out of the *medersa*, the smelly toilets on the right of the vestibule have an elaborate stalactite design on the ceiling. There is also a 10th century Andalusian ablution basin in the vestibule, decorated with eagles and Cordoban floral designs.

To the N of the Ben Youssef Medersa is an area of the medina which is worth exploring for an indication of the structure and working of the traditional Islamic city, unspoiled by the demands of the tourist industry which have so influenced areas closer to Djemaa El Fna. This area includes the **Zaouia of Sidi Bel Abbes**, one of the seven saints of Marrakech. He was born in Ceuta in 1130 (some authorities say 1145) and during his life in Marrakech, where he championed the cause of blind people, was patronized by Ya'qub al-Mansur. The shrine, recently restored, is strictly closed to non-Muslims. Nearby is the **Zaouia of Sidi Ben Slimane el-Jazuli**, a 14th century sufi.

Bab Agnaou, Saadian Tombs and El Badi Palace Bab Agnaou, meaning the gate of the blacks, marks the entrance to the kasbah quarter. To get to it, follow rue Bab Agnaou from Djemaa El Fna, or enter the medina at Bab Rob. The kasbah quarter dates from the late 12th century and the reign of the Almohad Sultan Ya'qub al-Mansur. Bab Agnaou is also Almohad. The gateway itself is surrounded by a series of arches within a rectangle of floral designs with a shell or palmette in each corner and an outer band of Kufic inscription.

The road from the gate leads to rue de la Kasbah, turn right along this and then along the first left. On this road is the much restored **Kasbah Mosque**, dating from 1190. It is almost square in shape. The minaret has the *darj w ktaf* and *shabka* (net) motifs on alternate sides, with a background of green tiles, above which is a band of coloured tiles. The square lantern also has geometric designs. The minaret is not as impressive as that of the Koutoubia Mosque but is worth noting en route to the Saadian Tombs. Inside, by the *mihrab*, the pillars sport 'recycled' capitals.

The entrance to these lies directly to the right of the mosque. The late 16th

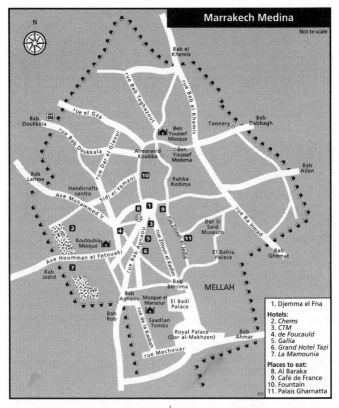

Marrakech Medina

Not to scale

N

Bab el
Khemis

Bab
Doukkala

rue el Gza

rue Bab Taghazout

rue Bab el Khemis

rue Bab Doukkala

rue Dar el Glaoui

Ben
Youssef
Mosque

Almoravid
Koubba

Ben
Youssef
Medersa

Tannery

Bab
Dabbagh

Bab
Ailen

Bab
Larissa

Handicrafts
centre

Sidi el Yamani

Ave Mohammed V

10

Rahba
Kedima

2

Koutoubia
Mosque

Ave Houmman el Fetouaki

8 **1** **9**

4

3

6

rue Zitoun el Kedim

rue Bab Agnaou

rue Zitoun el Jedid

Dar Si
Said
Museum

11

El Bahia
Palace

rue Ba Hmad

Bab
Ghemat

7

Bab
Jedid

Bab
Berrima

Bab
Agnaou

Mosque el
Mansur

El Badi
Palace

MELLAH

Bab
Rob

Saadian
Tombs

rue de la Kasbah

Royal Palace
(Dar al-Makhzen)

Bab
Ahmar

rue Mechouar

1. Djemma el Fna

Hotels:
2. Chems
3. CTM
4. de Foucauld
5. Gallia
6. Grand Hotel Tazi
7. La Mamounia

Places to eat:
8. Al Baraka
9. Café de France
10. Fountain
11. Palais Gharnatta

century **Saadian Tombs** (open 0800-1200 and 1400-1800) are the mausoleums for the dynasty's Sultans and their families, and were only discovered in 1917, having been sealed off by Moulay Ismail. There is a series of chambers and tombs off a small garden, with carved cedarwood and plasterwork which is in a remarkably good condition. The design is influenced strongly by the Andalusian tradition. The *mihrab* of the first main mausoleum is particularly impressive, and in this room is the tomb of Moulay Yazd. The second room contains the tomb of Ahmed al-Mansur, with finely carved columns. The second and older mausoleum was built for the tombs of Ahmed al-Mansur's mother, Lalla Messaouda, and Mohammed es-Sheikh, founder of the Saadians. In the garden and courtyard are the tombs of numerous princes and household members. As a small site the Saadian Tombs can become crowded with tour groups.

The **El Badi Palace** (open 0900-1200 and 1430-1730) was built by the Saadian Sultan Ahmed al Mansur Ad-Dahbi (the Golden) between 1578 and 1593, following his accession after the Battle of the Three Kings at Ksar el Kebir. To get to it, return to the Bab Agnaou and head right inside the ramparts, and then take the second right. This road leads more or less directly to Place des Ferblantiers. Pass through Bab Berima, the gate on the S side. The entrance to the palace is on the right.

The El Badi Palace was a lavish display of the best craftsmanship of the period, using the most expensive materials, including gold and onyx, but was largely destroyed in the 17th century by Moulay Ismail, who stripped it of its decorations and fittings and carried them off to Meknes. Little now remains except the palace's *pisé*-cement walls. The palace probably had a largely ceremonial purpose, being used for receptions. Past the mosque is the central courtyard, built above water channels connecting a number of pools. The largest of these even has an island. The ruins on either side of the courtyard were probably summer houses, that at the far end called the **Koubba el Hamsiniya** after the 50 pillars in its construction. The complex contains a small museum which includes the movable *minbar* from the Koutoubia Mosque. The scattered ruins of the palace, with odd fragments of decoration amidst the debris, include also stables and dungeons. To the S of the El Badi Palace is the **Dar al-Makhzen**, the modern-day Royal Palace, now one of King Hassan II's favourite residences.

Nearby, the **Musée Dar Al Funun Ashaabia**, 154 Derb Sahrige, rue Arste Moussa Riad Zitoune Kedim, T 426632, has audio-visual displays on various themes of Moroccan arts including dance, theatre and the marriage ceremony, each lasting between 20 and 45 mins.

The Southeastern Medina To get to the SE area of the medina follow rue des Banques from just past *Café de France* on the Djemaa El Fna. This leads into rue Zitoun Jedid. Off to the left is the **Dar Si Said**, the **Museum of Moroccan Arts and Crafts** (open 0900-1200, 1600-2100 in the summer, 1430-1800 in the winter, closed Tues) is on Riad Zitoun

Jedid, T 442464. This palace was built by Si Said, *Visir* under Moulay El Hassan, and half-brother of Ba Ahmed Ben Moussa, who built the El Bahia Palace. The museum includes pottery, jewellery, leatherwork from Marrakech and a collection of beautiful carpets from Chichaoua. It is particularly strong on Berber artifacts such as curved daggers, copperware, jewellery of silver, ivory and amber. The first floor has been made into an elegant salon with Hispano-Moorish decoration and some very elegant cedarwood furniture. The palace itself is small but with a cool and pleasant courtyard where a remarkable collection of old window and door frames are on display. They carry intricate decorations.

At 8 rue de la Bahia, between the El Bahia Palace and Dar Si Said, is **Maison Tiskiwin**, T 443335. This includes a shop, a café and a museum, the latter concerned with Moroccan rural culture and society, a collection put together by the Dutch art historian Bert Flint. There is an exhibition of craftsmen's materials and techniques from regions as far apart as the Rif, High Atlas and the Sahara, including jewellery and costumes, musical instruments, carpets and furniture. Note the nomad's tent from the Middle Atlas. The building itself, around a courtyard, is an authentic and well-maintained example of traditional domestic architecture.

Further to the S, the **El Bahia Palace** (Bahia means 'brilliant') (open 0800-1200 and 1430-1800) was built in the very late 19th century by the *Visir* Ba Ahmed Ben Moussa, or Bou Ahmed, a former slave who exercised considerable power under Moulay Hassan and Abd al-Aziz. The palace has the Andalusian-inspired decor of the period, although executed in a garish fashion which does not do justice to the craftsmanship of the city. It is a maze of corridors, passageways and staircases. Bou Ahmed was so hated that, on his death in 1900, his palace was looted and his possessions stolen by slaves, servants and members of his *harem*. The building is centred around a marble paved courtyard 50m x 30m, the walls covered with ceramic tiles and round the sides a glazed gallery which stood on wooden columns. There is a colourful garden known as the Grand Riad or Moorish Garden which was planted with fruit trees (bananas and oranges) cypress trees and fragrant flowers. The apartments of the favourite wife looked out on to this garden and also on to a smaller, private patio.

The *mellah*, the Jewish quarter, was created in 1558. This lies S of the El Bahia Palace and to the W of the El Badi Palace. This is an extensive quarter reflecting the community's historic

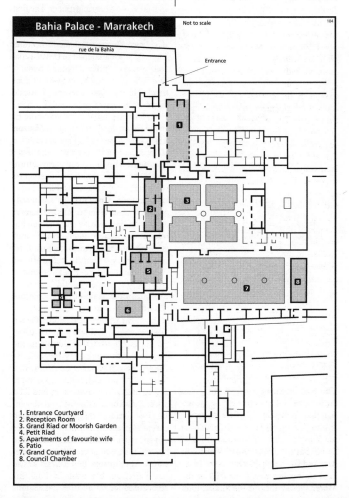

Bahia Palace - Marrakech   Not to scale   104

rue de la Bahia

Entrance

1. Entrance Courtyard
2. Reception Room
3. Grand Riad or Moorish Garden
4. Petit Riad
5. Apartments of favourite wife
6. Patio
7. Grand Courtyard
8. Council Chamber

importance to the city, when they were involved in the sugar trade and banking, as well as providing most of the jewellers, metalworkers and tailors. There were several synagogues, and under the control of their *rabbis*, the area had considerable autonomy. There are now few Jews left, but the quarter is still distinct in the cramped houses and narrow streets. Conditions here remain worse than in much of the medina, with unpaved roads and insanitary drainage. It is worth asking around to be let into one of the synagogues.

The Walls and Gates The extensive ramparts of Marrakech (20 gates and 200 towers stretching for 16 km) are predominantly Almoravid, excepting those around the Agdal Gardens, although extensively restored since. The reconstruction is a continual process as the *pisé*-cement walls, made of the distinctive earth of the Haouz plains, gradually crumble. The ramparts and gates are one of the distinctive sights of Morocco, and a tour in a horse-drawn *calèche* is recommended. All the gates are clearly named.

Bab Rob, near the buses and grand-taxis on the SW side of the medina, is Almohad, and is named after the grape juice which could only be brought through this gate. **Bab Dabbagh** (the Tanners' gate) on the E side, is an intricate defensive gate with a twisted entrance route and wooden gates which could shut off the various parts of the building for security. From the top of the gate there is a good view of the tanneries. It is possible to look around the tanneries. Note that hides are often laid out to dry on the banks of the nearby *oued*. **Bab el Khemis**, on the NE side, opens into the **Souq el Khemis** (Thur market) and an important area of mechanics and craftsmen. There is a small saint's tomb inside the gate building. **Bab Doukkala**, on the NW side by the bus station is a large gate with an *outrepassé* arch and two towers. The medina side has an *outre-*

passé arch and a cusped, blind arch, with a variation on the *darj w ktaf* motif along the top.

The Gardens The **Agdal Gardens**, stretching S of the medina, were established in the 12th century under Abd el-Moumen, and were expanded and re-organized by the Saadians. The vast expanse, over 400 ha, includes several pools, and extensive areas of olive, orange and pomegranate trees. They are in the main closed when the king is in residence, but are worth visiting at other times. Of the pavilions, the **Dar al-Baida** was used by Sultan Moulay Hassan to house his *harem*. The largest pool, **Sahraj el Hana** receives its coach-loads of tourists, but in between times is a pleasant place to relax, although not to swim.

From the medina and the Agdal Gardens, Ave de la Menara leads past the **Oliveraie de Bab Jedid** to the **Menara Gardens**. This is an olive grove, itself not very interesting but a good place with shelter from the sun for a picnic. At the centre is a rectangular pool with a good view of the Atlas Mountains, a picture on numerous postcards and brochures. The green-tiled pavilion alongside was built in 1866. Inside, above the small display of carpets and other Berber artifacts, is an impressive painted cedarwood ceiling.

The Jardin Majorelle, also called the **Bou Saf-Saf** (open 0800-1200 and 1400-1700 in the winter, 0800-1200 and 1500-1900 in the summer), is off Ave Ya'qub al-Mansur. This is a small tropical garden laid out by a French artist, Louis Majorelle. The buildings are a vivid blue, but the overall effect is worth seeing. There is also a small **Musée d'Art Islamique** in the grounds.

The Palmerie includes around 180,000 trees used mainly for wood. It is a good place for a drive or a *calèche* tour, but is gradually being expropriated by large villa and hotel developments. Take the Route de Palmeraie off the P24 to Fes to explore it.

Local information

Price guide

Hotels:

AL	over US$75	D	US$20-40
A	US$75	E	US$10-20
B	US$60-75	F	under US$10
C	US$40-60		

Places to eat:

♦♦♦	expensive	♦♦	average
♦	cheap		

● **Accommodation**

AL *Hotel Es Saadi*, Ave Kadissia, Hivernage, T 448811, similarly luxurious hotel built in 50s style and set in large and pleasant gardens, with a rec restaurant, bar, casino, nightclub, tennis and pool; **AL** *La Mamounia*, Ave Bab Jedid, T 448981, F 444940, is itself a monument, a place to visit, a converted patronized by the rich and famous, recently redecorated to the highest standard, everything completed to perfection, with little touches that will delight the visitor, 171 luxurious rm, 49 normal suites, 8 incredible themed suites, 3 villas, outstanding service, 5 restaurants serving stunning menus of the highest standard, 5 bars, casino, conference room, business centre, shops, fitness and beauty centre, *hammam*, excellent pool, tennis, squash, beautiful flower gardens, if you cannot stay there, visit for a coffee; **AL** *Palmerie Golf Palace*, T 301010, F 305050, in Les Jardins de la Palmerie, 77 ha site, 314 rm, incl 6 senior suites, 2 royal suites and 24 suites with sitting room, all rooms have balcony, a/c, direct dial telephone, satellite TV, radio, minibar and hair dryer, features incl 24-hr room service, 9 restaurants, 4 bars, baby sitter, crèche, travel agency, bank, hairdresser, laundry/dry cleaning, car rental, 15 km from airport and 10 km from train station, beautiful gardens, tennis, 18-hole golf course, minigolf, bowling, squash, horseriding, fitness centre with hammam, sauna, jacuzzi, massage and body-building, 5 pools (2 heated), very large conference centre with variety of rooms of different sizes, shopping arcade; **AL** *Sheraton Marrakech*, Ave de la Menara, T 448998, F 437843, 291 comfortable a/c rm and suites, Moroccan and international restaurants, pizzeria, pool restaurant, pool, tennis, shops, salon, very friendly atmosphere.

A *Hotel Atlas Asni*, Ave de Frabos, 304 rm and 18 luxury suites, 3 restaurants, pools for adults and children, safe parking; **A** *Hotel el Andalous*, Ave President Kennedy/Jnan el Harti Hivernage, T 448226, 200 double rm each with 2 queen size beds, bath, a/c, balcony, telephone and radio, authentic Andalusian style, 2 restaurants (Moroccan and international), pool, tennis, sauna, fitness centre; **A** *Imperial Borj*, 5 Ave Echouhada, T 447322, 187 rm, modern, conference centre, restaurant, bar and popular nightclub; **A** *Hotel Pullman Mansur Eddahbi*, Ave de France, T 448222, 450 rm, restaurant, pool, tennis; **A** *Hotel Safir Marrakech*, Ave President Kennedy, T 447400, F 448730, 280 rm, a fully equipped hotel with a disco, 2 tennis courts, bar, restaurant, shops, *hammam* and a pool surrounded with palm trees; **A** *Hotel Semiramis Le Meridien*, Route de Casablanca, BP 525, T 431377, F 447127, restaurant, bar, nightclub, tennis, and an excellent pool.

B *Hotel Agdal*, 1 Blvd Zerktouni, Gueliz, T 433670, 129 rm and 4 apartments, all with a/c, balcony, telephone, radio, bath, pool heated in winter, bar, restaurant, breakfast room with panoramic view, taxis only 10m, airport 4 km, *calèches* available at hotel entrance; **B** *Hotel Amine*, Route de Casablanca, T 434953 and 432083, around a lavish heated pool with ancient (100 years) palm trees, 112 rm a/c bath, telephone, radio, balcony, restaurant offers a superb selection of traditional Moroccan dishes, also international cuisine, poolside snackbar, shops; **B** *Hotel Tichka*, Route de Casablanca, Semlalia, T 448710, Tx 74855, 138 rm, beautifully designed and decorated, restaurant, International and Moroccan menus, bar, nightclub, tennis, good pool, shop, conference facilities.

C *Hotel Chems*, Ave Houmane El Fetouaki, BP 594, T 444813, Tx 72008, small, restaurant, bar and nightclub; **C** *Hotel Menara*, Ave des Remparts, T 436478, F 447386, typical Moroccan style hotel, situated half way between the medina and the European Centre, views over the ramparts to the High Atlas, 100 rm with bath, balcony, a/c, and central heating, telephone, Moroccan cuisine and French specialities, bar, TV room, garden, pool, tennis, free parking; **C** *Hotel le Tafilalet*, Ave Mohammed Abdelkrim El Khattabi, T 434518, Tx 72955, mock kasbah style, pleasant room, a good garden; **C** *Hotel Siaha Safir*, Ave President Kennedy, T 448952, F 448730, 243 rm, pool and hammam; **C** *Myriems*, 154 rue Med el Beql, a few mins from Djemma El Fna, rooms have a/c, TV, direct telephone and radio, 2 restaurants, pool and safe parking.

D *Hotel Amalay*, Ave Mohammed V, clean and modern; **D** *Hotel de Foucauld*, Ave El Mouahidine, T 445499, 33 rm, a good hotel with restaurant and bar, same management as the *Tazi*; **D** *Hotel Gallia*, 30 rue de la Recette, T 445913, clean, conveniently located just off the Djemaa El Fna (via rue Bab Agnaou), in an old building and some good rooms, plenty of hot water; **D** *Grand Hotel Imilchil*, Ave Echouhada, T 447653, Tx 74073, modern hotel with pool, restaurant and bar; **D** *Hotel Koutoubia*, 51 Blvd Mansur Eddahbi, T 430921, restaurant, central courtyard with excellent (when in use) pool; **D** *Hotel le Grand Sud*, 25 Blvd Mansur Eddahbi, modern, rec; **D** *Hotel Oudaya*, 147 rue Mohammed El Baqal, T 448512, F 435400, 15 suites, 77 rm, modern hotel with pool, restaurant and bar; **D** *Hotel Pacha*, 33 rue de la Liberté, T 438399, F 431326, highly rec small hotel with dated charm, bar and restaurant, on a quiet street; **D** *Grand Hotel Tazi*, rue Bab Agnaou, T 442152, Tx 74021, memorable rooms with extravagantly painted ceilings and furniture, one of the few bars in the medina, a very good Moroccan restaurant at average prices, and a pleasant pool, strongly rec and very convenient for the sights.

E *Hotel Ali*, rue Moulay Ismail, Medina, T 444979, F 433609, especially rec for those intending to go climbing/trekking in the Jbel Toubkal region as the guides are here, clean, comfortable and friendly, good Moroccan cuisine, adjacent to Djemma El Fna and only 5 mins' walk from buses to Asni; **E** *Hotel Toulousain*, 44 rue Tarik Ibn Ziad, Gueliz, T 430033, best cheap option in the *ville nouvelle*, quiet location around 2 courtyards; in this area also try *Hotel Oasis*, 50 Ave Mohammed V, T 447179, good but noisy, with restaurant and bar, clean rooms, some with shower; *Hotel des Voyageurs*, 40 Blvd Mohammed Zerktouni, T 447218, reasonable and central but *Oasis* is better choice; *Hotel Franco Belge*, 62 Blvd Mohammed Zerktouni, T 448472, similar; *Hotel CTM*, on the Djemaa El Fna, T 442325, good and clean rooms, some with a view of the square, often full.

There are cheap hotels in the medina, on the small alleys between rue Bab Agnaou and rue Zitoun el Kedim, to the S of Djemaa El Fna, of very variable quality. Always ask to see a room. Try **F** *Hotel Oukaimeden*, a basic place on the Djemaa El Fna; **F** *Hotel de France*, 197 rue Zitoun el Kedim, T 443067; **F** *Hotel Central*, **F** *Hotel Afriquia* with a good patio and roof terrace, and **F** *Hotel Nouazah* on the first left off rue Bab Agnaou; and **F** *Hotel El Atlas*, a friendly, efficient place on rue de la Recette.

Camping: *Camping Municipal* is off Ave de France, 5 mins S of the railway station, T 431844, with shop, showers and café, site of 2 ha, bar, laundry, first aid, electricity for caravans, petrol at 800m, quiet, clean and pleasant.

Youth Hostel: Rue El Jahed, Quartier Industriel, T 4432831, 80 beds, kitchen, meals available, bus 200m, train 700m, overnight fee MD20, IYHF cards only, open 1200-1400 and 1800-2200 in winter, 0600-2400 in summer.

● **Places to eat in Gueliz**

◆◆◆ *Al Fassia*, 232 Ave Mohammed V, T 434060, reservations rec, an excellent Moroccan restaurant on the main street, delicious desserts; *Le Jacaranda*, 32 Blvd Mohammed Zerktouni, T 447215, French food, strong on fish, closed Tues and Wed lunch time, bar; *La Trattoria du Gian Carlo*, 179 rue Mohammed El Bequal, T 432641, a very good Italian restaurant with an excellent selection of wines, in an art deco villa; *Le Dragon d'Or*, 10 bis Blvd Mohammed Zerktouni, T 433341, Chinese food; *Villa Rosa*, 64 Ave Hassan II, T 430832, a small Italian restaurant with terrace specializing in pasta and fish.

◆◆ *Rotisserie du Café de la Paix*, 68 rue Yougoslavie, Gueliz, T 433118, there is a garden in the summer, and reasonable grilled food all the year round; just opp is *Restaurant Bagatelle*, 101 rue Yougoslavie, T 430274, good French food served in the restaurant and vine shaded courtyard open 1200-1400 and 1900-2300; *Chez Jack'Line*, 63 Ave Mohammed V, T 447547, Italian, French and Moroccan dishes, good for pizzas; *Restaurant La Taverne*, 23 Blvd Mohammed Zerktouni, T 446126, fixed standard menus and a bar.

◆Top of the cheap range in the *ville nouvelle* is *Brasserie du Regent*, 34 Ave Mohammed V, T 448749; also try *Le Petit Poucet*, Ave Mohammed V, T 448238, bar and restaurant with basic but good French dishes; *Le Sinbad Café*, Place 16 Novembre, basic but tasty meals and breakfasts, good service; or *Café Agdal*, 86 Ave Mohammed V, T 448707, good for chicken, no alcohol.

● **Places to eat in the Medina**

◆◆◆*Restaurant Marocain du Mamounia*, in the *Hotel Mamounia*, Ave Bab Jedid, T 448991, reservations rec, lavishly decorated restaurant with one of the best introductions to élite Moroccan cuisine, an excellent *pastilla* (pigeon dish), music/folklore in the evening; *Restaurant La Calèche*, in the *Hotel Mamounia*, Ave Bab Jedid, T 448991, top-notch French food with a view over the hotel's famous gardens; *La Maison Arabe*, 5 Derb Ferrane, nr Bab Doukkala, T 422604, with a reputation for the best food in Morocco, expensive, reservations necessary; *Restaurant Riad*, rue Arset El Maach, T 425430, in the medina, with expensive but excellent Moroccan meals accompanied by folklore entertainment; *Restaurant Relais Al Baraka*, Djemaa el Fna, nr the police station, T 442341, Moroccan meals around a courtyard with fountain, convenient after sightseeing, reservations rec; *Restaurant Palais Gharnatta*, 56 Derb el Arsa, Riad Zitoun Jedid, T 445216, nr the El Bahia Palace, this restaurant offers Moroccan dishes at high prices, clients pay for the supposedly 16th century palace surroundings, reservations rec; *El Bahia*, 1 Riad Zitoun Jedid, similar arrangement with evening entertainment; *Restaurant Stylia*, 34 rue Ksour, T 443587, reservations rec, a 15th century palace, with variations on Moroccan traditional dishes.

◆◆*Restaurant de Foucauld*, in the *Hotel Foucauld*, Ave El Mouahidine, good *couscous* and *tagines* nr the Djemaa el Fna; *Restaurant Tazi*, in the *Grand Hotel Tazi*, rue Bab Agnaou, similar restaurant run by the same management, the cheapest licensed establishment in the medina; Buffet dinner in *Hotel Ali*, rue Moulay Ismail, nr the Djemaa El Fna massive choice and very reasonably priced; *Café-Restaurant Argana*, Djemaa El Fna, food with a view; *Restaurant Etoile de Marrakech*, rue Bab Agnaou, very good value set meals with view of Djemaa El Fna from the roof.

◆In the medina the most popular option is to eat at the open-air restaurants in the **Djemaa El Fna**. Each has a different variety of cooked food, some of which tastes very good. The conditions are, however, far from sanitary, and so it is best to go for the food cooked to order whilst waiting, as other dishes may have been around for some time. For a safer meal try the excellent value *Chez Chekrouni*, on Djemaa El Fna, left of the *Café de France*; the somewhat smelly *Café de Fath* which has very good *tagines*; or *Restaurant Toubkal*, in the opp corner. There are a series of cheap restaurants along Bani Marine, in between rue Moulay Ismail and rue Bab Agnaou, such as *Casse-Croûte des Amis*.

Cafés: one of the best places for a drink is beside the Djemaa El Fna: *Café-Restaurant Argana* has a good terrace view; even better is the *Café de France*, with several levels and an excellent panorama over the square, and the medina beyond, scattered with minarets. In Gueliz Ave Mohammed V and Blvd Mohammed Zerktouni meet at a roundabout with popular cafés on each side, incl the *Brasserie des Négociants* and *Café Renaissance*; *Boule de Neige*, on rue de Yougoslavie just off Ave Mohammed V, is a trendy place for pricey but excellent drinks, ice

---

Sweet almonds

The almond *Prunus amygdalus* is Morocco's second most important tree crop after the olive occupying an estimated surface area of over 100,000 ha with over 12 million trees. Morocco is the world's fifth largest producer of shelled, sweet almonds, after USA, Spain, Greece and Italy. The familiar edible kernel is consumed as it is or used in confectionery, as almond oil or as almond meal. Like all nuts, almonds provide protein and B vitamins, also small amounts of important minerals such as iron, calcium and phosphorus. They are high in vegetable fat.

Nearly 50% of the almond trees are self seeded. This is particularly so in the almond groves of the Rif, the valley of the Draa and around Imi-n-Tanoute SW of Marrakech which play an important part in the farming economy of these regions. Cultivated almond plantations exist around Meknes, Fes, Beni Mellal, El Kelaa des Sraghna and Marrakech where the most common varieties planted are Marcona, Fournat de Brèze, Naud, Non pareil, Ferranges and Ferra-duel. These well tended groves produce between 1,000 and 1,500 kg/ha and up to 2,000 kg/ha with irrigation.

cream and breakfasts; next door is *Pâtisserie Hilton*, with a full range of Moroccan sweets and cakes; the best is perhaps *Pâtisserie Zohor*, rue de la Liberté. For late night coffees or ice creams (most places close by 2130), try *Café-Glacerie Siroua*. Locals swear by *Café Zohor*, rue de la Liberté; *Café Firdaous*, Ave Mohammed V, also has an authentic local clientele.

● **Bars**

Piano Bar, at the *Hotel Mamounia*, Ave Bab Jedid, T 448981, 1800-0100, drinks are not cheap but the Western atmosphere and music a pleasant change; *La Renaissance*, Ave Mohammed V, go up the lift to the rooftop bar with the best view of the Gueliz; *Le Petit Poucet*, 56 Ave Mohammed V, no view but fairly cheap drinks; also try *Ambassadeurs*, 6 Ave Mohammed V; or *Haouz*, Ave Hassan II.

● **Banks & money changers**

ABM, 55 Blvd Zerktouni, T 448912; **Banque Al Maghrib**, Djemaa El Fna, T 442037; **Banque Populaire**, 69 Ave Mohammed V, T 434851; **BCM**, Blvd Zerktouni, T 434805; **BMCI**, Blvd Mohammed Zerktouni; **Credit du Maroc**, Ave Mohammed V, T 434851; **SGMB** 59 rue de Yougoslavie, T 448702; **Uniban**, rue Moulay Ismail, T 425285; **Wafabank**, 213 Ave Mohammed V, T 433840.

American Express: Voyages Schwartz, Immeuble Moutaouskil, rue Mauritania, T 433321.

● **Cultural & language centres**

American Language Center, 3 Impasse Moulin du Gueliz, weekly film, small library and bookshop; **Centre Culturel Français**, (open 0830-1200 and 1430-1830, except Mon), Route de la Targa, Gueliz, with a café, library and pleasant garden, has films, exhibitions and other cultural events.

● **Embassies & consulates**

French Consulate, rue Ibn Khaldoun, T 444006.

● **Entertainment**

Casinos: *Grand Casino de la Mamounia*, at the *Mamounia Hotel*, Ave Bab Jedid, T 444570, open from 2000 or 2100; *Hotel Es Saadi*, Ave Kadissia, T 448811.

Cinemas: the major cinemas showing films in French, are the *Colisée*, Blvd Mohammed Zerktouni; the *Regent*, Ave Mohammed V; try also the *Centre Culturel Français*, Route de Targa, Gueliz, T 447063, 446930.

Discos & nightclubs: *Disco Paradise*, at the *Hotel Pullman Mansur Eddahbi*, Ave de France,

T 448222, admission MD80, 2200-0700, a large disco with the latest equipment; *Cotton Club*, at the *Hotel Tropicana*, Semlalia, T 433913, admission MD60, 2100-0500; also try *L'Atlas* and *Le Flash* on Ave Mohammed V; *Le Diamant Noir* at the *Hotel Marrakech*, Ave Mohammed V; or *Temple de Musique* at the *Hotel PLM N'Fis*, Ave de France.

Folklore & fantasia: the *Cappa Club* at the *Hotel Issil*, the *Hotel le Marrakech*, Ave Mohammed V, and the *Club Mediterranée* all have large folklore displays but can be difficult to get into. The best bet is the *Restaurant Riad*. For fantasia, drive or take a taxi to *Chez Ali*, in the **Palmery** after the Tensift bridge, T 448187; *El Borj*, after the Tensift bridge, T 446376, *Zagora* Route de Casablanca, T 445237; *Ancien Casino de Marrakech*, Ave el Kadissia, T 448811, 'food and extravagant displays from 2100, admission MD100; *Restaurant Chaouia*, nr the airport, T 442915, displays of horsemanship, sword play, dance and music.

Hammams: try one of those on rue Zitoun el Kedim; or *Hammam Dar El Bacha*, rue Fatima Zohra, with amazing decor.

● **Hospitals & medical services**

Ambulance: T 15 (private ambulance service: 10 rue Fatima Zohra, T 443724).

Chemists: *Pharmacie Centrale*, 166 Ave Mohammed V, T 430151; *Pharmacie de Paris*, 120 Ave Mohammed V; *Pharmacie Bab Ftouh*, Djemaa El Fna, T 422678. There is an all night chemist, *Pharmacie de Nuit*, at rue Khalid Ben Oualid, T 430415.

Dentists: Dr Hamid Laraqui, 203 Ave Mohammed V, T 433216; and Dr E Gailleres, 112 Ave Mohammed V, both speak English.

Doctors: Dr Ahmed Mansouri, rue de Sebou, T 430754; and Dr Perez, 169 Ave Mohammed V, T 431030, both speak English.

Hospitals: *Hôpital Ibn Tofail*, rue Abdel Ouahab Derraq, T 448011; *Hôpital Avenzoar*, rue Sidi Mimoun, T 422793.

● **Places of worship**

Catholic: *Eglise des Saints-Martyrs*, rue El Imam Ali, Hivernage, for information T 430585.

Jewish: *Synagogue Bet-el-Gueliz*, Arset El Maash, for information T 447832, 447976.

Protestant: *Protestant Church*, 89 Blvd Moulay Rachid, T 431479.

● **Post & telecommunications**

Area code: 4.

Post Office: the Central PTT for post normally very busy, telegrams, poste restante and telephones is on Place 16 Novembre, Gueliz, the telephone service being particularly inefficient, slow and expensive, open till 2100. There is also a reasonable post/telephone office on the Djemaa El Fna.

● **Shopping**

The *souqs*, N of the Djemaa El Fna, are the best place to search for bargains in carpets and handicrafts, but a visit can be a tiresome experience as the tourist is besieged by traders and misled by absurd prices. Bargaining is a long activity requiring patience, and should be carried out without assistance from guides, whose commission will be added on to any price. *Souq Semmarin* is the main area with the largest boutiques, some with supposedly fixed prices, and can be more expensive. *Rahba Kedima*, off to the right, has some interesting small shops. Leather goods should be bought in *Souq Cherratin*, Moroccan slippers from the *Souq des Baboushes*, where they are often made as well as sold.

Coopartim Ensemble Artisanale, Ave Mohammed V, 5 mins walk from the Koutoubia Mosque, T 423835, can be treated as an exhibition of locally-made handicrafts, even some craftsmen working on the premises, but one can also buy at fixed prices.

Marrakech has numerous good jewellers, who sell a variety of traditional jewellery, including bracelets, necklaces and inlaid boxes, antique items, and less attractive European-style gold and silver. Amongst many small but good boutiques is *Tresorie du Sud*, rue El Moissine, T 440439.

Souqs which can be reached by excursion from Marrakech include Ourika (Mon), Amizmiz (Tues), Tahanaoute (Tues), Ouirgane (Thur), Setti Fatma (Thur), Asni (Sat) and Chichaoua (Sun).

Foreign newspapers can be bought from the stands along Ave Mohammed V, and in the large hotels. They normally arrive a day late. Books in French from Ave Mohammed V, particularly *Librarie Chatr Ahmed*, No. 19, T 447997.

● **Spectator sport**

The *Kawkab* (KACM) football club of Marrakech, one of the best in Morocco, can be seen at the Stade al Harti, rue Moulay El Hassan, Hivernage.

● **Sports**

Ballooning: take off behind *Oasis Restaurant*, MD2,000 for 1 hr.

Flying: *Royal Flying Club*, Aéroport Marrakech Menara, T 431769.

Go-Karting: at *Kart Hotel*, Sud Quad.

Golf: the *Royal Golf Club*, 6 km S off the Ouarzazate road (P31), T 444341, F 430084, is a large 18-hole course set in orchards, 6,200m, par 72, fee per round MD300, club hire MD100, open every day. *Palmeraie Golf Palace*, 18-hole, par 72, 6,214m, fee MD350, 15 km S of town.

Riding: at *Club de l'Atlas* (Haras Régional), Quartier de la Menara, T 431301; or there is another 4 km along the road to Asni, T 448529.

Skiing: call at *Skiing Club*, Ave Mohammed V, T 434026, the best site is 76 km from Marrakech at Oukaimeden.

Swimming: at the municipal pool in the *Moulay Abd es-Salam Garden*, rue Abou el Abbes, nr the Koutoubia Mosque. The large hotels have pools, the cheapest and most convenient for the medina is the *Grand Hotel Tazi*, on rue Bab Agnaou.

Tennis: *Royal Tennis Club de Marrakech*, eight courts, Jnane El Harti, rue Oued El Makhazine, T 431902. 30 tennis courts in hotels.

● **Tour companies & travel agents**

Menara Tours, 41 rue Yougoslavie, T 446654, has English speaking staff; also try *Atlas Tours*, 40 Ave al-Mansur Ad-Dahbi, T 433858; *Sahara Tours*, 182 Ave Abdelkrim El Khattabi, T 430062; *Comanov Voyages*, 149 Ave Mohammed V, T 430265; *Atlas Voyages*, 131 Ave Mohammed V, T 430333; *Wagons Lits Tourisme*, 122 Ave Mohammed V, T 431687. **Royal Air Maroc**, 197 Ave Mohammed V, T 436205.

Trekking: *TTM-Trekking Tour Maroc*, 107 rue saad Ben errabia Issil, T 4308055, F 4434520, offer ski trekking in Toubkal from 15 Jan-30 Apr, camel trekking by the Atlantic coast, walking in Toubkal, Saghro and Siroua, guides, meals and all camping equipment provided.

● **Tourist offices**

Office du Tourisme, Place Abd el-Moumen Ben Ali, T 448889; **Syndicat d'Initiative**, 176 Ave Mohammed V, T 432097, 434797.

● **Useful addresses**

Fire: rue Khalid Ben Oualid, T 16.

Garages: Peugeot: Toniel S A, rue Tarik Ibn Ziad; **Renault**: CRA, 55-61 Ave Mohammed V, T 432015; others are **Auto Hall**, rue de Yougoslavie; and **Garage Ourika**, 66 Ave Mohammed V, T 430155.

Police: rue Ibn Hanbal, T 19.

● **Transport**

Local Buses: T 433933, can be caught from rue Moulay Ismail, just off the Djemaa El Fna, and elsewhere along Ave Mohammed V and Ave Hassan II. No 1 is the most useful, running from Djemaa El Fna along Ave Mohammed V, No 3 and 8 run from the railway station to the bus station, via Djemaa El Fna, No 10 from Djemaa El Fna to the bus station, No 11 from the Djemaa El Fna to the Menara Gardens. **Bicycle/motorcycle hire**: *Hotel de Foucauld*, Ave El Mouahidine, T 445499; **Peugeot**, 225 Ave Mohammed V; several cheaper places in Bani Marine, the road in between rue Moulay Ismail and rue Bab Agnaou. **Calèches**: green-painted horse-drawn carriages, can be hailed along Ave Mohammed V, or from the stands at Djemaa El Fna and Place de la Liberté. There are fixed prices for tours around the ramparts, other routes are up for negotiation, but they are not normally prohibitively expensive, and this is a pleasant way to see the city. **Car hire**: MD2,000 for 3 days. **Avis**, 137 Ave Mohammed V, T 433727; **Europcar Inter-Rent**, 63 Blvd Mohammed Zerktouni, T 431228 and at the airport; **Euro Rent**, 9 Ave al-Mansur Ad-Dahbi, T 433184; **Hertz**, 154 Ave Mohammed V, T 434680, F 434680, airport T 447230; **La Royale**, 17 rue Mauritanie, T 447548; lesser known firms with more competitive rates are **Concorde Cars**, 154 Ave Mohammed V, T 431114 (speak English) and **SAFLOC**, 221 Ave Mohammed V, T 433388. **Taxis Petit-taxis**: are easy to find around the city, beware as many do not operate meters, and inflate their prices dramatically for tourists. From the medina to Gueliz should cost MD5-10 during the day, and MD8-15 during the late evening and night. Few journeys should cost much more than this. Major ranks are to be found in Djemaa El Fna, at the Gare Routiere by Bab Doukkala, and outside the *marché municipal*, Gueliz. **Grand-taxis**: are normally more expensive, can be found at the railway station and the major hotels. They also run over fixed routes, mainly to outlying suburbs, from Djemaa El Fna and Bab Doukkala.

Air Aéroport Marrakech Menara, T 447862, is 6 km W of the city, by the Menara Gardens, and clearly signposted from the centre. There are flights to Casablanca (2 a day), Ouarzazate (4 a week), Agadir (2 a week), as well as to Brussels (Fri), Geneva (Sun), Paris (Mon and Fri),

London (Sat and Tues), and Madrid.

Train The railway station is in Gueliz, on Ave Hassan II, T 447768. Although there are long-term plans for an extension of the line S to Agadir and Laayoune, at present ONCF operates only bus services to the S, connecting with the arrival of the express trains. Express trains for **Casablanca** (3 hrs) and **Rabat** (4hrs) leave at 0900, 1230, 1400 and 1900, and non-express services at 0700, 1705, 2050 and 0130.

Road Buses: run from the Gare Routière at Bab Doukkala, T 433933, which is easily reached by taxis and local buses. There is often a choice between a number of different companies, including CTM, with different prices and times. Long distance buses – when leaving Marrakech as there is more than one bus company make sure the number of the booth where the tickets are bought matches the bus stop number where you intend to catch the bus. Always be there in advance even if the bus does not leave on time. It is worth trying the bus driver with MD10 for a seat near the front. CTM departures are currently: **Ouarzazate** 0445, 0730, 1300 and 1700; **Er Rachidia** 0445; **M'Hamid** 0730; **Beni Mellal** 0630, 1900 and 2100; **Agadir** 0800 and 1830 (currently MD60 single fare); **Laayoune** 1900; and **Casablanca** 0630, 1230, 1630 and 1800. There are also private line services to **Beni Mellal** (19 a day), **El Kelaa des Srarhna** (17 a day), **Rabat** (13 a day), **El Jadida** (9 a day), **Essaouira** (6 a day), **Ouarzazate and Skoura** (5 a day), **Agadir** (4 a day), Safi (3 a day), **Taroudant** (2 a day), Fes, Tiznit, Tafraoute, Ouarzazate and Essaouira (all 1 a day), as well as to Asni, **Oualidia, Khouribga, Ifni** and **Demnate**. It is wise to call at the station the previous day as some services, notably across the High Atlas to **Taroudant** and **Ouarzazate**, leave early in the morning. There are CTM services to Paris every day except Fri and Sun at 1700, cost MD1150. The private line alternative leaves at 1200. CTM services for ˙**Agadir** and **Casablanca** can also be taken from Gueliz, in Blvd Mohammed Zerktouni, but places should be reserved a day in advance. Buses to the **Ourika Valley, Asni** and **Moulay Brahim** run from Bab Rob. Taxi: grand-taxis running over fixed routes, with fixed prices, leave from a variety of places around the city. For Ourika, Asni and Ouirgane leave from Bab Rob. For most other destination, including Chichaoua, Essaouira and Agadir, go to Bab Doukkala.

THE HIGH ATLAS

Marrakech is an ideal base from which to make excursions to the High Atlas, which provide welcome relief both from the hassle and the heat of the city, as well as having a distinct interest of their own. Transport for most of these is by bus or grand-taxi from the rough ground outside Bab Rob.

CHICHAOUA AND AMIZMIZ

Chichaoua is a small town, 100 km from Essaouira, at the intersection with the road to Agadir. There are garages, café-restaurants and a small Sun *souq* near the crossroads, and a *Centre Cooperative Ar-ti*...(closed Sun) where the carpets for ...town is well known are exhib... There are regular buses ...and-taxis (MD15) to and ...h. The road from Mar-...over flat plains and in through the western residential and industrial quarters of the city.

To Tamesloht and Amizmiz

Tamesloht, 3 km to the W of the S507, is famous as the home of the man of '366 sciences' who is credited with working miracles.

Oumnass is an attractive small, sand-coloured settlement. To the S the road crossed the Oued Nfis at the Cavagnac dam which permits a splendid view over the 7 km long Barrage Lalla Takerkoust. A further 21 km takes you to Amizmiz.

Amizmiz, 55 km SW from Marrakech at the end of the S507, is known for its acrobatic school which has existed since mediaeval times, and now trains the acrobats which appear in Marrakech and in Europe. It was founded by a *marabout*, Sidi Ahmed. There is also a semi-ruined kasbah, a former *mellah*, and an important Tues morning *souq*, specializing in carpets and pottery. The **F** *Hotel de France*, with attached bar, is adequate. There are regular buses (2½ hrs), and much quicker grand-taxis, to and from

Bab Rob in Marrakech.

ASNI, THE TOUBKAL NATIONAL PARK AND OUIRGANE

Asni has quite limited facilities, garage, telephone, police, post office, shops and youth hostel. There are regular grand-taxis from Bab Rob to Asni, as well as the Taroudant buses which leave from the *gare routière* at Bab Doukkala and call at Bab Rob. The bus takes 1½ hrs. The journey by car from Marrakech takes 1 hr. En route from Marrakech to Asni the S501 passes through the large village of **Tahanaoute** with a good *souq* on Tues and a *zaouia* to Moulay Brahim, who brings luck to childless women.

Moulay Brahim is a popular week-end stop for the people from Marrakech, small hotels and few cafés. The annual festival is Jun and Sept. Incorporate the visit with a trip to the gorge, an attractive and interesting stop. Hint – get a taxi uphill and so have the easier walking downhill. Taxis/buses to/from Asni and Marrakech.

Asni, a typical Berber village, is a busy village with houses in dark earth stacked in clusters around the green valley, plenty of cafés and small shops. It is a pleasant place to stop en route to Ouirgane, Tin Mal or Taroudant, or on to the Toubkal National Park, if one avoids the attentions of the jewellery sellers. The

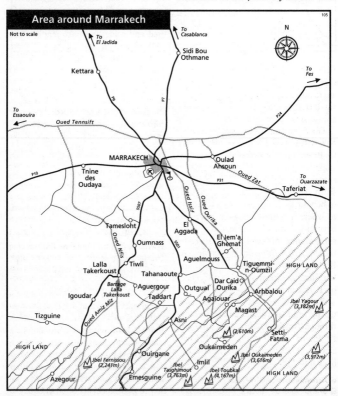

Area around Marrakech

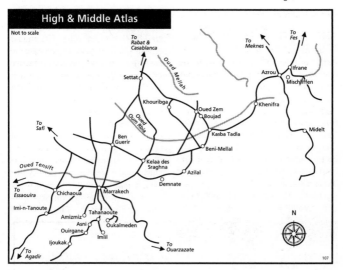

High & Middle Atlas

Not to scale

To Rabat & Casablanca

To Meknes

To Fes

Oued Mellah

Ifrane

Azrou

Mischliffen

Settat

Khouribga

Oued Zem

Boujad

Khenifra

To Safi

Oued Oum Rbia

Kasba Tadla

Midelt

Ben Guerir

Beni-Mellal

Oued Tensift

Kelaa des Sraghna

Azilal

To Essaouira

Chichaoua

Marrakech

Demnate

Imi-n-Tanoute

Amizmiz

Tahanaoute

Asni

Oukaïmeden

Ouirgane

Imlil

Ijoukak

To Ouarzazate

To Agadir

N

107

Sat market has become a tourist attraction but if you are there early it is pleasant to watch the day's events unfold. The small stalls selling lunches to the locals always smell very appetising.

Good walking from here along the Kik plateau to the W of Asni, N to Moulay Brahim and S to Ouirgane. The lower slopes are forested and the higher limestone plateau is indicated by a rocky scarp. The spring flowers are a delight to behold. Walk up the Tizi-n-Test road to where a mule track goes off right beyond a distinctive conical hill. Continue aiming for the plateau edge. Here there is a choice of going NE to Moulay Brahim or SW to Ouirgane. As these are long distances be prepared to take a taxi back to Asni for the return leg.

From Asni it is better to take a taxi up to Imlil and walk downhill back through Tinifine (17 km). After the Az-zif Imenane joins from the right cut across to Tansghart to the old mule track back into Asni.

● **Accommodation** The main option is the **D** *Grand Hotel de Toubkal*, T Asni 3, a con-verted kasbah, at far end of village to N of main square (buses, taxis and petrol) where road goes right to Taroudant, 19 comfortable rm, celebrated restaurant with local specialities, bar, pool only in summer and a delightful garden with fruit trees and rose bushes, good meals and a stork's nest on the roof for added interest. non-residents can use the pool for MD25, good value. **Youth hostel**, T 447713, on Route d'Amlil, at far end of village where the road goes out left to Imlil, take sleeping bags, blankets can be hired, can be cold in winter, 40 beds, quite spartan but beautiful setting, kitchen, overnight fee MD20, open all year, open to non-members.

● **Places to eat** Limited choice available. Eat expensively at *Grand Hotel de Toubkal* or in the centre of the village at the number of stalls and cafés cooking *harira* soup and *tagines*. This is the last place to stock up on basic supplies for a visit to the Toubkal region.

● **Transport** Buses/taxis to Imlil go from just S of youth hostel.

Toubkal National Park is reached by a track which leads off left in Asni, through the market. Take the left hand fork. For those without transport either hike or negotiate a grand-taxi which are easy to find especially on market day. It is possible to walk from Asni to *Imlil*, or to *Tachedirt*, which has a *Refuge Club Alpin Français*.

Imlil is 17 km SE from Asni. It is the start of the walks in this area. In the centre of village is the carpark/taxi area with the stone built CAF hut (places for 35) standing on the corner of the road, guides hut and Café du Soleil. Numerous small cafés and shops, good baker and a travel agent. Mules 'parked' to S of village, on left, before junction. There is a utilitarian route indicator of concrete on the right, should you be unsure of your direction.

Imlil is not connected by telephone. The locals who are used to walkers are generally anxious to provide accommodation. *Aït Idr Mohammed* in Targa Imoula, just through Imlil, has been recommended for accommodation and hire of mules and guides. In Imlil one can stay and eat at **F** *Café du Soleil*, a tiny and basic place; the **F** *Etoile de Toubkal*; or at the *Refuge Club Alpin Français*, which provides clean but minimal facilities. Mules and guides can be hired in Imlil, most easily in the *Refuge* or at *Ribat Tours*.

● **Walking** Options include the **Aremd** circuit, a refreshing hike through remote villages and past breathtaking views, and a walk to the **Lac d'Ifni**. Another is to walk to **Setti Fatma**, in the Ourika Valley. Much more challenging is to climb **Jbel Toubkal**, the highest mountain in North Africa at 4,167m. It is necessary to break the walk at the *Refuge Club Alpin Français* at Neltner, a simple dormitory place with no meals. In winter this is a difficult trek and full equipment is essential. A wise plan is to purchase specialist hiking books, such as Robin Collomb's *Atlas Mountains*, and maps, for the region, before arriving.

Ouirgane is a beautiful village about 1 hr drive from Marrakech in a dramatic valley location, on the S501. The almond blossom in spring is breathtaking. It can be reached by bus from Marrakech (the Taroudant service), or by grand-taxi from Asni. The two hotels in Ouirgane offer wonderful food and the opportunity to explore the valley in easy rambles. The **C** *Le Val de La Roseraie*, BP 769, T 432094, F 432095, 23 a/c rm, is a beautiful and peaceful hotel set in extensive and profusely flowering grounds, with two fine restaurants, bar, disco, nightclub, *hammam*, hydrotherapy centre, tennis, horse riding and pool; whilst the **D** *L'Hostellerie au Pont d'Ouirgane 'Auberge Au Sanglier Qui Fume'*, T Ouirgane 9, is an *auberge* run by a Frenchwoman, with 14 old style chalets amidst the gardens, a restaurant serving excellent French country food, a bar, tennis and a pool in the summer, as well as camping for those who have a meal in the restaurant. Cheap rooms opposite *Auberge Au Sanglier* have been recommended.

TREKKING IN THE HIGH ATLAS

This is a very attractive region and the route from Imlil to the summit of Jbel Toubkal is used by several thousand visitors each year. The other routes are less frequented and are consequently more peaceful.

The following suggested routes require adequate preparation, good maps and the correct equipment for safe and complete enjoyment. A good guide and mules would remove the strain. We recommend Hamish M Brown, 21 Carlin Graig, Kinghorn, Fife KY3 9RX, T 0159 22890422, for maps and sound advice. He has been walking in these mountains for over 30 years.

The best time for walking is after the main snows, when attractive spring blossoms appear just below the snow line. Mules cannot negotiate passes until Mar/Apr. Summers are too hot, visibility in the heat haze is poor. Nov-Feb is too cold and too much snow for walking although frozen ground is often more comfortable than walking on than the ever moving scree. Deep snows and ice present few problems to those with ropes, ice axes, crampons and experience. Without these – stay away in winter.

The route from Imlil to Jbel Toubkal

Imlil is the end of the surfaced road but it is possible to reach **Around** by car up the rough track. Takes about 45 mins to walk. *Café Lac d'Ifni* makes a good stop here. Sidi Chambouch is reached in another 2½ hrs, going steadily uphill. It is important to bear right after the *marabout* to find the initially very steep, but later steady slope up to the Nelter Refuge (3,207m). Allow a total of 4½ hrs from Imlil. Nelter Refuge, dormitory accommodation for 30 persons, US$5 per night. Better to book. Campers using level site below the hut can use the facilities.

To Jbel Toubkal by the S Cwm

This is the more usual approach for walkers. It is clearer on the map than it is on the ground ... First observe the route from the rear of the Nelter refuge and the large boulders on the skyline. These are a point to aim for. Leave the refuge and go down to the river. Cross over and up the other side is the main path to the foot of the first of the many screes. Take the scree path up to the bolders which can be reached in just over an hour. From there is a choice, the long scree slope to the N of the summit or the shorter, steeper slope to the S to the summit ridge. Either way allow 3½ hrs.

The summit is not attractive and one has to wonder who carried up the pieces of iron for the strange pointed structure on the top. The stone shelters make fairly comfortable overnight camping for good view of sunrise. Views are excellent if there is no heat haze, to the Jbels Saghro and Siroua (see page 364) but as the summit here (4,167m) is a plateau other views are limited. Be prepared for low temperatures at this altitude and for the bitter winds that blow 3 out of 4 days in the spring and autumn.

The descent is quicker, allow between 2 and 2½ hrs.

To Jbel Toubkal by the N Cwm

This route is certainly less congested but you will need a guide and/or a good map. Take the route N from the Nelter Refuge crossing the river after about 1 km near the small ruined building. Stike up towards the N cwm. The screes move here and the path is not very distinct although the direction is clear enough. The way is up the back of the cwm to the left, to the break in the craggy skyline and a col. The summit then lies to the S along the ridge. It is a long hard climb.

Allow at least 4 hrs for the ascent.

The Toubkal Circuit

Starting/ending at Asni The times are approximate and assume most equipment is carried by mule. Note that some of the high passes like Tizi-n-Ouanoumss may not be passable by mule until late Jun.

1. To Amskere (1,800m) Arrange transport to Imi Oughlad or to Aguersioual (about another 5 km) and from there a gentle walk to Amskere (2 hrs).

2. To Tacheddirt (2,300m) This walk follows the Oued Imenane towards its source (5 hrs). There is a CAF hut here.

3. To Azib Likemt (2,650m) This is not an easy day as the going is steep, the path winds and bends across the screes. The pass of Tizi Likemt (3,555m) is a well earned rest with excellent views of the way already travelled. Downhill is quicker but no more comfortable (8 hrs).

4. Azib Tifni (2,800m) A shorter leg, again uphill by the Assif Tifni. Keep to the right of the *oued*. Just 1½ km out of Azib Tifni a left hand track leads S as an alternative route to Amsouzerte. Continue along the *oued* to the berber village of Azib Tifni (4 hrs).

5. Amsouzerte (1,740m) This long leg leads up, out of the valley to the pass of Tizi-n-Terhaline (3,355m), the views as breathtaking as the ascent. The de-

scent, also very steep, swings round S and SE to Assifn-Tisqui, by Tiseldai (2,100m) which gives its name to the valley, Missour and Tagadirt down through more and more settlements and into the walnut groves around Amsouzerte (8 hrs).

The last section of this walk by the stream is particularly pleasant through the terraced fields. Rooms are available here in some of the unusual 3-4 storey houses. There are one or two shops and mule hire is possible. There is an option to spend a

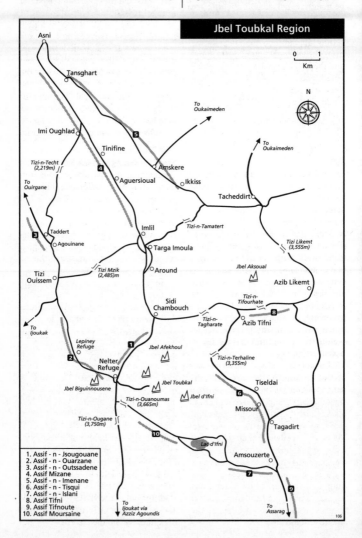

Jbel Toubkal Region

0   1
Km

N

1. Assif - n - Jsougouane
2. Assif - n - Ouarzane
3. Assif - n - Outssadene
4. Assif Mizane
5. Assif - n - Imenane
6. Assif - n - Tisqui
7. Assif - n - Islani
8. Assif Tifni
9. Assif Tifnoute
10. Assif Moursaine

second night here and visit the market town of Assarag, about 2 hrs S up the Assif Tifnoute, but only if it coincides with the Sat market.

6. Lake Ifni (2,290m) The route, gradually uphill, reaches Lake Ifni, which to be honest, is not such an inviting area of water as it appears on the map. Overheated walkers can take a swim before setting up camp on the lake shore (4 hrs). The lake once extended further W and there is a large area, about 1 km in length and 250m wide of round boulders, once part of the lake bed. Circular patches in these are clearings made by previous campers. Round the lake is a series of tidemarks showing earlier levels of the water.

7. Nelter Refuge (3,200m) A long steady ascent to Tizi-n-Ouanoumss (3,665m) takes a long morning. There is time then to admire the views before the short steep descent, much of it scree, down to the Nelter Refuge (see page 325) (6 hrs).

8. From this refuge the ascent of Mt Tobkal is made. It is a very popular climb/walk with some very arduous screes and some stiffer slopes. Allow a long day for the ascent and return to this base (7 hrs). See details above.

9. Around (1,920m) A gentle downhill gradient alongside the Assif n-Isougouane where the spring blossom on the walnut trees is magnificent, the steeper ascent being before the shrine of Sidi Chamhaouch (2,340m) and its tiny collection of stalls. At the time of the pilgrimage this shrine is very busy. Then on to Around, quite a big settlement after the tiny Berber villages (3 hrs).

10. Imi Oughlad (1,300m) a last long stretching of the legs. The country is certainly more gentle though the mule track up to the pass of Tizi Mzik (2,485m) is steep enough. From Tizi Oussem (1,850m) continue down to Assif n-Ourssadene which is followed N for 3-4 km. The track never reaches the *oued* bed but keeps along the contour and only gradually rises to go through the small settlements of Agouinane and Taddert before the last pass, Tizi n-Techt (2,219m) gives access to Imi Ourglad. It is here one wonders if the arrangements made for collection and return to Marrakech were really understood ...

Jbel Toubkal from Ijoukak

Ijoukak, on the S501 94 km out from Marrakech can be reached by bus. There are toilets and cafés here and rooms may be rented. Taking the bus a little further permits a walk to historic Tin Mal about 5 km off the road and a quiet walk back downstream to Ijoukak along the river most of the way.

This is an approach from the W and permits one to begin the walk along the Assif Agoundis with the plateau of Tazharhart to the N and return from Iziz Oussem with the same plateau to the S. The route up the Assif Agoundis is a steady climb and the walk along under the crests (provided the snow line is high enough) provides good views, and in spring a surprising number of flowers. The most commonly followed tracks lead eventually to the Nelter Refuge allowing keen scree scramblers to reach the summit of Jbel Toubkal and then on N to Imlil. After the section Imlil to Tizi Oussem, walked on most circuits, the route continues W over the Tizi n-Ouarhou to Tisgui and back to Ijouka. Allow 10-14 days for this longer circuit if taking in Jbel Toubkal summit.

Refuges run by CAF in Casablanca	height	places
Refuge d'Imlil	1,740m	38
Refuge du Toubkal	3,207m	30
Refuge de la Tazarhart	3,000m	22
Refuge de Tachdirt	2,314m	23
Refuge de l'Oukaimeden	2,630m	80
(restricted opening times)		

TIN MAL

Tin Mal is a ruined settlement high in the Atlas mountains, off the S501 from Marrakech to Taroudant. It was the holy city of the Almohad Dynasty, and it enables the non-Muslim to see the interior of a major mosque, with examples of 12th century Almohad decor intact amidst the ruins.

Tin Mal is 100 km from Marrakech, just past the village of Ijoukak. From Marrakech drive, or take a Taroudant bus as far as Ijoujak, where there are several basic cafés with rooms. Just after the village, on the right, is the **Talat n-Yacoub Kasbah**, the home of the Goundafis, who formerly ruled the area, and a ruined summer pavilion with a ribbed dome, and further along, on the left, another kasbah of the Goundafi family. Carry on walking, and across the river to the right can be seen the square structure of the **Tin Mal Mosque**. Cross the river on the next bridge (often impassable by car), and walk up past Tin Mal village to the mosque.

The town, the base of the Almohad revolt against the Almoravids, became a necropolis for its rulers, with the burial there of Ibn Tumart, Abd el-Moumen,

Handmade carpets

🕊 The visitor will be surprised at the number of carpets on display in the *souqs* of North Africa. There is a great variety of designs, materials and unusual colours. A carpet is a splendid memento of a holiday in North Africa and a better choice will be made with a little knowledge and by taking your time in making your selection. North African carpets, unlike Persian carpets, are best not considered as investments.

There are two main types of handmade carpet, the flat woven *kilims* and knotted carpets usually of wool on a cotton base.

Kilims are flat woven rugs and include tapestries with woven scenes. They have the great virtue of being cheap, light in weight and easily packed. Very decorative are the thin Bedouin rugs in bright reds and golds, while there are also coarse rag rugs made from scraps of material common in Egypt. Most valuable are the *kilims* made entirely of wool and dyed in natural colours or mixed fibres, some in very bright hues.

Handknotted carpets and rugs are more expensive than *kilims*. The number of knots per square centimetre determines the quality of a handknotted carpet, as does the materials of which it is constructed. The backing (the warp) may be of cotton, wool or silk and the knots of wool or silk. Coarse woollen material is used when knot densities are low, on average about 25 per centimetre, while the fine wools and silks require higher densities of up to 69 knots per centimetre, take longer to make and therefore cost more.

Designs for the handknotted carpets are very varied, though the best usually take their patterns from tile designs from the walls of the famous mosques. Often however designs are adapted from traditional patterns made popular elsewhere in the Middle East – Persian, Turkish and Caucasian being most widespread. Pleasing designs on small rugs follow the classical patterns of the tree of life, formal hunting scenes, the Persian garden, bird carpets and central medallions. Most small rugs were and to an extent are still produced as prayer mats and incorporate a triangular top portion to act as the indicator of the direction to Mecca copied from the *mihrab* in the wall of the mosque.

Abu Ya'qub and Abu Youssef. The tombs and the mosque became venerated as a pilgrimage centre, even after the Merinid destruction of 1275-6. The mosque dates from 1153-4, during the reign of Sultan Abd el-Moumen, and was built by the tomb of Ibn Tumart.

The mosque has a rectangular shape, with thick *pisé*-cement and stone and a low minaret of brick, unusually located behind the *mihrab*. The *mihrab* niche, with its stalactite dome, is built into the minaret, in between the door used by the *Imam*, and a room used to store the pulpit. Below the courtyard is a cistern

fed by two conduits. The mosque is decorated with plaster applied to the brick facing, and is simple as befits the conservative tastes of the period. The *mihrab* niche has a distinctive shape, accentuated by the configuration of two arches and rectangular frame surrounding it, with rosettes in the spaces between the arch and frame. Around this is a geometric pattern of interlacing 8-pointed stars and rectangles. The three windows above the niche are surmounted by a band of interlacing 6-pointed stars. The stalactite dome above once included plaques of Almohad floral decor, two of which remain

The most prolific producers of fine carpets and rugs are Egypt, Tunisia and Morocco, all of which have their own favourite colours and designs. It is best to buy a local speciality. The fact that carpets are slightly misshapen is not a sign of poor quality. Handlooms are all different and little credit is given in the traditional as opposed to tourist orientated weaving areas to mathematical accuracy. Indeed, in Morocco some Berber carpets are made deliberately out of square by women who make a portion of their carpet to reflect each separate month of their pregnancy. The nine-strip carpets bulge interestingly towards the central area !

Machine made carpets, normally to be avoided, can be distinguished by the fringe which will often have been sewn on later, or by the sides which are much neater and flatter than handmade rugs, and by the back which does not show the pattern very clearly and is quite smooth. Fold back the carpet for a close examination of the knots and pattern on the rear of the carpet to check the mathematical precision of weaving which gives away the fact that it is factory made.

Each carpet will have to be bargained for with patience and humour. The following pointers will help during this process. In Morocco carpets ought to carry a government seal indicating the price. In official handicraft shops fixed prices are generally the rule, though this might not make them cheaper than the souq for the avid bargainer. In Tunisia and particularly Morocco tourist guides will lead you to carpet shops which will give him a commission on your purchase. This is already included in the price. There is no need to be rushed in your purchase – the tale that the 'shop is closed tomorrow' is often a ploy used to clinch a sale. If possible take your carpet with you rather than let the shop arrange delivery to your hotel or your home address.

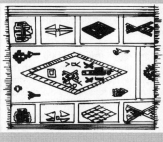
Traditional Moroccan carpet

in this dome. The remainder of the mosque includes a large number of arches and several areas of stalactite plaster work. Examples of the *darj w ktaf* and palmette motifs can be found, but little inscription. Stairs up lead to an impressive view over the valley.

THE TIZI-N-TEST AND THE ROAD TO TAROUDANT

The S501 from Marrakech to Taroudant, is one of the most spectacular routes in Morocco, winding its way up and then down through the High Atlas mountains, above the beautiful valleys of this region and past isolated villages, eventually reaching the Tizi-n-Test pass, with its breathtaking views across the Sous valley to the Anti Atlas mountains. There are buses between the two cities, although check that they are *par Tizi-n-Test*. Driving has been feasible since the road, a traditional trading route, was formerly opened in 1928, following the work of French engineers. Some of its sections are a bit scary, but it is a highly recommended experience, particularly when tied in with visits to Asni, Ouirgane and Tin Mal. Signs on the exit to Marrakech will indicate if the pass is open. The S501 joins the P32 from Taroudant to Ouarzazate.

OUKAIMEDEN

Oukaimeden, at 2,600m, the meeting place of the four winds, is Morocco's major ski resort, open Dec-Mar, with an extremely high ski lift up the 3,273m Jbel Oukaimeden (see page 466). The skiing is reputedly good, with a range of standards, although the slopes often become wet by the afternoon. There are instructors working in the resort, and a skiing shop is located beside the *Hotel de l'Angour*. Oukaimeden has one or two local shops with expensive tinned goods for sale. In winter hotels and restaurants open, in summer it is less busy and many places are closed. Daily bus from Marrakech in the winter. It is also possible to climb the Jbel Oukaimeden in a day.

Another option is to walk the piste which leaves the road S of Oukaimeden, and cross the hills to the S501 to S of Asni. In summer visitors can walk, climb and parasail while in spring the drive through the blossoming walnut and almond trees is breathtaking. Walk to see the prehistoric wall engravings on the rocky outcrop below the dam wall. Takes about 20 mins with the right guide.

There is also access by a beautiful mountain route taking the S501 as far as Tahanaoute (34 km) then the piste (only the first few km are surfaced) to Sisi Fahes (22 km) where there is an inn. Continue along, and up, the mountain track which gives access to the Oukaimeden plateau. North of Oukaimeden is Jbel Tizerag, 2,784m, with an easy track almost to the top. It is only 200m higher than the resort itself but the views are magnificent and those who have witnessed sunset from the summit consider it an unforgettable sight.

This is an interesting area for birdwatchers, as the altitude and vegetation both limit the range of birds. The Golden Eagle with a wing span of 2m is an uplifting sight as is the even larger Lammergeier. Booted Eagles are smaller but their aerial acrobatic displays are a delight. Look out on the lower reaches for Black Redstarts, noisy Red-billed Choughs, Blue Rock Thrushes and Black Wheatears.

One can still catch the occasional sight of the magnificent Barbary sheep.

To get to Oukaimeden, follow the S513 from Marrakech, branching off the Ourika valley just before Arhbalou. For accommodation the choice is between the **D** *Hotel Imlil*, T 459132, a comfortable place with restaurant, bar, and *après-ski* nightclub; E *Hotel de l'Angour* (also called *Auberge Chez Juju Oukaimeden*), T 459005, open all year (except Ramadan) has 8 rm, good restaurant with French cuisine, bar with cold beer, half-pension required but reasonable prices for clean sheets and hot showers; *Hotel Panoramique*, open all year has 14 rm and a dormitory with 20 beds; *Le Chouka*, only open in winter has 8 rm and a dormitory with 30 beds, restaurant, modern and comfortable; *Refuge of the Club Alpin Francais*, has space for 100, but not bunks for all, often has spaces for non-members, restaurant with reduced prices for the CAF members, very comfortable considering position, skiing equipment can be hired here, open all the year, bar room, games room, showers (sometimes with hot water), very clean. *Camping Oukaimeden*, small site, is open only to caravans, has electricity and petrol 1 km.

THE OURIKA VALLEY

The Ourika Valley is a beautiful area of green, terraced fields above the winding Oued Ourika, the most popular excursion for Marrakechis, particularly the young who can court here without police harassment. Buses and grand-taxis to Ourika leave from Bab Rob, Marrakech. It is worth going all the way to Setti Fatma, at the head of the valley. Once in Ourika, a good means of transport is a lift in the open top vans and lorries which speed along the valley. **NB** The valley has a problem with flooding, which campers should bear in mind.

Dar Caid Ourika is the first major settlement, with a Mon *souq* often crowded with tourists. Don't be confused by the field of donkeys which are local transport and not for sale. It also has a *zaouia* and a ruined kasbah. Some buses terminate here. The next big village is **Arhbalou**, which has one of the best hotels of the valley, the **C** *Hotel Ourika*, T 433993, 27 a/c rm, with good food, a pleasant atmosphere, nightclub and pool; also try the **E** *Auberge Ramuntcho*, T 446312, with a good restaurant, bar and pool. Three other good places to eat in Arbalou are *Hotel Restaurant Bar le Lion de l'Ourika*; *Bar Restaurant Amnougour*; and *Bar Restaurant Kasbah de l'Ourika*, all patronized by coach parties. There is also a shop selling antiques, carpets and ceramics, the *Musée d'Aghbalou*, just beyond the village.

The road ends at **Setti Fatma**, noted for its 100-year-old walnut trees, where there is a small market and a number of basic hotels, incl **F** *Hotel Café Atlas*, good rooms; also **F** *Hotel Azrou* and **F** *Hotel Asgaoua*. However the main part of Setti Fatma is further on, entailing a climb along the right hand side of the river. At the main village, cross over to the grassy area where the youth of Marrakech picnic and relax. There are a number of café-restaurants along the bank, **F** *Hotel Café Bouche de la Source*, provides basic rooms and cheap *tagines*; alongside, and

---

Blooming trees

Drifts of snow are common in the Atlas massifs but the drifts of blossom in early spring which clothe the slopes for a second time are much more attractive. There are over 12 million almond trees to delight with their pale pink and fragile white blooms in Jan and Feb. The roads from Marrakech to Agadir, the road from Agadir to Tafraoute and the whole region fed by the Oued Draa are breathtakingly beautiful at this season. These groves of self-seeded almonds have adapted to the environment, are resistant to drought and cold and provide, despite their low yields, an important source of income. While the early almond blossom here is in sharp contrast to the barren earth, the blossom on trees in the oasis gardens has a green backcloth. In addition there are almond plantations especially in the Haouz of Marrakech which are equally beautiful and show greater profits. Every year, in Feb, the Festival of the Almond Tree takes place at Tafraoute and the folkloric and cultural festivities are based on the theme of the blossoming almond trees, harbingers of spring.

marginally better, is **F** *Auberge des Routards/Restaurant les 7 Cascades*; beyond is the *Restaurant des Cascades*. The 7 cascades are a 30-min scramble up from Setti Fatma, following the path up behind the first café. There is a café perched up where the path ends, beside the first waterfall. Setti Fatma is also another good point to start a walking tour, with guides who will accompany tourists the 10 km to Tachedirt, where there is a *Refuge Club Alpin Français*.

Jbel Yagour has over 2,000 prehistoric rock carvings, but you will certainly need a guide and perhaps a mule from Setti Fatma.

TIZI-N-TICHKA, KASBAH TELOUET AND THE ROAD TO OUARZAZATE

The P31 from Marrakech to Ouarzazate, and its Tizi-n-Tichka pass, is a larger road and safer option than the route over the Tizi-n-Test, but is still an exhilarating experience with similarly stunning views, passing through the range of environments, from the Haouz plains, through the verdant foothills, to the barren peaks and the arid regions around Ouarzazate. The route is often lined with mineral and fossil sellers, and there are a number of café stops en route. Before the pass is the village of Taddert, with the French-run **E** *Le Noyer auberge*.

Just past the pass is a turning on the left leading to the **Kasbah Telouet**. This was the base of the el-Glaoui family, who from the late 19th century, under the brothers Madani and Thami controlled much of S Morocco, a dominance which continued under the French, who used them to establish control over the region. Thami el-Glaoui was a ruthless and powerful *pasha* of Marrakech as late as 1956. The kasbah itself is a vast, labyrinthine, decaying place, built by Thami el-Glaoui. A guardian will appear to unlock the door and show groups round part of the building. There are grand-taxis from the village of Irherm to

Telouet. From the pass the road sweeps down to Ouarzazate. The kasbah of Aït Benhaddou can be visited en route, or the next day as an excursion, see page 372.

To Lake Aït Aadel and Demnate At 16 km E of Marrakech, opposite the road to Zaouia Bou Sassi, take the minor road through Sidi Rahhal to Tazzerte where there are kasbahs belonging to the Glaoui family and on to the reservoir. It has an attractive setting, with the red of the High Atlas as a background. This is a popular picnic spot. Further on lies Demnate (see page 333).

BENI MELLAL AND ENVIRONS

BENI MELLAL

This is one of the major centres of central Morocco, with a population of 95,003 (1982), and an important *souq* on Tues. The town is scruffy but relaxed, and with adequate facilities for a pleasant stay. At the entrance to the town is the **Kasbah Bel Kush**, built in the 17th century by Moulay Ismail, but heavily restored in the 19th century. The main thing to do in Beni Mellal is to walk up from the town to the small and quiet gardens, which lie below the ruined **Kasbah de Ras el Aïn**, perched precariously on the cliffside. There is a nice café in the gardens.

● **Accommodation B** *Al Bassatine*, Route de Ben Salah, T 482227, 61 a/c rm, pool, restaurant, TV, direct telephone, private parking and conference facilities. Both **C** *Hotel Ouzoud*, Route de Marrakech, T 483752/3, with restaurant, bar, tennis and pool; and **C** *Chems*, Route de Marrakech, BP 68, T 483460, Tx 24891, 77 rm, with restaurant, bar, nightclub, tennis and pool, are a bit far out from the centre.

The more central options incl **E** *Hotel Gharnata*, Ave Mohammed V, T 483482, 14 comfortable rm, restaurant with European food, and a bar; **E** *Hotel de Paris*, Nouvelle Medina, T 482245, with a restaurant and bar; **E** *Auberge du Vieux Moulin*, Ave Mohammed V, T 482788, 9 rm, good restaurant and a bar. Much cheaper options are the **F** *Hotel des Voyageurs*, Ave Mohammed V, basic but satisfactory; the **F** *Hotel El Amria*, Ave des Forces Armées Royales, T 483531, simple; and the **F** *Hotel de l'Aïn-Asserdoun*, Ave des Forces Armées Royales, T 483493, a modern place with restaurant.

● **Places to eat** There are several cheap restaurants in the town centre, but one of the best places to eat is *Auberge du Vieux Moulin*, Ave Mohammed V; another on the same street is in *Hotel Gharnata*. A good place to drink a tea or coffee, or eat a delicious pastry, is the *Salon de Thé Azouhour*, 241 Ave Mohammed V; similarly good is *Salon de Thé El Afrah*, Place Afrique; there are several other good fruit juice shops, *laiteries* and *cafés* along the main street.

● **Sports Gliding**: *Centre Royal de Vol à Voile de Beni Mellal*, T 482095. **Light and Sporting Aircraft**: *Royal Aéroclub de Beni Mellal* at local airport, T 482095.

● **Tourist offices** A tourist office is located on the 1st flr of Immeuble Chichaoui, Ave Hassan II, T 483981.

● **Transport Road** CTM buses leave from the terminal on the Route de Marrakech. There are regular connections with Marrakech and 3 a day for Fes. From the bus station it is a 10 mins walk up Ave des Forces Armées Royales to the town centre.

EXCURSION TO BIN EL OUIDANE, AZILAL AND THE CASCADES D'OUZOUD

This region around Azilal, to the S of Beni Mellal, is predominantly Berber, a forested, mountainous area popular with walkers. The villages clustering around its slopes have adobe houses with added stone and woodwork. Skiing is popular from Feb to Apr, and there is good hiking in the Mgoun mountains. The Taghia ravine is a popular climbing site. There are a number of high altitude refuges.

The **Bin El Ouidane dam** and lake, 38 km S of the P24, is good for fishing, swimming, sailing and wind-surfing. Stay at the **E** *Auberge du Lac*, a clean and reasonable place with a restaurant serving Moroccan and European food, and which hires out boats for use on the lake.

28 km further on is **Azilal**, a small town with a Thur *souq*. Accommodation is available at the **E** *Hotel Tanout*, T 488281, 12 rm, restaurant. Azilal has a tourist office on Ave Hassan II, T 488334, and is connected by buses with Beni Mellal and Marrakech. Camping at Azilal, *Camping du Lac*, Bin el-Ouidane, T 442465, on site of 3 ha, bar, snacks, restaurant, showers, laundry, electricity for caravans, petrol station 30 km. The impressive **Cascades d'Ouzoud** which plunge some 100m are 41 km from Azilal. Ride W for 22 km along the S508 then take the right hand track for a further 19 km. For those without a car hire a grand-taxi from Azilal. The Cascades d'Ouzoud is a picturesque Middle Atlas site which has become very popular, particularly with young Moroccans camping in the summer. Camping is possible at various small sites. *Camping Cascades d'Ouzoud* in 4 ha of land, first aid, nearest petrol 32 km. There are also rooms at *Hotel Dar es Salam*, which has a reasonable restaurant.

The S508 continues towards Marrakech and gives an opportunity to visit **Demnate**, only a 10 km detour. This is one of the very old villages of Morocco, all painted white and carved out of the rock around an unusual kasbah in the middle of olive groves. Off the track beyond Demnate is Imi-n-Ifri, a natural cavern with impressive stalactites.

KASBAH TADLA

Kasbah Tadla was built in 1687 by the Alaouite Sultan Moulay Ismail. The town is a military garrison with a relaxed air but little to see. There is the kasbah, now crumbling and squatted by families of soldiers, as well as an old bridge with 10 arches over the Oum er Rbia, also built by Moulay Ismail. The **Jamia Mosque** on the main market square is from the same period. Nearby is a covered market and a small medina. The *souq* is on Mon.

● **Accommodation** The town has one reasonable hotel, the **D** *Hotel Bellevue*, just outside the town off the P24 from Fes to Beni Mellal, T 418731/2/3. There are three basic hotels in the centre: **F** *Hotel des Allies*, Ave Mohammed V, T 418171, is perhaps the best; the others are **F** *Hotel El Atlas*, rue el Majati Obad, T 418046; and **F** *Hotel Oum Rbia*, 26 Blvd Mohammed Zerktouni, with no shower. There are a few basic restaurants in the town centre. **Camping**: at El Ksiba just 30 km E of Kasbah Tadla in 2 ha, showers, electricity for caravans.

● **Transport Road** CTM buses leave at 1035 for Fes, 1145 for Marrakech, 1335 for Casablanca and 1705 for Beni Mellal, and private line buses from *Agence SLAC* for Beni Mellal at 1300, Boujad and Oued Zem at 1700, and Rabat at 0430, 0730 and 1300. These can all be caught from the agencies on the main street, Blvd Mohammed Zerktouni.

DETOUR TO BOUJAD, OUED ZEM AND KHOURIBGA

Boujad has a beautiful and historic medina, with cobbled streets and white houses, and had importance as a pilgrimage centre up to the 19th century, dating from the 16th century establishment of a *zaouia*, although much of the town was destroyed in 1785. The medina is dotted with shrines and mosques, most notably the **Shrine of Sidi Othman** and the **Mosque of Sidi Mohammed Bu'abid ech Cherki**, the town's founder. There is one hotel on the main square, Place du Marché, the **F** *Café-Hotel Essalyn*, and several cheap restaurants nearby. This is also from where regular buses and grand-taxis leave to Kasbah Tàdla and Oued Zem.

White gold from Morocco

Phosphates occur widely throughout the world but in great quantities capable of easy commercial exploitation at very few sites of which the USA, FSU, Morocco are by far the most significant. Morocco alone accounts for 66% of the world's recoverable phosphate reserves and more than 10% of world output. While the Government of Morocco is making every effort to use phosphates as raw materials for domestic industrialization, the importance of Morocco as a producer is the availability of the rock and its primary products for export. Approximately 75% of Moroccan output is sent abroad worth MD2,577 million (US$300 million) in 1994.

Of course, if the Western Sahara is taken into account, the Moroccan position as an owner of phosphates is much enhanced, lifting its reserves to perhaps 75% of the world total and adding a potential (but currently unused) capacity of 3 million metric tons to production.

The main areas of phosphate production in Morocco are generally far from tourist resorts. Of the 13 fields it is the Khouribga zone that is most significant with output from Beni Idir, Sidi Dachi, Sidi al-Maati, Mera al-Arech, Sidi Chennan and al-Borchi. Other fields exist at Ben Guerir, Youssoufia and Meskala. The railway system plays a part in moving phosphate rock to processing plants with lines between the coast at Casablanca, and Safi and the phosphate fields of the interior.

In the Western Sahara there is a vast SW-NE oriented swathe of phosphate rock at Bu-Craa from which a moving conveyor belt formerly – pre-Polisario's war with Morocco – carried rock to a treatment area S of Laayoune on the Atlantic coast.

At one stage in the mid-1970s Morocco attempted to force up the price of phosphate on the international market following the model of the oil producers in 1973-74. The move failed and Morocco suffered badly through new producers, some in the USA, entering the market. Primary commodities such as phosphates have in any case found markets difficult in the last decade as international trade became highly competitive. Even so, phosphates remain a vital natural resource for Morocco and will remain internationally important for many years yet.

Oued Zem (*Pop* 58,744 (1982)) is an uninteresting phosphates town with useful railway connections and a busy market in the centre. **F** *Hotel El Salam*, is very cheap and central; the other option is **F** *Hotel des Cooperatives*, on rue Rachid II. There are cheap restaurants in the centre. Trains to Casablanca leave at 0720, 0840 and 1500 and take between 2 hrs 15 mins and 3 hrs.

Khouribga (*Pop* 127,181 (1982)) is an important city, owing much to its central role in the phosphates industry, but is singularly lacking in any charm or appeal. There is one luxury hotel, the **A** *Hotel Safir*, T 492013, 493013, with restaurant, bar, tennis and pool; the best cheap hotel is the excellent value, clean and comfortable **F** *Hotel de Paris*, 18 Ave Mohammed V, T 492716; the only other is **F** *Hotel des Hotes*, 1 rue Moulay Ismail, T 493030, a basic and unfriendly place. Around the market, just off the main street, are a number of basic restaurants. Trains to Casablanca, with connections to Marrakech, El Jadida, Safi, Rabat, Fes and Tanger, leave at 0757, 0923, 1540 and to Oued Zem at 1228, 1931 and 2239.

The game of draughts - Moroccan style

For *La Kherbga*, Moroccan draughts, there is no need for a board or counters – the immediate environment provides all. A small pile of sand/ earth/dust is scraped together with the foot and patted flat with the hand. Into this 49 holes are pressed, 7 rows of 7 holes. Pieces used in the game are pebbles, date stones, dried dates or dried donkey droppings (evidence of own eyes in Sijilmassa), all easily available.

The purpose is to systematically eliminate the pieces of the other player in a style similar to our game of draughts. Despite being a 'game for two' all the group participates with well-meaning advice or noisy criticism of the mode of play.

THE MIDDLE ATLAS

KHENIFRA AND ENVIRONS

El Ksiba Continuing on from Kasbah Tadla, the P24 passes El Ksiba, just off to the S of the road. This is a pleasant place to stay. **E** *Hotel Henri IV*, excellent food, good rooms; or at *Camping Taghbalout*.

Khenifra is a relaxed Middle Atlas resort with a population of 38,840 (1982). It has a large Wed and Sun *souq*, and a reputation amongst Moroccans as a centre of prostitution. The town was the site of a large defeat for the French in 1914, at the hands of a local *caid*. The top place to stay is **B** *Hotel Hamou Azzayani Salam*, in new town, T 586020, Tx 41932, 60 a/c rm, restaurant, bar, nightclub, tennis and pool; a much cheaper option is the basic but clean **F** *Hotel-Restaurant de France*, Quartier Forces Armées Royales, T 586114; or the **F** *Hotel Voyageurs*, nearby. There is a tourist office at Immeuble Lefraoui, Hay Hamou-Hassan.

A popular excursion from Khenifra is to the tree-lined lake of **Aguelmane Azigza**, 24 km along the 3485. The road continues to the source of the Oued Oum er Rbia and Aïn Leuh, and then back onto the P24 just SW of Azrou. 96 km N of Khenifra, just off the 2516 to Rabat, is **Oulmes-Tarmilate**, a spa from where *Oulmes* sparkling mineral water originates. There is a hotel here, the **D** *Hotel les Thermes*, T 552355, 42 rm, restaurant, bar, and there are waterfalls just below at Lalla Haya. Back on the P24, in between Khenifra and Azrou, is **Mrirt**, with a large and fascinating Thur *souq*.

AZROU

Azrou is a small Berber market town and hill resort named after the rock around which it is built. The town has a relaxed air and good hiking in the wooded vicinity. The ruined kasbah was built by Moulay Ismail. The French built the **Collège Berbère**, which trained many of the civil and military staff of the Protectorate, as part of a divide and rule policy.

All buses, except those of CTM, arrive at a rough patch of land surrounded by food and fruit stalls, in front of the town's distinctive rock. The heart of the town, Place Mohammed V, is to the right on leaving the bus stop. There is a covered market near Place Mohammed V, whilst the *Ensemble Artisanal* (open 0830-1200 and 1430-1800), is situated off Ave Mohammed V, with a fixed price shop and a number of craftsmen working on the premises, look out for the Middle Atlas carpets. There is a large Berber *souq* held just above the town on Tues, with vegetables, textiles and some interesting Middle Atlas carpets, as well as traditional entertainment from musicians and others. The town also has a small pool for summer use.

• **Accommodation** In Azrou: A *Hotel Amos*, 10 km S of town towards Azrou, 66 rm, 8 suites, international and Moroccan cuisine, nightclub, pool, tennis, conference facilities. A pleasant hotel with a good view is the **D** *Hotel Panorama*, T 562010, 39 rm, rec restaurant and bar, good view. **E** *Hotel Azrou*, Route de Khenifra, T 562116, reasonable, 9 rm, restaurant and noisy bar. Best value for money is **F** *Hotel des Cèdres*, Place Mohammed V, T 562326, a clean establishment with hot water, communal showers and a good restaurant; also try **F** *Hotel Salam*, on a square off Place Mohammed V opp the *Hotel des Cèdres*; alongside the less rec **F** *Hotel Ziz* and **F** *Hotel Beau Séjour*. **Youth hostel**: T 563733, Route de Midelt, Azrou, BP147, to get to it follow the signs from Place Mohammed V, and turn left off the road to Midelt, clean and friendly, 40 beds, kitchen, overnight fee MD20, about 1 km from town centre.

• **Places to eat** The best meals are in the restaurant of *Hotel Panorama*; at the *Café Restaurant Relais Forestier*; or the restaurant of *Hotel des Cèdres*, both on Place Mohammed V, or at the cheaper places along the road to Marrakech and around the bus stop.

• **Banks & money changers** The Banque Populaire is on Place Mohammed V.

• **Transport Road** CTM buses depart from near Place Mohammed V, at 0730 for Casablanca, 0800 for Midelt, and at 0730 and 0800 for Meknes. There are other CTM or private line services from Azrou to Rissani, Er Rachidia, Marrakech, Khenifra and Fes, and numerous grand-taxis to Khenifra, Ifrane, Immouzer du Kandar, Meknes and Fes.

AIN LEUH, THE WATERFALLS AND AGUELMANE AZIGZA

At 19 km S of Azrou, a turning off the P24 leads to **Aïn Leuh**, a Berber village with a Wed *souq* important to the semi-nomadic Beni M'Guid tribe, a ruined kasbah from the reign of Moulay Ismail, and nearby **waterfalls**. 20 km S of this is the source of the Oued Oum er Rbia, with a footpath leading from the road to the numerous and impressive waterfalls, falling from a cliff into a dangerous pool. Further on again is **Aguelmane Azigza**, a crater lake ideal for swimming. The tree-lined spot has its devoted followers amongst Moroccan campers and is an ideal location. There is also accommodation in a café. The road continues to rejoin the P24 at Khenifra.

DETOUR TO MIDELT AND ON TO ER RACHIDIA

Midelt (*Alt* 1,525m) lies in the Middle Atlas mountains, a convenient stopping point en route from Fes, Meknes or Azrou to Er Rachidia and the Sahara, a town with a calm, friendly atmosphere and a large *souq* on Sun. In the town, the minerals and fossils of the region are energetically sold by the young and in shops. Also look out for the town's *excellent carpets*, which have the distinctive vegetable-dyed geometric patterns of the region. These can be found in the permanent market opposite the bus station. They can also be bought at a weaving school, the **Atelier de Tissage**, run by Franciscan sisters in a convent off the road to Tattiouine.

• **Accommodation D** *Hotel Ayachi*, rue d'Agadir, a few minutes from town centre, T 582161, 30 rm with bath, TV, radio and telephone, quiet, restaurant, nightclub, safe parking, and garden; there are several more

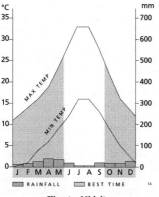

Climate: Midelt

°C / mm scale with MAX TEMP and MIN TEMP curves

J F M A M J J A S O N D

RAINFALL · BEST TIME

basic hotels, the best perhaps are *Hotel Minlal*, on the N entrance to the town, good restaurant; *Hotel Toulouse* in the centre; and *Hotel Roi de la Bière*, nr the S exit. The *Camping Municipal* is on the road to Er Rachidia.

● **Places to eat** *Restaurant de Fes*, 2 Ave Mohammed V, which has very good *couscous*; *Excelsior*, also in the town centre; *Brasserie Chez Aziz*, by the Er Rachidia exit.

A possible excursion is on the rough pistes of the Cirque Jaffar, to the W of Midelt, signposted from the town, and only possible for part of the year. The road (3418) initially follows the Oued Ikkis, a tributary of the Oued Moulouya, almost to Tattiouine from which one can take a mule track to the summit of Jbel Ayachi (3,737m) the highest peak in the Middle Atlas. The circuit takes a lower route just before Tattiouine, measured as 7 km from Midelt, provides some magnificent views and return to the P21 10 km W of Midelt. This journey is only possible after the snows have melted.

A short excursion N of Midelt goes along the S317 to Mibladene (10 km) and over the head of the Oued Moulouya where there are some attractive gorges, past the lead mines and on to Aouli. It is possible to continue over almost unmarked ground adjacent to the *oued* to Ksabi but for this a guide is recommended.

A longer excursion, a round trip of 260 km, leaves the P21 just 15 km S of Midelt, taking the left turn, the S329 towards Missour and eventually to Guercif. The region is known as the Aftis plain and is most attractive, orchards of olives, figs and tamarind trees among which are a number of *ksour*. In the gardens supported by water from the *oued* Bee-eaters, nightingales and olivaceous warblers breed. Jbel Missosur gradually rises ahead to the left. From Missour travel W rising up towards the Tazaouguart Pass, the bulk of Jbel Ouchilas (2,053m) blocking the view S. For those with 4WD El Borj can be reached from this road just after the *oued* cuts across the road. This road here is liable to be washed away after heavy rains. Beyond El Borj the track is very unreliable and those determined to see subalpine and orphean warblers must go carefully. The main road descends to Enjil after the pass, to the P20 and on to Taouerda and Zeïda. Zeïda stands by the Oued Moulouya and the area to the S is noted for hearing if not sighting the Dupont's lark at dusk.

Like all this plateau region the winters are very cold and the summers very hot and so the best time to visit is the spring. Here the spring is later, and May or even early June is recommended.

The P21 continues to Er Rachidia and into the Sahara, past the military fort at Aït Messaoud and the village of Rich, which has two small, unclassified hotels, *Salama* 14 rm, T 579343; *El Massira*, 7 rm, T 579340, before entering the spectacular **Ziz Gorge** and then Er Rachidia.

IFRANE, MISCHLIFFEN AND AN EXCURSION TO THE LAKES

Ifrane is a mountain resort developed by the French, which now has numerous large villas and chalets, as well as a royal palace and hunting lodge. When this is occupied by the king, the town becomes busy with staff and politicians. From the town there are good walks in the *cedar* *forests*, and a drivable excursion round the *dayats* (crater lakes). There is *skiing* at the nearby resort of Mischliffen.

● **Accommodation** The most luxurious hotel is the **A** *Hotel Michlifen*, BP 18, T 56607, F 566623, 107 rm, restaurant, bar, nightclub and pool, 2 conference rooms; **D** *Grand Hotel*, Ave de la Marche Verte, T 566407, 33 rm, dated style, comfortable and calm; **D** *Hotel Perce Neige*, rue des Asphodelles, T 566404, 566210, a friendly place, restaurant and bar. The budget alternative is **F** *Hotel Tilleuls*. **Camping**: *Camping International* is very busy in the summer but open all the year round, signposted from the town centre, in site of 6 ha, laundry facilities available, petrol only 2 km.

● **Places to eat** Good places to eat are *Café-Restaurant de la Rose*, 7 rue des Erables, T 566215; and *Au Rendez-Vous des Skieurs*, on the main street.

● **Useful services** There is a **Syndicat d'Initiative** information centre and a municipal swimming pool in the town, and regular buses from Ifrane to both Azrou and Fes, T 891694, F 891695.

Skiing at Mischliffen near Ifrane is from Jan to Mar with good but short slopes, sometimes with patchy snow cover. Hire equipment from the *Chamonix* restaurant in Ifrane and take a taxi to the resort. This is a small area with cafés and ski lifts but little else. During the summer the area is very popular with walkers.

Aaoua, Afourgan and Ifrah Dayats North of Ifrane, leave the P24 to the E for a tour of the *dayats*, lakes formed by solution of the limestone. There are five lying between the P24 and the P20: Aaoua, Afourgan and Iffer. Dayat Aaoua could be a scenic place to picnic but at present the lake is less than 25% capacity and there are no boats and few birds. **D** *Hotel Chalet du Lac*, Route de Fes, T Ifrane 0, an atmospheric hotel with French restaurant and bar, adjacent to lake, don't rely on it being open. The circular route also takes in Dayats Ifrah and Hachlaf before returning to Ifrane.

In good circumstances the *dayats* support coots, herons and egrets, look out for the black-winged stilt, and numerous reed warblers. The surrounding woodland, made up mainly of holm-oak and cedar, is alive with small birds, tits, chaffinches and short-toed treecreeper, and not-so-small birds like the jay and greater spotted woodpecker and a wide range of raptors including black and red kite, Egyptian vulture and booted eagle. In the woodland near Ifrane the Barbary apes can be seen and where the woodland gives way to more open plateau look out for the jackals.

Be warned, however, that when there has been a shortage of rain all the *dayats* dry up and the region is very disappointing.

IMMOUZER DE KANDAR

This is a small mountain resort, beautiful in spring with the apple blossom, a lively place during the **Fête des Pommes** in Jul, and with *souq*, Mon, in its ruined kasbah. It is a popular excursion from Fes, from where there are regular buses and grand-taxis. *Aïn Erreggada* is clearly signed to the W of the road, the approach from the centre of town near the taxis being the easier. Unfortunately due to the drought the opportunity to swim in the municipal pool, filled with spa water, is not available and the area currently looks very forlorn.

Just N of Immouzer de Kandar are the popular picnic/camping springs, *Aïn Seban* and *Aïn Chifa* clearly signed to the W of the road. In drought conditions they are less attractive.

● **Accommodation** **D** *Hotel Royal*, Ave Mohammed V, T/F 663080, 663186, 40 rm, TV lounge, restaurant and bar; the better value **D** *Hotel des Truites*, Ave Mohammed V, T 663002, a small and friendly place with a popular restaurant for 80 and bar; **E** *Hotel Chahrazed*, basic, central. **Camping**: at *Camping d'Immouzer*, S of town, only in summer, laundry, petrol 2 km.

● **Places to eat** ◆◆ *La Chaumière*, nr the southern exit of the town, with moderately-priced European food; the adjacent *Auberge de Chamotte*. ◆ *Hotel des Truites*, popular, pleasant atmosphere.

Southern Morocco

THE SOUTH OF MOROCCO is quite different from the centre and North, with the arid areas of the Sahara a great attraction to travellers. Morocco has its dunes, near Zagora and Erfoud, but the most beautiful features of the desert are the oases and fertile valleys, with the distinctive earth-built *ksour* and kasbahs, areas of housing clustered together behind impressive but crumbling fortifications. The Draa, Dades and Ziz valleys are memorable areas in which to explore the date palmeries and small villages, whilst the Dades and Todra gorges are striking natural formations, where the rivers descend from the High Atlas. The Sous valley has the historic town of Taroudant at its centre: at its mouth lies the modern city of Agadir, the most popular tourist destination in Morocco noted for its beach and fine weather conditions. To the South of Agadir there are more remote towns, where travelling becomes harder. The Western Sahara has been incorporated within Morocco, but resistance from the Independence movement Polisario continues around its borders with Algeria and Mauritania. At the moment it is still relatively undeveloped for tourists.

AGADIR AND ENVIRONS

AGADIR

(*Pop* 110,479 (1982); *Alt* 20m) The city of Agadir, lying on the Atlantic coast at the mouth of the Sous valley, takes the largest number of tourists in Morocco, and has perhaps the best facilities for them, with a vast number of hotels. Agadir has a vast expanse of sand stretching around the bay, and excellent weather conditions which enable tourists to swim and sunbathe for almost all of the year. Many of these tourists are on package holidays, based in whole or part in one of the larger hotels. Agadir is also an excellent entry

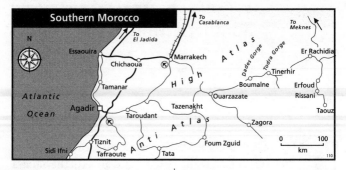

Southern Morocco

point to Morocco, with regular flights arriving at its new airport, Al-Massira, and can serve as a good base for exploring nearby regions, the Sous valley, the Sahara, the Atlantic coast, the Anti Atlas and High Atlas mountain ranges. Whilst the city has the relaxed air of beach resort, it has perhaps little which is distinctively 'Moroccan', as the old settlement was almost totally destroyed in the earthquake of 1960, and has been rebuilt and developed around its tourist potential, in the image of a European resort. There are not many places to visit in the city, nor is it a good place to shop, but the onward connections are good, particularly by bus from Agadir or nearby Inezgane.

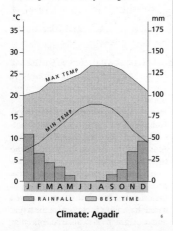

Climate: Agadir

History
Agadir under the Portuguese and Saadians The name Agadir, a shortened form in this case of Agadir n Irir, refers to the Berber word meaning 'a fortified granary'. Agadir was occupied by the Portuguese who built a fort on the site in 1503 which was known as Santa Cruz de Aguer. The Berber tribes of the Sous valley carried out a *jihad*, or holy war, against the colony, and the Saadian Emir of the Sous, Mohammed Echeikh El Mehdi, captured it in 1541, pre-empting the Portuguese departure from most of their Atlantic strongholds. His son, Moulay Abdellah El Ahalib, built the kasbah on the hill overlooking the city, the ruins of which still stand. With the development by the Saadians of the agricultural potential of the Sous valley, Agadir became an important trading centre in the 17th and 18th centuries, exporting sugar cane, olive oil, gold and spices, both from the immediate hinterland of the Sous valley, and further afield from the Sahara. However Agadir declined during the reign of Sidi Mohammed Ibn Abdellah, who preferred to develop Essaouira, to the N, and closed down Agadir's port.

Agadir in the 20th century In 1911 an incident occurred offshore, when a German gunboat appeared 'to protect German interests', in spite of the 1906 Algeciras treaty. This crisis was settled by negotiations between the French and Germans, recognizing France's rights in

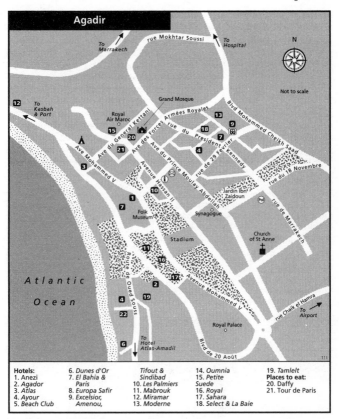

Agadir

To Marrakech

rue Mokhtar Soussi

To Hospital

N

Not to scale

To Kasbah & Port

Grand Mosque

Royal Air Maroc

Blvd Mohammed Cheikh Saad

Ave des Forces Armées Royales

rue du President Kennedy

Ave du General Kettani

Ave Mohammed V

Ave du Prince Moulay Abdellah

rue de 29 Février

rue du 18 Novembre

Avenue Hassan II

Route de Oued Souss

Jardin Ibn Zaidoun

rue de Marrakech

Atlantic Ocean

Folk Museum

Synagogue

Stadium

Church of St Anne

Avenue Mohammed V

rue Chaik el Hamra

To Airport

Royal Palace

To Hotel Atlas-Amadil

Blvd de 20 Août

Hotels:	6. *Dunes d'Or*	*Tifout &*	14. *Oumnia*	19. *Tamlelt*
1. *Anezi*	7. *El Bahia &*	*Sindibad*	15. *Petite*	**Places to eat:**
2. *Agador*	*Paris*	10. *Les Palmiers*	*Suede*	20. *Daffy*
3. *Atlas*	8. *Europa Safir*	11. *Mabrouk*	16. *Royal*	21. *Tour de Paris*
4. *Ayour*	9. *Excelsior,*	12. *Miramar*	17. *Sahara*	
5. *Beach Club*	*Amenou,*	13. *Moderne*	18. *Select & La Baie*	

Morocco, in exchange for territorial concessions in the Congo. The French occupied Agadir in 1913. They constructed the port in 1914, and enlarged it in 1930 and 1953. The town was completely destroyed by the earthquake of February 29 1960. The town was totally rebuilt to the S, planned on a Western influenced layout as a major tourist resort, with distinct functional zones separated by green swathes, with the large hotels kept well apart from the local population. The ruined kasbah was encased in concrete and engraved in the wall are some words by Mohammed V,

commemorating the dead which say, "If destiny desired the destruction of Agadir, its reconstruction depends on our faith and our determination." More obvious, above the kasbah, are the three large Arabic words translated as "God, Country, King". Much of the architecture of the city has the characteristic functional blocks of the period, with little influence of Moroccan design, except in the token embellishment of more recent constructions. The port which escaped total destruction was developed as the base for a large fishing fleet and as the centre of an industrial zone. The city has grown rapidly in size, population and prosperity.

ACCESS Air Agadir Al Massira Aéroport, T 839002, is 28 km from the city. The airport bus to Inezgane (MD3) then a local bus or grand-taxi (MD3) to Agadir, which will drop you off at Place Salam where a petit-taxi can be hired. A taxi from the airport costs MD150, be warned. **Road** From Rabat, Casablanca, El Jadida and Essaouira entrance to Agadir is via the P8, leading into Ave Mohammed V; from Marrakech and the P40 turn left along Blvd Mohammed Cheikh Saadi into the town centre; from the airport and Inezgane, and beyond along the P32 to Taroudant or the P30 to Tiznit and the S, one enters along either Ave Hassan II or Ave Mohammed V. **Bus**: there are ONCF buses from Marrakech, connecting with the trains from Rabat and Casablanca, which arrive on rue Ya'qub al-Mansur just off Place Lahcen Tamri, as do CTM and private line services. Some buses, however, go to Inezgane, connected to Agadir by Bus No 5, Bus No 6 or a grand-taxi.

Places of interest

Although Agadir is a new town its places of interest are not to be underestimated. The **beach** is Agadir's main asset, an excellent strip of sand and enjoyable swimming. It is clean and well provided with cafés. The beaches in front of the hotels are patrolled by 'guardians' who keep the sellers of glass beads, oranges, carpets and camel rides at a distance. On the more public beaches there is unfortunately no protection from the constant interruptions to your sunbathing as the sellers are very determined to be noticed and very thick skinned. This is a problem that those encouraging tourism have not yet solved. From the city centre walk down Ave du Prince Heritier Sidi Mohammed, turn right along Ave Mohammed V, and then left down to Blvd du 20 Août, which runs parallel to the beach.

The Port To get to the port take a petit-taxi for MD6, or Bus No 1 or walk along from the beach. The main reason for visiting, beyond any curiosity in Moroccan industry, is to sample the wares on offer at the small and excellent fish restaurants to the right of the port's entrance.

The Kasbah was built in 1540 to launch an attack on the Portuguese city, and was retained after the victory as a fortification against local insurrection. Whilst ruined by the 1960 earthquake, the ramparts and entrance way have been maintained in a reasonable condition, as Agadir's one historic site. The kasbah, which has a good view over Agadir, used to be a densely populated area, but was not resettled after 1960. It is reached by a winding road to the N of the centre, off Ave Mohammed V.

Architecturally the city is far from memorable, except for the marginal appeal of the modern **Grand Mosque**, on Ave des Forces Armées Royales, and the particularly ugly post office and shopping centre on either side of Ave du Prince Heritier Sidi Mohammed. Off Ave du Prince Moulay Abdellah is the dull **Jardin Ibn Zaidoun**. **The Folk Museum** (open 0930-1300 and 1430-1800), opposite the *Hotel Salam*, has a small but interesting display of local handicrafts from S Morocco, as well as occasional visiting displays. **La Vallée des Oiseaux**, lying between Ave Mohammed V and Blvd du 20 Août is a pleasant place to wander and listen to bird song.

Local information

Price guide

Hotels:			
AL	over US$75	D	US$20-40
A	US$75	E	US$10-20
B	US$60-75	F	under US$10
C	US$40-60		

Places to eat:			
♦♦♦	expensive	♦♦	average
♦	cheap		

● **Accommodation**

Any hotel on the two main avenues of Mohammed V and Hassan II has a problem of traffic noise, and the ordinary folk of Agadir go to work very early!

AL *Hotel Atlas-Amadil*, Route de l'Oued

Sous, T 840620, F 823663, 322 rm, beside the beach but further from the town centre, a reliable place, 3 restaurants, a wine bar, 2 bars, a coffee shop, nightclub, hairdresser, laundry, library, pool, tennis; **AL** *Europa Hotel Safir*, Blvd du 20 Août, T 821212, F 823435, 221 rm, Moroccan-influenced design and decor, 3 restaurants, 2 bars, business centre, art gallery, tennis, pool; **AL** *Hotel al Madina Palace*, Blvd de 20 Août, facing the sea, 165 rm and 40 suite with a/c, direct telephone, TV, heated pool, sauna, conference facilities, 3 restaurants, bar by pool, 24-hr room service; **AL** *Sheraton Hotel*, Ave Mohammed V, T 843232, F 844379.

A *Adrar*, Ave Mohammed V, T 840417, 174 rm, another package tour hotel, but the food is excellent even if it is crowded round the pool, useful rear access to beach area; **A** *Anezi*, Ave Mohammed V, T 840940, good position, 254 rm, terrace, gardens, pool, *hammam*, usual problems of road noise but cheerful, helpful staff a compensation here; **A** *Club PLM Dunes d'Or*, on beach, T 840150, Tx 81827, 450 rm, price incl all activities, famous tennis courts which host professional events, sauna, *hammam*, gym, horse riding, volleyball and basketball, 2 pools, 5 restaurants, 6 bars and a nightclub, constant activity, not the place for a rest; **A** *Hotel Sahara Agadir*, Ave Mohammed V, T 840660, F 840738, popular and luxuriously equipped with 300 pleasant rm, 4 restaurants, 2 bars, nightclub, hairdresser, sauna, *hammam*, tennis, horse riding and volleyball, children's and adult's pools; **A** *Sud Bahia*, rue Administration Public, T 841809, 246 rm with a/c, bath and phone, good restaurant, pool heated in winter, a short walk to the beach; **A** *Hotel Tamlelt-Agador*, Quartier des Dunes d'Or, T 841525, 659 rm, this complex links 2 hotels, the *Tamlelt* inspired by Moroccan medinas, the *Agador* by the kasbahs, luxurious establishment, large gardens, numerous fountains, 4 restaurants, a nightclub, hairdresser, several bars, 4 pools, not suitable for disabled; **A** *Transatlantique*, Ave Mohammed V, T 842083, F 842076, 208 rm with a/c, TV, some bargaining can be done here if the package tours have not taken all the places, friendly atmosphere despite the size, note our comment about traffic noise.

B *Agadir Beach Club*, T 840791, F 825763, 374 rm, luxurious rooms, nightclub, 2 bars, nightclub, laundry, hairdresser, tennis, magnificent pool; **B** *Aladin*, rue de la Jeunesse,

T 843228, F 846071, comfortable, small pool, serves a good breakfast; **B** *Hotel Club Salam*, T 840840, F 841834, on Ave Mohammed V, right in the centre of town and the best beaches, 50 bungalows and 150 double rm, restaurant for international and Moroccan dishes, serves an excellent breakfast, buffet bar at pool, visitor's comment: "This hotel needs to 'get a grip', even the curtains didn't fit the windows"; **B** *Hotel Jamal*, junction of Ave Hassan II and Ave General Kettani, T 842346, F 844367, 36 rm, restaurant, bar, rooftop terrace, small pool, lounge, off-street parking, used by tour groups but a long walk to the beach; **B** *Hotel Oasis*, just off Ave Mohammed V, T 843313-6, F 842260, excellent view, 132 rm, 2 restaurants, 2 bars, pool, sauna, *hammam*, nightclub, tennis and golf; **B** *Talborjt*, rue de l'Entraide, T 841832, pleasant garden setting.

C *Atlantic Ave Hassan II*, T 843661, clean, comfortable and cool courtyard for outside meals; **C** *Hotel Atlas*, Ave Mohammed V, T 843232, F 844379, 156 rm, and bungalows amidst the gardens, a rec and reasonably priced option, 2 restaurants, tennis, pool, nightclub; **C** *Karam*, rue de la Foire, T 844249; **C** *Hotel Oumnia*, Quartier des Dunes, T 823351, close to the beach, well-equipped and friendly; **C** *Palmiers*, Ave Sidi Mohammed, T 843719, rec at this price range.

D *Aït La'ayoun*, rue Yacoub El Mansour, T 824375, popular at this price range and can be fully booked, plenty of hot water, reports of unclean rooms, bus stop outside reduces chances of a good sleep; **D** *Hotel Ayour*, 4 rue de l'Entraide, T 824976, modern, comfortable, pool; **D** *Hotel Itrane*, 23 rue de l'Entraide, T 821407; **D** *Hotel Mabrouk*, Blvd du 20 Août, T 840606, 40 rm, nearer town centre, reasonable place, pool and bar; **D** *Hotel Miramar*, Ave Mohammed V, T 840770, a pleasant, quiet place nr the port, reasonable restaurant; **D** *Hotel Royal*, Ave Mohammed V, T 840675, 73 rm/bungalows amidst pleasant gardens, with bar, restaurant and pool; **D** *Hotel Sindibad*, Place Lahcen Tamri, T 823477, small and popular place on a busy square with bar and adjoining restaurant, even phone in rooms.

E *Hotel De La Baie*, rue Allal Ben Abdellah, T 823014, reasonable and convenient; **E** *Hotel El Bahia*, rue El Mehdi Ibn Toumert, T 822724, 823954, breakfast available, the traveller hang-out, very friendly, recently renovated with spotless, well-equipped rooms;

E *Hotel Excelsior*, rue Ya'qub El Mansur, T 821028, nr the bus station but otherwise not brilliant and rather noisy, hot communal showers; **E** *Hotel Moderne*, rue El Mehdi Ibn Toumert, T 823373, quite good and quiet; **E** *Hotel Paris*, Ave Kennedy, T 822694, fairly clean, quiet, recently redecorated, rooms round a cool courtyard, shared hot showers; **E** *Hotel Petite Suede*, Ave Hassan II, T 840779, 840057, a friendly place with reasonably priced and comfortable rooms.

F *Diaf*, rue Allal ben Abdellah, T 825852, adequate, hot water supply unreliable; **F** *Hotel Select*, behind *Restaurant Salam*, rue Allal Ben Abdellah, shower outside, reasonable and convenient; **F** *Hotel Tour Eiffel*, rue Allal Ben Abdellah, small and simple; *Hotel Amenou*, 1 rue Ya'qub al Manour, T 823026, clean and welcoming; *Hotel Tifawt*, rue Ya'qub al-Mansur, T 824375, quite basic.

Cheaper accommodation can be found at: *Anezi*, Ave Mohammed V, T 840940; *Nejma*, Ave des Forces Armeés Royales, T 841975 and *Yasmine*, rue de la Jeunesse, T 842565.

Camping: *Camping Caravaning International d'Agadir*, Blvd Mohammed V, T 840374, a well-equipped and reasonably priced place nr the centre, with showers, site of 3½ ha only 300m from beach, pool, laundry, first aid, snack bar, restaurant, grocery shop, shade but no grass, electricity for caravans, petrol only 500m, bus to railway station and airport, very crowded in summer; *Camping Taghazout*, Km 12, N of town on road to Essaouira, also full in summer.

● **Places to eat**

◆◆◆ *La Tour de Paris*, Ave Hassan II, T 840906, closed Sat, reservations advised, an elegant restaurant in the town centre with *nouvelle cuisine* and traditional French dishes, the large outside terrace is ideal for watching the crowds go by, 4-course tourist menu MD170, all main dishes MD80-90; the *Golden Gate*, Blvd du 20 Août, T 840820, 2 restaurants with excellent fish dishes, especially the turbot, bar, live music, but too few customers makes this a place with little atmosphere, main dishes MD95-110.

◆◆ *Restaurant Daffy*, rue des Oranges, set menus, incl good value *mechoui*, *pastilla* and *tangia* specialities; *Restaurant Copenhagen*, Prince Moulay Abdellah, Danish food in Agadir may be bizarre but this is the place for it; *Restaurant Marine Heim*, Ave Mohammed V,

T 840731, excellent German food and drink centred around fish, friendly and efficient; *Via Veneto*, Ave Hassan II, T 841467, high quality European food and a very popular place, reservations advised; *Restaurant la Tonkinoise*, Ave du Prince Heritier Sidi Mohammed, reasonable Chinese food; the *Miramar*, Italian food; *Le Jardin d'Eau*, Blvd du 20 Août, T 840195, very good French food and Moroccan dishes, particularly the lamb *mechoui*, reasonable prices; *Darkhoum Restaurant Marocain*, Ave du General Kettani, T 840622, reservations advised, below the *Hotel Sud Bahia*, Moroccan decor, food and music; *Restaurant du Port*, T 843708, a seafood restaurant by the port with mixed reports; *Pizzeria Annamunda*, Ave du Prince Heritier Sidi Mohammed, music and Italian food.

◆The *Resto Poissons* restaurants by the port have cheap and excellent fresh fish, open 1230-2030, standards and reasonable prices maintained through hectic competition. Take a petit-taxi there for MD5, or Bus No 1; in another good area try *Restaurant Sindibad*; *Restaurant Mille et Une Nuits*, N end of rue 29 de Fevrier, which has good Moroccan main courses and salads; *Restaurant Chabib*, rec for a cheap *tagine*; or *Restaurant Coq d'Or*, all on Place Lahcen Tamri; nearby there are 2 good fish restaurants on rue du 29 Février; and the satisfactory *Café-Restaurant Select*, in *Hotel Select* on rue Allal Ben Abdellah; *Chez Redy*, Ave du Prince Heritier Sidi Mohammed, has standard fare, lots of alcohol and a lively atmosphere.

Cafés: *Oufella's*, rue Allal Ben Abdellah adjacent to *Hotel Select*, is a *pâtisserie* with a good selection of cakes, sweets and drinks.

● **Bars**

Try *Corniche Restaurant Bar*, by the beach, with bands each night.

● **Banks & money changers**

ABM, Ave Prince Heritier Sidi Mohammed, T 841567; **Banque du Maroc**, Ave du General Kettani, T 840172; **BCM**, rue des Administrations Publiques, T 840808; **BMAO**, Ave Hassan II, T 820425; **SGMB**, Ave du General Kettani, T 840281; **SMDC**, Ave Al Mouquaouma, T 821676; **Wafabank**, 43 Ave du General Kettani, T 840496.

American Express: Voyages Schwartz, Ave Hassan II, T 822894.

● **Beaches**

The N end of the beach is quieter than the

centre or S where hotels increasingly dominate the skyline. The busier areas have more amenities – sunbed hire, camel rides! and watersports and also more hassle.

Sunbed hire around MD20-30/day, incl toilet/shower facilities where available. Most of the private sunbed hire units have snack bars and restaurants.

● **Embassies & consulates**
Belgium, Holidays Services, Ave Hassan II, T 824080; **Finland**, Good Year, Ave Hassan II, T 823821; **France**, Blvd Mohammed Saadi, T 840826; **Italy**, rue de Souvenir, T 843093; **Spain**, rue Ibn Batouta, T 822126; **Sweden**, rue de l'Entraide, T 823048; **UK**, rue des Administrations Publiques, T 827741.

● **Entertainment**
Cinemas: this is good and inexpensive entertainment, MD4 for a cheap seat and MD6 in the balcony. Try *Cinema Sahara*, opp *Restaurant Sindibad* at N end of Ave 29 Feb; *Cinema Salam*, Ave Hassan II, going S beyond the stadium, nr *Hotel les Cinq Parties du Monde* or *Cinema Rialto*, nr the municipal market.

Discos & nightclubs: are plentiful in the large hotels but they are of variable quality, try the *Tan Tan*, at the *Hotel Almohades*, Blvd 20 Août, T 840233, 840096; the *Byblos*, at the *Club PLM Dunes d'Or*, on the beach front, T 820150 (open 2130-0500), admission MD60, popular and the drinks are reasonable; *Black Jack Disco*, at the *Hotel Agador*, T 841525 (open 2130-0500), admission MD60.

Excursions: *Sahara Tours*, Ave General Kettani, T 840634, 840421, organize a range of excursions outside Agadir starting at MD130, incl visits to Taroudant, Marrakech, Tafraoute and Essaouira, usually incl at least one meal. Other agents in the same building also organize trips to Immouzer des Ida Outanane, Tata and Akka, and imine.

Folklore: *Sahara Tours*, Ave du General Kettani, T 840421, 840634, organize evening meal and folklore excursions out of Agadir, better than the tame displays at the Agadir hotels.

Massage: a professional massage is available at *Hotel Anezi*, 25 mins for MD100, enter the hotel and turn right to the relaxation rooms in the massage area and hairdressing area, no booking required, closes at 1900 so go no later than 1800.

● **Hospitals & medical services**
Ambulance: T 15.

Chemists: *Pharmacie*, Municipalité d'Agadir, T 823349, open all night.

Hospital: *Hôpital Hassan II*, Route de Marrakech, T 841477; *Red Cross*, T 821472.

● **Places of worship**
Catholic: *Eglise Saint Anne*, rue de Marrakech, T 822251.

Jewish: *Synagogue Beth-El*, rue Afghanistan.

Muslim: *Mosque Mohammed V*, Ave 29 February; *Mosque Liban*, Sidi Med Talborjt, plus 50 other mosques in the vicinity.

Protestant: *Temple*, 2 rue Chouhada.

Synagogue: *Beth-El*, Ave Moulay Abdellah.

● **Post & telecommunications**
Area code: 08.

Post Office: the PTT is located on the corner of Ave Prince Heritier Sidi Mohammed and Ave du Prince Moulay Abdellah.

● **Shopping**
Handicrafts: Agadir has no shortage of handicrafts for sale, notably from the traders displaying their wares along the paths and roads leading from the big hotels to the beach. The quality of these goods is, however, questionable, and the prices often exorbitant. Similarly, the fixed price shops, around the shopping centre located between Ave du Prince Moulay Abdellah and Ave Hassan II, and along Ave Sidi Mohammed, are expensive, although their prices are often in fact negotiable. The best display and most reliable, although inflexible, prices, are to be found as with most Moroccan cities, at the *Centre Artisanal Cooperative* in rue du 29 Février.

General: for more general shopping try the Moroccan quarter rather than the expensive tourist quarter. Perhaps the best stock is held by the supermarket *Uniprix*, Ave Hassan II, (open 0830-1230 and 1430-1930), which also does handicrafts. There is a number of good beer and wine shops on Ave Mohammed V, right from Ave du General Kettani. European newspapers can be bought from stalls outside the major hotels and on Ave Hassan II. There is a bookshop, the *Crown English Bookshop*, in the shopping centre off Ave du Prince Moulay Abdellah.

Souq: the best days for Agadir's *souq* are Sat and Sun. It is located on rue Chaïr el Hamra

Mohammed ben Brahim, which is left turn off Ave Mohammed V on the S edge of the city. Agadir's souq is not very impressive in comparison with places such as Taroudant.

Tailor: take this opportunity to have a suit made (male or female) in 48 hrs. Depending on the quality of material and depending on how well you can bargain, prices range from MD1,000-1,400. Try *Chez Najib*, 34 rue Imam Sahili, T 823065.

● **Sports**

Flying: *Agadir Flying Club*, at Agadir Airport.

Golf: at *Royal Club de Golf*, 12 km from Agadir, between Inezgane and Aït Melloul, T 241278, F 844380, green fees MD220 for par 36, 9-hole course and club hire MD160, course recently completely renovated, set in beautiful grounds, snack bar and play area for children, weekends can be very busy; *Club Les Dunes*, more central, on Route d'Inezgane, T 834690, F 834649, green fees MD220 for 9 holes and MD340 for 18 holes, club hire MD160. Set in beautiful landscaped gardens of 107 ha, huge driving range, pitching green with bunkers, pro shop, minimum handicap of 28 for men and 32 for ladies, proper dress required, best to book in advance, caddy compulsory, prices subject to change.

Horse riding: *Royal Club Equestre*, 7 km Route d'Inezgane; *Ranch les Pyramides*, 8 km Route d'Inezgane, experienced riders at 0745 costs MD200, beginners at 0945 also MD200; *Ranch REHA*, 17 km Route d'Essaouira; *Club de l'Etrier*, 5 km Route d'Inezgane, expect to pay MD250 for 2 hrs, bring your own hard hat.

Shooting: Clay pigeon shooting – Quartier Anza.

Surfing: is very popular on this Atlantic coast, but watch the currents. Try location 'Banana' 12 km N, 'Mystery' 23 km N and 'Killer' 25 km N.

Swimming: apart from the sea, a pool by the beach front, turn off Ave Mohammed V by the Syndicat d'Initiative.

Tennis: 120 clay courts at *Royal Tennis Club d'Agadir*, Ave Hassan II, T 23395, 23738, 14 courts.

Yachting: *Yacht Motor Club*, Port d'Agadir.

● **Tour companies & travel agents**

Air France, 287 Ave Hassan II, T 842546, 825037; *Atlas Tours*, 50 Ave Hassan II, T 841913; *Atlas Voyages*, rue de l'Hotel de Ville, T 821284; *Comanov Voyages*, 5 bis Ave Mohammed V, T 840669; *Fes Voyages*, 9 rue de la Foire, T 821553; *Globus*, Ave Mohammed V, T 842860; *Menara Tours*, 341 Ave Hassan II, T 821108; *Royal Air Maroc*, Ave du General Kettani, T 840145/840793; *SoussTourisme*, 20 Ave des Forces Armées Royales, T 841386; *Sud Voyages*, Blvd Mohammed V, T 840746; *Wagons-Lits Tourisme*, 26 Ave des Forces Armées Royales, T 823528; *Top Voyages*, Ave Hassan II, T 823394.

● **Tourist offices**

Office du Tourisme, Immeuble A, Place Prince

Beach sports approximate prices (MD)		
Catamaran for 2 people	1 hr rent	250
Catamaran	1 hr lesson	300
Windsurfer	1 hr rent	100
Windsurfer	1 hr lesson	150
Surf board	½ day rent	300
Belly board	1 hr rent	00
Kayak	1 hr rent	100
Water ski	10 mins	130
Water ski	10 x 10 mins	1,200
Jet ski	20 mins	300
Jet ski	10 x 20 mins	2,500
Catamaran	6 x = day training course (check personal insurance)	2,000
Windsurfer	6 x = day training course (check personal insurance)	1,500
Surf board	6 x = day training course (check personal insurance)	1,500

Heritier Sidi Mohammed, T 822894, 841367 (open Mon-Fri 0800-1500 (Jun-Sep), 0800-1200 and 1430-1830 (Sep-Jun); **Syndicat d'Initiative**, Ave Mohammed V, T 840307.

● **Useful addresses**
Fire: T 15.

Garages: Citroên and Peugeot, Sed-Souss, Ave El Mouqaouama, T 820619; **Mitsubishi and Fiat**, Auto-hall, rue de la Foire, T 843973; **Land Rover**, Maghred-A Industrie, Ave Hassan II, T 842386; **Renault and Berliet**, rue Cadi Ayad, T 820707; **Volvo, Mercedes, Fiat** and **Isuzu**, Ata, Ave El Mouqaouama, T 820177.

Police: rue 18 Novembre, T 19.

● **Transport**
Road Bus: ONCF buses, T 841207, leave from rue Ya'qub al Mansur, connecting with the trains at **Marrakech**, departures 0440, 0800, 0930, 1930, 2030. CTM and private line services leave from the same place. There are private line services to **Marrakech** (5 a day), **Casablanca** and **Taroudant** (4 a day), **Essaouira** and **Tiznit** (3 a day), **Safi, Tata, Tan-Tan** and **imine** (2 a day), **Akka, Tafraoute, Rabat, Meknes, Fes, Oujda, Taza** and **Tanger**. Local buses to the airport, **Inezgane** (5 and 6) and **Tarhazoute** (12 and 14) leave from Place Salam.

Local Bus: from Blvd Mohammed Cheik Saadi, No 5 and 6 go to Inezgane, Bus No 1 goes to the port. Place Salam is a good place to pick up services. **Bicycle/motorcycle hire**: there are several individuals hiring bicycles, mopeds and motorbikes from Blvd du 20 Août, but they can often be rather expensive. **Car hire**: Afric Car, Ave Mohammed V, T 840750; **Agadir Voitures**, Immeuble Baraka, rue de Paris, T 22426; **Avis**, Ave Hassan II, T 841755, and at the airport, T 840345; **Budget**, Ave Mohammed V, T 840762; **Hertz**, Bungalow Marhaba, Ave Mohammed V, T 840939, and at the airport, T 839071; **Inter-Rent Europ-car**, Ave Mohammed V, T 840367; **Lotus Cars**, Ave Mohammed V, T 840588; **Tiznit Cars**, Ave Hassan II, T 20998; **Tourist Cars**, Ave Mohammed V; **Week-End Cars**, Ave Mohammed V, T 20567. **Taxis**: Agadir is quite a wide spread city and therefore its plentiful petit-taxis, painted orange, can be useful, particularly to get to the kasbah or the port, insured for 3 passengers, metered, cannot go outside town limits, prices +50% after 2000. Grand-taxis are blue, insured for up to 6 pas-

sengers, operate within town limits and further afield. A taxi from the airport will cost MD100. Grand-taxis leave for various destinations, particularly Inezgane and Taroudant, from Place Salam. Taking a Grand-taxi or bus to/from the airport is more difficult as both methods require a change in Inezgane.

Air Agadir Al Massira Aéroport is 28 km from the city, on the road to Inezgane, T 839003/6. Take a grand-taxi, or as bus from Place Salam. There are 3 flights a day to Casablanca, 2 a day to Marrakech, 6 a week to Laayoune, 2 a week to Tanger and Las Palmas, 1 a week to Dakhla and Ouarzazate, as well as regularly to European cities. The loudspeakers at the airport are impossible to understand. Watch the departure boards with care.

EXCURSION NORTH TO TARHAZOUTE AND IMMOUZER DES IDA OUTANANE

The coast to the N offers the potential for rewarding excursions, and some limited opportunities for staying out of the city. Although this potential is gradually being realized by developers, the area remains idyllic and tranquil, with the **Paradise Beach** and others stretching 30 km to the N of Agadir. To the E the **Paradise Valley** is a beautiful gorge and river basin, dotted with palm trees and waterfalls, leading up into the mountains.

Tarhazoute is the main settlement on this area of the coast, 19 km N of Agadir. The village is being developed with the construction of many homes, but remains a relaxing place to enjoy the superb beach. To get here, catch Bus 12 or 14 from Place Salam in Agadir. It is possible to rent cheap rooms in private houses, normally for a week minimum. The official camp site is to the S, with a café and basic facilities, an official site is nearby. Near the camp site is the best restaurant, *Taoui-Fik*, other cafés are around the village. 6 km to the S of Tarhazoute is Tamrakht, in a banana grove, and a good place to buy them.

Immouzer des Ida Outanane 12 km N of Agadir at Aourire, just before Tamrakht, a road turns off to the right and then forks right again in the village to Immouzer (50 km). This route, which is well metalled but narrow in places, winds steadily upwards through a green steep-sided valley past local traders selling fossils at roadside stalls. After approx 15 km it descends into Paradise Valley, through a beautiful gorge with possibilities of camping, although beware of flooding. Stop on the way at

Café-Restaurant Tafrite, a good restaurant 30 km from the main road. The spectacular scenery continues for the rest of the ascent through hillsides dotted with beehives until at the end of this valley, 61 km from Agadir, at an altitude of 1,160m, is the small market town of Immouzer des Ida Outanane, named after the confederation of Berber tribes in this area. There is a bus from Place Lahcen Tamri in Agadir at 1400. Camping is possible near the

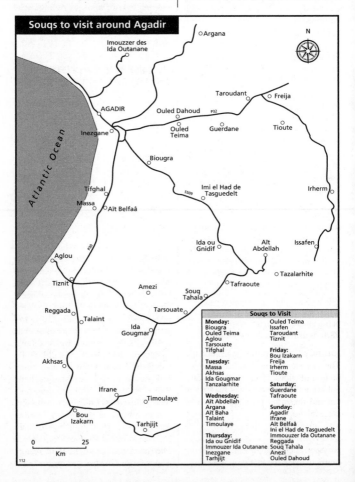

Souqs to visit around Agadir

Atlantic Ocean

Argana
Imouzzer des Ida Outanane
AGADIR
Ouled Dahoud — P32
Taroudant — Freija
Ouled Teima   Guerdane   Tioute
Inezgane
Biougra
Tifghal
Massa — Aït Belfaâ
Imi el Had de Tasguedelt
Irherm
Aglou
Ida ou Gnidif   Aït Abdellah   Issafen
Tiznit   Amezi   Souq Tahala   Tafraoute   Tazalarhite
Reggada   Talaint   Tarsouate
Akhsas   Ida Gougmar
Ifrane   Timoulaye
Bou Izakarn   Tarhjijt

0 — 25
Km

Souqs to Visit

Monday:
Biougra
Ouled Teima
Aglou
Tarsouate
Tifghal

Tuesday:
Massa
Akhsas
Ida Gougmar
Tanzalarhite

Wednesday:
Aït Abdellah
Argana
Aït Baha
Talaint
Timoulaye

Thursday:
Ida ou Gnidif
Immouzer Ida Outanane
Inezgane
Tarhjijt

Ouled Teima
Issafen
Taroudant
Tiznit

Friday:
Bou Izakarn
Freija
Irherm
Tioute

Saturday:
Guerdane
Tafraoute

Sunday:
Agadir
Ifrane
Aït Belfaâ
Ini el Had de Tasguedelt
Immouzer Ida Outanane
Reggada
Souq Tahala
Anezi
Ouled Dahoud

Café de Miel near the foot of the cascades, but the best option is the **C** *Auberge des Cascades*, contact via Agadir agent T 842671, F 821671, a wonderful hotel with 27 rm, terrace or balcony, with bath, excellent food in the restaurant, no TV, bar, tennis, pool lined with pomegranate and pear trees and a delightful, tiered garden full of colourful flowers, fruit and olive trees located in peaceful surroundings above the waterfalls, recently extended with 9 spacious new, well equipped rooms, this hotel has a beautiful geranium flanked terrace shaded by fig trees from which there are wonderful views of the mountains to the W, dinner menu MD169, breakfast MD48, all major CCs and TCs taken, at present bookings have to be made via an agent in Agadir, but a direct phone link is likely soon.

The village, which has a *souq* on Thur, is known for honey production, with a honey festival in May. To reach the foot of these celebrated waterfalls which lie below the village turn left in the main square (signposted) and descend for 4 km past the *Café de Miel* and the *Restaurant Amelon*. This road, although a little rough in places, is driveable with care. Although they have been reduced in volume in recent years, the falls are popular for both sightseeing and bathing. The village is also a good place for bird watching and walking, be it rambles in the immediate surrounds, or more strenuous walks further afield. Make sure you have sufficient petrol for the round trip before leaving the P8 at Aourire.

Journey from Agadir to Essaouira

The 173 km on the P8 route N to Essaouira provides a journey of contrasts, following the coast for about the first 70 km and thereafter travelling some distance inland, often through hills covered with argane trees. Although there are good views back over Agadir beach and port soon after climbing the hill from the centre of town, the first part of the jour-

ney is an otherwise unattractive drive through an industrial area. After 12 km, however, beyond the turning to Immouzer at Aourire, the attractive beaches around Tamrakht come into view, followed by those at Tarhazoute at 19 km. Northwards from here the road often stays close to the shoreline which alternates between outcrops of rock and deserted sandy bays, with some very picturesque views entering and leaving the small settlement of Aghrod. The lighthouse and viewpoint at Cap Rhir is reached after 40 km at a point where the most westerly point of the High Atlas falls over 360m to the sea. There are opportunities for bird watching around a lagoon as the road swings inland along the wide estuary valley of Asif Ait Ameur past the banana plantations to **Tamri**, a small village with a scattering of shops and cafés. There is a last chance for panoramic views of the coast as the road climbs out of Tamri and then descends again towards the left turn at 89 km to the resort and shrine at Point Imessouane and the clifftop viewpoint of **Point d'Igui-n-Tama**. Look, too, for the **Gouffre d'Agadir Imoucha** at Km 77, a ravine over 1 km long cutting into the plateau from the sea; you can find it by walking W across the fields. Soon **Tamanar**, said to be the capital of the argane tree, is reached. This town offers accommodation at a small hotel, *L'Etoile de Sud*, some cafés, including *Café Argan*, a reasonable option for a cheap snack, and an assortment of shops, *tajine* stalls and petrol stations. From here the P8 soon descends to cross the two parts of the Oued Iguezoulen, passing a left turn to Plage Tafadna, and then climbs through many bends around the side of Jbel Amsittene (905m) to the village of Smimou where you will find a few cafés and petrol. Here a road leading E by the side of Jbel Amardma to Souq el Tnine and Sebt des Ait Daoud offers an interesting detour into the mountains of the Haha region. After a further 24 km a turning to the left

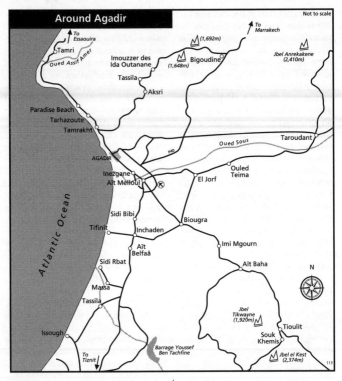

Around Agadir

Not to scale

To Essaouira

To Marrakech

Tamri

Oued Assif Amer

Imouzzer des Ida Outanane

(1,692m)

Bigoudine

(1,648m)

Jbel Anrekakene (2,410m)

Tassila

Aksri

Paradise Beach

Tarhazoute

Tamrakht

Oued Sous

Taroudant

AGADIR

P40

Inezgane

Aït Melloul

El Jorf

Ouled Teima

Atlantic Ocean

Sidi Bibi

Biougra

Tifinit

Inchaden

Imi Mgourn

Aït Belfaâ

Sidi Rbat

Aït Baha

Massa

N

Tassila

Jbel Tikwayne (1,920m)

Tioulit

Issough

Souk Khemis

Barrage Youssef Ben Tachfine

To Tiznit

Jbel el Kest (2,374m)

113

leads you 12 km to the **Marabout of Sidi Kaouki** on the coast. The best route into Essaouira is then via the P8 and P10 main roads; the alternative via Diabat starts promisingly enough but then degenerates into a poor quality track.

Journey from Agadir to Marrakech (268 km)

This is a very busy road through some very striking country. Shortly after leaving Agadir the road climbs to begin the long journey across the western extension of the High Atlas. This is the northernmost region in which the argane tree survives. Argane oil is sometimes being offered for sale at the roadside. Its keeping properties are very poor. Here the argane trees and the browsing goats are common but once N of the village of Argane these trees disappear to be replaced by juniper. The Tizi Maachou pass, 1,700m, is not as spectacular as those to the E but has the advantage of being open to traffic all the year when the others are closed due to snowdrifts. Imi-n-Tanoute is an administrative centre, market Mon, where the 'short cut' to Marrakech leaves in a NE direction.

Journey from Agadir to Tafraoute

This follows the S509 and is a distance of almost 170 km. While the best way is to drive oneself with freedom to stop and photograph there are frequent louages and service buses no 8 and 13 cover this route. **El Kolea**, a dirty and dusty settlement, has all the necessary services.

Despite the grime this is popular with Moroccans from Agadir. It is said the water from the central fountain has curative properties and is taken home by these visitors. By contrast **Biougra** is neat and clean with trees set into the tiled pavement along the central dual carriageway. Between the two settlements the busy road winds across an almost level plain through agricultural land which produces citrus or vegetables under plastic. Eucalyptus trees line much of the route.

From here the land slowly rises up, gently undulating, lots of cereals and poorer areas for grazing and argane, very little farming under plastic. Workings in the huge limestone quarry on the left throw white clouds across the land. Beyond **Imi Mgourn** the first foothills are encountered and the road rises up with good views towards **Aït Baha**, but there is nowhere to pull off safely to admire the view. The first of the fortified settlements are up here. Driving requires great concentration as large stretches of this narrow winding road are being repaired or certainly need repair after damage by heavy rain and neglect. At least with these conditions it won't be suitable for use by tour coaches – don't you believe it!

At Aït Baha, the usual just adequate services, *souq* on Wed, 92 km still to go to Tafraoute, there is a road S to Tanalt. This makes an interesting detour of 100 km, the first 64 km being surfaced. There are three villages of note and an opportunity to strike N into the massif just before Aougounz. From Tanalt to Tioulit the scenery is very attractive but the track is exceedingly rough so don't begin what you cannot finish.

In Aït Baha the hotels are basic with communal wash basins, squat WC, and no showers. Pay about MD50 per rm at **Tafraoute** and MD35 at **El Massira**. Both are on Blvd Mohammed V. The former may have nicer rms but the latter is slightly cleaner. Most cafés/restau-

rants are on the main street and serve food which is adequate but not special. There are 2 buses a day to Agadir departing at 0600 and 1800, MD12, take 1½ hrs. A Grand-taxi to Agadir will cost MD15. Taxis also to Tanalt.

There are one or two small villages on the main route such as **Hadz Aït Mezzal** and many abandoned villages high up the slope with the new village much lower now that conditions are safer. As the road swings over the cols there are good views. Here is the time to consider a stop for a drink. Look out now for *Café du Moulin*, *Café Imhiln* and *Café Aïn Alla* all around 60 km from Tafraoute and if you miss these *Café Madou* in **Aguerdn'tzek**, right in the centre of village where most of the tourists stop. Shortly beyond **Tioulit** (note the *agadir* which can be visited) is a sign off S to Souq Khemis Ida ou Gnidif. Take this short detour, only 4 km, if you don't intend to come this way again. The Thur *souq* is very traditional and the visiting country folk most colourful. Try the bread if opportunity allows. Other days it is very quiet. Returning to the main road there will be time to admire the quite unusual landforms where the strata is at an angle of $45°$, the ochre mosque in Sidi M'Zar and the circular threshing places before the junction of road and then track to Igherm appears on the left. The road then sweeps down into the **Ameln Valley**. For details of the Ameln valley, see page 396, for information about Tafraoute, see page 396.

Journey from Agadir to Tiznit

Follow the signs from Agadir towards the airport, 20 mins on a quiet day, then take the P30 S to Tiznit. This is a good straight and fast road through rich agricultural land with plenty of places for petrol and coffee. Bus no 14 also follows this route. Tifnite to the W is a beach resort.

Sidi Rbat and **Massa** are signed on the right at 46 km from Agadir. Follow the 7128 W across the flat coastal plain

Old crafts and contemporary kitsch

In contrast to other Arab countries, traditional craft industries in Morocco have survived and continue to flourish today. Across the Middle East during the 19th century the craft guilds went into sharp decline as imported manufactured goods became readily available with the development of industry and shipping in Europe.

In Morocco, Resident General Lyautey made respect of traditional crafts a priority. Well aware of the enormous damage done in neighbouring Algeria, Lyautey wanted to preserve the artistic heritage of Morocco. As of 1913 any new building which might have an effect on the appearance of Morocco's historic cities had to be approved by the Residence's Fine Arts Department. Craft specialists were recruited from Europe, among them Prosper Ricard, the author of a monumental study on Moroccan carpets. The Fine Arts Department collected examples of old carpets and in 1919 official standards were established, helping traditional carpets to compete with cheaper machine made copies. Similar detailed studies were done on ceramics and leather work, embroidery and jewellery. Researchers patiently catalogued both the city crafts, generally based in the specialized souqs and workshops and to a certain extent open to outside influences and domestic rural production (weaving, basket making and pottery), the work of women during the quiet times of the agricultural year.

Moroccan craftwork had pride of place in numerous French colonial exhibitions, a version of the 'Empire made' policy being promoted. Museums were opened to display the best examples of craftwork – notably the craft museum at the Kasbah des Oudaias in Rabat (see page 100) which was set up by Prosper Ricard and Dar Batha in Fes (see page 270). The craft preservation policy, despite being imbued with a strong sense of paternalism, maintained and even stimulated traditional skills.

aiming for the small protective hills at the coast. The large and still spreading agricultural settlement of Sidi Ouassi looks very prosperous and this connecting road is very busy – service bus No 1 and many louages. Take the right turn marked to Sidi Rbat with a deep *oued* to the right hand. The road surface stops very suddenly after 3 km becoming more holes than surface but this does not deter the louages or the bus. It is a most pleasant ride, apart from the bumps (probably quicker to walk), along the side of the Oued Massa way below to the left for the last 5 km to the mouth and the Oued Massa Nature Reserve. There is also access at the next junction S via the 7128 to Tassila where one turns right to Sidi Ouassi.

As the water of the Oued Massa is held back by large sandbanks a lagoon has formed. This water, the vast reed beds it supports, the massive fringing dunes to the SW, the sandbanks at the mouth and in the water course and the mud banks to the N provide a selection of habitats making this a very interesting and important area for both bird and land animals. The P30 S from Agadir gives access. The best times to visit are between Feb and Apr and between Sep and Nov. There are birds over-wintering here but in summer it is very quiet. The estuary is home (temporary or permanent) to crane, avocet, spoonbill, great flamingo, osprey, and night, squacco and purple heron. Coots make up the greatest numbers. One of the few surviving groups of the endangered bald ibis (*Geronticus eremita*) live here. Certainly not an attractive creature but not deserving to be hunted almost to extinction. Oued Massa is the most southerly location for the pochard, the male's dark red

The work of the artisan is often said to lack creativity and be repetitive, a mere reproducing of ancestral models. Yet a variety of influences are visible in Moroccan crafts. The blue and white pottery of Fes has clear design links with Chinese porcelain brought to Morocco by Dutch and English merchants, while embroidery motifs can be traced back to Andalucía and the Balkans. Craftwork has been a source of inspiration for contemporary Moroccan artists such as Férid Belkahia whose geometric motifs on stretched skins and wood recall Touareg designs.

Tastes have changed, the balance between shape and utility is shifting, under the pressure of tourist demand and changes in local taste itself where the plastic container and machine woven carpet are considered to be 'modern'. *Savoir faire* is difficult to hand down to school educated children and what were once highly functional objects are reduced to the status of 'traditional items'. Nevertheless, as the work of a number of contemporary Moroccan designers shows, the old techniques are still there. See the work of Marrakech designer Med Hjlani. Modern plastics have made their appearance in traditional basket work, metal waste is recycled in handsome lanterns and table lamps while old perfume bottles are sheathed in delicate metal arabesques.

Although for many, artificial flowers and gilt wall clocks mean 'we are city dwellers' there is an increasing interest in the craft heritage. In family villas in Casablanca or Rabat, inherited *déniajates* (embroideries) and ceramics are displayed with pride in a contemporary setting. A red Ribati carpet is the essential floor covering for the *salon marocain* – the living room in the modern Moroccan home. Generations of artisans (and Prosper Ricard) would be happy to see their work still so much in demand.

head so familiar in northern Europe. Several kinds of raptor are attracted by the populations of birds including small groups of ospreys calling in or over-wintering. This National Park also offers shelter to a selection of mammals and reptiles. A week's excursion can be organized from MD2,000, see Nature Trek and Sunbird Tours in Information for travellers (page 476).

Detour to Barrage of Youssef Ben Tachfine

Turn E to the barrage which holds back the water of the Oued Massa, clearly signed, on a smooth surfaced road, which cuts through a plain of quality wheat with some argane on the higher slopes. An old *agadir* stands deserted high up on the right with the new village lower by the road. The route goes over the actual dam wall, with lovely views in all directions.

This is another good area for bird watching but don't block the road. Instead take the track which goes left just beyond the dam wall. The main road continues SW to Tiznit through Souk el Arba des Ersmouka back to the P30, again through cereal country. Information about Tiznit is found on page 392.

Journey from Agadir to Taroudant

The buses No 11 and 20 from Inezgane cover this route. This is an interesting 73 km which improves as it continues. The initial part is very built up other than the incongruous sight of dromedaries grazing adjacent to the Agadir bypass. The first signs of farming, some fields of cereals, appear at 10 km from Agadir and the first of the many plastic greenhouses at 13 km from Agadir. Whatever the time of day traffic is very

Islamic and vernacular architecture in Southern Morocco

Small towns such as Taroudant, tucked away in the middle Sous valley, display a marvellous variety of architectural features. On the surface the buildings seem to visitors to be uniformly 'Islamic', with a scattering of minarets, high-walled houses, narrow streets and clattering lock-up workshops.

In reality the towns and villages contain at least four elements – local, universal Islamic, French colonial and contemporary characteristics all welded together, sometimes in quite unsuitable ways. Note the off-the-peg school houses in each village which are partly prefabricated and absolutely uncompromising in their modernity against the adjacent roughcast village buildings.

Elsewhere the grafting of new onto old building styles has been less confrontational. In Taroudant the new mosque on the eastern edge of the town illustrates good neighbourliness in an architectural sense. The mosque was begun in 1986 and completed in the mid-1990s latterly using private funds after the government budget failed to provide sufficient financial resources for completion of the project. The new mosque will be rather bigger than the old jama' kebir (Great Mosque) and is clearly modern in shape, with concrete, steel and block construction, but has incorporated into it a deal of traditional ornate plaster work. There is also a wealth of green tilework on the roof and all the arches are designed to conform to the local pointed configuration. It is worth a visit (from the outside only!) to see how modern materials can be successfully used in a traditional design.

In the town of Taroudant many of the buildings which seem to be local date in fact from the colonial period and by detail of foundations, materials and style are more French than Moroccan except for the imposition of Moroccan taste and usage. Look out for the wall-top corner palm tree decorations and painted marks on the front surfaces. Moroccans love to use coloured glass in house windows with geometric designs and green tilework on doorways and windows is another expression of local taste.

In Taroudant visit the *Hotel Palais Salam*, which incorporates a wonderful mixture of southern Moroccan features – multiple split level accommodation, geometric window screens, balconies, salons and ancient and contemporary water features – all for the price of a cup of coffee!

slow, in both directions, giving an opportunity to see what is going on, peer down the side streets and admire the bright garments of the women. This is a 60 km per hour area but one is very unlikely to reach this speed. Traffic crawls through **Temsi** but clears at **El Jorf** and speed restriction ceases. In season the sweet smell of orange blossom is very strong and the road is lined with bright wild flowers. The first argane trees are spotted to the E of El Jorf with thin cereals underneath. **Ouled Dahoud** is an attractive town, pink and ochre buildings, blue doors with white edgings. The covered market (Sun) lies to the S of the road, the stalls covered against the later heat of the day. Some attempts have been made here to replant the once distinctive eucalyptus trees which lined the road. **Ouled Teïma** is a large town at a busy cross road, junctions to N and S. The new tall buildings, mainly 4-storey with lock-up shops beneath line the main street. All is neat and tidy with places clearly marked, market, various ministries, hospital etc. Again the ladies' outer garments are extremely colourful. Market day (Mon) attracts a strange mixture of people. Major agricultural products in season are oranges and potatoes. Not surprisingly the whole area seems to be devoted to citrus fruit. Right until mid-summer the High Atlas to the N have a covering of snow, such a contrast to the dry plain. Beyond Ouled Teïma the plain of the Oued Sous, one of Morocco's most productive regions, lies ahead.

INEZGANE

Inezgane (*Pop* 17,592 (1982)) lies 13 km S of Agadir and is almost a suburb of it now. It is primarily a transport hub, very busy every day of the week with taxis, local buses and coaches to Casablanca, Rabat, Tiznit, Marrakech, Taroudant (1 hr), Ouarzazate and Laayoune, amongst other places, with far more services than Agadir. This is likely to be the main reason for staying overnight, for there is little of interest in the town, and the buses make it extremely noisy. It is, however, the true Morocco, of streets choked with traffic, sheep on the road, goats grazing, women in bright garments carrying their packages on their heads, men in *jellabahs* in the cafés. All long-distance buses and Grand-taxis stop along the wide, busy main street lined by bus agents, including CTM, small shops and cheap restaurants. At the end of this is the main square, with the local bus stands. Off to the right of the square is a relaxed and mildly interesting covered market, with the main market day on Tues.

Inezgane provides access to the mouth of the Oued Sous, an important place for bird watchers. Out of town going towards the airport there is a track on the left or from the S of the town there is another access. Both lead along the N bank to the coast. This is a busy area so an early start is recommended. The best visiting times are Feb-Apr and Sept-Nov when many varieties of gulls and terns are in residence. The surrounding area has colourful residents which include the black-headed bush shrike, the great grey ahrike, brown-throated sand martin and moussier's redstart.

● **Accommodation** The best hotel lies just outside Inezgane, the **C** *Hotel Club Hacienda*, Route de l'Oued Sous, T 830176, with bar, restaurant, nightclub, tennis, pool and horse riding; also rec is the **D** *Hotel-Restaurant les Pergolas*, T 830841, along the road to Agadir, with 23 rm, a bar and a highly-rec restaurant serving French food; **D** *Hotel Provencal*, nearby, T 831208, 44 rm, bar, restaurant and pool; **D** *Hotel les Pyramides*, Route de l'Oued Sous, T 834705, a quiet place with 20 rm, a pool, restaurant, bar and horse riding; and **D** *Hotel Hagounia*, 9 Ave Mokhtar Sousi, T 830783, with 48 rm with shower and wc, located on the road just before the town centre. Grouped around the main square are nine cheap hotels, preferably choose the **F** *Hotel El Merjane*, which is cheap and clean with communal facilities.

● **Places to eat** There is no shortage of restaurants, but a good inexpensive one is the ◆*Café-Restaurant Bateau de Marrakech*, on the main square. Try ◆*Café/restaurant* adjacent to *Hotel Hagounia* right in the centre for a view of the activity. There are plenty more adjacent to it. Also rec is *Saada* on Blvd Moulay Abdallah opp the stadium.

● **Transport Road** Buses and Grand-taxis are abundant. Bus No 22 to the airport; Nos 5,6 and 7 to Agadir; to Taroudant and Tata (3 a week leaving at 0630), to Laayoune/Dakhla (daily), Tiznit and Goulimine (several daily).

Aït Melloul across the Oued Sous is to be avoided, and this can now be done by using the Agadir bypass. Not only is it dirtier than most Moroccan towns it is also very crowded and the road surface is appalling.

TAROUDANT AND ENVIRONS

TAROUDANT

Taroudant (*Pop* 36,000) is nicknamed by the locals 'grandmother of Marrakech', and indeed it has some of the character of the more famous city, although on a smaller scale and with a far more relaxed air. The small medina is enclosed by impressive red earth walls and is focused on two intimate and friendly squares, in between which lie a range of interesting *souqs* selling handicrafts for which Taroudant is famous. Although without any distinctive monuments, the town is well worth a visit, and after Agadir, feels far more 'Moroccan'. Taroudant is also a good base, with Agadir and the coast to the W, the High Atlas and the Tizi-n-Test pass to the N (see page 330), the Saharan oases of Tata and Akka to the S (page 360), and the routes to Ouarzazate and the Draa, Dades and Ziz valleys to the E (see page 364). It is also well provided with good hotels and restaurants, and has a handicrafts and folklore fair in Apr.

Taroudant has always been a major population and marketing centre of the fertile Sous valley and has played a strategic role, although rarely achieving any national prominence. The town was conquered by the Almoravids in 1056, but under the Almohads had greater independence. From 1510 the Saadians gave greater prominence to Taroudant, when their first leader, Mohammed al Quaim, was based here as Emir of the Sous. Even after the Saadians gained control of Morocco, Taroudant remained for a while their capital. Taroudant supported Moulay Ismail's nephew in his rebellion, and when the Sultan overcame the town in 1687 he extracted his revenge by slaughtering the population and destroying much of the town. Decline set in, which continued into the 18th and 19th centuries. In the early years of the French protector-ate Taroudant harboured the rebel Sultan El Hiba and was consequently sacked by the colonial forces. The French neglected Taroudant after this, and the town now remains little more than a regional market.

ACCESS Buses from Inezgane, Agadir, Marrakech and Ouarzazate deposit their passengers either at Place Talmoklate or Place Assarag. The town is small enough to walk around, although there are petit-taxis, painted light brown, and horse-drawn *calèches*, around the town.

Places of interest

The Souqs in Taroudant are excellent and this is likely to be an easier place to shop or appreciate handicrafts than the central and northern cities, whilst offering more variety than elsewhere S of Marrakech. The busiest days are Thur and Sun, the *souq* days, bringing in people from the villages, but much of it operates during the week. The *souqs* lead off from Place Assarag, beside the bank, and weave across to Place Talmoklate. Notable specialities of Taroudant amongst its excellent handicrafts are jewellery, some of it antique or mock antique, limestone sculptures, and the excellent carpets of the region. There are numerous small stalls to shop at, as well as bigger tourist shops, of these *Ali Baba*, 95 Joutia, T 852435, is friendly. Off the other side of Place Talmoklate is an area of small stalls, notably selling spices, herbs, medicines and pottery.

The Walls and Kasbah The Saadian *pisé* walls interspersed with towers are still intact and are worth following around the town, preferably by *calèche*. They are broken by five gates, at least one of which can be mounted for a view over gardens and olive groves. En route they pass the kasbah, now looking like a more densely-populated and poor area of the town, but in fact it was once a fortress for Moulay Ismail. Outside the walls are the tanneries, left from **Bab el Khemis**, a smelly area understandably located beyond the medina, where skins of a variety of animals are still cured by traditional methods.

Local information
● Accommodation
AL *Hotel la Gazelle d'Or*, Route d'Amezgou, T 852039/48, F 852537, 2 km outside the town, one of the two most luxurious, exclusive and expensive hotels in Morocco, with 30 individual bungalows set amidst beautiful gardens and orange groves, as well as two restaurants, bar, tennis and pool,

C *Hotel Palais Salam*, Route d'Ouarzazate, T 852312, F 852654, 144 rm in a beautiful 18th century palace and bungalows amidst gardens, three restaurants, bar, tennis, pools, car and bicycle hire. We rec this.

D *Hotel Saadiens*, Borj Oumansour/Annasim, T 852589, small and friendly, in the medina with 57 rm, restaurant, bar, tea room, pool, parking.

E *Hotel Taroudant*, Place Assarag, T 852416, old, French run, friendly atmosphere, 37 good rm around a verdant courtyard, with roof-terrace, excellent bar, and a very good restaurant selling reasonably priced and large meals.

F *Hotel de la Place*, Place Talmoklate, cheap, very small rooms, cold water only; **F** *Hotel El Warda*, Place Talmoklate, noisy but cheap;

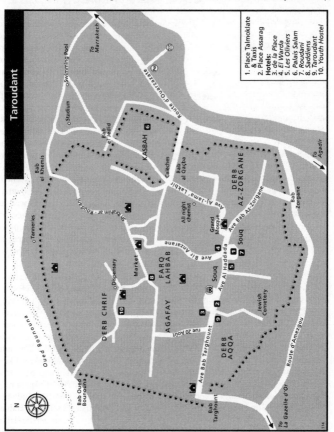

Taroudant

1. Place Talmoklate & Taxis
2. Place Assarag

Hotels:
3. de la Place
4. El Warda
5. Les Oliviers
6. Palais Salam
7. Roudani
8. Saadiens
9. Taroudant
10. Youth Hostel

To Marrakech
Swimming Pool
Stadium
Route d'Ouarzazate
Bab el Rbatis
Bab el Khemis
KASBAH
Bab el Jedid
Caleches
Bab al Qasba
Tanneries
Sh'rahim ar-Rouah
Ave Al-Jama'Labbir
All night chemist
Grand Mosque
Bab Zorgane
DERB AZ-ZORGANE
To Agadir
Dispensary
Market
FARQ LAHBAB
Ave Bir Anzarane
Souq
Souq
Ave Al Haddada
Jewish Cemetery
DERB CHRIF
AGAFAY
rue 20 Aout
Ave Bab Targhount
DERB AQQA
Route d'Amezgou
Oued Boujnoudna
Bab Oued Boujnoudna
Bab Targhount
To La Gazelle d'Or

N

The Moroccan souq

The *souq* or bazaar economy of Morocco, continues successfully to exist in most towns and cities. Why this should be the case when for many years it has been a key part of the economic and political systems within Morocco. Traditional activities in financing trade and social organizations were helped by the bazaar's successful role in running international commodity trade. Since the 1960s there has been little 'modernization' of the Moroccan *souq* by way of adoption of trading practices normal in the industrial societies of the world.

Why do the *souqs* in Morocco flourish? Part of the explanation is straight forward. Moroccan governments, with few exceptions, have left the merchants of the *souq* to run most of their traditional trading operations. Also Morocco's third world economy is much more favourable to the bazaar than modernized economic systems. The bazaar is at the top of the commercial hierarchy in Morocco and so it is to the bazaar that the benefits of economic activities come and thus the bazaar merchants prosper accordingly.

In traditional society, the bazaar is an important source of lending. Islamic cultures demand that the transfer of money is organized in ways that avoid obvious payment of interest. In Morocco standing crops are bought from farmers before harvest or capital is repaid by the delivery of products at harvest time. A variety of other means are used to get round the ban on taking interest from loans. Some forms of lending from the bazaar are far more expensive than direct interest-tied credit from other sources. Non-Muslim bazaar merchants are not of course impeded by the taboo within Islam on taking interest on loans made to third parties. In Morocco the merchants of the *souq* still provide agricultural investment and provide seasonal farm credits.

Bazaar economies thrive best where there are low average incomes, say where purchases are for foodstuffs, traditional clothing/textiles and locally manufactured materials. The link between a strong bazaar and low living standards is seen clearly in Morocco. Morocco has a dynamic *souq* system, assisted by large populations still living in and around the bazaars. Fes, Marrakech, Tanger, Rabat and Meknes are all prime instances of this bazaar-old town strength. Morocco has modest average living standards, with US$900 per head. Once Morocco becomes richer and has mass consumption of 'international' products, the role of the bazaar will weaken since it lacks the space for showrooms and the technical expertise to handle modern goods.

Bazaars survive best when they have long-standing indigenous manufacturing industries based within them. The more individual and highly prized the goods manufactured, the more competitive the individual or national bazaars will be. In Morocco there are leather goods and woollen rugs developed as internationally traded commodities. Also a prosperous tourist industry brings an income estimated at US$800 million each year, of which a proportion, possibly as high as US$250 million, is expended in the purchase of traditional hand-made goods from the country's various *souqs*.

It might be judged by visitors looking into Moroccan society that, economic factors aside, the vibrant bazaar culture, with all its human colour, noise and bustle makes Morocco far richer than those countries which have, in the process of 'modernization', lost their traditional *souqs*.

F *Hotel les Oliviers*, just off Place Talmoklate, clean, only cold water; **F** *Hotel Roudani*, Place Assarag, reasonable, hot water, makes it slightly better than *Hotel de la Place*.

A new field study centre located within the medina with special facilities for vegetarian travellers has private apartments and dormitories. Contact in UK: *Naturally Morocco Ltd*, T/F 01276 233279.

Camping: there is an unofficial area of camping in front of the police station, Route d'Ouarzazate.

● **Places to eat**

◆◆◆ *La Gazelle d'Or*, Route d'Amezgou, T 852039, reservations necessary, one of the best Moroccan restaurants, with a diverse menu incl an excellent pigeon *pastilla* and desserts; *Hotel Palais Salam*, Route d'Ouarzazate, T 852312, reservations rec, for lavish Moroccan cuisine, specialities should be ordered in advance.

◆◆*Hotel Taroudant*, Place Assarag, T 852416, big portions of good French-Moroccan cuisine; *Hotel Roudani*, good Moroccan food; *Hotel Saadiens*, a rec place for reliable Moroccan cuisine.

◆*Restaurant Tout Va Bien*, Place Talmoklate, upstairs, with good prices and food, particularly *couscous*; *Café-Restaurant Dallas*, Place Assarag, is fine and cheap but with dodgy *couscous*; *Restaurant Sindibad*, Place Assarag, is also good; other cheap places are located between the two main squares.

Cafés: in Place Assarag there is a large café with seating on the square, a pleasant place to relax; and several on Place Talmoklate, incl the excellent *Pâtisserie El Ouarda*.

● **Bars**

In *Hotel Taroudant*, Place Assarag, T 852416, a small friendly bar with a good atmosphere and low prices; of another class is the cocktail bar at the *Hotel Palais Salam*, Route d'Ouarzazate, T 852312.

● **Bank & money changers**

Banque Populaire, Place Assarag.

● **Entertainment**

Hammams: there is a *hammam*, nr the *Hotel Taroudant*, another is off Place Assarag opp.

● **Hospitals & medical services**

Doctor: Dr Ahmed Iben Jdid, T 852032 (clinic), T 853626 (home).

● **Sports**

Cycle hire: MD13/hr.

Tennis: *Tennis Roudani*, nr the *Hotel Palais Salam*.

● **Tourist offices**

Syndicat d'Initiative, Maison de Jeune de Téromo.

● **Transport**

Road Bus: bus agencies are located on Place Assarag and Place Talmoklate, although some of the services leave early in the morning. There are regular buses to **Inezgane** (1 hr), and other services to **Ouarzazate** (5 a day, 3 hrs), **Tata** (3 a week), **Casablanca** and **Agadir** (4 a day). A bus leaves for **Marrakech** via the spectacular Tizi-n-Test pass at 0400, taking 9 hrs. There is another service to **Marrakech** via the less impressive route through Agadir. **Taxi**: Grand-taxis are a practical option to Inezgane and Agadir, entailing a change at Ouled Teima.

There is a minor road from Taroudant to Agadir which goes to the N of Oued Sous. At present the surface is very poor and there are roadworks at frequent intervals where necessary repairs are in progress. It is a very busy rural road, lots of intensive farming, lots of cereals, small amounts of plastic, small areas of citrus, and lots of slow moving agricultural machinery. This is not a reasonable alternative to the main P32 but for an insight into the non-touristic part of Morocco, it is fascinating.

NORTH TO JBEL AOULIME AND JBEL TICHKA

The piste to Tanefacht and Souq el Had d'Imoulass starts at the N of the town, winds its way across the *oued* and then strikes N. This is a very rough road but gives access to some splendid walking country fortunately not yet discovered by the safari groups.

This area around Taroudant, once argane forest though now much has disappeared, is an interesting environment. Spring is, as always in Morocco, a good time to visit. The crested lark, a ground nesting bird, is common but being well camouflaged less often noticed. Not so the moussier's redstart, a magnificent cardinal red underside from beak to tip of his tail. Other interesting birds include the stone curlew, the little owl and the red-necked nightjar, all more likely to be heard than seen. The black-shouldered kite and the dark chanting goshawk, an extremely rare raptor from tropical Africa, can perhaps be spotted in the vicinity of Taroudant. Less exotic birds like the spotted flycatcher and the spotless starling suffice most visitors.

DETOUR SOUTHWARDS TO TIOUTE, IRHERM, TATA AND BEYOND

Just 7 km E of Taroudant, a road (7084) leaves the P32, and follows a 171 km route across the Anti Atlas mountains and down into the Sahara at Tata.

Tioute is the first stop. It is 33 km from Taroudant on the road S. It has a splendid palmery and a newly restored kasbah founded in the 16th century by El Oumara Chaurafa Essaidine, over-

---

The Argane tree – the tree of the flying goats

Visitors to this particular area of Morocco might be forgiven in thinking that the trees are full of flying creatures. The creatures are goats but though they are perched on the extended boughs of the argane tree they climb, they do not fly.

The argane tree is found today only in this small region of Morocco between Agadir and Essaouira and eastwards along the Sous valley beyond Taroudant and in parts of Mexico.

At first glance one could mistakenly think that the area was under olive cultivation. The trees are well spaced and the average height is the same, around 4m, although some specimens reach 20m. The short trunk, however, is thicker, perhaps 8m in girth. In fact it is not one trunk but a fusion of stems and the canopy of clumps of argane can spread to 40m. The trees grow very slowly but live a long time, with an estimated average lifespan of 125 years.

The wood from the tree is extremely hard and makes excellent charcoal and the small pale green leaves set among vicious spines make nutritious fodder. The small greenish flowers are produced in spring and sometimes in autumn and the resulting fruit, something like a wrinkled yellow plum, appears between May and Sep. Don't be tempted to try one. The fruit is much prized. The fleshy cover makes a rich, longlasting cattle cake, while being particularly rich in sugar the juice can be fermented to produce an alcoholic drink.

The oil from the kernels within the hard shell is used by the local population who have acquired the taste. It is honey coloured with a nutty flavour. It is used in cooking, in the preparation of sweets and mixed with almond paste and honey it makes a delicious 'butter'. A bowl of argane oil into which hot bread is dipped is served at most meals.

The goat herders collect the fruits from the ground. Officially they are forbidden to beat the trees to make the fruits fall. Some fruits are dislodged by the feeding goats, in other cases the stones which are spat out by the goats who have eaten the pulp and the stones which have travelled through the animal's digestive system are collected. The nuts can be stored for years, providing food in times of scarcity. The women produce the oil in small quantities because it cannot be stored. They break the shell, roast the kernel often using the shell casing, grind the kernels into a paste which is mixed with tepid water and from this squeeze the oil. The work is tedious and the yield is very low, estimated at about 2 kg of oil for every 100 kg of kernels. The oil's reputation as an aphrodisiac is widespread.

looking the seven small villages. At this time affluent merchants came from as far as Fes, Marrakech and the southern Sahara to trade. *Restaurant Kasbah Tioute*, T 851048, is highly recommended for lunch, ask for the chicken tajine served in traditional style. This is a spectacular journey, rarely travelled beyond Tioute by tourists, but worth it for devotees of wilderness, and now passable by car, although spare parts and petrol are less plentiful in this region.

93 km from Taroudant the road reaches **Irherm**, which has a Wed *souq*, a petrol station, and the *Café de la Jeunesse*, with basic accommodation. Irherm **market** still has a high proportion of copper utensils, the trade and production of these going back to the time when the saharan caravans passed through here. Do not be persuaded to take the route SW from Irherm to Tafraoute, it is in a dreadful condition and is a journey you are unlikely to complete except on a desert motor bike. The track NE to Talioune is in a similar condition, 86 km of bumps, potholes and road that has slipped away. The 104 km to Tata by comparison is much better. Enquire in Irherm before you set off as the recom-

mended route is directly S to Tagmoute rather than the track heading SE. From Tata, the options are to travel E to Foum-Zguid and Zagora, along the Jbel Bani mountain range, or W along the P30 through a series of oases to Bou Izakarn, and connect with the Agadir-Tiznit-Laayoune road. There are four buses a week between Taroudant and Tata via Irherm, and daily buses between Tiznit, Bou Izakarn and Tata.

Tata is the principal town of the region, a pink settlement built around an oasis. The oasis to the N of the town, with its scattered housing and several *ksour*, is cultivated by the Berber-speaking population who wear distinctly Saharan clothing. At the centre of the town is a garden square, and nearby are all the facilities, the bank, the post office and basic café-restaurants. Office du Tourisme, T 802075, Syndicat d'Initiative et de Tourisme, Chambre de Commerce, T 673583. The best place to stay is at the **B** *Tata Hotel de Sables*, in centre of town, 50 double rm with bath, restaurant, bar, pool and private parking; **E** *Hotel de la Renaissance*, 96 Ave des Forces Armées Royales, T 802042, 45 rm with bath/wc, on the edge of town, with the town's top

The famous "flying goats" grazing in the branches of an Argane tree

The khattara – an endangered species

There is a great urgency in the problem of conservation or rescue of traditional Islamic technologies. Quite apart from man-made disasters, the processes of weathering on mud brick, from which many Islamic traditional constructions are made, are considerable. The abandonment of the *khattara* at Marrakech is comparatively recent and is an example of how whole sectors of traditional technology can be exposed to destruction by man's neglect, natural erosion and silting.

The *khattara* is an underground water canal which taps the water table in the foothills and carries the water considerable distances to the village and its associated cultivated fields. The *khattara* certainly illustrates the virtues of traditional Islamic technology and the advantages it possesses are considerable. There is no foreign-exchange requirement for its initial construction. It has a long life cycle and once it has been completed, it will keep flowing, given simple, low-cost maintenance. It will run continuously day and night and, except in a few cases, throughout the four seasons. The *khattara* needs no power other than that provided by the force of gravity and is a 'friendly' influence on the water table. It takes water only as there is a flow in the water table and is thus different from the extraction of water by motor pumps in wells that cause a reduction of the aquifer. In addition there is no way these channels can pollute the aquifers. The *khattara* carries water from areas where water is available to areas where water is in demand and offers great benefits in the arid and semi-arid parts of Morocco. The *khattara* can run for long distances underground and so evaporation losses are kept low. There is another particular advantage of the *khattara* which is apparent at the present time. *Khattaras* are 'local' in all senses. Survey, construction and maintenance, together with supply of men and equipment, can all be done from local sources.

Government encouragement of constructing pumped wells in the catchment of the *khattaras* has a dramatically bad impact especially if pumping is sustained over an extended period. An option still remains for the authorities to conserve the output of existing *khattaras*. The choice is also available for the construction of new units, while the technology of their construction is still local knowledge. The future of the *khattara*, as with so many other kinds of traditional technologies is uncertain and, at worst, is at great risk of extinction.

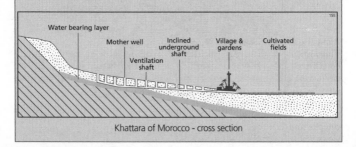

Khattara of Morocco - cross section

restaurant; the other options are the **F** *Hotel Sahara*; and the **F** *Hotel Salam*, both basic.

East from Tata There are police checks along this route, and it may be necessary to get a permit: check with the police in Tata. Transport is by 4WD vehicle, or by hitching a lift on a lorry. 70 km E from Tata, **Tissint** has five *ksour* and is known for its excellent dates. **Foum Zguid** has a Thur *souq*, basic accommodation, and buses to Ouarzazate. There is a rough road from Foum Zguid to Zagora.

West from Tata The village of **Akka** lies 70 km W of Tata, in a large oasis, with an interesting old quarter, with a petrol station, 2 primitive cafés and basic accommodation at the **F** *Hotel-Café Tamdoult*. Akka, like Irherm, was an important stopping point and trading place on the great caravan route through the Sahara in the 19th century, vying in importance with Sijilmassa. On market days, Thur and Sun, the place is a little more lively. Further on, another 80 km, **Foum El Hassan** is another oasis. The rock carvings in the town centre have gone. The nearest are 4 km from the town, up the track into the mountains. Here and at a spot some 20 km out of the village (you will need local directions and even better a guide) are some remarkable carvings of animals, illustrating wildlife once found in these parts – giraffes, elephants, rhinos and antelope are easily recognized. These have been given dates from around 2000 BC. The carvings of camels are later additions.

At 55 km E of Foum El Hassan a piste goes N to Souq Tnine d'Adai and **Id Aissa** also known as **Amtoudi** (26 km). This is well worth the journey, which can be achieved in a car with reasonable clearance. Here is found a very well preserved *agadir* and because of this attraction a number of tourists. It is possible to clamber around inside this storage complex and on to the top to admire the views. The *oued* further N has some wa-

terfalls. It is a little less than 5 km through the oasis from the village and makes a very pleasant place for a picnic and with luck a swim. Id Aissa offers a restaurant with basic facilities and a simple campsite by the *oued*, which considering the isolation, is very welcome. It may even be possible to hire a donkey here to save the scramble up to the *agadir*.

Tarhijit has a *souq* on Thur but is really only lively when the dates are being marketed.

From the village of **Timoulay Izder**, petrol available, a road leads 10 km to **Ifrane de l'Anti Atlas**, an historic settlement surrounded by a number of *ksour*, spaced around the slopes of the mountain bowl. Ifrane had a large Jewish population, the *mellah* once held over 500 homes hence its old nickname of Old Jerusalem. Jewish families still revisit the necropolis just to the N on higher ground beyond the bend in the river, so this is still a special place for them. The village has an interesting *souq* on Sun morning. There are three places to stay, marginally the best is the **F** *Hotel Anti-Atlas*; the others are the **F** *Café-Restaurant de la Poste*; and the **F** *Café du Paix*. Back on the main route, **Bou Izakarn**, 14 km from Timoulay Izdar, lies on the junction with the Agadir to Laayoune road, with regular transport to Goulimine and Tiznit, and a Fri *souq*. The **E** *Hotel Anti-Atlas*, T 874134, 10 rm, on the road to Goulimine, has a restaurant, pool and garden, and is a pleasant place to stay. The cafés at the junction have been recommended. From here there are buses and Grand-taxis to Ifrane de l'Anti Atlas.

The piste N from Ifrane is not even to be contemplated – except as a 59 km walk to Teffermit about halfway along on the Tiznit to Tafrouate road.

TAROUDANT TO TAZENAKHT

The road from Taroudant to Tazenakht incorporates all ranges of scenery – intensive oasis agriculture, nut orchards, vines, dry farming of cereals, argane culture, expanses of gravel desert grazed by goats and camels and extensive views from the winding road through the Anti Atlas. The landforms on the N side have sharp lines, making a distinctive skyline. Oulad Berrehil is off to the E. Here is a large house, once the home of an ancient chief. Take the time to ride down and have a look. After 52 km a road N to Marrakech over the Tizi-n-Test takes much of the traffic and the next section, though the road is not really wide enough for two vehicles to pass, is easier driving.

Further along the P31 **Aoulouz**, about 30 km E of the junction to Tizi-n-Test, is a beautiful spot. There is easy access to the Oued Sous. Take the track to the right when approaching from the W which goes right down to the water's edge. There are good places to stop and view the surroundings, even stop and picnic. In good years there is water in the *oued*. Here while the women use this water to wash the clothes there may be an opportunity to see a rare bald ibis (see birds, page 50).

The barrage which controls the flow of the *oued* lies 4 km W up a clearly signed track. It cannot however be approached officially, the road sign says closed to civilians. Further upstream some 21 km is a second barrage.

The road E climbs up to Iouzioua Ounneine, a settlement no longer than its name, over a pass of 1,050m which provides good views to the SW. Up here look out for restaurant *Noukia*, better than average, a good place for a coffee on a long journey.

Taliouine is a pleasant town, improved without doubt by the presence of a magnificent kasbah to the S of the road. Here one can find a pharmacy, post office, telephone, police, mechanics,

taxis, cafés and hotels. There is petrol (Ziz) at the E end of town beyond the triumphal arches. Most tours call in so photographs can be taken of the kasbah and discrete shots of the women doing their washing in the *oued*. They then call in at the best hotel, *Ibn Toumert*, for coffee or lunch. You are recommended to do the same. **A** *Hotel Ibn Toumert*, T 535130, F 535131, 100 rm with bath, a/c and heating, breakfast MD39, lunch menus MD112 or MD140, pleasant hotel, lovely surroundings, adjacent to recently deserted kasbah to the S of the road and E of the *oued*. There is also in town *Hotel/Café Renaissance* and *Auberge/Restaurant Souktana* on the N side of the road, just W of the road junction to *Hotel Ibn Toumert* and E of *oued*, small, clean, lovely small garden surrounds it, also does camping, rec for good food, especially tagines, availability of guides, mules, tents for walkers etc. *Hotel/Camping Siroua* to S of road on W side of the town. *Hotel de la Poste* is to be avoided. *Auberge Askaoun* just 1 km out of town towards Tazenakht is better but "kind of lonely".

From Taliouine there is a road S to Irherm and a minor road N to Askaoun. Taliouine is recognized as a starting point for walks into the Jbel Siroua.

WALKING IN THE JBEL SIROUA (A)

Allow a week to do this in comfort. Mar and Apr are good months for walking here provided the snow cover is lifting. A minor road leaves Taliouine on the N side between the bus station and the Oued Zagmouzine to the village of Akhfame. A track also leads there beside the *oued*. Here there are some splendid examples of old *agadirs* or granaries, a gentle walk. The slope steepens to climb up through a pass to the village of Tamgout and the Oued Ouamrane. Keep with the valley travelling N, in places it has quite steep sides, to the village of Atougha passing the sheep/goat herders' huts (this area is used as summer pasture) and on up the cwm towards the plateau. Jbel Gueliz (2,905m) and Jbel Siroua (3,304m) can be reached from here and there is a number of smaller peaks on the plateau commanding good views S. Instead of a direct return it is possible to follow a more easterly route in the next major valley, through Tagouyamt and eventually back to the P32 (see also walking in Jbel Siroua (B) on page 367).

Continuing E, the road climbs steeply out of the town. Look back to the S and see the old deserted settlement right on the top of the hill. Look N and see terraced slopes, tiny walls to hold back the soil, cereals and fruit trees. The pass provides good views down over the plain, intensive cultivation in valleys, usual oasis gardens behind the walls, cereals, olives, almonds, pomegranates, figs, vines taking advantage of the aspect and altitude which tempers the climate and takes away the fierceness of the summer heat. Beyond on the top of the plateau the soil is very thin suitable only in places for dry farming producing poor cereals. There is a small, not very special, café on top of this first climb out of Taliouine. You ought to have stopped in the town.

Between Taliouine and Tazenakht are two high passes, Tizi-n-Taghatine (1,886m) and Tizi Ikhsane (1,650m) with a small settlement of Tinfat boasting another imposing kasbah, midway between. The highest pass, Tizi-n-Taghatone incorporates some of the nicest of the scenery on this route, a mixture of landforms, terracing with small trees, spacious, views on all sides, and the road, though not perfect, allows time for eyes to do a little wandering. In truth it is a better journey going E-W as the snow capped Atlas make a better backdrop, to the right and straight ahead.

The pattern of farming does not alter much. On some of the very straight sections between Taroudant and Ouarzazate it is argane trees underplanted with wheat as far as the eye can see.

There are a few long straight sections, though from the map these are not obvious. Some sections are in poor condition, the irregular surface being a little more than a car wide and sides dropping steeply away into mud that has been churned by heavy vehicles in the winter and has then baked hard. It gives the impression that the road has not been serviced since the French left.

Between the passes there is patchy shifting cultivation and little else. These passes are not very spectacular in themselves as they are just lifting the road to the top of the next major rise which is not high enough for good views. At the top of the lower pass, Ikhsane, a man has a small hut from which he is selling plain terracotta pottery. One has to admire his determination. Beyond Ikhsane after another very straight stretch of road is **Kourkouda**, by the well are a few stalls with pottery and fossils, another with a few carpets, painted rams' horns and sheets of selenite, a form of calcite.

Tazenakht is at an important junction though much of the town stands to the NW of the road. Triumphal pillars announce the entrance to the town just before the junction off E to Foum Zguid. Adjacent to the arch is Petrol Afrique with a small clean restaurant. At this junction one will find louages and petite taxis on the left, bus station, pharmacy on right, Café Essaadi, Hotel/restaurant Senajaga, basic rooms, very cheap, and telephone. Market Fri. *Hotel Etoile*, in the centre by the taxi stand, is a very run down motel, damp and unpleasant. *Hotel Zenaga* is the only place fit to stay in, rooms vary and so do prices, hot water in evening only. The Shell petrol station is on the left by the *oued* the triumphal arch which marks the far end of the town. Tazenakht also has a bank, a number of carpet shops with even a Cooperative of Carpets Café, shops for general supplies like coke and biscuits, and a mosque.

TAZENAKHT TO FOUM ZGUID

This is a journey of 87 km, along the S510 E and then S. There are buses to/from Foum Zguid to Ouarzazate, 3 or 4 times a week, all stopping at Tazenakht. The journey with no delays takes 65 mins by car or taxi.

For the first 22 km the road goes E through some quite startlingly rugged landforms with particularly high peaks to the S. Once over the Tizi Taguergoust, 1,640m, the view opens to the SE, basins with small villages, abandoned *ksour*. The signs of progress are obvious. This is no longer a drive into the unknown and primitive S, for alongside the road all the way to Foum Zguid there are domestic water supply pipelines, electricity and telephone wires.

At 22 km there is a turn to Bou Azzer and Arhbar, small poor villages depending on mining (cobalt). The road beyond these becomes a poor track going E to Zagora and a shorter and much worse track going NE to Agdz.

This is an area of transhumance, the animals being moved to better pasture as the year progresses. This is no longer the chaotic and picturesque scene described by earlier travellers. Progress is the blue Ford Transit van (all the vans are blue) adapted to carry the animals and the belongings. These do the job much more quickly, a group of 3 or 4 vans, returning for another load, can soon move the full flock and all the people. If you see this quaint spectacle note that sheep, packed in so they barely have room to stand, are well behaved but the goats are so unpredictable they have to be tied down. What an uncomfortable journey they must have.

For a considerable distance the road runs alongside a very sandy *oued*, the Asif n'Aït Douchchene, orleanders bloom by the water and in the occasional oasis there are fruit trees. Elsewhere the soil cover is thin and as already mentioned is only used for pasture for part of the year. The vol-

canic nature of the landscape is clearly indicated by the presence of one or two fine volcanic plugs.

Zaouiat Sidi Blal is a small settlement 57 km N of Foum Zguid with a large water tower and a smaller minaret on the mosque. Most of the settlement is to the left (E) and the *oued* to the right (W). Most obvious features are the cemetery, the large school and new palm gardens being laid out. The *marabout* on the road by the *oued* has a high dome rather than a hemispherical one, and is cream in colour. There are neat oases gardens fed by irrigation channels producing mainly cereals. Beyond the *oued* extends the plain of dark flat stones.

Amazzer has an old *ksar* perched up on the right three storeys and more high. It, like all the houses, is made of mud. The big *oued* is alongside the road; here orleanders bloom. The oasis gardens grow palms, pomegranates, and cereals. There are lots of small settlements like Aït M'rabte, many with abandoned *ksour* and oases, far more than marked on the maps. In every case the all important oasis gardens contain vegetables, usually beans, and cereals among the palms.

The village of **Tassetiste** is 35 km from Foum Zguid where one of the main village activities appears to be washing clothes in the *oued* using cut down oil drums and colourful plastic buckets.

The village of **Alougoum** has a large oasis and beyond can be seen the return of the argane tree on the extensive flat plain.

The turn off to Zagora (120 km) is a far from pretty village of **La Hamid** just N of our destination, where the Jbel Bani to the W is highest (1,635m) and to the E rises as a steep saw-toothed edge to 1,503m. The *oued* has cut a gorge through here and the road now runs alongside. The settlement of La Hamid continues into **Foum Zguid** which has a small petrol station at the entrance to

The Ait 'Atta – a Moroccan tribal group

The Ait 'Atta of southern Morocco – centred on the Jbel Sargho in a tribal territory of 55,000 sq km – occupy a broad band of terrritory running from the northern rim of the Sahara Desert through into the High Atlas Mountains. They are semi-nomadic herders, moving from their own settled agricultural areas according to the season with their sheep to new pastures. The Ait 'Atta are famed for their brave resistance, until 1934, to the French colonial authorities, being among the last of the tribal groups to submit.

The Ait 'Atta are a Berber tribe and even recently were unable to communicate in either Arabic or French. Heads of tribe are elected by a mixture of rotation between families and acceptability of the individual candidates. Although Muslim, the Ait 'Atta followed their own customary law and had a complex system of local courts and a central appeal court in their capital – Agharm Amazdar.

Forms of economic and social dependency were traditionally imposed by the tribes of the Ait 'Atta on Jews, black slaves and other minority groups. The ending of slavery in the recent past, the migration of most Jews after the creation of Israel in 1948 and a changing economy through drought and development meant that the Ait 'Atta tribesmen in modern times became economically weaker than some of their former dependants and have lost control over them. Their, as in the cases of many other tribes, systems of law and economic survival are now in doubt as is the viability of the tribal structure that sustained them in the difficult terrain on the rim of the Sahara.

the village on the E side, before the *oued*. There are rooms available over the garage. The main town is surprisingly large and surprisingly busy but has little to recommend it. There are one or two poor cafés such as *Lac Iriki* on the W side, *El Far* by the *oued*, a bank and some lock-up shops. The market (Thur) held in the central square trades in household goods, light metal and plastic goods.

From the triumphal arch at the S of the town it is 151 km to Tata.

TAZENAKHT TO OUARZAZATE

The P32 road climbs up to Tizi-n-Bachkoum 1,700m. Nothing grows here in the very poor soil. There is, at the summit, a good view to the W and even a place to pull off but the inevitable group of small children is waiting.

Anezal stands by a large *oued* of the same name. Often tourist mini-coaches are parked at the café here which is good for a rest and a drink. This has an important animal market.

WALKING IN THE JBEL SIROUA (B)

Anezal is one of the recognized starting points for walks to the W into the Jbel Siroua. It is possible to walk from here via Tizi-n-Melloul (2,506m) and Tizi-n-Tleta (2,502m) across to Askaoun, Aoufour and Aoulouz, coming down to the main road by the barrages above Aoulouz (see page 364). Askaoun is also connected by track to Taliouine giving an alternative rendezvous on the P32. (For Walking in the Jbel Siroua (A) see page 364.)

To the right of the road between Anezal and Tiouine is a huge *oued* with tributaries which eventually lead into the barrage to the E of Ouarzazate. The road goes alongside this for 20 km all the way to Tiouine. Here there is an old ruined fortress on the right and new buildings on the left. Manganese is mined in hills to the right. The road descends to cross the big Oued Iriri just N of Tiouine. This *oued* also drains into the same large barrage of Mansour Eddahbi. There are two junctions where roads go N to Marrakech which is 178 km away over the Tizi-n-Tichka. Beyond these the road is far busier. Roadside sales on this exceedingly straight road lined with eucalyptus trees include pottery, dyed desert roses, amythyst and polished stone. The village of Taborhat is at the junction where the road goes off SE to Zagora. In this last stretch into Ouarzazate the road climbs up and gives to those sitting on the right of the bus a lovely view down into the settlement of Taborhat below, views right into the square courtyards and across to the mosque. The car driver gets a better opportunity to see this when travelling E.

OUARZAZATE

(*Pop* 20,000; *Alt* 1,160m) Ouarzazate's primary attraction is not in the settlement itself, an unexciting town and military garrison with a crumbling *ksar*, but as a base for exploring the Saharan re-

gions, and as a transit point en route to the desert. For this, it is well-equipped and a pleasant enough place to stay.

Located at the confluence of three rivers, Ouarzazate is in a strategic location, and has been garrisoned since the Almohad period. A tribal war in the late 19th century left Ouarzazate in the hands of the el-Glaoui family, and the kasbah became the power base from which they expanded control over the S. The town was chosen by the French in 1928 as a military garrison and administrative centre – the buildings from this period straggle along the main street. Around and above them are the large hotels, which have been built in recent years, giving Ouarzazate a prosperity unusual in this region. This is compounded by the role of the town and its immediate vicinity as a film location. From the point that *Lawrence of Arabia* was filmed at Aït Benhaddou, this area

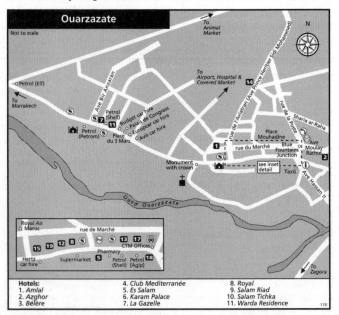

Ouarzazate

Hotels:	4. Club Mediterranée	8. Royal
1. *Amlal*	5. *Es Salam*	9. *Salam Riad*
2. *Azghor*	6. *Karam Palace*	10. *Salam Tichka*
3. *Bélère*	7. *La Gazelle*	11. *Warda Residence*

has become a popular director's choice, and there is now a permanent studio nearby. Ouarzazate hosts a handicrafts fair in May and a *moussem* in Sept. Popular with bird watchers. In spring when the almond blossom is at its best around the ochre/red buildings of the town and the snow still covers the summits of the High Atlas Ouarzazate has a magic which is hard to beat.

ACCESS Air The airport is at Taorirt, NE of Ouarzazate, T 882345. **Road** Access is by the P31 NW from Marrakech; and by the P32 W from Taroudant; E to Boumalne, Tinerhir and Er Rachidia on the P32; and SE on the P31 to Zagora. **Bus**: the CTM bus terminal is on a square on the main street, Ave Mohammed V, private line buses arrive at Place 3 Mars, and grand-taxis on Place Mouahidine. Most of the important buildings are located on or near Ave Mohammed V.

Places of interest

The town is proud of its mosque, the first stone of which was laid by King Mohammed V in 1958. The main days for the town market are Sun and Tues, but beyond this the main point of interest in Ouarzazate is the **Kasbah Taorirt**, located E of the town centre along Ave Mohammed V. This was an el-Glaoui kasbah, built in the 19th century, reaching its height of importance in the 1930s. The kasbah would have housed the extended family of the chief, his servants and followers, as well as a community of tradesmen, artisans and cultivators, gathered together in a continuous area of building for common security. The kasbah is partly ruined, but is still occupied, on its rear side, by some of the poorest people in Ouarzazate in a maze of narrow passageways, small houses and shops. The area of the kasbah adjacent to the road has been maintained (open 0830-1200 and 1500-1800 Mon-Fri, 0830-1200 Sat). This would have been the quarters

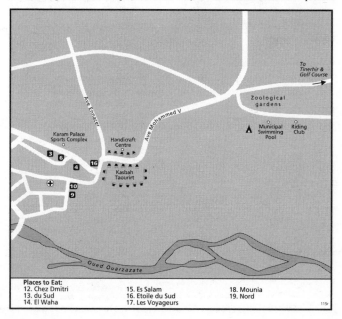

Places to Eat:

12. Chez Dmitri	15. Es Salam	18. Mounia
13. du Sud	16. Etoile du Sud	19. Nord
14. El Waha	17. Les Voyageurs	

of the family and immediate associates, and includes a courtyard and several reception rooms. Upstairs are a small dining room and salon.

Opposite the kasbah in the *Ensemble Artisanal* (open 0800-1200 and 1300-1800 Mon-Fri, 0830-1200 Sat), T 883449, which has a number of sculptors working on the premises, as well as a selection of local handicrafts. The local woollen carpets of the Ouzgita Berbers are worth looking out for. In the town centre there is also a *Coopérative Artisanale des Tissages de Tapis*, another fixed price shop. *Atlas Studios*, where film work is regularly in process, is open to public view (0800-2000), and is located 3 km from the centre, along the road to Marrakech. Outside Ouarzazate, to the E, the Barrage al-Mansur, is a large manmade lake with the partly ruined **Tamdaght Kasbah**. To the S, off the P31, lies the **Kasbah Tifeltout**, over 300 years old, the mud-brick walls remain intact, now used as a pleasant hotel, with good food and magnificent views, T 882813.

Local festivals

Each Aug the people of Ouarzazate celebrate the popular *moussem* of Sidi Daoud.

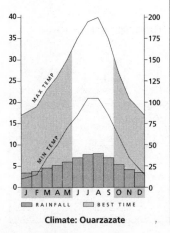

Climate: Ouarzazate

Local information
● Accommodation

A *Hotel Bélère*, 22 Ave Moulay Rachid, T 882803, F 883145, 270 rm and 11 suites, a/c, pool, tennis, restaurants with Moroccan and International menus, nightclub, cool, spacious, excellent facilities, helpful manager, second best hotel in town; **A** *Berber Palace*, T 883105, F 883615, 211 rm, well appointed with usual pool, bar, choice of restaurants, even a *hammam*; **A** *Hanane Club*, Ave Erraha, T 882555, F 885737, part of the new hotels complex, 53 rm incl 7 suites, all have TV, telephone and mini-bar, a/c, restaurant has 200 spaces, Moroccan and international menus, pizzeria has 50 spaces, American bar, nightclub for 200-250, pool, *hammam*, tennis, shops; **A** *Hotel Karam Palace*, Blvd Prince Moulay Rachid, T 882225, luxurious, 150 rm, restaurant, bar and pool, riding, tennis, built in style of kasbah; **A** *Hotel Riad Salam*, Ave Mohammed V, T 883735, F 882760, 2 converted kasbahs, luxuriously equipped, 14 suites, 63 rm, with TV, restaurant, bar, spectacular pool with waterfall, as well as a sauna, massage, horse riding and tennis, shops, conference facilities; **B** *Tichka Salam*, off Ave Mohammed V, 101 rm, T 882416, F 882766.

C *Hotel Azghor*, Blvd Prince Moulay Rachid, T 882612, above the town, a good place with 150 rm, a restaurant, bar, nightclub and pleasant pool; **C** *Hotel Zat*, Aït Gief, T 882521, F 885550, 60 rm, a quieter hotel on the outskirts, with an excellent restaurant, a bar and pool.

D *Hotel la Gazelle*, Ave Mohammed V, T 882151, a good option with 30 rm, an excellent bar-restaurant, small pool, a little out of town on the Marrakech road.

E *Hotel Es Salam*, Ave Mohammed V, T 882512, a well-run hotel, some of the 50 rm are poorly lit; **E** *Hotel Royal*, 24 Ave Mohammed V, T 882258, a friendly place with good super clean rooms with bath, lots of hot water (MD10) and fair prices.

F *Hotel Atlas*, 13 rue du Marché, T 882307, behind the main street, cheap and satisfactory; **F** *Essada*, rue de la Poste, T 883231, only has cheapness to recommend it.

Camping: *Camping Municipal*, T 882578, is on the Tinerhir exit of the town, a friendly place with running water, café and simple restaurant, pool, showers, electricity for caravans, grocery shop and petrol 800m away, the site is small, only 1 ha, and a bit expensive but the facilities are good. *Camping Imlil* has been rec at MD5 pp and MD10/tent.

● Places to eat
◆◆◆*PLM Hotel Zat*, Aït Gief, T 882521, a very good restaurant; *Le Palais Vert*, Aït Kdif, opp the *PLM Hotel Zat*, T 882428, with Moroccan decor, specializes in local food; *Restaurant Waha*, T 882354, rather too far out of town for standard of food and price; *Chez Dmitri*, on Ave Mohammed V, in the town centre, is an excellent bar-restaurant, once the focus of Ouarzazate, serving excellent European/Italian food, with a good *lasagne*; further out from the centre is the rec restaurant of the *Hotel la Gazelle*, Ave Mohammed V, T 882151.

◆The cheapest places are along rue du Marché and nearby streets, *Restaurant Es-Salam*, Ave du Prince Heritier Sidi Mohammed, is a reasonable cheap option for Moroccan food; *Restaurant El-Helah*, 6 rue du Marché, is a good second choice.

● Bars
The best place for a drink is *Chez Dmitri*, Ave Mohammed V.

● Banks & money changers
Banque Populaire, Ave Mohammed V; **BMCE**, Ave Mohammed V.

● Hospitals & medical services
Chemist: *Pharmacie de Nuit*, Ave Mohammed V, T 882708, also on Ave Al-Mouahidine.

● Post & telecommunications
The PTT is on Ave Mohammed V.

● Shopping
Although much of the material on show is geared to the tourists who pass through each day to glimpse the kasbah, useful items like films, batteries for cameras, sun cream, writing paper and stamps can be obtained. In town there is the supermarket on Blvd Mohammed V which even sells alcohol.

● Sports
Bird watching: see Mansour Eddahbi Dam below.

Golf: *Ouarzazate Royal Golf Club*, 9 holes, par 36, T 882653, F 883344, green fees MD150, open every day.

Sporting Club: *Hotel Karam*, T 882225.

Riding Club: to E of town beyond kasbah.

Swimming: at major hotels and municipal pool. That at the *Hotel Bélère* is very good, for MD30/50 you can use pools as a non resident.

● Tour companies & travel agents
Ksour Voyages, Place du 3 Mars, T 882997; *Palmiers Voyages*, Place de la Poste, T 882617; *Top Voyages*, Hotel Karam, T 883645, for excursions in the region.

● Tourist offices
Ave Mohammed V, opp the CTM bus terminal, T 882485 (open 0900-1200 and 1430-1830 Mon-Fri). **Syndicate d'Initiatives et du Tourisme**, Kasbah de Taourirt.

● Useful addresses
Fire: T 15.
Police: Ave Mohammed V, T 19.

● Transport
Local Car hire: **Budget**, Ave Mohammed V, on the road to Marrakech, T 882892; **Hertz**, Blvd Mohammed V, T 882048; **Inter-Rent**, Place du 3 Mars, T 882035; other agencies around Place du 3 Mars include **Dani Car**.

Air There are flights from the Taourirte airport, NE of the city, T 882348, to Casablanca and Marrakech (4 a week) and Agadir (1 a week). International flights to Europe (mainly Paris) in season.

Road Buses: to Marrakech cross the High Atlas by the impressive Tizi-n-Tichka pass. There are also several services a day to Zagora, E to Boumalne, Tinerhir, Er Rachidia, and W to Taroudant and Inezgane. CTM buses leave from the terminal on Ave Mohammed V, private line buses from the nearby Place du 3 Mars. **CTM** buses from Ouarzazate: Marrakech 0830, 1130, 1230, 2100; Agadir 1200; Casablanca 2100; M/Hamid 1230; Zagora and Agdz 1230; Er

Flights Ouarzazate – arrivals	
Mon	Paris/Orly
Wed	Casablanca
Thur	Casablanca
Fri	Paris/Orly and Casablanca(2)
Sat	Marrakech
Sun	Casablanca (2)

Flights Ouarzazate – departures		
Mon	Jeddah	0010
	Casablanca	0700
	Paris/Orly	1245
Wed	Casablanca	1900
Fri	Casablanca	0700
	Paris Orly	1245
Sat	Marrakech and	
	on to Jeddah	0235
Sun	Casablanca	0700
	Marrakech	1630
	Paris/Orly	1640

Rachidia and Tinerhir 1030. **Taxi**: from Place
Mouahidine go to Skoura, Boumalne and Zagora
amongst other destinations.

EXCURSION TO THE MANSOUR EDDAHBI DAM

To the E of town the Oued Draa has been
dammed to form a huge lake in this
semi-desert area extending over 20 km in
length and varying in width as a number
of tributaries such as the Oued Dades
and Oued Ouarzazate join the main valley. A few roads from the P32 lead down
towards the northern shore. One is
signed into a gated reserve, and another,
to be avoided, into the Golf Club. Access
to the southern shore is more difficult
and access to the dam itself is prohibited.
Bird watchers come here to see the wintering and migrating ducks and waders.
Spoonbills and Greater Flamingoes
make spectacular visitors.

To get to the island in the barrage
contact Omar Aouzaale BP206, 45000,
Ouarzazate. He can also be contacted at
Club Med on T 890080 or T 882650. The
only useful time to do this trip is spring
or autumn. To get to the waterside at the
gated reserve just say you are a tourist
or wave your binoculars and you can go
through.

EXCURSION TO TIFELTOUT

Take the road W from Ouarzazate and at
7 km turn SE. Here is the village of
Tifeltout with a splendid kasbah, much
better than the one in Aït Benhaddou.
There is clear evidence of restoration and
expansion. It stands alongside the Oued
Igissi, the water from which is directed
into a series of complicated irrigation
channels. There are other kasbahs along
this road, all interesting to see but none
quite as spectacular as the first. At a main
junction take the road N 5 km back to
Ouarzazate through an area of expensive
and spacious new villas.

EXCURSION TO AIT BENHADDOU

Aït Benhaddou is 30 km from Ouarzazate

and its fame has spread far and wide. The
kasbahs here are scattered around a dramatic hillside location and coach after
coach drives up, pauses for a photograph
to be taken and then returns.

The junction from the P32 after 22
km from Ourzazate is clearly signed and
a large *marabout* with ridged cupola and
crenelated edges on the tower is a prominent landmark to make sure you don't
miss your way. The road which is of fair
quality follows the valley with the *oued*
on the right. The first village is Tisser-
gate, marked out in plots, the sandy soil
growing cereals and onions, beans, citrus. A roadside seller takes advantage of
the tour coaches and tries to sell large
pieces of selenite. After a further 10 km
the old kasbah comes into view on the
right, in a bright green cultivated area.
Quite a spectacular situation. The newer
houses are set further away across the
oued. The red towers of the kasbahs provide vantage points for views across the
area and the old village also includes a
large *agadir*, or store house on the hill-
top. Guides will show tourists around
the kasbahs, which have been given
UNESCO 'World Heritage' status.
These old buildings are intricately decorated and well preserved.

This was a strategic location on the old
route from Marrakech to Ouarzazate
since the 16th century, but with few people
living there now. The village attracts day-
trippers from Ouarzazate, because of both
its intrinsic appeal and its role in the film
industry, with *Lawrence of Arabia* and
Jewel of the Nile filmed here, as well as *Jesus
of Nazareth*, for which part of the settlement was actually rebuilt.

You will have seen much more spectacular places, for example nearby Tifeltout. So far the area is not really spoilt
by tourists, with no huge car parks, no small
children or souvenir sellers, presumably
visitors stop, photograph and go.

● **Accommodation & places to eat** At the
entrance to village on the right is first **E** *Café-
Restaurant la Kasbah*, with 8 dormitory rm

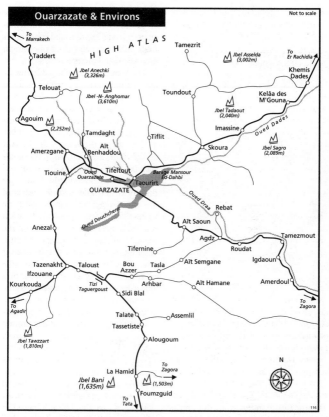

Ouarzazate & Environs

Not to scale

To Marrakech

HIGH ATLAS

Taddert

Jbel Anechki (3,326m)

Telouat

Agouim (2,252m)

Amerzgane

Tiouine

Anezal

Tamdaght

Aït Benhaddou

Tifeltout

Oued Ouarzazate

OUARZAZATE

Oued Douchchene

Tamezrit

Jbel Asseida (3,002m)

To Er Rachidia

Khemis Dades

Kelâa des M'Gouna

Jbel -N- Anghomar (3,610m)

Toundout

Tiflit

Jbel Tadaout (2,040m)

Imassine

Skoura

Oued Dades

Jbel Sagro (2,089m)

Barage Mansour Ed-Dahbi

Taourirt

Oued Draa

Rebat

Aït Saoun

Tamezmout

Tazenakht

Ifzouane

Kourkouda

Taloust

Bou Azzer

Tizi Taguergoust

Sidi Blal

Jbel Tawzzart (1,810m)

Tifernine

Tasla

Arhbar

Talate

Tassetiste

La Hamid

Jbel Bani (1,635m)

Agdz

Roudat

Aït Semgane

Aït Hamane

Assemlil

Alougoum

To Zagora

(1,503m)

Foumzguid

To Tata

Igdaoun

Amerdoul

To Zagora

N

To Agadir

and a bar-restaurant; or **F** *Auberge-Restaurant Al Baraka*, a small place with a restaurant and 5 fairly average rm to let with primitive washing arrangements, or sleeping possibilities on the roof or in the tent in front, standards here are low; there is a camping site nearby. These two places are fine for lunch, neither is cheap but the food is served quickly and cheerfully. We rec *La Kasbah* as being the better of the pair. *Auberge Ouidame* is signed down to the right at the entrance to village but has nothing better to offer, being described as "chilly and uninviting".

The road continues to the ford at Tamdaght with a *Café-Restaurant Casbah* adjacent to the Oued Mellah. There are accounts of guides carrying tourists over the *oued* here on their backs for outrageous sums of money. Just take off your shoes and paddle across. From here there is a little used track up to Tourhat alongside the Ouid Asif Ounila.

DETOUR TO ZAGORA AND THE DRAA VALLEY

The Draa Valley The road to Zagora is spectacular, first winding its way across the Jbel Anaouar mountains, and then down along the Draa valley, a strip of intense cultivation of settlement, a band of vivid colour weaving through the desert. The P31 is a good road, with frequent villages en route, but it is worth allowing adequate time and taking sufficient water. There are regular buses and grand-taxis connecting Ouarzazate, Agdz and Zagora, but one's own transport will enable visits to the numerous smaller and less spoilt oases and villages that are passed.

Agdz is the first major settlement of the valley, with a Thur *souq*. The buses, often full, pass through here, and there are grand-taxis. No banks here. It is possible to stay at the **F** *Hotel-Café-Restaurant de Draa*, with 17 rm, breakfast provided, a friendly place, price includes hot shower (evenings only); or **F** *Kissane*, Ave Mohammed V, 29 rm. *Camping la Palmeraie*, also rents rooms, very clean, with hot showers all day long and a simple restaurant. The village has carpet and pottery shops, and the palmery nearby is a pleasant place to wander.

ZAGORA

Zagora is the main town of the valley, an administrative centre, the best place to stay and the destination of most tour groups. Unfortunately the influx of tourists has encouraged some inhabitants to be over enthusiastic in their attempts to make sales. It dates from the 13th century when it was founded by an Arab tribe. Although Zagora is itself an unexciting settlement it is an excellent location to explore the nearby areas of the valley, with paths through the date palmeries and to the various *ksour*. Particularly pleasant is the **Amazrou date palm oasis** across the river, where there is also some accommodation. In Amazrou there is a former Jewish kasbah, where their traditions of silverwork are still carried on. Above Zagora and within walking distance are two hills, from where there is an excellent view over the valley and towards the dunes. Nearby are the ruins of an 11th century Almoravid fortress.

During the *mouloud*, there is a major

religious festival held in Zagora, the *Moussem of Moulay Abdelkader Jilala*. The town's market days are on Wed and Sun. Look out for the blue cloth worn by the men of the desert tribes, called in the tourist literature 'blue men'. The *souq* is an important place for the exchange of produce and livestock for the surrounding region. *Camel excursions* can be organized, try *La Fibule du Draa*, 2 km to the S in Amazrou at MD140 for camel and meals.

The fact cannot be ignored – the people of Zagora have woken up to the possibilities of tourism. They see the visitors, no doubt correctly, as having a great deal more money than they do and are determined to extract some for themselves. While most often this is done in a cheerful and friendly manner, bargaining and offering worthwhile services, we are increasingly hearing tales of unpleasant harrassment verging on to bullying tactics and examples of sharp practice. You are advised to take only official guides and to make travel arrangements into the desert through your hotel or agencies they recommend.

Local information
● Accommodation

For a small town, Zagora has a reasonable selection of hotels. Among the more expensive places, choose between the modern **A** *Hotel Reda*, Route d'Amazrou, set nr to the Oued Draa at the S of the town in the palmerie, T 847249, F 847012, 155 rm, restaurant, bar, tennis and 2 pools. **A** *Hotel Riad Salem*, Ave Mohammed V, T 847400, F 847551, at entrance to the town, 60 double rm and 4 suites, with shower and telephone, restaurant with international and Moroccan cuisine, pool and private parking; **A** *Hotel Tinsouline*, at N end of town between Ave Hassan II and Oued Draa, T 847124, F 847042, 88 rm.

Also **D** *Grand Hotel Tinsouline*, T 847252, 90 reasonable rm, central position, beautiful gardens, a good restaurant, bar and excellent pool; and the **D** *Hotel-Restaurant Kasbah Asma*, T 113, along the M'Hamid road towards Amazrou on E side of and adjacent to Oued Draa; **D** *La Fibule du Draa*, T 847318, 26 rm, 1 km to the S in Amazrou, across Oued Draa and on right before irrigation channel, an

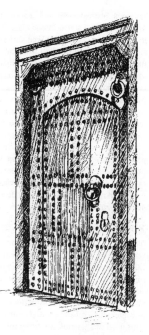

Typical Moroccan door - note two knockers, high one for male callers. Note also smaller door inserted into main door.

idyllic and relaxing little place with pool and rec restaurant-bar.

The cheaper places incl the **E** *Hotel de la Palmeraie*, Ave Mohammed V, nr road junction to S of town, T 847008, friendly with 16 rm, restaurant, popular bar, newly decorated rooms with basin MD80, rooms with bath MD100.

F *Hotel Vallée du Draa*, Ave Mohammed V, T 847210, basic but adequate, with restaurant, very central, rec; **F** *Hotel-Café-Restaurant des Amis*, Ave Mohammed V, friendly, clean and with a reasonable restaurant, hot water evenings only, only MD30.

Camping: at *Camping d'Amazrou*, 1 km to the S in Amazrou, basic and friendly; *Camping la Montagne*, further to the S, in site of 1 ha, friendly and with a pool, restaurant, groceries, electricity for caravans, petrol at 1 km, on bus route; *Camping Sindibad*, beside the *Grand Hotel Tinsouline*, in a small palmery with a small restaurant and pool, also rooms available MD50 with toilet and hot shower, pleasant setting but rooms are very damp; *Camping Tagounit*, in site of 0.8 ha, snacks, groceries, pool, showers, laundry, electricity for caravans; *Camping de Zagora*, restaurant, groceries, electricity for caravans, petrol nearby.

● **Places to eat**

Incl *Grand Hotel Tinsouline*, T 22; and the cheaper *Hotel de la Palmeraie*, Ave Mohammed V, T 08; *Restaurant Timbuctou*; *Café-Restaurant Essahara*; or *Restaurant l'Afrique*. The best place is a 1 km walk away in Amazrou: *La Fibule du Draa*, reasonably priced and not to be missed. Drink at the *Hotel de la Palmeraie*.

● **Useful addresses**

Anything of any importance is on Ave Mohammed V which has most of the town's facilities, incl the grand-taxi park, the bus station, post office, the *Banque Populaire*, *Pharmacie Zagora* and the best shops and the *souq*. Bicycles can be hired in Ave Hassan II.

Tamegroute lies 20 km SE from Zagora on the left bank of the Oued Draa and is visited mainly because of the *zaouia*, or **monastery**, founded in the 17th century, headquarters of the influential Naciri Islamic brotherhood, which had great importance in the Draa region until recently, and is visited by scholars from the Islamic world. The outer sanctuary and library are open to public view (closed 1200-1500), the latter containing a number of impressively old *korans* and 12th century antelope hide manuscripts. Whilst there, the village is interesting to explore, a close-knit area of old housing typical of the region, with potters at work producing the characteristic green and brown pottery, and a *souq*, main day Sat. It is possible to stay in Tamegroute, at the **F** *Hotel Said Naciri*, a welcoming place; or the **F** *Hotel-Restaurant Riad Dar Nousri*, a reasonable establishment with 18 rm, restaurant, pool and garden. There is a daily bus, and grand-taxis, to Tamegroute. South of Tamegroute are the **Tinfou dunes**, popular with tourists seeking the stereotypical desert view. There is a small inn, the **F** *Auberge du Repos des*

Sables, which is popular amongst independent travellers, and boasts an impressive collection of art for sale.

M'Hamid can be reached by bus or by a negotiated grand-taxi from Zagora. It is a 90 km drive S along a reasonable road through the desert, the main reason for the excursion, an impressive view of stony desert interspersed with verdant oases. M'Hamid has basic facilities, cafés and accommodation, a Mon *souq*, and dunes nearby. A visit on Mon gives an opportunity to see the 'Blue men' who frequent the market and who gather at the end of the day when occasionally there is folk dancing, known as **Ahouach** dancing. M'Hamid is a good place from which to arrange short camel rides. There is very poor accommodation and food at **F** *Hotel Sahara*, T 9, 10 rm, separate shower or camping 2 km from the town. A second small hotel is being built. Hire of camel MD275 and Land Rover MD1,200 per day available.

FROM ZAGORA TO RISSANI

A rough track exists E from Zagora to Rissani, just S of Erfoud. **NB** This is a difficult journey only to be undertaken in a 4WD vehicle. Ask at the hotels for details of the vans and lorries covering the routes. There is a better route to Rissani which is generally passable with a sturdy car, but 4WD vehicles are recommended (see page 59). Drive 60 km N from Zagora and turn E across the Oued Draa through the small oases of Nkob (42 km from junction) and Mellal towards Tazarine (75 km from junction) a small settlement which offers petrol, shop, camping and **F** *Hotel Bougafer*, T 10, 40 rm, restaurant, very basic. Grand-taxi from Zagora to Rissani via Tazzarine is MD100 per person, or MD600 for the whole taxi! 4WD vehicle with driver from Zagora to Rissani is MD900 and takes 6 passengers. Here the black top ends and although there are signs that the old road is being upgraded and in places a new road is under construction there are 31 bumpy,

dusty km of *piste* to cross. Back on the smoother surface pass through the tiny oasis settlement of Tiguerna (128 km from junction), the airstrip where anti-locust spray planes are parked before reaching the more major oasis settlement of Alnif with two hotels, **F** *Hotel Restaurant Bougafer*, very basic, fairly clean, well meaning staff and opp the similar **F** *Gazelle du Sud*. Meals provided at both places. Mechanics, petrol and shop available. With just 90 km to go to Rissani, small villages such as Achbarou with shops and a café and after a further 30 km Maoisis with school, petrol and café *Levée de Solei* are passed, before crossing the dry river bed and turning S the last 3 km into Rissani.

FROM ZAGORA TO FOUM ZGUID

This is another difficult journey best attempted with the correct transport and with accompanying vehicles. Much of the road is a very poor surface and 124 km in these conditions are not to be undertaken lightly. The thrill of the open spaces, the wide horizons and the faint prospect of sandstorms makes this a journey to remember but tedious to describe.

OUARZAZATE TO ER RACHIDIA

Immediately E of Ouarzazate the land viewed from the road is barren with hillocks of reddish brown rock. On the right is the Barrage of al Mansur Eddahbi. No vegetation appears until the Oued Izerki provides water for cereals, olives and fruit trees. The Royal Golf Course is a landmark. It has traditional style villas beside the water and overlooking it and/or the green golf course. It certainly improves the area.

The large oasis fed by the Oued Idelssan has irrigated gardens with palms, olives, cereals. It has a lovely setting with the snow capped mountains to the N. Oued Hajag crosses the road on the W of Skoura. The small settlement here has a white square mosque with white square cupola. The road rises up through the red houses of mud and the oasis gardens.

The **Skoura oasis** is more interesting than the village at its centre: a large palmery surrounded by kasbahs and *ksour*. Before the village, to the left of the road, is **Kasbah Amerhidl**, the largest of Skoura's kasbahs, with a particularly decorative design. The village also includes two kasbahs formerly occupied by the el-Glaoui family, **Dar Toundout** and **Dar Lahsoune**. Skoura village has a *souq* on Mon and Thur, a few basic restaurants, and the **F** *Hotel Nakhil*, a somewhat primitive establishment.

The older part of the town is to the N, providing all the usual services, petrol (Ziz), small shops in arcades on both sides of the road include bakers and pharmacy. If you stop groups of children and youths will want to take you to the kasbahs. *Café Atlas* is clean and fairly welcoming. An alternative is *Café de Sud*. After the construction of the bypass road to the W, new buildings now fill in the space in among the palm trees. There are plenty of kasbahs to walk around, some better than others. Avoid those visited by coach parties and you will avoid the demanding children as well. Take just a little care as it is sometimes difficult to see if a building is inhabited or not!

The road surface to the E of Skoura is again 1½ cars wide with a rough and sharp edge. Most of the village centres along this route suffer from even narrower badly maintained roads forcing both passing vehicles to pull off and swamp the villagers with clouds of dust. They rarely reduce speed however. On the E side of Tizi-n-Taddert the road widens and has a tidy edge. **Imassine**, just E where the road crosses the Oued Dades, there are 2 small coffee shops, *Des Amis* and *Salem*. The number of new houses in *Aït Ridi* perhaps indicate money from abroad. This is the beginning of the rose growing area. All the fields have hedges of roses, but there are no flowers to be seen because as soon as the bud opens the petals are picked.

The Dades valley has a similar if less dramatic appeal than the Draa valley. There is a belt of productive agricultural land beside the river, and a series of earth-built and crumbling *ksour* stretching from Skoura to Boumalne, flanked by arid mountains on either side. Skoura and El Kelâa des M'Gouna are practical excursions from Ouarzazate, or can be visited en route to Boumalne and the Gorges du Dades.

Road surface approaching Boumalne is awful, just one car wide and falling away sharply. There is quite a deal of traffic. For the last 20 km to Boumalne there is a line of settlement which stretches along the Dades valley, in some places being three of four blocks deep, which indicates the wealth of the area. Behind the houses is a string of prosperous oasis gardens with dilapidated kasbahs popping up at intervals.

Cafe de Salam on N side of road at 24 km E of Skoura is more than adequate for a coffee stop.

El Kelâa des M'Gouna is a neat town. Beyond Skoura, this is another area of *ksour* along the valley, including another el-Glaoui kasbah. The village, which has a Wed *souq*, banks, police, small shops for provisions, petrol, is known for the production of rose water, with a rose water factory, and a rose festival in late May/early Jun with dances and processions under a shower of rose petals. The children at the roadside will try to sell bunches of roses and garlands of rose petals. Here is an opportunity to see the women of the Aït Atta tribe who are considered to be the most beautiful in Morocco. Their beauty is set off by make-up and jewellery. It is possible to stay at the **C** *Hotel des Roses du Dades*, T/F 836007, 102 rm, above the town at 1,927m, the cool interior gives welcome relief from the heat, reasonable restaurant, bar, tennis, horse riding and a good pool; or the much more basic but friendly **F** *Hotel du Grand Atlas*, Ave Mohammed V, T 37, 12 rm, communal showers.

THE GORGES

Oued Dades and Oued Todra both descend from the High Atlas mountains through narrow and spectacular gorges that are attractive excursions from Boumalne and Tinerhir. Both gorges offer options for walking up into the hills beyond, but most people choose just to walk in the gorge and enjoy the scenery from the pleasant vantage point of the restaurants located nearby.

BOUMALNE

Boumalne is a small town, with a market on Wed, and a reasonable selection of hotels. The town has grown from a very basic settlement to its current size mainly in the second half of the 20th century. In the Muslim cemetery there is a *koubba* to Sidi Daoud, who is commemorated in an annual festival, when bread is baked from flour left at the grave, and fed to husbands to ensure their fertility.

● **Accommodation A** *Kasbah Tizzarouine* is an experience not to be missed, this beautiful new complex is situated on the plateau which dominates the small town of Boumalne and overlooks the Oued Dades responsible for cutting the famous Dades Gorge, into the traditional architecture has been incorporated all modern comforts, there is a difficult choice between sleeping in a truly underground room (troglodyte) which is cool in summer and cosy in winter or in a nomad tent which relies on the breeze to keep one cool, there are 'normal' rooms of international standard for the less adventurous, Moroccan cuisine is served, there is a huge tent for entertainments, ceremonial occasions – or for conferences, contact Lemnaouar Mohammed, T 830690, F 830256; **C** *Hotel Madayeq*, T/F 830763, 100 rm, comfortable, a/c, good restaurant, bar and rooftop pool, only reception is very off-hand, once past them it is sunshine all the way; **E** *Auberge de Soleil Bleu*, off to the right before the *Hotel Madayeq*, T 830163, 12 rm with bath, good restaurant, camping permitted, treks organ-

Ecologically adapted: village architecture in the High Atlas

Life is hard in mountain areas everywhere, and the High Atlas is no exception: every year, the village communities see their share of snow and wind, violent thunderstorms and drought. Communications in many places are still by mule track. To protect themselves from the elements, the people of this beautiful but often tough land have developed an architecture splendidly adapted to their environment.

The best known examples of traditional architecture in Southern Morocco are the spectacular kasbahs and *ksours* of the Dades, Ziz and Draa valleys, often set in spectacular locations. Hikers in the High Atlas are likely to stay one or two nights in a flat roofed village home, maybe an extension of an old *tighermt* or fortified granary. Access may be via a courtyard, with steep stairs leading up from dark stables on the ground floor into rectangular rooms with windows and painted ceilings in which guests are received.

Although some building is in stone, the main construction material is *tabout* (packed earth, referred to in French as *pisé*). In this very 'ecologically friendly' method of building, the local heavy clay, slightly dampened, is excavated and poured between wooden formwork to be packed down to produce a small section of wall. The wooden boards are moved horizontally, and the process is repeated until a whole layer of wall is complete. In this way, the *mablem* or master builder and his team can construct walls up to 20m high with no particular stability problems. The clay is 'quarried' from the actual construction site, or close by.

The rooms in these village houses tend to be narrow. Although in the upper storeys sundried bricks or stones may be used for the walls, brick vaulting is rarely used, and as there are few large trees, ceilings are made of short branches and trunks functioning as beams. Then a thick layer of *ifsy*, a wild plant with woody

ized into High Atlas and Jbel Saghro; **E** *Hotel-Restaurant Vallée des Oiseaux*, T 830764, a new place with 12 comfortable rm and a restaurant, journeys can be arranged here into the mountains; **F** *Hotel/Restaurant Chems*, T 830041/830089, 10 double rm and 5 single rm, breakfast MD20, open only in summer; **F** *Hotel-Restaurant Salam*, T 830762, opp the *Hotel Madayeq*, a friendly and helpful place which provides free transport to Aït Oudinar in the gorge, and organizes skiing, trekking, 4WD, mountain bikes, contact Douad in Boumalne, 15 rm, communal showers, heating, rooftop terrace and restaurant with local food; **F** *Hotel Adrar*, opp the *souq*, T 04 830355, 27 rm around a courtyard, with restaurant.

• **Places to eat** The best restaurant in town is at the ◆◆◆*PLM Hotel Madayeq*, T 31, 32; cheaper options are the ◆◆ *Hotel-Restaurant Salam*, rec for regional specialities; and the ◆*Café Atlas*, in the centre, good for for food or just a tea or coffee; just outside Boumalne, on the Er Rachidia road, *Restaurant Chems* is highly rec, with reasonable prices and a pleasant terrace.

• **Transport Road** There are grand-taxis from Boumalne to Tinerhir or Ouarzazate. There is a variety of vehicles available for the journey up into the gorges, including grand-taxis, vans, Land Rovers and lorries. Msemrir, beyond the gorges, is also possible by local transport.

EXCURSION TO THE GORGES DU DADES

The 6901 leaves the P31 at Boumalne and follows the Oued Dades through limestone cliffs which form the striking Gorges du Dades. The principal destination is the section of the gorges following Aït Oudinar, but the track continues up into the High Atlas, with public transport as far as Msemrir. There are very basic *pistes* into the mountains, and around into the Gorges du Todra.

Just beyond Boumalne is **Aït Arbi**, where there are a series of striking *ksour* above the road. The road continues past areas of unusual rock formations,

stems, is placed on top of the beams. This layer is covered in turn with packed earth. The roof terraces are particularly well made, with a slight slope draining water down towards wooden spouts.

Windows in Berber village dwellings are generally situated low down in the walls, as furniture is also low and much activity, including cooking, takes place at floor level. In older buildings, window frames may be of wood. More recent constructions have windows fitted with glass, protected by wrought iron grills purchased from the city blacksmith. Sometimes ceilings are covered with painted designs – and the most modern homes will have fully plastered inside walls. Occasionally the master builders will ornament parts of a façade with geometric designs.

Few, if any, High Atlas dwellings can be precisely dated (the same is also true for the great kasbahs of the *oueds* mentioned above). Rather, like certain Japanese wooden buildings, where rotting parts are replaced, the earth buildings of the Chleuh Berbers, always in use, are constantly being repaired – especially as the flat roofs are not the ideal solution in a land of heavy snowfall. This of course means that a building left empty is destined to crumble and disappear.

The High Atlas regions have an architecture which has evolved from the very specific circumstances of the mountains. The simple red brown cubes of the village buildings merge into the landscape, wonderfully adapted to housing people and animals, and providing storage space for crops. The question is how this architecture will change (and survive) as the economy of the mountains changes. A great effort will be necessary for new buildings, satisfying new demands, to achieve the same simple beauty of ancient Berber houses.

through Tamnalt and Aït Oudinar, where there is basic accommodation. The valley narrows after Aït Oudinar, creating the most striking area of the gorges, where the cliffs are in vivid shades of red. The road/track continues alongside the *oued* as far as Msemrir just beyond which it branches. The right hand branch goes E across the pass (2,800m) and continues in theory, linking with the 6902 through the Gorges du Todra, and up into the High Atlas. The gorges and crags offer a good environment for golden and bonelli's eagles and lammergeiers, and the scree slopes for blue rock thrushes. At very high altitudes the wheatear is a surprising spotting.

● **Accommodation** In Tamnalt accommodation and food are available at the **E** *Hotel-Restaurant Kasbah*. But the best place in the gorges is the **E** *Auberge des Gorges Dades 'Aït Oudinar'*, with a restaurant; there is camping nearby. Further on is the **F** *Café des Peupliers*, with 3 rm and camping and the **E** *Kasbah de la Vallée de Dades*, with 6 rm and a restaurant. At Aït Hammou there is the **F** *Café-Hotel Taghea*, with several rooms but no electricity. Basic accommodation is available at Msemrir.

The track SE which leaves the P32 just E of Boumalne gives easy access into the desert environment. It rises steadily to Tagdilt and provides an experience of the desert and possibilities for spotting desert birds and, less likely, desert fauna.

BOUMALNE TO TINERHIR

From Boumalne to Tinerhir there are attempts to 'forest' the area and stabilize the land, though the tiny trees only 0.5m high are taking some time to establish.

Boumalne du Dades

Not to scale

To Dades Gorge

To Ouarzazate

To Tinerhir

Oued Dades

Scarp

Bivd le Prince Héritier

Grand Taxis

Fax

Petrol (Shell)

Military Area

Petrol (Total)

Remains of old Kasbah

N

Hotels:
1. Adrar
2. Almander
3. Chems
4. Kasbah Tizzarouine
5. Madayeq
6. Salem
7. Soleil Bleu
8. Vallée des Oiseux

Places to eat:
9. Ahbab Rest/Café
10. Bougafer Rest/Café
11. Dades Rest/Café

117

The lower peaks of the Anti Atlas foothills to the N are now closer, a clear line. It is through these that the gorges have been cut. On the S is the Jbel Saghro. Climb up out of Boumalne over the pass and then down to cross the *oued* and on to **Imiter**. At **Timadriouine** a track leads S to mines (silver) which can be seen from the road and N to Arg Sidi-Ali ou Bourek. A number of ruined *ksour* stand in the valley at Imiter, some quite tall. There is sparse pasture land between.

Asir is the first village of this long oasis and the buildings along the road are continuous, showing no break between here and Tinerhir.

Tinerhir is a modern administrative centre alongside a large oasis and older settlement, ideal for visiting the Gorges du Todra, but in itself a pleasant and interesting place to stay. It is set amidst some of the most beautiful landscapes of southern Morocco. There is a stark contrast of barren mountains and verdant oases. View best seen from the Kasbah el-Glaoui – see below. The oasis settlement is a walk away behind the town, and a visit here is recommended. Hire a guide for MD35. The main part of the settlement was previously the Jewish quarter and has olive and fruit trees intercropped with grains and vegetables, and is interspersed with *ksour*. The main population is the Aït Atta tribe, often divided into small clans. Above the

town and oasis is the massive ruined **el-Glaoui kasbah**, officially closed but normally possible to enter. There is a Tues *souq*, behind the *Hotel Todra*. PTT is on Place Principale and the *Banque Populaire* on Ave Mohammed V.

At present Tinerhir is undergoing some changes to the main square where the travel agent, small shops, restaurants and cafés are situated. Once this is complete vehicle movement, parking and ability to hear oneself think will improve.

● **Accommodation B** *Hotel Bougafer*, Blvd Mohammed V, T (04) 833200/80, F 833282, 2 km W of town, new, comfortable, clean, good pool, but footsteps and door slamming echo through building; **C** *Hotel Sargho*, T 834181, F 834352, on the Ouarzazate road, with the appearance of a *ksar*, 62 comfortable rm, a restaurant, bar and pool; **D** *Hotel Tomboctou*, Ave Bir Anzane, T 834604, F 833505, MD10 extra for secure car parking; **E** *Hotel Todra*, 32 Ave Hassan II, T (04) 834249, 30 rm, restaurant, over-priced; **F** *Hotel Oasis*, Place Principal, cheap, clean, central, welcoming, upstairs restaurant with good food and views over town; **F** *Hotel El Salam Saada*, Place Principal, basic. **Camping**: there are 3 camping sites 8 km along the road leading to the gorges, rec are *Camping Atlas*, T 834209, small and friendly with a restaurant, also has rooms, hot showers, lovely views over the 'oued' from the terrace and constant loud music, MD9 pp, MD13/car or van; *Camping des Poissons Sacres*, with restaurant; *Camping du Lac*, bar, restaurant, more expensive;

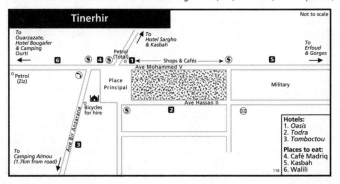

Tinerhir

To Ouarzazate, Hotel Bougafer & Camping Ourti ←

To Hotel Sargho & Kasbah

To Erfoud & Gorges →

Petrol (Total)

Shops & Cafés

Ave Mohammed V

Petrol (Ziz)

Place Principal

Military

Bicycles for hire

Ave Hassan II

To Camping Almou (1.7km from road)

Not to scale

Hotels:
1. Oasis
2. Todra
3. Tomboctou

Places to eat:
4. Café Madriq
5. Kasbah
6. Walili

Camping Almo, MD8 pp, is in centre of town, on S of road, very secure, with pool and shop, only open in summer; *Camping Ourti*, S of road at W end of town beyond *Hotel Bougafer*, very secure, restaurant, bungalows, pool but quite a walk from town. All sites have electricity for caravans.

• **Places to eat** ◆◆ *Hotel Sargho* has the best restaurant; *Hotel Todra*, 32 Ave Hassan II; and *Hotel Oasis*, Place Principal are a little cheaper; *La Gazelle d'Or*, in the town centre is also good; *La Kasbah*, Ave Mohammed V, T 13, a friendly place with delicious food. A good café is ◆*Chez Habib*.

• **Transport Road** Buses and grand-taxis to all locations, including Ouarzazate, Boumalne and Er Rachidia, leave from Place Principal. *Grand-taxis* and vans run from Place Principal to the gorge. Hotel staff can organize trips to the gorge for MD55.

EXCURSION TO THE GORGES DU TODRA

The Gorges du Todra are more spectacular than the Gorges du Dades, particularly popular in the evening when the rocks are coloured in bands of bright sunlight and dark shadow. There are places to stay near the narrowest part of the gorge, a highly recommended break from the activity of the major towns. Just N of Tinerhir as the road climbs up, is the village of Aït Ouaritane. There are many good views but few safe places to stop. It is one of the best places to see the neat strips of crops in the oasis gardens – viewed from above.

8 km from Tinerhir are the camping sites already mentioned, in an idyllic location beside a pool and palmery. 6 km further on is the most visited section of the gorge, where the high cliffs leave just enough space for the road and river. It is a particularly photogenic sight at sunset, and is also excellent for birdwatching. There is a small toll to pay for taking one's car up beyond this point. Worth it at ten times the price. Heed the directions of the man by the stream who will guide you through the shallower parts. People who ignore his advice and get

stuck have to wait a surprisingly long time before they are pushed back to dry land.

Just before the gorge are the three hotels: the **F** *Hotel Restaurant El Mansur* is very basic with shared rooms but is the cheapest option, it also has a restaurant and some camping space; further on the E *Hotel des Roches* has 10 good rm and a restaurant in a ceremonial tent; the E *Hotel Yasmina*, T (04) 833013, newly extended with 12 'Moroccan' rm, and a large and recommended restaurant in a traditional black tent, often used by tour groups. Camping here by arrangement. Sleeping on roof (mattress provided) is MD20 per person and includes a hot shower. **NB** Hot water is only provided when the generator is working to produce light – so have your shower in the evening. Take a torch.

The more adventurous will want to continue beyond the narrow confines of this gorge. The village of Tamtatouche is a walk of about 4 hrs considering the steady climb. A few lorries returning from the *souq* use this route and would provide a lift which will prove to be a very slow, very dusty and very bumpy ride. With 4WD many of the smaller villages to the N can be reached. By far the greatest danger to walkers are the fleets of Fronteras and squads of adapted motorbikes using these routes. Connections can thus be made westward with the Dades Gorge or N to Imilchil (see page 316). The 'short cut' of 42 km W to M'semrir from Tamtatouche which reaches a height of 2,800m is particularly rough. These journeys are not to be undertaken without careful planning.

EXCURSIONS SOUTH FROM TINERHIR

The village of **Aït Mohammed** stands to the SE of Tinerhir and is clearly visible from the main road. It stands on the minor road which goes along the *oued* to **El Hart-n'Igouramène**. A track due S leads into the Jbel Saghro aiming for the village of Iknioun which nestles under the central heights.

The road from Tinerhir keeps to the S of the imposing Jbel Tisdafine. At 10 km from town a track to the right goes to Alnif (63 km) and a connection with the desert road from Erfoud to Zagora.

FROM TINERHIR TO ER RACHIDIA

Buses run from Tinerhir to Er Rachidia, or from Tinejdad, en route, across to Erfoud. There are grand-taxis from Tinerhir to Tinejdad, Tinejdad to Goulmima, and Goulmima to Er Rachidia. **Tinejdad** is a Berber and Haratin town in a large oasis, with some significant kasbahs, notably the **Ksar Asrir**; and the **F** *Hotel-Restaurant Tizgui*, with basic accommodation and food. There is an amazing number of bicycles in Tinejdad, every child seems to own one so be particularly careful when sessions change at school. You are unlikely to find many cyclists beyond the town limits as the road surface is so bad. The central square offers a post office, the town gardens, town hall, telephones, taxis and Total petrol. There is a weekly *souq*. *Café Alfat*, *Café Assagm* and *Café Ferkla* are possibilities. This is a long town which takes a while to drive through. There are some very large buildings in the centre and some pleasant new homes to the W end. *Café Oued Ed-Dahab* stands N of Tinejdad at the junction with the road to Erfoud. It is a good place to stop offering cold drinks and juice but you may find the place overrun with people from Safari tours. We counted a convoy of 13 campervans there.

The road from here goes due N, leaving the palms of the oasis gardens for dry farming cereals on the level plain and aiming for a gap in the scarp, a gorge cut by the Oued Rheris. This is an extension of the scarp through which the gorges of Dades and Todra are cut. The settlement of Goulmima has a striking position. The P32 on which it is situated approaches across the plain and make use of where the *oued* has cut through the scarp.

There is a lot of new property on the outskirts well served with water, electricity and telephone. The centre of Goulmima is similar to Tinerhir, a large number of *ksour* around an extensive palmerie. Much of the town is to the N of the road in the main oasis. The older low grey buildings are made of local mud and none is as high as the palm trees. The newer buildings are a pleasant shade of ochre and tend to be higher.

Approaching the centre after passing through the usual mechanics and carpenters on the outskirts the road becomes wider. There are ministry buildings on both sides, a hospital on the left, village gardens on the right desperately in need of some attention. Opposite the garden is a bus station and a walled area for Grand-taxis which extends about 200m into town. Agip petrol station on the left before the market square. Market day Mon. The market square, with two entrances from the road, is opposite **F** *Hotel Gheriz*, T 783167, with 10 reasonable rm, restaurant with good food. In this area are situated the pharmacy, telephone boutique and after 50m *Petit restaurant* advertising sandwiches, with chairs under the trees, all on the right. In the arcade of shops you will find another café, telephone, shop for stamps and postcards, *Restaurant Badou* and beyond up on the left the covered *souq*. *Camping Tamaris*, on a site of 4 ha, showers, petrol station 100m.

There is very little space for the orchards between the town buildings and the scarp. It is a very narrow strip, perhaps 200-300m. Leaving the town beyond the library and the swimming pool the scarp is very close on the left. After the Ziz petrol station the road sweeps up and over the *oued* via a high bridge which indicates the flow that can be expected. The road climbs up sharply between the gardens, through the scarp, pause here and take in the view back. It is most spectacular. Unfortunately finding somewhere safe to stop and take in this amazing view is not easy.

There is a road N from Goulmima leading to the villages of the High Atlas, only suitable for 4WD. It is 'surfaced' for the 55 km to **Amellago** from where it is possible to circle back to the Todra Gorge and/or the Dades Gorge. There is a road SE to Gaouz (4 km) and eventually to Touroug on the road to Erfoud.

The last 58 km to Er Rachidia are up on the plateau where the Jbel Timetrout runs parallel to road on the N side. It is very poor land, scrappy pasture for large flocks of sheep and goats and in places dromedaries herded by nomads in black tents. Traditional farming has seen some changes. The herder rides a motor bike!

Water is provided at evenly spaced drinking and penning areas. An added interest is a distinctive butte clearly visible and gradually approached for about 30 km.

ER RACHIDIA AND THE ZIZ VALLEY

ER RACHIDIA

ACCESS Buses from **Aéroport Er Rachidia**, T 572350, stop at the bus station off Ave Mohammed V, the main street, and the grand-taxi park opposite.

Er Rachidia (*Pop* 27,040), previously known as Ksar Es Souq, took its new name from the first Alouite leader, Moulay ar-Rashid. It was established by the French, initially by the Foreign Legion, as a military and administrative centre, a role it retains today. The town has little of interest for the visitor, beyond a **19th century** *ksar* near the Erfoud exit. However Er Rachidia is a convenient stopping point at the meeting of routes to Ouarzazate, Erfoud, Figuig and Fes, and is such is reasonably well equipped and with a relaxed atmosphere. The town, an important local *souq*, has its biggest market days on Sun, Tues and Thur. The grid iron street pattern, so typically French, makes orientation simple. The main road Ave Moulay Ali Cherif leads down to the new bridge over the Oued Ziz. Set behind the new white painted buildings the older mud-walled dwellings still exist.

● **Accommodation B** *Hotel Kasbah Tizimi*, Route de Jorf, T 576179, F 577375, 34 double rm, breakfast MD33, lunch MD110, needs some shaded parking; **B** *Hotel Kenzi el Ati*, T 577372, F 577086 has 110 rm and 8 suites, breakfast MD45, lunch and dinner MD180, opened 1995; **B** *Hotel Kenzi-Rissani*, Ave de la Marche Verte (direction Erfoud), T 572186, F 572585, pleasant location on the town's outskirts, 60 rm, restaurant, bar, disco, tennis and pool, open to non-residents for MD50 daily; **B** *Khasbah Asma Route de Rissani*, between Erfoud and Rissani, 40 rm with bath and 2 suites, pool, safe parking, restaurant serves Moroccan and international cuisine, friendly atmosphere; **D** *M'daghra*, rue Allal Ben Abdallah, T 574047, 29 rm; **D** *Hotel Oasis*, 4 rue Sidi Abou Abdellah, T 572519, a modern place with 46 rm, restaurant and bar; **E** *Hotel Lamada*, Ave Moulay Ismail, T 576097, 24 rm; **E** *Hotel Meski*, Ave Moulay

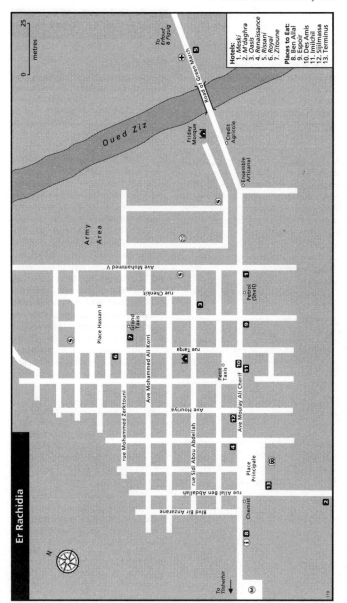

Er Rachidia

Hotels:
1. Meski
2. M'daghra
3. Oasis
4. Renaissance
5. Rissani
6. Royal
7. Zitoune

Places to Eat:
8. Ben Allal
9. Espoir
10. Des Amis
11. Imilchil
12. Sijilmassa
13. Terminus

Oued Ziz

Army Area

Friday Mosque

Credit Agricole

Ensemble Artianal

Road Green March

To Erfoud & Figuig

Ave Mohammed V

rue Chenkit

Place Hassan II

Grand Taxis

rue Targa

Petit Taxis

Ave Mohammed Ali Korri

Ave Moulay Ali Cherif

Ave Houriya

rue Mohammed Zerktouni

rue Sidi Abou Abdellah

rue Allal Ben Abdallah

Blvd Bir Anzarane

Place Principale

Chemist

To Tinhrhir

Petrol (Shell)

0 25 metres

Ali Cherif, T 572065, next to tourist information office, 25 comfortable rm with restaurant, café and pool; **F** *Hotel Essaada*, Ave Moulay Ismail, T 576317; **F** *Hotel Renaissance*, 19 rue Moulay Youssef, T 572633, 15 clean rm, people are helpful and friendly, restaurant, has limited choice but good quality food; **F** *Hotel Sable d'Or*, Ave Mohammed V, T 576348, 10 rm, good value for money at this grade, good views too which are free; **F** *Royal*, 8 rue Mohammed Zerktouni, T 573068, 21 rm, 31 beds, ask when you get to Place Hassan II; **F** *Zitoune*, 25 Place Hassan II, T 572449, 10 beds in 7 rm, very basic, no hot water. *Hotel Atlas*, Ave Mohammed V, very cheap so don't expect much, camping – electricity and shower at extra cost, pick up a 4WD car with guide from this hotel, ask for Abdoul Oudai or ring him before in Er Rachidia on T 572486; *Hotel Farah Zouar*, T 576146; *Hotel Merzouga*, 114 Av Mohammed V, T 576532, 14 rm, primitive. **Camping**: 2 km along the Erfoud road there is a basic municipal camp site with a pool, 6 ha site, laundry, showers, electricity for caravans, petrol 20m.

● **Places to eat** ◆◆*Hotel Oasis*, 4 rue Sidi Abou Abdellah, T 572519, 572526, has a good and clean licensed restaurant serving Moroccan food; *Restaurant Lipton*, Ave Moulay Ali Cherif, good food throughout the day and night; *Restaurant Imilchil*, Ave Moulay Ali Cherif, T 572123, good traditional Moroccan food in a licensed establishment. ◆The most economic place is *Restaurant Sijilmassa*, Ave Moulay Ali Cherif, with a simple but good menu; *Hotel-Café la Renaissance*, 19 rue Moulay Youssef, T 572633, is reliable, with excellent *couscous*. There are other cheap places along Ave Mohammed V.

● **Bank & money changers** Banque Populaire, Ave Mohammed V.

● **Hospitals & medical services Chemist**: (all night) Blvd Moulay Ali Cherif.

● **Post & telecommunications Area code**: 05. **PTT**, just off Ave Mohammed V nr the *Banque Populaire*.

● **Shopping** The *Complexe Artisanal*, nr the bridge, has a selection of fixed-price goods.

● **Tourist offices** Ave Moulay Ali Cherif, T 572733 (open 0830-1200 and 1400-1800).

● **Useful telephone numbers Police**: T 19; **Fire**: T 15.

● **Transport To & from Er Rachidia Air** There is a weekly flight to Fes, and from there to other destinations, from Aéroport Er Rachidia, T 572350. **Road Bus**: buses leave from the bus station off Ave Mohammed V, T 572760, with several a day for Erfoud and Rissani (2 hrs), Midelt (3 hrs), Tinerhir (3½ hrs), Fes (9 hrs), and Meknes (8 hrs), and one each morning to Figuig (8 hrs). **Taxi**: there are frequent grand-taxis to Erfoud, Meski and Tinejdad, the park is opp the bus station.

EXCURSION NORTH FROM ER RACHIDIA

The P21 N to the **Gorges of Ziz** is a short and very interesting detour. It is a very attractive route, even the blocks of new housing to the N of the town has been enclosed in walls to resemble a kasbah. For the first 20 km it follows the Oued Ziz, note where caves have been cut into the cliff, for use as storage then the western shore of the Barrage de Hassan Addakhil which was completed in 1971. This body of water ensures a more regulated supply of water to Er Rachidia and the oasis gardens requiring irrigation, controls any flooding of the Oued Ziz (see what happened to the shrine of Moulay Ali Cherif, page 390) and is noted as a rest haven for migrating birds. The evening sun accentuates the unusual landforms of the area, the hard bands with screes between. Beyond here are the Gorges of Ziz, a spectacular ride in a narrow defile 2 km in length, an attraction in their own right. Small settlement, picnicking and camping, where the road crosses the river at the bridge is 29 km from Er Rachidia. On the return journey take the road which goes to the dam wall and follow it across the irrigation channels and through the oasis gardens of Tirhiourine. Keep to the surfaced road and eventually turn right on the P32 back to Er Rachidia.

EXCURSION TO MESKI

Meski, lying to the W of the Erfoud road about 18 km S of Er Rachidia, also known as Source Bleu, was developed by the

French Foreign Legion. It is a springwater pool surrounded by palms, and a popular camp site, the *Camping de la Source Bleu*, T 249, MD5, which in the summer has a lively atmosphere but can become overcrowded. Its restaurant is not recommended being very overpriced. The **Meski Ksar** is 485 years old and the ruins make an attractive silhouette above the incised gorge. **The source** is well worth a visit, and there is frequent transport to and from Er Rachidia. To get the best advantage of this spectacular gorge, when approaching from the N, turn off the P32 as soon as the gorge comes into sight on the right of the road. There is a track marked by a small cairn which goes across to the edge of the gorge and turn left along the edge. There is space and time to stop anywhere to admire the view and the peace. Eventually the track reaches the better road into Meski. Turn right on this and go to the source. Avoid paying for parking unless you intend to camp, by stopping at the top where the buses turn, and walk down. The café is not recommended. Take precautions against mosquitoes here.

The water here is said to aid conception and women bathe here in the pool and light candles in the cave hoping to cure their barren state.

DETOUR ALONG THE ZIZ VALLEY

The Tafilalt From Meski, the P21 follows the Ziz valley S, often called the road to the ksour. This is another of the memorable valleys of the S, a succession of *ksour* alongside a heavily cultivated riverside area, with on either side the vast stony expanses of the Sahara. It encompasses an area 16 km wide and 20 km in length. Many of the settlements of the valley were destroyed in the flood of 1965. The southern stretches of the Ziz valley, a region known as the Tafilalt, are particularly fertile, and historically of considerable importance. This was due in part to its location on the trans-Saharan trade routes, with the town of Sijilmassa a

major mediaeval population centre, whose rapid decline has not yet been fully explained. In the 8th and 9th centuries the region was a separate kingdom, and became known as a centre of religious unorthodoxy – of the Kharajite Berber heresy and later of Shi'ism. The present Alawite Dynasty of Moroccan Sultans originated in Rissani. From 1916 to 1931 French control of the region was challenged and effectively thwarted by local forces. Nowadays it is still noted for its production of figs and olives and dates (not very special) but particularly for the tamarind trees. The galls off the tamarind contain tannin used for curing leather, a high quality product, the word *tafilete* actually meaning high quality Moroccan leather.

If you have time take a 4WD and a guide along the small roads by the river through the small settlements rather than 'speed' along the P21. Here you will see a great contrast between the green

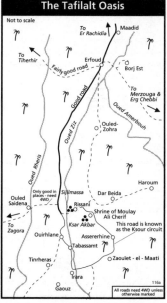

The Tafilalt Oasis

Not to scale

To Er Rachidia
Maadid
To Tiherhir
Fairly good road
Erfoud
Borj Est
To Merzouga & Erg Chebbi
Oued Amerbouh
Good road
Ouled Zohra
Oued Ziz
Oued Rheris
Haroum
Only good in places – need 4WD
Sijilmassa
Dar Beida
Ouled Saidena
Rissani
Shrine of Moulay Ali Cherif
To Zagora
Ksar Akbar
This road is known as the Ksour circuit
Ouirhlane
Assererhine
Tabassamt
Tinrheras
Zaouïet - el - Maati
Irara
Gaouz
All roads need 4WD unless otherwise marked
116a

fertile ribbon of palms and oasis gardens and the surrounding scorched landscape. In each loop of the river stands a *ksar* or fortressed village made of mud brick guarding the valley and providing protection for the village and also supervision for the trade in slaves and precious metals that used this route. Look out for the circular threshing floors where they can find sufficient level land, one or two in each village. **Zouala** is particularly attractive. Take the *piste* to the right hand side and descend steeply down to be alongside the *oued*. During the descent the road levels where it is cut into the hillside, there are soaring crags above and the water way below, a lovely environment for birds as many habitats.

An interesting point, if the ladies wear black they are bedouin, if they wear black with a coloured band they are Berber and if they are dressed in bright coloured garments and are more heavily veiled, they are going visiting.

Aoufouss, try *Café Saada* on the right, sit under trees on the opposite side of road.

Borj Yerdi, 14 km N of Erfoud has some interesting saltwater geysers. The water is red being very rich in iron too and experiments are underway to see what, if anything, can benefit from this type of water.

North of Erfoud to the E of the road stands the *ksar* of **Maadid**. Here it is said the streets are so narrow and the arrangement so complicated that only locals can find their way in and, more importantly, out. Take a guide if you visit.

Erfoud (*Pop* est 7,000) is the administrative centre of the Tafilalt, built in the 1930s, and an excellent base for exploring the valley and nearby desert areas. On the other side of the river from the town is the **Borj Est**, a military fort – no admittance, but get a taxi up to the top for the view – overlooks the village and the date palms, shadows of their former glory, the Tafilalt oasis and the desert. There is a *souq* on Sun in the town centre, and a Date Festival in Oct. Take a visit to the interesting **Marmar Marble Factory**. Here they polish a black rock estimated to be about 650 million years old embedded with fossilized shells known as goniatites (ammonites), making an interesting decoration. It isn't really marble as in a true marble the shells would have been metamorphosed to oblivion. The slabs, rather reminiscent of tomb stones, appear in all the hotels and bars in town. The main quarries are

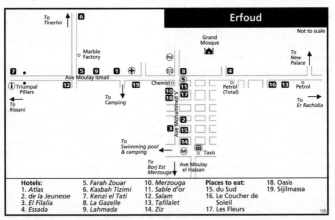

Hotels:		Places to eat:	
1. Atlas	5. Farah Zouar	10. Merzouga	18. Oasis
2. de la Jeunesse	6. Kasbah Tizimi	11. Sable d'or	19. Sijilmassa
3. El Filalia	7. Kenzi el Tati	12. Salam	15. du Sud
4. Essada	8. La Gazelle	13. Tafilalet	16. Le Coucher de Soleil
	9. Lahmada	14. Ziz	17. Les Fleurs

120

Sijilmasa – entrepot extraordinary

Visitors to Sijilmasa today will find it hard to imagine the earlier greatness of this settlement. The position was ideal for trade, the exchange of livestock and other local produce from the surrounding zones. The inhabitants of the pre-desert and the Sahara itself met here with the men from the valleys in the High Atlas and regions even further N.

But this was not the real basis of the town's prosperity. It stood at the northern end of one of the few trans-Saharan crossings and acted as a staging post for the huge caravans which carried salt to the never satisfied inhabitants of Sudan and Ghana who willingly traded it for inedible gold. It was also within an estimated 10-day journey to Fez or the Mediterranean coast. Sijilmasa was able to accommodate a caravan which would mean providing water and fodder for thousands of camels and provisions for hundreds of traders and possibly slaves. Sijilmasa could be that hospitable because it had the one essential – water. It stood on a broad alluvial plain, the Tafilalt, between two fairly dependable water courses, the Oued Ziz, the more reliable flowing to the E, and the Oued Rheris on the W, both with their source in the High Atlas. The water was stored in cisterns and carefully distributed to the agricultural land. In summer the supply was supplemented from wells and by the traditional *khattaras* (see box, page 362), man-made sloping underground channels designed to transfer water from a distant aquifer to the town. No wonder this was **the** place to rest before or after the 2-month long and dangerous trans-Saharan journey.

Sijilmasa was large, with extensive suburbs. One traveller estimated its size as half a day's walk across. There was room to spread, and it did, with gardens and separate dwellings distributed over the plain and the centre with four mosques and other splendid buildings encircled by a smart high wall of stone and brick and no less than a dozen gates. And today it is, as Walter Harris described it "miles of shapeless ruins".

out of town on the road to Merzouga, near the *Hotel Salam*.

● **Accommodation** B *Hotel Salam*, Route de Rissani, at entrance to town, T 576665, F 576426, modern, well-equipped in traditional style, 100 rm, 45 deluxe suites, bar, exchange, a good restaurant, pool (not always!), shops, gardens, private parking, vehicle and driver hire incl 4WD vehicles with guides, used by tour groups, ask for Abdoul Oudai or ring him in Er Rachidia, T 572486 to book in advance; C *Hotel Farah Zouar*, Ave Moulay Ismail, T/F 576230, 30 a/c rm, restaurant serving typical Moroccan food, very good views from terrace; D *Hotel Tafilelt*, Ave Moulay Ismail, T 576535, F 576036, 64 a/c rm, bar, restaurant, pool and garden; D *Hotel la Gazelle*, Ave Mohammed V, T 576028, 9 rm, hot showers, good apart from noisy rooms at the front, a reasonable restaurant; F *Hotel Ziz*, 1 Ave Mohammed V, T 576154, 39 rm round courtyard, some with showers, good licensed restaurant, hire of Land Rovers to see sunrise over dunes etc; F *Hotel el Filalia*, 36 Ave Mohammed V, T 576033, 15 rm, communal shower, cheap restaurant; F *Hotel-Restaurant de la Jeunesse*, Ave Mohammed V, basic, with restaurant; there is also **camping**, with basic facilities and a pool, no shade, not rec.

● **Places to eat** ◆◆◆*Kenzi el Ati*, eat here in luxury; ◆◆ *Hotel Salam*, Route de Rissani, T 576426 offers the best meals; ◆◆ *Kasbah Tizimi*, rec; ◆◆ *Restaurant Sijilmassa*, Ave Moulay Ismail, very popular; ◆There are cheaper meals at the excellent *Hotel-Restaurant de la Jeunesse*; and the rec *Café-Restaurant les Fleurs*; as well as at the *Restaurant-Café du Sud*; *Restaurant Merzouga*; and *Hotel-Bar Ziz*, all in Ave Mohammed V.

● **Useful services** The post office, a branch of the **Banque Populaire**, and the bus station are located in the town centre on Ave Mohammed V.

• **Telecommunications Area code**: 05.

• **Transport** There are buses each day to Er Rachidia and on to Meknes. Transport onwards to Rissani is by bus, Grand-taxi, or by a hired Land Rover.

ERFOUD TO RISSANI

Rissani, 22 km S of Erfoud, birthplace of the Alaouite Dynasty is a modern village close to the site of the ruined town of Sijilmassa. It includes a 17th century *ksar*, housing most of the population, and a street with a bank and cafés. It is possible to stay at **C** *Hotel Asmaa*, T 575494, with 34 rm; **E** *Hotel-Café-Restaurant Sijilmassa*, Place Massira Khadra, T 575042, 10 rm, modern and clean, nearest to the ruins and the mechanics, over-priced; or the **F** *Hotel El Filala*, T 575600, 18 good size rooms but often dirty. The village has an interesting *souq* on Sun, Tues and Thur, and there are several handicraft shops.

Sijilmassa was once the Berber capital of the Tafilalt region, and a major trading centre. It was founded in 757 by the Arab leader Musa ben Nasser, and its location on the major Sahel to Europe trade route, from Niger to Tanger, gave it considerable importance and prosperity, trading in gold. Its fame grew as did its size. The ruins, little of which remain, are between the town and the river. The kasbah was kept up by Moulay Ismail, but the Aït Atta tribe destroyed the town in 1818. The current Alawite Dynasty settled in the surrounding region in the 13th century before gaining the Moroccan Sultanate in the 17th century. The ruins are of historical interest only and the 'guides' are ill informed. The fanciful tales of earthquake destruction must be discounted.

THE KSOUR CIRCUIT

To the SE of Rissani is the **Zaouia of Moulay Ali Sherif**, the founder of the Alawite Dynasty. This is a new building as the previous one was destroyed by flash flood. Non-muslims may not enter and are prevented therefore from viewing the beautiful glazed tilework, the central courtyard with fountain and surrounded by palms. He was buried here in 1640. Adjacent to this is the **Ksar d'Akbar**, a ruined Alawite palace from the 19th century quite unhappily derelict – but no doubt has some tales it could tell of the rejects of important families it accommodated and the vast treasures it stored. Whilst 2 km to the S is the **Ksar Ouled Abd el-Helim**, well worth the visit. It was built in 1900 by Moulay Rashid, elder brother of Moulay Hassan, as a governor's residence. It is quite magnificent, its decorated towers, monumental gateway and cloistered courtyards providing a little grandeur in the oasis. It deserves its name of 'Alhambra of the Tafilalet'. *Getting there*: there is a daily bus to Er Rachidia, and a Land Rover taxi each Thur along the rough piste to Zagora. There are lorries and Land Rover taxis from the village centre to Merzouga.

Tinrheras – the advantage of visiting this southerly *ksar* is the splendid view from the walls, the *hammada* to the S and the panorama of the oasis to the N. It stands at an altitude of 770m.

Merzouga, 61 km SW from Erfoud, has one attraction, the huge dunes 50m high called **Erg Chebbi**, a vast pile of sand stretching into the Sahara. There is little else, beside the other tourists and a small village with a Sat *souq*, but then the calm and wilderness is part of the appeal. A short walk across the dunes is a must once there. There are also camel excursions organized by the *Auberge La Grand Dune*, and some good bird watching in the adjacent Dayat Merzouga when it has water, particularly the greater flamingo which makes up for being less pink by being larger. Other birds attracted to the body of water so far into the desert include redshanks, sandpipers and godwits. This desert environment is interestng for the bird watcher, despite the paucity of specimens while the adjacent oases, by comparison, are bristling with birds both breeders and those calling in while migrating. It is surprising that the desert can support birds, such as the desert warbler, desert sparrow, mourning wheatear and hoopoe amd desert larks while Egyptian vultures and desert eagle owls hunt these and the desert animals. The *piste* continues S to Taouz. A taxi from Rissani, changing at Merzouga will cost MD40.

● **Accommodation** It is possible to stay at Merzouga, although accommodation is often taken early in the day. The options incl the **D** *Auberge-Kasbah Derkaoua*, nr the dunes at Erg Chebbi, BP 64, full board, very good French-Moroccan licensed restaurant, pool. **F** *Hotel Merzouga*, a friendly place with good food; **F** *Café des Amis*; **F** *Auberge la Grand Dune*, has hot showers; and **F** *Café-Restaurant de Palmeraie*, all basic places with dormitory accommodation.

ERFOUD TO TINEJDAD

The distance is 90 km. The first part has a good surface road but this is frequently lost under the blowing sand. Take care. The water for irrigation brought in the concreted channels is fed from the tiny barrage to the W of Erfoud called Moulay Brahim.

The mud brick houses beside the oasis are very smart. They have a stepped design on the corner of the walls, blue painted window frames and sometimes blue doors. The main crops in the oasis

are palms and olives. There are some efforts to fix the sand and prevent it invading the cultivated area.

Jorf by contrast is a surprise. The road in the centre of the village is a disgrace falling away at the sides to dust and quantities of litter blows about in the wind. There is a café at Jorf but one is not encouraged to stop, and Ziz petrol.

This region has a particular method of transporting water from the subsoils of the foothills on both N and S, a system using *katarrah* or underground channels accessed by frequent wells (see box on Katarrah, page 362). Once you recognize the signs the mounds of spoil from the diggings (each with a central access aperture) can be seen, line after line from the foothills to the oasis gardens.

The central section of this journey is very barren, the occasional herd of dromedaries searching for fodder and the even more occasional flock of goats.

Touroug, 39 km from Tinejdad has a very long oasis, mainly to the N of the road, the green of the palm a welcome sign. The few houses line the road where a new mosque is under construction.

The road climbs up to 929m and then slowing descend to Tinejdad between some interesting mounds of rock – decaying volcanic material to the oases of **Mellab** and **Igli**. In truth this road needs the distant snow-capped Atlas to add interest and perspective to the route.

The Deep South

HERE IS yet another face of Morocco – the deep south. The mind conjures up old caravan trade routes, lines of camels on the distant horizon, small green oases and lots of empty space. They are all here. This region includes many places not yet touched by the general tourist being too far from 4-star comforts. It includes splendid scenery and delightful villages at the end of long dusty, bumpy tracks. It offers lots of space in a changing landscape, expanses of wilderness inhabited by people who are welcoming to visitors but who expect their privacy to be respected, stone agadirs built for protection and security, mud villages clinging to the hillside, even a decaying Spanish enclave. The western border is marked by beaches of white sand and magnificent Atlantic breakers.

TIZNIT

About 90 km to the S of Agadir, is Tiznit, an important garrison and market town, with pinkish brown houses surrounded by large *pisé* walls of red mud, well worth a wander after an overnight stop. One theory is that it may have been established originally by Fatima Tiznitia, hence the name, who discovered a spring here. Another is that it derives its name from Lalla Zninia. The main town was founded in 1882 by Moulay Hassan, the 17th Sultan of the Alawite Dynasty. He enclosed a number of separate *ksour* within the walls. It was the first base for El Hiba's insurrection against the French from 1912, following the example of his father Ma el Ainin in 1910. There are just over 5 km of walls with 36 towers and although there are eight gates in all, the three most important are Bab Ouled Jarrar, Bab el Aouina and the Gate of the Three Windows – a later addition by the French.

It retains its oasis atmosphere and is well known for the numerous craftsmen, masters in the art of producing silver jewellery. The Souq des Bijoutiers on the right between Place du Mechouar and the town walls is still famous. The fibulas, bracelets, rings, anklet and breast decorations are very attractive. See section on jewellery and dress, page 62.

ACCESS From N or S by bus or taxi you will be dropped at the Place du Mechouar, the central square, once the parade ground for the garrisons here.

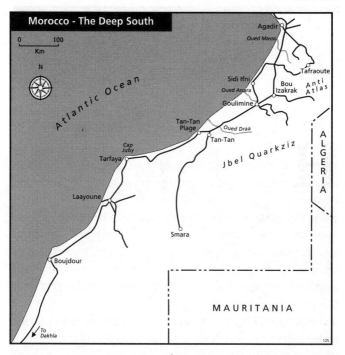

Morocco - The Deep South

Places of interest

The town *souq* (open air) is on the Tafraoute exit, with its main days on Thur and Fri. There is an interesting jewellery *souq*. Along rue de l'Hôpital from the square is the **Grand Mosque** with a minaret reminiscent of the Sahelian style, with protruding perches. These are to assist the dead as they climb to paradise. Adjacent to this is the **Source Bleu de Lalla Tiznit**, named after the town's saint, a reformed prostitute for where she died a spring appeared. From **Bab Targua**, on the N side of the town, it is possible to get onto the walls and walk W to the next gate. Good views. There are two religious festivals in Tiznit in Aug, the Moussem of Sidi Abderrahman, and the acrobat's Moussem of Sidi Ahmed ou Moussa.

The new mosque, buff with green tiles and a green cupola is a distinctive landmark, very useful as it stands on the junction of the road to Sidi Ifni.

The nearest beaches are at Sidi Moussa d'Aglou, deserted for most of the year when the sea is cold and the Atlantic waves are ferocious. In summer though it is crowded as the Moroccans camp out on the beach. There is a primitive camp site and a couple of places to eat. It is possible to go S from here to join up with the road to Sidi Ifni, a peaceful walk of some 30 km across the sand dunes and by deserted beaches.

Local information
● Accommodation

The top two hotels in Tiznit are the **D** *Hotel de Tiznit*, rue Bir Anzaran, on the edge of the town, T 862411, 862119, 40 rm, with the *Anzli Club* nightclub, restaurant, bar and good pool.

E *Hotel Mauretanie*, rue Bir Anzarane, T 862092, easier to park here than in the town

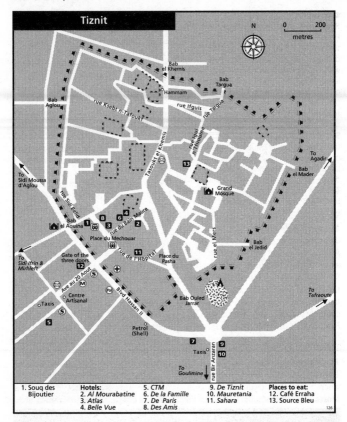

1. Souq des Bijoutier	**Hotels:**	5. *CTM*	9. *De Tiznit*	**Places to eat:**
	2. *Al Mourabatine*	6. *De la Famille*	10. *Mauretania*	12. Café Erraha
	3. *Atlas*	7. *De Paris*	11. *Sahara*	13. Source Bleu
	4. *Belle Vue*	8. *Des Amis*		

Map caption: **Tiznit** — N, 0 200 metres

centre; **E** *Hotel de Paris*, Ave Mohammed V, T 862865, 20 rm, fine restaurant, set menu lunch MD130, dinner MD260, breakfast MD36.

F *Hotel Atlas*, Place du Mechouar, T 862060, clean and reasonable, good restaurant; **F** *Hotel des Amis*, Place du Mechouar, satisfactory; **F** *CTM Hotel*, nr the bus terminal, T 862211, friendly with bar and restaurant.

The following are unclassified and cheap: *Hotel des Amis*, Place du Mechouar, T 862129, fairly clean, good view from the roof; *Hotel Belle Vue*, rue du Bain Maure, T 862109, better than average for this range; *Hotel Sahara*, rue de l'Hôpital, T 862498, as a last resort; *Hotel Al Mourabatine*, again as a last resort.

Camping: no shade and no grass, MD5 pp and per car, shop, showers, first aid, electricity for caravans, petrol at 250m, MD10 per caravan/campervan, water and electricity available at extra cost.

● **Places to eat**

There is good food at the ◆◆*Hotel de Paris*, rec; ◆◆*Hotel de Tiznit*, rue Bir Anzaran; and cheaper but still tasty meals at the ◆*Hotel Atlas*, Place du Mechouar; and the *Café-Restaurant du Bon Acceuil*, on the same square.

● **Useful services**

Around the square are a tourist information office, the **Syndicat d'Initiative**, T 869199, banks and post office, as well as hotels and cafés.

● **Transport**

Road Most buses and grand-taxis arrive at Place du Mechouar, the focal point of the town. There are private line buses from Place du Mechouar, including several services a day which go to Tata, Agadir, Marrakech, Casablanca, Tafraoute, Sidi Ifni and Goulimine and on to Laayoune. Buses to Tafraoute depart at 0700 and 1500, MD15, 3 hrs. **CTM** bus leaves from the nearby **Bab Ouled Jarrar** at 0530 for Casablanca (MD100) via Agadir, Essaouira, Safi and El Jadida. At 0900 there is a bus timetabled to Tanger (MD250) and taking 16 hrs. This goes via Agadir, Marrakech, Casablanca and Rabat. Grand-taxis leave from Place du Mechouar, with Land Rover taxis from the Tafraoute road. Grand-taxi to Sidi Moussa beach (MD5), and Sidi Ifni (MD18).

West of Tiznit (17 km) is the beach of **Sidi Moussa d'Aglou**, with a long sand strip, dangerous swimming due to the huge Atlantic waves and strong currents and a small troglodyte village of fishermen's families. There is good accommodation at the **F** *Motel d'Aglou*, 15 cabins and a restaurant; and a camp site open only in summer; as well as good food at the *Café-Restaurant Ouazize* which also has rooms.

TIZNIT TO TAFRAOUTE

The 7074 road to Tafraoute is due W from Tiznit, reaching **Assaka** after 16 km where the road winds down to the *oued*. Most of the settlement lies to the N of the road at a higher level and the mosque with its separate minaret is quite unusual. Most maps mark this as a good view – you will see why. Just beyond Assaka, across the second branch of the *oued* is a road to Anezi. This is one route to Tanalt but not the best though the countryside as far as Anezi is most relaxing.

The turning to **Sidi Ahmed ou Moussa** is to the S of the road at 40 km from Tiznit. This is the home of the famous acrobats in the red pantaloons (see box, page 395). **Tirhmi** is the next village where another route to Anezi is signed after which the road climbs up, affording very good views, up to the impressive Col du Kerdous at 1,100m. Take advantage of the lovely scenery, visit **B** *Kerdous Hotel*, Km 54, route Tiznit à Tafraoute, T 862063, F 862835, 39 rm, with a/c, telephone, radio and TV, restaurant has Moroccan and international dishes, 2 bars, large terrace taking advantage of the views, exchange, shop and secure parking.

The route S to Ifrane (de l'Anti Atlas), marked just before the village of Tifermit, is only for the very determined. The road swings N at Tizourhane where there are a couple of places adequate for a coffee and continues towards the Ameln Valley and Tafraoute through a series of oases, some with basis services.

Red pantaloons

A flash of red pantaloons from under the white *jallabah* – you are in the presence of a member of the Sidi Hamid ou Moussa sect. Closer inspection, perhaps not to be recommended, may show that the pantaloons sport a green strip down each side.

The members of the Sidi Moussa sect are travelling acrobats. For the few coins thrown on the mat and perhaps a place to sleep for the night they will perform great acrobatic feats, regardless, it seems, of the danger. These entertainers travel from village to village, calling in on market day to bring the 'blessing' of their saint under whose protection they survive.

The greatest number congregate in the Djemma el Fna (see Marrakech, page 302) where their amazing sense of balance and their agility entertains the crowds. Human columns and pyramids are built and destroyed, individual contortionists twist, cartwheel, and pirouette into tortuous positions with amazing speed. Think carefully before you buy red pantaloons of what may be expected of you.

TAFRAOUTE AND THE AMELN VALLEY

Tafraoute (*Alt* 1,000m) is the most rewarding town of this area of the Anti Atlas mountains, located in the attractive Ameln Valley, with its unusual rock formations and beautiful villages. The pink and red granite boulders contrast with the green of the almond trees and palms in the small oases which are situated at intervals along the valley. Even the buildings in the villages are painted pink.

Tafraoute has the most dramatic position, set in a rock amphitheatre. It is the modern administrative centre of this green valley and the best base for exploration. There is a large almond festival here, the Fête des Amandes, in Jan-Feb, and a *souq* on Wed. The town has a post office, a hospital, telephones and a *Banque Populaire*, on Place Hassan II, as well as a branch of the *BMCE*. Tafraoute market is an excellent place to pick up handicraft bargains. Visitors should on no account omit a visit to **La Maison Touareg**, Ave Mohammed V, T 800210, which behind its unprepossessing exterior has an amazing range of good quality carpets and other leather, metal and pottery goods, and very friendly staff. Safari and camping trips can be arranged here. It is also the only place to change money in the evening and at weekends.

- **Accommodation C** *Hotel Les Amandiers*, T 800088, F 800343, built in local style, is the most luxurious here, but offers little for the price other than a view of the Jbel El Kest, located on a rock above the town, with 60 a/c rm, TV, a restaurant, bar and pool; **D** *Hotel Salama*, T 800026, F 800448, town centre, new, comfortable, rooms with shower and WC, salon de thé, rec; **E** *Hotel Tafraoute* in the town centre nr the petrol station is the best bargain, with hot water, clean rooms and friendly staff; the nearby **F** *Hotel Redouane*; and **F** *Hotel Tanger*, by the *oued*, is slightly cheaper and has hot showers, are basic places with minimal facilities and hygiene standards, but friendly staff and good food. **Camping**: the site along the Tiznit road, is reasonably equipped and has a café, very popular with motor caravaners.

- **Places to eat** *Hotel les Amandiers* has the best restaurant and the only bar, *Restaurant Etoile du Sud* which caters for large groups, is cheaper and often good; cheaper still are the *Hotel Tanger*; and the *Café Atlas* (*Café Etoile d'Agadir*), the latter with excellent value meals of local specialities. *Snack Sportive* is excellent value in the cheaper range.

- **Tour companies & travel agents** Contact Famille Aït Sidi Brahim at *Erg Tours*, T 221890, F 229993 or call in to Maison Touregg. Safari tours in 4WD vehicles into the desert can be arranged – short circular tours and long routes

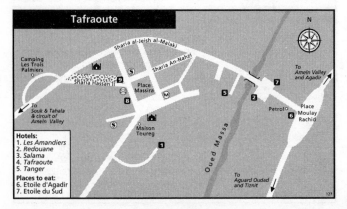

Tafraoute

Camping Les Trois Palmiers

Sharia al-Jeish al-Malaki

Sharia An-Nahzi

Sharia Hassan II

Place Massira

To Souk & Tahala à circuit of Ameln Valley

Maison Toureg

To Aguard Oudad and Tiznit

Oued Massa

Petrol

Place Moulay Rachid

To Ameln Valley and Agadir

N

Hotels:
1. Les Amandiers
2. Redouane
3. Salama
4. Tafraoute
5. Tanger

Places to eat:
6. Etoile d'Agadir
7. Etoile du Sud

across the extreme S of the country to Tata, Akka and Foum Zguid. Costs MD1,000/day for 5 people with vehicle, driver, food etc. Also organizes camel/4WD desert trips for up to 14 days.

● **Transport Road** Most buses from Inezgane and the N pass through Tiznit and along the 7074. There are several buses a day from Inezgane and Tiznit, and even one from Casablanca. Grand taxis, often Land Rovers, connect Tafraoute with Tiznit. Transport out to the villages is difficult. There are two buses a day, other options will be hitching, or bargaining with grand taxi drivers.

The Ameln Valley, or Valley of Almonds, is scattered with villages in between areas of irrigated agriculture, producing argane oil (see page 360) and almonds. Many of the men work elsewhere, returning for holidays or retirement, and are known for their participation in the grocery trade.

The Ameln Valley Circuit There are said to be 25 villages in this valley, most of them precariously positioned on the S facing slopes of Jbel El Kest. They seem to be stuck on to the mountainside and on to each other. The older grey

settlements which were constructed of mud and are now mainly in ruins, are higher up above the agricultural land where springs emerge from the mountainside. The newer sections of the village are lower, and the houses which are often 2 or 3 storeys high are coloured a dark red.

Leave Tafraoute travelling W, the road by the camp site, and follow the 7074, the old road to Tiznit. There are a number of villages, **Adaï** in particular being very picturesque. The houses are small with red walls painted cream along the top, the window and door surrounds are also picked out in cream colour. These neat houses are set in the orchard among the fruit trees, really lovely among the blossom in spring. The rock formations caused by weathering are most unusual, reminiscent of onion rings. After 15 km there is a crossroads, the road right is unmade and goes down to a ford and through the village of Souq el Had Tahala. Better to take the next right keeping to the surfaced road, the

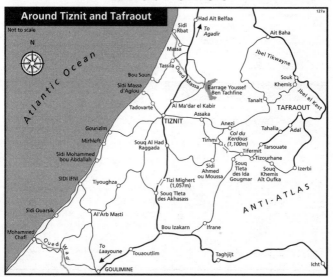

Around Tiznit and Tafraout

Not to scale

Atlantic Ocean

ANTI-ATLAS

7148. This way you pass a dozen or so of the villages either on the road like **Taguenza** or high up to the left like **Annameur**. It is much more interesting to walk the upper track that connects these villages in the knowledge each has access down to the main road.

Opposite **Asgaour** the road swings

The souq mentality

✍ An enduring characteristic of all *souqs* is their use of pricing through bargaining for every transaction, however large or small. This bargaining, so unfamiliar to the European, has brought rather differing responses. On the one hand bargaining is seen as a sign of the efficiency of the *souq*. Each separate business transaction is done with the finest of margins so that prices are very sensitive and really reflect the value. Contrary opinions strongly maintain that, far from being efficient, bazaar transactions only maximize profits for the seller for each article sold rather than getting the best potential profit flow. *Souqs* or bazaars thus actually act as a brake on the expansion of commerce as a whole. They also rely on the ability of the seller to exploit the absence of quality controls, trade mark conventions and other types of consumer protection. In these situations, the seller treats each transaction as an opportunity to cheat the customer. *Souqs* are, in this view, places where the buyer must be doubly wary since short measure, adulteration of goods and falsification of origin of goods for the benefit of the seller is normal. By definition this system can operate only in countries like Morocco with minimal regulatory régimes and where consumer information is unorganized.

When shopping in Morocco the best advice is to be fully aware that the system is designed to work to the seller's advantage.

round to the right and up to Tafraoute but it is necessary to bear left to continue the circuit along the road signed to Aït Melloul. A further 15 km of road passes more of the Ameln villages, in particular **Oumesnate**. and **Tizerht**. Oumesnate is a popular call as there is a traditional house open to visitors. The blind owner speaks French as well as Arabic and does a good guided tour.

To the S of Tafraoute just 3 km on the new road to Tiznit, is **Agard Oudad**, an interesting village built below a rock named after Napoleon's horse. From here you should get a guide to show you the *'les Pierres Bleus'*. These are rocks and mountain sides painted in various colours by the Belgian landscape artist Jean Verame, known for performing art projects on a massive scale. This is an impressive and vast piece, one of the truly memorable sights of Morocco, even if it has faded a little since 1984.

Continue S taking the left turn on the 7075 to Souq Tlet de Tasserit, a tiny settlement. The piste to the E leads to the N end of the gorges while the road S continues for a further 5 km, becomes good grade piste for about the same distance and ends up at the S end of the gorges. Either way the route through the gorge, often referred to as a canyon, threads through the oases, bypasses ancient *agadirs* and provides a fascinating, if somewhat strenuous, day. Places of interest here include ancient (and modern) Tarhat, the oasis of Tizerkine deep in the gorge and the *zaouia* at Temguilcht.

GOULIMINE (GUELMIM)

Goulimine has become a major stop on the tourist network, a regular excursion from Agadir. This is because of its camel *souq*, on Sat morning, which is, however, nowadays geared almost totally towards the demands of the tourist industry, with the nomadic tribesmen distinguished by their blue clothing, the 'blue men', in dutiful attendance. The market is along the road to Tan-Tan. More genuine, however, are the religious festivals, or *moussems*, held in Jun (at Asrir) and Aug, when Touareg nomads are in plentiful supply. From the 8th century Goulimine was an important trading post on a route swapping Saharan salt and West African gold. From the 12th century the town declined, but still retained some importance, with a large camel market. The town is located in an area of calm wilderness, but it is likely that the traveller will move on fairly quickly. There is a **kasbah** above the market.

The tourist brochures recommend a visit to the thermal springs at Abaynou and the oases of Asrir and Aït Boukha to the E of town – but there are better

examples of these features elsewhere in this huge country.

● **Accommodation** E *Hotel Salam*, junction of Route de Tan-Tan and Ave Hassan II, T 872057, F 872673, friendly, 27 rm, bar and restaurant; F *L'Ere Nouvelle*, Blvd Mohammed V, basic, clean, reasonable restaurant, friendly staff; F *Hotel Bir Nazarene*, cheap, cold water only; F *Hotel Oued Dahabi* on Place Bir Nazarene; F *Hotel La Jeunesse*, Blvd Mohammed V, opp *Hotel L'Ere Nouvelle*. **Camping**: signposted from Place Hassan II, is not rec.

● **Places to eat** ♦♦Eat at *Hotel Salam*. ♦Try *Café March Verte*, *Café Le Diamante Bleu*, *Café Jour et Nuit* with little to choose among them.

● **Useful services** In the village there is a bank and post office. Tourist office, 3 Residence Sahara, Blvd d'Agadir, T 872545. The grand-taxi stop is on Place Bir Nazarene, and the café-restaurants on Place Hassan II; nearby is the bus stop.

● **Transport** Express buses leave to Marrakech. Buses to Sidi Ifni dep at 1500, MD13, takes 1½ hrs (taxi will cost MD16); several buses a day to Tiznit (MD20) and Tan Tan (MD28).

Goulimine

Hotels:
1. Bir Nazarene
2. la Jeunesse
3. L'Ere Nouvelle
4. Oued Dahabi
5. Salam

Places to eat:
6. Café Jour et Nuit
7. Café Le Diamante Bleu
8. Café Marche Verte

128

CIRCULAR TOUR TO SIDI IFNI

Take the 7064 from the centre of Tiznit, by the large mosque, go via the small settlement of Souq el Arba du Sahel, and on to the coast with a long slow sweep down to Gourizim, a lovely small bay, stony beach, crashing Atlantic rollers. The road turns S where small fishing boats are pulled up on the shore edge at the side of the bay. The track from here permits a walk N to Sidi bou Ifedail and Sidi Moussa d'Aglou. It is 7 km to Mirhleft, once the border between Morocco and Spanish Sidi Ifni. There is an old fortified settlement on the hill to the left hand side, neatly cultivated land in the *oued* with small regularly shaped fields and one or two café/restaurants on the road at the coast. The huge Atlantic waves attract the surfers while the wide open spaces attract the motorcaravan owners for whom there is a water point on the track to the beach. **Mirhleft** is a long settlement with a number of new dwellings. *Hotel Mirhleft* has very little to recommend it. There are other hotels, even more basic. Access to the beach is difficult as the cliffs are very high.

Further S the beaches have more sand. Sidi Mohammed bou Abdallah 27 km before Sidi Ifni is determined not to be missed, an interesting sea-stack with an arch eroded through stands in the middle of the bay – very photogenic. Camping permitted here. Nearby, also very prominent, is the *marabout* of Sidi Mohammed. Plage Aftas, another resort (small hotel only open in the season), lies between here and Sidi Ifni which has a most disappointing approach down the hill through the far from attractive newly built Moroccan suburbs.

Sidi Ifni is one of the strangest towns in Morocco, a crumbling port town with a distinctive Spanish feel, and some unusual architecture. It was occupied by the Spanish from 1476 to 1524, and again from 1860, as a consequence of the Treaty of Tetouan. Sidi Ifni was always an enclave, surrounded by Morocco from 1860-1912 and from 1956-1969, and between 1912 and 1956 by the French Protectorate. The town had a port and an airstrip, and a role as a duty free zone. The economic survival of the town was based on the fact that the border was open to trade. In the 1960s Morocco grew tired of the continuing Spanish presence, and forced Spain into negotiations from 1966. The enclave was returned in 1969. Sidi Ifni is a wonderfully relaxing place to stay and wander for a few days, but after that its ghost town feel can get oppressive.

The **Plaza de España**, renamed Place Hassan II, is the centre of the colonial town, a once pleasant garden and fountain surrounded by bizarre Art Deco buildings: the dilapidated church, which is now the tribunal, the crumbling town hall, the very faded Spanish consulate which opens 1 day a month,

the *Hotel Belle Vue*, and several others. From there a promenade winds down the cliff to the none too clean beach. This is a long and often deserted strip with excellent swimming. To the S is the defunct Spanish port, an odd offshore construction on a concrete island linked to the mainland by a cable car. The Moroccans have built a new port nearby. The main *souq* on Sun on the old airfield is very disappointing. There is a large *moussem* in Jun.

● **Accommodation** E *Hotel Belle Vue*, 9 Place Hassan II, T 875072, an old building, 14 rm in need of decoration, restaurant and bar; E *Hotel Aït Ba Hamran*, rue de Plage, T 875267, 20 rm, restaurant and bar, a sad, dead place; E *Hotel Suerta Loca*, T 875350, is by far the best in town, friendly, clean, excellent food, with some lovely new rooms with shower and wc overlooking the sea, a popular hang-out in the evening, downhill from Place Hassan II. **Camping** (mainly motor caravans): site, signposted from the town centre, is basic, no shade but quite secure. **Youth hostel**: Complex Sportif, T (10) 3402, 40 beds, kitchen, overnight fee MD15.

● **Places to eat** Excellent food at the *Hotel Suerta Loca*, otherwise try *Hotel Belle Vue*, *Hotel Aït Ba Hamran*, or nr the market, the cheap and basic *Café-Restaurant de la Marine* and *Café Tafoukt*, rue El Adarissah. **Bars**: the two bars are at the *Hotel Belle Vue* and the depressing *Hotel Aït Ba Hamran*.

● **Transport** There are regular grand-taxis between Sidi Ifni and either Tiznit (MD18) or Goulimine (MD16), as well as daily buses which leave from opp Banque Populaire, to Agadir, Tiznit departs 0700, MD16, 2½ hrs, and Goulimine departs 0630, MD13, 2 hrs.

From Sidi Ifni there is a rough piste S to Foum Assaka. This crosses two large *oueds*, neither of which can be forded after heavy rain.

Continuing the round trip the road from Sidi Ifni to Goulimine is 57 km of misery, an inferior country road through inferior land. The red soil supports a few argane trees but little else. The triumphal arch with its green glazed tiles on the outskirts of Goulimine is a welcome relief.

The alternative route to Goulimine is the P30/S512 via Bou Izakarn, a fast road with a good surface and quite busy. It has many interesting features, ruined ksour, new settlements, expanses of cereals, women herding sheep and on the poorer land yet more argane trees. The highest pass is Tizi Mighert after the long straight road to Souq Tleta des Akhasass.

Tan-Tan was the starting point for the Green March into the Spanish Sahara, now incorporated into Morocco as the Western Sahara, albeit with an ongoing conflict with the local Independence movement, the Polisario. The town is a dull administrative centre, with duty-free shops and a fishing port. A visit to Tan-Tan to see the fishing fleet is recommended. The blue cloth worn by the formerly nomadic inhabitants of this area is sold in the *souq*. There is a beach 25 km away, with some good fish cafés.

● **Accommodation** Travellers who decide to stay have very little choice, *Hotel Amgala*, and *Hotel Etoile du Sahara*, are now closed and E *Hotel Dakhla*, is far from satisfactory. Only C *Hotel Royal* nr northern main square can be rec, nice and quiet, rooms have bath and wc. Camping possible on beach.

● **Places to eat** Best places are at or nr

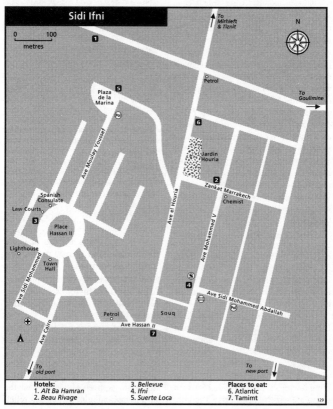

Sidi Ifni

0   100
metres

To Mirhleft & Tiznit

N

Plaza de la Marina

Pol

To Goulimine

Petrol

Jardin Houria

Ave Moulay Youssef

Ave el Houria

Zankat Marrakech
Chemist

Spanish Consulate

Law Courts

Place Hassan II

Lighthouse

Town Hall

Ave Mohammed V

Ave Sidi Mohammed

Ave Sidi Mohammed Abdallah

Pol

Petrol

Souq

Ave Hassan II

Ave Cairo

To old port

To new port

Hotels:	3. Bellevue	Places to eat:
1. Aït Ba Hamran	4. Ifni	6. Atlantic
2. Beau Rivage	5. Suerte Loca	7. Tamimt

129

northern main square. Southern main square less satisfactory.

● **Bank & money changers** BMCE, Ave Hassan II, T 877277.

● **Transport Air** There are flights from Aéroport Tan-Tan, Place Blanche, 9 km out of the town, T 877143, 877164, to Laayoune and Casablanca (1 a week). The *Royal Air Maroc* office is on Ave de la Ligue Arabe, T 877259. From Tan-Tan the onward options are to Laayoune, or inland to Smara. **Road** There are buses, grand-taxis and Land Rover taxis on from Tan-Tan. Several buses a day to Goulimine (MD25), Tizuit (MD40) and Tarfaya/Laayoune (MD60, 4 hrs). Taxis to Tan-Tan port (MD10).

Tarfaya lies SW of Tan-Tan, just off the road to Laayoune. A grand-taxi from Laayoune to Tarfaya takes 90 mins and costs MD40. On the way into the town several wrecked ships are passed. The town is an oppressively quiet place with a few old sand blown Spanish colonial buildings. Spanish from 1916 as Villa Bens, capital of the S zone of their protectorate of Morocco from 1920 to 1956, and prior to that, between 1878 and 1895, it was a British trading post known as Port Victoria. The post office is the prominent building in the centre. The market is near the mosque. The **Dar Mar** is a square structure just off the beach, supposedly British. There is also an abandoned church and colonial buildings. There is not much in the way of facilities in Tarfaya, although there are basic cafés, which do snacks and

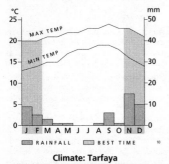

Climate: Tarfaya

harira, and a few shops. **F** *Hotel-Café Tarfaya* is at the end of the main street nr the port.

LAAYOUNE

Laayoune, with a population of 93,875 in 1982 and known before as El Aioun, was the capital of Spanish Sahara, and is the provincial capital under the Moroccans. The Moroccan government, to underline their claim to the region, have carried out an extensive programme of development, establishing facilities and constructing buildings unrivalled S of Agadir, and settling a large population from Morocco in the town, in addition to the big military garrison. Beyond the political curiosity of seeing the effect of post-colonialism, there is little to do in the town. It is, however, a strangely calm place, and not unpleasant to stay in.

ACCESS Hassan I Aéroport is 2 km outside the town, T 893346/7. There are taxis into the town, although it may be necessary to wait a while. For the energetic, it is a manageable walk. The CTM buses arrive on Ave de la Mecque, in the centre, the ONCF buses at the stadium a little further out.

Places of interest
The Place du Mechouar is interesting architecturally, a square with large canopies, with an exhibition space commemorating the Green March in 1975, and the modern **Grand Mosque** alongside. There is also a bird sanctuary, the **Colline des Oiseaux**, a calm place with some interesting species, on rue Okba Ibn Nafi, opposite the *Hotel Parador*. The Malhfa, on Blvd Kairouan, off Ave de la Mecque opposite the *Hotel Massira*, is the main market area. Below the town is the lagoon, a beautiful spot, but not for swimming in. See **Travel agents** below for excursions.

Local information
● **Accommodation**
A *Hotel Al Massira*, 12 Ave de la Mecque, BP 12, T 894225, Tx 28801, comfortable, 72 rm,

The flooding of the Sahara (by boat to Timbuktu)

Though we find cause now to smile at this proposition, available knowledge at the time supported the case of the Scottish engineer Donald Mackenzie. He proposed that a significant part of the Sahara be flooded with water from the Atlantic Ocean thus allowing access by boat to the outskirts of Timbuktu. The advantages to trading would be considerable. The success of the scheme hung on the engineer's firm belief that the Sahara was mainly below sea level. This was based on the widespread deposits of salt (dried sea water?) in that area. The only major works involved cutting through the sand barrier, just a few km wide, in the coastal region near present day Laayoune. This breached, there would be no hindrance to the flooding. Whereas one can be wise after the event more research would have revealed no land below sea level and much above 150m. The project certainly fired the imagination of the Victorians but it is just as well that no backers were forthcoming.

restaurants, bar, nightclub, tennis and pool, often taken by tour groups; **A** *Hotel Parador*, rue Okba Ibn Nafih, BP 189, T 894500, Tx 28800, 31 rm, small, luxurious, restaurant, popular bar, tennis, good pool.

C *Hotel Nagjir*, Place Nagjir, a fork on Ave de la Mecque, T 894168/9, Tx 28019, with a bar, restaurant, nightclub.

D *Hotel El Alya*, 193 rue Kadi Ghallaoui, T 893133, Tx 20087, 32 rm, restaurant, rather gloomy, building requires attention, no hot water, try bargaining; **D** *Hotel Lakouara*, Ave Hassan II, nr the market, T 893378/9, 40 rm with shower and wc, in a sleepy faded establishment.

F *Hotel Marhaba*, Ave de la Marine, 36 rm, with wash basins, communal shower, not very friendly but the best cheap option, clean rooms, hot communal showers, roof-terrace, above a café; **F** *Hotel Rif*, in a square opp rue Cheikh Maalaouine, T 894369.

Youth hostel: *Complexe Sportif*, Sakiat Al-hamra, T 3402, 40 beds, kitchen, overnight fee MD20.

● **Places to eat**
Hotel Parador, rue Okba Ibn Nafih; and the *Hotel Al Massira*, Ave de la Mecque and Place Nagjir have good restaurants and there are several cheap restaurants on Ave Mohammed V and end of Ave de la Marine nr *Hotel Marhaba*; *Snak Fes* on Ave Hassan II, with reasonable and nourishing food.

● **Banks & money changers**
Banque Populaire, Ave Mohammed V; **BMCE**, rue Mohammed Zerktouni; **Wafabank**, 5 Ave Mohammed V, T 893598.

● **Entertainment**
Hammam: an experience not to be missed, MD10, spotlessly clean.

● **Tour companies & travel agents**
Agence Massira Tours International, 20 Ave de la Mecque, BP 85, T 894229, who organize excursions to Tarfaya for fishing, to Laayoune Plas International, 20 Ave de la Mecque, BP 85, T 894229, who organize excursions to Tarfaya for fishing, to Laayoune Plage and to Oasis Lamsaid, and hire out Land Rovers and drivers; *Bureau du Tourisme du Sahara*, Oum Saad, T 894224; *Agence de Voyages Sahara*, rue Kadi Ghellaoui, T 894144. **Royal Air Maroc**, 7 Place Bir Anzarane, T 894071/77.

● **Tourist offices**
Ave de l'Islam, BP 471, T 892233/75.

● **Transport**
Local Car hire: Comptoir Sakia Al Hamra, Quartier Industriel, Sahat Dchira, T 893345; **Ouled Abdellah**, Assurance Ouled Abdellah, T 893911, **BTS**, T 894224.

Air Hassan I Aéroport is 2 km outside Laayoune, T 893346/7, with flights to Casablanca and Agadir (1 a day), Tan-Tan (1 a week), Las Palmas (2 a week), Dakhla (3 a week).

Road CTM buses leave from Ave de la Mecque, by *Agence Massira Tours International*, services to Boujdour/Dakhla, Smara/Tan-Tan and Agadir/Marrakech. ONCF services to Agadir and Marrakech, from near the stadium. Bus to Boujdour/Dakhla departs 0800, to Tan-Tan at 1200. **Taxi**: grand-taxi from the roundabout at the end of Ave Hassan II, by the market, go to Agadir (MD150) and Marrakech

(MD220). For grand-taxis to Tarfaya and Tan-Tan go by petit-taxi across the river to the *police controle* on the road out to the N, and pick one up there.

AROUND THE WESTERN SAHARA

Laayoune Plage and Port To get to Laayoune Plage, it will probably be necessary to hire a whole grand-taxi, as the regular services go to the port, which is a distance from the beach. However, the beach itself is not very clean. It is possible to stay at the **F** *Maison des Pêcheurs*. Laayoune Port, which no longer has ferries to the Canary Islands, is a phosphates port located 25 km from Laayoune, MD6 by grand-taxi. It is a sand-swept settlement with a few semi-operational café-restaurants, but little else.

Smara The town of Smara lies 225 km along the new road from Tan-Tan. There is not much to attract the traveller along this route except a liking for long desert journeys. There are daily buses and taxis on this route. The settlement of Abattekh about 75 km from Tan-Tan is the best place for a coffee break. Laayoune is 240 km to the SW. Buses there are less frequent. There are two flights a week to Laayoune. Royal Air Maroc at airport T (08) 892188.

Smara is situated in one of the most inhospitable regions of southern Morocco. It was built by Sheikh Ma el-Anin (The Blue Sultan and known for masterminding the resistance to the French and Spanish) in 1884-5 and stood astride the great caravan route to Mauritania. It was a grandiose scheme, a town built from the local black granite on a rocky prominence some 6m higher than the rest of the stone strewn plateau. Here stood the larger kasbah with the mosque (never completed) which was based on the Mezquita in Cordoba. The circular cupola, arcades and some of the pillars survive today. There was also a library and a Koranic school for Sheikh Ma el-Anin was a scholar, grain silos, a hammam and living quarters. The isolated, smaller kasbah was some 100m away.

When visited by Michel Vieuchange (see page 405) it was deserted, the nomads of the Rio de Oro using it only as shelter as they passed by with their caravans. He visited the mosque (six bays) and a minaret (poised to send the call to prayer to the four corners of the Sahara), and the large kasbah (four high wooden doors with pointed arches and iron facings). Many of the deserted dwellings were roofless.

Today it has petrol, banks, post office, hammam and half a dozen hotels, plus restaurants/cafés on the main street, Ave Hassan II. The best hotel is **E** *Maghrib el Arbi* on Ave Hassan II. Try **F** *Hotel Erraha* and **F** *Hotel Atlas* both on the same street to the right of *Maghrib el Arbi* or *Sakia el Houria* also on Ave Hassan II adjacent to the bus station.

Dakhla (*Pop* 6,500) is over 1,000 km S of Agadir and almost on the Tropic of Cancer. For those who wish to continue along the coastal road, there are lorries making the journey to Dakhla, and an ONCF bus service leaving Laayoune at 1200. **Boujdour** has a fishing port and beach. Dakhla is in a beautiful location with impressive beaches and cliffs. It was formerly called Villa Cisneros and was built on a spit protruding from the coast. Today it is a minor military and administrative centre with fishing (sea bass) and surfing.

● **Accommodation C** *Hotel Doumss*, 49 Ave el Wallaa Dakhla, new, clean, comfortable, bar, rooms with bath/wc; **D** *El Wahda*, Ave el Wallaa Dakhla, new, reasonable, bargain to reduce rates, rooms with bath/wc. Basic accommodation, incl the **F** *Hotel Imlil* and **F** *Sahara*, nr the *souq*, both with communal facilities; also try the *Pensión Atlas* or the *Hotel Bahia*; there are a basic restaurants around the town. Free camping possible on beach opp city entrance, secure. **Camping**: *Moussa-Fire*, 7 km N of town at hot springs, MD10 pp.

● **Places to eat** Many small cafés/restaurants nr souq. Best is restaurant in *Hotel Sahara* with good, cheap local food.

● **Useful services** There is a tourist office at 1 rue Tiris, T 898228, and a travel agent, *Dakhla Tours*, on Ave Mohammed V, T 141. **Bank**: BMCE, Ave Mohammed V. The **Royal Air Maroc** office is on Ave des PTT, BP 191, T 897050.

● **Transport Air** From Aéroport Dakhla, 5 km from the town, T 897049; direct flights to Casablanca, Agadir and Laayoune (1 a week). **Road** Bus to Agadir departs 1200, MD350, takes 18 hrs, reservation rec. Convoys to Mauritania leave Tues and Fri. **RAM**, Ave des PTT, T 897050.

Mauritanian border There is a road S of Dakhla to the border with Mauritania. All formalities in Dakhla, allow whole day to cross border, camping at border, customs minimal, convoys to border once/twice a week.

Destination Smara – the forbidden city: a journey by Michel Vieuchange

Assisted by his brother Jean he spent a year of study and preparation for this essential journey, essential to him, his dream. On 11 September 1930 he exchanged his European clothes for the disguising white robe, thick veil and heavy jewellery of a Berber woman and placed his destiny in the hands of tribesmen with whom he could barely communicate. He moved into a land without government, where aggressive tribesmen fought, where a European, an infidel was worth as much as a ransom or as little as the garments he wore. The agony of his journey ought not to be contemplated but he accepted without question the restrictions of the enveloping garments, the overpowering heat, the numbing cold, the lice, the unpalatable water, the desperation of thirst, the irregular, unusual meals and the worst, the pain of walking on badly damaged feet unused to such demands. His guides argued and delayed him, cheated him and stole his belongings, changed their route, their minds and the price they required for their services but he would not turn back. They bent him double and prised him into a camel's pack basket to hide him from enquiring eyes and he urged them on. He risked three short hours in Smara on 2 November while his guides, terrified of discovery, protested, twitched and urged him away. He had succeeded. The joy was his.

The return journey was shorter but no more comfortable as men and animals were exhausted. Michel's search for 'the chance of action and the spice of danger' was over. He succumbed to dysentery and died shortly after reaching Agadir, a journey of almost 1,500 km. He was 26 years old.

Mauritania

MAURITANIA lies at the crossroads of the Sahara desert, the Sahel and Sub-Saharan Africa and has historically played a crucial role in the entire region. Home to the Almoravids who swept up through 11th century Morocco to conquer Andalucía and the ancient Empire of Ghana, Mauritania was also a crucial transit zone for Trans-Saharan trade, and the Islamization of West Africa. Contact with Europeans dates from the 15th century when first the Portuguese, then the Dutch, British and French traded with the Moors along the Atlantic coastline and later along the Senegal River valley. Despite this trade, the interior of Mauritania was virtually inaccessible to Europeans until the French managed, with great difficulty, to occupy the country earlier this century. The cultural impact of the French had little effect on the Arabo-Berber Moors, the majority of whom remained nomadic until the devastating droughts of the 1970s. Today the settled majority of the population which includes large minorities of African descent, live in the capital Nouakchott, in scattered desert towns, or in towns and villages along the more fertile southern region bordering the Senegal River valley. Despite enormous changes over the past few decades, western influence is minimal compared to elsewhere in the Maghreb and West Africa, while the strength of traditional Islam among the Moors and Africans has prevented the rise of radical Islamism.

There is very little physical provision made for the traveller but those who are adventurous enough to place Mauritania on their itinerary will be rewarded with a dramatic travel experience.

Indeed for the intrepid traveller, and desert enthusiasts more generally, Mauritania's austere but visually stunning Saharan-Sahelian setting has much to offer including ancient caravan towns, beautiful oases, Neolithic ruins, wild life sanctuaries and hundreds of kilometres of unspoilt beaches. Moreover, the almost total absence of hustlers, even in the large cities, makes Mauritania a particularly relaxing and safe place to travel, for both men and women.

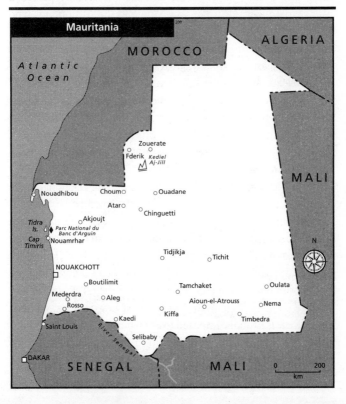

BASICS

OFFICIAL NAME al-Jumhuriyah al- Islamiyah al-Muritaniyah (Islamic Republic of Mauritania)

NATIONAL FLAG Green field with large yellow crescent and star, placed centrally.

OFFICIAL LANGUAGE Arabic

OFFICIAL RELIGION Islam

INDICATORS *Population*: (1994) 2.3 million. *Urban*: 54%. *Religion*: Muslim 99.4% (mainly Malekite), Christian 0.4%. *Birth rate*: 48 per 1,000. *Death rate*: 16 per 1,000. *Life expectancy*: 45/51. *GNP per capita*: US$480.

THE LAND

GEOGRAPHY

Mauritania has a surface area of 1,026,000 sq km, more than twice the size of neighbouring Morocco but half the size of Algeria. It spreads 1,287 km from N to S and 1,255 km from W to E. Its coastline on the Atlantic runs for 666 km from the delta of the Senegal River in the S to Cap Blanc in the N.

Borders

Relations with Morocco were particularly fraught during the first decade of independence on account of Moroccan claims to Mauritania as part of the former's nationalist project for a 'Greater Morocco'. Morocco eventually granted recognition of their southern neighbour in 1969 but Mauritania's withdrawal from the war with Polisario in 1979 marked a new decline in relations. The subsequent frequent ebbs and flows in the relations between the two countries have been linked to accusations that Mauritania has allowed Polisario freedom to operate in their territory, while in turn Mauritania has accused Morocco of encouraging Mauritanian political dissidents to destabilize the country, and of supporting Senegal in the crisis of 1989-90. More generally the Moroccan occupation of much of the Western Sahara including the border area adjacent to Nouadibou is a constant reminder of Moroccan territorial ambitions. Mauritania has no border disputes with Algeria in the NE, though Morocco has frequently claimed that Saharoui forces have operated from Algerian territory through Mauritania in their guerrilla war. There is a long international border with Mali which is geometric and permeable. In the S, Mauritania's uneasy border with Senegal runs along the N bank of the Senegal River. Although relations with Senegal have historically been very close, in the aftermath of the events of 1989 war nearly broke out between the two neighbours. Since 1992, however, when diplomatic relations were restored, there has been a substantial improvement, although the question of Haplulaar Mauritania refugees in Senegal has still not been entirely resolved to date.

Major regions

The landscape in Mauritania is unspectacular in respect of altitudes, especially in comparison with Morocco and Algeria. It is formed by three large regions of rather uniform relief. In the N is a vast territory of low altitude, broken only by the occasional rocky ridge and sand covered areas where dune series are aligned roughly NE-SW. The highest point in the region is the peak of **Kediel Aj-Jill** at 915m. In the central zone, extending E to the border with Mali, is a vast basin where the rock series form scarp slopes facing towards the centre separated by gravel plains. Sand dune cover, in places highly ridged and attaining heights of 90m, is general in this area, with low points where salt lakes are found. The interior is at altitudes of little more than 220m with the coastal plains below 45m. The Mauritanian S is a narrow strip made up of the basin of the Senegal River, with richer sedimentary soils. Overall the topography is constrained, with the bulk of the country lying well below 100m.

Rivers

The arid centre and N carry few streams other than temporary *oueds* in spate after storms. Most drainage is internal to salt lakes or indeterminate see page areas. Very little water reaches the sea. The exception to this is the S where the Senegal River drains the better-watered Mauritanian side of the basin in streams such as the Gorgol Al-Abiad and the Wadi Guélaour. The Senegal River is entirely within Senegalese territory and cannot be counted as a Mauritanian river but is considered as an international resource shared by member states of the OMVS (l'Organisation pour la mise en valeur du fleuve Sénégal), Guinea, Mauritania, Mali and Senegal.

CLIMATE

Other than the region of the Senegal River valley, Mauritania receives negligible rainfall and is profoundly arid. Rainfall at Nouakchott comes erratically but principally between Jul and Sep and is less than 150 mm on average. Further N rainfall is even less, an average of less than 125 mm at Atar and 35 mm at Nouadhibou. In the S, the N rim of the Senegal valley at sites such as Kiffa, receive 365 mm on average and the immediate river banks such as Selibaby approximately 390 mm. Most rain in the S falls in summer between Jul and Sep.

Temperatures in Mauritania are extreme. The coast benefits to a small extent from proximity to the sea as at Nouakchott, though temperatures of 45°C have been recorded there. In the centre and E, Saharan conditions prevail with very hot daytime temperatures but cold nights. The S has more tropical thermal conditions of the savanna type with less extremes both season to season and between day and night temperatures. Maxima run at 25°C in Dec against 30°C in Jun and minima at 18°C in Dec against 23°C in Jun at Rosso, for example.

The prevailing winds are the NE Trades, which are dry. In summer a shift in wind belts brings South Westerlies to the area and rainfall principally for the S region. Travellers should be ready to cope with the hot dry wind from the E, the **harmattan** in Dec, Jan and Feb, which pushes up temperatures and leads to rapidly diminishing relative humidity.

FLORA AND FAUNA

Animal life is, of course, sparse in the desert but look out for leopards, jackals, wild boar, antelopes, gazelles and ostriches. The most interesting areas are the coast, and for birdlife particularly visit Parc National du Banc d'Arguin.

AGRICULTURE

Mauritania was traditionally a country of nomads. Until recent years and the terrible effects of the Sahelian droughts, it is estimated that 85% of the population was pastoral nomads who specialized in various kinds of herding. Camel nomads tended to travel the greatest distances, while nomads who specialized in cattle, mainly in the Sahel, tended to move shorter distances. Both of these types of herding were combined with the more traditional herding of sheep and goats. Land use is registered in forms of pasture. The S is savanna grasslands with occasional trees, merging gently into the Sahel, or 'rim' of the Sahara, where thin grasslands and drought resistant shrubs survive eventually fading out N into patchy scrub in areas where annual rainfall averages less than 150 mm per year. Here in the large regions of the centre, N and NE pasture is scant and confined to temporary pastures receiving erratic rainfall or to *wadi* basins. In recent years of drought all the pastures have been depleted by lack of rain and overgrazing.

Land use (1991)	(%)
Arable and orchards	0.2
Forests and woodlands	4.2
Pastures and meadows	38.0
Desert	57.6

Source: *Encyclopaedia Britannica*

Apart from the region along the Senegal River only a tiny proportion of the country is under permanent forms of cultivation – less than one quarter of 1%. The cultivated area is almost entirely in the S, in the region of the Senegal River. The tiny cultivated areas in the N and W are predominant in the oases or in the beds of rain-fed *oueds*.

Land tenure

In the past the complex land tenure system strongly reflected the hierarchical nature of Mauritanian society. In the case of the nomadic Moors, if pasture was not owned as such, access was determined by the position a given group occupied in the social hierarchy. The Hassan dominant warrior tribes collectively controlled most of the nomadic zones, while the few wells that existed were dug and owned by tribes of religious scholars known as *zawaya* who were obliged to provide water for the warriors. A third group, who were mainly herders, paid tribute to the warriors in return for access to water and pasture. The numerous palmeries situated in the oases of Adrar and Tagant were owned by *zawaya* individuals and families, as were the main zones of cultivation under Moorish control in the S. The oases and fields were tended by slaves and ex-slaves (*haratin*), as the Moors disdained physical labour associated with agricultural work. In the S, in the areas where African groups predominated, elite African lineages owned most of the land.

During the colonial period the tenure system was slightly modified. The French encouraged free access to pasture, and built a large number of wells. The colonial administration did little, however, to change the land ownership system, which persisted into the independence period. Eventually, in 1983, after the devastating droughts of the previous decade, the government introduced sweeping land reforms. These reforms, which were designed to resolve the problems caused by increasing competition over land and water, became the source of considerable inter-ethnic tension.

Potential

Mauritania started its national life at Independence with a very poor and basic economy. However, the raw material resources are promising. In particular iron ore near Zouerate and copper deposits in Akjoujt, could provide the basis for a large scale extractive industrialization programme once political security and management of the economy is improved.

Despite setbacks caused by the drought, and economic mismanagement, the existence of natural resources suggests that the potential for dramatic improvement is considerable. Aside from the resources already mentioned, offshore the fish resources of the Atlantic within the country's economic zone are enormous. At the same time, provision of more reliable water supplies for arable farming offer prospects for the country being able to feed itself. The small population at some 2 million is a constraint on national economies of scale but also means that the state is not yet faced with an insurmountable problem of population growth and numbers.

CULTURE

PEOPLE

The **population** of Mauritania was estimated at 2.3 million in 1995 against 1.86 million in the 1988 census. Growth is tending to rise slightly towards 2.8% as the fertility rate goes up. The crude birth rate is rising and the crude death rate is much improved but life expectancy at 45 years for males and 51 years for females remains poor.

ETHNIC GROUPS

The country's position on the interface between the Wet Equatorial and Arid

Sahara zones is matched by its parallel situation as the meeting point for two worlds: one Arabo-Berber, the other African. Today, the Arabo-Berber Moors – who call themselves *bidan* (the whites) – constitute with the *haratin* (ex-slaves mainly of African origin) the majority of the population. They speak *hassaniyya*, an Arabic dialect, and until recently shared a nomadic way of life.

All Moors belong to a particular tribe in a ranked hierarchy. In the pre-colonial period the Hassan warrior and raider tribes of Arab descent were supreme and tribute and taxes were paid to them by other social groups in return for protection, access to pasture and passage through territory under warrior control. Another powerful social category, known as *zawaya* (marabouts), was comprised of tribes of religious specialists (Islamic scholars, judges, mystics, saints, healers) of Arab and Berber descent. In addition to religious activities, these tribes owned most of the herds and slaves, organized agricultural enterprises, the caravan trade and were responsible for digging many of the wells. A lower rung in the hierarchy was occupied by tribes of *zenaga*, herding specialists.

The French occupation modified the social hierarchy. From the 1950s, tributary payments ceased and many of the *hassan* became involved in herding or commerce. On the other hand, *zawaya* tribes, with a background in religious learning and trade were the first to take advantage of the colonial education system and the commercial opportunities offered by the introduction of the market economy. Although some warrior tribes have considerable power in Mauritania today, all religious leaders, and most politicians and entrepreneurs come from a *zawaya* background.

Apart from a very small minority of Lebanese traders and professionals, of whom some are Christian, the remainder of Mauritania's present day population is composed of several Muslim African minorities – the Halpulaar, Soninke, Wolof, Peul and Bambara. With the exception of the Peul, who are cattle nomads, all the other African groups are by tradition agriculturalists living mainly in the S of the country, along the Senegal River valley, in Gudimaka and in the regions bordering Mali.

The precise demographic breakdown of the different ethnic groups is hard to establish due to the politically sensitive nature of this question in Mauritania. At Independence the *bidan* and *haratin* together made up about 75% of the population. This proportion has increased in recent years with the expulsion of African Mauritanians, and the return of Moors from Senegal during 1989.

Beyond their cultural and linguistic differences each ethnic group shares an adherence to Sunni Islam and follows the Maliki legal school. This common religious tradition and shared religious identity is emphasized in the naming of Mauritania as an Islamic Republic, and is frequently held up as the one key factor uniting the diverse population within the state. Indeed, although the Arabization policies of the Moor elite have become a source of increasing inter-ethnic tension, inter-ethnic religious alliances have remained important.

DISTRIBUTION AND DENSITY OF THE POPULATION

A sign of the effects of the drought and modernization is the growing urbanization of the country, with 48% of the population now living in towns and cities in contrast to a mere 25% some 10 years ago. The main towns are Nouakchott, the capital, with 480,408 people in 1992, Nouadhibou (formerly called Port Etienne) with 72,305, Kaedi 35,241, Kiffa 29,292 (1988) and Rosso 27,783 (1988).

A second feature of population distribution is the concentration of more than 90% of people in the southern zone where rainfall totals more than 100 mm per year – roughly S of the Nouakchott-Nema road. Here densities are comparatively high at five people per km sq but the national average is a mere two people per km sq. There is a slight seasonal bias to population distribution with the semi-nomads gathering in their millet and fruit growing lands of the S for the period of rainfall and agricultural activity but spreading N in search of pasture later in the year. In the N the two plateau areas of Adrar, N of Atar, and Zouerate are centres of small, relatively densely settled, districts.

AGE GROUPS

Mauritania, in common with most developing nations, has a youthful population. No less than 45% of Mauritanians are under 15 years of age, 50% in the principal working age group between 15-59 and only 5% 60 years and over.

LITERACY

Literacy among adults, probably exaggerated by official statistics, is 38%, with a far greater proportion of men (50%) than women (26%) having had schooling. School participation rates are very low with a mere 10% of children attending at primary level.

INCOME PER HEAD

Mauritania is among the poorest (about 32nd in UN rank) countries of the world with income per head put at US$480 in 1994. While Mauritania seems to have avoided the very worst effects of maldistribution of income, there is a skew that benefits the new urban elite and those of the traditional leadership who also control land and water ownership.

HISTORY SINCE INDEPENDENCE

Mauritania became independent in 1960. In many respects, the new state was a French colonial artefact in which different and potentially antagonistic ethnic groups had been thrown together. At the time of Independence the majority Moorish population were divided among themselves: some supported the pre-Moroccan Nahda party, founded in 1958, while others, including the future President Mokhtar Ould Daddah, opposed Moroccan claims on the region and favoured Mauritanian independence. Although a considerable proportion of the African minorities supported Ould Daddah's party, the AJM (l'Association de la Jeunesse Mauritanienne), others pursued an African nationalist line, and looked to the S for their political inspiration.

The Ould Daddah government

Mokhtar Ould Daddah, elected premier in 1959, became president of Mauritania in 1960. He replaced the long standing multiparty system with the PPM (le Parti du Peuple Mauritanienne) which remained the sole legal party until the coup d'état of 1978. Ould Daddah, from a prestigious maraboutic family, was an astute diplomat who, at least initially, attempted to steer a middle course between the demands of Arab and African nationalists. He placed great emphasis on Mauritania as the the link between Arab and African worlds. The first in a series of inter-ethnic conflicts erupted in Nouakchott in 1966 and in subsequent years Ould Daddah also faced protests from Moorish students and trade unionists who demanded reforms including nationalization of the mining industry and the creation of a national currency. After serious unrest in 1968, 1969 and 1971, Ould Daddah introduced a series of reforms, which met the demand of the protesters, many of whom then joined the PPM.

In foreign affairs, the Ould Daddah régime attempted to pursue a nonaligned stance, and enjoyed good relations with most African states. This position was partly imposed by the refusal of virtually every Arab state, except Tunisia, to recognize Mauritania in 1960. By the end of the decade, however, most Arab régimes, including Morocco, had recognized Mauritania, thus paving the way for the latter's entry into the Arab League in 1973. During the 1970s Ould Daddah, who had enjoyed close relations with Algeria, switched alliances to support Moroccan claims to the former Spanish Sahara. Indeed, Mauritania was persuaded to make its own claim on the S part of the colony – the Rio de Oro or the Tiris Al-Gharbia – and, when Spain withdrew in 1976, Mauritania, after a short period of tripartite administration with Spain and Morocco, took over the Tiris Al-Gharbia.

The Polisario Front, the western Saharan national liberation movement which, with Algerian backing, was fighting for the right of the western Saharans to self-determination, decided to direct its major military effort against Mauritania, by far the weaker of the two occupying powers. By 1978, after attacks on Zouerate and even Nouakchott, the Mauritanian government accepted a ceasefire in return for withdrawal from the Tiris Al-Gharbia. The presence of 9,000 Moroccan troops added to the considerable domestic unrest and, in Jul 1978, Ould Daddah was overthrown by a military coup led by Lieutenant-Colonel Mustafa Ould Saleck. A succession of governments followed, until Colonel Mohammed Khouna Ould Haidallah took power, initially as Prime Minister in 1979, then as President in 1980.

In mid-1979, after a 9 month truce, the Polisario Front attacked Mauritania again, forcing the Haidallah government to negotiate a peace agreement – the Algiers Agreement – with the Polisario Front's government-in-exile, the Saharan Arab Democratic Republic, renouncing all claims to the western Sahara. Mauritania did not actually recognize the Republic until 1984, largely because of Moroccan

pressure. Morocco, in response, occupied the region itself and began to support Mauritanian exile groups.

Tensions between the two countries arose intermittently as Morocco extended its control over the western Sahara during the 1980s, particularly when Morocco's defensive wall system abutted against the railway line from Zouerate to Nouadhibou after 1987. Morocco also regularly accused Mauritania of allowing the Polisario Front's guerrillas to use Mauritanian territory in organizing attacks on Moroccan forces. Relations between the two countries were eventually normalized when both joined the Maghreb Arab Union (UMA), a regional unity agreement signed in Marrakech by Morocco, Mauritania, Algeria, Tunisia and Libya in early Feb 1989. Earlier, in 1983, Mauritania had joined a mutual support treaty arrangement with Algeria and Tunisia.

Internally the Haidallah régime continued to have constant problems. In spite of introducing a number of reforms including the abolition of slavery, the introduction of the Sharia in 1980, and land reform in 1983, by 1984 Ould Haidallah had alienated most Mauritanians. In Dec 1984, the chief-of-staff of the armed forces Colonel Maaouiya Ould Sid'Ahmed Taya took power.

Although initially welcomed by Mauritanians, the Ould Taya régime rapidly ran into problems. Several of Ould Taya's plans, such as the Arabization programme, closer integration into the Maghreb and wider Arab world, and the policy of permitting Moor entrepreneurs to buy land in the Senegal River valley, were viewed with great disquiet by African Mauritanians. In 1987, a failed coup attempt on the part of Halpulaar army officers led to three executions and life imprisonment for many others. Another alleged coup attempt in 1988 by pro-Iraqi Ba'ath elements in the army was met with further oppression by the régime.

During Ramadan 1989, anti-Moor riots and looting erupted in Senegal. As reports of these reached Mauritania, massacres of Senegalese and other West African nationals took place in Nouakchott and Nouadibou. These in turn led to massacres of Moors and *haratin* in Dakar. The subsequent international airlift repatriated over 200,000 Moors and *haratin* to Mauritania and over 60,000 Senegalese. In the backlash more than 50,000 African Mauritanians, mainly Halpulaar and Peul, took refuge in Senegal. Mauritania and Senegal broke off diplomatic relations, and by early 1990 were on the brink of war. The crisis strengthened the alliance between Mauritania and Iraq, the sole Arab state to lend their unequivocal support to Mauritania during the conflict. In return the Mauritanian government lent its tacit support for Saddam Hussain in the Gulf crisis, a position that led to serious problems with the allies, notably Saudi Arabia and Kuwait who were hitherto principal donors of aid to Mauritania.

In Apr 1991 Ould Taya, in a bid to shore up his credibility, announced, possibly under pressure from France, his decision to implement a series of democratic reforms.

MAURITANIA IN THE 1990s

GOVERNMENT

Mauritania is an Islamic republic. A new constitution was adopted following a referendum in Jul 1991 which provided for a two chamber national assembly to replace the military rulers in 1992. The new constitution, which aside from references to Islam was largely inspired by the constitution of the French Republic, was approved overwhelmingly in the referendum, although black and Islamist politicians, who had recommended a boycott, accused the government of falsifying the figures. Nonetheless, political parties were allowed to form and elections were promised for the following year. A general amnesty was announced after the referendum for all political dissidents who had opposed the military régime. In subsequent months more than 16 political parties formed, all of whom, except the Islamist party (Umma), who had opposed the referendum, were granted official recognition. The first open presidential elections were held in 1992, in which Ould Taya, the incumbent, defeated Ould Daddah, the younger brother of the former president. The results were contested by the main opposition parties who boycotted the legislative and senatorial elections, allowing Ould Taya's party to dominate the 2-chamber National Assembly. In spite of continuing to question Ould Taya's legitimacy, the main opposition groups agreed to participate in local municipal elections in Jan 1994 when they did fairly well, particularly in the two major cities.

Despite its obvious flaws, Mauritania's democratization process has had positive effects, notably the creation of a free press, the easing of ethnic tensions and the reconciliation with Senegal, and has been heralded as one of the rare success stories in the region. The French in particular, disturbed by the debacle in Algeria, and instability in Mali, have given support to Ould Taya who they consider a stable force. This French seal of approval has led to the gradual international rehabilitation of Mauritania, which in turn has been a key factor in restoring internal confidence in the Ould Taya regime. Hence, while 1994-95 has witnessed a certain amount of unrest; the arrests in Sep 1994 of the Islamists, and the subsequent riots in Jan 1995 after a 25% rise in the price of bread followed by the brief arrest of main opposition leaders, such events have posed little real threat to the régime to date.

In this respect the arrests of the

pro-Iraq Bathists in the autumn of 1995 were seen by observers of the Mauritanian political scene as further signs of the régime's rapprochement to the West, and a gesture towards moderate forces within the country's elite. Here it is also worth noting that the last couple of years have seen the progressive weakening of the main opposition as many of the factions making up the party have gone over to the president's party and increased the presidential majority. Legislative elections are excepted in Oct 1996 and the opposition will participate for the first time. Presidential elections are scheduled for 1998 and Ould Taya intends to stand again. It seems likely that Ould Taya and his political party, the PRDS (Parti Républicain Démocratique et Social), will continue to dominate the political scene in the foreseeable future.

ECONOMY

Traditional agriculture

As many as 90% of the Moors were engaged in various forms of pastoral nomadism until the early 1970s. During the droughts of the 1970s, many herds, particularly camels, were sold at rock bottom prices to urban based entrepreneurs who hired the former nomads as salaried herders. A fair proportion of the country's 4.8 million sheep, 3.1 million goats, 1.0 million cattle, 1.0 camels and 155,000 asses remain, however, in the hands of nomads. Camel nomads are nowadays mainly found in the N and E, while cattle nomads, mainly Peul, are found in the Assaba and Gorgol regions. The Sahelian drought reduced animal numbers by an estimated 45% but there has since been a recovery. The nomadic herdsmen retain as many animals as they can and dispose of them only when they need money or when the pastures will no longer support the herds. The animal trade can be seen at Kaedi, Kiffa, Timbedra and Nema where the dealers and

exporters are centred. In recent years the government has attempted to rehabilitate and modernize the pastoral sector and the World Bank has funded a project for pastoralist associations.

The country is not self-sufficient in grain and the loss of farmers from the land during the drought and the fighting by Polisario in the N made the situation worse. In the S, sedentary rainfed or flood based agriculture is undertaken by *haratin* or African farmers in the Senegal River belt, where the main crops are millet, vegetables and pulses. In the Adrar and Tagant date palm oases continue to produce important harvests. The palmeries are owned by Moors but tended by *haratin* who keep a share of the produce and are nowadays often paid a salary. Farming in the N is possible only with irrigation water withdrawn from cistern water-stores or from wells dug into the beds of *oueds*.

Modern agriculture

Some attempts have been made to improve the quality of pastoralism. The French colonial administration set up wells and fodder points in the N zone to help ensure fewer disputes over land and water. A veterinary service was also set up which brought about significant improvements in the quality of animals. Some small scale development works were attempted in the oases and a rational system of marketing and taxation was established. Some of this structure was lost as a result of Independence and the drought. The new government of Mauritania attempted to pursue food self-sufficiency as a goal and concentrated its efforts on the Senegal River area. Rice became the main crop on the 300,000 ha Golgol project which used water drawn from the Senegal River at Kaedi. The construction of a series of dams in the early 1980s made irrigated agriculture possible on a wide scale and attracted the interest of Moor entrepreneurs. Tensions between the latter and black farmers have been a major source of ethnic unrest in recent years. In spite of the introduction of irrigated agriculture Mauritania still spends over 30% of its available foreign exchange on imported foodstuffs.

Agricultural production 1994

	(tonnes)
Sorghum	114,000
Pulses	17,000
Rice	59,000
Dates	22,000
Vegetables	15,000
Millet	7,000
Maize	6,000

Source: *FAO*

Energy/petroleum

Mauritania produces neither coal nor petroleum and its electricity output of 165 million kwh is produced with imported fuels. A refinery produces 827,000 tonnes per year of petroleum products, inadequate to fulfil domestic demand. Imports of crude oil and products account for 9.2% of the country's total import bill.

Economic plans

A series of economic development plans has been adopted by independent Mauritania, beginning in 1963 with the first 4-year plan. Funds for the plan came from revenues earned from mining operations and from foreign aid, notably from Spain and China. The plan went far from smoothly and by 1966 it became inoperative. In practice, the various plans involved taking on foreign debt and the need for state management of large scale ventures which eventually overwhelmed the abilities of the government. The problems were exacerbated in 1972 by nationalizations of most trade activities. The impact of the Sahelian drought after 1973 brought the economy into an increasingly depressed state. This was worsened by the war in the western Sahara. Aid from the EU and Arab countries did little other than enable the country to survive. Mauritania is presently in the midst of an extensive World Bank/IMF Structural Adjustment programme and in late 1992, the Ougiya was devalued 28%.

Contrary to fears, the devaluation has not led to uncontrollable inflation and, with the resumption of financial aid from Saudi Arabia and the Gulf States, the Mauritanian economy now seems healthier than in recent years.

Industry

The principal industry in Mauritania is mining. The iron ore extracting industry is based on the Kediel Aj-Jill deposits which are limited and reaching exhaustion. Other low grade ores occur E of Zouerate but require large investments in new plant at a time of low profitability for iron ore exports. The iron industry is controlled by SNIM (Société Nationale d'Industrialization Minier). The Akjoujt copper mine began output in 1973 based on modest reserves of 28 million tonnes. Copper concentrate is carried to Nouakchott by a specially constructed road from a mining town at Akjoujt. The company, Somima, was less than successful as a result of internal difficulties and falling prices for copper on the world market. It was also nationalized and amalgamated in the state-owned SNIM. A shut-down occurred in 1978 but the mine has now reopened. Since 1991 gold is also being mined in Akjoujt by the Australian company, Morag. The mining industry produced 9.4 million tonnes of iron ore and 3,240 tonnes of gypsum in 1993. Other small scale industry relies on processing animal and food products.

Economic trends

Growth in the economy has been at about 5.5% per year in the last decade, obviously hindered badly by war, the Sahelian drought and internal mismanagement of the economy. National income was worth only US$1,109 million in 1992 and is still growing inadequately to outstrip the increase in population. Agriculture dominates the economy despite mining and the expansion of government services in recent years.

Structure of GDP (%)
Agriculture 23.7
Mining 9.1
Manufacturing 11.1
Public Utilities/Construction 6.7
Transport 6.5
Other Services 42.9

Source: *Encyclopaedia Britannica*

Economic Indicators

Most economic indicators are adverse, including inflation at 9.4% (1993) and foreign debt at US$1.86 billion, far exceeding the annual value of total GDP.

Economic indicators (Mauritania)					
	1989	**1990**	**1991**	**1992**	**1993**
GDP (UM billion)	118.0	125.0	135.6	100.2	125.5
Inflation (1985=100)	93.8	100.0	105.6	116.3	...
Exports (UM million)	37.45			37.0	34.6
Imports (UM million)	29.17			35.3	32.4
Balance of Trade (UM million)	+8.28			+2.3	+2.2
Foreign Debt (US$ billion)	1.86	0.99		1.86	2.5

US$1 = 132.56 Mauritanian Ouguiya

Source: IMF, EIU, *Encyclopaedia Britannica*

Nouakchott and Environs

NOUAKCHOTT, capital since 1958, is located on the Atlantic coast and offers the best access both to the desert and to the Sahel. It struggles against the encroaching Sahara, is the government and administrative centre and has the best hotel, hospital and educational facilities.

Pop 480,408 (1992), more recent estimates vary but are usually between 400,000-500,000. *Alt* 1m.

HISTORY

HISTORY

Construction of Nouakchott began in 1958 as an extension of an old **ksar**, or fortified town, and a French military post. It was made capital of the newly independent Mauritania in 1960. Before this the French colony had been governed from St Louis in Senegal. Nouakchott was chosen as capital because it was in a neutral zone situated outside the areas associated with the most powerful Moorish tribes. At that time Nouakchott was some distance from the Sahara, but desertification has brought arid, sandy conditions to the edge of the city. Indeed Nouakchott with its pervasive dust, orange sand dunes, sandy streets and herds of camels gives the impression of a city not just trailing off into the desert but inhabited by it. The general impression is of a yellow haze/fog hanging over the town, particularly to the E. If it wasn't for the pleasant sea breeze that refreshes Nouakchott in the late afternoon, it would be easy to forget that the Atlantic Ocean only lies 6 km away. For the traveller arriving from overseas, Nouakchott is unsophisticated, with very few of the facilities and services normally associated with a capital city. However, in the last couple of years concerted efforts have been made to give Nouakchott at least the appearance of a capital. Hundreds of kilometres of the dilapidated roads within the city have been cemented. New

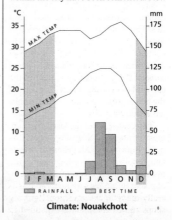

Climate: Nouakchott

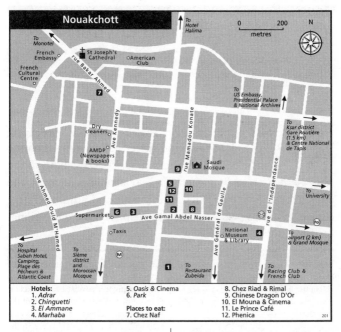

Hotels:		5. *Oasis & Cinema*	8. Chez Riad & Rimal
1. *Adrar*		6. *Park*	9. Chinese Dragon D'Or
2. *Chinguetti*			10. El Mouna & Cinema
3. *El Ammane*		**Places to eat:**	11. Le Prince Café
4. *Marhaba*		7. Chez Naf	12. Phenica

routes have been created and the road from town that runs E and links to the Route de l'Espoir has been widened to two lanes. It is also likely that before the end of the century a major project will be mooted to give Nouakchott a modern capital centre with the associated facilities. This will involve the destruction of some of the most run down buildings in central Nouakchott, along a section of Ave Gamal Abdel Nasser. Demolition of some of the dwellings here, built in the early 1960s to house the civil servants of the new republic and now virtual slums, has already started.

The changes over the last 2 years are most impressive. New shops specializing in high quality Mauritanian objects and jewellery have opened along the main roads in the city centre and choice of places to eat has widened. More generally many of the traditional grocery shops run by locals have expanded to become small-scale supermarkets.

Like the rest of the country, Nouakchott has a somewhat sleepy air, a city waiting for something to happen to it. Do not rely on the few traffic lights being obeyed. Traffic discipline is poor. The city is relaxed, the people are shy but not unfriendly, but has little to occupy the traveller after 2 or 3 days.

Originally designed for 12,000, Nouakchott's population has swollen as drought has forced people to migrate to the capital to escape from the difficult economic conditions prevailing in the interior. As a consequence there are vast areas of shacks on all sides of the city, some made only from waste packaging materials and containers. Many recent migrants use tents. Nouakchott has one of the worst cases of over-urbanization in Africa, with high unemployment and great shortages of basic services and utilities, as well as the housing dilemma.

One of the major problems regarding housing is the highly speculative land market: not only do the criteria governing the granting of allotments often favour those least in need, but once land is distributed there is a tendency for people to resell or rent at exorbitant prices. These problems became so severe during the 1980s that people, especially women, often would set up constructions overnight on publicly owned land in an attempt to force the government to grant title to such land. Eventually when this phenomena became so popular that entire settlements – known as *gazra* – sprang up virtually overnight, the government began to grant the illegal tenants official title. At the other – luxury – end of the market planning seems equally anarchic with luxury villas springing up. More generally the capital's property market has been the source of several vast fortunes for many Mauritanian private speculators involved in the construction of the city in the 1960s.

On the whole life for rural migrants to the capital is difficult as jobs are hard to come by; the civil service works on a patronage basis and contacts are needed to gain jobs in this already overstaffed sector, while industry is minimal. Although huge disparities of wealth do exist, the continuing strength of traditional networks which ensure the redistribution of wealth in return for socio-political support means that few go hungry.

The city of Nouakchott is located in a flat, sandy area close to the sea, and is centred around an older Moorish town, the ksar, and the modern town centre which has wide streets but few impressive buildings. Most of the larger public buildings are little more than functional. The city is, however, the location of most of the country's important commercial and industrial corporations and is the main political centre. Nouakchott has a very shallow economic base, with few vigorous economic concerns, perhaps a consequence of its hasty planning and construction.

The city has a large and interesting market area, as well as a long and pleasant beach, where travellers can take an invigorating swim or watch local fishermen at work. The construction of an international port has made Nouakchott the country's second most important port, but in an economic backwater like Mauritania that is not saying much.

ACCESS **Air** The airport, 3 km to the E, now hosts a newly opened international terminal which has a café, shops and a bank. The old international terminal is now used for domestic flights only and has minimal facilities, a drinks counter, a small shop, and a *bureau de change* which is occasionally open. There is no airport bus service. Travellers must rely on a taxi to the centre, 10 mins away, which may cost as much as UM300, after hard bargaining.

Road Taxi from Rosso, the SE or the Adrar terminate at the *Gare Routière* in the Ksar area of the city, not far from the airport. Either take a taxi, or ask directions to where the yellow and green minivans labelled *Transports Urbaines* will stop.

LAYOUT The airport and *Gare Routière* are in the Ksar district of the city. Ave Gamal Abdel Nasser is the main thoroughfare running into the centre and on to the sea. The intersection with Ave Kennedy marks the city centre, or what there is of it. Ave Kennedy runs from the government, diplomatic quarters and *quartiers chics* in the N to the market and residential areas in 5ième district to the S.

PLACES OF INTEREST

The City Centre Just off Ave Kennedy is the large covered **Central Market** selling a large variety of goods. It is best to visit here early in the day. There is a women's centre behind the market. Along Ave Général de Gaulle is the **Maison du Parti et de la Culture**, containing the **National Museum** (1000-1200 Tues-Sat and 1430-1745 Tues-Sun), with ceramic and historical exhibits. There are few architecturally impressive buildings in Nouakchott. Perhaps one should see the two main mosques, one donated by Saudi Arabia and the other by Morocco but do not attempt to enter mosques uninvited.

The Cinquième district The most interesting area of Nouakchott is the 5ième district, an area of economic housing and popular commerce. A 5 min minibus ride away from the city centre, it is an enjoyable place to wander. The main target will be the market, a rambling area full of stalls selling everything from fruit and vegetables to handicrafts.

The Ksar is the old Moorish town of the Nouakchott area which was destroyed by a 1950 flood and rebuilt. It is a run-down area, with some traders, notably sellers of rugs. There is also a women's rug school, the **Centre National du Tapis**, rue Ghary, perhaps an expensive place to buy carpets but an interesting place to visit. On the road S to Rosso is the **Centre Artisanal**. It is a good place to look at and buy handicrafts. Along this road and the route to the Adrar are large areas of shanty town accommodation.

Tevragh Zeina, which means in hassaniyya 'the most beautiful place', is the area that lies N of Ave Kennedy. It is here, and in the adjoining *quartier chic* of Las Palmas, that the Mauritanian élite have constructed their immense villas, and is worth a visit if only to gain an idea of the huge disparities of wealth that exist in Mauritania.

LOCAL INFORMATION

● Accommodation

Nouakchott's hotels are very expensive, the grades indicating the price and facilities but not the general rundown, shabby conditions which prevail everywhere, and give little opportunity for economizing without misery. The **A** *Monotel Dar el Barka*, behind the French Embassy, BP 1366, T 53526, is perhaps the best of this limited choice, with pool, bar, restaurant and a/c rooms, all major CCs; **A** *Hotel Halima*, opp Russian Embassy in Tevragh Zeina, PO Box 5144, T 57920, F 57922, 30 rm

and 4 suites, restaurant, bar (no alcohol), no pool, small shop, charming staff, collection from and delivery to airport, all major CCs.

B *Hotel Marhaba*, BP 2391, T 51838, 51686, Marba, a/c rooms with TV, also suites, lunch/dinner at UM1,500-2,000 and breakfast at UM500-800 in the restaurant, as well as a bar, snack bar, *bureau de change*, a small handicrafts stall and a pool.

C *Hotel El Ammane*, Ave Gamal Abdel Nasser, BP 13, T 52178, F 53765, reasonable rooms, adequate restaurant with breakfast for UM300-400 and meals for UM1,500-2,000; **C** *Park Hotel*, BP 150, T 51444/6, a/c rooms with balconies, a bar selling non-alcoholic drinks, reasonable restaurant with breakfast for UM300; **C** *Sabah Hotel*, BP 452, T 51552, 51564, Tx 821, is located 100m from the beach and 6 km from the town, with 40 reasonable a/c rooms and suites, a covered pool, a poor restaurant, disco, free transport to/from airport (ask at the *Sabah* café), and transport to/from town.

D *Hotel Chinguitti* next to *Restaurant Phenica*, T 53537; **D** *Hotel Oasis*, Ave Général de Gaulle, BP 4, T 52011, restaurant and reasonable but overpriced a/c rooms.

E *Hotel Adrar*, is a dirty, smelly, shabby place doubling as a brothel, which although it is comparatively cheap and quite friendly, is only for the hardened traveller with a streak of madness.

Camping: is possible and permitted on the beach, 6 km W of the city, which is comparatively secure and safe. Camping costs UM500 pp. Huts which sleep five or six available for UM3,000. Common rooms available for lounging in but be very careful as the tea and coffee so readily served is very expensive and causes unpleasant situations.

● Places to eat

◆◆◆ Restaurants in the hotels incl *Monotel*, said to serve the best food in the city but is commensurately expensive and certainly not busy; *Hotel El Ammane* serves excellent continental food and is one of the most popular establishments in town; *Le Dragon d'Or*, opp Saudi Mosque, T 53211, serves Chinese food; *Park Hotel* also has a reasonable conventional menu at slightly cheaper prices. ◆◆ *Chez Naf* serves western food and some Lebanese dishes, a bit pricey, but clean and friendly with reasonable food and delicious ice creams; *Restaurant Phenica*, T 525-75, standard European/Middle Eastern food, reasonably good and popular; *El Mouna* situated opp the *Phenica* is slightly cheaper and less rec; *Rimal*, Ave Gamal Abdel Nasser, serves Lebanese food, has pleasant terrace; *Sindibad*, across from the downtown market, has a wide range of cheap dishes; *Chez Riad* serves reasonable Lebanese food at good prices; *Zubeida* is a good Moroccan restaurant, although it is not very cheap. ♦ there are few cheap places to eat, but try along Ave Kennedy where a multitude of cheap Shawarma restaurants has opened in the last 2 years; *Le Palmier*, nr the market is economical; *Le Prince* nr *Park Hotel* serves good food, popular with locals, even pizza is available.

● **Bars**
Are only found at the *Monotel* and the *Hotel Marhaba* where alcohol is not served. Alcohol can only be ordered at the *American Club* and the *Racing Club*.

● **Airline offices**
Air Afrique, BP 51, T 252084; **Air Algérie**, Ave Gamal Abdel Nasser, T 252059; **Air Mauritanie**, Direction Commerciale, Ave Gamal Abdel Nasser, BP 41, T 52211/2, F 53815; **Iberia**, Ave Gamal Abdel Nasser, BP 727, T 52654; **Royal Air Maroc**, Ave Gamal Abdel Nasser, T 53564; **UTA**, Ave Gamal Abdel Nasser, BP 662, T 53916.

● **Banks & money changers**
Banque Arabe Africaine en Mauritanie (BAAM), Imm. Afarco, Ave Gamal Abdel Nasser, BP 622, T 52826; **Banque Al Baraka Mauritanienne Islamique (BAMIS)**, Ave du Roi Fayçal, BP 650, 4944, T 51424, F 51621; **Banque Arabe Libyenne Mauritanienne (BALM)**, Ave Gamal Abdel Nasser, BP 626, T 52142, F 53382; **Banque Internationale pour la Mauritanie (BIMA)**, Ave des Dunes, BP 210, T 52363; **Société Mauritanienne de Banque (SMB)**, Ave Gamal Abdel Nasser, BP 614, T 52602.

● **Embassies & consulates**
The few embassies in Nouakchott include **Algeria**, T 52182; **Egypt**, BP 176, T 52192; **France**, BP 231, rue Ahmed Ould M'Hamed, T 51740; **Germany**, BP 372, T 51394; **Libya**, T 52552; **Morocco**, BP 621, T 52304; **Senegal**, BP 611, T 52106; **Spain**, BP 232, T 52080; **Tunisia**, T 52124; **USA**, BP 609, T 52068.

The nearest embassies for other countries are in Dakar, Senegal: **Canada**, BP 3373, T 210290; **Italy**, BP 348, T 220076; **Japan**, BP 3140; and the **UK**, BP 6025, T 217392, Tx 548.

● **Entertainment**
Cinemas: there are three choices for films, normally in French or Arabic, the *Cinéma Oasis*, the *Cinéma El Mouna* opp, and the *SNC Theatre*, nr the post office.

The French Cultural Center also occasionally shows films at its cinémathEque, and also has an excellent video lending library. There are numerous video rental stores in Nouakchott, the quality of films, however, is often very poor.

Nightlife and live music: with the ban on alcohol and the need to get special licenses to hold public events, Nouakchott's night life leaves much to be desired. However, for the visitor who happens to be in town on a public holiday there are usually live concerts that feature Mauritanian and occasionally foreign musicians. These events offer a chance to hear the unusual but haunting music performed by Mauritanian *griots* (hereditary musicians) and meet Mauritanians. Apart from such events, most night life takes place behind closed doors, at weddings, baptisms and private parties which are well worth going to if one is lucky enough to be invited.

● **Hospitals & medical services**
Hospital: T 252135.

● **Laundry & dry cleaners**
Available at *Monotel* and *Hotel Marhaba* are very expensive. Better value from the various *blanchisserie* around the market and the dry cleaner in Immeuble el Mamy on Ave Kennedy.

● **Post & telecommunications**
Area code: 2.

PTT, Ave Gamal Abdel Nasser (0800-1230 and 1400-1830) for post, poste restante and telex. For telephones use the *Monotel*, the *Hotel Marhaba* or the cheaper *cabine telephonique* found throughout the city. Fax can be sent/received at *Monotel* and many *cabine telephonique*.

● **Shopping**
Antiques: there are some new antique shops on the section of Ave Gamal Abdel Nasser that goes to the hospital and on Ave Kennedy/rue Bakar Ahmed. Look with care, bargain with skill for the beautiful chests, rugs, etc.

Books and newspapers: try *Gralicoma* or SLIM nr the market for books, or the boutique in the *Monotel*, or the AMDP situated in Immeuble el Mamy on Ave Kennedy for a wide range of press. The AMDP also sells French language books, although prices can be high. The French Cultural Centre sells French books on Mauritania at very reasonable rates, and also has an excellent specialist library on Mauritania. Another useful library collection is located at the Catholic Church.

Food: there are two supermarkets nr the *Hotel El Ammane* in Ave Gamal Abdel Nasser, which sell imported foreign foodstuffs at inflated prices.

Handicrafts: the best place to get bargains is the open market in the Sième district. Look for engraved silverware, beads, neolithic arrow heads, dyed leather cushions, carpets, wood carvings, hand-crafted leather tobacco pouches and local-style pipes. The various markets are also good for buying cloth such as the colourful locally dyed *melafhas* worn by Moorish women and the richly dyed and embroidered *bazin* cottons used to make up the *boubous* worn by Moorish men and African Mauritanians. Buying cloth can also provide an interesting opportunity for meeting Moorish women who run the stalls. Higher quality items can be bought in the *Centre Artisanal*, such as copper and silver jewellery, daggers, carpets, wooden boxes and chests; or from the dealers in front of the *Hotel El Ammane*. *L'Artisanat Feminin* (0800-1100 and 1600-1800 Sat-Thur), opp the central market, is a women's cooperative selling clothes, purses, pillows, leather cushions and tents. *Le Grand Marché* and *Le Souk*, off Ave Gamal Abdel Nasser, sell leather goods. The *Centre National du Tapis* in rue Ghary has a selection of expensive carpets.

● **Sports**
Fishing: the area is good for fishing, but equipment is difficult to find.

Softball: Fri at 0900, ask at the American Embassy.

Swimming: there are pools at the *Monotel*, the *Marhaba* and the *Sabah*, as well as the sea at the Plage des Pêcheurs.

● **Tourist offices**
Direction à l'Artisanat et au Tourisme, off Ave General Nasser, BP 246, T 53337, ext'n: 368, 322, 374; Société Mauritanienne du Tourisme et de l'Hôtellerie (SMTH), BP 552, T 2353.

● **Useful addresses**
Car repair: this is most likely to be in the Ksar

district of the town. Try *Peyrissac*, on Ave Gamal Abdel Nasser, T 52213.

Police: T 17.

● **Transport**
Local Car hire: Avis, T 51713; Cotema, T 52352; Europcar T 51136; Lacombe, T 52221. **Taxis**: are no longer the ubiquitous green and yellow. Beware as there are some surprisingly decrepit vehicles. Your driver (and vehicle) may be from Senegal or Guinea. Green and yellow minivans, labelled **Transports Urbaines**, run over the city along fixed routes, and are very cheap, often overcrowded and subject to frequent stops by the police. There are no buses from the airport to the town centre, taxis are the only option and will entail serious bargaining. Taxi from airport UM1,000-1,500; local taxi trips UM100-200.

Air Air Mauritanie has international flights to **Casablanca, Dakar, Rome (via Tunis), Paris,** and **Brussels,** and domestic flights to towns throughout the country. Times are very variable. Check locally. To **Dakar** by Air Mauritanie on Thur and Sat, £100 (equivalent) for 21 day open return; to **Paris** by Air Afrique direct flight twice a week (Air Afrique, Ave Gamal Abdel Nasser, T 53564). To **Nouadhibou**, daily (UM8,300); also **Aioun-el-Atrouss,** Fri (UM8,500); **Atar**, Sat, Mon, Thur (UM7,100); **Kaedi,** Wed (UM6,100); **Kiffa,** Tues (UM7,200); **Nema,** Fri (UM11,300); **Tidjikja,** Tues (UM8,400); **Selibaby,** Wed (UM7,200); **Zouerate,** Tues, Thur (UM10,100). Return flights are same day and cost double price of single ticket.

Road Transport to **Nouadhibou** is difficult as there is no direct road. The most practical way is by aeroplane. A cheaper option is by truck, which can be picked up from the 5ième district of Nouakchott. Trucks and *bâches* (converted pick-up trucks) leave from this district to Nouadhibou, Atar and Kaedi.

EXCURSIONS

Plage des Pêcheurs and the Wharf The Wharf is a small, old port, now mainly used by small-scale fishermen and artisans, with deep sea fishing and facilities available for hire. The best time to visit is around 1600 when the fishing boats return. This is a good place to buy fish. It has recently been developed as a small modern port. The Chinese built port, S of the wharf, is also worth a visit although access can sometimes be difficult. Fishing also takes place at the Plage des Pêcheurs, which is also a pleasant place to wander or swim. After the little sightseeing that Nouakchott has to offer this is the main place to spend time, a long, unspoilt beach stretching into the distance. To get there follow the black top road W from the Ave Kennedy/Ave Gamal Abdel Nasser intersection or get a green Renault taxi costing UM25.

The North

THE COAST NORTH from Nouakchott to Nouadhibou, a distance of 525 km, contains some excellent beaches and some spectacular flora and fauna. It passes Cap Timirist and the *Parc National du Banc d'Arguin*, a huge reserve for migrating birds.

THE COAST FROM NOUAKCHOTT TO NOUADHIBOU

In this unusual country there is no black top road connecting the two main towns. Even the *piste* N from Noukchott to Nouadhibou is frequently undefined. Few vehicles (mainly lorries carrying water/fuel and trucks piled high with goods and passengers, few private cars) make this journey and most (perhaps 20-30 trucks a day) use partly *piste* and, depending on the tide, the 3m band of firm sand exposed on the shore. It is recommended to take a guide if aiming for Nouadhibou as particularly further N there are numerous vehicle tracks over a very wide area and the route to Bou Lanouar where one turns W for Nouadhibou is certainly not as clear as the maps indicate. Only 4WD vehicles stand a chance of completing the journey. It is possible, but quite unnecessary, to do this journey in 2 days. Allow 3 full days with 2 nights camping en route.

Officially one needs an authorization to take a vehicle out of the town and this may be asked for at the road check on the town's outskirts – but not of course if you drive up the beach from beside the *Sabah Hotel*.

Nouamghar, 155 km N of Nouakchott, a collection of about 200 shanties, is the major village of the Imraguen, a group of about 800 coastal dwellers who depend for their livelihood on fish, particularly mullet, the main season for which is Oct-Dec. The sea here is very shallow, the net is positioned into a semi-circle and the fish are driven into the net by hitting the water with large flat boards. The dolphins, frequent visitors to this coast, are always in evidence at this time. While it is romantic to assume that the dolphins are there to assist the fishermen, the more likely explanation is that they are only there for the food. Boats may be hired here but **Iwik** further N is a better place from which to visit the islands for bird watching.

The **Parc National du Banc d'Arguin** is a very significant site for aquatic birds migrating between Africa and Eurasia. They include broad-billed sandpipers, black terns, flamingoes, white pelicans, spoonbills, herons, white herons and cormorants. Some birds remain and breed here in this tranquil and food-rich environment. The birds often inhabit the offshore sand islands, thus a boat is required for proper birdwatching. The

Shipwreck

🦶 Despite the beauty and tranquillity of the Banc D'Arguin, Tidra Island and Cap Timiris the numerous sand flats hidden beneath the rising tides were a dangerous trap for ships in the past and the Mauritanian and neighbouring Western Saharan coastlines are punctuated by numerous shipwrecks. The most famous of these is undoubtedly the 'Meduse', which was part of a fleet travelling to Senegal when the territory was returned to France after the Napoleonic wars of the early 19th century. The fate of the occupants of the ship, whose passengers included women and children was dire; many perished in a march across Mauritanian territory, while the men cast adrift in the infamous 'raft' immortalized in Gericault's famous painting now hanging in the Louvre 'The raft of the Meduse' mostly died in massacres that took place on the raft. The fate of the Meduse caused an enormous scandal in France, not least because the treasure that the ship was said to be carrying destined for the coffers of Senegal was lost somewhere off the coast. The myth of this lost treasure still attracts treasure hunters, although to date no one has succeeded in locating the gold.

If other shipwrecks were less dramatic, the fate of the marooned sailors left much to be desired. If they survived they were likely to be captured and enslaved by Moorish tribes who specialized in combing the coast for goods run ashore in the course of shipwrecks. If the sailors were lucky enough to escape or be ransomed by British or other foreign representatives based in Mogador (now Essaouria in Morocco) whose remit included organizing the release of the unhappy western captives, they frequently wrote or dictated narratives of their 'adventures'.

Nowadays Mauritania's coast continues to be dotted with shipwrecks although today the wrecks are more likely to be linked to fraudulent insurance claims than the hazards of the ocean and weather or poor navigation.

main entrance to the park is at Nouamghar. The man who sells the tickets is in one of the smarter shacks. Entrance UM800 per day. Just say for how many days. Once in the park – which is really no more than a strip of coast, much of it quite swampy, backed by a huge area of desert – one is free to ride. We recommend you to take a guide who will navigate across the erg rather than the very poor quality *piste*.

Trips to sail round the islands are best arranged from **Iwik**, another small collection of shacks 60 km N of Nouamghar. The main island is **Tidra** but there are many smaller ones too. It is necessary to consider the weather. The sailing boats can only operate if there is a wind but the birds are only there if it is calm ... so try to book on a day with a light breeze. The boat which can take 4-6 passengers will cost, after some hard bargaining, about UM10,000 for 4-6 hrs. Be firm too about the time scale as the boat owner will return you sooner if he can. There is much to observe without landing. Special permits are required to land on the islands and to walk among the birds. These are only given to genuine ornithologists. Restrictions to protect the birds from visitors in the breeding season do not appear to operate. Permits may be granted at Iwik but make enquiries both at the tourist office in Nouakchott and at the park entrance in case the routine has changed – it is too far to go back. For specialist tours to this area see page 440.

There are some cabins for visitors near the manager's house in Iwik although the two main camping spots are both N of Iwik, at **Cap Tafarit**, noted also for fishing, though jackals can be a problem here and **Cap Tagarit**, only 8 km further N, which is much prettier and has fewer jackals.

NOUADHIBOU

Pop 59,198 (1988), *Alt* 8m.

History

Nouadhibou, formerly called Port Etienne, is Mauritania's second city and the capital of the Dakhlet-Nouadhibou (Baie du Levrier) region. It is the most northerly settlement in Mauritania, on the coast, on the sheltered side of a peninsula shared with Moroccan western Sahara but administered in the whole by Mauritania. This is a very barren area of coast. Nouadhibou is the country's main port, with economic activities centred around iron ore and fishing, for this is one of the richest fishing grounds in the world. Although the fishing industry has been plagued by mismanagement, in the last 2 decades several substantial fortunes have been made by Mauritanians involved in this potentially lucrative sector. Nouadhibou lies at the terminus of the iron ore railway line from Zouerate, which brings in vast amounts of this raw material, which is then exported in large ore carriers, from Port Minéralier which

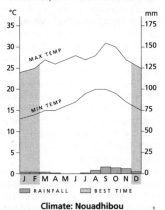

°C / mm

Climate: Nouadhibou

RAINFALL   BEST TIME

is S of the city centre. The state-controlled iron-ore company, *SNIM*, runs the railway, the port and Cansado, an autonomous settlement for company employees, 6 km S of the town on the peninsula tip. There is a substantial West African immigrant population, who arrive in Nouadhibou as the last stop, before the border with Morocco. Many seek to stow away on boats to the Canary Islands or Europe.

ACCESS The train from Choum or Zouerate arrives at Port Minéralier, S of the city centre. Taxis or the police will take travellers from the train into town. Arriving at the rather tumbledown airport (aptly described as just a more level piece of erg between Nouadhibou and La Gouèra), the city centre is a short taxi ride away, taking 5-10 mins and costing UM30-50. Coming in by road there is a customs post about 16 km N of Nouadhibou. It is not always easy to get through here and travellers report that sometimes 'presents' are demanded in return for the car documents.

Places of interest

The town, such as it is, has one main street running NS with minor ones parallel and alleys connecting across. To the N is a large area of shanty dwellings. The town has no real centre except the point on the main road at the taxi stand where there are some 2-storey buildings, banks etc. There are half a dozen restaurants and the liveliest area is around the shops. The town is unusual in Mauritania, because of its mix of ethnic communities, European and Far Eastern workers, particularly Korean, at the port and West Africans looking for work or a passage to Europe. This is reflected in the shops and restaurants around Nouadhibou. The Paris to Dakar rally passes through each Jan. Near the airport are the ruins of Tcherka, formerly occupied by the Canary Islanders. South again are the ports for cargo and fishing while the harbour to the E is noted for its 150 or so rusting hulks out to sea. South again another 6 km is Cansado where Mauritanians and expatriates have beach huts – perhaps slightly less run down than Nouadhibou. Further S again is Port Minéralier where the train line from Zouerate terminates and the iron ore is loaded on to boats.

There is no swimming in the bay to the E as it is polluted. Swim instead off the W coast. Monk seals can be seen off shore here but there are more on the W coast where they come out of the water. Between 50-100 such seals have been counted. Cap Blanc at the southern tip of the peninsula has a lighthouse, and good views.

It is possible to go on the W side of the peninsula where there is a very attractive beach with bays and headlands and a huge wrecked freighter. This attractive area which sometimes gets good surf, at other times provides good swimming. The bottom is very rocky. The Atlantic coast N along the peninsula has some spectacular cliffs. You will need a car to get there. It is not possible to go further N than **La Gouèra**, an old Spanish fishing village, as this is occupied by the Mauritanian army. **Take great care** on the W side of the peninsula. Although the beach itself is not mined do not venture on the dunes behind the beach or the land as far E of the central border.

There are no maps available of the area but the restaurant *Le Surf* has some amazingly detailed maps of Cap Blanc peninsula on the wall.

Local information
● **Accommodation**
Nouadhibou has several good hotels, some of which serve alcohol. Try the **B** *Sabah Hotel*, near the airport, BP 285, T 45317/77, F 45499, with pool, disco and bar.

D *Hotel du Maghreb*, Blvd Median, BP 160, with breakfast at UM200 and lunch/dinner at UM1200, and a bar; the more economic **D** *Hotel des Imraguens*, 1 km from the centre, BP 160, T 2272, with 21 rm, restaurant and nightclub; and the **D** *Hotel Niabina*, rue Sonney, BP 146, T 45983. Apparently the Catholic Mission also has accommodation.

In Cansado, the iron ore company runs a good hotel, the **C** *Hotel Oasian*, Cansado, BP 42, T 2700, on coast, views of bay, 36 rm, three suites, TV, phone, frig, with a restaurant, bar and pool.

● **Places to eat**
Seafood is a popular speciality. Try ◆◆◆*Le Surf* in *Hotel Oasian* for shellfish; ◆◆*Le Marin* is good for fresh fish; *Le Cabana*, in the Port de Pêche, near the town centre, is a good bet for fish and other food. There are a number of bars selling alcohol in Nouadhibou.

● **Banks & money changers**
Banque Al Baraka Mauritanienne Islamique (**BAMIS**), BP 205, T 45663/4, F 45665; Banque Arabe Libyenne Mauritanienne (**BALM**), T 45132, F 45133.

● **Sports**
Fishing: Nouadhibou has good fishing all year, particularly of sea bass, sea bream, ray, umbrine and trout. Surf casting is very popular and there are fishermen in the port that will take enthusiasts out for a negotiated price. However, serious fishers will want to go to the *Centre de Pêche Sportive*, in the Baie de l'Étoile, 15 km N of Nouadhibou. This is a residential centre, with excellent opportunities for fishing, mainly surf casting, for an immense variety of species. The centre has eight double rooms, a restaurant, vehicles, staff and guides. *Air Afrique* organizes package tours to the centre, including the air ticket, lodging, meals and fishing gear, from Nouakchott or Paris, and varying in length from a few days to weeks. Contact: Service Tourism, **Air Afrique**, 29 rue du Colisée, F 75008, Paris, T 42257169.

Swimming: there are good beaches on the peninsula.

● **Transport**
The easiest way to get to Nouakchott is by aeroplane, a cheaper way is by truck. However, as there is no road this is a problematic route. **Local** Nouadhibou has taxis to the airport, as well as to Cansado and Port Minéralier.

Air Air services from Nouadhibou include **Air Mauritanie** to Atar, Zouerate, Nouakchott (daily by airbus 300, takes 35 mins, costs UM8,300 single) or Las Palmas, and **Iberia** to Las Palmas. There may also be *Aeroflot* flights.

Train The trains to Choum or Zouerate leave from Port Minéralier.

THE ADRAR REGION

If there is only time for one tour, then perhaps the Adrar should be the destination, as it offers some of the most dramatic scenery and two historic towns.

The Adrar region is a large massif of mountains, plateaux, dunes and canyons in the N of Mauritania, with some breathtaking desert scenery. It is one of the most interesting areas of the country, an historic area of settlement, and a region where nomads have traditionally lived. Indeed, the Adrar has been occupied since Neolithic times, as stone tools and other remains testify. Its warriors were known throughout the area, and it was the base of an Emirate until French colonization. More recently, the Adrar was known as a centre of opposition to the rule of the republic's first president, Ould Daddah. There is a number of oases, several associated with historic sites and towns. In the months of Jul and Aug, many families and individuals originally from the region descend on the oases of Adrar for the date harvest, known as *guetna*, which is a major social occasion not to be missed if you are travelling through Adrar during this period. In the oases and gorges crops are cultivated for local consumption, including millet, sorghum, barley, tomatoes and green vegetables, but dates dominate. However, as in much of Mauritania, the towns and cultivated areas

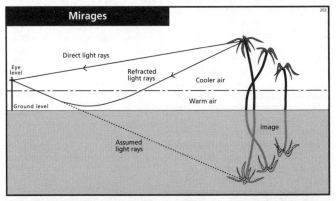

Mirages

202

Direct light rays

Eye level

Refracted light rays

Cooler air

Ground level

Warm air

Image

Assumed light rays

Mirages – illusions in the desert

A mirage is a type of optical illusion caused by the refraction (bending) of rays of light as they pass through air layers of varying temperatures and densities. The most common mirage occurs in the desert where what appears to be a distant pool of water, perhaps surrounded by palm trees turns out, to the disappointment of the thirsty traveller, to be only another area of dry sand.

The rays of light that come directly to the eye show the palm trees in their correct position. The rays of light that travel through the warmer, less dense air travel faster as they meet less resistance and change their direction. They bend nearer to the ground but are assumed to have come directly to the eye so the brain records the trees and the blue sky as reflections in a pool of water.

The rays are real, just misinterpreted, thus a mirage can be photographed but that does not, alas, make the shimmering 'water' available to quench the thirst.

are often threatened by encroaching sand. Cut into the plateaux are some impressive canyons, and there are some interesting ancient rock paintings. Travel to the Adrar can be by aeroplane to Atar (from Nouakchott or Nouadhibou), by taxi or private vehicle from Nouakchott. The only other possibilities, for the adventurous, are the train to Choum and then a taxi to Atar, or across the deep desert from Tidjikja, Nema or Ouadane, in a camel or 4WD vehicle convoy.

Akjoujt, although not actually in the Adrar, is the first town en route from Nouakchott to Atar, and stands at the end of the black top road. The 250 km black top road itself is of a poor quality, but will be passable by most vehicles in about 6-9 hrs. This town, which is the administrative centre of the Inchiri region, is based around the mines for the copper resources discovered in 1941, notably at Guelb Moghrein, which have since closed down. There are shops, tea houses and fuel at Akjoujt. The track from Akjoujt to Atar is not black top, but there are taxis.

Terjit and **Oujeft** could be visited en-route to Adrar, or as an excursion from Atar. Terjit, signposted to the right of the *piste* before Atar, is worth visiting, with its tree-lined hot and cold springs, where swimming is pleasant. A further 35 km S of Terjit is Oujeft, a scenic oasis with verdant palmeries and interesting archaeological relics.

ATAR

Pop 16,326 (1976), *Alt* 226m.

This is the capital of the Adrar region, an old oasis settlement lying on the route of the historic salt caravans, and an important marketing centre for the nomads of the region, with an historic core, the ksar. The town has had a considerable colonial influence, and in fact there are still French there, at the Inter-Arab Ecole Militaire, for Atar is also a military

base. Atar is a pleasant, relaxed town and a good base for exploring the surrounding region. There is a petrol station and basic provisions shops. Walk along the dike that separates the town from the rural area, and from the beautiful date palm groves that surround the town.

Places of interest

Atar is divided into an interesting **ksar** area with narrow streets, and a modern area of wider streets and bigger buildings. The **market** between has a small selection of things to buy, including leatherware, jewellery and rugs. There are also workshops for leather, jewellery and metal work in the surrounding areas of the town. Near the hotel is a **French fort** dating from WW2, as well as a contemporary military school. Exploration of the date palmery is interesting because of the use of traditional systems of irrigation. The locals enjoy the walk along the dike at sunset. This can be reached from either the town or the palmeries, or from the grounds of the hotel.

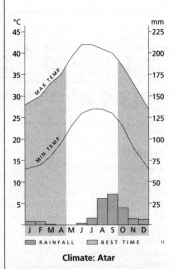

Climate: Atar

Local information

● Accommodation

Atar has a good hotel, the **D** *Hotel des Almoravides*, which has a/c rooms with bath, restaurant and non-alcoholic drinks bar, with a set meal at UM800 and breakfast at UM200. Ask directions from the town centre. There is also a basic and run down rest house near the centre. Apparently it is also possible to stay at the Catholic Mission.

● Places to eat

Apart from the hotel, basic meals can be had at establishments in the old part of town. The situation there changes quickly in these cheap places so be selective.

● Transport

Air Atar is connected by air with Nouakchott. Flights on Sat, Mon, Thur UM7,100 single. Taxis to/from the airstrip cost UM500.

Road A place in a taxi to Nouakchott costs UM2500, with driving time approximately 8 hrs. There are also taxis to Choum to meet the Zouerate-Nouadhibou trains, along a rough but just passable track. Land Rovers make the run to Chinguetti, these cost UM700 outside and UM1,000 in the cab. They wait till they are full and therefore do not leave every day, but one can take a Land Rover alone and immediately for UM9,000. The journey takes 1 hr. Places are also available on the twice-weekly food lorry to Chinguetti. The track to Chinguetti and on to Ouadane is not an easy one. A car and driver can be hired for 1 day, the itinerary fixed by the client, cost UM15,000. Travellers with their own 4WD vehicle will probably need a guide to get to Amogjar, Chinguetti or Ouadane. For those with less time, there are some feasible short excursions from Atar. As well as Terjit, Oujeft and Amogjar which can mainly be reached only by personal transport, there are the ruins at **Azougui**, which can be reached by taxi costing UM50/100.

EXCURSIONS

Azougui lies along a scenic route, 15 km to the NW of Atar. This oasis has the ruins of a citadel, dating from the Almoravid period of the 11th and 12th century, when it was capital of the Adrar. This was the base for conquests of the empire of Ghana, notably Aoudaghost, and the establishment of the powerful Moroccan Dynasty that toppled the Idrissids. Close to the citadel is the Almoravid Imam Hadrami's necropolis.

Amorgar (or Amogjar) is a mountain pass 70 km along the track from Atar to Chinguetti, the summit of the Adrar plateau which has impressive views. A day excursion from Atar is a spectacular experience, passing through dramatic mountain scenery. En route there are fortifications marking Mauritania's period of involvement in the W Sahara war. Near the pass itself, to the left of the track are rock paintings of suns, giraffes, cows and hunters. These are of great antiquity but still discernable. The verdant landscape depicted in the paintings indicates how the environment of the region has changed. 6 km further on, on the right, are some more curious rock paintings. From the rock paintings, return to Atar or continue along the rough *piste* to Chinguetti.

CHINGUETTI

Mauritania's most famous historic city, Chinguetti dates from the 13th century. Named 'Shinqit' in Arabic, a name also used for the whole country before the French colonization. It is located on the salt caravan route. It was both a Moorish capital and a religious centre famous around the Islamic World, and reckoned to be Islam's seventh city. It was the point where the pilgrims from the region gathered for the caravan across Africa to Mecca. Chinguetti was known for its poets and Islamic scholars, and still has an important mosque and libraries. The town is now declining both in status and in physical terms with erosion, being literally worn away by or covered with the sand. The visitor arrives first in the newer area of the town. The fort in Chinguetti, originally occupied by the Foreign Legion, was used in *Fort Saganne*, a French film from the early 1980s. Near the fort there is also a curious non-functional solar demonstration pump, and the police station, where travellers are required to register.

Camels – ships of the desert

There are two kinds of camel, *Camelus Dromedarius*, the Arabian camel with one hump and *Camelus Bactrianus*, the Bactrian which has two. Arabian camels, found in North Africa, though only as domestic animals, are about 3m long and about 2m high at the shoulder. They range in colour from white to black.

They are not the most attractive of creatures, looking particularly ragged and scruffy at the spring moult. Large bare leathery areas on legs and chest look like some serious skin complaint but are normal and act as cushions when the animal kneels down.

Interesting physical characteristics which allow these animals to survive in the desert include hairs inside the ear opening as well as the ability to close the nostrils between breaths, both preventing sand penetration; thick eyebrows to shade the eyes from the sun's glare; a pad of skin between the two large toes on each foot forming a broad, tough 'slipper' which spreads the animal's weight over a larger area and prevents sinking in the loose sand; the ability to store a reserve of fat in the hump and to go for days without water. Each eye has three eyelids, the upper and lower lids have very long eyelashes to protect the eyes from sand whipped up by desert winds, while a third, thinner lid blinks away dust from the eyeball. The skin inside a camel's mouth is so tough that cactus thorns do not penetrate, hence a camel can eat anything, 'even its owner's tent'.

Camels can go for many days without food as the hump can store up to 35 kilos of fat as emergency rations. They can go without water for even longer, depending on the weather and the kind of food available. As camels do not sweat but instead function at a higher body temperature without brain damage, their demands of fluid are less. At a water hole they drink only enough to balance their body moisture content.

Less pleasant characteristics include a most unpredictable nature, especially in the mating season, which includes nasty habits like using its long sharp teeth to bite people and other camels, viciously kicking with the back legs, spitting and being generally awkward. When a camel stands up it moves in a series of violent jerks as it straightens first its hind legs then its front legs. When a camel walks, it moves both the legs at one side at the same time, giving a very rolling motion which can give the rider travel sickness.

Camels are unwilling beasts of burden, grunting and groaning as they are loaded and generally complaining at being made to lie down or stand up. Once underway though, they move without further protest.

These large, strong beasts are used to pull ploughs, turn water wheels and carry large loads for long distances across difficult terrain. They can carry up to 400 kg but usually the load is nearer 200 kg. Despite moving at a mere 6 or 7 km an hour, camels can travel 100 km in a day. They also provide their owners with hair for cloth, rich milk and cheese, dried dung fuel and eventually meat, bones for utensils and hides for shoes, bags and tenting.

The Arabian dromedary, bred for riding and racing, is of a slighter build but can cover 160 km in a day and reach speeds of up to 15 km per hour.

Across the *wadi* is the old town, with its impressive stone buildings. It is still owned today mainly by members of the Idaw'ali and Laghlal *zawaya* tribes. The 16th century mosque is famous and quite striking, but closed to non-Muslims, although views of it from around the town should satisfy the curiosity. Its minaret has five pinnacles, each surmounted by the *oeufs d'autruche* (ostrich eggs). The principal Koranic library has some 1,300 ancient manuscripts, some as old as the 3rd century. The market displays some interesting items to buy, including ancient tools and arrow heads.

● **Accommodation** Accommodation is in the basic **E** *Maison du Bien Etre*, the even more basic *Auberge des Caravanes*, or with local people who will share what little they have. There is nowhere to eat, but food can be bought at the market stalls or shops.

● **Transport** Travel on to Ouadane is over a rough desert *piste* that leaves the *piste* from Atar just before the town. Follow either the 120 km *Piste* du Dhar Chinguetti, or the *Piste* du Batha over sand dunes. Both require a 4WD vehicle, the latter a guide too. There are few vehicles making the journey.

OUADANE

In a country of ruins Ouadane is one of the most impressive, a hillside of stone buildings in a dramatic landscape above a beautiful palmery. It is rewarding at the end of the long journey from Atar via Chinguetti, but only the dedicated travellers will make it. The town of Ouadane dates from either the 9th or the 12th century, according to different accounts. Some of its earliest inhabitants were the Berber Idawalhaj tribe. Today Ouadane is still home to Idawalhaj families as well as members of the Kunta and Amgarish tribes. Ouadane soon became an important and prosperous camel caravan centre, located as it was between the West African states and the trade routes to the N. These caravans were mainly taken up with salt, dates and gold. Even the Portuguese recognized its economic impor-

tance, setting up a significant trading post in the 15th century. However, Ouadane's location in the N of Mauritania meant that it suffered more than most places from the conquests of the powerful Moroccan Dynasties, the Saadians and the Alawites.

There are beautiful views from Ouadane's hill location, over the oasis, palm groves and surrounding desert areas. The ruins include a mosque and the Ksar el Klali. Also don't miss the Richat hole, a large spiral hole made by a meteorite. It lies to the N of Oudane. Other than basic rest house accommodation in Ouadane, which may be available, travellers will be dependent on the hospitality of the locals.

TINLABBE

Whilst in Ouadane travellers should not miss the opportunity to visit the cave dwellings and rock paintings of Tinlabbé, 7 km NW of the town. Ask directions in Ouadane. It's a long, hot walk but worth it.

THE FAR NORTH

Mauritania reaches a considerable distance N, its joint border with Algeria and Morocco is parallel with Laayoune in Morocco and In Salah in Algeria. In this immense area of generally low-lying land known as Tiris, and renown throughout the region for its fertile pastures, the massif of Kediel Aj-Jill at 915m is conspicuous. The towns associated with the exploitation of the iron ore in this massif are the only settlements in the region.

Choum can be reached by a rough, bumpy, but often spectacular taxi journey of 120 km from Atar. The only reason to go to Choum is because of the Zouerate to Nouadhibou train line. Choum has basic tea tents/houses where travellers wait for the train.

Zouerate, 190 km N from Choum, with the associated settlement of Fderik, and formerly Fort Gouraud, used to be on the western caravan route across the

Sahara. It has grown to a population of 22,500 (1992), as a town devoted to iron ore mining, the centre of that activity in Mauritania, and at the end of the long iron ore railway to Nouadhibou. There is little of interest in the town, but for those visiting, the mining company runs a hotel and restaurant. Transport runs as far as the town, but onward travel is impossible because of problems in the western Sahara. There are flights to Nouakchott on Tues and Thur, UM10,100 single.

Bir-Moghrein, formerly called Fort Trinquet, used to be a caravan post. It has a rest house and rock paintings which ought not to be missed if you have got so far. Located 400 km N from Zouerate, one needs **permission from the police** in Nouakchott to go this far.

ZOUERATE, CHOUM AND NOUADHIBOU

The state iron ore company has a railway line between the iron ore mines at Zouer-ate and the port at Nouadhibou. It runs two daily trains each way. These trains are, at 2.5 km, the longest in the world. The train consists mainly of open wagons of iron ore. However there is often, but not always, a passenger wagon attached, tickets being reasonably priced, about UM300. Many Mauritanians choose to travel for free on top of the iron ore rubble. Indeed this is the only means when a passenger wagon is not laid on. This is a most dramatic way to travel, perhaps one of the world's memorable journeys, if not just for the serious discomfort of the swirling invasive dust, and at night, the biting cold. Take warm clothes and preferably a blanket or sleeping bag, a plastic sheet to lie on, a scarf to wrap tightly round the mouth and eyes, and food and water. The train also stops at Choum, with one of the services leaving at about 1800 for Nouadhibou. The taxi will take its passengers to the train. The train journey from Choum to Nouadhibou takes about 12 hrs.

The South

SOUTHERN MAURITANIA which experiences winter rains in varied proportions encompasses very diverse regions, dunes and sandstone plateaux with villagers dependent on livestock rearing, small areas of cereal cultivation and bare rock outcrops. In the extreme South the Senegal River valley contains areas of sedentary agriculture, even irrigation.

THE ROUTE DE L'ESPOIR

The Route de l'Espoir, the Road of Hope, was built by the Brazilians. It connects the S and SE of the country to Nouakchott. The building of this road means that it is now significantly quicker for the people of these regions to reach the capital. As a consequence, migration from the rural areas, where livelihoods are difficult to maintain, has rapidly increased to the capital where there is the dream of gainful employment, but the reality of great hardship. Along the road lie a succession of towns, of varying interest, but with the advantage of comparatively frequent transport. It is possible to complete the Route de l'Espoir to Nema in 2 days, but why go so fast? Off the road there are interesting detours to the Tagant region, the Koumbi Saleh archaeological site, and the desert religious centre of Oualata with its beautiful houses.

The first region that the road passes through lies mainly to its S is known as Trarza or the Gibla. Although the pervasive orange sand dunes of the region make it hard to believe, before the droughts of the 1970s this region, which extends to the Senegal River was famous for its rich gum Arabic forests and variety of pastures. Home to one of the four emirates that dominated much of Mauritania in the pre-colonial era, Trarza continues to be renowned for its religious traditions. Of notable interest are several villages of the Idawa'li tribe which are situated to the N of Lake R'kiz and form the spiritual centre of the Tijaniyya Sufi order. Although access is difficult to these villages Ma'ta Moulana and Boubacr in particular are worth a visit. A word of caution here; as in other sensitive religious zones it is important for people to behave respectfully and be dressed modestly. Further S Lake R'kiz is a major agricultural zone which is popular with ex-patriates based in Nouakchott who often go there at weekends to hunt wild boar.

Boutilimit is the first town along the road, 265 km and 2 hrs from Nouakchott. It was founded in the 19th century by a religious scholar and mystic, and remains today one of the most renowned centres for religious learning in the region with several *medressa* still functioning. This century it had fame as the birthplace of the country's first president, Mokhtar Ould Daddah. The town is now also known as the location of an Institute for Higher Islamic Studies, an important centre in West Africa. Boutilimit has a large **market**, which is worth seeing as the town is known for its craftwork, particularly silverware and rugs.

After **Aleg**, the centre of the Brakna region but an unexciting place where taxis often stop for tea breaks, the next major settlement is **Kiffa**, population: 29,292 (1988), the main town, administrative centre and market of the Assaba region. The town is connected by an air service with Nouakchott each Tues, UM7,200 single. It has little to see except a reasonably interesting market, with some local handicrafts for sale. However the town does have accommodation, at the **D** *Hotel de l'Amitié et du Tourisme à Kiffa*, BP 46, T 233, a well-run place with electricity but no a/c, and clean, basic rooms with just a mattress, and a separate shower room. The alternative is to stay with local people.

From Kiffa two routes lead off to the N. It is not a great problem to find transport along the 120 km deviation NE to **Tamchaket** but **Tagdawst**, the archaeological site of the Sanhadja Berber capital of Aoudaghost, 40 km further, is only reachable by those with their own transport. This was a very important trading city, through which passed large caravans of horses and bullocks from Morocco from at least 500 BC, and which attained greater prosperity with the arrival of the camel as a transport animal from the 3rd century AD. The city retained its importance until 1050, when it was captured by the empire of Ghana, and by the Almoravids under Yahya Ibn 'Omar, in 1054. Archaeologi-

cal excavations have revealed that the town had been rebuilt on successive levels as the sand covered it, notably in the 16th and 17th centuries, but was then abandoned. The site is not very rewarding to the visitor.

The second route N from Kiffa is to Tidjikja – a rough route not to be undertaken lightly. See Tidjikja, page 437.

Aioun-El-Atrouss, 210 km E of Kiffa along the main road, is a well established town, the administrative centre of the western Hodh area, with a hotel, bank, post office and shops, and some attractive sandstone houses. There are flights from the town's airstrip to Nouakchott Fri morning, contact Air Mauritanie in Nouakchott UM9,500 single, or the distance can be covered by public transport in 2 days. There is accommodation at the **D** *Aïoun Hotel*, BP 41, T 90079, 90060, a quiet friendly place which was built in the mid-1980s in the hope that the Paris-Dakar would pass through annually!, simple rooms with bath, supposed to have electricity and a/c, but both are unreliable.

A wander amongst the houses is pleasant, whilst there are good views from the rocks that ring the town. A very scenic area with some strange rock formations. There is an interesting market with a good line in beads.

The *piste* S from Aioun-El-Atrouss goes to Mali, about 180 km. There is a customs post on the border. Problems are reported of 'fines' of up to US$40 per person for not spending a minimum of UM10,000 per day while in Mauritania. Appeals to the chief of police might save you.

Timbedra, which has an important animal market, lies 170 km E of Aioun-El-Atrouss and it may be possible to get a lift from vehicles en route to Mali. **Koumbi Saleh** is 70 km SE of Timbedra along a quite reasonable track. This is Mauritania's most important archaeological site. Koumbi Saleh was once one of the most populous cities of the world, as capital of the empire of Ghana from the 3rd century. It included two distinctive settlements, a royal town and a large area of residential districts and mosques, the two connected by further houses. It is the main residential district that is the archaeological site to be seen, revealing impressive stone houses and one of the large mosques.

Nema, 106 km beyond Timbedra, is the capital of the eastern Hodh region, an area of the Kunta people, and known for its use as a place of exile for political prisoners. The town marks the end of the Route de l'Espoir, although there are plans to continue this to Mali. Nema has many houses built from stone and clad with clay, in a similar but less decorative style than Oulata (see below). The town has a petrol station, police, a bank, a post office, shops, a market, and an airstrip with weekly flights to Nouakchott on Fri UM11,300 single. Camel convoys still leave for the Saharan regions to the N, and it is a good place to arrange transport and vehicles. The long taxi journey to Nouakchott will probably have to be taken in sections, perhaps changing vehicles in Aioun-El-Atrouss and Kiffa. There is an occasional and very slow bus which makes the journey to Nouakchott. There is no hotel, but accommodation with the family of Sass Ould Moulay Abdelmalek, Commerçant, BP 27 is recommended, which will probably cost UM550 plus meals, as arranged, ask in the town for 'Maison Sass' or 'Commerçant Sass'. All passport formalities must be carried out at the police station in Nema for entry into Mali or Senegal. At Adel Bagrou there are customs but no problems are encountered there.

Oualata, 95 km N of Nema, is a mediaeval fortified settlement which has had great importance as a Saharan caravan post and Islamic centre, with a famous **Koranic school** that is still running, and includes an important library. The **Muslim cemetery** at Tirzet is nearby. Oualata is built on a high terrace, an impressive location. Most striking in Oualata are the houses, which were traditionally heavily ornamented, with intricate decorations executed in gypsum and different colours of clay. Many of these older houses have been abandoned, and the art has declined. However the interiors and studded wooden doors are impressive. Sensitivity over photography should be borne in mind, as this town is also used for internal exile, and indeed the police must be visited on arrival. There is no accommodation in Oualata other than with families. There are some vehicles which make the journey from Nema, particularly after the flights from Nouakchott arrive.

THE TAGANT REGION

The Tagant Region is a dramatic area of stony plateaux with impressive views, prehistoric rock paintings, archaeological remains, palmeries, and some interesting old forts and towns which are now being over-run by sand. The name itself means 'forest' in the Zenaga language, implying the environment was more verdant in the past. Although very appealing, the Tagant is a difficult region to visit. Travellers will find it easiest to use the weekly flight from Nouakchott to Tidjikja (despite uncertainties about day or time of departure). Public land transport is difficult although the road has recently been repaired, the best option being a *taxi-brousse* from Nouakchott, or closer at hand from Aleg or Magta-Lahjar. For those with their own 4WD vehicles, turn off the Route de l'Espoir at Sangarafa, 20 km E after Magta-Lahjar. From Sangarafa there is a rough sandy track to Tidjikja. The fuel supply is unreliable in the region.

TIDJIKJA

The capital of Tagant, this is a small town, with a busy market but few facilities for tourists except the airstrip. Flights on

Tues to Nouakchott, UM8,300 single. There is a **French colonial fort** built by Xavier Coppolani, assassinated here in May 1905, and near the town there are remains from the Neolithic period, including arrowheads and pottery. Tidjikja was founded in 1680 by Idaw'ali exiles from the Adrar. The historic area lies on the NE bank of the *wadi*, with an old mosque, housing and Tidjikja's celebrated palm groves dating from the original settlement. Although some of the houses are vacant or ruined, the Tagant region's impressive architecture is highly evident in Tidjikja. The houses are built from stone with clay added. The buildings have flat roofs, palm-trunk waterspouts, narrow rooms and elevated latrines carved into stone. The distinctive features are the decorative niches with carved geometrical designs, and gargoyles on the roofs. The historic quarter is threatened by sand.

To the SW of the *wadi* is the modern area, with a bank, post office, shops, a hospital and a petrol station. Tidjikja has a lake but we do not recommend swimming. 4WD vehicles can be hired in Tidjikja, for a 40 km drive to Rachid, or for the 200 km, more expensive, journey to Tichit. This is the starting point of the 470 km to Atar, only negotiable by high clearance 4WD vehicles in convoy with guides. There is a basic rest house in Tidjikja, otherwise accommodation must be with locals.

Rachid lies 40 km to the N of Tidjikja, and is an impressive fort settlement with rock engravings, ruined buildings and a delightful palmery. In Jul/Aug many natives of Rachid who live elsewhere descend on the town for the *guetna* or date harvest. It was a bedouin citadel built by Kunta in the 18th century, a refuge for those who would rob caravans. Access is mainly by private 4WD vehicle.

TICHIT

200 km to the E of Tidjikja, Tichit is very difficult to get to, but fascinating in ar-

chitectural and social terms, and worth visiting whilst it struggles on as a functioning settlement, a ghost of its impressive past. Tichit is a fortified caravan town founded around 1150 AD, from when it was a stopping point on the route between West Africa and the Sahel, and Morocco and the Mediterranean, and a large city. It has declined rapidly, with encroaching sand, changing economic circumstances and rapid emigration.

Now only a handful of families remains. These families reflect the traditional complex ethnic diversity of Tichit and its position as a transit point for Moor tribes nomadizing in the region. They include the Masena, blacks who speak Aser; Abid, former slaves often still working in similar situations and Haratin Moors, slaves liberated much earlier.

The old houses are impressive structures built from local rock, often using colouration and carvings, of a similar style but more elaborate than in Tidjikja. Green, white and red stone is used, and the ornamental niches are quite beautiful. There are also distinctive wooden doors. However, many of the houses are partly ruined and poorly maintained. The town mosque is worth seeing, although much of its fabric dates from frequent repairs. The surrounding area has other ruins and ancient rock paintings. There is an archaeological site nearby at Akreijt. Palm groves stretch S from Tichit, with a date harvest in Jul.

● **Transport** From Tidjikja, this is very difficult, with lifts only possible after the arrival of flights at the airstrip. A chartered flight continuation from Tidjikja is an expensive option. For motorists a 4WD vehicle, plentiful petrol (there is none in Tichit) and a guide are essential. The route is straightforward to Leckcheb, and then much more difficult over a bad *piste* and dunes to Tichit. From Tichit those with time and petrol could follow a 400 km long *piste* to Oulata, along an old caravan route.

THE SENEGAL VALLEY

South of the Route de l'Espoir is a more fertile area, firstly dry savanna and bush, and nearer the river Senegal irrigated crop lands, producing rice and millet. The region is mainly populated by black people speaking languages other than Arabic although in recent years the Moor and Haratin populations have increased.

Rosso, with a population of 27,783 (1988), is the administrative centre of the Trarza region, an area of mixed ethnic groups reflecting a diverse environment in which agriculture and cattle-rearing are dominant. It is an uninteresting town, only normally visited for travel to, or from, Senegal. There is a basic rest house/restaurant, the **E** *Hotel Trarza*, with 9 rm, and a Catholic mission. There is a black top road to Nouakchott, which was rebuilt after the floods of 1950, a dull journey, although look out for encampments of nomads. Taxis take approximately 3 hrs to Nouakchott, and can be found at the *Gare Routière*, 500m N out of the town. Horse-drawn *calèches* carry people from the town centre. The airstrip has no scheduled service.

From Rosso there is a ferry to the Senegal bank of the river, every 20 mins from 0700-1230 and 1500-1700, taking 3 mins, due to frequent waits due to heavy traffic. There is a black top road from the river to Dakar, with frequent taxis. As relations between Mauritania and Senegal have been strained the border has on occasion been closed.

Mderdra is 20 km from Rosso, reachable for those with 4WD vehicles. Traditionally a gum arabic centre, it is now famous for inlaid wooden chests made for nomads, and silverware.

Keur Massène, W of Rosso, located in the river Senegal delta, close to the ocean. Keur Massène is a village with an eight bungalow *campement de chasse*, or hunting centre, run by *Air Afrique*. This offers surf-casting on the ocean as well as shooting of a wide variety of wildfowl. Contact: Service Tourisme, *Air Afrique*, 29 rue du Colisée, F 75008 Paris, T 42257169, or the Nouakchott office, BP 51, T 52084.

Bogué is an unremarkable town on the river Senegal. However, it is well connected, with a recently constructed paved road covering the 60 km distance S from Aleg on the Route de l'Espoir. A *pirogue*, an open boat, takes foot passengers across the river to the Senegalese Isle à Marfil.

Kaedi, *pop* 30,515 (1988), is the largest town in the Valley region and the economic centre of the E, linked by 100 km of *piste* to Bogué. It has an airstrip with a regular link to Nouakchott on Wed, UM6,100 single, and a rest house. The town is best known for its large market, one of the most interesting in the country and with good handicrafts. The Italian-designed hospital of Kaedi recently won an Aga Khan architectural award. Kaedi is the capital of the Gorgol region, an economically diverse area with strong agriculture, fishing and cattle-rearing sectors.

Selibaby is the capital of the Guidimakha region, where the Soninke people live. Many of the migrant West African labourers and marabouts in France are Soninke. Remittance money sent home to Gudimakha is often used to build spectacular mosques. Soninke culture has a reputation for being very conservative and hierarchical. It is an area of savanna and sub-tropical forest producing a wide variety of crops. The town has an airstrip, with a service to Nouakchott on Wed, UM7,200 single.

Information for travellers

BEFORE TRAVELLING

ENTRY REQUIREMENTS

● **Visas**

Visas are required for most visitors. Exceptions include France, Italy and some African countries. The difficulty may be finding an embassy. Visas require two forms, two passport photographs and a return air ticket as evidence of intention to limit stay. A letter from your Travel Agent will not do but a letter from a Mauritanian may be useful. In Paris the cost is FF122, one is asked to go in person but postal requests are accepted. Time to process the visa here varies from immediate to 24 hrs, or, alas, a refusal and a suggestion to try in Rabat. There is a problem for overland travellers who may have to buy an air ticket to get the visa then return to the travel agency for a refund. Available also in Bonn, Brussels, Madrid and Rabat (reported to be cheaper than in Paris). Some travellers have obtained visas at the border, but this a very unreliable option. It is possible to get visas in neighbouring countries such as the Canary Islands and Morocco, but one will need a letter of introduction from one's own embassy. French embassies are often helpful in African countries without a Mauritanian embassy. Mali, for example, does not have a Mauritanian embassy. Mauritanian embassy in Dakar (see below) requires letter of introduction from own embassy, takes 2 days to produce visa and charges £5-6 equivalent. For visa renewals go to the Commisariat Centrale, on Ave Gamal Abdel Nasser, in Nouakchott.

Entry into Senegal and other African countries Visas for Senegal are not available in Nouakchott nor at the river crossing, but are available on arrival at the airport in Dakar. The French embassy in Nouakchott provides visas for a number of Francophone African countries, takes 24 hrs usually with no fuss.

Departure Provided you retain all receipts for financial transactions and are in no great hurry, leaving is no problem.

● **Vaccinations**

Travellers no longer require certificates of immunization against Yellow Fever and Cholera, but protection against these is advisable on health grounds anyway (see **Health** page 490). There are mosquitoes and anti-malarial medication is also recommended.

● **Tourist information**

That little information that there is can be had from either the **Direction à l'Artisanat et au Tourisme**, off Ave Gamal Abdel Nasser, BP 246, Nouakchott, T 53337, ext'n: 368, 322, 374; or the **Société Mauritanienne du Tourisme et de l'Hôtellerie (SMTH)**, BP 552, Nouakchott, T 52353. It is probably better to go to one of the travel agents below.

● **Specialist tour companies**

These include **Agence-Dayna Voyages et Tourisme**, Ave Gamal Abdel Nasser, and **Inter Tour**, Ave Gamal Abdel Nasser, BP 708, T 53217. One of the most helpful is **Adrar Voyages**, BP 926, Nouakchott, T 51717, F 53210 (0800-1230 and 1500-1830 Sat-Wed, 0800-1230 and 1500-1700 Thur). This company offers pre-arranged tours, and tours designed for the customer, primarily centred around desert safaris and watersports, with guides, vehicles, food and accommodation laid on. On a daily basis desert safari costs are approximately: vehicle, driver, food and fuel – UM45,000. A sample week-long tour takes in Nouakchott, Akjoujt, Atar, Chinguetti, Azougui and Terjit. **Adrar Voyages** in conjunction with Sodetour also runs safaris and fishing holidays along the coast, through the Parc National du Banc d'Arguin to Nouadhibou. The company works with a number of travel agents in France, Italy, Switzerland and South America. Staff speak French, Arabic and English.

WHEN TO GO
● **Best time to visit**
The heat is most manageable between Nov and Feb, but even then it can be uncomfortable. Avoid Jul to Oct for visiting the Senegal Valley.

● **Climate**
Mauritania has a Saharan climate in the N and centre, hot and very dry with hardly any rain. The rain that does fall comes between Jul and Oct, although it is rarely above 30 mm. The hottest season is May to Sep, with peak temperatures between 40 and 45°C. Night temperatures in the desert can be as low as 13°C in Nouakchott. These cool night temperatures occur mainly in Dec to Feb. The coast is a little, but not much, cooler. The S, near the Senegal River, has a more humid climate.

HEALTH
● **Staying healthy**
Visitors must be immunized against Yellow Fever to enter the country, however, certificates are rarely checked if visitors arrive from Europe or the US. They should also be immunized against polio, typhoid, meningitis, hepatitis B, and take appropriate anti-malarial pills, particularly in the S. Water should be boiled or sterilized. Mineral water is a fairly cheap alternative. On long journeys it is essential to drink sufficient water. Protection from the sun is essential throughout the year. Travel insurance with full medical cover is of course recommended, traffic accidents are frequent. There is a reasonable hospital in Nouakchott, with French doctors as well as several private medical clinics with French, Russian or Lebanese doctors. For emergency dental care there are several Lebanese dentists with private practices around Ave Gamal Abdel Nasser in Nouakchott.

● **Further health information**
Visitors are recommended to read the section on Health, see page 489

MONEY
● **Banks**
There are no western banks, but a number of Mauritanian banks: the **Banque Centrale de Mauritanie** (BCM), **Banque Arabe Africaine Mauritanienne** (BAAM), **Société Mauritanienne de Banque** (SMB), **Banque Internationale pour la Mauritanie** (BIMA), **Banque Mauritanienne pour le Développement et le Commerce** (BMDC) and **Banque Arabe Libyenne-Mauritanienne pour le Commerce Extérieur et le Développement** (BALM). Banks are easy to find in Nouakchott and Nouadhibou, but very rare elsewhere except in Atar, Aioun-El-Atrouss, Kaedi, Kiffa, Nema and Rosso. Banks are open 0800-1300 every day except Fri and Sat.

● **Cost of living**
In comparison with Morocco, Egypt or Tunisia, Mauritania is an extremely expensive country. Distances to be covered are long and prices high, with travellers often having to resort to air travel. A day's travel can be upwards of UM2,800. There is little choice in hotels, which are also highly priced, often above UM1,500 for quite basic accommodation. Meals in Nouakchott or Nouadhibou restaurants are similarly exorbitant. Local meals are cheaper.

● **Credit cards**
These are not normally accepted outside the few large hotels, or airlines. American Express has no representation in Mauritania.

● **Currency**
A **currency declaration** no longer has to be made at the place of entry. Make a record of financial transactions and keep them safe. Mauritanian currency cannot be taken out of the county. There is no restriction on foreign currency, in fact officially one should have sufficient funds for the duration of the stay and a return journey (or air ticket).

The Mauritanian currency is the Ouguiya (UM), pronounced 'oogeeya', which equals five khoums. It is unlikely that visitors will come across anything other than 5, 10 and 20 UM coins, and 100, 200 and 1000 UM notes.

Regulations and money changing There is no limit, within reason, on bringing foreign currency into the country. The receipts from money changing should be kept in case they are needed on departure. As it is difficult to find banks outside the main towns plan well ahead. In town Bureaux de Change are everywhere. A black market does not exist, and there are limited possibilities for informal transactions, but not at greatly preferential rates. Most Western currencies are acceptable but it is safest to stick to US, UK, German or, preferably, French, currency as you get 10% more for changing cash than changing TCs. For exchange rates for March 1997 (see page 12).

● **Eurocheques and Travellers' cheques**

Although it is possible to cash TCs in Nouakchott, cash is more convenient, dollars and French francs are more useful than sterling, and can be cashed in an emergency when banks are closed.

GETTING THERE

● **General note**

It is both difficult and expensive to get to Mauritania. European flights are mainly restricted to services from Paris and Las Palmas. There are limited flights from nearby African countries. Overland travel is straightforward from Senegal, difficult from Mali and Morocco and almost impossible from Algeria. There are no scheduled shipping routes.

AIR

Mauritania has only two international airports, at Nouakchott and Nouadhibou. Travellers will find the facilities quite primitive. Taxis wait outside both airports for the short trip into the centre – they tend to charge exorbitant prices. There are connecting flights from both these airports to regional airports.

International services are limited, with no direct flights from the Americas. From New York **Air Afrique** flights are via Dakar. There is a service four times a week between Paris and Nouakchott run by **Air Afrique/Air France**, which takes 5 hrs. **Aeroflot** runs an occasional service from Moscow or Budapest to Nouadhibou. **Air Afrique** runs a weekly service between Nouakchott and Jeddah. **Tunis Air** to Nouakchott each Tues. Sabena flies direct from Brussels each week. Dakar-Nouakchott takes 40 mins and the flight along the coast is fabulous.

Within Africa There are services between Nouakchott and Algiers (**Air Algérie**), Banjul and Casablanca (**Royal Air Maroc, Air Mauritanie** and **Gambia Airways**), Niamey and

Ndjamena (**Air Afrique**), daily to Dakar (**Air Afrique, Air Mauritanie** and **Air Sénégal**, although the last is unreliable) and three times a week to Las Palmas in the Canary Islands (**Air Mauritanie** and **Iberia**). From Nouadhibou there are links with Bissau (**Aeroflot**), Conakry (**UTA**) and twice weekly with Las Palmas (**Air Mauritanie**).

ROAD

The main road approach is from Dakar in Senegal, across the river Senegal ferry at Rosso. There is a black top road from Dakar to the river. There is a very unpredictable ferry running from 0700-1230 and 1500-1700. The crossing takes 5 mins but there can be quite a wait due to heavy traffic. There is also a reasonable black top road from Rosso to Nouakchott. This takes 3-4 hrs by taxi and costs £15-20 equivalent. Relations between Mauritania and Senegal are somewhat strained, and the border has on occasion been closed. Along the Senegal riverbank there is a black top road, on the Mauritanian side an unmade track. It is possible to cross at other points up the river, notably between Matam and Sive. The customs can be difficult and there are numerous police checks targetted at taxis and trucks which may be carrying West African immigrants.

Entry from Mali into Mauritania is quite possible although the roads are of a poor quality. Many travel from Aioun-El-Atrouss, across the border to Nioro. Another route is from Nema to Nara in Mali. Travellers should get their passports stamped in the last Mauritanian town.

Due to the Western Saharan conflict it is difficult to enter from Algeria, via Tindouf, the Polisario stronghold, but it is worth checking the current situation at the time of travel.

From Dakhla in Morocco the road is a good surface and there are one or two convoys a week to the border, depending on volume of traffic, where all formalities must be concluded. Camping is available at the border and while the customs are more interested in vehicles than people and are happy to accept 'gifts', no serious problems have been reported. Once sufficient vehicles have been processed on the Moroccan side, the Mauritanians send a guide to conduct them through the mined no-man's land on to Nouadibou where formalities are completed. The customs here are more welcoming than those in Rosso. It is advised to hire a guide if driving S to Nouakchott as there is no defined road.

● **Motoring**

Drivers will need to have an **autorisation d'importation** to bring a car into the country. For information contact the Direction des Douanes, BP 183, Nouakchott.

● **Taxi and bus**

By taxi the route from Dakar to Nouakchott, via Rosso, will take about 11 hrs, changing at the border. There are both car and minivan taxis, as well as lorries, running from Rosso to Nouakchott which terminate at the *Gare Routière*. There are also taxis which make the journey from the Malian border.

SEA

There are no regular ferry services to or from Mauritania, but from the major port of Nouadhibou it is occasionally possible to arrange passage on cargo vessels to Las Palmas in the Canary Islands, and further afield to Casablanca and Dakar (Senegal). Contact the Port Autonome de Nouadhibou, BP 236, Nouadhibou, T 2134. Similarly, ask around in Las Palmas, Casablanca or Dakar.

CUSTOMS

There are no taxes. Importation of alcohol is strictly banned.

ON ARRIVAL

● **Clothing**

The most appropriate clothing is light cotton, covering the whole body, with a scarf to wrap around the face as protection from blowing sand and sun on journeys, sunglasses and headwear. Women should avoid exposing arms and shoulders in respect of religious sensibilities.

● **Hours of business**

Banks are open 0800-1300 Sun-Thur, Government offices 0800-1500 Sat-Wed and 0800-1400 Thur, Private offices 0800-1230 and 1500-1700 Sat-Thur, and shops 0800-1230 and 1500-1700 Sat-Thur.

● **Official time**

Mauritania is in the same time band as Morocco and the UK, always on GMT.

● **Photography**

This is allowed without a permit, but there is sensitivity about official and military buildings and installations. Be discrete when taking photographs in Nouakchott and along the Sengal River. The largest hotels in Nouakchott will sell film but its age must be checked. Better to bring your own supplies.

● **Safety**

Crime in Nouakchott and the rest of the country is relatively scarce. There are frequent roadblocks in Mauritania, when the police attempt to read passports and ask irrelevant questions. There is normally a checkpoint at the entry to each town, and the police will often accompany travellers to the central police station for registration. Some police like to write in one's passport, which can be annoying after several towns. Vehicle searches do occur. Women will find in Mauritania less hassle than in Morocco, although there may be a lot of curiosity. It is perhaps unadvisable to travel alone. Hints: cover hair to minimize unwanted attention, don't offer to shake hands with a man unless he does so first and avoid lying on the back or stomach in public.

● **Shopping**

For handicrafts and many other items, purchase is by haggling, which is usually good natured and less exploitative than in Morocco. Trading in Western goods can get the traveller a good deal. A few shops and cooperatives are listed for Nouakchott. Otherwise the best place to shop is in the markets, which in different areas will reflect the local handicraft and other industries.

Best buys At the upper end of the market are carpets and wooden chests, but prices are much above the usual range in North Africa. Try for jewellery and the colourful cloths that Mauritanian women wear. In some areas interesting Neolithic artifacts, such as tools and arrow heads, are sold.

● **Tipping**

Tipping is rarely demanded and it is up to the client in restaurants and hotels. 10% is reasonable.

● **Weights and measures**

Mauritania uses the metric system. See conversion table on page 496.

WHERE TO STAY

● **Hotels**

There are few hotels in Mauritania, particularly outside Nouakchott and Nouadhibou. Few are anything to write home about, and most are over-priced.

Hotel classifications

AL US$75+. International class luxury hotel. All facilities for business and leisure travellers are of the highest international standard.

A US$75+. International hotel with air conditioned rooms with WC, bath/shower, TV, phone, mini-bar, daily clean linen. Choice of restaurants, coffee shop, shops, bank, travel agent, swimming pool, some sport and business facilities.

B US$60-75. As A but without the luxury, reduced number of restaurants, smaller rooms, limited range of shops and sport.

C US$40-60. Best rooms have air conditioning, own bath/shower and WC. Usually comfortable, bank, shop, pool.

D US$20-40. Best rooms may have own WC and bath/shower. Depending on management will have room service and choice of cuisine in restaurant.

E US$10-20. Simple provision. Perhaps fan cooler. May not have restaurant. Shared WC and showers with hot water (when available).

F under US$10. Very basic, shared toilet facilities, variable in cleanliness, noise, often in dubious locations.

● Camping

This is legal in most places, but there are no organized sites.

● General

There are no **Youth hostels** in Mauritania. The Peace Corps is mentioned in some guides as a possible source of accommodation. Please note this is NOT the case. Some trainees/volunteers may put people up if they meet them, but this is not a reliable source. The *Maison du Passage* just outside Kiffa does not have accommodation, and that in Chinguetti is closed. Accommodation is occasionally possible at **Catholic Missions**. In many towns the only source of accommodation is **local hospitality**. Gifts such as biros, lighters, or small Western items are the usual means of recompense.

FOOD AND DRINK

● Food

Travellers should not go to Mauritania expecting a taste sensation. The food, much of which is imported, is often dull. It is often difficult to get fruit and vegetables outside Nouakchott and Nouadhibou, indeed food supplies are difficult in the interior and travellers should be prepared with their own back-up. Mauritanian food is dominated by lamb, beef, camel, chicken, with rice, *couscous* and pasta. However, fish and seafood, which are excellent and cheap are available along the coast. Look out for *poutarge*, mullet eggs, which is a delicacy in France. Lobster cooked in Senegalese style is also very popular. Dates are easy to find. The fruit in the S is varied and good. Travellers can purchase plenty of expensive imported tinned food in both Nouakchott and Nouadhibou. Take your vitamin tablets with you as it is difficult to eat a balanced diet.

● Drink

Mauritanians drink a lot of tea, served sweet in small glasses, which is drunk quickly so the glass can be passed on for the next person to use! *Zrig*, milk mixed with water and sugar is also popular for locals and lethal for visitors, avoid it. Canned and bottled soft drinks, and mineral water, can be bought in most towns. Never drink water except from a bottle which is unsealed in your presence. *Alcohol* is officially banned in Mauritania, but is available in a few large hotels in Nouadhibou, and at the American and French clubs in Nouakchott.

● Where to eat and drink

In Nouakchott and Nouadhibou there are restaurants in the hotels and outside, primarily serving European food. Prices can be as expensive as in Europe. Elsewhere there are tents serving basic food, although hygiene is often inadequate.

Restaurant classifications

Given the variations in price of food on any menu our restaurants are divided where possible into three simple grades: ♦♦♦ expensive, ♦♦ average and ♦ cheap.

GETTING AROUND

AIR

This is one of the best means of getting around the country, with fares only two or three times that of the taxis, whilst the services are, of course, far quicker. **Air Mauritanie** runs a reasonably good network, although services can be cancelled or delayed at short notice. There are daily or twice daily services between Nouakchott and Nouadhibou. There is a weekly service connecting Nouadhibou with Atar, and another with Zouerate. There are three services a week between Atar and Nouakchott, two a week between Zouerate and Nouakchott, two a week connecting Nouakchott with Tidjikja and Kiffa, and another two with Selibaby and Kaedi, and a weekly service between Nouakchott, Aioun-El-Atrouss and Nema. The airline's offices are at Ave Gamal Abdel Nasser, BP 41, Nouakchott, T 52211, and BP 10, Nouadhibou, T 45022.

TRAIN

Mauritania has only one railway line, which runs from the NE iron ore town of Zouerate to the port of Nouadhibou. The train is primarily for transporting iron ore, it is slow and very long. The operating company normally attaches a basic passenger compartment, but many Mauritanians travel for free in the open trucks on top of the piles of iron ore. This is a very cold and extremely dusty way of travelling, so take warm clothing and a scarf to cover the mouth and eyes. There are two trains a day either way. These can be taken from Zouerate or Nouadhibou, or either way from Choum, mid-way along the line, between the Moroccan border and the town of Atar. See also page 430.

ROAD

The main road in the country is the Route de l'Espoir, from Nouakchott through Kiffa and Aioun-El-Atrouss to Nema, although even this is narrow and pot-holed in parts. There are also adequate roads from Rosso to Nouakchott, Nouakchott to Akjoujt and Aleg to Bogué. There is, incredibly, no black top road from Nouakchott to Nouadhibou, nor for that matter, anywhere else in the country. Consequently public transport is limited, infrequent, very slow and expensive, and driving in one's own vehicle is difficult.

OTHER LAND TRANSPORT
● **Bicycles/motorcycles**
Although these are impractical in Mauritania, one occasionally encounters cyclists, motor-cyclists.

● **Bus**
These run along the Route de l'Espoir, between Nouakchott and Nema. They are very slow, uncomfortable and infrequent, but much cheaper than the shared taxis. Buses leave from the *Gare Routière* in Nouakchott.

● **Car hire**
Car hire in Mauritania is expensive and limited to Nouakchott and Nouadhibou. There is a **Europcar** at Nouakchott airport. In some places, such as Atar, Land Rovers can be hired, with or without a driver.

● **City minibuses**
In Nouakchott the best means of transport, and a fairly cheap one at that, is the green and yellow *transports urbaines* minibuses that hurtle around the city. Travellers will need to ask locals where to wait. Each minibus has a boy hanging out the back door, who takes the money and knows the route.

● **City taxis**
In Nouakchott and Nouadhibou are not as standard in appearance as in many cities, but are usually fairly recognizable. There is a base price, but prices are in general negotiable as there are no meters.

● **Hitchhiking**
Most transport in Mauritania will require payment.

● **Motoring**
It is important to bear in mind that there are very few black top roads in Mauritania. Those in the desert can become hazardous and difficult to follow because of drifting sand, those in the S can become waterlogged because of rain. Coastal routes are dangerous because of sandbanks and tides. Thus a 4WD vehicle, careful planning, and all necessary equipment, are essential prerequisites of a journey. Stock up on petrol, oil, water and food, and carry a first aid kit and shelter at all times, as well as a repair kit with all essential spare parts, shovels, ropes and sand ladders. When one is stuck in sand, let out air from the tyres. In a breakdown, stay near the vehicle. Inform the authorities in each settlement of the route to be followed, and in the deep desert it is preferable to travel in

convoy and to hire a guide. Take into account that there is little help on hand for motorists with problems. See main introduction, page 59.

Nouakchott to Atar (8 hrs) is fairly straightforward, as is Nouakchott to Kiffa, Aioun-El-Atrouss and Nema, and Nouakchott to Rosso. The track from Atar to Choum is rough but possible, that from Atar to Chinguetti and Ouadane is very difficult. Nouakchott to Nouadhibou is not black top, indeed it runs along the beach for part of the distance. This route is not advised for the independent motorist.

● **Taxis brousses**

These are normally large Peugeot 504 estates, which take nine passengers. They will leave when nine passengers are assembled. There are standard fares, about which the drivers are normally honest. If in doubt, check with the police. Journeys will be interrupted by frequent tea stops, in addition to the prayer stops. The taxi driver will normally pay for the tea. Drivers and passengers are quite casual about deciding to stop for the night under a tent, and equally casual about transferring passengers from one car to another. It is relatively straightforward to get taxis between Nouakchott and Rosso, Nouakchott and Atar, and along the Route de l'Espoir, between Nouakchott, Kiffa, Aioun-El-Atrouss and Nema. There are also services in the Senegal Valley area.

● **Trucks and Land Rovers**

Off the black top roads, trucks and Land Rovers act as taxis, notably between Nouakchott and Nouadhibou. Trucks and minivans also follow the same routes as the *taxis brousses*, but are less comfortable and slower.

COMMUNICATIONS

● **Language**

Arabic is the main language, and has the status of official language. The form of Arabic spoken in Mauritania is Hassaniya. In the S a number of African languages are spoken by a substantial minority, including Wolof, Pulaar and Soninke. Other languages are spoken by migrants from Mali, Senegal and other West African states. Due to the linguistic diversity of the state French is often used as a language of communication between the different linguistic groups. English is rarely spoken.

● **Postal services**

There are large *PTTs* (post offices) in Nouakchott and Nouadhibou, and smaller offices in regional centres such as Nema, Aioun-El-Atrouss, Kiffa, Kaedi, Rosso and Atar. Post from and to Mauritania is very slow. Postcards are UM50, letters UM100. Letters can be received *poste restante*, although it is perhaps best to use just Nouakchott *PTT Centrale* for this. DHL have an office next to *Hotel Marhaba* in Nouakchott.

● **Telephone services**

The Mauritanian telephone system is connected by satellite with the international system, but it is not cheap to call overseas. 1 min to the UK costs approximately £1 = UM200. It is easiest to call from the large hotels or *cabine telephonique*.

International code: 222.

Code for Nouakchott: 2.

ENTERTAINMENT

● **Media**

Daily papers, and some aged international newspapers, are available in Nouakchott. There is an extremely lively local press published in French. The best are *'Mauritanie Novelles'* and *'Le Calame'*. The state owned radio service, run by the *Office de Radiodiffusion et Télévision de Mauritanie*, broadcasts in French, Arabic, Wolof, Toucouleur and Sarakolé. The BBC World Service (Africa) can be picked up for part of the day on long wave frequency. There is a basic TV service broadcast in colour which began in 1984 and runs a service in the evenings only. In the main cities TV is very popular, particularly satellite channels such as MBC, CNN and Canal Horizons. Senegalese TV is also tuned into frequently.

● **Sports**

There are almost no sporting facilities in Mauritania. The most likely activities are swimming and fishing. The latter is a popular activity because of Mauritania's rich fishing grounds and a great variety of fish is caught by enthusiasts. **Air Afrique** and **Adrar Voyages** organize a number of packages, at, for example, Keur Massène (see page 439), Baie de l'Étoile (see page 428) and Banc d'Arguin (see page 425). Wildboar hunting in area around Lake R'Kiz (see page 435).

HOLIDAYS AND FESTIVALS

1 Jan: New Year's Day
26 Feb: National Reunification Day
8 Mar: Women's Day
1 May: Labour Day
25 May: Organization of African Unity Day
10 Jul: Armed Forces Day
28 Nov: Independence Day
12 Dec: Restructuration Day

The dates of the Islamic religious holidays and the fast, Ramadan, are celebrated on different dates each year as they are calculated according to the moon (see page 27). Approximate dates for 1997:

12 Jan: Beginning of Ramadan
8 Feb: Aïd es Seghir (end of Ramadan)
18 Apr: Aïd el Kebir
7 May: Islamic New Year
16 Jul: Prophet's Birthday

Information for travellers

BEFORE TRAVELLING

ENTRY REQUIREMENTS

● **Visas**

No visas are required for full passport holders of the UK, USA, Canada, Australia, NZ, Canada, Ireland and most EU countries. On the aeroplane or boat, or at the border, travellers will be required to fill a form with standard personal and passport details, an exercise to be repeated in almost all hotels throughout the country. From the point of entry travellers can stay in Morocco for 3 months.

Visa Extensions will require a visit to the **Immigration** or **Bureau des Etrangers** department at the police station in a larger town, as well as considerable patience. An easier option is to leave Morocco for a few days, preferably to Spain, if not to Ceuta or Melilla.

● **Vaccinations**

None required unless travelling from a country where yellow fever and/or cholera frequently occurs. It is advised to be up to date with polio, tetanus, typhoid and hepatitis protection. See Health, page 489.

● **Passport loss**

Report immediately to police giving number and date and place of issue. The last hotel at which you stayed will have this information on the registration form but it ought to be carried separately. Getting fresh documents may entail a trip to Casablanca.

● **Tourist offices**

Many towns have an **Office du Tourisme** (Tourist Office) and a **Syndicat d'Initiative** (Information Office). These are rarely of much use, and will normally only have the fairly general official brochures, and addresses for hotels and restaurants. They may be of most use in arranging excursions and getting the services of an official guide.

WHEN TO GO

● **Best time to visit**

This will depend on requirements. Sun seekers congregate in the N between Apr-Oct and move S in the winter to places like Agadir. For sightseeing, from Marrakech S the heat can be oppressive during the day from Jun to Sep. Routes from Tanger are busy in summer with returning migrant workers from Europe in overloaded cars and are best avoided as is Tanger itself with day-trippers from Spain. Worst on Wed.

● **Climate**

In general Morocco is pleasant all the year round. Some of the coastal towns can be humid, particularly near rivers. Desert and pre-desert areas are obviously dry and hot, but from Dec to Feb can get cold at night. Equally, whilst the mountain areas are cold at night and during the winter, they can get quite hot during the summer days. Occasional but heavy showers occur turning the dry river beds into dangerous flash floods and snow blocks the high passes in winter. See Climate, page 76.

HEALTH

● **Staying healthy**

Morocco is well provided with fairly reliable

chemists, dentists, doctors and hospitals, although none is free. Addresses are to be found in this guide book, or via larger hotels, the **Syndicat d'Initiative** or the **Office du Tourisme**. For ambulances T 15. Most standard medicines can be obtained in medium and large-sized towns. In general Morocco is a clean and fairly low risk country – the worst experience being diarrhoea. Tap water is generally good, but the short-term visitor may wish to play safe by buying the very cheap bottled mineral water. Some rivers and oases have bilharzia, making drinking or bathing hazardous. Travel insurance, including coverage for health risks, is advised. Tampons can be bought at general stores in towns and cities.

● **Further health information**
Read the section on Health, see page 489 and be prepared for some stomach upsets due to heat and a change of diet.

MONEY

● **Banking hours**
Are 0830-1130 and 1500-1630. In the summer and during the fast month of Ramadan they are 0830-1400. There are also separate *bureaux de change* in the major cities, mainly of **BMCE**, often open for longer hours (0800-2000), which in theory give the same rates of exchange but charge different amounts of commission. There are several different banks in Morocco, with **BMCE, Credit du Maroc, Wafabank** and **Banque Populaire** all widespread. The latter is often the only bank in southern towns. Banking in Morocco is a slow, tortuous process, with several different desks for different purposes.

● **Changing money**
There is a fixed exchange rate for changing notes and no commission ought to be charged for this. A small commission will be charged for changing TCs.

● **Cost of living**
It is possible to live in Morocco for US$25-30 a day. Accommodation, food and transport are all cheap, and there is a lot to see and do for free. Imported goods, notably cosmetics, toiletries and electrical goods, are expensive. Top quality hotels, restaurants, nightclubs and bars are similar to Europe. Rabat, Casablanca and Agadir are the most expensive places while goods in remote rural areas cost more. There are plenty of things to buy in Morocco, and the prices, if you bargain, can be quite reasonable. Sample prices: bottled water MD10, beer MD10, tea/coffee MD6.

● **Credit cards**
These are widely accepted at banks, top hotels, restaurants and shops, but it is wise to check first. *American Express* are represented by *Voyages Schwartz* in Morocco, with limited services.

● **Currency**
The major unit of currency in Morocco is the **dirham** (in this Handbook: MD). 1 **dirham**=100 **centimes**. There are coins for 1 (very rare), 5, 10, 20 and 50 **centimes**, and for 1 and 5 **dirhams**, as well as notes for 5 (quite rare), 10, 50, 100 and 200 **dirhams**. Currency is labelled in Arabic and French. Most transactions are in cash. To the complete confusion of travellers, many Moroccans refer to **francs**, which equal 1 centime, and **reals**, which equal 5 centimes, but these only exist in speech. For exchange rates for Jun 1995 see page 12.

● **Currency regulations**
Foreign currency may be imported freely.

● **Eurocheques**
These are accepted in Morocco, and can be a good way to make sure one will not run out of money. Try at banks with the *Eurocheque* sticker.

● **Travellers' cheques**
These are usable in Morocco, although the traveller may be sent from bank to bank before the appropriate one is found. Use TCs from a bank/company that will be familiar to the cashiers, and preferably with UK, US, French or German currency, although this is not an absolute rule. Some hotels and shops will exchange TCs.

GETTING THERE

AIR

There are numerous scheduled and charter flights to Morocco, and reasonably convenient and quite cheap flights on from Spain or Gibraltar. A number of airlines fly to Morocco, and flights are fairly cheap, but only when bought outside Morocco. There are over 50 agents using scheduled flights to Morocco. The state airline, **Royal Air Maroc**, is a reliable and not over-priced company which has large international and national networks. Its main services go through Casablanca. The main

airports are at Casablanca (Anfa and Moham-
med V), Rabat/Sale, Tanger, Oujda, Fes, Al
Hoceima, Marrakech, Agadir, Ouarzazate and
Laayoune. A rail shuttle links Mohammed V
with Casablanca and Rabat. Airlines – Royal
Air Maroc, departures from Heathrow, Termi-
nal 2, London-Casablanca daily except Wed
with internal connections on domestic net-
work; London-Tanger on Mon, Wed, Fri and
Sat. Departures from Heathrow, Terminal 1, to
Agadir on Fri, Casablanca on Mon, Tues, Wed,
Thur and Sat.

British Airways services to Morocco are
operated by the independent carrier GB Airways who offer regular direct scheduled services from Heathrow to Casablanca and Tangier
and from Gatwick to Agadir and Marrakech.
Regular direct services from Gibraltar to Casablanca and Marrakech are also available.
These flights are expensive. For further information and reservations T 0345 222111.

Charter – from Dublin to Agadir by Budget
Travel, 134 Lower Baggot St, Dublin 2, Ireland,
T 00 353 1 6613122, F 6611890 and Sunway
Travel Ltd, Main St, Blackrock, Co Dublin, Ire-
land, T 00 353 1 28868828, F 2885167.

Charter – from UK by Cosmos, Tourama
House, Holcombe Rd, Helmshore, Rossendale,
Kent BR2 9LX, T 0181 4643444, F 1081
4666640 from Gatwick and Manchester to
Agadir; Goldenjoy Holidays, 36 Mill Lane,Lon-
don, NW6 1NR, T 0171 7949767, F 0171
7949850 from Gatwick to Agadir; Inspirations,
Victoria House, Victoria Rd, Horley, Surrey, RH6
7AD, T 01293 822244, F 01293 821732 from
Heathrow to Tanger, Fes, Casablanca, Agadir,
Marrakech and Ourzazate, Gatwick to Agadir
and Tanger and Manchester to Agadir; First
Choice Holidays, London Rd, Crawley, West
Sussex, RH10 2GX, T 01293 560777, F 0129
3588680 from Gatwick or Manchester to
Agadir.

● **From Europe**

Most of the major European airlines fly to
Morocco, including **Air France**, **Iberia** and
British Airways. The most competitive from
UK are normally **KLM** and **Royal Air Maroc**
(205 Regent St, London W1, T 0171
4394361). The latter also has flights from
Amsterdam, Athens, Barcelona, Bastia, Bor-
deaux, Brussels, Copenhagen, Dusseldorf,
Frankfurt, Geneva, Lisbon, Madrid, Málaga,
Marseille, Milan, Munich, Nice, Paris, Rome,
Stockholm, Strasbourg, Toulouse, Vienna and
Zurich. **Air France** and **Royal Air Maroc** offer

cheap flights from Paris. Charter flights or
package holidays bought in Europe can be a
cheap alternative, particularly to Tanger or
Agadir.

● **Fly-boat**

It is possible to get a flight to Gibraltar, Almería
or Málaga, and then continue by boat to
Melilla, Ceuta or Tanger. **British Airways** have
London-Gibraltar-Morocco flights which can
be booked in Morocco at their Tanger office,
83 rue de la Liberté, T 935211, or via **Menara
Tours** in either Casablanca or Marrakech.
Flights to Málaga are particularly cheap if one
shops around and takes a standby.

● **From the Americas**

Royal Air Maroc flies between Casablanca,
Montreal and New York.

● **From Africa and the Middle East**

In North Africa all the national carriers fly to
Casablanca. **Royal Air Maroc** runs regular
services between Casablanca and major cities
in the other countries, including 6 a week from
Algiers, 8 a week from **Tunis** and 4 a week
from **Cairo**. From the Canary Isles (Las Palmas)
there are direct flights to Agadir and Laayoune.
There are 2 flights a week between Casablanca
and **Nouakchott**. Elsewhere in Africa there
are flights from Casablanca to Abidjan,
Bamako, Conakry, Dakar and Libreville, and in
the Middle East to Abu Dhabi, Jeddah and
Riyadh.

TRAIN

Train travel to Morocco is a relatively cheap
option for those under 26, and a convenient
way to tie in a visit to Morocco with a short
stay in Europe. For those under 26 an **InterRail**
ticket bought in any participating European
country includes the Moroccan train network,
and a reduction on the Algeciras-Tanger ferry.
Travelling through Spain often entails extra
cost, as there are supplements to be paid on a
number of trains. **British Rail International**,
London Victoria Railway Station, T 0171
8342345 (enquiries), T 0171 8280892 (tickets), only sell tickets to Algeciras, about £214
return. **Eurotrain**, T 0171 7303402, and
Campus Travel, their agents for people under
26, T 0171 8284111, sell tickets from London
Victoria to Tanger, including both ferry crossings. These are very reasonably priced from
£250 return, and enable the traveller to stop
off at any point on the fixed route for any
length of time within the 2 month validity of

the ticket. Try **Rail Shop** at 179 Piccadilly, London, W1V 9DB, T 0189 1515477. Trains to Morocco from London via France and Spain and across to Tanger. Euro-Rail is valid in Morocco. Rail entry from Europe is only through Tanger. Rail entry from Algeria in more settled times is at Oujda.

ROAD

● Car

See below for car ferries.

Import of private cars Tourists/foreigners/visitors are allowed temporary import of a private vehicle for up to 6 months in total (be it one or several visits) per calendar year. **Documents required are**: car registration documents and Green card from insurance company, valid in Morocco which will be inspected at the border along with International Driving Licence (or national licences). The car will be entered in the drivers' passport, and checked on leaving the country, to ensure that it has not been sold without full taxes being paid. It should be noted that some car hire companies do not allow customers to take cars into Morocco from Europe. The minimum age of driving is 21. Car entry is not possible from Mauritania. From Algeria, in more peaceful times, the crossing points are Oujda and Figuig.

On arrival complete customs form **D 16 bis** called 'Declaration d'importation temporaire' and specify the intended duration of stay. Visitors arriving at the border without valid recognized insurance cover may take out a short-term policy available at any frontier post. The **Moroccan Insurance Bureau** is: Bureau Central Morocain d'Assurances rue Mostafa el Maani Casablanca. A customs carnet is required for a trailer caravan but not for motor caravans. If using a vehicle or caravan of which you are not the owner carry with you a letter of authorization signed by the owner. Customs officials may require a detailed inventory in duplicate of all valuable items but routine items of camping equipment need not be listed.

● Bus

There are regular coach services to Morocco from Paris and other French cities. From London Victoria there is **Eurolines/Iberbus** to Algeciras, which takes 2 days, T 0171 7300202. Leaves Mon and Fri, adult £143 return, under 26 £129 return. Coach services use the Algeciras-Tanger ferry.

SEA – FERRIES

The many sea routes from Europe to Morocco provide relatively cheap travel. The principal passenger arrival point is Tanger. Other scheduled passenger services run to the Spanish enclaves of Ceuta and Melilla, as well as to the Moroccan towns of Mdiq, near Ceuta, and Nador, near Melilla. Contact Southern ferries, 179 Piccadilly, London W1V 9DB, T 0171 4914968, F 0171 4913502.

● Between Algeciras and Tanger

The main ferry route between Spain and Morocco is the Algeciras/Tanger passenger and car service, operated jointly by **Trasmediterranea** and **Isleña de Navegación**. This is very convenient for onward rail or bus transport from Tanger. Algeciras has regular bus services from Gibraltar and Málaga, both towns having cheap flights from UK. Algeciras has a train service from Madrid, and tickets can be bought from London to Algeciras or Tanger. The ferry terminal, near the town centre, has a ticket office and money changing facilities. There are similar facilities in the Tanger terminal. The ferry takes 2-3 hrs, and there are normally between 6 and 10 services a day, either way, with some seasonal variation. **NB** Although services usually leave late one should allow at least an hour to clear the police and customs, particularly in Tanger. Be cautious about scheduling onward journeys on the same day, in view of the delays. The passenger fare one way is currently around MD200 (MD100 for children), with cars from MD600 and bicycles from MD200. It is cheaper to buy a return in Tanger than two singles, if applicable. Tickets can be bought at either terminal or at numerous agents in both towns.

The ferries are often dirty and crowded with the usual bars, restaurants, cafés and lounges, as well as a *bureau de change*. When travelling from Algeciras to Tanger all passengers must have their passports stamped by Moroccan border police whilst on the boat. **NB** This ferry service is booked solid in summer and around Muslim feast days. The conditions on board at that time **would prevent any chance of escape** in an emergency from overcrowded cabins where seats, aisles, corridors and exits are piled high with the passengers' unwieldy baggage.

The **hydrofoil service** runs Mon-Sat and takes 1 hr. Contact **Transtour**, T 956 665200.

● Between Algeciras and Ceuta

The connection between Algeciras and the Spanish enclave of Ceuta, which lies E of

Tanger and N of Tetouan, is cheaper and quicker, but onward travel from Ceuta is more difficult than from Tanger, and accommodation is more expensive. Ferries are run by the same companies from the same terminal in Algeciras. There are between six and nine services every day except Sun, when there are five, the journey taking 1½ hrs. Passenger fares are from MD146/2,200 Ptas, children 4-12 half price, car fares from MD600/9,000 Ptas, bicycles and motorbikes from MD150/2,300 Ptas. It is possible to buy tickets at either terminal or from numerous agents. Ceuta is a comfortable if unexciting place to stay, but more expensive than Morocco, except for some duty free goods. There is a reasonable number of transport options from the scruffy town of Fnideq, just in Morocco, and there is a *bureau de change* at the border. It can take a while to pass through the border. There is also a faster (30 mins) but more expensive and slightly less frequent **hydrofoil** (£30/6,000 Ptas return), 6 Mon-Sat, 4 on Sun, between Algeciras and Ceuta. Contact T 956 509139 or **Stirling Travel**, Gibraltar 71787.

● **Between Málaga or Almería and Melilla**
A long distance service from Málaga and Almería, leaving at 1300, plies to the Spanish enclave of Melilla. Fares are from 2,530 Ptas for passengers, 7,300 Ptas for cars, and 2,900 Ptas for bicycles and motorbikes.

● **Between Sète and Nador or Tanger**
Comanov, Companie Morocaine de Navigation, run car and passenger ferry services from Sète in the S of France to Nador, adjacent to Melilla and Tanger. Passenger fares are from MD1,390 (Nador) and MD1,200 (Tanger), car fares from MD1,700 (Nador) and MD1,340 (Tanger), bicycles and motorbikes from MD620 (Nador) and MD490 (Tanger). These are relatively luxurious services, running every 4 days between Nador and Sète from Jun to Oct, and daily between Tanger (leaving 1800) and Sète (leaving 1900) a journey of 36 hrs. The vessel is called the Marrkech, has a capacity of 634 passengers and 220 cars. There are 185 fully a/c cabins, 118 in star class and 67 tourist, medical services on board, swimming pool, clay pigeon shooting, children's play area, cinema, nightclub, cafeteria has wide choice and restaurant. **Comanov** are at 7 Blvd de la Résistance, Casablanca, T 302412,

F 308455; 43 Ave Abou El Alaâ El Maâri, Tanger, T 932649, F 306138; Immeuble Lazaar Beni Enzar, BP 89, Nador, T 608538, F 608667; **SNCM Ferryterranee**, 4 Quai d'Alger, BP 81, 34 202 Sète Cedex, France, T 67747055, F 490545; **Compagnie Charles Leborgne**, 6 Quai François Maillol, 34 202 Sète Cedex, France, T 67745055, F 67743304. Bookings also through **Continental Shipping and Travel**, London, T 071 4914968.

Between Gibraltar and Tanger Direct services from Gibraltar run daily and take 2½ hrs. 1995 fares were single MD250/£18, return MD390/£28. Tickets can be purchased in Tanger from **Med Travel**, Ave Mohammed V, T 935872/3, and in Gibraltar from **Exchange Travel**, 241 Main St, T 76151/2, F 76153 and Tour Africa, 2a Main St, Gibraltar, T 77666, F 76754. Day tour travellers take precedence over booked return tickets – be warned. **NB** See note regarding overcrowding on ferries from Algeciras to Tanger which also applies here.

● **Between Gibraltar and Mdiq**
There is a weekly (Thur) catamaran service in summer between Gibraltar and Mdiq, a small town S of Ceuta, with regular transport to Tetouan. Contact **Seagle**, 9B George's Lane, Gibraltar, T 76763.

● **Between Faro and Tanger**
There are three car and passenger ferries a week from Faro, in Portugal, to Tanger, taking 9-10 hrs. Contact **ACP Viages**, 49A Rua Rosa Araugo, Lisbon, T 01 560382, or **Comanov**, 43 Ave Abou El Alaâ El Maâri, Tanger, T 932649, F 932320.

SEA – CRUISES

There is a commercial port at Casablanca, and some cruises stop here but there are no scheduled services. **CTC** from Tilbury and Greenock calls in at Casablanca, **CTC** from Greenock and Liverpool calls in at Tanger. **CTC Cruise Lines**, 1 Regent St, London, SW1Y 4NN, T 0171 896 68888. **Cargo Ship Voyages**, Strand Cruise Travel Centre, Charing Cross Shopping Concourse, Strand, London WC2N 4HZ, call in at Casablanca, Ceuta and Melilla; **Costa Cruises**, 45/49 Mortimer St, London W1N 8JL, T 0171 3232200, F 0171 3234566, call in at Casablanca and Agadir; **P&O Cruises**, 77 New Oxford St, London WC1A 1PP, T 0171 8002222, F 0171 8001280, the Victoria, Oriana and

Canberra call in at Tanger, Casablanca and Agadir; **Crystal Cruises**, 11 Quadrant Arcade, Regent St, London W1R 6JB, T 0171 2879040, F 0171 4341410, call in at Casablanca; **Airtour Cruises**, Wavell House, Holcombe Rd, Helmshore, Rossendale, Lancs, BB4 4NB T 0170 6260000, a number of their cruises call in at Agadir and less frequently into Tanger and Casablanca. **Holland American Line**, 77-79 Great Eastern St, London EC2A 3HU, T 0171 7291929, F 0171 8311410, call in at Casablanca. **Fred Olsen Cruise Lines**, White House Rd, Ipswich, IP1 5LL, T 0147 3292222, F 0147 3292345, call in at Tanger and Agadir; **Cunard Line**, South Western House, Canute Rd, Southampton SO14 3NR, T 0170 3716608, F 0170 3225843, call in at Casablanca and Agadir.

SEA – CARGO

The main ports are Al Hoceima, Tanger, Kenitra, Mohammedia, Casablanca, El Jadidia, Safi, Essaouira, Agadir, Tan-Tan, Laayoune, Dakhla, Mdiq and Asilah.

CUSTOMS

Visitors may take in, free of duty, 400 grammes of tobacco, 200 cigarettes or 50 cigars and such personal items as a camera, binoculars, a portable radio receiver, computer or typewriter.

● Pets

Europeans may take their pet to Morocco. It will need a health certificate no more than 10 days old and an anti rabies certificate less than 6 months old.

● Prohibited items

It must be stressed that travellers must not support the exploitation of the wildlife and should be aware that some items openly for sale in Morocco cannot be legally imported into the UK and EU. This includes products made from tortoise shell, snake skin, lizards and many fur products. It is too late to save these creatures but buying such products puts the sentence of death on others. Visitors should certainly not purchase live animals as export from Morocco and import into EU and USA is in most cases illegal and is punishable by large fines and confiscation. There are severe penalties for possession of or trade in narcotic drugs: 3 months to 5 years imprisonment and/or fines up to MD240,000.

ON ARRIVAL

● Airport information

The principal destination is the much improved **Aéroport Mohammed V**, which is at **Nouasseur**, 30 km SE of Casablanca, T 339100. From here there are trains to Casablanca and regular bus services to both Casablanca (40 mins) and Rabat (90 mins). They drop and collect passengers at the CTM terminal in Casablanca, off Ave des Forces Armées Royales, and in Rabat in front of the *Hotel Terminus*, on Ave Mohammed V. There are also more expensive grand-taxi services. The airport terminal includes a restaurant, bar, post office, a BMCE *bureau de change* and agencies for the larger hotels, tour companies and car hire companies.

Agadir is the next major destination as large numbers of tourists fly there direct. **Aéroport Agadir Al Massira**, is a modern construction 28 km from the city, T 839002, with connections by bus and grand-taxis.

Other important international airports are: **Aéroport Marrakech Menara**, 6 km from Marrakech, undergoing improvements; **Aéroport Les Angads**, 15 km from Oujda; and **Aéroport Boukhalef**, 15 km from Tanger. There are also some international flights to **Aéroport Charif Al Idrissi**, Al Hoceima; **Aéroport Fes Saiss**, Fes; **Aéroport Hassan I**, Laayoune; **Aéroport Taorirt**, Ouarzazate; and **Aéroport Rabat-Sale**, 10 km from Rabat. All airports are well-connected by buses or grand-taxis.

● Airport tax

There are no airport taxes. On entry into Morocco vehicles and larger electronic equipment will be entered in the passport, to prevent resale without paying taxes which can be as high as 100%.

● Conduct/clothing

Morocco is more relaxed than many Muslim countries and therefore it is possible to wear clothing that exposes arms and legs in coastal resorts. However, to minimize hassle, women are advised to cover themselves away from the hotel compounds at social occasions and visits in traditional rural areas. Full coverage of limbs and head is recommended when travelling in the heat. Winter temperatures can be low and night temperatures in the desert and at altitude are low all the year round so carry extra garments.

● Electricity

Most of the country runs at 220V, although some areas are on 110V. International adaptors are a good investment.

● **Hammam**

These are public baths where most Moroccans wash, relax and gossip and are worth a visit. The *hammam* is a succession of hot steamy rooms with plentiful water, and masseurs and assistants on hand. Men and women will either have separate premises or hours. Foreigners may be less welcome in some *hammams* than others – it is worth asking at the hotel, youth hostel or campsite for a recommendation.

● **Hours of business**

Working hours are normally 0900-1200 and 1400-1800. There are different working hours for summer and during Ramadan. On Fri the midday break is normally longer to allow for prayers.

● **Laundry**

Laundries and dry-cleaners are available everywhere, cheapest in the medina, where they are speedy but of varying quality. Hotels are expensive but reliable.

● **Monuments – entry**

Entrance fee to government run sites is always MD10 – except at Volubilis, MD20.

● **Official time**

Morocco follows GMT all year round, 1 hr behind the UK and a surprising 2 hrs behind Spain in summer.

● **Photography**

Many people, including Moroccans, dislike being a subject for a photograph, and it is very unwise to photograph women. People like water-sellers, musicians, animal tamers and camel owners expect to be paid for posing while small children will get in the way and then demand remuneration. Take great care near military or sensitive installations. Protect your camera from the dust and heat. Films are available for purchase in Morocco, but can be of variable quality. If possible purchase where the film has been properly stored or only recently imported. In selecting films and the camera to take remember that the sunlight is bright and the main subjects are likely to be buildings and scenery.

● **Safety**

Security Morocco is neither the most dangerous nor the safest country in the world. If reasonable precautions are taken the risk can be minimized. It is advisable never to carry valuables or large amounts of cash and to carry money and documents securely, ie in a money belt. Camp-sites are notoriously insecure places while hotels are normally much better. Never leave valuables in the car, and preferably entrust the car to a **gardien** for a small fee. Most importantly travellers should trust their personal instincts, and not go anywhere with anyone who seems suspicious or overly keen.

Airports and ports can be chaotic due to complicated bureaucracy and lack of order. Baggage is normally hastily checked. All papers should be correct otherwise even greater delays will occur. The traveller often arrives confused and insecure, particularly at the bustling port of Tanger, and this a favourite time for pickpockets and con-artists to strike. Do not believe a word the latter say, but go immediately to the hotel, railway or coach station already chosen.

Guides Travellers are likely to be hassled by guides often posing as 'students' or 'friends', and extreme caution should be taken in accepting help from these people, as it will lead to considerable expense (whatever the initial fee) and possible personal danger. The worst places are Tanger, Fes, Meknes and Marrakech. These people are often extremely skilled at the job, and have considerable linguistic abilities. Travellers will be well advised to use an official guide from the tourist office or manage without. The only medinas where guides may be necessary are Fes, Meknes and Marrakech. A much less threatening variation on the *faux guides* is the children in S villages who ask for money or presents, or who offer their help in exchange for a small remuneration.

Hashish Throughout Morocco, although particularly in the Rif, travellers will be offered hashish. It should be borne in mind that hashish dealers often tip off the police, and that there are considerable risks involved, despite the attraction of the cheap prices. The charity **Prisoners Abroad** supports a number of travellers who succombed to the temptation – be warned.

Police Throughout the country the police are normally helpful to tourists, and there is no problem approaching them for directions. The traveller will have more dealings with the grey-uniformed **Sûreté** than the khaki-uniformed **Gendarmerie**.

Women should be careful when travelling in Morocco, and preferably should not travel alone. Hassle from Moroccan men can be quite heavy-duty.

● **Shopping**

Many of the main tourist towns now have fixed price shops, although some of these can be negotiated despite the label. The best is the *Ensemble Artisanal*, run by the government, which is normally a good guide to the range of products available, although it is a bit expensive. The best bargains, and the more authentic experience, are to be had in the *souqs*, the areas of traditional shops found in most historic cities. Similarly cheap and interesting are the markets which are held on a daily or weekly basis in large villages and towns throughout the countryside, as well as specialist markets in larger urban centres.

Best buys include leather goods, pottery. metalwork and woodwork. Essaouira has excellent carved cedarwood products. Pottery is best in Safi and Fes. In leather, belts and *baboushes* (slippers) are cheap. Jewellery was traditionally the preserve of Jews, but despite their emigration good pieces can still be bought. Carpets are excellent and come in a variety of forms, from basic rugs, to vast silk carpets, and reflect regional traditions. It is worth inspecting the weave closely. Chichaoua and Taroudant are good places to buy.

● **Tipping**

It is normal to tip waiters in cafés, restaurants and bars, who often receive a very low basic pay. In some more expensive restaurants service is included in the bill. Tipping is also advisable for porters on buses and trains and in hotels. It is optional with taxi-drivers, but recommended (10%) when the meter is being used.

Do not tip for taxi journeys where the meter is not being used, as the negotiated price will be generous anyway. For handling baggage in hotels tip around MD2-3, MD3-5 on buses and MD5 on trains and in airports.

● **Tourist information**

Most towns in Morocco have an Office de Tourisme and larger towns also have a Syndicat d'Initiative et de Tourisme (Information Office). The standard of information varies and is best represented by the booklets available. They offer to find official guides, again of very variable standard. See entries for individual towns.

● **Weights & measures**

Morocco uses the metric system. See conversion table on page 496.

WHERE TO STAY

● **Hotels**

Rooms are normally easy to find except in some popular places in peak seasons. The most difficult place all year round is Casablanca, where cheap rooms go early in the day. It is wise to reserve rooms in the top hotels in most cities. In almost all hotels, the night's accommodation ends at 1200, although some will be flexible in view of travel plans, and most will look after bags between 1200 and a later departure. On arrival at the hotel it will be necessary to fill a form giving name, occupation, address, date of arrival in Morocco, passport details, etc. Hotels in Morocco cover a wide range from the super luxurious like the *Mamounia* in Marrakech and the *Gazelle d'Or* in Taroudant, to absurdly cheap and small establishments that have little more than a bed and ceiling. At the cheapest end the hotels (also called *auberges* and *pensiones* in some places) are basic rather than miserable. Moroccan hotels are classified in a number of starred bands from five down to 1B, with the remainder, the cheapest places, unclassified. It is advisable to see the room before agreeing to stay in all but the five and four star hotels. Unclassified hotels are often found in the old part of town, the medina, where there is often a problem with water. The more expensive hotels are normally in the new town.

● **Youth Hostels (auberges de jeunesse)**

11 in total affiliated to the IYHA, and a cheap option for anyone with a YHA card, are found in the largest cities: Casablanca, Rabat, Fes, Meknes and Marrakech, as well as at Azrou in the Middle Atlas and Asni in the Grand Atlas. The headquarters is in Meknes, in Ave Oqba Ibn Nafi. Overnight charge MD20-40, use of kitchen MD2, maximum stay 3 nights, priority given to people under 30 years of age. Opening hours: summer 0800-1000, 1200-1600 and 1830-2400; winter 0800-1000, 1200-1500 and 1800-2230. *Moroccan Federation of Youth Hostels*, Parc de la Ligue Arabe, 15988 Casablanca, T 220551, F 226777.

● **Refuges**

In the High Atlas there are a number of refuges run by *Club Alpin Français*, BP 6178 Casablanca 01, T 270090, F 297292, have refuges where hikers may rest and use the basic sleeping and cooking facilities. Rates depend on category and season but about MD15-50 per night.

Hotel classifications

AL US$75+. International class luxury hotel. All facilities for business and leisure travellers are of the highest international standard.

A US$75+. International hotel with air conditioned rooms with WC, bath/shower, TV, phone, mini-bar, daily clean linen. Choice of restaurants, coffee shop, shops, bank, travel agent, swimming pool, some sport and business facilities.

B US$60-75. As **A** but without the luxury, reduced number of restaurants, smaller rooms, limited range of shops and sport.

C US$40-60. Best rooms have air conditioning, own bath/shower and WC. Usually comfortable, bank, shop, pool.

D US$20-40. Best rooms may have own WC and bath/shower. Depending on management will have room service and choice of cuisine in restaurant.

E US$10-20. Simple provision. Perhaps fan cooler. May not have restaurant. Shared WC and showers with hot water (when available).

F under US$10. Very basic, shared toilet facilities, variable in cleanliness, noise, often in dubious locations.

● Camping

Sites are found all over Morocco. Security can be a problem, as can the climate. Sites are often poorly equipped, and far from the town centre, whilst they are often not much cheaper than basic hotels. Casual camping is allowed with the permission of the local authority or the landowner if they can be located. You are advised to use the established sites, preferably those which are guarded. The tourist board quote 87 camping and caravaning sites providing 41,000 places in well chosen locations. Rates around MD15 per person and MD15 per car/caravan. Cultural Tourism Service for Young People and Rest Centres have about 20 rest centres specially for young tourists, contact, 6 rue Soumaya, Rabat Agdal, T 672772, F 670388.

FOOD AND DRINK

● Food

Most Moroccan towns have cafés, some of which offer *croissants*, *petit-pain* and cake, occasionally soup and basic snacks. Restaurants will be divided into **medina** and **ville nouvelle** establishments, the former cheap and basic, the latter normally more expensive. Restaurants may be limited to larger settlements, those with a tourist appeal, or on major roads. Fast food outlets occur in larger cities. **Laiteries** and snack bars will make up sandwiches to order. Beyond these options there are food stalls and open air restaurants in every village, town and city serving various types of soup (normally the standard broth, *harira*), snacks and grilled meat. The best place for the adventurous open air eater is the Djemaa El Fna square in Marrakech, which is full of stalls in the evening. Another good place is near the port in Essaouira, where fresh fish are grilled. Obviously there is a greater risk of food poisoning with this type of food, so it is better to go for dishes that are cooked as one waits, or that are on the boil.

Moroccan food in restaurants can often be simple, centred around meat, and somewhat dull for vegetarians. Real Moroccan cuisine, in top restaurants, or in houses, is excellent, and worth seeking out. The following are the main specialities:

Couscous is Morocco's most famous speciality, steamed granules of semolina cooked with various combinations of meat and vegetables. In some houses and restaurants this is reserved for Fri, the holy day, a very approximate equivalent of Sun lunch.

Harira: a staple soup, the exact composition varying according to availability of ingredients, normally involves vegetables, meat and chick peas. This is a filling and tasty snack available for a few dirhams in most restaurants and at many stalls or cafés.

Kebab and Kefta: the main meat in cheaper restaurants are *kebabs*, made of beef, mutton or lamb, which are also called *bro-*

Restaurant classifications

Given the variations in price of food on any menu our restaurants are divided where possible into three simple grades: ♦♦♦ expensive, ♦♦ average and ♦ cheap.

chettes. Minced meat, called *kefta*, is also common. These are often served with chips (*frites*).

Mechoui involves mutton roasted on a spit, and is often eaten at festivals. In restaurants order in advance.

Pastilla is most famous in Fes. This sweet layered pastry dish usually made with pigeon, saffron and almonds often has to be ordered in advance.

Salads are good, although risky, (see Health, page 492) in cheaper establishments. The local combination is called, unsurprisingly, *salade marocaine*, there is also *salade verte*, *salade des tomates* and *salade nicoise*. Finely chopped tomato and onion are a popular accompaniment to *kebab* or *kefta*.

Sweets, Morocco has good pastries, although the quality varies. Distinctive are the coiled sticky sweets eaten at the daily breaking of the Ramadan fast. Try the yoghourt made in the local *laiterie*. Fresh *fruit* is excellent, and cheap, in season. Oranges are particularly cheap, as are prickly pears, sold off barrows.

With *tagines*, meat, fish or vegetables are stewed in a conical ceramic utensil, with combinations of potatoes, olives, lemon, prunes and spices. This very tasty dish is found in the top restaurants and roadside cafés, and will often involve local ingredients.

The speciality of Marrakech is *Tangia*, a tall ceramic pot in which meat is baked in butter, spices and olives for hours, normally in the embers of the fire at the local *hammam*.

Dishes for Ramadan. At sunset the fast is broken with a rich and savoury *harira* (see above), *beghrir* (little honeycombed pancakes served with melted butter and honey) and *shebbakia* (cakes turned in oil and covered in honey).

● **Drink**

All over Morocco the main drink apart from water is **mint tea** (*thé à la menthe* or *thé marocain*) a cheap, refreshing drink which is made with green tea, fresh mint and masses of white sugar. The latter two ingredients predominate in the taste. **Coffee** is most commonly drunk black and strong, although the preferred strength can be requested. *Café au lait* (with milk) is common. For a half-way version ask for *demi-demi* or *nus-nus*. Prices in cafés are fixed by the government according to the quality. **Fruit juices** are excellent, notably the freshly squeezed orange juice (*jus d'orange*) available in most cafés. Similar, although

less common, is grapefruit juice (*jus de pamplemousse*), and lemon juice (*jus de citron*), the latter to be taken with sugar. Altogether different are banana juice (*jus de banane*) and apple juice (*jus de pomme*), as these are in fact a sort of milk shake. Similar, delicious, although a bit less common are almond juice (*jus d'amand*) and avocado juice (*jus d'avocat*). Very good cafés may have strawberry juice (*jus de fraise*), pineapple juice (*jus d'ananas*), raspberry juice (*jus de framboise*), and a mixed cocktail (*panaché* or *mélange*).

Soft drinks are also common and popular, often called collectively *limonades*. There are many varieties, including *Coca-Cola* and *Pepsi-Cola*, both of which seem to taste different in Morocco, and lemonade, such as *7-Up, Sprite* and the local *Cigogne*. Still mineral water (*eau naturel*) is almost always *Sidi Harazem* or *Sidi Ali*. There is also fizzy mineral water (*eau gazeuse*).

Despite its Islamic status, Morocco is fairly relaxed about **alcohol** which officially is only for sale to non-Muslims. Imported lager, wine and spirits are readily available. Morocco also makes its own wine and beer, which are of course cheaper. The wine, in red, rosé and white, can often be quite good, particularly *Guerrouane* from Meknes, Morocco's main producing area. There are also some very poor wines. Moroccan beers, *Stork, Flag Pils* or *Flag Special* are all inoffensive lagers.

GETTING AROUND

AIR

Royal Air Maroc and its subsidiary **Royal Air Inter** serves the country's major cities. The head office is at Aéroport Casa-Anfa, Casablanca, T 02 912000, F 02 912397. The network includes Agadir, Al Hoceima, Casablanca, Dakhla, Er-Rachidia, Fes, Laayoune, Marrakech, Ouarzazate, Oujda, Rabat, Smara, Tanger, Tan-Tan and Tetouan.

TRAIN

The **ONCF** rail service is limited by the physical geography and recent development of Morocco. There are 1,900 km of railway lines. The principal routes are: Casablanca-Rabat-Kenitra; Casablanca-Meknes- Fes- Oujda; Casablanca- Marrakech; Casablanca- Tanger; Casablanca-Oued-Zem; Casablanca-El-Jadida. At present the track is single except between Kenitra and Casablanca and delays occur, but

	Agadir	Al Hoceima	Beni Mellal	Casablanca	El Jadida	Er Rachidia	Essaouira	Fes	Laayoune	Marrakech	Meknes	Nador	Ouarzazate	Oujda	Rabat	Safi	Tanger
Al Hoceima	1019																
Beni Mellal	467	564															
Casablanca	511	536	210														
El Jadida	419	632	271	99													
Er Rachidia	681	616	375	545	506												
Essaouira	173	887	370	351	252	745											
Fes	756	275	291	289	388	364	640										
Laayoune	649	1740	1116	1160	1066	1330	822	1396									
Marrakech	273	758	196	238	197	510	176	485	922								
Meknes	740	335	278	231	328	346	580	60	1389	467							
Nador	1095	175	628	628	727	510	979	339	1736	822	399						
Ouarzazate	375	992	398	442	399	306	380	687	1024	204	652	816					
Oujda	1099	293	632	635	731	514	983	343	1748	826	403	104	820				
Rabat	602	445	260	93	190	482	442	198	1251	321	138	535	528	541			
Safi	294	792	351	256	157	683	129	545	943	157	486	884	361	888	347		
Tanger	880	323	538	369	468	608	720	303	1529	598	287	1086	811	609	278	625	
Tetouan	892	278	536	385	484	602	736	281	1541	675	258	437	820	555	294	641	57

Morocco: distances by road between major cities (Km)

in general the service is speedy and reliable, particularly if the traveller picks the special rapid services. Between Casablanca, Kenitra and Rabat there are regular **Trains Navettes Rapides**. For Rabat the train is more convenient than the bus.

The network has three branches from Sidi Kacem; S through Kenitra, Sale, Rabat, Mohammedia, Casablanca, Settat and Marrakech; E through Meknes, Fes, Taza and Oujda; N to Asilah and Tanger. A weekly service uses freight lines from Oujda to Bouarfa, on the E flank of the country, N of the Figuig crossing into Algeria. In addition, **ONCF** buses connect with its trains, from Tnine Sidi Lyamani (just S of Asilah) to Tetouan, from Taourirt (in between Taza and Oujda) to Nador, from Khouribga to Beni Mellal, and from Marrakech to Agadir, Laayoune and Dakhla. Most train stations have *consigne* (left luggage depots) but normally only for locked baggage.

First class compartments are spacious and generally quieter than second class. Second class train fares are little more expensive than the Compagnie de Transporte Marocaine, CTM buses, and compartments are very comfortable. 'Economic' compartments are very basic and crowded, but quite feasible for the budget traveller. The trains normally have a drinks and snacks trolley.

BUS

Morocco has a highly competitive bus service. The government company, **Compagnie de Transporte Marocaine (CTM)**, has a 24 hr information service 'Allo CTM' on (02) 449424 for Casablanca or (02) 449254 for other towns. This company is by far the most reliable and comprehensive. It runs to a fixed timetable. Its buses leave on time and do not dawdle en route. Except for a few so-called 'rapid' services with videos, the private companies are normally cheaper and less comfortable, and far slower. The private companies do however reach some small places which CTM ignores, and will follow more difficult routes, such as the spectacular road over the High Atlas mountains and the famous Tizi-n-Test pass, between Taroudant and Marrakech.

Bus travel is confusing. Some towns have one terminal for all buses while others have separate terminals for CTM and private companies. Others have different terminals for different lines and destinations. Where tickets do not specify seats it is worth buying early to avoid competition for the best places. Luggage will be stowed in the boot or on top of the bus, it is normal to tip the man for this job. For early morning buses it is worth buying tickets in advance.

Most larger towns have local urban buses which are very crowded, when pick-pocketing is a great danger. The buses are cheap, but then so are petit-taxis. The buses are perhaps only necessary for getting around Fes, Marrakech, Rabat and Casablanca, and for visiting outlying sites of interest, beaches and airports.

CAR

Morocco has a good road network, and plentiful petrol stations and mechanics, except in mountainous and desert areas. A 4WD vehicle is advisable for more adventurous exploration off the major roads in the Sahara and the mountains. Mountain roads are narrow and winding and should be approached with caution. The only fast, wide route is the toll road between Rabat and Casablanca. Roads are not heavily congested, there are few private cars, but numerous taxis, buses and lorries that thunder down the roads at dangerous speeds. Driving and parking in town is relatively easy, although some roads within the old medinas are extremely narrow. Employ a **gardien** to guard the car when parking in cities. The only cities with traffic problems similar to western conurbations are Rabat and Casablanca. Night driving is more dangerous. Always drive with a good spare tyre.

Motorway links Casablanca and Rabat, toll of MD15; and Rabat and Kenitra, toll of MD10.

● P = main trunk road, mainly hard top. S + secondary regional road, mostly hard top.

● *piste* There are almost 10,000 km of surfaced main road and several thousand km of classified but unsurfaced roads known as *pistes* which can be negotiated with care by an ordinary car but for which 4WD is recommended. They should certainly not be attempted by motor caravans or caravans.

● Bad weather can affect travel. Snow blocks roads in the Atlas and the Rif. Landslides occur after heavy rain. Enquire at your last stop for in prolonged bad weather road reports are given twice daily on the radio.

● Petrol prices per litre: super and lead free MD8, ordinary MD7, diesel MD4. Lead free petrol is becoming more widely available but so far only in the larger towns. If you leave the main roads fill up the fuel tank at every opportunity.

● The highway code is international. Road signs are in Arabic and French. Speed is limited to 120 kmp on the motorway, 100 kph on main roads, 40-60 kph in towns (watch the signs). The wearing of seat belts is compulsory ... if there is a belt. Don't be afraid to use the horn to warn animals, pedestrians, cyclists of your approach.

● Red and white lines on the kerb mean no parking.

● Tyre repairs. Prices vary, expect to pay MD40 as a foreigner in a hurry in town centre at busy time of day or MD10 for a local repair in a small village if you have time to wait.

● Warning triangles are not compulsory but are advisable. They should be placed at least 10m behind a parked/broken down vehicle.

● Police are empowered to levy on-the-spot fines for contravention of traffic regulations. Fines vary between MD5 and MD10 according to the offence.

● In the case of an accident report to the police in the town where this occurs and obtain a written report, otherwise the insurance is invalid.

Car hire is relatively easy in Morocco. There are international agencies and smaller and local firms, in most large towns. It is possible to arrange one-way hire. Before leaving the agency check that the car is fully equipped with all the necessary spares. Prices begin at MD200 per day plus MD2 per km or MD800 per day unlimited distance. The cheapest car is almost always the *Renault 4*, which is quite suitable for rough Moroccan roads.

● **As a matter of self preservation** do not agree to take a hire car other than in daylight – light to check the car and more important light to see the way in a strange car in a strange country.

• Be prepared to pay for the petrol already in the tank of your hire car – as much as US$58. You will need Moroccan dirhams except at an office which takes credit cards. For instance Agadir airport had cash for cash exchange only, no TCs.

● **Important addresses**

Royal Automobile Club, Rabat, T 780511; Touring Club du Maroc, 3 Ave des Forces l'Armées Royales, Casablanca, T 265231, F 262386.

Branch offices of Touring Club du Maroc: 41 Blvd Mohammed V, Meknes, T 522055; 45 Place Patrice Lumumba, Rabat, T 27548; 5 Terrasse Rensshause, Tanger.

Agents of Touring Club du Maroc: Villa Dourcet, Place de la Mosquee, Agadir; Tadia Voyages, Beni Mellal; Agency de Voyage Mortier, 41 rue de Beyrouth, Fes; Cabinet Chelly, 20 rue de Marrkech, Khouribga; Syndicate d'Initiative, Municipal Camping Site, Ave de France, Marrakech; 28 Ave Mohammed V, Sidi Kassem.

Facilities of Touring Club du Maroc: visitors who can show membership of clubs affiliated to the AIT may obtain all touring information free of charge. The TCM will also make all the necessary arrangements with the customs authorities on behalf of visitors for extension of carnets de passage etc. It issues itineraries free of charge.

OTHER LAND TRANSPORT

● **Bicycles/motorcycles**

These can be hired in the larger towns. Cycling is a tough but rewarding option in Morocco, with four mountain ranges to confront, where mountain bicycles are particularly suitable on the pistes. There is no shortage of mechanics for either bicycles or motorbikes, as both are popular with Moroccans. Security will be more of a problem. City centres have **gardiens** who wear blue coats and tin badges and guard cars, motorbikes, mopeds and bicycles, for a small fee (bicycles normally MD1-2). Trains, buses, grand-taxis and trucks will take travellers' bikes for a small fee.

● **Motorcycle hire**

Scooters and Yamahas: try **Golden Tours**, Ave Mohammed V, Agadir, T 840362, F 825692; Casablanca, T 447734, F 447737; Marrakech, T 449161, F 435257; Ouarzazate, T 885858.

● **Hitchhiking**

Hitchhiking is possible, although it usually involves some payment. This is one of the main

Hiring a car

Sample prices for hire one week low/high season, unlimited distance, fully insured, booked in advance in UK.

Group A Renault 4	£225/239
Group B Fiat Uno	£259/269
Group C Peugeot 205	£379/389
Group D Peugeot 309	£389/395
Group E Renault 19	£399/405
Group F Renault 21	£539/549
Group G Mercedes 190E	£699

See car hire details town by town.

Sample prices unlimited mileage (MD)

	3 days	7 days	Insurance	CWD	PAI	
Group A	1,962	3,437	4,500	45	20	Renault 4/Fiat Uno
Group B	2,400	4,200				Renault 5/Peugeot 106/205
Group C	2,826	4,949	6,000	60		Fiat Tipo
Group E	3,768	6,594				Peugeot 306
Group F	5,139	8,995	8,000	100		Peugeot 405 a/c
Group G	5,520	9,660	12,000			Feroza 4X4
Group H	7,710	13,496				Volvo 940
Group I	6,615	11,578				Cherokee

ways to get around the more isolated mountain and desert areas. Vans and lorries will pick up passengers for a bargained price. **NB** Hitch-hiking is unadvisable for women on their own.

● **Taxis**

Grand-taxis run over fixed routes within cities, between different towns and cities, or from urban centres to outlying settlements. There is a fixed price for each route, and passengers pay for a place, with six in a Mercedes and nine in a Peugeot. The taxis wait until they are full, but each passenger has the right to pay for the remaining places in order to leave sooner or have more space.

Between towns, grand-taxis are quicker than trains and buses and normally only a little more expensive. Each town has a taxi rank, where someone will point travellers to the first car leaving for the appropriate destination.

Petit-taxis are used within a town, have a limited range, are normally small or medium sized saloons, and colour coded, blue in Rabat, red in Casablanca and buff in Marrakech. Officially they are metered, with an initial fare (MD1 in Rabat, MD5 in Casablanca) followed by increments for time and distance, and a 50% surcharge in the late evening and during the night. Petit-taxis may pick up to three passengers which makes fare calculation confusing. For taxis that are not metered, it will be necessary to estimate one's own fare. As a general rule most city centre journeys should not be more than MD5. Tipping is welcomed. Taxi drivers have very variable standards of French.

COMMUNICATIONS

● **Language**

The official and predominate language is Arabic. A large minority, particularly in rural regions speak Berber, which has three distinct dialects, based in the Rif, the High Atlas and the Sous valley. Many Arabs and Berbers also speak Spanish and French, the latter being the language in which much business and politics is carried out, and the main vehicle for tourists. Street signs are in Arabic and French, and occasionally in tourist towns in English. English is becoming increasingly popular as a foreign language.

● **Postal services**

Letters to or from Europe can take up to a week. Posting letters is relatively easy, with the *PTT Centrale* of each town selling the appropriate stamps; a card to UK costs MD1.5. It is best to post the letter in the box inside or just outside this building as these are emptied more frequently than those elsewhere. For those without a contact address to receive letters, instruct that they should be addressed clearly, with the surname underlined, to: Poste Restante, PTT Centrale, the town, Morocco. Each *PTT Centrale* will have a **post restante** section, where letters are kept for a number of weeks. There is a small charge on collection. Post offices are open 0800-1200 and 1500-1800 Mon-Fri in the winter, 0800-1500 in the summer. Some travellers use *American Express* offices to collect mail, in Morocco this is c/o *Voyages Schwartz*. Postage costs to Europe are MD3.5 for a letter and MD3.2 for a post card.

● **Telephone services**

Teleboutiques clearly marked in blue, rather like a shop are very plentiful. They are nearly always supervized to give information and change. Generally more than one even in a small settlement. The machines takes range of coins and are easy to use – international calls no problem. For internal calls put in several MD1 coins and dial the region code, followed by a 6 figure number. For overseas calls, put in at least 3 MD5 coins, dial 00 and wait for a musical sequence before proceeding. Most call boxes only accept the 'silver all over' coins. Calls can also be made at the **PTT Centrale**, or the *Telephonique* cabins where generally the number is given to the telephonist who dials it and then calls out a cabin number where the call is waiting. It is simpler but more expensive to phone from a hotel.

Calling Morocco from abroad the code is **212**.

Regional codes:

02 – Casablanca

03 – Settat, Beni Mellal, El Jadida, and Mohammedia

04 – Essaouira, Ouarzazate, Marrakech and Safi

05 – Er Rachidia, Erfoud, and Meknes

06 – Fes, Sefrou, Nador, Figuig and Oujda

07 – Rabat/Sale, Kenitra, Sidi and Kacem

08 – Agadir and the south, Laayoune, Goulimine, Taroudant and Tan-Tan

09 – El Hoceima, Tetouan and Tanger

To call a mobile phone the code is always 02 what ever area it may be in.

Fax and telex facilities are available from luxury hotels and the main PTT offices.

Useful numbers for any region: **Police**: T 19. **Fire Service**: T 15. **Highway Emergency Service**: T 177.

ENTERTAINMENT

● Newspapers

Moroccan newspapers are produced in Arabic, French and Spanish. Although some represent opposition parties criticism of the monarchy is rare, as there is strict government control. In French *Le Matin du Sahara* and *Maroc Soir* are the most pro-government, whilst *L'Opinion*, *Liberation* and *Al Bayane* are more independent. These newspapers are cheap and give an insight into Morocco and its politics, but will have limited interest for the traveller. Coverage of overseas news is limited. Foreign newspapers are available in larger towns and cities. *The Guardian* and *Herald Tribune* (International editions) and *Le Monde* reach Rabat and Casablanca in the evening, *Le Figaro*, which is printed in Casablanca, the same morning.

● Radio

BBC World Service Radio broadcasts on short wave (see page 474 for frequencies), although reception can be difficult in the night and morning. The commercial radio station *MIDI-1* gives news and music in Arabic and French. The state radio service is predominantly in Arabic and French, but has an afternoon slot in English. Northern areas can pick up broadcasts from Gibraltar, Spain and Portugal.

● Sports

Flying Moroccan Federation of Light Aviation and Aerial Sports can be contacted at Complex Sportif Prince Moulay Abdellah, Rabat, T 708347, F 706958. There are 11 Royal aeroclubs: at Tanger, T 934371; Marrakech, T 447764; Fes, T 644167; Kenitra, T 772183; Rabat, T 724222; Beni Mellal, T 482095; El Jadidia, T 350582; Safi, T 622614; Agadir; Casablanca (Tit-Mellil), T 350760; Casablanca (Anfa), T 350760.

Freshwater fishing Licences can be obtained from the Ministry of Water and Forest, 11 rue du Devoir, Rabat (also offices in most large towns) on a daily or annual basis for fishing in the rivers. A special licence must be obtained for fishing in the reservoirs and other artificial lakes. Fishing is not permitted anywhere between sunset and sunrise. Information regarding restrictions such as closed seasons, catch limits, sale of catch and forbidden areas will be provided with the permit. Trout in the *oueds* and particularly in the swifter gorge section are considered the best sport though in some *oueds* the construction of storage barrages

which prevent upstream movement have reduced the fish population. Pike, black bass, perch, roach, carp, eels and barbels can be caught in the lakes.

Gliding (*vol à voile*), the centre for this is at Centre Royal de *Vol à Voile* de Beni Mellal, T 482095.

Golf was introduced at the beginning of the century and has become a national passion in Morocco. It is the King's favourite sport. Major competitions attract international attention. The most famous is the Hassan II trophy played at Rabat. There are currently 14 courses designed by masters such as Robert Trent Jones and Jack Nicklaus and there are plans to double that number in the next 5 years. These courses have superb facilities and their settings, all magnificent, are as varied as the courses themselves. Without exception these courses are maintained in superb condition. The snows of the Atlas form a backdrop to the course at Marrakech; the game is played amid ancient oaks in Rabat, on golden dunes at Agadir, by the tamarisk and heather at Cabo Negro; in Meknes the golfers perform in the heart of the city by the Royal Palace. All courses are open to the public though evidence of handicap is required. Check locally for regulations, green fees and opening hours. The Royal Moroccan Golf Federation is at the Royal Dar es-Salam Golf Course in Rabat, T 755960, F 751026.

Agadir – The Dunes Golf Club, T 834690, F 834649. There are three 9-hole, par 36

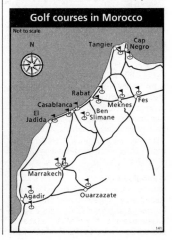

Golf courses in Morocco

Not to scale

courses here. The Eucalyptus, the blue course, 3,174m, is ideal for warming up. Hole 8 with its hilltop green has a distracting view SE over Inezgane. The Wadi or yellow course of 3,050m requires more skill while the Tamarisk, the red course, the longest at 3,204m, is even more demanding, the last hole fortunately sloping down to the green and the club house.

Agadir – Royal Golf Club, Km 12, Route Aït Melloul, T 241278, F 844380, is 9 holes. This is another par 36 course, 3,600m long, with fairways between pines, eucalyptus and shrubberies of mimosa. The undergrowth here is very dense. The greens are broad and hole 3 (par 5) with a water hazard is reported to be particularly challenging.

Ben Slimane Royal Golf Club, Ave des Forces Armées Royales, T 328793, 9 holes, 3,100m, par 36. This has an immense lake which stretches the length of the course and the surrounding trees are pine, eucalyptus and cork oak. Hole 8 requires concentration as the green is situated on a small island in the lake.

Cabo Negro Royal Golf Club, T 978303, F 978305, overlooking the Mediterranean 18 km from Tetouan. Currently it is 9 holes, 3,087m, par 36, but it is soon to be extended. The course was designed by Hawtree and Sons and revised by Cabell B Robinson and water

plays an important part in the plan, being a serious hazard on hole 3 and hole 5 which is crossed by a stream.

The Tanger Royal Golf Club, BP 41 Tanger, T 944484, F 945450, the first in the country, was inaugurated in 1917 and has since been updated retaining as far as possible the original characteristics devised by the architects Cotton and Pennink. The 18 holes (5,545m, par 70) weave their way through pine trees, cypresses and eucalyptus. It climbs and dips, hole 5 having an unexpected hill to contend with. From the summit the views over the rooftops of Tanger to the sea are rewarding.

The Marrakech Royal Golf Club, BP 634, Ancienne Route de Ouarzazate, T 444341, F 430084, is 18 holes, 6,200m, par 72. This was built in the 1920s by the Pasha of Marrakech, making it one of the longest established clubs in the country whose guests have included Churchill, Lloyd George and Eisenhower. It has been frequently renovated and improved and is one of the favourite courses played by King Hassan II. In addition to the cypresses, eucalyptus and palms on the course there are olive, orange and apricot trees. In the background rise the snow covered Atlas mountains. It is advised to concentrate on the course rather than the scenery as there are a

Golf – what it costs			
Name of Club	**Green fee**	**Club hire**	**Closed on**
Dar es Salaam	MD400	MD100	Monday
Royal Golf d'Anfa	MD200	MD100	Monday
Agadir – The Dunes	MD220 (9) MD160 MD340 (18)	none	
Agadir – Royal Golf	MD220 (9) MD160 MD340 (18)	none	
Ben Slimane Royal Golf	MD200	n/a	none
Cabo Negro	MD300	n/a	none
Tanger Royal Golf	MD200	MD70	Monday
Marrakech Royal Golf	MD300	MD100	none
Marrakech Palmeraie	MD350	MD200	none
Ouarzazate Royal Golf	MD150	n/a	none
El Jadida Royal Golf	MD300 MD350	weekday MD75 weekend	none
Mohammedia Royal Golf	MD220	MD100	Tuesday
Meknes Royal Golf	MD200	MD100	Monday
Fes Royal Golf	MD400	MD100	Monday
Settat Royal Golf	MD200	MD80	none
Golf d'Amelkis	MD300	n/a	none

NB Prices are subject to change without notice.

number of hazards, hole 15 requiring particular vigilance.

The Palmeraie Golf Club, Marrakech, Les Jardins de la Palmeraie, PB 1488, T 301010, F 302020, 18 holes, 6,214m, par 72. This course was designed by Robert Trent Jones Snr and is considered his 18 hole masterpiece. It was opened in 1993. Amidst the thousands of palm trees he set seven lakes, created sand filled bunkers, wove fairways and as the centrepiece to his whole design added a magnificent Moorish style club house. Described as sumptuous.

The Ouarzazate Royal Golf Club, T 882653, F 883344, 9 holes, 3,150m, par 36 is situated at the edge of the Sahara desert with the snow clad peaks of the spectacular High Atlas lying to the N. The fairways with their slopes and embankments wind through the broken terrain between palm trees and around the large lake at the last hole. There are plans to extend this course to 18 holes.

El Jadida Royal Golf Course, Km 7, Route de Casablanca, T 352251/2, 18 holes, 6,274m, par 72. This course was designed by Cabell B Robinson making full use of the attractive natural surroundings. There are fragrant pines and eucalyptus, tamarisk and mimosa, a lake, the dunes and the sea.

The Mohammedia Royal Golf Club, Casablanca, T 324656, F 321102, 18 holes, 5,917m, par 72. There are lines of pines and eucalyptus to greet you at the first hole, gorse and acacias at the second while hole 9 is defended by a bank of flowers. But the major factor to contend with throughout the whole length of the course is the wind whipping in from the Atlantic.

Anfa Royal Golf Club, Casablanca, 9 holes, 2,710m, par 35. This is a fascinating course in the heart of the city, sharing the land with the race track, set out with skill and imagination. Skill and imagination are both required to play the course as the fairways wind between the flower beds and clusters of pines and palms.

Meknes Royal Golf Club, El Mhancha, T 530753, F 550504, 9 holes, 2,707m, par 36. This is a city centre course, the centre of the ancient city of Sultan Moulay Ismail, with the roofs of the medina as a background, ancient ramparts where the club house is situated and a garden of plum, orange, olive and apricot trees. An entrance to the Royal Palace stands close to green 4. This is a small but enchanting course with floodlighting facilities permitting playing at night.

Fes Royal Golf Club, Route d'Ifrane, T 763849, 9 holes, 3,168m, par 37. This course began life as an olive grove. Cabell B Robinson accentuated the terrain and produced undulating fairways and deceptively sloping greens. The lake, divided into three sections, makes some interesting features, but by far the most important for the golfer are the bunkers which come in three sizes, huge, giant and monumental, the largest covering 1,200m sq. There are plans to double the size of this popular course.

Dar es-Salam Royal Golf Club, Rabat, T 755864/5, F 757671, is really three courses. The Green course of 9 holes, 2,170m, par 32; the Blue course, 18 holes, 6,205m, par 72 and the Red course, 18 holes, 6,702m, par 73. All the courses were laid out with imagination and a flair for the luxurious. The Green course is the most relaxed, described as a course to entertain with holes of only par 3 and par 4. The Blue course is certainly colourful with beds and banks of cultivated and wild flowers in season. There are water features and clumps of majestic eucalyptus trees. This is a course which 'cannot be taken for granted'. The Red course is the gem. Here the Hassan II trophy is fought for each year. Scoring less than 70 here is something few professionals manage to achieve. The trees alongside the fairways and the cunningly set bunkers make accurate driving essential. The water is another feature/hazard with the 172m hole 9 played over the heads of the water lilies to the green placed on a small island and hole 12 restricted too by this element. The reflection of a series of Roman columns originally from Volubilis must not be allowed to distract.

Hang Gliding (*vol libre*), to practice hang gliding one must contact the Delta Club, 'Aigles de l'Atlas' at Rabat-Sale airport or 21 bis Ave Allal Ben Abdellah Passage, Passage Karrakchou, Rabat, T 708347.

Hiking There are considerable opportunities for climbing and hiking, and in areas such as the Toubkal National Park in the High Atlas, guides are available. For walking the best period is Apr to Oct, but in the high summer keep to the high valleys which are cooler and where water can be obtained. Tents will be adequate in summer but indoor accommodation is necessary in autumn in the shepherds' huts or staying with the locals. The use of mules/donkeys to carry the heavy packs is becoming more common – and the hire of these animals less difficult. Specialist maps and guides will be useful to hikers.

Hunting and Fishing Wild boar in the countryside around Asni and Amizmiz; partridge and quail in the Ourika valley; pike, perch, roach, carp and trout in lakes and rivers. All foreigners wishing to hunt in Morocco must produce a valid hunting permit and permit to carry firearms from his country of origin, and three photographs. A permit to hunt will be given which lasts 30 days and cannot be extended. It is compulsory to take out an insurance by a Moroccan company for this visit. There are several game reserves including Arbaoua and Ben Slimane. For import of hunting dogs, see page 454.

Parachuting There are three clubs run by the Le Parachute Club de Maroc. Contact 1 rue Roger Harman, Plateau, Casablanca.

Riding is a good way to explore the High Atlas. The main centres are to be found at Rabat, Casablanca, Agadir, Meknes, Fes, Oujda, Ouirgane and Tanger but most towns have stables.

Skiing and mountain sports are being developed in Morocco at a number of sites in the Middle and High Atlas mountain ranges. The best places are the Mischliffen resort near Ifrane, in the Middle Atlas just S of Fes, and the skiing centre of Oukaimeden, S of Marrakech in the High Atlas. Both have ski lifts and good slopes, as well as equipment for hire and instruction. Mountain Information Centre of Ministry of Tourism, 1 rue Oujda, Rabat, T 7701280, has details of escorted and individual cross-Atlas treks. Overland skiing is now very popular. The best time is from beginning of Feb to end of Apr. The lower snowline rises rapidly from 2,500m on the N face to 3,000m on the S face and later in the year it will be necessary to keep to these northern facing slopes. National Assoc of Mountain Guides and Monitors (ANGAHM) BP 47, Asni Marrakesh.

There is a small number of equipped ski resorts in Morocco.

In the Middle Atlas, only 18 km from Ifrane, is the natural amphitheatre of the crater of **Mischliffen**. This is an attractive region situated in the cedar forest at an altitude of about 2,000m but the ski runs are short, only 100-200m. There are ski lifts but not the auxiliary services one expects at a European ski station as it is only open 40-60 days a year from end of Dec to end of Feb. **Access**: from Meknes take the P21 S 14 km beyond Azrou then take

the left turn. From Fes take the P24 SW to Ifrane (61 km). Follow the S309 for 8 km turning W via the Tizi-n-Tretten pass to Mischliffen. **Slopes**: red track, difficult, a slope of 215m; Black track, difficult, a slope of 215m; Blue track, fairly easy, a slope of 200m; Yellow track, easy, a slope of 200m. In addition to the paths there are possibilities of individual tracks around the crater. **Lifts**: Pomagal ski system, length 463m, gradient 193m, goes from the depth of the crater and serves the Red track at its highest point. The other lift of 232m, serves the Yellow track. **Accommodation**: at the northern part of the ski station there are some shelters and mountain lodgings. The most important shelter belongs to the Ministry of Youth and Sport and is fully equipped to accommodate over 100 skiers.

There are two ski stations near **Azrou** in the foothills of the Middle Atlas, **Habri** 15 km from Azrou and **Hebri** 20 km from Azrou. The maximum height here is 2,000m and the runs are between 50m and 200m in length, ideal for beginners. The snowfall here is very irregular and at best lies from Nov to Mar. It remains a little longer at Hebri. **Access**: the two stations are within 9 km of each other and reached by surfaced road from Azrou by following the P21 for 12 km then turning left. **Lifts**: Pomagal ski system is 400m long with a gradient of 156m at Hebri and 226m long with gradient of 68m at Habri. **Accommodation**: see Azrou, page 336.

Oukaimeden at an altitude of 2,600m in the High Atlas just 27 km S from Marrakech is Morocco's major resort. It provides a rich variety of ski runs at altitudes of between 2,220m and 2,730m accessed by five teleskis. Throughout the season there are courses for beginners and for professionals organized by the Moroccan Centre for Skiing and Alpinism. **Access**: take the S513 S from Marrakech for 43 km turning W just before village of **Arhbalou**. There is a steady climb up the Lekak valley to Aït Lekak and on to Oukaimeden. The settlement, lying mainly to the right of the road, is built on the hillside in terraces each connected by a service road. One track swings N round and behind the village up to Jbel Tizerag (2,784m). The other track leads S to the ski lifts, the furthest of the five extending up the side of Jbel Oukaimeden, 3,273m. Snow is expected from end of Nov to early Apr, turning granular by end of Feb. The fields are suitable for training beginners and others have facilities for competitions. The NW slopes offer 2,872m

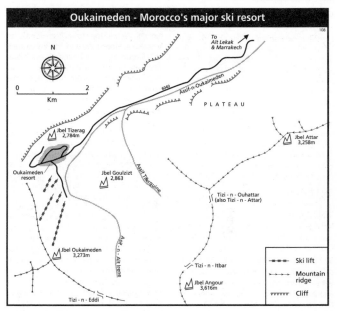

Oukaimeden - Morocco's major ski resort

108

of medium obstacles with gradients varying from 200m-300m. The slopes to the E side of the Jbel Oukaimeden are classified in 5 distinct itineraries from the 'great descent' of 630m starting at the peak to the smaller ones serviced by the big and medium ski lifts. **Slopes**: of note are those from the Jbel Attar (3,258m) with a gradient of 630m giving a very good run and those on the Tizi-n-Itbir of 3,308m. Jbel Attar lies 4 km directly E of Oukaimeden and Tizi-n-Itbir SE in the track beyond the ski lifts. Smaller runs of 270m facing the station offer more leisurely activity. **Lifts**: the mechanical lifts are claimed to be the highest in Africa, a small ski lift for beginners on a gradient of 50m with a capacity of 300 skiers per hour, a medium ski lift with a gradient of 150m over a run of 296m with a capacity of 400 skiers per hour. Cost MD0.5, a big ski lift with a gradient of 400m over a run of 1,100m serving 5 slopes with a marked run. At the top of the ski lift is a refuge called the Schuss, for a rest and time to admire the magnificent views of the Atlas and the plain of Marrakech. Capacity of 200 skiers per hour and cost of MD2.5. There are two ski jumps, one suitable for competitions and allows jumps of 40m-50m and a smaller one

which is suitable for ski schools with jumps of about 20m. **Accommodation**: there are four small hotels and a refuge. See page 330 for details.

Other, smaller ski-stations, without equipment, include: **Hayane Mountain** in the Middle Atlas has an altitude of 2,400m and offers many ski slopes. Snow sometimes lasts here until the end of Apr. Continue S from Azrou along the P21 for 8 km beyond Timahdite.

Jbel Bou Iblane is at the extreme E end of the Middle Atlas, directly S of Taza. There is a long crest of 70 km with the highest peak at 3,190m. To the S and E a higher range includes Jbel Bou Naceur at 3,340m, the highest summit in the Middle Atlas. These northwesterly slopes, with the advantage of facing the Atlantic, receive their first snows in Oct above 2,300m. The snowline extends quickly down to 2,000m and often 1,800m within the space of a month. Snow remains here until May. The S facing slopes have less reliable accumulations of snow. Tracks are very fast and long and skiers may choose their own destination and route towards the summits, in the pass or in the forests. The Taffert refuge, a forestry hut, at 1,968m although not central for the Jbel Bou

Iblane offers a good point for journeys out into the region and particularly the lower cedar clad slopes. The refuge stands on the track going NW to Fes where it crosses Oued Zloul. **Slopes**: of notes are: Tizi Bou Zabel (2,300m), difficult, reaching 300m. In the E of Tizi Bou Zabel the first peak of Jbel Bou Iblane (1,976m) goes down to 700m. The central summit of Jbel Bou Iblane (3,050m) has an inclination of 700m. Mousa ou Salah the highest peak of the range has an inclination of 700m. L'ich Askor (2,507m), a challenging slope with a difficult inclination and L'ich'n Maalem (2,450m) are both recommended by the Moroccan Nationalist Tourist Office.

Azourki in the High Atlas has snow for up to 6 months in the year on the N facing slopes. This region where the high relief is distinguished by three parallel chains has many summits over 3,000m while Jbel Ighil M'Goun (4,071m), the ultimate peak, lies to the western extreme. **Access**: East from Marrakech by the P24 to Tamelelt (53 km) and just beyond the S508 goes to Azilal (108 km). Here a track (possible by car but better with 4WD) goes on to Ait Mohammed and Tamda. It turns NE under the lee of Jbel Azurki to Zaouia Ahanesal. The route from Beni Mellal picks up the S508 (20 km) towards Azilal and takes the track round the Bin el-Ouidane barrage through Ouaouizarht, Tilougguit and on to Zaouia Ahanesal. These two tracks connect and on it stands the Azourki shelter at the foot of the northern slope. The irregular terrain offers opportunities for average skiers on the various slopes and steep runs for good skiers. There are many slopes suitable for beginners in what is some of the prettiest scenery (if one has time to notice). Itineraries for cross country skiing are available at the refuge.

Toubkal in the High Atlas has snow from Dec to May. Many ski tracks begin at the Neltner refuge. For access to this region see page 188. Considering the difficulty of access and the paucity of accommodation this is an area for the experienced and determined. There are no marked routes.

Jbel Ayachi, highest point 3,737m, in the Middle Atlas with access from Midelt. The track SW from the centre of Midelt is in good condition and after 15 km reaches the base of the slope. The track continues a further 30-40 km to other slightly higher slopes. The summit of this range has snow by Dec and generally due to the NE aspect skiing is possible until the following May.

Tlata Ketama in the Rif Mountains. Access via the P39 from Chaouen or Al Hoceima to Ketama then S on the S302 for 8 km. The summits here reach 2,456m. Snowcover is less regular here but skiing is generally possible for about 10 weeks per year. Further details from Royal Moroccan Federation of Skiing and Mountaineering, Parc de la Ligue Arabe, BP 15899, Casablanca, T 203798, F 474979.

Surfing Royal Moroccan Surfing Federation, T (2) 259530, F (2) 236385.

Swimming Large towns have municipal pools but these can be crowded. In the summer the luxury hotels are very tempting, with their pools. There are occasional cheaper establishments with facilities. There is some good sea swimming, but beware of currents.

Tennis Morocco has an international tournament in Agadir, and excellent tennis facilities at larger hotels and tennis clubs.

Watersports centres are found in Agadir and Mohammedia. Essaouira is excellent for surfing. Equipment can normally be hired. Salt and fresh water fishing is popular.

● **Spectator sports**

The major cities have arenas with Basketball, Handball, Athletics and Football. Check the local press for details. Football is seriously popular, with kick-arounds in the most remote locations, and an excellent standard on beaches and in town pitches. The national team qualified for the 1986 and 1994 World Cups. The national league is strong, with particularly strong teams at Casablanca (WIDAD and RAJA) and Marrakech (KACM).

● **Television**

Satellite TV in some hotels provides Sky and other overseas channels. The few houses with TVs receive the state run channel, with programmes in Arabic and French. Others who have a decoder can get the commercial TV station.

HOLIDAYS AND FESTIVALS

1 Jan: New Year's Day
3 Mar: Coronation of King Hassan II – celebrated with processions/ dancing
1 May: Labour Day
23 May: National Day
9 Jul: King's Birthday and Youth Day
14 Aug: Allegiance Day
6 Nov: Anniversary of Green March
18 Nov: Independence Day

The dates of the Islamic holidays and the fast, Ramadan, vary each year, as they are calculated according to the moon. Ramadan is strictly observed by most Moroccans, and it is advisable not to eat or drink in public during this period in the daytime. The breaking of the fast each evening is a very sociable and entertaining time, particularly when invited to a house.

Approximate dates in 1997:

12 Jan: Beginning of Ramadan
8 Feb: Aïd es Seghir (end of Ramadan)
18 Apr: Aïd el Kebir
7 May: Islamic New Year
16 Jul: Prophet's Birthday

● Festivals

There is a number of large *moussems* throughout the country, gatherings to pay homage to a holy man. There are also a number of festivals to mark the seasons or to celebrate local resourse. They attract very large crowds. Your attendance at the festivals will be welcome, at the *moussem* less so. The opportunity to see and observe the traditional costumes, the dancing, the processions, the fantasias and to hear the music and singing ought not to be missed.

February
Tafraoute – *Festival of the almond blossom*

April
Immouzer des Ida Outanane – *Honey festival*

May
El Kelâa Mgouna – *Rose festival*
Sale – *Festival of wax*

Moussem Moulay Bousselham
Tan-Tan (end May)

June
Ouarzazate – *Desert symphonies*
Sefou – *Cherry festival*
Marrakech – *Festival of Folk Art*
Larache – *Moussem Moulay Abdeslam ben M'chich*

July
Goulimine – *Camel festival*
Essaouira
Ida or Tanane near Agadir – *Honey festival*
Setti Fatma (Ourika)

August
*El Jadida – *Moussem of Moulay Abdellah*
*Meknes – *Moussem of Moulay Idris*
Asilah – *Cultural festival*
Saïdia – *Festival of popular music*

September
Imilchil – *Engagements festival*
Tissa (Fes) – *Horse festival*
Fes – *Moussem of Moulay Idris al Ashar*

October
Erfoud – *Date festival*
Fes – *Festival of Sacred music*
Sale – *Wax Fair* at Sale

December
Agadir

* = major moussem

Rounding up

ACKNOWLEDGEMENTS

StJohn Gould who was responsible for much of the original material; Royal Air Maroc for travel assistance; Malcolm Hachemi who produced the chapter on eastern Morocco after some very gruelling travelling; Kenneth Longhurst for substantial additions to the text and maps on the region south and east of Casablanca; Justin McGuinness (our man in the Maghreb) for his many contributions to travel and background' Geoff Moss for his excellent illustrations; Diana Stone for correcting and adding to our material after her visit to Mauritania; Alfred Molonj, Heilenbeckeweg 2, 40625 Dusseldorf; Paul Flindall, 9 Woodlands Rd, Ashton-under-Lyme, Lancs; Mr and Mrs Cardholm, Tunvägen 4, S-261, 75 Asmundtorp, Sweden; Hans-Jochen Baethge, Amselweg 9, D-23611 Bad Schwartau, Germany; Andrew Highfield of Carmarthen for his contribution to the wildlife section and recommendations for further reading; Tim Eyre, Nottingham; Frank Schaer, Australia; Richard D'Olivo, Jersey; Piergiorgio Pescali and Higuchi Yasuko of Cologno, Italy; Nick Scrannage, Rickmansworth; Thomas Tolk, Bonn, Germany who gave us details from his 1,800 km cycle ride.

READING AND LISTENING

MOROCCO

BOOKS

Anthropology and society

Crapanzano, V (1980) *Tuhami: Portrait of a Moroccan*, University of Chicago Press; Deshen, S (1980) *The Mellah Society*, University of Chicago Press; Drummond Hay, J (1846) *Western Barbary, its wild tribes and savage animals*; Dwyer, K (1982) *Moroccan Dialogues: Anthropology in Question*, John Hopkins University Press: Baltimore; Gellner, E (1969) *Saints of the Atlas*, Weidenfeld & Nicolson: London; Mernissi, F (1985) *Beyond the Veil: Male/Female Dynamics in Modern Muslim Society*, London, Al Saqi; Mernissi, F (1994) *The Harem Within – Tales of a Moroccan Girlhood*, Bantam Books, New York, £5.99; Warnock, E *A Street in Marrakech*, Doubleday; Westermarck, E (1926) *Ritual and Belief in Morocco*, MacMillan: London, 1926.

Archaeology and monuments

Broadman J and Robertson M (OUP), *The Mosaics of Roman North Africa*, ed Ashmole B; Burckhardt, T (1992) *Fez: City of Islam*, Islamic Texts Society: Cambridge;

Landau, R (1969) *The Kasbahs of Morocco*, Faber and Faber: London; E Lennox Manton (Seaby) *Roman North Africa*; Paccard, A, *Traditional Islamic Craft in Moroccan Architecture*, Editions Atelier; Parker, R (1981) *A Practical Handbook to Islamic Monuments in Morocco*, Baraka Press: Virginia.

Food

Benkirane, F *Moroccan Cooking, the best recipes*, useful; Bennani-Smirès, *Moroccan Cooking*, very good; Carrier, R *Taste of Morocco*, Arrow, London; Dinia, H (1993) *La Cuisine Morocaine*, ed Ribat al Fath; Guinaudeau, Z *Traditional Moroccan Cooking – recipes from Fes*, pub Serif, £8.99; Wolfert, P *Good Food from Morocco*, John Murray.]000

Historical travelogues

Cunninghame-Graham, RB (1898) *Maghreb el Acksa: A Journey in Morocco*; Harris, W (1921) *Morocco That Was*, Eland Books; Ibn Khaldoun (1967) *The Muqaddimah: An Introduction to History*, Routledge, translated from the Arabic, London; Lewis, W (1983) *Journey into Barbary*, Black Sparrow Press: Santa Barbara; Maxwell, G (1983) *Lords of the Atlas* Century; Meakin, B (1901) *The Land of the Moors*, London; Wharton, E (1920) *In Morocco*, MacMillan: London.

History

Abun-Nasr, JM (1971) *A History of the Maghreb in the Islamic Period*, Cambridge University Press; Barbour, N (1965) *Morocco*, Thames and Hudson; Blunt, W (1951) *Black Sunrise*, Methuen. The life and times of Mulai Ismail, Emperor of Morocco 1646-1727; Bovill, EW (1968) *The Golden Trade of the Moors*, OUP; Douglas, N *Fountains in the Sand*, OUP; Flaubert, G *Salammbo*, Penguin Classics; MacKenzie, D (1911) *The Khalifate of the West*, Simpkin Mashall. He was the founder of the British Settlement at Cape Juby; Oliver and Fage, *A Short History of Africa*, Pelican; Porch, D (1986) *The conquest of Morocco*, Jonathan Cape; Porch, D *The Conquest of the Sahara*, Papermac.

History books on Rabat and Sale – in French

Les Corsaires de Salé, Coindreau R, ed La Croisée des Chemins, 1993; Rabat, le Temps d'une Ville, Ducrot L, and Lakhdar K, ed Eddif, 1992; Rabat, Repères de la Mémoire, Mouline S, ed Ministère de l'Habitat, 1991; Rabat-Sale, Vingt Siècle de l'Oued Bou-Regreg, Chastel R, ed La Porte, 1994; Sale, Repères de la Mémoire, Mouline S, ed Ministère de l'Habitat, 1993.

Politics

Amnesty International (1989) *Morocco File*, Amnesty International: London; Hodges, A (1983) *Western Sahara: the Roots of a Desert War*, Croom Helm; Rogers, PD (Reprinted 1989) *A History of Anglo-Moroccan Relations*, London.

Short stories and novels

Bowles, P (1982) *Points in Time*, Arena; Bowles, P *Sheltering Sky*, Granada; Bowles, P *Their Heads are Green and Their Hands Are Blue*, Abacus; Bowles, P *The Spider's House*, Arena; Bowles, P *Two Years Beside the Strait: A Tangier Journal, 1988-89*, Peter Owen; Bowles, P *Without Stopping*, Papermac; Burgess, A *Earthly Powers*, Penguin; Charhadi, D *A Life Full of Holes*, Grove Pres; Chraibi, D (1972) *Heirs to the Past*, Heinemann: London; Choukri, M (1987) *For Bread Alone*, Grafton: London; Gysin, B *The Process*, Paladin; Hughes, R (1979) *In the Lap of the Atlas*, Chatto & Windus: London; Jallounn, Tahar Ben (1988) *The Sand Child*, 1988, Quartet.

Travel accounts

Canetti, E (1978) *The Voices of Marrakech*, Marion Boyars; Dumas, A *Tangier to Tunis*, Peter Owen; Mayne, P *A Year in Marrakech*, Eland Books; Romanelli, S (1989) *Travail in an Arab Land*, first published in 1792 translated from the Hebrew. University of Alabama Press, Tuscaloosa and London. He is a little hard on the Arabs but then if you were stranded in Morocco for 4 years due to a lost passport you might feel the same; Twain, M (1958) *Traveling with the Innocents Abroad*, University of Oklahoma Press; Vieuchange, M *Smara: The Forbidden City*, Ecco Press, New York, reprint 1987. A heartbreaking account of a painful and fatal journey.

Trekking and skiing

Brown, H *Great Walking Adventure*, Oxford Illustrated Press; Camminelli, Claude *Ski dans le Haut Atlas de Marrakech*; Collomb,

RG (1987) *Atlas Mountains, Morocco*, West Col, gives some very sensible hints and very thorough data about the walks in the Atlas. Even if access is easier, the accommodation has changed for the better and some provisions can now be acquired on the way, the mountains have not changed; Dickinson, M (1991) *Long Distance Walks in North Africa*, Crowood Press; Fougerolles, A *La Grande Traverse du Haut Atlas*; Fougerolles, A *Le Haut Atlas Central – Guide Alpin* with many good diagrams and maps; Peyron, M *La Grande Traverse de l'Atlas Marocain*; Peyron, M *Grand Atlas Traverse*, Goring: West Col; Smith, K *Atlas Mountains: A Walker's Guide*, Cicerone Press; Winter, Bert and Mabel (1989) *The Rogues' Guide to Tangier*, Tanger.

Wildlife

Bergiers, P and Bergier, F *A Birdwatcher's Guide to Morocco*, Prion Ltd, Perry. This is a slim but useful guide to the best localities in Morocco for bird observation. Good site maps and fairly comprehensive species list; Blamey, M and Grey-Wilson, C (1993) *Mediterranean Wild Flowers*, Harper Collins. Beautifully illustrated and comprehensive guide to the flowers of this region. Biased towards coastal localities and not particularly easy for the non-specialist to use. Many Moroccan endemics are not described. Highly recommended nonetheless; Cremona, J and Chote R, (1989) *The Alternative Holiday Guide to Exploring Nature in North Africa*, Ashford. Difficult to obtain, but a very good general introduction to the flora and fauna of North Africa. Insufficiently detailed for the specialist, however, but good coverage of Moroccan wildlife, including that of desert regions; Haltenorth, T and Diller, H (1980) *Collins Field Guide to the Mammals of Africa including Madagascar*, London. Although continent-wide in scope, contains a considerable amount of useful data on mammals in Morocco; Heinxel, Fitter and Parslow *The Birds of Britain and Europe with North Africa and the Middle East*, Collins; Hollom, PAD, Porter, RF, Christensen, S and Willis, I (1988) *Birds of the Middle East and North Africa*, Poyser, Staffs. This is the definitive guide to the birds of this region but must be used in conjunction with a guide which covers birds in Europe such as Peterson, Mountford and Hollom, A *Field Guide to the Birds of Britain and Europe*; Le Berre, M (1989) *Faune du Sahara*, Editions Raymond Chabaud-Lechevalier, Paris. Three volumes. Volume I covers reptiles, amphibians and fishes; Volume II mammals and Volume III birds. In French. Inaccurate and incomplete in places, this is nonetheless an invaluable guide; Ploquin, P and Peuriot, F (1992) *Maroc: Faune & Grands Espaces*, Editions Daniel Briand, Toulouse. Very much a glossy coffee table book, but contains excellent photographs of wildlife habitats and a good range of mammal, bird and reptile species, so can prove useful in assisting identifications. In French, although an English edition is also available. This is the only book in this list that you might be able to obtain in Morocco itself, as it was published in association with the National Office of Tourism; Polunin, O and Huxley, A *Flowers of the Mediterranean*, Chatto and Windus; Schleich, HH, Kastle, W and Kabisch, K (1996) *Amphibians and Reptiles of North Africa*, Koeltz, Germany. An extremely expensive (£125) reference with detailed distribution data and descriptions. One for the specialist.

MAPS AND TOWN PLANS

Simple town plans are printed in the brochures available from tourist offices, others are available from street kiosks in Tanger, Rabat, Casablanca, Fes, Meknes, Marrakech and Agadir. Maps of Morocco as a whole are best bought before reaching the country, notably from *Stanfords* in Long Acre, London, T 0171 8361321. Try the *Michelin* or the *Hildebrand* road maps. Topographic maps suitable for hiking are sometimes available from the **Division de Cartographie**, Ave Moulay Al Hassan, Rabat. Others are sold in the hiking base, Imlil.

Maps available for the High Atlas

1:100,000, Beni Mellal, Imilchil, Azilal, Zawyat Ahnsal, Tinerhir, Talwat, Skours, Qalat Mgouna; 1:50,000, Beni Mellal, Taghzirt, Tizi-n-Islay, Wawizaght, Tilougguit, Aziylal, Aït Mhammed, Zawyat Ahançal, Demnat, Tifni, Abachkou, Talwat, Aït Tamlil.

Maps available for Jbel Toubkal

1:100,000, Amizmiz, Oukaïmeden Toubkal, Telouat; 1:50,000, Tahanawt, Larbat Tighdiwine, Had Zaraqtane, Azgour, Amizmiz, Toubkal, Tala Yacoub, Taliwien, Assarag.

MAURITANIA

BOOKS

Abeille, Barbara (1979) *A Study of Female Life in Mauritania*, USAID: Washington DC – study for American aid organization; Calderini, Simonetta; Cortese, Delia; Webb, James, LA jnr (1992) *Mauritania* (World Bibliographical Series Vol 141), Clio Press: Oxford – a comprehensive bibliography of sources in European languages; de Chassey, Claude (1984) *Mauritania 1900-1975*, L'Harmattan: Paris – introduction to the country; Gerteiny, Alfred G (1981) *Historical Dictionary of Mauritania* (African Historical Dictionaries No 31), Scarecrow Press: Metuchen (NJ) – basic historical facts, people and places; Gerteiny, Alfred G (1967) *Mauritania*, Pall Mall: London – useful summary of Mauritania, its geography, history and people; Handoff, Robert E (ed) (1990) *Mauritania: A Country Study*, US Government Printing Office: Washington DC – official study in this comprehensive series, covers most aspects of the country in some detail; Hudson, Peter (1990) *Travels in Mauritania*, Virgin Books: London – a very readable account of a recent visit to Mauritania; Moorhouse, Geoffrey (1986) *The Fearful Void*, Penguin: Harmondsworth – aborted trans-Saharan journey; Norris, H T (1986) *The Arab conquest of the western Sahara*, Longman: Harlow – draws on local sources to describe the process of Arabization, and the structure of society in the past; Ould Daddah, Mokhtar (1973) *Mauritania: A Land of People*, Centre d'Information et de Formation: Nouakchott – dated and superficial propaganda from the then president; Stewart, C C (1973) *Islam and Social Order in Mauritania: a case study from the nineteenth century*, Clarendon Press: Oxford – a biography of a 19th century sheikh who founded Boutilimit; Stone, Diana, 'The Moors of Mauritania' in Carmichael, P (1991) *Nomads*, Collins and Brown: London – focussing on a group of contemporary camel nomads; Toupet, C, 'Nouadhibou (Port Etienne) and the Economic Development of Mauritania', in Hoyle, B S/Hilling, D (eds) (1970) *Seaports and Development in Tropical Africa*, London – for those with a fascination for ports; Westebbe, Richard M (1971) *The Economy of Mauritania*, Praeger: New York – comprehensive but dated guide to the depressed economics of the country.

MAPS AND TOWN PLANS

There are no useful town plans of Nouakchott or Nouadhibou. Other towns are easy to explore in a few minutes. For maps of Mauritania the choice in the UK is limited to a few undetailed large-scale sheets available at well-stocked map specialists. Michelin 953 gives an overall view. The French (IGN) map costing £7.50 (must be ordered from Stanfords bookshop in London) has also been recommended. In Paris, very detailed small scale maps are sold at IGN, 107 Rue la Boétie, 75008 Paris.

SHORT WAVE RADIO GUIDE

The BBC World Service (London) broadcasts throughout the region. Frequencies are shown in the accompanying table overpage.

Useful addresses

EMBASSIES

MOROCCO

Algeria
8 rue des Cèdres, El Mouradia, Algiers

Australia
2 Phillis Lane, N Curl, Sydney, NSW,
T 6496019

Austria
Untere Donaustrassse 13/15, 1020 Vienne,
T 2142568

Belgium
Blvd Saint-Michel, 29 Brussels 1040, T 02
7361100

Canada
38 Range Rd, Ottawa, T 2367391

Denmark
Oregarrds Allé 19, 2900 Hellerup, Copenhagen, T 624511

Egypt
10 rue Salah el-Din, Zamalek, Cairo,
T 3409677

Eire
53 Raglan Rd, Ballsbridge, Dublin 4,
T 6609449

France
5 rue le Tasse, 75016, Paris, T 4050 6879

Germany
Gotenstrasse 7-9, Badgodesberg 5300,
Bonn, T 228 355044

Greece
14 rue Mousson, Palaio Psychio, Athens,
T 6474209

Italy
Via Lazzaro Spallanzani 8/10, 00161 Rome,
T 4402524

Netherlands
Oranje Nassaulaan 1-1075, Amsterdam,
T 736215

Norway
Parkveien 41, Oslo, T 22556111

Saudi Arabia
BP94392, Riyad, T 4811858

Spain
Serrano 179, Madrid, T 4580950

Sudan
PO Box 2042 Amarat, St No 1, Khartoum

Sweden
Kungsholmstorg 16, Stockholm, T 544383

Switzerland
22 Chemin François-Lehmann, Grand Sa-
connex, Geneva, T 981535

Tunisia
39 rue du 1 Juin, Tunis, T 783801

UAE
Said Ali Saloih Villa, Area Manasser, Al
Nehyan St, Abou Dhabi, T 4339973

UK
49 Queens Gate Gardens, London SW7,
T 0171 5815001/4627979

USA
1601 21st St NW, Washington DC 20009,
T 202 4627979

MAURITANIA

There are also embassies in China, Gabon,
Germany, the Ivory Coast, Nigeria, Russia
and Zaire.

Algeria
BP 276, El-Mouradia, Algiers

Belgium
Ave Colombie 6, Bruxelles, T 322 6724747

Egypt
c/o the Senegal Embassy, 46 Abdel Moneim
Riad St

France

69 rue du Cherche Midi, 75006 Paris,
T 45482388

Libya
BP 4664, Tripoli

Mali
BP 135, Bamako

Morocco
30 Ave d'Alger, Rabat

Senegal
37x Blvd General de Gaulle, BP12284,
Dakar, T 226238, F 226268, just opp Gen-
damerie base at Colobane, open daily
0830-1500 except Fri 0800-1400

Spain
Calle Velázquez 90, Madrid, T 3415757007

Tunisia
Route du Hilton, Notre Dame, Tunis

UK
nearest is the embassy in Paris

USA
2129 Leroy Place NW, Washington DC
20008, T 2441491

CONSULATES

MOROCCO

Spain
Ave de Francisco 4, Algeciras, T 56673698
and Ave de Andalucía 63, Málaga,
T 52329962

USA
437 Fifth Ave, New York, 10016, T 212
7582625

NATIONAL TOURIST OFFICES OVERSEAS

MOROCCO

Australia
11 West St, Sydney, NSW 2060, T 9576711

Belgium
66 rue du Marché-aux-Herbes, Brussels
1040, T 027361100

Canada
2 Carlton St, Suite 1803, Toronto, Ontario
M5B 1K2, T 4165982208

France
161 rue Saint-Honoré, Place du Théâtre-
Français, 75001 Paris, T 42604724

Germany

59 Graf Adolf Strasse, 4000 Dusseldorf,
T 49211370551/2

Italy
23 Via Larga, 20122 Milan, T 392
58303633

Japan
Tokyo, T 813 32517781

Portugal
rue Artilharia 7985, 1200 Lisbonne,
T 3885871

Spain
Calle Quintana 2 (2°e), Madrid, T 5427431

Sweden
Sturegaten 16, Stockholm 11436, T 66099

Switzerland
Schifflande, 5, 8001 Zurich, T 2527752

UK
205 Regent St, London, T 0171 4370073

USA
20 East 46th St, Suite 1201, New York NY
10017, T 2125572520

SPECIALIST TOUR COMPANIES

MOROCCO

Africa Explored
Rose Cottage, Summerleaze, Magor, New-
port, UK NP6 3DE – overland camping
expeditions and safaris which include a
3-week comprehensive circular journey
from Tanger called Morocco Encountered,
visiting the main cities and main sites costing £295 and a shorter 2-week, Morocco
Encountered costing £250 with a flight
back from Marrakech. Their 22-week Trans
African expedition begins in Morocco and
goes on through Mauritania to Nairobi.

Alpinschule of Innsbruck
In der Stille 1, A-6161 Natters, Innsbruck,
Austria – organize walking tours based on
Taroudant. The walks are not too strenuous
and participants are taken to and from the
walk by Landrover.

The Best of Morocco
Seend Park, Seend, Wiltshire SN12 0NZ,
UK, T 380 828533 – offer unlimited flexi-
bility using quality hotels.

The British Museum Traveller
46 Bloomsbury St, London WC1B 3QQ – is
part of the British Museum and provides
accompanied tours to discover the splen-

dours of ancient civilizations, many of the sites being not generally open to the public, it advertises a 9-day accompanied tour of the Royal Cities of Morocco.

Exodus Walking Explorer

9 Weir Rd, London SW12 0LT, T 0181 675550 – 7-23 day treks supported by guides and mules in the High Atlas. Winter treks in the Jbel Sahro.

Explore Worldwide

1 Frederick St, Aldershot, Hants GU11 1LQ, T 0125 2344161 – offers small exploratory accompanied travels. On offer are 8 days in the Jbel Siroua including Taroudant; 15 days trekking in the High Atlas attempting an ascent of Mt Toubkal; 15 days in the sparsely populated Jbel Saghro; 15 days exploring the mountains, desert and coasts in winter; 15 days visiting the Imperial Cities of Marrakech, Rabat, Fes and Meknes then moving on into the great sand sea. This group attempts to make the impact of tourism positive – by taking small groups, dealing with local suppliers for transport and food and controlling litter and waste disposal.

Guerba – Africa in close-up

Guerba Expeditions Ltd, Wessex House, 40 Station Rd, Westbury, Wiltshire, BA13 3JN, T 0137 382661/858956, F 01373 858351 – tours and treks including 15 day High Atlas Trail, beginning in Marrakech with a climb of Mt Toubkal.

Insight Travel

Insight International Bldg, 26 Paradise Rd, Richmond, Surrey, TW9 1SE, T 0181 33229000 – are operators offering combined trips to Morocco with Spain and Portugal.

Inspirations, Morocco

Inspirations East Ltd, Victoria House, Victoria Rd, Horley, Surrey, RH6 7AD, T 0129 3822244, F 0129 3821732 – very reliable, offer special interest section birdwatching, trekking, sport, but their advertised tailor-made travels can only be made up from the areas/hotels they use.

Jasmin Tours

High St, Cookham, Maidenhead, Berks SL6, 9SQ, T 0162 8531121, F 0162 8529444 – escorted tours to Casablanca, Rabat, Fes, Zagora, and Marrakech. Advertised as cultural tours.

Morocco Bound Ltd

Triumph House, 189 Regent St, London W1R 7WE, T 0171 7345307, F 0171 2879127 – guided tours, Land Rover tours, horse riding, short breaks. They can organize individual journeys using the hotels in their brochure.

Morocco Made to Measure (CLM)

4a William St, Knightsbridge, London, SW3 1JJ, T 0171 2350123, F 0171 2353851 – made to measure itineraries, horse riding, trekking, birdwatching, cultural tours, golf, tennis. A reliable firm that knows its Morocco.

Nature Trek

Chautara, Bighton, Hampshire – offer natural history and bird watching tours in S Morocco.

Prospect Music and Art Tours

454-458 Chiswick High Rd, London W4 5TT, T 0181 9952163 – accompanied tours with experts in art and art history, archaeology and architecture.

Rambler Holidays

Box 43, Welwyn Garden City, Herts, AL8 6PQ, T 0171 7331133

Specialist – Golf International

36 Mill Lane, London NW6 1NR, T 0181 4524263, F 0181 2083894 – they have agents in Rabat and Mohammedia.

Sunbird Tours

PO Box 76, Sandy, Bedfordshire, SG19 1DF, T 01767 682969 – Sunbird and Sunbirder tours cater both for the keen birdwatcher happy to be out from dawn to dusk and also for those wishing to combine birds with other interests. Their Morocco – the world in miniature, is 14 days in a small group (max 16) taking in every habitat. Their Morocco – an early winter break, is 7 days in the region around Agadir.

Trafalgar Travel

5 Bressenden Place, Victoria, London, SW1E 5DF, T 0171 8288143.

MAURITANIA

Encounter Overland

267 Old Brompton Rd, London SW5, T 0171 3706845; Backerstr 52, Postfach CH8026, Zurich, T 01 2971112; Schipholweg 101, PO Box 360, 2300 Leiden, Netherlands – cover Mauritania and the W Desert in their itineraries.

Explorator

16 Place de la Madeleine, 75008 Paris, T 42666624 – organizes birdwatching in the Parc National du Banc d'Arguin.

Dragoman Overland Expeditions

T 0728 861133 – include Mauritania in their trans-African trips.

Language for travel

Arabic It is impossible to indicate in the Latin script how Arabic should be pronounced so we have opted for a very simplified transliteration which will give the user a sporting chance of uttering something that can be understood by an Arab. An accent has been placed to show where the stress falls in each word of more than two syllables.

For both Spanish and French the gender of nouns has been given in brackets. In Spanish masculine is *el* and feminine *la* with plurals *los* and *las*. In French the plural of both *le* (masculine) and *la* (feminine) is *les*.

Spanish is spoken more or less as it appears. Bear in mind that *z*, and *c* before *e* and *i* are a soft *th*, *h* is silent, *ll* is pronounced *y* as in million, *ñ* as *ny* in onion and *v* almost like the English *b*.

French unlike Spanish, does not have the final letter of the word pronounced unless accented as in *marché*.

ARABIC NUMERALS

١	1	١٠	10	١٩	19	٨٠	80
٢	2	١١	11	٢٠	20	٩٠	90
٣	3	١٢	12	٢١	21	١٠٠	100
٤	4	١٣	13	٢٢	22	٢٠٠	200
٥	5	١٤	14	٣٠	30	٣٠٠	300
٦	6	١٥	15	٤٠	40	٤٠٠	400
٧	7	١٦	16	٥٠	50	١٠٠٠	1000
٨	8	١٧	17	٦٠	60		
٩	9	١٨	18	٧٠	70		

NUMBERS

	Arabic	French	Spanish
0	sífr	zéro	cero
1	wáhad	un (m) une (f)	uno (m) una (f)
2	tnéen	deux	dos
3	taláata	trois	tres
4	árba	quatre	cuatro
5	khámsa	cinq	cinco
6	sítta	six	seis
7	sába	sept	siete
8	tamánia	huit	ocho
9	tíssa	neuf	nueve
10	áshra	dix	diez
11	ahdásh	onze	once
12	itnásh	douze	doce
13	talatásh	treize	trece
14	arbatásh	quatorze	catorce
15	khamstásh	quinze	quince
16	sittásh	seize	dieciséis
17	sabatásh	dix-sept	diecisiete
18	tmantásh	dix-huit	dieciocho
19	tissatásh	dix-neuf	diecinueve
20	ishréen	vingt	veinte
30	tlaatéen	trente	treinta
40	arba'éen	quarante	cuarenta
50	khamséen	cinquante	cincuenta
60	sittéen	soixante	sesenta
70	saba'éen	soixante-dix	setenta
80	tmanéen	quatre-vingts	ochenta
90	tissa'éen	quatre-vingt dix	noventa
100	mía	cent	cien
200	miatéen	deux cents	doscientos
300	tláata mia	trois cents	trescientos
1,000	alf	mille	mil

GREETINGS

	Arabic	French	Spanish
Hello!	assálamu aláikum	bonjour	buenos días
How are you?	keef hálek?	comment ça va?	¿como está?
Well!	kwáyes	très bien	muy bien
Good bye!	bisaláma	au revoir	adiós
Go away!	ímshi, barra	allez vous en!	¡márchese!
God willing!	inshállah	si Dieu le veut	si Dios quiere
Never mind	ma'lésh	ne t'inquiète pas	no se preocupe
Thank God!	hamdulilláh!	Dieu merci!	¡Gracias a Dios!
Yes/no	naam, áiwa/la	oui/non	sí/no
Please	min fádlek	s'il vous plaît	por favor
Thank you	shukran	merci	muchas gracias
OK	kwáyes	d'accord	vale
Excuse me	ismáh-lee	excusez-moi	perdón

DAYS

	Arabic	French	Spanish
Sunday	al-áhad	dimanche	domingo
Monday	al-itnéen	lundi	lunes
Tuesday	at-taláta	mardi	martes

	Arabic	French	Spanish
Wednesday	al-árba	mercredi	miércoles
Thursday	al-khemées	jeudi	jueves
Friday	al-júma	vendredi	viernes
Saturday	as-sébt	samedi	sábado

FOOD

	Arabic	French	Spanish
banana	mouz	banane (f)	plátano (m)
beer	bírra	bière (f)	cerveza (f)
bread	khubz	pain (m)	pan (m)
breakfast	futóor	petit déjeuner (m)	desayuno (m)
butter	zíbda	beurre (m)	mantequilla (f)
cheese	jíbna	fromage (m)	queso (m)
coffee	qáhwa	café (m)	café (m)
dessert	hélwa	dessert (m)	postre (m)
dinner	ásha	dîner (m)	cena (f)
drink	mashróob	boisson (f)	bebida (f)
egg	baid	oeuf (m)	huevo (m)
fish	sámak	poisson (m)	pescado (m)
food	akl	nourriture (f)	comida (f)
fruit	fawákih	fruit (m)	frutas (f)
lemonade	gazóoza	limonade (f)	limonada (f)
lunch	gháda	déjeuner (m)	comida (f)
meat	láhma	viande (f)	carne (f)
menu (fixed price)	ká'ima	menu (à prix fixe)	menu (del día) (m)
milk	lában	lait (m)	leche (f)
olive	zeitóon	olive (f)	olivo (m)
restaurant	restaurán	restaurant (m)	restaurante (m)
salt	méleh	sel (m)	sal (m)
soup	shórba	potage (m)	sopa (f)
sugar	súkar	sucre (m)	azúcar (m)
tea (tea bag)	shay (shay kees)	thé (m)	té (m)
water (bottled)	móyyah (botri)	l'eau (f) (en bouteille)	agua (f) (embotellada)
wine	khamr	vin (m)	vino (m)

TRAVEL

	Arabic	French	Spanish
airport	al-matár	aéroport (m)	aeropuerto (m)
arrival	wusóol	arrivée (f)	llegada (f)
bicycle	bisiclét/darrája	vélo (m)	bicicleta (f)
birth (date of)	youm al-meeláid	date de naissance(f)	fecha de nacimiento (f)
bus	autobées	autobus (m)	autobús (m)
bus station	maháttat al-autobées	gare routière (f)	estación de autobuses (f)
car	sayára	voiture (f)	coche (m)
car hire	sayárat-ujra	location de voitures (f)	alquilar de coches
customs	júmruk/gúmruk	douane (f)	aduana (f)
departure	khuróoj	départ	salida (f)
duty (excise)	daréebat	droit (m)	derechos (m)
duty free	bidóon daréeba	hors-taxe	libre de impuestos
engine	motúr	moteur (m)	motor (m)
fare	ujrat as-safr	prix du billet (m)	precio del billete (m)
ferry (boat)	má'diya	ferry/bac (m)	barca (f)
garage	garáge	garage (m)	taller (m)

here/there	héna/henák	ici/là	aquí/allí
left/right	yesáar/yemeén	à gauche/droite	a la izquierda/derecha
left luggage	máktab éeda al-afsh	consigne (f)	consigna (f)
map	kharéeta	carte (f)	mapa (m)
oil (engine)	zeit	huile (f)	aceite (m)
papers (documents)	watá'iq	papiers d'identité(m)	documentación (f)
parking	máwkif as-sayyarát	parking (m)	aparcamiento (m)
passport	jawáz	passeport (m)	pasaporte (m)
petrol	benzéen	essence (f)	gasolina (f)
port	méena	port (m)	puerto (m)
puncture	tókob	crevaison (f)	pinchazo (m)
quickly	sarée'an	vite	de prisa
railway	as-sikka al-hadeedíya	chemin de fer (m)	ferrocarril (m)
road	trik	route (f)	carretera (f)
slowly	shwai shwai	lentement	despacio
station	mahátta	gare (f)	estacíon de trenes (f)
straight on	alatóol	tout droit	todo recto
surname	lákab	nom de famille (m)	apellido (m)
taxi	taxi	taxi (m)	taxi (m)
taxi rank	maháttat at-taxiyát	station de taxis (f)	parada de taxis (f)
ticket	tázkara	billet (m)	billete (m)
ticket (return)	tázkara dhaháb	billet de retour (m)	billete de ida
	wa-eeyáb		y vuelta (m)
what time is it?	is-sa'a kam?	quelle heure est-il?	¿qué hora es?
train	tren	train (m)	tren (m)
tyre	itár	pneu (m)	neumático (m)
visa	fisa, ta'shéera	visa (m)	visado (m)

COMMON WORDS

	Arabic	French	Spanish
after	bá'ad	après	después
afternoon	bá'ad az-zohr	après-midi	tarde (f)
Algeria	Aljazáyer	Algérie (f)	Argelia (f)
America	Amréeka	Amérique (f)	América (f)
and	wa	et	y
bank	bank	banque (f)	banco (m)
bath	hammám	bain (m)	baño (m)
beach	sháti al-bahr	plage (f)	playa (f)
bed	seréer	lit (m)	cama (f)
before	qabl	avant	antes de
Belgium	Belg	Belgique (f)	Bélgica (f)
big	kebéer	grand	grande
black	áswad	noir	negro
blue	ázrag	bleu	azul
camp site	mukháyyam	terrain de	camping (m)
		camping (m)	
castle	kál'ah	château (m)	castillo (m)
cheap	rakhées	bon marché	barato
chemist shop	saidalíya	pharmacie (f)	farmacia (f)
church	kenéesa	église (f)	iglesia (f)
closed	múglaq	fermé	cerrado
cold/hot	bárid/sukhna	froid/chaud	frío/caliente
consulate	consulíya	consulat (m)	consulado (m)
day/night	youm/lail	jour (m)/nuit (f)	día (m)/noche (f)
desert	sahra	désert (m)	desierto (m)
doctor	tebeeb	médecin (m)	médico (m)
Egypt	Masr	Egypte (f)	Egipto (m)

embassy	sifára	ambassade (f)	embajada (f)
England	Ingiltérra	Angleterre (f)	Inglaterra (f)
enough	bás	assez	bastante
entrance	dukhóol	entrée (f)	entrada (f)
evening	mássa	soir (m)	tarde (f)
exchange (money)	tabdéel	change (m)	cambio (m)
exit	khuróoj	sortie (f)	salida (f)
expensive (too)	kteer	cher (trop)	caro (demasiado)
film	feelm	pellicule (f)	película (f)
forbidden	mamnóoh	défendu	prohibido
France	France/Francia	France (f)	Francia (f)
full	melyán	complet	lleno
Germany	Almáni	Allemagne (f)	Alemania (f)
good (very good)	táyeb, kwáyes	bien (très bien)	bien (muy bien)
great	ákbar	formidable	magnífico
green	khádra	vert	verde
he/she	húwa/híya	il/elle	él/ella
house	mánzel	maison (f)	casa (f)
hospital	mustáshfa	hôpital (m)	hospital (m)
hostel	bait ash-shebáb	auberge (f)	hostal (m)
hotel	fúnduq/hotéel	hôtel (m)	hotel (m)
how far to..?	kam kilometri...	... est à combien de km?	¿Cuántos km a..?
how much?	bikám	c'est combien?	¿cuánto es?
I/you	ána/inta	je/vous	yo/usted
information	malumát	renseignements (m)	información (f)
is there/are there?	hinák	y a-t-il un ..?	¿hay un ..?
Italy	Itálya	Italie (f)	Italia (f)
key	miftáh	clef (f)	llave (f)
later	ba'déen	plus tard	más tarde
Libya	Líbiya	Libye (f)	Libia (f)
light	nour	lumière (f)	luz (f)
little	sghéer	petit	pequeño
market	sook	marché (m)	mercado (m)
me	ána	moi	me
money	flóos	argent (m)	dinero (m)
more/less	áktar/akál	plus/moins	más/menos
morning	sobh	matin	mañana (f)
Morocco	al-Maghreb	Maroc	Marruecos (m)
mosque	mesjéed	mosquée (f)	mezquita (f)
near	karéeb	près	cerca
Netherlands (Dutch)	Holánda	Pays-Bas (m) (hollandais)	Países Bajos (m) (holandés)
newspaper	jaréeda	journal (m)	periódico (m)
new	jedéed	nouveau	nuevo
not	mush	ne...pas	no
now	al-án	maintenant	ahora
oil (heating)	naft	mazout (m)	aceite combustible(m)
open	maftooh	ouvert	abierto
pharmacy (see chemist)			
photography	taswéer	photographie (f)	fotografía (f)
police	bulées/shurta	gendarmerie (f)	policía (f)
post office	máktab al-baréed	poste	correos (m)
price	si'r	prix (m)	precio (m)
red	áhmar	rouge	rojo
river	wádi, wed	rivière (f),fleuve (m)	río (m)
roof	sat'h	toit (m)	techo (m)
room	górfa	chambre (f)	habitación (f)

sea	bahr	mer (f)	mar (f)
shop	dukkán	magasin (m)	tienda (f)
shower	doosh	douche (f)	ducha (f)
small	sghéer	petit	pequeño
Spain	Espánya	Espagne (f)	España (f)
square	maidán	place (f)	plaza (f)
stamp	tábi'	timbre poste (m)	sello (m)
street	shári	rue (f)	calle (f)
Sudan	as-Sóodan	Soudan (m)	Sudán (m)
Switzerland	Esswízi	Suisse (f)	Suiza (f)
synagogue	kenées	synagogue (f)	sinagoga (f)
telephone	teleefóon	téléphone (m)	teléfono (m)
today	al-yóom	aujourd'hui	hoy
toilet	tualét	toilette (f)	servicio (m)
tomorrow	búkra	demain	mañana
tower	qasr	tour (f)	torre (m)
Tunisia	Toónis	Tunisie (f)	Túnez (m)
United States	al-wilayát al-muttáhida	Etats-Unis (m)	Estados Unidos (m)
washbasin	tusht	évier (m)	lavabo (m)
water(hot)	móyya (sukhna)	eau (chaude)	agua (caliente) (f)
week/year	usboo'/sána	semaine (f)/an (m)	semana (f)/año (m)
what?	shenu?	quoi?	¿qué?
when?	ímta?	quand?	¿cuándo?
where (is)?	wain?	oú (est)?	¿dónde (está)?
white	ábyad	blanc	blanco
why	laih	pourquoi	¿por qué?
yellow	ásfar	jaune	amarillo
yesterday	ams	hier	ayer

Moroccan recipes – dishes to produce when you return home

Delightful desserts – Moroccan Oranges

Take one orange per person, remove all the peel and pith. Slice very thinly, arrange on a plate, sprinkle with orange blossom water and dust each circle of oranges lightly with cinnamon.

Moroccan Mint Tea

This is a delight as much for its ceremonial preparation and serving as it is for the refreshing taste. It ought to be served from an ornate silver teapot and poured with flourish (and skill) from a great height into individual glasses each in a silver holder.

1½ tbsp of green tea
sprigs of fresh green mint – *menth viridis*
lump sugar to taste

Use a heated teapot. Pour a little boiling water over the green tea in the pot to begin the infusion. Add the fresh mint and the lump sugar and a further litre of boiling water. Allow to infuse for at least 5 mins. Serve to friends in congenial surroundings.

Yoghurt with cucumber and mint

This is a very pleasant way to start a meal on a hot day.

1 large cucumber peeled and diced or coarsely grated
1 or 2 small cloves of garlic
salt and pepper to taste
4 tbsp of chopped fresh mint
½ litre of yoghurt

Sprinkle the diced or grated cucumber with salt and leave for 20 mins. Crush the garlic and mix with a little of the yoghurt.
Mix in the rest of the yoghurt, the seasoning, most of the chopped mint and the drained cucumber. Before serving add 6 small ice cubes and decorate with the rest of the mint.
Dill weed can be substituted for the mint – to good effect.

Stuffed vine leaves – hot or cold

Fresh vine leaves are softened by immersing in boiling water for 2 or 3 mins. tinned vine leaves are usually preserved in salt and must be soaked for at least 15 mins, drained and soaked again to remove the salt. Each leaf is placed veins upward and the filling placed in the centre of the leaf. The stalk is folded over first then the outside edges. The leaf is rolled up and secured with a cocktail stick until ready for cooking.

Fillings:
100g long grain rice
250g minced lamb
1 large onion (chopped)
3 tomatoes (skinned and chopped)
2 tbsp of parsley (chopped)
3 tbsp olive oil
2 cloves of garlic
3 tbsp lemon juice
½ tsp pepper
½ tsp cinnamon
½ tsp salt
½ tsp allspice
Tomato concentrate (optional)

Soak the rice in cold water. Mix all the ingredients except the garlic and the lemon juice together in a bowl and use to fill vine leaves as above. Line the base of a large pan with discarded vine leaves or tomato slices and place layer upon layer of vine leaves inside, sprinkling with lemon juice and pieces of garlic. Cover with ¼ litre of water and simmer for 2 hrs, adding more water as required. Serve hot or cold. Additional flavours include dill weed, crushed mint, rosemary.

Bright Eggs

Shelled hardboiled eggs are coloured with saffron to an unusual shade of yellow and served just like that before a meal.

Couscous

Couscous can be considered the national dish of the Maghreb and it appears almost daily at the main meal. Its origin is Berber. At one time the wheat for couscous would be ground for each family by the miller to its own specification. Today most Moroccans buy their couscous ready made but the really good host/hostess still makes his/her own couscous – of course, as follows.

Spread the coarse semolina in the base of a large shallow dish, gently add water and stir until the moisture is evenly spread. Over this sprinkle fine semolina flour and roll the mixture in the palm of the hand, adding more water or more fine semolina flour until each separate piece of wheat is coated. Use the first couscous sieve with the coarse mesh and shake and break up the mixture till it all goes through. Repeat the process with the medium mesh again breaking up any larger pieces with the palm of the hand to help them through. Shaking the mixture in the small mesh sieve removes the too fine material and leaves the finished couscous. Put water to simmer in the base of the couscous steamer and the slightly dampened couscous in the colander above and allow to steam. After 30 mins remove the colander and place the contents in a shallow bowl, sprinkle it with water and using a fork break up any lumps so each grain is separate. Return the couscous to colander and steam for a further 20 mins.

Couscous is served with countless savoury dishes and many of these can be cooked in the base of the steamer while the semolina is being cooked above it.

To serve with the couscous
1 kilo of meat (lamb, beef or chicken)
2 onions (chopped)
2 turnips (chopped)
2 large carrots (chopped)
2 tbsp olive oil
pinch of saffron
pinch of ginger
cumin
salt and pepper to season
The above items are started in the base of the steamer before the couscous is begun.
3 fresh tomatoes, sliced
3 red peppers, seeds removed, sliced
chopped herbs are added 20 mins before the meal is to be served.

The cooked couscous is mixed with oil or butter and piled in the centre of the dish, the pieces of meat are placed in the centre with the vegetables and the liquid poured over the top.

Brochettes/Kofta

Moroccans serve *brochettes* which are just a smaller version of the Maghrebi *kofta*. They are an integral part of the meals on skewers cooked on the street.
1 kilo of beef or lamb (very finely minced)
2 large onions (finely minced)
2 tbsp parsley (finely chopped)
seasoning to include: oregano, coriander, cumin, cayenne pepper, salt.
Mix the ingredients into a dough and shape into sausage shapes on to flat skewers ready for grilling. Sometimes egg is used to bind the ingredients together.

Tagine (pl Touajen)

These spicy mixtures of pieces of meat and fruit are very popular dishes and many hotels produce very good versions of this unusual dish.
In every case the long slow cooking (at least 2 hrs) brings out the flavour.

a) Lamb with apricots

1 kilo of lamb cut into cubes
2 onions (chopped)
250g dried apricots (soaked)
50g ground almonds as thickening
seasoning to include salt, pepper, cinnamon, coriander, cumin, ginger.
water to cover
grilled or roasted sesame seeds can be used as a garnish.

b) Lamb with prunes

1 kilo of lamb cut into large pieces (retain any bones to cook in the stew, often part of the leg bone with meat attached is included)
2 onions (chopped)
300g prunes (soaked) If using tinned prunes

add the juice instead of water making a very rich gravy.

50-80g almonds (whole or sliced)

seasoning to include cinnamon, cumin, coriander, ginger, salt and black pepper

water (or prune juice) for stewing.

NB It is better to add the soaked prunes after the first hour and the tinned prunes just long enough before serving to heat through.

450g of cooking apples (cored and sliced, but not peeled) can be substituted for the prunes though this produces a much blander dish. On no account must the apples be allowed to disintegrate – the peel is left on for this reason.

450g of quinces (cored and sliced but not peeled) and a little extra ginger makes an interesting alternative fruit.

2 tbsp of honey in any of the above fruit dishes gives an unusual added sweetness. The variation with prunes is said to be a speciality of Fes.

c) Chicken T'Faia

2 kilos of chicken (jointed)

2 onions (finely chopped)

3 tbsp parsley (finely chopped)

3 tbsp olive oil or butter

salt and pepper to season

spices to include ginger, cinnamon, saffron (optional)

water to cover

6 whole hard boiled eggs coloured yellow with saffron

100g blanched almonds (fried)

The meat is slowly cooked in a tagine in the usual way. The hard boiled eggs and fried almonds are used to garnish the dish before serving.

Lamb can be used instead of chicken in this dish.

d) Chicken Q'dra

2 kilos of chicken (jointed)

3 large onions (finely chopped)

2 tbsp parsley (finely chopped)

2 tbsp melted butter or olive oil

season with salt, black pepper, cumin, saffron, cinnamon

250g chickpeas (soaked)

100g blanched almonds

½ lemon to squeeze over chicken before serving

water as required

The meat, chickpeas, oil, seasoning and ¼ of the onion is simmered in the tagine for 1½ hrs. The rest of the onion, the almonds and the parsley are added for the last 30 mins.

Black-eyed peas or white bean can be use instead of the chickpeas and lamb instead of chicken.

250g of green or back olives (best without stones) can be added a few minutes before serving.

e) Kofta and Eggs

750g minced lamb

2 tbsp parsley (finely chopped)

1 tbsp fresh mint (finely chopped)

1 tbsp fresh marjoram (finely chopped) or tsp dried marjoram

seasoning to include salt, cayenne pepper, cumin, allspice and cinnamon

3 tbsp melted butter or olive oil

6 eggs

Place all the ingredients except the eggs and oil in a blender until a smooth texture is produced. Roll into small walnut size balls and fry in the hot oil until brown. Cover with water and simmer gently for 20-30 mins until tender. Remove from the heat. Immediately break the eggs over the cooking meatballs without damaging the yolks and allow the heat of the meal to cook the eggs. Serve at once.

Moroccan Pies

The pastry for these pies is made from a dough (see below) and takes a little skill to produce. Today *fila* pastry readily available frozen is almost as good. If you are offered home made Moroccan pastry take this as a special treat.

Moroccan pastry: for this is required a special dough and a special tray. The dough is made from semolina (durum wheat), flour, water and salt. Leave it to stand for an hour then knead well, adding lukewarm water to make a really soft paste.

The tray is silver plate on copper and is warmed face-down over the fire.

To produce a sheet of this special pastry allow a little of the dough to run over the warm tray covering its surface. As the film of dough dries carefully remove the sheet and place it on a damp cloth. A little practice is required here! Repeat the process heating the tray each time, until all the paste is used and covering the sheets with a damp cloth so they do not become brittle. 250g of semolina flour makes about 16 pastry sheets.

Bstilla or *pastilla* is a common dish in the Maghreb and particularly popular in Morocco when entertaining special guests.

6 pigeons or 2 chickens
1 onion (grated)
3 tbsp parsley (finely chopped)
2 tbsp melted butter or olive oil
seasoning to include salt, black pepper, allspice, cinnamon, ginger
9 eggs
16 sheets of pastry
150g chopped blanched almonds fried in butter until golden
sugar and ground cinnamon to garnish.

Stew the chickens in seasoning, oil and a little water and dismember when cooked. Chop the meat and retain the stock.

Heat 8 beaten eggs and 130 ml of stock to make a thick filling for the pie.

Grease an oven dish about 30 cm in diameter with melted butter and line the base and sides with 6 sheets of pastry brushing with melted butter between each layer. Sprinkle the sixth layer with almonds, cinnamon and sugar and add half the egg/stock filling. Cover with 4 sheets of pastry brushed with melted butter as before. Place the pieces of chicken and the rest of the egg/stock filling and cover with the remaining pastry sheets, brushed with butter. Join the pastry from the sides to the top sheets. Paint with the beaten egg (egg no 9) and sprinkle with sugar and cinnamon. Bake for 40 mins at 170°C and 10-15 mins at 200°C until crisp and golden brown.

SPICES AND HERBS

The section of the *souq* selling spices and herbs is attractive not only for the mixture of delightful aromas which bombard one's sense of smell, but also for the amazing displays constructed by the spice sellers making use of the fine changes in colour tones and interesting textures.

Spices and herbs, the dried flavoured parts of various plants, have always been used to season food and drink. Some of the spices on display in the *souq* are local but others, being tropical, have been transported great distances. They have little nutritional value but their judicious use adds greatly to the attraction of the food.

The Arabic names for the more common herbs and spices are:

Allspice (*kebab es-seeny***)**
Dried almost-ripe berry of the pimento tree. Taste resembles a mixture of spices (cinnamon, cloves and nutmeg), hence the name. Used in baking and preserving.

Basil (*rihan***)**
More than one type of dried basil is on offer. The common basil with a small leaf is less fragrant and tastes stronger, the larger leaved varieties have more fragrance and a warmer, sweeter flavour. Try before you buy. Used to flavour meat and used widely on salads.

Bay leaf (*warra randa***)**
From the sweet bay tree, grown locally, used for marinating meat and removed (sometimes not) before serving.

Cardamom (*habbahan***)**
Related to the ginger plant, highly aromatic. Sometimes the whole dried fruit is ground and sometimes only the seeds.

Cayenne (*shatta***)**
A very strong pepper, usually orange/red, ground dried fruits of capsicum.

Celery salt (*boudra caraffs***)**
Celery seed is very small, light brown in colour and tastes like the parent plant, warm rather than hot and slightly bitter. Used for stews and soups.

Chervil leaves (*kozbarra***)**
Pale green dried leaves with a delicate aroma for fish, salads and egg dishes.

Chilli (*filfil ahmar***)**

Cinnamon (*erfa***)**
Powdered form used in cakes and pastry and in sticks in *tagine*. It is powdered bark.

Cloves (*orumfil***)**
Small reddish-brown flower bud with distinctive aroma and hot taste (unfortunately reminds one of the dentists), adds zest to savoury dishes.

Coriander (*kosbara*)
Morocco is a major source of this seed which has a fresh and gentle peppery flavour.

Cumin (*kamoon*)
Morocco is a noted source of this seed. In powdered form it is mixed with salt and sprinkled on grilled meat.

Dill (*shabat*)
Excellent with cucumber and yoghourt as a cold soup, and in lamb tajine.

Fennel (*shamar*)
Tastes rather like aniseed.

Ginger (*ginzabeel*)
The underground stem is dried and ground to produce the pleasant, sharp tasting spice used to add flavour to savoury sauces and sweet dishes too.

Gum Arabic (*mystica*)
Really Gum Acacia produces a colourless thickener for sauces and other dishes.

Horseradish (*figl baladi*)
The dried and ground root of large perennial plant belonging to the mustard family .Also sold as a preserve or relish. Exceedingly hot to taste.

Mace (*bisbassa*)
A yellow/orange spice pleasantly fragrant and with a gentle warm taste formed from the dried and ground aril hich forms between the nutmeg and the outer fleshy covering.

Marjoram (*bardakosh*)
Native to Morocco, belongs to the mint family. Has a sharp, warm taste and a pleasant smell.

Mint (*naanaa*)
The use of fresh mint in tea is widespread. Tea drinkers say they can tell the origin of the mint by the taste of the tea. Those with particularly sensitive taste buds have fresh mint sent to them from their favourite regions.

Mixed spice (*ras el hanout*)
Is the shopkeeper's section and is basically of ground cloves and cinnamon.

Oregano (*zaatar*)
Native to Morocco, a member of the mint family, strongly aromatic with a warm/bitter taste.

Paprika (*filfil ahmar roumi*)
Morocco is a major source of this spice which is not as hot as its colour would suggest.

Peppercorns (*filfil eswed*)
White pepper from dried seeds of unripe fruit and black from ripe.

Rosemary (*hassa liban*)
Mediterranean perennial shrub, related to mint. Powerful, slightly bitter taste, for stews and as a beverage.

Saffron (*zaa'faran*)
The three stigmas from the centre of the purple crocus, used to colour food such as rice and fish a bright yellow. The smell is sweet but the taste is not. The best quality is imported from Iran.

Sage (*maryameya*)
Dried leaves of the aromatic perennial herb.

Savory (*stoorya*)
An annual Mediterranean herb, related to mint, in salads and for seasoning meat.

Sesame (*semsem*)
One of the oldest herbs known. It varies in colour from almost black to pure white. A sweet tasting seed (rather like nuts) which used to flavour the *halva*. Thought to have mystical powers – hence "Open sesame" in the story of Ali Baba.

Tarragon (*tarkhoun*)
An aromatic herb. The bright green leaves are used fresh in salads. The leaves and flowering tops are dried. It has a taste rather like aniseed.

Turmeric (*korkom*)
Orange/yellow spice belonging to the ginger family, used for its colour and its warm/bitter taste in pickles and preserves, and in egg and fish dishes.

Health

WITH THE FOLLOWING advice and precautions, you should keep as healthy as you do at home. Despite the countries being part of Africa where one expects to see much tropical disease this is not actually the case, although malaria remains a problem in some areas. Because much of the area is economically under-developed, infectious diseases still predominate in the same way as they did in the West some decades ago. There are obvious health differences between each of the countries of North Africa and in risks between the business traveller who tends to stay in international class hotels in large cities and the backpacker trekking through the rural areas. There are no hard and fast rules to follow; you will often have to make your own judgements on the healthiness or otherwise of your surroundings.

There are many well qualified doctors in the area, a large proportion of whom speak English or French but the quality and range of medical care is extremely variable from country to country and diminishes very rapidly away from big cities. In some countries, such as Mauritania, there are systems and traditions of medicine rather different from the Western model and you may be confronted with unusual modes of treatment based on local beliefs. At least you can be reasonably sure that local practitioners have a lot of experience with the particular diseases of their region. If you are in a city it may be worthwhile calling on your Embassy to obtain a list of recommended doctors.

If you are a long way from medical help, a certain amount of self medication may be necessary and you will find that many of the drugs that are available have familiar names. However, always check the date stamping and buy from reputable pharmacists because the shelf life of some items, especially vaccines and antibiotics is markedly reduced in hot conditions. Unfortunately many locally produced drugs are not subjected to quality control procedures and can be unreliable. There have, in addition, been cases of substitution of inert materials for active drugs.

With the following precautions and advice you should keep as healthy as usual.

Make local enquiries about health risks if you are apprehensive and take the general advice of European and North American families who have lived or are living in the area.

BEFORE YOU GO

Take out medical insurance. You should have a dental check up, obtain a spare glasses prescription and, if you suffer from a longstanding condition such as diabetes, high blood pressure, heart/lung disease or a nervous disorder, arrange for a check up with your doctor who can at the same time provide you with a letter explaining details of your disability (in English and French). Check the current practice for malaria prophylaxis (prevention) for the countries you intend to visit.

For a simple list of 'Health Kit' to take with you, see page 12.

INOCULATIONS

Smallpox vaccination is no longer required. Neither is cholera vaccination, despite the fact that the disease is endemic in Mauritania and Algeria and also occurs in Morocco and Tunisia. Yellow fever vaccination is only required for Mauritania although in the other countries, particularly Algeria and Libya, you may be asked for a certificate if you have been in an area (Sub-Saharan Africa for example) affected by yellow fever immediately before travelling to North Africa. Cholera vaccine is not effective which is the main reason for not recommending it but occasionally travellers from South America, where cholera is presently raging, or from parts of South Asia where the disease is endemic may be asked to provide evidence of vaccination. The following vaccinations are recommended:

Typhoid (monovalent): one dose followed by a booster in 1 month's time. Immunity from this course lasts 2-3 years. Other injectable types are now becoming available as are oral preparations marketed in some countries.

Poliomyelitis: this is a live vaccine, generally given orally and the full course consists of three doses with a booster in tropical regions every 3-5 years.

Tetanus: one dose should be given with a booster at 6 weeks and another at 6 months and 10 yearly boosters thereafter are recommended.

Children: should, in addition, be properly protected against diphtheria, whooping cough, mumps and measles. Teenage girls, if they have not yet had the disease, should be given rubella (German measles) vaccination. Consult your doctor for advice on BCG inoculation against tuberculosis. The disease is still common in the region. North Africa lies mainly outside the meningitis belt and the disease is probably no more common than at home so vaccination is not indicated except during an epidemic.

INFECTIOUS HEPATITIS (JAUNDICE)

This is common throughout North Africa. It seems to be frequently caught by travellers probably because, coming from countries with higher standards of hygiene, they have not contracted the disease in childhood and are therefore not immune like the majority of adults in developing countries. The main symptoms are stomach pains, lack of appetite, nausea, lassitude and yellowness of the eyes and skin. Medically speaking there are two types: the less serious, but more common, is hepatitis A for which the best protection is careful preparation of food, the avoidance of contaminated drinking water and scrupulous attention to toilet hygiene. Human normal immunoglobulin (gammaglobulin) confers considerable protection against the disease and is particularly useful in epidemics. It should be obtained from a reputable source and is certainly recommended for travellers who intend to live rough. The injection should be given as close as possible to your departure and, as the dose depends on the likely time you are to spend in potentially infected areas, the manufacturer's instructions should be followed. A new vaccination against hepatitis A is now generally available and probably provides much better immunity for 10 years but is more expensive, being three separate injections.

The other more serious version is hepatitis B which is acquired as a sexually transmitted disease, from a blood transfusion or injection with an unclean needle or possibly by insect bites. The symptoms are the same as hepatitis A but the incubation period is much longer.

You may have had jaundice before or you may have had hepatitis of either type before without becoming jaundiced, in which case it is possible that you could be immune to either hepatitis A or B. This immunity can be tested for before you travel. If you are not immune to hepatitis B already, a vaccine is available (three shots over 6 months) and if you are not immune to hepatitis A already then you should consider vaccination (or gamma globulin if you are not going to be exposed for long).

MENINGITIS

This is a 'significant risk' in Mauritania. Protection against meningococcal meningitis A and C is conferred by a vaccine which is freely available.

AIDS

In North Africa AIDS is probably less common than in most of Europe and North America but is presumably increasing in its incidence, though not as rapidly as in Sub-Saharan Africa, South America or Southeast Asia. Having said that, the spread of the disease has not been well documented in the North African region; the real picture is unclear. The disease is possibly still mainly confined to the well known high risk sections of the population i.e. homosexual men, intravenous drug abusers, prostitutes and children of infected mothers. Whether heterosexual transmission outside these groups is common or not, the main risk to travellers is from casual sex, heterosexual or homosexual. The same precautions should be taken as when encountering any sexually transmitted disease. In some of these countries there is widespread female prostitution and a higher percentage of this population is likely to be HIV antibody positive. In other parts, especially high class holiday resorts, intravenous drug abuse is prevalent and in certain cities, homosexual, transsexual and transvestite prostitution is common and again this part of the population is quite likely to harbour the HIV virus in large measure. The AIDS virus (HIV) can be passed via unsterile needles which have been previously used to inject an HIV positive patient but the risk of this is very small indeed. It would, however, be sensible to check that needles have been properly sterilized or disposable needles used. The chance of picking up hepatitis B in this way is much more of a danger. Be wary of carrying disposable needles yourself. Custom officials may find them suspicious. The risk of receiving a blood transfusion with blood infected with the HIV virus is greater than from dirty needles because of the amount of fluid exchanged. Supplies of blood for transfusion are now largely screened for HIV in all reputable hospitals so the risk must be very small indeed. Catching the AIDS virus does not necessarily produce an illness in itself; the only way to be sure if you feel you have been put at risk is to have a blood test for HIV antibodies on your return to a place where there are reliable laboratory facilities. The results may not be ready for many weeks.

COMMON PROBLEMS

ALTITUDE

Mountain sickness is hardly likely to occur in North Africa, even in the High Atlas. A not-too-rapid ascent is the sure way to prevent it. Other problems experienced at moderate altitude are: sunburn, excessively dry air causing skin cracking, sore eyes (it may be wise to leave your contact lenses out, especially in windy and dusty areas) and stuffy noses. Many travellers, as long as they are physically fit, enjoy travelling in the mountains where it is generally cooler and less humid and there are fewer insects.

HEAT AND COLD

Full acclimatisation to high temperatures takes about 2 weeks and during this period it is normal to feel a degree of apathy, especially if the relative humidity is high. Drink plenty of water (up to 15 litres a day are required when working physically hard in hot, dry conditions), use salt on your food and avoid extreme exertion. Tepid showers are more cooling than hot or cold ones. Large hats do not cool you down but prevent sunburn. Remember that, especially in the mountains, there can be a large and sudden drop in temperature between sun and shade and between night and day so dress accordingly. Clear desert nights can prove astoundingly cold with a rapid drop in temperature as the sun goes down. Loose fitting cotton clothes are still the best for hot weather; warm jackets and woollens are essential after dark in some desert areas, and especially at high altitude.

INSECTS

These can be a great nuisance. Some, of course, are carriers of serious diseases such as malaria and yellow fever. The best way of keeping insects away at night is to sleep off the ground with a mosquito net and to burn mosquito coils containing Pyrethrum. Aerosol sprays or a 'flit' gun may be effective as are insecticidal tablets which are heated on a mat which is plugged into the wall socket (if taking your own check the voltage of the area you are visiting so that you can take an appliance that will work. Similarly check that your electrical adaptor is suitable for the repellent plug).

You can use personal insect repellent, the best of which contain a high concentration of Diethyltoluamide. Liquid is best for arms and face (take care around eyes and make sure you do not dissolve the plastic of your spectacles). Aerosol spray on clothes and ankles deters mites and ticks. Liquid DET suspended in water can be used to impregnate cotton clothes and mosquito nets. Wide mesh mosquito nets are now available impregnated with an insecticide called Permethrin and are generally more effective, lighter to carry and more comfortable to sleep in. If you are bitten, itching may be relieved by cool baths and anti-histamine tablets (care with alcohol or driving) corticosteroid creams (great care – never use if any hint of sepsis) or by judicious scratching. Calamine lotion and cream have limited effectiveness and anti-histamine creams have a tendency to cause skin allergies and are therefore not generally recommended. Bites which become infected (commonly in dirty and dusty places) should be treated with a local antiseptic or antibiotic cream such as Cetrimide as should infected scratches. Skin infestations with body lice, crabs and scabies are unfortunately easy to pick up. Use Gamma benzene hexachloride for lice and Benzyl benzoate for scabies. Crotamiton cream (Eurax) alleviates itching and also kills a number of skin parasites. Malathion lotion 5% is good for lice but avoid the highly toxic full strength Malathion used as an agricultural insecticide.

INTESTINAL UPSETS

Practically nobody escapes this one so be prepared for it. Some of these countries lead the world in their prevalence of diarrhoea. Most of the time intestinal upsets are due to the insanitary preparation of food. Do not eat uncooked fish or vegetables or meat (especially pork), fruit with the skin on (always peel your fruit yourself) or food that is exposed to flies. Tap water is generally held to be unsafe or at least unreliable throughout North Africa with the exception of large cities in Morocco. Filtered or bottled water is generally available. If your hotel has a central hot water supply this is safe to drink after cooling. Ice for drinks should be made from boiled water but rarely is, so stand your glass on the ice cubes, instead of putting them in the drink. Dirty water should first be strained through a filter bag (available from camping shops) and then boiled or treated. Bringing the water to a rolling boil at sea level is sufficient but at high altitude you have to boil the water for longer to ensure that all the microbes are killed. Various sterilising methods can be used and there are proprietary preparations containing chlorine or iodine compounds. Pasteurized or heat treated milk is now widely available as is ice cream and yoghurt produced by the same methods. Unpasteurized milk products including cheese and yoghurt are sources of tuberculosis, brucellosis, listeria and food poisoning germs. You can render fresh milk safe by heating it to 62°C for 30 mins followed by rapid cooling or by boiling it. Matured or processed cheeses are safer than fresh varieties.

Diarrhoea is usually the result of food poisoning, occasionally from contaminated water (including seawater when swimming near sewage outfalls). There are various causes – viruses, bacteria, protozoa (like amoeba) salmonella and cholera organisms. It may take one of several forms coming on suddenly, or rather slowly. It may be accompanied by vomiting or by severe abdominal pain and the passage of blood or mucus when it is called dysentery. How do you know which type you have and how do you treat it?

All kinds of diarrhoea, whether or not accompanied by vomiting, respond favourably to the replacement of water and salts taken as frequent small sips of some kind of rehydration solution. There are proprietary preparations consisting of sachets of powder which you dissolve in water or you can make your own by adding half a teaspoonful of salt (3.5 grams) and four tablespoonfuls of sugar (40 grams) to a litre of boiled water. If you can time the onset of diarrhoea to the minute, then it is probably viral or bacterial and/or the onset of dysentery. The treatment, in addition to rehydration, is Ciprofloxacin 500 mgs every 12 hrs. The drug is now widely available as are various similar ones.

If the diarrhoea has come on slowly or intermittently, then it is more likely to be protozoal i.e. caused by amoeba or giardia and antibiotics will have no effect. These cases are best treated by a doctor, as is any outbreak of diarrhoea continuing for more than 3 days. If there are severe stomach cramps, the following drugs may help: Loperamide (Imodium, Arret) and Diphenoxylate with Atropine (Lomotil).

The lynchpins of treatment for diarrhoea are rest, fluid and salt replacement, antibiotics such as Ciprofloxacin for the bacterial types and special diagnostic tests and medical treatment for amoeba and giardia infections. Salmonella infections and cholera can be devastating diseases and it would be wise to get to a hospital as soon as possible if these were suspected. Fasting, peculiar diets and the consumption of large quantities of yoghourt have not been found useful in calming travellers diarrhoea or in rehabilitating inflamed bowels. Oral rehydration has on the other hand, especially in children, been a lifesaving technique. As there is some evidence that alcohol and milk might prolong diarrhoea, they should probably be avoided during and immediately after an attack. There are ways of preventing travellers diarrhoea for short periods of time when visiting these countries by taking antibiotics but these are ineffective against viruses and, to some extent, against protozoa, so this technique should not be used other than in exceptional circumstances. Some preventives such as Enterovioform can have serious side effects if taken for long periods.

MALARIA

This disease occurs in all the regions covered by this book, with the exception of Tunisia. The disease is, however, only common in Mauritania and Libya with some limited transmission occurring, seasonally in coastal Morocco and central Algeria. Despite being nowhere near so common as in Sub-Saharan Africa, malaria remains a serious disease and you are advised to protect yourself against mosquito bites as described above and to take prophylactic (preventive) drugs where and when there is a risk. Start taking the tablets a few days before exposure and continue to take them 6 weeks after leaving the malarial zone. Remember to give the drugs to babies and children and pregnant women also.

The subject of malaria prevention is becoming more complex as the malaria parasite becomes immune to some of the older drugs. This phenomenon, at the time of writing, has not occurred in North African countries other than Mauritania and so the more traditional drugs can be taken with some confidence. Protection with Proguanil (Paludrine) two tablets per day, or Chloroquine two tablets per week will suffice and at this dose will not cause any side effects. In Mauritania where there is Chloroquine resistance, both drugs should be taken. You will have to find out locally the likelihood of malaria and perhaps be prepared to receive conflicting advice on how to prevent yourself from catching it. You can catch malaria even when taking prophylactic drugs, although it is unlikely. If you do develop symptoms (high fever, shivering, severe headache, sometimes diarrhoea) seek medical advice immediately. The risk of the disease is obviously greater the further you move from the cities into rural areas with limited facilities and standing water.

PSYCHOLOGICAL DISORDERS

First time exposure to countries where sections of the population live in extreme poverty or squalor and may even be starving can cause odd psychological reactions in visitors. So can the incessant pestering, especially of women which is unfortunately common in some of these countries. Simply be prepared for this and try not to over react.

SNAKE AND OTHER BITES & STINGS

If you are unlucky enough to be bitten by a venomous snake, spider, scorpion, lizard, centipede or sea creature try (within limits) to catch the animal for identification. The reactions to be expected are fright, swelling, pain and bruising around the bite, soreness of the regional lymph glands, nausea, vomiting and fever. If in addition any of the following symptoms supervene, get the victim to a doctor without delay: numbness, tingling of the face, muscular spasms, convulsions, shortness of breath or haemorrhage. Commercial snake bite or scorpion sting kits may be available but are only useful for the specific type of snake or scorpion for which they are designed. The serum has to be given intravenously, so is not much good unless you have had some practice in making injections into veins. If the bite is on a limb, immobilize it and apply a tight bandage between the bite and body, releasing it for 90 secs every 15 mins. Reassurance of the bitten person is very important because death by snake bite is in fact very rare. Do not slash the bite area and try and suck out the poison because this kind of heroism does more harm than good. Hospitals usually hold stocks of snake bite serum. Best precaution: do not walk in snake territory with bare feet, sandals or shorts.

If swimming in an area where there are poisonous fish such as stone or scorpion fish (also called by a variety of local names) or sea urchins on rocky coasts, tread carefully or wear plimsolls. The sting of such fish is intensely painful and this can be helped by immersing the stung part in water as hot as you can bear for as long as it remains painful. This is not always very practical and you must take care not to scald yourself but it does work. Avoid spiders and scorpions by keeping your bed away from the wall and look under lavatory seats and inside your shoes in the morning. In the rare event of being bitten, consult a doctor.

SUNBURN AND HEAT STROKE

The burning power of the sun in North Africa is phenomenal, especially at high altitude. Always wear a wide-brimmed hat and use some form of sun cream or lotion on untanned skin. Normal temperate zone suntan lotions (protection factor up to seven) are not much good. You need to use the types designed specifically for the tropics or for mountaineers or skiers with a protection factor (against UVA) between seven and 15. Certain creams also protect against UVB and you should use these if you have a skin prone to burning. Glare from the sun can cause conjunctivitis so wear sunglasses, especially on the beach.

There are several varieties of heat stroke. The most common cause is severe dehydration. Avoid this by drinking lots of non-alcoholic fluid and adding some salt if you wish.

OTHER AFFLICTIONS

Athletes foot and other fungal infections are best treated by exposure to sunshine and a proprietary preparation such as Tolnaftate.

Dengue fever is not common in North Africa but there have been cases of this virus transmitted by mosquito bites producing severe headache and body pains. There is no treatment: you must just avoid mosquito bites.

Filariasis causing such diseases as elephantiasis occurs in Mauritania and again is transmitted by mosquito.

Hydatid disease is quite common in Algeria but can be avoided by keeping well clear of dogs, which is good advice in any case.

Intestinal worms do occur in insanitary areas and the more serious ones, such as hook-worm, can be contracted by walking bare foot on infested earth or beaches.

Leishmaniasis causing a skin ulcer which

will not heal is also present in most of the North African countries. It is transmitted by sand flies.

Prickly heat is a common itchy rash avoided by frequent washing and by wearing loose clothing. It can be helped by the regular use of talcum powder to allow the skin to dry thoroughly after washing.

Schistosomiasis (bilharzia) occurs particularly in Morocco and can easily be avoided because it is transmitted by snails which live in fresh water lakes so do not swim in such places or in canals.

Rabies is endemic throughout North African countries. If you are bitten by a domestic animal try to have it captured for observation and see a doctor at once. Treatment with human diploid vaccine is now extremely effective and worth seeking out if the likelihood of having contracted rabies is high. A course of anti-rabies vaccine might be a good idea before you go.

WHEN YOU RETURN HOME

Remember to take your anti-malarial tablets for 6 weeks. If you have had attacks of diarrhoea, it is worth having a stool specimen tested in case you have picked up amoebic dysentery. If you have been living rough, a blood test may be worthwhile to detect worms and other parasites.

FURTHER HEALTH INFORMATION

The following organisations give information regarding well-trained English speaking physicians throughout the world: International Association for Medical Assistance to Travellers, 745 Fifth Avenue, New York, 10022; Intermedic, 777 3rd Avenue, New York, 10017.

Information regarding country by country malaria risk can be obtained from the World Health Organisation (WHO) or the Ross Institute, The London School of Hygiene and Tropical Medicine, Keppel Street, London WCIE 7HT which publishes a strongly recommended book entitled *The Preservation of Personal Health in Warm Climates*. The organisation MASTA, (Medical Advisory Service to Travellers Abroad), also based at The London School of Hygiene and Tropical Medicine, T 0171 6314408, F 0171 4365389, will provide country by country information on up-to-date health risks.

Further information on medical problems overseas can be obtained from Dawood, Richard (ed), *Travellers Health, How to Stay Healthy Abroad*, Oxford University Press, 1992, costing £7.99. We strongly recommend this revised and updated edition, especially to the intrepid traveller heading for the more out of the way places.

General advice is also available in *Health Advice for Travellers* published jointly by the Department of Health and the Central Office of Information (UK) and available free from your Travel Agent.

The above information has been prepared by Dr David Snashall, Senior Lecturer in Occupational Health, United Medical Schools of Guy's and St Thomas' Hospitals and Chief Medical Officer, Foreign and Commonwealth Office, London.

TEMPERATURE CONVERSION TABLE

°C	°F	°C	°F
1	34	26	79
2	36	27	81
3	38	28	82
4	39	29	84
5	41	30	86
6	43	31	88
7	45	32	90
8	46	33	92
9	48	34	93
10	50	35	95
11	52	36	97
12	54	37	99
13	56	38	100
14	57	39	102
15	59	40	104
16	61	41	106
17	63	42	108
18	64	43	109
19	66	44	111
20	68	45	113
21	70	46	115
22	72	47	117
23	74	48	118
24	75	49	120
25	77	50	122

The formula for converting °C to °F is:
$$°C \times 9 \div 5 + 32 = °F$$

WEIGHTS AND MEASURES

Metric

Weight
1 Kilogram (Kg) = 2.205 pounds
1 metric ton = 1.102 short tons

Length
1 millimetre (mm) = 0.03937 inch
1 metre = 3.281 feet
1 kilometre (km) = 0.621 mile

Area
1 heactare = 2.471 acres
1 square km = 0.386 sq mile

Capacity
1 litre = 0.220 imperial gallon
      = 0.264 US gallon

Volume
1 cubic metre (m³) = 35.31 cubic feet
            = 1.31 cubic yards

British and US

Weight
1 pound (lb) = 454 grams
1 short ton (2,000lbs) = 0.907 m ton
1 long ton (2,240lbs) = 1.016 m tons

Length
1 inch = 25.417 millimetres
1 foot (ft) = 0.305 metre
1 mile = 1.609 kilometres

Area
1 acre = 0.405 hectare
1 sq mile = 2.590 sq kilometre

Capacity
1 imperial gallon = 4.546 litres
1 US gallon = 3.785 litres

Volume
1 cubic foot (cu ft) = 0.028 m³
1 cubic yard (cu yd) = 0.765 m³

NB 5 imperial gallons are approximately equal to 6 US gallons

Glossary

A

Aghlabid
Adjective of Aghlabite

Agora
Market/meeting place

Aïd/Eïd
Festival

Aïn
Spring

Affanes
Woollen slipper used by nomads

Abbasids
Muslim Dynasty ruled from Baghdad 750-1258

Aghlabites
Orthodox Muslim Dynasty in Tunisia and eastern Algeria 800-909

Alawite
Present rulers of Morocco since 1666

Alcazaba
Fortress

Almohads
Second Berber dynasty in this region of North Africa, 1130-1269. Name is a corruption of *Al-Muwahidun* translated as unitarians

Almoravids
First Berber dynasty in this region of North Africa, 1054-1147. Name is a corruption of *Al-Murabidun* translated as from the *ribat* or monastery

Andalucía
Moorish Spain

Arabesque
Geometric pattern with flowers and foliage used in Islamic designs

Assif
See oued

Azib
Seasonal shelter – originally just for animals

B

Bab
City gate

Bâches
Converted pick-up truck

Bahri
North/northern

Baladiyah
Municipality

Baksheesh
Money as alms, tip or bribe

Baraka
Blessing, charm from a holy person or site

Barbary
Name of North Africa 16th-19th centuries

Barboushe
Soft, flat leather slipper

Basilica
Imposing Roman building, with aisles, later used for worship

Bayoud
Fungal disease of date palm

Bazaar
Market

Bedouin
Nomadic desert Arab

Beni
Sons of (tribe)

Berber
Indigenous tribe of North Africa

Bey
Governor (Ottoman)

Bidonville
Shanty town

Bir
Well

Borj
Fort or tower

Burnous
Man's cloak with hood – traditional wear

C

Caftan
Long flowing robe, male and female versions

Caid
Official

Calèche
Horse drawn carriage

Calidarium
Hot room

Capital
Top section of a column

Caravanserai
Lodgings for travellers and animals around a courtyard

Chaouia
Berbers of the Aurés

Chechia
Man's small red felt hat

Chotts
Low-lying salt lakes

Couscous
Steamed semolina

D

Dar
House

Darj w ktaf
Carved geometric motif of intersecting arcs with superimposed rectangles

Dayat
Freshwater lake

Dechra
Earth coloured terraced hamlets topped by fortress silos

Deglet Nur
High quality translucent date

Delu
Water lifting device at head of well

Dey
Commander (of janissaries)

Djemma
Main or Friday mosque

Dour
Village settlement

E

Eïd
see Aïd

Erg
Sand dune desert

F

Fantasia
An extraordinary war exercise, in which men on horseback perform the most extraordinary feats and fire their *moukhala* (old powder charged rifles) during a frantic gallop in perfect synchronization. The horsemen gallop towards the 'audience' and at the very last second draw their mounts to a standstill

Faqirs
Muslim who has taken a vow of poverty

Fassi
A person or item from Fes

Fatimids
Muslim dynasty 909-1171 AD claiming descent from Mohammed's daughter Fatimah

Fondouk/Funduq
Lodgings for goods and animals around a courtyard

Forum
Central open space in Roman town

Ful/Fuul
Beans

G

Gare Routière
Bus station

Garrigue
Mediterranean scrubland – poor quality

Gargum
Paste made from shellfish in Roman times

Ginan
Small garden or tree embayment

Gymnasium
Roman school for mind and body

H

Habous
Religiously endowed land in Morocco

Hafsids
Berber dynasty 13th-16th century in present day Tunisia and Algeria

Haïk
Piece of cloth worn by women

Hamada
Stone desert

Hammam
Bath house

Hara
Jewish quarter in Tripoli

Harem
Women's quarters

Harira
Soup

Harmattan
Mauritanian hot dry wind from east that raises temperatures and reduces humidity

Hassi
Well

Henna
Dye used on hair and hands

Hoddud
Imaginary line or sacred frontier dividing harem from rest of household

I

Idrissid
Dynasty founded by Moulay Idriss I 788 AD

Idrissids
The first Arab dynasty in this region of North Africa, founded by Moulay Idris I (788-794)

Imam
Muslim religious leader

J

Jallabah
Outer garment with sleeves and a hood – often striped

Jami'
Mosque

Janissaries
Elite Ottoman soldiery

Jbel
Mountain or mountain range

Jihad
Holy war by Muslims against non-believers

K

Kasbah
Castle/Fort

Kharejite
Followers of Ali (seceders) who regarded God as the sole arbitrator in the choice of Islamic leader

Khattara
Underground water channel

Kilim

Woven carpet
Kif
Hashish
Kissaria
Covered market for craftsmen
Kofta
Meat dish
Koubba
Dome on tomb of holy man, also special room in houses in Ghadames
Ksar (pl Ksour)
Fortified village
Kufic
Angular style of Arabic writing

L

Limes
Border region protected by militarized farmers
Liwan
Vaulted arcade

M

Maasras
Traditional olive press
Mahboub
Coins worn as jewellery
Maghreb
Western Arab world – Morocco, Algeria and Tunisia
Malekite
Section of Sunni Islam
Maqbara
Cemetery
Maqsura
A railed enclosure or screen once placed in front of the prayer niche
Maquis
Mediterranean scrubland – often aromatic
Marabout
Muslim holy man/his tomb
Marinids
Berber dynasty 13th-15th centuries, strongest in Morocco
Maristan
Hospital

Mashrabia
Wooden screen
Mashreq
Eastern Arab world
Mastaba
Tomb
Mausoleum
Large tomb building
Mecheoui
Moroccan meat dish (mutton)
Mechour
Large open space used for important ceremonies
Medersa (pl Medressa)
School usually attached to a mosque
Medina
Old walled town, residential quarter
Mellah
Jewish quarter of old town
Menzel
House
Merinids
Third Berber dynasty in this region of North Africa, 1248-1420. From this dynasty Merino sheep were named
Mihrab
Recess in wall of mosque indicating direction of Mecca
Minbar
Pulpit in mosque, generally of wood, moved into position when required
Minaret
Slender tower of mosque from which the muezzin calls the faithful to prayer
Mosque
Muslim place of worship
Moulid/Mouloud
Religious festival – Prophet's birthday
Moussem
Religious gathering
Muezzin
Priest who calls the faithful to prayer
Mullah

Muslim religious teacher
Murabtin
Dependent tribe

N

Necropolis
Cemetery

O

Oasis
Watered desert gardens
Ottoman
Major Muslim Empire based in Turkey 13th-20th centuries
Oued
Water course – more usually dry
Ouled
Tribe/children
Outrepassé
Horse-shoe shaped arch

P

Pasha
Governor
Phoenicians
Important trading nation based in eastern Mediterranean from 1100 BC
Piscine
Pool
Pisé
Sun-baked clay used for building
Piste
Unsurfaced road

Q

Qibla
Mosque wall in direction of Mecca
Qasr
see Ksar

R

Rabbi
Head of Jewish community
Ramadan
Muslim month of fasting
Reconquista

Christian campaigns to re-capture Iberian territory from Muslims

Reg
Rock desert

Ribat
Fortified monastery

S

Saadian
Second Arab dynasty in this region of North Africa, claiming descent from the Prophet, 1554-1659

Sabil
Public water fountain

Saggia
Water channel

Sahn
Courtyard or patio in a mosque

Sarcophagus
Decorated stone coffin

Salat
Worship

Serais
Lodging for men and animals

Serir
Sand desert

Shahada
Profession of faith

Shergui
Hot, dry desert wind

Sidi
Mr/Saint

Skala
Walkway along rampart

Souq
Traditional market

Suani
Small walled irrigated traditional garden

Sufi
Muslim mystic

Sunni
Orthodox Muslims

T

Tagine (pl Touajen)
Stew

Taifa
Sub-tribe

Taksira
Strenuous massage for men at hammam

Tamashek
Language of Touareg

Tariqa
Brotherhood/Order

Tesserae
Small, regularly shaped plain and coloured tiles used to produce designs in a mosaic

Tizi
Mountain pass

Touareg
Nomadic Saharan dwellers, noted for men's blue face covering

Tourbet
Private cemetery

Troglodyte
Underground dweller

V

Vandals
Empire in North Africa 429-534 AD

Visir
Governor

W

Wattasids
Fourth Berber dynasty in this region of North Africa, 1420-1554

Wikala
Merchants' hostel

Wilaya/Wilayat
Governorate/district

Z

Zaouia
Shrine/Sennusi centre

Zayyanids
Berber dynasty NW Algeria in 13th century

Zellij
Geometrical mosaic pattern made from pieces of glazed tiles

Zenata
Tribal confederation which controlled northern Morocco in the late 10th century until the Almoravids came

Zeriba
House of straw/grass

Tinted boxes

MAURITANIA

INFORMATION FOR TRAVELLERS

Illustrations

504

Index

Maps

MAURITANIA

INFORMATION FOR TRAVELLERS

Map Symbols

Administration

International Border	
State / Province Border	
Disputed Border	
Neighbouring country	
Neighbouring state	
State Capitals	□
Other Towns	○

Roads and travel

Main Roads (National Highways)	R 15
Other Roads	
Jeepable Roads, Tracks	
Railways with station	

Water features

River	*Oued Bou Regreg*
Lakes, Reservoirs, Tanks	
Seasonal Marshlands	
Salt Lake	
Sand Banks, Beaches	
Ocean	
Ferry	

Topographical features

Contours (approx), Rock Outcrops	
Mountains	
Gorge	
Escarpment	
Palm trees	

Cities and towns

Built Up Areas	
Main through routes	
Main streets	
Minor Streets	
Pedestrianized Streets	
One Way Street	
National Parks, Gardens, Stadiums	
Fortified Walls	▲ ▲ ▲
Airport	✈
Banks	Ⓢ
Bus Stations (named in key)	🚌 🚌₁ 🚌₂
Hospitals	⊕
Market	Ⓜ
Police station	Pol
Post Office	✉
Telegraphic Office	☏
Tourist Office	ⓘ
Key Numbers	1 2 3 4 5
Bridges	⌣
Mosque	🕌
Cathedral, church	✝ ✝
Guided routes	

Other symbols

Pyramid	▲
National Parks and Bird Sanctuaries	♦
Camp site	Λ
Motorable track	
Walking track	
Archaeological Sites	⫶
Places of Interest	○
Viewing point	❀

Footprint Handbooks

All of us at Footprint Handbooks hope you have enjoyed reading and travelling with this Handbook, one of the first published in the new Footprint series. Many of you will be familiar with us as Trade & Travel, a name that has served us well for years. For you and for those who have only just discovered the Handbooks, we thought it would be interesting to chronicle the story of our development from the early 1920's.

It all started 75 years ago in 1921, with the publication of the Anglo-South American Handbook. In 1924 the South American Handbook was created. This has been published each year for the last 73 years and is the longest running guidebook in the English language, immortalised by Graham Greene as "the best travel guide in existence".

One of the key strengths of the South American Handbook over the years, has been the extraordinary contact we have had with our readers through their hundreds of letters to us in Bath. From these letters we learnt that you wanted more Handbooks of the same quality to other parts of the world.

In 1989 my brother Patrick and I set about developing a series modelled on the South American Handbook. Our aim was to create the ultimate practical guidebook series for all travellers, providing expert knowledge of far flung places, explaining culture, places and people in a balanced, lively and clear way. The whole idea hinged, of course, on finding writers who were in tune with our thinking. Serendipity stepped in at exactly the right moment: we were able to bring together a talented group of people who know the countries we cover inside out and whose enthusiasm for travelling in them needed to be communicated.

The series started to grow. We felt that the time was right to look again at the identity that had brought us all this way. After much searching we commissioned London designers Newell & Sorrell to look at all the issues. Their solution was a new identity for the Handbooks representing the books in all their aspects, looking after all the good things already achieved and taking us into the new millennium.

The result is Footprint Handbooks: a new name and mark, simple yet assertive, bold, stylish and instantly recognisable. The images we use conjure up the essence of real travel and communicate the qualities of the Handbooks in a straightforward and evocative way.

For us here in Bath, it has been an exciting exercise working through this dramatic change. Already the 'new us' fits like our favourite travelling clothes and we cannot wait to get more and more Footprint Handbooks onto the book shelves and out onto the road.

The Footprint list

Footprint T-shirt

The Footprint T-shirt is available in 100% cotton in various colours.

Mail Order

Footprint Handbooks are available worldwide in good bookstores. They can also be ordered directly from us in Bath (see below for address). Please contact us if you have difficulty finding a title.

The Footprint Handbook website will be coming to keep you up to date with all the latest news from us (http://www.footprint-handbooks.co.uk). For the most up-to-date information and to join our mailing list please contact us at:

Footprint Handbooks
6 Riverside Court
Lower Bristol Road
Bath BA2 3DZ, England
T +44(0)1225 469141
F +44(0)1225 469461
E Mail handbooks@footprint.cix.co.uk